Outdoor Recreation

ENRICHMENT FOR A LIFETIME

Hilmi Ibrahim

Whittier College, Professor

Kathleen A. Cordes

San Diego Miramar College, Professor Emeritus

Second Edition

Sagamore Publishing

Champaign, IL

Production Manager: Janet Wahlfeldt

Interior Design: Christina Cary

Cover Design: K. Jeffrey Higgerson

Cover Photo: Jane Lammers

Interior Photos: Jane Lammers

Editor: Susan Moyer

Library of Congress Catalog Card Number: 2002108169

ISBN1-57167-495-0

Printed in the United States.

DEDICATED TO

TO MY CHILDREN AND GRANDCHILDREN
H.I.

AND

TO ED AND RITA CORDES
K.C.

CONTENTS

INTRODUCTION

This book is written with a number of objectives in mind. Most importantly, it tries to avoid duplicating what other books on outdoor recreation do. This book attempts to look at outdoor pursuits first as a sub-phenomenon of the larger recreation and leisure phenomenon, but with an added touch, that of the natural element, with its psychological influence and social significance. These two points will be elaborated on in Part One.

Part One provides two views of nature. The first is based on the experiences and values of the original inhabitants of the New World. The second is derived from the values of members of Western civilization who were transplanted into the New World after its discovery and colonization. These two views are not necessarily incompatible. For despite the exploitation of nature that began with the early European settlers, there were, and still are, those whose love of nature is evident in their writings, advocacy, and leadership. The early transcendentalists, naturalists, and practitioners were ahead of their time. Today the field of psychology shows us why nature is so appealing and soothing to human beings. Since we need nature for our well-being, effective management of our natural resources is a must. Psychology aside, effective managers should be equipped not only with managerial skills but also with a thorough understanding of the socioeconomic factors that have a direct bearing on outdoor recreational pursuits.

Part Two provides the reader with a description of the resources available to the outdoor adventurer. There are four categories of resources—federal state, local, and private. While these categories prevail in the United States, Canada has a very similar arrangement. Other countries are included in this volume to give an idea of how pervasive the quest for outdoor adventures is globally. Also this information will acquaint the reader with the problems facing the manager and the users of recreation resources everywhere.

Part Three is devoted to examining the management of outdoor resources as well as outdoor education. Both future managers and recreation participants would definitely benefit from knowing the policies, procedures, and even the problems of management of outdoor recreation.

An epilogue is provided that expresses our hopes for a bright and prosperous future for outdoor recreation. The appendices provide pertinent information such as a listing of federal and state agencies dealing with outdoor recreation as well as professional and voluntary associations concerned with outdoor pursuits. Finally, the index is provided for the reader.

Acknowledgments

We are grateful to Jane Lammers for her assistance, encouragement, and patience. Besides her diligent work on the manuscript, she contributed the majority of the photographs used in this volume. Thank you, Jane.

In the course of the preparation of the manuscript, many friends, colleagues, and others have helped us. We wish to express gratitude to the following: Heather Nabours, John Strey, Jim Palmer, Dave Sanderlin, Rick Matthews, Mary Ellen Vick, Ray Young, Barbara Himes, and the many organizations that provided us with data and material.

We are grateful to the assistance we received from Darlene McCracken, Nicole Kiselicka, Bianca Urquidi and Lori Ginoza during the writing of the manuscript.

Our many thanks go to Joseph Bannon, for his encouragement and to Douglas Sanders for his patience and diligence.

We also would like to thank our editor, Susan Moyer, for her help and support, and our reviewers, whose comments helped improve the manuscript. They are:

Professor Brenda K. Blessing,
Missouri Western State University

Dr. Craig Kelsey,
University of New Mexico

Professor Phyllis Ford,
Greenbough Programs

Professor Wayne Allison,
Lock Haven University

Professor O. J. Helvey,
Cumberland College

Professor Jack B. Frost,
California Polytechnic University-Pomona

H.I.
K.C.
July 2002

OUTDOOR RECREATION

— ENRICHMENT FOR A LIFETIME —

PART ONE

The Fundamentals of Outdoor Recreation

The first part of this book is devoted to examining the foundations of outdoor recreation, which include the historical, spiritual, social, psychological, and economic factors that led to its rise in the Western world, particularly in the United States and Canada. Chapter 1 gives an overview of these foundations. Chapter 2 focuses on the spiritual attitudes of Americans toward the outdoors, one aspect of which is the Native American relationship to nature. How outdoor recreation emerged is the result of the change in values and the teaching and leadership of a few people. Some of these teachers and leaders are presented in Chapter 3. Chapter 4 discusses the psychology of the natural environment, and Chapter 5 concentrates on the social aspects of outdoor experiences. The economics of outdoor recreation are discussed in Chapter 6.

1 | FOUNDATIONS OF OUTDOOR RECREATION

In this book we use the term outdoor recreation to encompass the organized free-time activities that are participated in for their own sake and where there is an interaction between the participant and an element of nature. Surfing is an outdoor recreational activity where there is interaction between the participant and water, an element of nature. Football is not an outdoor recreational activity under our definition, for although it is an organized recreational activity, nature plays a minimal role in it. Nature plays a more important role in mountain climbing or cross-country skiing than it does in football.

Although predicated on play and part of the growing sphere of leisure activities, recreation differs from both play and leisure in that it is basically organized and takes place mainly in groups. At the core of recreation is play, and at the core of outdoor recreation is involvement with the natural environment. On the other hand, leisure is defined as the state of mind that allows an individual to participate in certain activities, and availability of free time is an important contributor to both recreation and outdoor recreation.

Recent studies have shown that ritual among humans played, and still plays, an important role, not only in establishing social order but also as a vehicle of creativity and expression. Ritual seems to have added to the importance and significance of both leisure and recreation. Elaboration on play, ritual, and outdoor recreation follows.

HUMANS, PLAY, AND RITUAL

Hardly anyone disagrees that humans tend to play. Some may argue that play is witnessed among the young of the human race only, but empirical evidence negates such a claim: some adult activities that may not be considered as play by everyone are in fact play activity, albeit somewhat sophisticated play. Such sophistication results from both the maturation of the individual and the complexity of modern societies. Studies show that many of the original activities of adults in some primal societies were very similar to children's play (Wood, 1871, Roth 1902, Blanchard & Cheska, 1985). Complexity in many activities provides us with much of today's recreation (Turner, 1982).

Outdoor recreation, the activities that are the main focus of this volume, is practiced by most members of complex, modern urbanized and industrial societies. Most Americans and Canadians camp, ski, and go on organized picnics. In previous societies, only the well-to-do could afford to do so. They were the ones whose value system not only allowed but also encouraged enjoyment of picnics and going camping and skiing. While the reasons for the shift that allowed everyone to recreate are societal, be they economic or political, the reason for participation, by wealthy or commoner alike, is based on the tendency to play and, to a great extent, to ritualize.

Play

Some researchers claim that the tendency to play may have a deeper niche in human behavior than was once believed. Humans share this propensity with the upper mammals (deVore, 1965; Lancaster 1975; & Marano, 1999), and there may be a genetic imprint, or a chemical code, that propels us in this direction (Eisen, 1988). In order to understand this tendency, an explanation of the structure of the human brain and its evolution is a must.

The simple elementary brain, which is labeled the reptilian brain, is surrounded by a more complicated brain known as the limbic system or the old mammalian brain. While the elementary brain handles basic functions of self-preservation and preservation of the species through hunting, homing, mating, fighting, and territoriality, the old mammalian brain is identified with mothering, audiovocal communication, and play. Experiments have shown that when the limbic system was severed in some small animals, they reverted to reptilian behavior, which is void of play (lbrahim, 1991:1).

The third brain, called the new mammalian brain or the neocortex, surrounds the old mammalian brain and is divided into two hemispheres, each responsible for the opposite side of the body. According to Ornestein and Thompson (1984:34), hemispheric specialization took place at the time when humans were becoming bipedal and using their front limbs in tool making. With the enlarged brain, more complicated processes took place, including the construction and storage of symbols. Mental processes utilizing the two hemispheres can be roughly divided into two groups: processes that help in maintaining order in everyday activities such as language, and others that pertain to insight, imagination, and artistic expression. Sagan (1977) asserts that while the left hemisphere is responsible for the first group, the right hemisphere is responsible for the second.

In the early 1940s, brain research led to the assumption that a drive for arousal in both humans and animals helps to avoid boredom (Berlyne, 1960). Others today are advocating that a "hormonal code" or "genetic programming" initiates, propels, and, to a lesser degree, regulates play (Eisen, 1988). The evidence comes from observation of animals and humans. In the case of animals, it is evident that the higher the animal on the evolutionary scale, the greater the time devoted to play, at least among the young. Among humans, Sutton-Smith suggested that Neuroimaging studies of the brain may reveal a ludic center located somewhere in the Frontal Lobe (Marano, 1999).

Although play varies from species to species among primates, Lancaster indicated that field observers were impressed with the amount of time and energy spent in play by their juveniles (1975:49). For instance, young chimpanzees spend over 50 percent of their waking hours in play. Play behavior is the first seen in the early morning and the last seen before young baboons retire. The same is observed among young howlers and bonnet macaques (de Vore, 1965).

Evidence of a biological base for the tendency to play among young humans comes from the sequence of children's play forms, regardless of their social or cultural background. The sequence of manipulative, repetitive, relational, make-believe, and rule-governed play is remarkably stable across diverse populations, which points toward a possible universal blueprint for play (Wolf, 1984). Others are finding similar regularity (Edwards, 2000).

But play is not the only element in the rise of organized recreational activities among the members of a given society. Rituals play an important role as well. The first scholar to bring to our attention the link between play and ritual is historian Johan Huizinga. He believed that play is the basis of culture and that ritual assisted in the process of bringing about civilized life.

> Now in myth and ritual the great instinctive forces of civilized life have their origin: Law and order, commerce and profit, craft and art, poetry, wisdom, and science. All are rooted in the primeval soil of play (1950:5).

At the time of Huizinga's writing, the concept of instinctive play was not quite palatable to many scholars of play. The idea that ritual might also be instinctive was equally unacceptable. In the last few decades, however, research on the brain has lent some credence to Huizinga's advocation that there seems to be some biological basis for both play and ritual (Marano, 1999).

In between these two extremes, our biological nature and our cultural orientation, many attempts were made to explain play in terms of psychology and sociology. All these attempts underscored the multifaceted nature of play. Human development and societal sophistication were aided by another tendency in creating an array of the human activities we call recreation.

Ritual

Scholars are just now beginning to understand the role of ritual in human life. Ritual refers to a set or series of acts, with a sequence established by tradition and stemming from the life of a people. Thanksgiving dinner in America, for example, is a tradition with an original purpose that some may have forgotten, yet it is celebrated year after year (with a new element added, a football game to be watched on television). And although the original meaning of the activity may be forgotten, humans ritualistically repeat the activity with great passion. Some scholars believe that it is the repetitiveness that matters and not the activity itself, on the assumption that ritualization has a biological basis in humans and animals.

Ritualization refers to the stylized, repeated gestures and posturing of humans or animals. Ritualization is based on rhythmicity and formation, two biological principles that are essential for survival. Rhythmicity is observed in the alteration of systole and diastole (higher reading and lower reading of blood pressure, respectively) and in the cycle of wakefulness and sleep. Formalization is the tendency to stabilize inner compulsions as well as output by putting things in order—a tendency that paves the way for the act we call ritualization. Rhythmic, formalized, and ritualistic activity give life stability not only for the young, but for the adult as well.

Simple ritualization evolved into complex rituals which, in turn, expanded to five modes as proposed by Grimmes (1982). While decorum, magic, and liturgy are not usually connected with outdoor activities, ceremony and celebration can be. A *ceremony* is a ritual that requires that one surrender to the demands of authority. Examples of nature ceremonies in many societies will be provided in Chapter 2. *Celebration* is the ritual most related to play. Here one participates for the sake of participation and not for an external end. Celebration has permeated human life since early times, including the celebration of nature, as will be seen in the examples given in Chapter 2.

Deegan (1989:5) states that participatory ritual is deeply rooted in social interaction in America. Participatory rituals exhibit three common characteristics. These are social activities

1. requiring participation and face-to-face contact;
2. with a matrix of roles, statuses, and culture; and
3. organized by a set of rules for ritual action.

For our purposes, we want to know, for instance, what propels a person to go fishing or hunting year after year during the long weekend designed to celebrate the birth of a president? Is it the tendency to play? Or is it the tendency to ritualize? If the tendencies to play and to ritualize are biologically based, why is it that not all Americans of the same age and sex go fishing on that occasion? Another person may spend the long weekend alone watching nature programs on television, and a third may spend it hiking in the woods. A

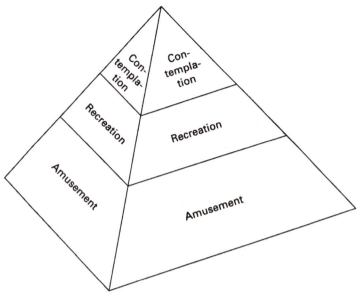

Figure 1.1 Hierarchy of leisure

presentation of two more concepts that affect our outdoor experience is important at this point: leisure and recreation.

LEISURE OR RECREATION

When it comes to adult behavior during free time, analyzing the situation becomes rather complicated. For instance, when camping, is the individual playing, recreating, or at leisure? One does not hear or see terms such as outdoor leisure, or therapeutic play, yet the American lifestyle is full of outdoor recreation, community recreation, and therapeutic recreation. What is the difference? Conceptual differentiation among the definitions for play, recreation, and leisure is necessary at this point. In this work, play refers to activities of the young partaken by choice. On the other hand, recreation refers to organized activity in which an adult participates during free time. The emphasis in leisure is on the state of mind that allows the adult to participate in an activity of his or her choice during the time freed from work or civil or familial obligations.

The state of mind, by itself and in itself, is not easily discernible to the casual observer, but the engagement in a recreational activity is. Recreation gained greater attention at the beginning of this century in the United States because it revolves around the most easily observed feature of the leisure phenomenon, the activity. The other two elements, the state of mind and freed time, were not essential in recreational programs. The activity became central to the thinking of social reformers such as Jane Addams, who advocated that the lack of these activities led to social ills such as delinquency and truancy. In fact there are still attempts in that direction, recreation as rehabilitation, not only where adolescents are concerned (Mahoney & Stattin, 2000) but also for the physically disabled (Pati et al,1999).

The philosopher Aristotle, who paid serious attention to the leisure phenomenon "qua" a phenomenon and not as a method to combat social ills, may help us understand the nature of leisure. Aristotle believed that leisure encompasses three subsets of activities: contemplative, recreative, and amusive activities. Leisure can be seen as a pyramid, the bottom third of which encompasses amusive activities, on top of which are recreative activities, which is topped by contemplative activities (see Figure 1.1.).

In outdoor settings all three levels can be achieved. On the first level we would enjoy watching animals as they go about their lives. On the second level, backpacking and hiking are pursued. On the third level the study of nature is an important aspect of contemplation. One of the elements in pushing for the building of America's first city park, Central Park of New York City, was the concept of contemplation (Taylor, 1999).

The Emergence of Outdoor Recreation

Contemplation is only one form of leisure that Americans came to enjoy, the other forms being recreation and amusement. Although free time was being gained by the new settlers of North America, that free time did not transform into leisure easily. Leisure, as a state of being, was fought vigorously by the strict Calvinists of colonial America. Puritan requirements led the colonists to live without the "mispence of time," adhering strictly to the observance of the Sabbath. They tolerated no pagan festivities, no licentious plays and spectacles, no violations of the Sabbath.

Whatever open space there was then in the early settlement of North America was used as commons, pasture land, or training grounds in hunting. The term commons describes a piece of land to be shared and enjoyed by all members of the community. By the mid 1700s, the open space was used for recreational pursuits and other amusements. The Dutch settlers in New York, who were less restrained in their religious beliefs, organized a few recreational activities after the Sunday service over the objection of church leaders. Also, wealthy Southerners began to socialize and to recreate on the Lord's Day. By the middle of the 1700s the American lifestyle included many recreational activities, among which were pursuits in natural settings such as hunting, fishing, skating, sleighing, and tobogganing. Resorts became fashionable among the wealthy of that era.

Despite the proposal to the Continental Congress of 1774 to prohibit extravagance and dissipation such as horse racing,

gaming, and cockfighting, outdoor recreation increased steadily after the Revolutionary War, particularly on the frontiers. With America's westward expansion, the frontier people found in hunting, horse racing, rail tossing, and tomahawk hurling the needed release from a life of hard work and isolation. These were also occasions for get-togethers where ritualistic activities such as husking and quilting bees took place.

In the meantime, American cities were growing, and the need for open space was being felt. Chicago preserved a site for outdoor recreation near Fort Dearborn in 1839, but it was New York that built the first city park in 1853. Central Park was designed by Frederick Law Olmsted and Calvert Vaux. According to Taylor (1999) Central Park was a source of conflict between the elite, the middle class, and the working class. The first group sought the park as a tool of social control, the second group looked as it as a place for art, nature, and beauty, and the third group wanted active leisure. Olmsted later planned San Francisco's Golden Gate Park, Philadelphia's Fairmount Park, Boston's Franklin Park, and the District of Columbia's Rock Creek Park. More on the father of America's city parks later.

The second half of the nineteenth century witnessed a surge in organized sport such as baseball, basketball, and football, and in outdoor recreational pursuits such as hunting and fishing. Depletion of wildlife became a concern, and in 1887 two prominent sportsmen, Theodore Roosevelt and George Bird Grinnell, editor of *Forest and Stream Magazine*, formed the Boone and Crockett Club to deal with conservation issues on the national level.

Conquering the wilderness during the western expansion meant the destruction of many of America's forests, to which Franklin B. Hough, head of the 1870 census, sounded the alarm. In 1876 the U.S. Congress authorized him to study the issue, and his reports led to the creation of the Division of Forestry in the U.S. Department of Agriculture in 1881—the forerunner of today's U.S. Forest Service, U.S. Department of Agriculture.

Meanwhile, many of the states on the eastern seaboard began to establish game preserves. Deer parks were established to preserve this popular game animal. The concept of preservation reached its pinnacle in 1872 with the establishment of America's first national park.

Although there were two earlier precedents for national preserves, at Hot Springs, Arkansas, in 1832 and Yosemite Valley, California, in 1864, the concept of a national park was born with Yellowstone in 1872. The significance of this event was in the change in public policy from allowing private exploitation of America's natural resources to the setting aside of public land for protection and public enjoyment. In 1890, a bill was passed in the U.S. Congress creating Yosemite National Park. Two years later, naturalist John Muir formed the Sierra Club to explore, preserve, and enjoy the mountains of the West Coast of the United States.

The concept of preservation spilled over into America's forests when President Harrison created a 13-million-acre forest preserve in 1891 to which President Cleveland added 20 million acres in 1897. Gifford Pinchot enhanced our knowledge of forests as the first American to study forest management in Europe. In 1896, the Division of Biological Survey was created in the U.S. Department of Agriculture to administer wildlife refuges. It became the forerunner of the U.S. Fish and Wildlife Service, Department of the Interior, when it was combined with the Bureau of Fisheries, U.S. Department of Commerce, in 1940.

President Theodore Roosevelt appointed a National Conservation Commission in 1908, which put together an inventory of America's natural resources. He also took executive actions to preserve vast federal lands as forest preserves, wildlife refuges, and national monuments. Eight years later, in 1916, the National Park Service was established, and in 1924 the first Wilderness Area was designated in the Gila National Forest. The same year witnessed the first National Conference on Outdoor Recreation. Three years earlier, opening of the Appalachian Trail ushered in a new concept in outdoor recreation. Illinois became the first state to establish a state park system in 1909, followed by Indiana in 1919. The first national conference on state parks took place in 1921, and five years later the Federal Recreation Act made some public domain lands available to states for parks.

During the Depression years, and despite the economic conditions, Americans saw the opening of their first scenic parkway, the Blue Ridge Parkway. The Tennnessee Valley Authority was created to provide the needed energy to vitalize the region and to control floods, but it also created many opportunities for outdoor recreational pursuits.

In the 1940s, the Bureau of Land Management was formed to control most federal real estate. The Flood Control Act of 1944 charged the U.S. Army Corps of Engineers with providing recreation on many of the reservoirs it built. A 1948 amendment to the 1944 Surplus Property Act provided for the transfer of surplus federal lands at 50 percent of fair market value for use as state and local parks and recreational areas.

The Outdoor Recreation Resources Review Commission and the resultant Bureau of Outdoor Recreation were created in the 1950s. Motivated by the ORRRC report, many state and local governments passed laws for bond issues to acquire more open space. In 1962, the National Park Service began a ten-year mission renovation program. The U.S. Forest Service began Operation Outdoors for the purpose of revitalizing its offerings.

The 1960s witnessed the passage of many federal acts, the impact of which is felt today on outdoor recreation. Among these is the Multiple Use-Sustained Yield Act, which formalized multiple use in national forests and added outdoor recreation to the statutory list of activities provided on these lands. Other federal legislation passed in the 1960s included the Land and Water Conservation Act, the National Wilderness Preservation System

Act, and the Federal Water Project Recreation Act, all of which provided significant funds for federal grants to be matched by equal state and local funds for outdoor recreation areas. The National Trails System Act and the National Wild and Scenic Rivers Act embodied new and significant concepts for outdoor recreation in America.

Significant acts for outdoor recreation were passed in the 1970s, too. The Volunteers in the Park Act authorized the National Park Service to utilize volunteers in its system. Also of significance was the Youth Conservation Corps Act, which employed youth in both the National Park Service and the U.S. Forest Service. A new approach was tested at that time, which was the addition of urban recreation areas to the National Park Service, for example, the Gateway National Recreation Area in New York City and the Golden Gate National Recreation Area in San Francisco. Revenue-sharing programs of the 1970s helped in the establishment of many state and local parks.

According to Clawson (1985:79), a major development at that time was the great expansion of privately owned, privately financed, and privately operated outdoor facilities. These include ski areas, water sport areas, amusement parks, campgrounds, and resorts in outdoor settings. Another important development was the application of new technologies to outdoor settings, the results of which were the modem activities of scuba diving, snowmobiling, and recreational vehicle camping.

Today, thanks to the insight of a few persons and to the foresight of America's legislators, Americans are enjoying a lifestyle that includes many opportunities for active and contemplative recreation in outdoor settings.

A parallel movement for the provision of outdoor recreation areas was taking place in Canada (see Chapter 11). Canada and the United States and, to some extent, Australia led the world in this movement. It took the rest of the world almost another one hundred years to try to catch up with these three societies. Leisure and recreation (including outdoor pursuits) are becoming an important part in the lifestyles of many of today's world citizens. The following factors have led to this development.

Leisure and Recreation: A Human Right

In 1948 the General Assembly of the United Nations adopted the Universal Declaration of Human Rights. The member nations at that time agreed to the following principle:

> Every citizen has the right to rest and leisure, including reasonable limitation of working hours, and periodic holidays with pay ... and ... the right to freely participate in the cultural life of the community, to enjoy the arts. ...
>
> (U.N. 1978)

This statement by the U.N. represents the culmination of many human endeavors to achieve such a right. It may have begun with the Sixth Right, which evolved among the Ancient Israelites. The first five rights were the Right to Live, the Right of Possession, the Right to Work, the Right to Clothing, and the Right to Shelter. The Sixth Right included a provision for a Sabbath. Although the Sabbath was originally for rest and worship, it provided the opportunity for recreation activities that took place at later dates among the Israelites (Ibrahim & Shivers, 1979:55).

The ancient Greeks were also interested in the idea of leisure. The free men among them took it seriously and sent their offspring to schole, the institution where the young would learn the arts of graceful living, music, philosophy, art, and gymnastics. As mentioned earlier, it was their philosopher Aristotle who underscored leisure as an important ingredient of the good life.

Ibn Khaldun, the Arab philosopher of the fourteenth century, went as far as claiming the desire for leisure as the fifth layer of a five-layer schema of human desires, the first of which is bodily appetites, followed by the desire for safety and calm, the desire for companionship, and the desire for superiority (lbrahim, 1988). The fifth and last of these desires would be satisfied with the United Nations resolution quoted previously. Many nations are working to provide the same right. But the resolution alone did not contribute to the rise of leisure pursuits in today's world.

Increased Free Time

Although time freed from civic and familial obligations began with the rise of the leisure class, as suggested by Veblen (1953), leisure in its "pure" form, as a state of being, did not materialize until very recently. The Sabbath was observed as a day of rest from labor among the Israelites and early Christians, albeit as a day devoted to worship. Labor time was measured by the day that started at sunrise and ended at sundown, leaving little or no free time to speak of. Conditions became worse with the coming of the Industrial Revolution, which initially emphasized production over human happiness.

The movement to reduce work hours among labor began in the United States when, in the early 1800s, Boston machinist Ira Stewart formed the Grand Eight-Hour League of Massachusetts (Viau 1939:25). Much later, the World Labor Organization passed a bill for 40-hour workweeks and a 12-day annual vacation in 1966. Both France and Great Britain had adopted a 40-hour workweek in 1919, which became the standard for many of the industrialized nations.

The standard for paid annual vacation adopted in most of the industrialized nations was two weeks initially, and it has reached four weeks in some of these nations today (Samuel, 1986). Recently, France decreed a five-week vacation for its citizens. Adding to free time is the sometimes compulsory retirement from work. Paid retirees are now a fact of life in most countries, not only among those who served in industry but also in services and trade. Productivity in industry, services, and trade continues at a very high level, thanks to the increased use of machines in the twentieth century, which has made even more free time available to people. Assist-ing in the increase of free time is both industrialization and automation. Although some scholars decry the decline of leisure (Schor, 1991), the demand for more free time continues (Boggis, 2001).

Industrialization and Automation

Initially the Industrial Revolution created unpleasant conditions for those who became pegs in its machinery. Emigration to industrial centers led to crowded conditions in the cities of western Europe and North America. These slum dwellers included many children who worked long hours. Even when the conditions improved, industrialization revolved around tedious repetitive small tasks for the individual worker, and the need for outlets became very apparent. A need for outlets that "would exercise the workers' creative energy and provide a sense of achievement and accomplishment became pressing for people ..." (MacLean et al., 1985:44). Recreation, including outdoor pursuits, provided the required outlets. Many social reformers worked on providing facilities and programs of recreation. The Playground Association of America was organized in 1906. It was renamed the Playground and Recreation Association of America in 1911, became the National Recreation Association in 1930, and merged with other associations in 1965 to become the National Recreation and Park Association. The association published *Playground Magazine,* now *Parks and Recreation.* The need for such an organization grew as the world's population shifted from the countryside to urban cities.

Urbanization

In the mid 1800s there were 85 cities in the United States. Most people lived in the country. By 1910 the number of American cities with populations over 100,000 increased to 50. In Canada there were 20 communities with populations over 5,000 by the mid 1800s; by the turn of the century there were 62. The trend is not limited to North America or western Europe. Today there are 83 cities in the world with populations over one million. Only 18 are in

Europe, and nine are in North America. There are 39 in Asia, seven in what used to be the Soviet Union, seven in South America, and three in Africa.

Urban life itself may have increased the need for recreational outlets, including outdoor ones. More importantly is the role that urbanization plays in modernizing, meaning not only economic growth, but cultural and social changes as well. Services such as education, both formal and informal, are easier to provide in urban centers. Improved literacy rates lead to more sophisticated demands, one of which is the demand for recreation outlets. As will be shown in Chapter 5, The Social Aspects of Outdoor Experiences, the higher the education acquired, the more the demand for recreation and for outdoor pursuits in particular. There are calls today for the provision of recreational activities, particularly in the outdoors, for the urban centers of the World (Griffiths, 2001). But since most outdoor facilities are located away from urban centers, those who are interested in partaking of an outdoor pursuit must find not only the time but also the means to get there. Mechanized transportation is a fact in modern life.

Transportation

The steam engine was mounted on vehicles and propellers that had tremendous impact on recreation in North America and abroad: the train and the steamboat. Among the first transportation systems that encouraged outdoor recreation on a large scale is the railroad. The Train Excursion, which was organized on Easter Day of 1844, provides a good example of the role of mass transportation in outdoor pursuits. The Excursion, from London to the seaside resort of Brighton, created popular excitement (Lowerson & Myerscough, 1977:32). In the United States, the steamboat carried people and horses to racing centers along the Mississippi River in the antebellum era. The railroad helped transport people to the growing athletic events, both on the intercollegiate and professional levels after the Civil War. The same was taking place in Canada.

But it was the invention of the internal combustion engine that helped in the explosion of outdoor recreation. In the last decade of the nineteenth century, the automobile was introduced, and Henry Ford converted it into a means of popular transportation. While auto racing became the leisure activity revolving around this new tool initially, outdoor facilities, being large, were being built outside urban centers, and the masses used their automobiles to get to golf courses, ski resorts, campgrounds, fishing spots, and hunting lodges.

It was not until World War I that the airplane became commercialized. Today it has become the carrier for millions of people seeking rest and recreation in spots that in times past were frequented only by the privileged few. Tourism has become an important international business. Within the United States and Canada, another important means of recreational travel has evolved: the RV (recreational vehicle). Its sales peaked in 1972, at 540,000 a year in the United States, then leveled off and saw a drastic drop until 1985, when sales began to pick up again (Barker, 1986:15). Also, pleasure boats have seen a surge in popularity. They may represent a status in life that indicates some form of prestige. This is a function of social mobility.

Mobility

The mere provision of a vehicle such as an RV or a boat does not automatically mean that its owner will visit a park or engage in an outdoor pursuit. Mobility has a psychological dimension as well as a social dimension. The social dimension refers to the movement of an individual from one status to another. Upward mobility leads to improvement in status, downward mobility moves a person to a lower status, and horizontal mobility leads to a new and different status that is similar to the old one. Mobility is a phenomenon that is seen in open societies, the ones that allow for changes in one's status. This creates a psychological dimension that not only allows but also prompts the individual to go after the benefits to be accrued from the new, upward status, such as the type of recreation and the life-style enjoyed by the members of the desired "class." People seek higher pay, longer vacations, and the ability to afford an RV and/or a pleasure boat for both psychological and social reasons. Perhaps the article in *Transportation Quarterly* is the testimony that travel associated with leisure activities has become increasingly important (Lawson, 2001).

SUMMARY

In this work, outdoor recreation is defined as the organized free-time activities that are participated in for their own sake and where there is an interaction between the participant and an element of nature. Such activities are predicated on the tendencies to play and to ritualize. Both of these tendencies have biological roots as well as evolutionary dimensions. Observation of play among animals, particularly the higher forms, along with the studies of the human brain show how profound the tendency to play is. Meanwhile, the tendency to ritualize is seen in ceremonies and celebration of many human societies. Also, outdoor recreational pursuits are affected by a recent phenomenon, leisure, which describes the state of mind that allows a person to participate in an activity solely for the sake of that activity during the time freed from civic and familial obligations.

The need for recreational outlets overcame the objection of those who considered such pursuits as wasteful, if not sinful, among the early European settlers of the New World. Open spaces that were allocated for meeting, grazing, and training of hunters evolved into parks. Fear of wanton destruction of the vast, yet limited, natural resources on this continent led to the rise of a preservation movement which led to the establishment, for the first time in human history, of natural areas allocated for the enjoyment of extant and future generations. A concept of federally designated national parks, born in the United States with the establishment of Yellowstone National Park, is adopted by many nations today.

Expansion of outdoor recreational opportunities required the establishment of many agencies at the federal, state, and local levels. This was in response to demands that were accelerated by 1) the adoption of the Universal Declaration of Human Rights by the General Assembly of the United Nations in 1948, which includes the right to leisure and recreation; 2) an increase in free time for almost every citizen in many countries regardless of social class and life-style; 3) the advent of industrialization and automation, which allowed for more free time; 4) an increase in urbanization with the resultant increase in the need for outdoor recreational outlets; 5) the provision of adequate means of transportation that takes the desiring person to the spot of his or her choice; and 6) mobility with its social as well as psychological dimensions that, in the case of upward mobility, drives one to seek recreational pursuits that correspond to the newly acquired status.

REFERENCES

Barker, R. (1986, February 24). On the road to recovery: RV makers rev up for a strong year. *Barons, 15*, 28-30.

Berlyne, D. E. (1960). *Conflict, arousal and curiosity.* New York: McGraw-Hill.

Blanchard, K., & Cheska, A. (1985). *The anthropology of sport: An introduction.* South Hadley, MA: Bergin and Garvey.

Boggis, J. J. (2001). The eradiction of leisure, new technology, *Work and Employment, 16*(2).

Clawson, M. (1985). Outdoor recreation: Twenty-five years of history, Twenty-five years of projection. *Leisure Sciences, 7*(I), 73-99.

Deegan, M. J. (1989). *American ritual dramas: Social rules and culture meanings.* Westport, CT: Greenwood Press.

deVore, I. (1965). *Primate behavior.* New York: Holt, Reinhart and Winston.

Edwards, C. P. (2000). Children's play in cross cultural perspective. *Cross Cultural Research, 34*(4), 318

Eisen, G. (1988). Theories of play. In G. Gerson et al. (Eds), *Understanding leisure*. Dubuque, IA: Kendall-Hunt.

Griffiths, J. (2001). Playing for time: The importance of recreation in society. *The Ecologist, 31(4)*, 52.

Grimmes, R. (1982). *Beginnings in ritual studies*. Landham, MD: University. Press of America.

Huizinga, J. (1950). *Homo ludens*. New York: The Beacon.

Ibrahim, H. (1991). *Leisure and society: A comparative approach*. Dubuque, IA: Wm. C. Brown.

Ibrahim, H. (1988). Leisure, idleness and ibn khaldun. *Leisure Studies, 7*, 51-58.

Ibrahim, H., & Shivers, J. (1979). *Leisure: Emergence and expansion*. Los Alamitos, CA: Hwong Publishing.

Lancaster, J. B. (1975). *Primate behavior and the emergence of human culture*. New York: Holt, Rinehart and Winston.

Lawson, C. T. (2001). Leisure travel/activity decision: Time and location differences. *Transportation Quarterly , 55(3)*, 51.

Lowerson, J., & Meyerscough, J. C. (1977). *Time to spare in Victorian England*. Hassocks, Sussex: Harvester Press.

Mahoney, J. L. & Stattin, H. (2000). Leisure activities and adolescent antisocial behavior: The role of structure and social context. *Journal of Adolescence, 23(2)*, 113.

Marano, H. E. (1999). The power of play. *Psychology Today, 32*, 36.

McLean, J. J., Peterson, & Martin, W. D. (1985). *Recreation and leisure: The changing scene*. New York: Macmillan.

Ornestein, R., & Thompson, R. (1984). *The amazing brain*. New York: Houghton-Mifflin.

Roth, W. C. (1902). *Games, sports and amusements*. Brisbane, Australia: G. A. Vaughan, Government Printer.

Pati, A. B. et al, (1997). Recreation/ leisure interest of inpatients rehabilitation clients, *Physical Therapy, 79(5)*, 78.

Sagan, C. (1977). *The dragons of Eden*. New York: Random House.

Schor, J. B. (1991). *The overworked Americans: The unexpected decline of leisure*. New York: Basic Books.

Taylor, D. E. (1999). Central Park as a model for social control: Urban Parks, social class and leisure behavior in nineteenth century America. *Journal of Leisure Research, 31(4)*, 420.

Turner, V. (1982). *From ritual to theatre: The human seriousness of play*. New York: Performance Arts Journal Publication.

United Nations (1978). *Human rights: A compilation of international instruments*. New York: United Nations.

Veblen, T. (1953). *The theory of leisure class*. New York: New American Library.

Viau, J. (1939). *Hours and wages in American organized labor*. New York: George Putnam and Sons.

The Washington Post, (1998, June 30). See E. p.1, 11

Wolf, D. D. (1984). Repertoire, style, and format: Notions worth borrowing from children's play. In P. Smith (Ed.), *Play in animals and humans*. Oxford, England: Basil Blackwell.

Wood, J. (1871). *The uncivilized races of man*. Hartford, CT: J.B. Burr.

2 | NATURE AND THE SPIRITUAL LIFE

One aspect of American outdoor recreation is a person's respect for, and, in some cases, even reverence for nature. This reverence is characteristic of some of the early leaders who laid the foundation for preservation of federal lands, and it is an important part of American Indian cultural and spiritual heritage. In this chapter we will explore American Indian reverence for nature and address Western attitudes toward nature.

Historically, respect for nature was challenged by American cultural values as seen in the Industrial Revolution during the latter half of the nineteenth century and on into the beginning of the twentieth century. In recent years there has been a movement toward a renewed reverence for nature due to the influence of the ecology and health movements, and due to a spiritual reawakening. The origins of the modern reverence for nature are traced to the philosopher Jean-Jacques Rousseau, who popularized the notion that the world in its natural state is closer to the truth (Clark, 1969). Contemporary writers like Thomas Berry in *The Great Work (2000)* and *The Dream of the Earth* (1990) and George Sessions in *Deep Ecology for the 21st Century* (1995) advocate a spirituality that includes a fresh respect for the universe and a more harmonious relationship with nature.

As North Americans penetrate the new millennium with a rekindled sense of spiritual interest, the study of recreation's connections with the spiritual will be among the most important emerging areas of research in the field, and park and recreation professionals will increasingly need to manage leisure resources to accommodate the support of spiritual benefits (Zuefle, 1999:48-49). This area of research emerged into the mainstream of public land management during a 1992 multiperspective focus group session of public land managers and other experts to discuss spiritual values and the rapid increase in the use of public lands to refresh the human spirit (Iverson, 1997). The study of spiritual connections with natural places is of vital importance in achieving a complete and balanced view of the diversity inherent in the outdoor recreation experience.

The editors of *Nature and the Human Spirit: Toward an Expanded Land Management Ethic* (Driver et al, 1996) cite three broad trends that have reawakened people's awareness of the connection between nature and the human spirit. First, there has been a shift to a faster-paced life in urban areas where there is a perceived loss of predictability and control; second, there is a widespread orientation toward physical activity, nutrition, and the nurturance of more satisfying relationships aimed at a sense of fitness and inner peace; and third, there is an increased concern for the natural environment and the contribution that environment makes to the quality of life. Practitioners and visionaries alike call for an expanded land management ethic that adds to the foundation set by Aldo Leopold. For many, this expanded base includes the deeper spiritual and psychological meanings of land.

A Spiritual Relationship to Nature

The origins of the relationship of nature and the spirit are tracked by archeologists and anthropologists to the dawn of human civilization when much of the world was predicated on the worship of a single earth goddess who communicated a sense of harmony among all living things (Gore, 1993:260). When we focus on American history as it relates to nature, the spiritual emphasis plays an interesting role, particularly when we refer to the leisure experience. The first stage was an early relationship with nature. American Indians celebrated and ritualized nature, making efforts to achieve harmony and continuity with its many forces and its animal and plant life. The second stage occurred with the arrival of the pioneers. Eager to begin a new life in a new country, the pioneers felt compelled to conquer nature. The third stage was a time of dualities. The wilderness was less threatening, and with more leisure time available, transcendentalists began a philosophical movement back to nature. But during this stage, industrialization resulted in the exploitation of American lands. Fortunately, foresighted citizens sought the protection of significant public lands, which today provide a setting for a reawakening of the process of spiritual refreshment.

Spirituality

Spirituality, often mistakenly used interchangeably with *religion,* can be thought of as a personal belief in, or a search for a reason for one's existence; a greater or ultimate reality, or a sense of connection with God, nature, or other living beings. This differs from *religion*, which is commonly perceived as organized and institutional in nature; a group experience with accepted beliefs and traditions (Zuefle, 1999:28). When the two become entangled, authors often err by using the term *religion* to describe both activities. It is imperative that public park and recreation professionals understand the difference. Outdoor programs that include spiritual benefits, for example, involve individuals with and without specific religious faiths, whereas programs that focus on specific religious practices may well be in violation of federal and state constitutions. In abiding by state and federal requirements, some experts agree that in recent years physical wellness has been emphasized, and now we are in the beginning stages of the realization that individuals have spiritual wellness needs that pertain to the out-of-doors experience and that people are actively seeking inner peace at special places (Bunting, 1989:35). Spiritual resources that can be found in the nature experience help to provide a route-finding system that enables people to navigate life's journey. Certainly bookshelves in bookstores do not lack in ways that we begin that search, with many references to experiences in nature as gateways to the inner life and the spiritual journey.

Leisure offers time for contemplation and meditation in which human values can be established and enriched. Educator and leader in the profession Jay B. Nash (1886-1965) deemed the highest form of recreational participation to be those activities in which the participant was most fully involved emotionally, physically, and creatively. The spiritual aspect of life, according to one specialist in the field (Kaplan, 1979:190), "opens us to the interdisciplinary, fusionary, holistic prospect of leisure that invites emotional, unforced, free adventuresome levels of experience." Another authority (Kraus,1984:335-36) finds that "leisure provides the arena in which personal values are shaped and in which the individual may reach the highest potential of which he or she is capable. Beyond the purely practical and purposeful goals that characterize work, it [leisure] offers a vision of life carried on for its own sake, in celebration of all that is vital and generous in people. William R. H. Stevens, a writer on leisure and religion, found that the essential spirit of leisure is that of celebration. ". . .Real joy is a condition of the spirit deeper than the mere fleeting experience of pleasurable sensation (Kaplan, 1979:187)."

Spiritual forms or aspects of leisure, then, are not limited to special philosophies or church programs. One of the most significant outcomes of the camp experience is the development of spiritual feelings and values. In this sense Mitchell and Meier (1993:173) define *spiritual* as connoting a keen appreciation of nature as well as a kinship with one's fellow beings and an orderly universe. *Religious* groups have used camps for spiritual settings for years, but *spiritual* experiences do not necessarily occur at formally arranged times or in specifically designated places. These experiences may occur when the senses are unusually heightened, such as when immersed in the wilderness, where the scent of pines, the fragrance of wildflowers, the dazzle of soft light at sunset, or the caress of a gentle wind that rustles through the trees provide opportunities to experience the deep beauty and complexity of life's mysteries and mystique.

There are two sides to the spiritual or sacred life: the personal, ecstatic side that individuals are at a loss of words to adequately describe, and the communal part, which may be celebrated year after year through oral histories, rituals, ceremonies, and customs (Beck & Walters, 1988:6). The camp experience can nurture both sides of this spiritual life. One can have an individual peak experience in which the wholeness of life is experienced in a mystical fashion while making an arduous ascent to the top of a mountain or while feeling the refreshing mist of a cascading waterfall. Group members may have a communal experience around the blazing campfire in which a unity of spirit and connectivity with others is achieved that elevates the group to a more intense spiritual experience. In each case something of the mystery of life is revealed, albeit for a brief moment.

American Indians experienced a rich spiritual life that permeated their entire life, both individually and communally. Their experience is germane to outdoor recreationists in that they lived close to nature and spent much of their lives in the out-of-doors. Their spiritual life continuously celebrated nature in its diverse aspects. They, too, sensed the mystical in nature that we will later see hikers and backpackers, for instance, refer to as some of life's most profound experiences.

American Indians and the Native American Experience

American Indians view themselves as part of a delicate and balanced universe, not as its masters. In their world view, all life forms and natural elements are connected, interrelate, and interplay: no part of nature is considered more important than another. They further believe, generally, that only humans can upset this balance on earth. Everything is naturally alive, and ceremonies serve to maintain harmony with the pervasive powers of nature, stressing the relationship of people with the cosmos. Chief Luther Standing Bear of the Oglala Sioux found that "only to the white man was nature a wilderness and only to him was the land infested with wild animals and savage people. To us it was tame. Earth was bountiful and we were surrounded with the blessings of the Great Mystery" (Stegner, 1990:35).

Most American Indians have two common beliefs that play significant roles in their sacred practices: first, a belief in a knowledge of unseen powers, and second, a belief in the knowledge that all things in the universe are dependent on each other. Unseen powers might be worshiped in elaborate ceremonial dance. The mysterious powers of nature, such as the way the seasons change, are often marked by collective rituals and ceremonials that recognize the spirits of the seasons and share the good they bring. The rituals provide order and systematize the way in which the society, the natural environment, and the unseen worlds meet and come together. The rituals provide a physical expression of a mystical experience. In this manner the participants come closer to understanding the mysteries of life. Historically the American Indian ritual cycle has contained many celebrations and liturgies that focus on harmony with nature.

Harmony with Nature

By living in harmony with nature, American Indians seek unity with a fundamental life force inherent in everything. For the Hopi Traditionalists, it is referred to as *Techqua Ikachi* which means "blending with the land and celebrating life (Mails, 1997:1)." Ceremonies, rites, and songs serve as aids. Rituals transform the mysterious into something more tangible. It is glorified and celebrated rather than explained. Rituals are not simple, crude, or barbaric; they are complex, pervasive, remarkable human processes that are central to life. Whether as straightforward as prescribing how meals are shared, or as intricate as how major events are marked, rituals give us ways to be playful or explore our lives. They provide human beings with ways of dealing with forces that seem beyond comprehension and control, and they help us make connections and transitions (Imber-Black & Roberts, 1997:1-2).

For example, puberty ceremonies among the Sioux were closely linked to nature. A young male would travel to a hilltop, forest, or remote shore in order to participate in his initiation ceremony or vision quest. Alone, he would contemplate and seek the aid of a spirit guide who would assist him in dealing with nature's spiritual life force. Fasting and thirsting for several days, he would suffer hardships while waiting for a vision or hallucination to appear. An honored animal with supernatural powers might appear, teaching a song or providing special instructions to aid the young initiate's personal power for the rest of his life. If these visions in nature were particularly intense, the young man might be called upon to be a shaman—a spiritual leader—for his people.

Another example is the Apache girl's puberty ceremony, where the earths creation, the creation of humankind, and the relationship of earth and humans are symbolically recreated. This momentous ritual extends over four days and four nights and honors the youth's entry into womanhood as she ritualistically represents Mother Earth or White Painted Woman.

NATURE, DANCE, AND CEREMONY

Human motion has served as a powerful medium in the American Indian celebration of nature. Through ritualized dance, the spiritual body transcends itself into a prayer for rain, a cure for one who has lost touch with the forces of nature, or a means to celebrate creation or to express gratitude for nature's gifts. Ceremonial dance may shape the circumstances of nature if focused appropriately on the receptive powers of animals. Through the interaction of forces, something more arises. Ritual dancers outwardly imitate entities of the natural world, but inwardly endeavor to transform themselves into these entities.

For example, the Yaqui deer dancer does not simply represent the image of a deer in the Deer Dance but seeks to transform himself into the deer itself. By doing so he honors his brother the deer while requesting that it willingly allow itself to be sacrificed by the hunter so that humankind might live. Since this native American does not try to dominate nature, his relationship to the deer is one of intimacy and courtesy (Cordes, 1990:4). Similarly, when a buffalo was killed, Lame Deer and Richard tell us, "We apologized to his spirit, tried to make him understand why we did it, honoring with a prayer the bones of those who gave their flesh to keep us alive, praying for their return, praying for the life of our brothers, the buffalo nation, as well as our own people" (1972:111).

To encourage animals to return and regenerate as game, the Alaskan Eskimos of Nunivak Island held a dance and feast in honor of the souls of game animals. Throughout the year hunters saved the bladders of the animals for a symbolic burial at the conclusion of the annual ceremony so that the animals could return to earth as game. Some American Indians

The largest known serpent-effigy mound in the world is found at Serpent Mound State Park in southern Ohio. The mound exemplifies American Indian ritual artifacts that express veneration of wild creatures.

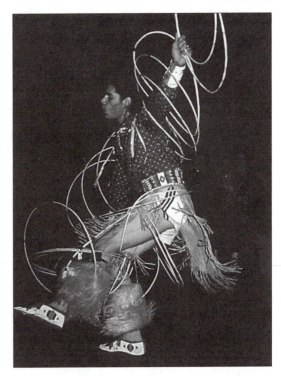

To many tribes, the hoop symbolizes the world or the universe. Time and even the seasons move in a circle.

utilized animal fetishes, which are objects of any material worn or cherished to ward off evil or attract good fortune. Their use dates from pre-Columbian times. To the Zunis of the Southwest—among the most skillful carvers of fetishes—the objects represent the "Breath of Life." Mother Earth, rain, and all of the life-giving forces upon which humans depend are represented by various fetishes. The living power believed to exist in the fetish provides support for the person wearing it.

An animal fetish worn over the heart during the hunt, for example, magically provides aid to the hunter through the charms quality of instinctiveness. The fetish's heart will overcome the heart of the animal preyed upon, ultimately causing the prey to weaken by charming its senses. Likewise, any phenomenon of nature can be associated with an animal analogous to that phenomenon. Lightning, for example, is personified by the snake. Both strike

instantly, may cause disastrous results, and are easily illustrated by a zigzag design. Since the snake is more closely aligned to lightning than is a human, but more closely related to humans than is lightning, the ritualized activity is directed and transmitted to the more mysterious and remote powers of nature through animals (Cushing, 1988:9,15, 39). In fact, the serpent fetish or ritualized image has been observed in all quarters of the earth. To some the snake is a "symbol of intelligence, of immortality, of protection against the power of evil spirits, and of a renewal of life and the healing powers of nature" (Bourke, 1984:412).

The Hopi Snake Dance is one of the most ancient snake ceremonies still performed. During the August ceremony on the Hopi mesas in Arizona, members of the Hopi snake clan collect snakes from the four cardinal directions: North, South, East, and West. After several days of private rituals, members dance in the plaza wearing short kilts painted with zigzag lines of lightning, each carrying a snake, referred to as elder brother, in his mouth. After the snakes are properly blessed they are released to return to the four sacred directions of the earth accompanied by the Hopi prayer for rain. Rain-laden August clouds often bypass the semiarid Hopi mesas, but after the ceremony the skies generally open to pour down rain, filling dry washes with wild, muddy water (Fergusson, 1988:150, 162-67; Fewkes, 1986:294-95;).

Nature, Architecture and the Cosmos

A culture's relationship with nature may be evident in its sense of space. The ancient ancestors of the Pueblo people, who lived in Arizona, Colorado, Utah, and New Mexico, ritualized their relationship to the land, which represented the divine. This outlook is evident in their architecture, which manifests balance and harmony with the landscape. The *kiva* or ceremonial center of the Pueblo represents the sacred center of the world. A symbol of the supernatural order of the universe, the kiva is described by an Acoma account as a sacred model of the world. Trees were symbolized by the four pillars that supported the roof, each pillar pointed in one of the four sacred directions, the sky is represented by the walls, and the Milky Way is represented by the beams of the roof. Kivas were originally built in a circular shape so the ceiling could take on the appearance of the sky. Correspondingly in the Navajo hogan, the door faces east to the rising sun with the fireplace centrally located, symbolizing the cosmic center. Smoke rises through the hole in the ceiling so that the incense will rise to the gods (Hadingham, 1984:150; Highwater, 1982:122-124).

Observatories were built by ancient peoples to record the movement of the solar system. Some of the observatories can be visited today in Hovenweep National Monument in Utah, Casa Grande National Monument in Arizona, and Chichen ltza in Mexico. Winter and summer solstices and

This five-story, 20-room cliff dwelling built by the Salado Indians around 1100 A.D. manifests balance and harmony with the land. The site in northern Arizona is protected by Montezuma Castle National Monument.

fall and spring equinoxes were observed by sungazers through alignments with geological features such as mountain peaks, caves, and rock formations. Rock art such as that of the Chumash Indians of California appears to represent the sun, moon, stars, eclipses, and comets. Chumash priests held daily rituals to interpret the behavior of the sky. The event causing the greatest apprehension was the winter solstice. Fearing that the sun might not choose to return, the entire community would gather for midwinter ceremonies. The high priest, personifying the "Image of the Sun," would impersonate the sun's rays. Ceremoniously he would anchor a wooden shaft into the ground as an emblem of the axis of the world. Capped with a stone disc symbolizing the sun, it was positioned so that only the shadow of the stone would appear on the ground during both solstices. At the appropriate time he would strike it with a magic stone and

Structures such as this one in Chaco Culture National Historical Park in New Mexico provide evidence of the celestial observations of Pueblo pre-Columbian civilization.

recite an incantation designed to pull the sun back toward the earth.

THE WESTERN VIEW OF NATURE

When agriculture replaced hunting and gathering as the dominant form of subsistence, there was a radical change in the way people responded to their natural surroundings. As westerners departed from wild nature, their view of nature revolved more around the belief that humans are superior to all other life forms and that the universe exists to serve the needs of human beings. Value began to be placed on those life forms that demonstrated usefulness to humans (Sessions, 1995:158-159). Ritual was relegated to an inferior position and was not incorporated intentionally into the predominant technological society.

Even basic ritualistic symbols were considered too simple for the language-bound mentality of Western people. European America was cut off from rhythmic-natural expressiveness, and most of the population tended to neutralize, rather than ritualize, nature (Highwater, 1982:144-48). Thinking became more linear, with high value placed on logic, organization, critical thinking, and judicious planning (Gernes, 2000:33). Granted, there are many positives in the advancements of human society, nonetheless, many believe that the loss of the link between people and nature is a negative outcome (Garvey, 1990:48).

The Movement Away from Ritual and Nature

The movement away from ritual and nature started long ago in both East and West. By the time the cultures of Egypt and the Far East arose, ritual had become highly structured and formalized visually to influence an observer, not the participant. As priesthood developed in Egypt, Greece, and Rome, the concern was with the organization of a sociopolitical structure, no longer with the power in nature but with the hierarchy (Highwater, 1985:40). The original impulse, which had given rise to the ritual, receded and ritual came to express literal ideas. For instance, during the Hellenic Age, dance had symbolically expressed the humanistic value system, while in the Middle Ages it transformed into a source of entertainment. By the time of the Renaissance, ballet emerged as an art form. Early Western architecture also turned away from nature. For example, departing from early temples, the Greek temple was a place to worship human-conceived divinity rather than nature's divinity (Highwater, 1982:124). Although balanced artistically, the temple was not viewed as a part of nature.

When the new culture of America unfolded, pioneers generally had an antagonistic attitude toward the wilderness. For them the wilderness posed dangers, and the major value to them of the forest was seen as a source of wood for shelter and warmth. Contrasting with the American Indian outlook, the pioneers believed that civilization, not nature, conveyed the sacred life-style. In Europe and America, the ensuing romantic period dissolved some of these antagonistic attitudes toward nature by recognizing nature's seductive splendor, mystery, and spiritual potential. During this period, life was more comfortable and nature less intimidating. Philosopher Jean-Jacques Rousseau (1712-1778) is credited with leading the return to the notion that primal peoples were rational in seeking harmony with nature. He was not at all convinced that the technological advancements of Western society were an improvement in the social condition. This transitional period opened the door to the romantic movement and later to Transcendentalism, a movement that established nature as the vehicle to life consciousness and greater spiritual wisdom.

In the eighteenth century, a few Europeans began to recognize the charm of the lakes and mountains of Switzerland. Mountains had been previously seen as an obstacle or nuisance, inhibiting travel and communication; and their recreational potential was not developed. In fact, only a few European contacts with the mountains were recorded in history prior to this period. In 1340 the poet Petrarch climbed a mountain to see the view from the top. Leonardo da Vinci (1452-1519) wandered around the Alps to study botany and geology, and developed and maintained a constant interaction in the study of nature throughout his career. The Flemish artist Peter Brueghel (1525-1569) painted the Alps in an inspired fashion ahead of his time (Clark, 1969; Marani, 2000:304).

Recorded, too, was Saint Francis of Assisi's (1181/82-1226) special relationship with nature, and his belief in the equality of all creatures rather than human domination over creation (Sessions, 1995:100, 160). Dutch philosopher Baruch Spinoza (1632-1677) drew upon ancient Jewish pantheistic roots of aligning God with nature, but few other instances are noted. Spinoza's beliefs that humans can only obtain happiness and dignity by identifying

The outdoor experience can be more spiritual than physical as the beauty of nature inspires awe in the recreationist's soul and, at times, a sense of the deeper truths in life.

themselves with all of nature inspired future environmentalists as well as eighteenth century Romantics, including English poet William Wordsworth (1770-1850) whose poems and essays expressed a new attitude toward nature (Sessions, 1995:162-163, 168). Reflecting the increase in harmony with nature, the layout of English gardens began to evolve away from rigid walkways to more natural maze-like paths. And the practice of taking walks in the countryside became fashionable, in part inspired by Wordsworth, who took them frequently. Intellectuals, poets, and philosophers followed his lead (Clark, 1969).

Rousseau as a man was moved by the lakes and alpine valleys of Switzerland. His total absorption in nature was a mystical experience that ultimately had a profound effect on the Western mind

A spontaneous celebration of nature.

because it inspired him to set forth a new philosophy. In advocating for a return to nature to discover the ultimate source of reason, Rousseau opened his contemporaries to the beauty of nature. His original thinking caused him to be persecuted, and eventually he sought refuge on an island in Lake Bien around 1765, where he had a mystical experience. Listening and watching the rhythmic waves he surrendered himself completely to nature; he became at one with the experience. In a mystical fashion, he lost all consciousness of an independent self, and later realized that existence is nothing more than a succession of moments perceived through the senses. He said, "I feel, therefore I am." He believed the qualities of beauty and innocence he observed in nature were also present in human beings. He believed that "natural man" was virtuous, and he is credited with leading the return to the notion that primal peoples were rational in seeking harmony with nature. Rousseau's theories

are propounded in his treatise, "A Discourse In The Origins Of Inequality Among Men" (Clark, 1969; Marceau, 1998; 372-373).

Twenty years after Rousseau wrote his landmark treatise, the islands of Tahiti were explored, which seemed to confirm that the simple, natural existence of the natives was superior to the squalor that existed among the eighteenth century European communities. This attractive goodness of natural living, and the ability of a human being to completely surrender to nature in a mystical experience as Rousseau's, was a precursor of a reappearance of nature as a divinity. The common denominator was a desire to probe the depths of the soul and return to nature, which was acclaimed as the ultimate source of reason (Janson & Janson, 1997:672; Marceau, 1998:372). The early proponents of this belief, Rousseau, Wordsworth, German poet and natural philosopher Johann Wolfgang von Goethe (1749-1832), and English lyrical poet Samuel Taylor Coleridge (1772-1834), sought to approximate nature with Truth. Later, during the Romantic era, these concepts were embraced by a larger group of philosophers and artists.

Other significant breakthroughs in the nature movement occurred. The impressionist painters, in their efforts to depict the natural reflections in ripples of water, strove to paint an impression of sunlight. This attempt at pure depiction of the impression, first captured by Claude Monet (1840-1926) and Pierre Renoir (1841-1919), was an innovation in painting that suited painting outdoors. To capture the natural, the artists were completely immersed in the out-of-doors, the natural subject matter of their paintings. During the period of Post-Impressionism that followed in the late nineteenth century, Paul Gauguin (1848-1903) traveled to Tahiti and other South Pacific islands to capture the unspoiled natural life, where he could paint scenes of natural men and women. Although nature alone was no longer the subject matter, a return to the aesthetic primitive art allowed for a more personal

Pioneers brought a new view of nature. The wilderness was to be conquered and tamed. Today, the open spaces in land managed by the BLM in Wyoming are enjoyed by those traveling on the Oregon National Historic Trail. Reliving the experience of the past, modern travelers have a tendency to ritualize the camping experience with picnics, evening songs, and by telling stories.

spiritual expression of man's connection with nature.

Nature was the single most important source of inspiration for Art Nouveau artists and designers in Europe and North American between 1890-1914. Motifs from the natural world such as flower stalks and buds, vine tendrils, and insect wings, decorated buildings, furniture, glass, jewelry, ceramics, and textiles. In New York, Louis Comfort Tiffany (1848-1933), one of the greatest glass artists of his time, transformed colorful images of plants and insects into luminous glass creations that celebrated the natural world. While some designers conventionalized natural forms by creating abstract curvilinear patterns, others copied nature in a realistic manner, often to convey a sense of spiritual affinity with the natural world. Even American modern dancer Loie Fuller (1862-1928), who used cloth veils in a dance to trans-

form herself into a flower, inspired the artists who were exploring the metamorphosis and the idea that humankind was no longer above nature, but inextricably part of it (Janson & Janson, 1997:768-770; Greenhalgh & Griffith, 2000:2,4,10).

In the United States, a nineteenth century movement of New England writers and philosophers was based in a belief in the essential unity of all creation. The Transcendentalist movement, founded by Ralph Waldo Emerson (1803-1882) and Henry David Thoreau (1817-1862), viewed nature as a means to transcend everyday life to encounter the divine (see Chapter 3). This philosophy influenced future naturalists (discussed in Chapter 3) to attempt to preserve the American wilderness (Clark, 1969). However, people caught up in the economic expansion in America persisted in utilizing all the resources that nature provided in an effort to achieve a better life on earth. In general, western society continued to view nature as a means to an end with little thought given to the potential repercussions. Several elements of the present-day contemporary reverence for nature, referred to as "nature religion," trace their roots to these eighteenth and nineteenth century artists and philosophers. These elements are as follows (Clark, (1969):

1. Value exists in the simple life.
2. Walking is both a spiritual and physical exercise.
3. Mountains are viewed as sacred places, and clouds are sources of divine inspiration.
4. There is a healing power in nature.
5. Natural man is virtuous and in general sympathizes with the humble and downtrodden.
6. Nature equals truth.
7. As a result of total absorption in nature, one can lose one's sense of identity and become enraptured.

Modern authors such as Catherine Alabanese, Thomas Berry, Charles Cummings, Jamake Highwater, Jack Kornfield, Dolores LaChapelle, George Sessions, and Gary Snyder refer to the Western separation of humans from nature, and the need for a renewed reverence for the earth. Thomas Berry (1990:180-183) believes that this reverence for nature is important to our planet's survival. He joins another environmentalist, Gary Synder (1995:459-460), in the belief that we can relearn this attitude from the American Indians, who are overwhelmingly in support of a full and sensitive acknowledgment of nature. The American Indian was immersed in nature, in contrast to modern society's experiences in nature, which are usually brief and sandwiched between urban experiences.

Dolores LaChappelle (1995:62) explains that the Western European industrial culture developed a limited kind of practicality. In rationalizing their world, they developed the left side of the brain.

American Indians knew that their relationship with the natural world, however, called for a more holistic approach that would allow nonhumans to commune with humans. Rituals, ceremonies, and festivals present a sophisticated spiritual technology that allows humans to transcend the limitations imposed by the structure of language, normally associated with the left hemisphere of the brain. They allow the whole being—the rational and the spiritual—to connect with others and the nonhuman world through the use of the right and left hemispheres of the brain. By connecting with the world in various ways, we learn to respect the complexity that is inherent in the unity of the whole.

In turning to American Indians for inspiration, Jamake Highwater (1985:19-26) notes that contemporary dancers added natural movement and ritualization to dance. Finding ballet too standardized, dancers like Fuller (discussed earlier in this chapter) and Isadora Duncan (1877-1927) led the way to a free movement form. The new *modern dance* revived the oldest form of dance as a means to provide expression for that which cannot be externalized by rational means. Today ballet and modern dance companies utilize indigenous themes involving nature as a basis for choreography (Heth, 1993:170). Like the Yacqui deer dancer, performers did not simply imitate but became the dance by transforming themselves into the idea, the feeling, or the emotion. Ritual can also serve as a tool for learning to think logically, analogically, and ecologically as we move toward a sustainable culture (LaChappelle, 1995:62).

As seen in world literature, feelings of connectedness and/or relationship are nurtured through encounters with nature (Dustin, 1994:95). While the spiritual life may initially be focused on self-transformation and wise human relationships, Jack Kornfield (2000; 262-266) believes that these relationships ultimately lead to a oneness with the mountains. This oneness comes from a sense of selflessness that means taking a hard look at our habits, including consumerism, as they relate to our interconnections with the earth and all life on earth. Transformations of this magnitude are not automatic. To learn to lose our human-centeredness, outdoor educators may help by encouraging students to connect with something in nature. Along these lines, John Seed, an environmental leader, developed a group meditation, called Council of All Beings, that is practiced around the world. Participants spend time meditating and connecting with a particular part of the earth, for instance waterfowl or rivers or mountains. Later, in a group session, individuals speak for the part of the earth they represent. A representative of waterfowl, for example, perhaps of the Canadian geese, may speak of the flock's difficult seasonal migration because the places of rest and refreshment, the wetlands, are disappearing. Or a participant who personifies a river of life may tell of its sadness in carrying wastes and toxins. The representative of the mountains may talk about the steady peace it feels and offers to all who come to see it.

The goal is not to reenact American Indian rituals or return to a pioneer state of wilderness but to recognize that modern technological knowledge neglects the natural experience that humans actually yearn to experience. Increased visitations to national parks and wilderness areas may be in part attributable to this search for the natural, this longing. Catherine Albanese (1990:197-198) asserts that a call to the natural has grown out of an innate concern for the environment. She finds that more Americans are celebrating nature, and that a modern nature religion is growing. Charles Cummings (1991) refers to a similar phenomenon as eco-spirituality, or the reverence for life in all its diversity, including balance with nonliving things, by those with and without religious affiliation.

Citizens of the United States are again participating more intimately with nature. About 30 million Americans, for instance, belong to environmental organizations or maintain interest in environmental protection. There is also a growing public interest in outdoor-oriented travel (Honey, 1999:19).

One 1994 study found that 77 percent of North American consumers had taken a vacation involving nature, outdoor adventure, or learning about another culture, while estimates that track the development of ecotourism indicate an annual growth rate of 10 to 30 percent (Honey, 1999:6-7). Statistics indicate that the units of the National Park System as a group are now the largest tourist destination in the world (Tolbert, 2001:29). From 1980-1990, visitors to the National Park System in the United States rose by 20 percent, from about 190 million to more than 250 million (Honey, 1999:10). Now it receives nearly 290 million annual visitors, inclusive of visitors from abroad. In some cases, outdoor recreational activities provide more than the recreational and physical values of the activity—they provide a forum in which activities may become ritualized events allowing attainment of a spiritual level of oneness with nature. These outdoor activities may become a person's own vision quest in nature. And the event is not necessarily planned or anticipated. It could occur after a tiring day of hiking on a backpack trip or while enjoying a quiet moment of reflection on the grassy banks of a small stream. One hiker (Monczunski, 1990:39) described his experience as follows: "I was there under the blue sky. And I could only be there by being related to everything else that was there. Not only related, but really part of it, an extension of everything else. So I was not so significant, not so separate, not so egotistical, not so important, not so self-derived. I surrendered into it and was part of it."

Simply embarking on a journey may somehow signal newfound freedom, a liberation of spirit, an openness, and a willingness to experience (Leshner, 2001:27). Inspired and with insights deepened, one is more at peace. As one backpacker expressed it, "You walk, eat, sit, sleep. And when you've covered some miles, you realize you've learned as much about yourself as about the land you've crossed— and that what you've explored has been the geography of the soul. You may learn that Walt Whitman was right when he said, 'Now I see the secret of making the best persons. It is to grow in the open air and to

| Meditating in a giant redwood.

eat and sleep with the earth!,'" (Temple, 1990:42).

Today's outdoor rituals may be anachronistic: relating hunting to American Indians, survival skills to mountain men, or horseback riding to cowboys. Or a participant in the midst of nature's beauty may develop an acute awareness of its sights, sounds, and smells. A surfer may admire the power of the ocean, a climber may prepare for a gathering storm, and a birder may recognize a species vanishing into extinction. An intimacy with nature, with the mysteries of life, and even with the past can be achieved. Deeper experiences or spiritual occasions do not necessarily occur at formally planned times, but often unfold when the senses rise to unusual heights of perception (Meier & Mitchell, 1993:173). Experiences may come during periods of meditation focused on a single delicate flower in the wild, under a vast canopy of stars, or at the moment of reaching the summit of a mountain. These are times when awareness may reflect everything with total clarity and brightness, and when one's whole attitude towards life can be transformed (May, 1982:51).

The outdoors can bring us back to a natural order (Rolston, 1986:103). We return to basics, and are in contact with *creation*, which is at the root of the word *recreation*. While testing our prowess in the outdoors, we may be participating in our own individual nature ritual. As activities in nature become ritualized, the meaning of the activity becomes more important than the activity itself. The outdoors becomes a cathedral to the sacredness of nature. One backpacker writes, "I try to memorize the view, to lock this feeling inside my head" (Temple, 1990:44-45). The ego is lost in nature's magnificence as recreation merges with creation. "The happiest man," wrote Emerson, "is he who learns from Nature the lesson of worship" (Temple, 1990:42).

Clearly more than amusement is found in outdoor activities. Family backpack trips and camp-outs held every year at the same time are referred to as a yearly ritual and create deep family bonds. Through outdoor experiences, a common reality is shared. Various roles are assumed by the participants. Moreover, many organized camps plan daily activities which highlight the spiritual experience. Supplementary activities include (Meier & Mitchell, 1993:174):

1. grace before meals
2. outdoor vespers
3. sunrise services
4. cabin devotions or meditations before taps
5. attendance at religious services
6. group discussions
7. singing of hymns

A "wilderness cathedral" or "woodland chapel" located in a natural amphitheater, on a hilltop with a view of a valley, in a clearing surrounded by trees, or beside a gently flowing stream can set the stage for inspired thought (Meier & Mitchell, 1993:175). The ceremonial campfire may also serve as a significant spiritual event to campers. Typically these planned events start with a light mood, progress to a more serious tone, and focus on beauty and serenity of the group's experience together in nature. Some camps ceremonially mix partially burned wood and ashes from last year's campfire with the first fire of the year (Meier & Mitchell, 1993). Alternatives to the traditional fire include beams from flashlights, artificially colored lights, and slide presentations when laws or one's ethics prohibit building a fire.

The very nature of camp draws campers out of themselves and encourages spiritual growth (Drovdahl, 1991:26). Stepping out of their routine, campers at a campfire or those on a quiet hike have the opportunity to reflect. They may be surrounded by trees, mountains, sky and creatures, all elements in life not created by humans, yet related in an internal way. This environment is a natural theater for spiritual reflection or sense of gratitude for the life within, around, and beyond us (Brothers, 2000:7). Nature is a philosophical, psychological, scientific, economic, aesthetic, and recreational resource, and the great outdoors, as a spiritual resource, works on the recreationist's soul.

SUMMARY

In the past, Western civilization believed it had progressed beyond nature by outgrowing the experiences of primal peoples, leaving them behind and viewing their primitive experience less valuable than the focus and priorities of civilized society. The American Indian appears to symbolize harmony with nature. Authentic ceremonials on the reservations are religious observations, performed in the same spirit as religious ceremonies held anywhere in the world, and pervading all these ceremonies is the principle of living in harmony with nature. Today, the Westerner is seeking a more harmonious relationship with nature. The outdoor experience of the hiker, camper, or outdoor adventurer is often far more than that of a fun adventure; it has the capacity to offer spiritual renewal and awakening to many, and is even a life-altering, profound experience for some.

REFERENCES

Albanese, C. (1990)., *Nature religion in America*. Chicago and London: The University of Chicago Press.

Beck, P., & Walters, A. (1988). *The sacred*. Tsaile, AZ: Navajo Community College Press.

Berry, T. (1990). *The dream of the earth*. San Francisco: Sierra Club Books.

Berry, T. (2000). *The great work*. NY: Random House.

Bourke, J. (1984)., *Snake dance of the Moquis*. Tucson, AZ: The University of Arizona Press.

Brothers, J. (2000, October). You can lead a more joyful life. *Parade Magazine*, 6-8.

Bunting, C. (1989). The compatibility of physical education and outdoor education. *Journal of Physical Education, Recreation and Dance, 60*(2).

Clark, K. (1969). *The worship of nature (Civilization, Episode II)*. BBC Television Distributors.

Cordes, K. (1990). *Values of another culture through dance and ceremonials*. Proceeding of the International Conference on the Global Village. Miami, FL: Barry University.

Cummings, C. (1991). *Eco-Spirituality*. Mahwah, NJ: Paulist Press.

Cushing, F. (1988). *Zuni fetishes*. Las Vegas, NV: K. C. Publications.

Driver, B. L. et al. (1996). *Nature and the human spirit*. State College, PA: Venture Publishing, Inc.

Drovdahl, R. (1991, May). Touching the spirit. *Camping Magazine, 63*(7).

Dustin, D. (1994). Managing public lands for the human spirit. *Parks & Recreation, 29*(9), 92-96.

Farb, P. (1968). *Man's rise to civilization*. New York: E. P. Dutton and Co.

Fergusson, E. (1988). *Dancing Gods: Indian ceremonials of New Mexico and Arizona*. Albuquerque, NM: University of New Mexico Press.

Fewkes, J. (1986). *Hopi snake ceremonies*. Albuquerque, NM: Avanyu Publishing.

Garvey, J. (1990). The stories we live. *Notre Dame Magazine, 19*(1), 40-45.

Gernes, S. (2000). Soul at play. *Notre Dame Magazine, 29*(2), 33.

Gore, A. (1993). *Earth in the balance: Ecology and the human spirit*. New York: Penguin Books USA Inc.

Greenhalgh, P., & Griffith, M.. (2000). *Art nouveau*. Washington, D.C.: National Gallery of Art.

Hadingham, E. (1984). *Early man and the cosmos*. Norman, OK: University of Oklahoma Press.

Heth, C. (ed.). (1993). *Native American dance: Ceremonies and social traditions*. Washington, D.C.: National Museum of the American Indian Smithsonian Institution with Starwood Publishing, Inc.

Highwater, J. (1985). *Dance rituals of experience*. New York: Alfred van der Marck Editions.

Highwater, J. (1982). *The primal mind*. New York: Penguin.

Honey, M. (1999). *Ecotourism and sustainable development*. Washington, D.C.: Island Press.

Imber-Black, E., & Roberts, J. (1997). *Rituals for our times*. New York: HarperCollins Publishers, Inc.

Janson, H., & Janson, A. (1997). *The history of art*. New York: Harry M. Abrams, Inc., Publishers.

Kaplan, M. (1979). *Leisure: Lifestyle and lifespan*. Philadelphia: W. B. Saunders.

Kornfield, J. (2000). *After the ecstasy, the laundry*. New York: Bantam Books.

Kraus, R. (1984). *Recreation and modern society*. Glenview, IL: Scott, Foresman and Company.

LaChapelle, D. (1995). Ritual: The pattern that connects. In G. Sessions (Ed.), *Deep ecology for the 21st century* (pp. 58-63). Boston: Shambhala Pub, Inc.

Lame Deer, J., & Richard, E. (1972). *Lame Deer: Seeker of visions*. New York: Washington Square Press.

Leshner, M. (2001). Why travel? *Westways, 6*(4), 26-27.

Mails, T. (1997). *The Hopi survival kit*. New York: Media Holdings, Inc.

Marani, P. (2000). *Leonardo da Vinci*. New York: Harry N. Abrams, Inc.

Marceau, J. (ed.). (1998). *Art: A world history*. London: DK Publishing, Inc.

May, G. (1982). Will and spirit: *A contemplative psychology*. San Francisco: Harper San Francisco.

Meier, J., & Mitchell, A. V. (1993). *Camp counseling: Leadership and programming for organized camp*. Dubuque, IA: William C. Brown Communications, Inc.

Monczunski, J. (1990). What the hermits know. *Notre Dame Magazine, 19*(1), 33-39.

Rolston, H. (1986). *Beyond recreational value: The greater outdoors preservation-related and environmental benefits*. President's Commission on Americans Outdoors, Literature Review. Washington D.C.: U.S. Government Printing Office.

Sessions, G. (1995). Ecocentrism and the anthropocentric detour. In G. Sessions (Ed.), *Deep ecology for the 21st century*. (pp.356-375). Boston: Shambhala Pub., Inc.

Stegner, W. (1990, April). *It all began with conservation*. Smithsonian Associates. Washington, D.C.

Snyder, G. (1995). The rediscovery of Turtle Island. In G. Sessions (Ed.), *Deep ecology for the 21st century*. (pp. 454-462). Boston: Shambhala Pub., Inc.

Temple, K. (1990). "Over the Rise." *Notre Dame Magazine* 19(1):40-45.

Tolbert, G. (2001). "Promoting User-Friendly Tourism to U.S. National Parks." *People, Land & Water* 8(7):29.

Zuefle, C. (1999). "The Spirituality of Recreation." *Parks & Recreation* 34(5):28-48

3 VISIONARIES AND PIONEERS

The early Americans, including the Puritans and pioneers, ordinarily had an antagonistic attitude toward nature and wilderness, believing that it was to be tamed and conquered. The major value of the forest was to cut it down to provide wood for homes and shelters. These early attitudes began to change through the efforts of a few who recognized nature's mystery and spiritual potential. The romantics moved toward greater harmony with nature. Also, life in the mid-nineteenth century became more comfortable and nature less intimidating. Romanticism paved the way for transcendentalism, a philosophy that viewed nature as the vehicle to inspire intuitive thought that lifted the consciousness to greater spiritual wisdom. This mode of thought influenced future naturalists toward the preservation of the American wilderness.

THE TRANSCENDENTALISTS

As a mode of perception, transcendentalism became an indefinable movement of abstract American intellectual thought. It intrigued New Englanders during the mid-nineteenth century, some of whom were turning to an inner world and exploring oneness with the universe. To them natural objects commandeered significance, and if used properly they reflected universal spiritual truths. Two of the leading tran-scendentalists, Emerson and Thoreau, will be presented here. Both believed that human beings have the potential to transcend materialism. Emerson defined transcendentalism simply as "belief in the Higher Law of God" (Wolf, 1974:125). Henry David Thoreau expounded on Emerson's idea that when one is close to nature something happens to his or her perceptions. Inspired by Emerson, Thoreau lived close to nature in order to experience and express his own heightened senses. His writings focused on nature, describing what he beheld and, then, generalized about overlying implications. Emerson, on the other hand, focused his perceptions on the human being, using deductive logic and philosophical abstractions (Ronald, 1987:2). Many characteristics of Emerson's and Thoreau's transcendentalism, such as the trust in organic form, the correspondences between elements of the natural world, the concern with people's relationship to the environment, and the institution of being solitary, are echoed by naturalists today and continue to exert great influence on today's naturalism and wilderness preservation.

Ralph Waldo Emerson (1803-1882)

Born in Boston, Ralph Waldo Emerson became one of the most famous, original nineteenth century thinkers, and one of the most quoted American writers. He endured the loss of his father and sister at an early age, which undoubtedly affected his writing. Drawn to nature, Emerson began to feel a profound affection for it and for the solitude it could provide him, which sustained him for the rest of his life. He proclaimed, "Nature is loved by what is best in us" (Atkinson, 1950: 411). At 14 he received a grant from his father's church and entered Harvard College. Appointed "President's freshman," he was provided free board. Here he began writing his journals, which became his constant companion for some 50 years. These gave rise to literary material in lectures, essays, and books. Upon graduation, Emerson joined his brother William in teaching and operating a finishing school in his mother's home. It was an unhappy time for him; his journals were filled with discouragement and self-doubt. He wrote to a friend who was also teaching: "How my heart bleeds for you! Better tug at the oar, dig the mine, or saw wood; better sow hemp, or hang with it, than sow the seeds of instruction (Gilbert, 1914:124)."

Descended from eight generations of ministers, Emerson enrolled in the Divinity School at Harvard, and once licensed, his teaching stopped. He married Ellen Tucker whose health was delicate, and after only 17 months of marriage she died of tuberculosis. Afterward Emerson resolved that he was not in sympathy with some of the doctrines of his church, and as a result he resigned his post and sailed for Europe. The trip revived him, and upon his return he met and married his second wife, Lydia. Soon he suffered the death of two of his beloved brothers. Later, Emerson and his wife lost the eldest of their four children to scarlet fever.

After his return from Europe, Emerson spent an allotted portion of each day walking in the woods and along the rivers with his eyes open to the natural surroundings. Occasionally he preached and lectured to enthusiastic audiences on the moral and psychological interaction between nature and the human spirit. In Concord he became involved in local affairs and was a respected and valued member of the community. His presence made Concord a significant intellectual and cultural center.

Emerson helped to organize a discussion group whose members called themselves "transcendentalists." Serving as their first literary proponent, Emerson envisioned a unity of nature, humans, and God; he believed that through the use of intuition, a heightened awareness could be reached that would transcend one's thoughts to a grander level of ultimate (transcendental) understanding. Through natural phenomena he believed one could intuitively understand human relationships to the universe, its components, and to God (Ronald, 1987). While transcendentalist notions were expressed by others, Emerson's literary style set him apart. In his first book, *Nature* (1836), he enumerated the values of nature:

> "If a man would be alone, let him look at the stars. The rays that come from those heavenly worlds will separate between him and what he touches. One might think the atmosphere was made transparent with this design, to give man, in the heavenly bodies, the perpetual presence of the sublime. Seen in the streets of cities, how great they are! If the stars should appear one night in a thousand years, how would men believe and adore; and preserve for many generations the remembrance of the City of God which had been shown! But every night come out these envoys of beauty, and light the universe with their admonishing smile" (Atkinson, 1950: 5).

In 1840 he helped to found and later edited a magazine called *The Dial*. Surviving only until 1844, it proved to be an excellent way for younger members of the transcendentalist school, including Henry David Thoreau, to express their ideas. During the same productive period, Emerson's *Essays*, derived from his lecture series, were published in two volumes (1841, 1844) and his reputation grew. During the American Renaissance in literature (1835-65), when Emerson was in his prime, he was recognized as a leading lecturer and author. His other publications included *Poems*

(1846), *Representative Men* (1849), *The Conduct of Life* (1860), *May Day* (1867).

In "Nature" in *Essays: Second Series* (Atkinson, 1950: 408) Emerson wrote:

> It seems as if the day was not wholly profane in which we have given heed to some natural object. The fall of snow-flakes in a still air, preserving to each crystal its perfect form; the blowing of sleet over a wide sheet of water, and over plains; the waving rye-field; the mimic waving of acres of houstonia, whose innumerable florets whiten and ripple before the eye; the reflections of trees and flowers in glassy lakes; the musical, steaming, odorous south wind, which converts all trees to windharps; the crackling and spurting of hemlock in the flames, or of pine logs, which yield glory to the walls and faces in the sitting-room—these are the music and pictures of the most ancient religion.

Inspiration and many ideas for his writings came to him on his long afternoon walks in the Concord hills. An observer of nature, he was not generally an active participant. On some occasions he hunted, but his friends implied that he never shot a living thing. Emerson enjoyed his excursions to the mountains with members of the Adirondack Club and later in life he took a trip to California where he met John Muir (described later in this chapter). The two men drew close, but Muir believed that Emerson was by 1871 only a ghost of what he had once been (M.V.D., 1931:140).

Henry David Thoreau (1817-1862)

Henry David Thoreau, who was introduced to the transcendentalists by his long-time friend Ralph Waldo Emerson, is regarded a classic writer and cultural hero. He established the tradition of nature writing that was later developed by naturalists John Burroughs and John Muir. His pioneer studies of the human uses of nature deeply effected conservationists including Benton MacKaye, founder of the Appalachian Trail. In searching for a spiritual dimension in a commercially expanding society, Thoreau demonstrated "the value of leisure, contem-plation, and a harmonious appreciation of and coexistence with nature" (BCD, 1998:3). Although he oscillated between a transcendental and scientific examination of nature, it was this alliance between contemplative thoughtfulness and close observation and speculation that became the pattern for his prose and essays. Neither style was as notably sentimental nor as romantic as Audubon's or Muir's writings (to be discussed later in his chapter).

The third of four children, Thoreau was born and raised in a beautiful setting in Concord, Massachusetts. During his early years he shared his mother's love of the out-of-doors and developed an affinity for hunting, fishing, and solitude in nature. He especially admired the pond called Walden. His family contributed to his education at Harvard, where he also received aid from a beneficiary fund for needy students. While in college he was granted a leave in order to teach and to assist his father, a pencil manufacturer. Originally christened David Henry, he reversed his names at age 20, demonstrating an early act of independence. After graduation he was unsure of his goals, and teaching appeared to be a means to support himself. He soon resigned after he was coerced into flogging students who lacked discipline. Thoreau returned to the family business of pencil making, which gave him leisure for his reading, studying, and walking. In 1837, after reading Emerson's *Nature*, he began to write about nature in his journal, which he kept throughout his life (Benet, 1966:84-90). Living simply, he found wealth in enjoyment rather than in possession. In later, more successful years he wrote in his journal,

> "Ah, how I have thriven on solitude and poverty! I cannot overstate this advantage. I do not see how I could have enjoyed it, if the public had been expecting as much of me as there is danger now that they will. If I go abroad lecturing, how shall I ever recover the lost Winter?" (Teale, 1962:73)

Thoreau opened a school with his brother John, and they introduced field trips for nature study, an innovation in American education. In 1839 the two brothers took a 13-day vacation voyage on the Concord and Merrimack Rivers, a journey Thoreau later immortalized in his writings. By 1841 the school closed due to his brother's ill health. He met Emerson at one of his lectures, and Emerson invited him to his home and introduced Thoreau to other transcendentalists. They appreciated Thoreau's freedom of thought. An acquaintance, Nathaniel Hawthorne, believed that Thoreau retained a wild and original nature and observed that he led a life similar to the American Indians (Harding, 1954:2,6). Thoreau did study the wisdom of Indians, and later described in *The Maine Woods* a camping trip with an Indian friend, and how Thoreau had learned from him.

As Thoreau read widely—from the explorations of Audubon to Hindu philosophy—his appreciation of solitude, meditation, and contemplation deepened. In solitude, he acquired an observant intimacy with nature, but he was not a lone woodsman. For Thoreau, nature also provided a lavish setting for wilderness excursions, where relationships with others were developed (Schildgen, 2001:74). He enjoyed the company of others, and his contemporaries attest that he was gregarious. The bachelor, Thoreau, had proposed marriage in 1840, but the engagement was broken upon the insistence of his fiance's parents. For a time, he lived with the Emersons, working as a handyman. Upon the death of his brother, he shared his loss with Emerson, who had just lost his son, and in their sorrow the friendship grew. Emerson and others encouraged Thoreau to lecture and write, and in 1845 Emerson gave him land on the northwest shore of Walden Pond. After building a cabin, Thoreau entertained many guests and welcomed children. He often took short walks into Concord for a meal with his family. Thoreau also practiced meditation, and spent long hours observing, recording, and writing about nature. When strangers insisted on joining him on his nature walks he complained, "They do not consider that the wood-path and the boat are my studio, where I maintain a sacred solitude and cannot admit promiscuous company" (Strong, 1988:11).

During Thoreau's two-year stay at Walden, he, the abolitionist who helped send enslaved Americans north on the Underground Railroad, was arrested for his past refusal to pay a poll tax in protest against slavery. After only one night in jail, a disgusted Thoreau was released after someone, probably his aunt, paid the tax. He argued that people should follow their own conscience, not the dictates of an immoral government. He retold the story in his essay "Resistance to Civil Government" (later called "Civil Disobedience" and "On the Duty of Civil Disobedience") which appeared a few years later in an obscure magazine. Leaving Walden forever, he spent the summer of 1847 at Emerson's home, while Emerson was away in Europe. Thoreau then returned to his father's home and the family atmosphere with the first draft of his book *A Week on the Concord and Merrimack Rivers* complete. This book about his trip into the wilderness with his now-deceased brother was released in 1849 at his own risk in an edition of 1,000 copies. When it sold poorly, he remarked, "I have now a library of nearly nine hundred volumes, over seven hundred of which I wrote myself" (Strong, 1988:14). An unfavorable review, probably due to his unorthodoxy in religion, criticized Thoreau's assertion that the Sacred Books of the Brahmins were not inferior to the Bible.

In his book, *Walden,* published in 1854, Thoreau strove to describe nature and demonstrate that civilized people could escape the evils of competition. *Walden* sold slowly but steadily and became a classic in later years. Four books, published after his death and derived in part from journeys taken during the five years following his Walden experience were: *Excursions* (1863), *The Maine Woods* (1864), *Cape Cod* (1865), and *A Yankee in Canada* (1866). Drawing on these same experiences, he wrote "Ktaadn" [sic] and the "Maine Woods,"

"Excursion to Canada," and "Cape Cod," which appeared in *The Union Magazine* (1848), *Putnam's Monthly* (1853), and *Putnam Monthly* (1855) respectively.

Adopting a more conventional life after Walden, Thoreau made a living as a self-taught surveyor and he worked in the family business. He continued to enjoy his walks and lectured occasionally. In later years, Thoreau became more of a scientific observer of animal behavior, the life cycle of plants, and features of the changing seasons. His most important scientific observation and contribution was presented in a lecture and article entitled, "The Succession of Forest Trees." Some speculated that his resolve to count tree rings one bitterly cold winter day may have precipitated his early death at age 44 (Strong, 1988:15-16), apparently from tuberculosis. His final words, "moose" and "Indian", indicate his final thoughts were about his beloved wilderness (R.W.A., 1936:494-95). Emerson delivered a long eulogy and described Thoreau as someone who was a pleasure to walk with, was physically fit, a good swimmer, runner, skater, and boatman, and knew the country like a fox. According to Emerson, Thoreau's study of nature inspired his friends, who appreciated hearing of his adventures and seeing the world through his eyes. Reading, writing, and the study of wildlife were the only occupations that really suited him. Thoreau's statement, "In wildness is the preservation of the world," that first appeared in "Walking" (1862 republished in *Excursions*) became the motto of the wilderness society years later (Teale, 1962:59).

Thoreau spiritualized his experiences with wilderness and nature and through his writings influenced future naturalists and the destiny of North America. Living at a time when trees were appraised in terms of board feet, and not as shelters for birds or animals, he feared that human naturalness and oneness with the ecosystems would vanish. Thoreau was a visionary in concluding that there was a need to preserve parcels of wilderness for the people, and he helped to lead the intellec-

tual revolution that found nature and wilderness attractive as opposed to threatening and disagreeable (Bolton, 1954:126-32; Vickery, 1989:45). To many, Thoreau is considered the father of the environmental movement. The following selection is taken from *The Maine Woods* (1965:87-88):

> It is difficult to conceive of a region uninhabited by man. We habitually presume his presence and influence everywhere. And yet we have not seen pure Nature, unless we have seen her thus vast and drear and inhuman, though in the midst of cities. Nature was here something savage and awful, though beautiful. I looked with awe at the ground I trod on, to see what the Powers had made there, the form and fashion and material of their work. This was the Earth of which we have heard, made out of Chaos and Old Night. Here was no man's garden, but the unhandseled globe. It was not lawn, nor pasture, nor mead, nor woodland, nor lea, nor arable, nor wasteland. It was fresh and natural surface of the planet Earth, as it was made forever and ever...

In the same book, his essay "The Moose Hunt" describes his feelings after observing a moose hunt:

> Strange that so few ever came to the woods to see how the pine lives and grows and spires, lifting its evergreen arms to the light—to see its perfect success; but most are content to behold it in the shape of many broad boards brought to market, and deem that its true success! But the pine is no more lumber than man is, and to be made into boards and houses is no more its true and highest use than the truest use of a man is to be cut down and made into manure. There is a higher law affecting our relation to pines as well as to men. . . .I saw the tops of the pines waving and reflecting the light at a distance high over all the rest of the forest, I realized that the former were not the highest uses of the pine.

The Naturalists

Although naturalism began with the French philosopher Jean-Jacques Rosseau, on this continent, two great men led the natural movement. One of them was John Audubon, the other John Muir. Rachel Carson, a great woman, distinguished scientist, and accomplished writer of the twentieth century, was the first to alert the nation to the damage suffered by the environment as a result of our chemical technology of the 1900s. Their devotion to understanding, depicting, preserving. and writing about nature led to a more intimate understanding of nature and the outdoors.

John James Audubon (1785-1851)

Early conservationist, artist, ornithologist, and perhaps the most popular naturalist of North America, John James Audubon explored the Ohio and Mississippi rivers, the wilderness of Kentucky, the dunes and lagoons of the Texas coast, the palmetto groves of Florida, and the wild coast of Labrador. Writing in his journals, he personalized and revolutionized the study, illustration, and description of birds and mammals.

Born the illegitimate son of a French naval officer, merchant, and slave trader, the four year old, originally named Jean Rabine, and his younger (also illegitimate) half-sister were taken to France and adopted by Captain Audubon and his legal wife in 1794. Audubon's real mother, Jeanne Rabine, a Creole girl who had worked on his father's sugar plantation in Santo Domingo (Haiti), died shortly after his birth there. In France his stepmother encouraged his early attraction to nature. He also learned to fence and dance, and to play the violin and flute. Later in life, with his flute Audubon was capable of imitating the songs of birds he observed, and he began to sketch them. Not showing much interest in scholarly work, he was sent to Paris to study drawing. Although the ability to draw eluded him at the time, he developed a desire to illustrate birds as they appeared in the forest, not in profile as they appeared in books (Audubon, 1960:14-15; Elman, 1977:80-84). His

attempts to do so always reminded him of his father's admonition that "all things possessing life and animation were difficult to imitate" (Fisher, 1949:15).

Believing that Audubon could learn English and enter a profitable trade in the United States, his father suggested that Audubon tend their farm in the United States near Philadelphia. The move was also a strategic one to keep the young Audubon out of a bloody conflict during the French Revolution. He considered himself the master of the farm at age 18, despite his father's hired agent, and continued to develop his fascination with nature and birds. It was at this time that the son changed his baptized name Jean-Jacque Fougere to the anglicized John James.

Using a vivid personal narrative rather than dry impersonal experimental reports, Audubon explained his methods of observation of wildlife in their natural surroundings. He began to conduct scientific investigations with the birds he sketched and skillfully mastered how to closely examine birds and mammals without alarming them. He handled nestlings without causing the adult birds to abandon them, developing a method used by twentieth century field biologists. In one of his experiments he tied threads as leg bands to phoebes for identification. In this manner he discovered that many of them returned in the spring to their fledgling region after winter migration. Little did he know that 100 years later, a Bird Banding Society would be formed to repeat his test in order to gather exact data on migratory species in every part of the American continent (Elman, 1977:85-86). Later, in his *Ornithological Biography*, he described one of his experiences observing nature:

> . . .rambling along the rocky banks. . .
> observing the watchful King-fisher
> perched on some projecting stone over
> the clear water of the stream. Nay, now
> and then, the Fish Hawk itself, followed
> by a White-headed Eagle, would make
> his appearance, and by his graceful
> aerial motion, raise my thought far above
> them into the heavens. . . There it was
> that I studied the habits of the Pewee;

and there I was taught most forcibly, that to destroy the nest of a bird or to deprive it of its eggs or young, is an act of great cruelty (Elman, 1977; 85-86).

After a quarrel with his father's hired agent, Audubon borrowed money from his fiancee's uncle, and in 1805 set sail for France, where he remained for a year visiting family, hunting, and drawing his first known bird sketches. He may have served in the French navy before returning to Pennsylvania with Ferdinand Rozier, who had agreed to work as a partner on the Mill Grove estate. They invested in a lead mine, which proved to be a bust. Audubon spent more time studying birds, and taught himself to wire dead birds into lifelike positions for his sketches. In New York as an apprentice in business, he met Samuel L. Mitchell, future founder of the Lyceum of Natural History, now the New York Academy of Sciences. Together they went on excursions to prepare bird and mammal specimens.

Disenchanted with life at Mill Grove, Audubon and Rozier opened a retail store in Louisville and eventually in Henderson, Kentucky. Audubon made a brief return to Pennsylvania to marry Lucy Bakewell, and soon struck up a friendship with Daniel Boone. Later he met ornithologist Alexander Wilson, who was known for his drawings of birds. Samuel Mitchell believed that Audubon's art was superior to Wilson's and urged him to consider his own professional potential, but Audubon continued to try his luck in business. After failed attempts, he traveled to Missouri still in the pursuit of business success. En route, the weather proved to be bitterly cold, with ice forming on the Mississippi River. On the trip Audubon taught his dispirited partner how to winter camp and expressed his exhilaration in observing the great snow-white birds lying on the ice. This proved to be a turning point in his career. Audubon sold out to his partner and journeyed back to Kentucky on foot, writing of his adventures, which were published later in his *Ornithological Biography*. In his journal he wrote, "Winter was just bursting into spring when I left the land of lead mines. Nature leaped with joy, as it were, at her own new-born marvels, the prairies began to be dotted with beauteous flowers, abounded with deer, and my own heart was filled with happiness at the sights before me" (Audubon, 1960: 23-31).

In Kentucky Audubon attempted several different enterprises, his last being a steam grist and lumber mill with his wife's brother that proved too elaborate for the needs of Henderson. Jailed for debt, he was released on the plea of bankruptcy, but grew increasingly despondent after the death of an infant daughter Rose, poignantly felt after their first daughter Lucy's death only a few years earlier. To support his wife and two sons, Audubon created charcoal portraits on commission until he found work as a taxidermist in Cincinnati in the new Western Museum. His wife persuaded him to devote himself to his artistic talents, and thereafter, his life course took aim. In 1820 Audubon explored the lands along the Ohio and Mississippi rivers for birds with a student, Joseph Mason. Settling in New Orleans, he supported the undertaking and raised money to send for his family by painting portraits and teaching archery, dance, and music. Accompanied by Mason and his sons, he traveled the swamps and forests to Natchez, where he drew full time. Enhancing watercolor application by using various media to express textures, Audubon developed his signature-style and Mason drew many backgrounds.

Determined to have his work published, Audubon went to Philadelphia with a large portfolio of work. Finding the cost of publication prohibitive, he made plans to travel to Europe, where engraving cost far less. Before departing, he visited Mitchell, now president of the Lyceum of Natural History who introduced Audubon to this society. Audubon's drawings were highly praised and he was elected to the Lyceum membership. His credibility grew after his reading of two papers to this prestigious society. Later his fellow Americans nominated him a fellow of the American Academy of Arts and Sciences.

During Audubon's 1826 voyage to Europe, the ship's crew would sometimes lower him onto the water in a small boat so that he could collect specimens. Once in Liverpool, Audubon was favorably received, and he acquired the initial subscriptions for his four-volume book *Birds in America*. These and later subscriptions would make possible the long publication of his 435 prints. After his exhibition of drawings at the Royal Institution of Liverpool, Audubon was declared an American genius. In Edinburgh, he received a regal reception and Audubon was elected to its Royal Society. Many other honors came to him during his stay in England, including his election to the Fellowship in the Linnean Society. Having garnered enough subscriptions, publication of *Birds of America* (1827-38) was underway. The monumental achievement, done in double elephant folio—27 by 40 inches—would result in the largest set of books ever published. All of the engravings were life-size, set in copper, and in color. Set in their natural environment, there were more than a thousand individual birds depicted as well as thousands of American flowers, trees, shrubs, insects, and animals from Labrador to Florida and from Louisiana and Maine to the Great Plains.

After spending three years in England, Audubon was reunited with his family and continued to search for new species to augment his growing project. During a visit to Washington, D.C. in 1830, President Andrew Jackson received him, and the House of Representatives became an early subscriber. Other original subscribers included Daniel Webster, Henry Clay, the kings of France and England, as well as many important libraries of the Western World. During this successful decade, Audubon teamed with Scottish naturalist William MacGillivray to write the five-volume text for *Birds of America,* called *Ornithological Biography* (1831-39), and *A Synopsis of Birds of North America* (1839). The content of the first, which provided a description of the habits of the birds he drew, gave an interspersed account about life in America during this turbulent period. Today Audubon's writings are recognized as a literary treasure (National Audubon Society, 2001:1). With his reputation now established internationally as a naturalist and artist and the foremost naturalist in the United States, the Audubon family chose to settle in New York (Elman, 1977:100-107; Fisher, 1949:70-71).

Still not content, Audubon entered into two new projects. These included his seven-volume Octavo or miniature edition of *Birds of America* (1840-44) and a new three-volume work *Viviparous Quadruped of North America* (1845-48) with an accompanying three-volume text (1846-53). The critically and commercially successful "miniature," produced under the guidance of Audubon and his son John, was entrusted to J. Bowen, a Philadelphia lithographer. The later companion book on mammals was done in collaboration with scholar and friend John Bachman with the aid of his sons, whose first wives were Bachman's daughters. Audubon's son John did the artistic work for over half of the 155 plates, while his other son Victor contributed by managing the sales and designing many of the backgrounds (National Audubon Society, 2001:2). *Viviparous Quadruped of North America* was the first book of its kind in America and without rival in Europe. Naturalists immediately accepted it as a standard and authoritative work (Fisher, 1949:74).

Throughout 1843, Audubon traveled and discovered species for the *Quadrupeds*. During an eight-month expedition to the upper Missouri River and the Yellowstone country, he chased the great Buffalo herds, but never realized his dream of reaching the west coast. At a later date, his comprehensive notes from this trip were published by his granddaughter in *Audubon and His Journals*. At the age of 60, Audubon's eyesight began to fail and an eventual stroke disabled him further. By the time of his death at his estate *Minnie's Land* in Upper Manhattan, his family fortunes were diminishing.

The National Audubon Society was formed in 1886 in Audubon's honor by George Bird Grinnell, editor of *Forest and*

Stream. Attracting the distinguished support of John Greenleaf Whittier, Oliver Wendell Holmes, and others, some 50,000 members joined within a two-year period (Fox, 1981:152). Audubon's enjoyment of the physical process of exploring the wilderness, tracking down each new species of bird and observing, recording and cataloging it, marks him as one of the finest artist-naturalists of the romantic era in America, earning him his nickname, "The American Woodsman." Renowned ornithologist Elliott Coues said, "Audubon and his work are one; he lived in his work, and his work will live forever" (Fisher, 1949:76).

John Muir (1838-1914)

John Muir was born in Dunbar, Scotland, and immigrated with his father, brother and sister to Wisconsin at the age of 11. The rest of his family followed later. His mother, kindly and compassionate, and his father, an unbending religious zealot, brought the family to the United States to seek a less discordant religious environment. The eldest of three sons and the third in a succession of eight siblings, Muir was expected to do heavy farm labor from dawn to nightfall. In his book, *The Story of My Boyhood and Youth* (1913), Muir recounted his harsh experience while digging a 90-foot-deep well. After he struck sandstone at 10 feet, his father was advised to blast the rock. Lacking the skills or the money to do it, he decided to send his son down in a bucket equipped with mason's chisels to do the work. Relentlessly chipping from morning to night, day after day for months, in a space about three feet in diameter, Muir finally struck water at 80 feet. In the process, carbonic acid gas that had settled at the bottom nearly killed him.

Experiencing the awe of the neighboring wilderness provided young Muir with some retreat from the harsh living, however, and he acknowledged in later years that it was on the farm site at Fountain Lake that he first conceived of the idea of wild lands to be set aside by governments for their scenic and educational value (Downing, 1992:2). Although Muir rejected the religious fanaticism of his father, his spiritual roots profoundly influenced his thinking and writing in later years. Taking issue with the Christian concept of dominion over natural resources, Muir saw the spirit in everything natural and became a pioneer of the idea that wilderness should exist for the value of its existence alone (Leshuk, 1998:1-2). Finding beauty intrinsic to his natural surroundings, he described the Wisconsin groves of oak as a summer paradise for song birds, saying, "Nature's fine love touches, every note going straight home into one's heart" (Muir, 1975: 137-38).

Inventive and hungry for knowledge, Muir made an arrangement with his father that he could read early in the morning before it was time for his chores. Rising at one o'clock, the zero-degree weather made a fire necessary. Fearing that his father might object to the cost of firewood, which took valuable work time to chop, he invented a self-setting sawmill. Neighbors encouraged him to take some of his inventions to the State Fair in Madison. Muir had a successful showing that resulted in some local fame, a position in a machine shop, and the favorable notice of university authorities. As a student at the University of Wisconsin he selected a practical course of studies and disregarded the regimen required for a degree. Between work and study he had only four hours to sleep each night, so he invented a bed that set him on his feet every morning at the hour desired. At his desk he arranged his books in order so that they would automatically open themselves up on a rack and then close according to schedule. After closing, each book would reposition itself in the appropriate slot as the next would appear.

The day after commencement, Muir and two of his college mates headed out on a long botanical and geological excursion down the Wisconsin River Valley through Minnesota and Iowa. These travels pulled at his heart as he waited for a response to his letter of application from the University of Michigan, where he hoped to continue his studies. Muir, a pacifist by nature, had also registered for the Civil War draft.

His number was passed in the early drawings and he decided that if his number was not drawn that fall while he worked for his brother-in-law that he would head to Canada for the "University of the Wilderness (Wilkins,1945:39). In Canada, Muir "entered at once into harmonious relations with Nature" (Wolfe, 1945:91). Returning after two years in Canada, his ability to take on odd jobs in factories led to quick promotions due to his inventions of labor-saving equipment. He became foreman-engineer at an Indianapolis carriage factory until an industrial injury nearly blinded him. Convalescing for weeks in a dark hospital room, he finally recovered his sight. This convinced Muir that he should be true to himself and he decided to follow nature and the inventions of God (Muir, 1975:247-48, 260, 274-86).

On September 2, 1867, Muir began a thousand-mile walk to the Gulf of Mexico. His journal entries recorded his observations about the forests, flora, and geography. He also wrote of his experiences with the inhabitants and of his personal reflections on human responsiveness toward nature. Edited and published posthumously, these observations appear under the title *A Thousand-Mile Walk to the Gulf* (1916). Once he reached the Gulf, he sailed to Cuba and then on to Panama, where he crossed the Isthmus and sailed up the West Coast, landing in San Francisco in March 1868. Immediately Muir sought directions into the wilderness of the Yosemite Valley, where he worked on a ranch and continued his explorations while studying botany and geology of the new state park. Muir's reflections, written at the age of 31, appeared four decades later in perhaps his best-loved book *My First Summer in the Sierra* (1911). And in an earlier publication, *The Mountains of California* (1894), he shared his enthusiasm of the unknown, portraying his climb on Mount Ritter located in the middle portion of the High Sierra:

> Its height above sea level is about 13,300 feet, and it is fenced round by steeply inclined glaciers, and canyons of tremendous depth and ruggedness, which render it almost inaccessible. But difficulties of this kind only exhilarate the mountaineer. . . .In so wild and so beautiful a region was spent my first day, every sight and sound inspiring, leading one far out of himself, yet feeding and building up his individuality. Now came the solemn, silent evening. Long blue, spiky shadows crept out across the snow-fields, while a rosy glow, at first scarce discernible, gradually deepened and suffused every mountain-top, flushing the glaciers and the harsh crags above them. This was the alpenglow, to me one of the most impressive of all the terrestrial manifestations of God. At the touch of this divine light, the mountains seemed to kindle to a rapt, religious consciousness, and stood hushed and waiting like devout worshipers. Just before the alpenglow began to fade, two crimson clouds came streaming across the summit like wings of flame, rendering the sublime scene yet more impressive; then came darkness and the stars.

During this period, Muir, who had learned of Emerson and Thoreau at the University of Wisconsin, acted as interpreter of natural history when Emerson visited Yosemite in 1871. Muir would later name a mountain in the Yosemite region in Emerson's honor (Teale, 1954:162). By this time, he had already discovered living glaciers in the Sierra and, contrary to the popular belief of the times, theorized that Yosemite Valley was produced by glaciation rather than by a devastating earthquake. As Muir became known throughout the country for his scientific writing, other famous men made their way to his pine cabin. He became publically known for his writings in 1874 when a series of magazine articles entitled *Studies in the Sierra* was launched. His enchantment with nature did not end in the Sierra, however. In 1879 Muir took his first of seven journeys to Alaska, where he became one of the first white men to discover the area now known as Glacier Bay. In Alaska, his adventures included discoveries and observations of plants, fish, animals, birds, rivers, mountains, and glaciers.

A new turn in his life occurred in 1880 when Muir married Louie (short for Louisiana) Wanda Strentzel and leased, and later bought, a part of the Stentzel fruit ranch. After 10 years of prudent farming in Martinez, California, he saved $100,000. With enough to support his wife and two daughters, he could devote himself to his true ambitions, his hikes and observations. Supportive of his fight for conservation and travel, his wife encouraged him to go to the mountains for his health. Muir had no feeling for haste and could sit for hours studying the flowers. He was known to have taken 10 hours to walk 10 miles because he stopped so frequently to study or ponder (W.F.B., 1934:37).

Returning to his work as an advocate for wilderness and forest preservation, Muir wrote many articles about the need to transfer Yosemite back to the federal government and rename it a national park. He also introduced bills to save the majestic Sequoia trees. By 1890, Yosemite, Sequoia, and General Grant (now King's Canyon) were all national parks. The next year, his book, *Our National Parks,* was released. In 1903, Muir who had helped persuade President Benjamin Harrison to set aside 13 million acres of forest and President Grover Cleveland to set aside another 21 million acres, camped with President Theodore Roosevelt during his tour of the American West. Together, they laid the foundation of Roosevelt's innovative and notable conservation programs (Downing, 1992:6). Between Presidents Roosevelt, Wilson, and Taft, Muir's influence could be gauged by the designation of over 50 national parks, 200 national monuments, and 140 million acres of National Forest (White, 1996:6). While Muir credited Robert Underwood Johnson, an editor of *Century Magazine*, as the "originator of Yosemite," Muir himself is credited with saving the Grand Canyon and the Petrified Forest and with assisting in the establishment of Sequoia, Yosemite, Mount Rainier, Crater Lake, Glacier, and Mesa Verde national parks, as well as 12 national monuments (Ford, 1989:42). Two of these, the Grand Canyon and Olympic Peninsula, later became national parks. Deservedly, Muir is often called the Father of the National Park System, while his work toward preservation later became the mission of the National Park Service.

In order to protect the newly created Yosemite National Park, Johnson and others suggested to Muir that an association be formed. On May 22, 1892, Muir helped to found the Sierra Club in San Francisco and served as the club's first and singular president for 22 years. In his invitational letter, he expressed his hope that this Club would be able to "do something for wilderness, and make the mountains glad" (Downing, 1992:5-6). Although the club gained national recognition for its efforts to reserve and preserve scenic and forest areas first in California and then across the Nation, Muir lost his last major battle when Congress in 1913 authorized the Hetch Hetchy reservoir in the valley adjacent to Yosemite Valley. Both were part of the Yosemite National Park (see Chapter 7). To Muir, who felt that a journey into the Yosemite Valley itself was an inherently spiritual experience, the loss of this beautiful land was most certainly a heartbreak. Yet, the resilient man pulled his attention to a long-deferred book on Alaska. Optimistically, Muir wrote to Johnson, the long-drawn-out battle-work for Nature's gardens has not been thrown away. The conscience of the whole country has been aroused from sleep, and from outrageous evil compensating good in some form must surely come (Wilkins, 1995:243).

The public conscience was so thoroughly aroused that wilderness preservation grew in popularity, and Muir was "enshrined at its heart" (Wilkins, 1995:243). His great contribution to wilderness preservation lay in his ability to successfully promote the revolutionary idea that wilderness had spiritual as well as economic value (Ryan, 1990:12). And his own deepest insight was perhaps in finding the inner oneness in all of nature, pointing out that no particle of nature is ever wasted. In the wilderness, Muir believed, one could appreciate fellow creatures, realizing one's part in a harmonious whole. He said, "In God's wildness lies the hope of the world, the great fresh, unblighted, unredeemed wilderness" (Grossman & Bearwood, 1961). Other books written by John Muir were: *Stickeen* (1909) and *The Yosemite* (1912). Published posthumously were *Travels in Alaska* (1915), *The Cruise of the Corwin* (1917), and *Steep Trails* (1918).

Rachel Carson (1907-1964)

Scientist and ecologist Rachel Carson was employed by the United States Fish and Wildlife Service from 1936 to 1952. As a talented writer she was capable of transforming her government research into poetic prose. Together her books *Under the Sea-Wind* (1941), *The Sea Around Us* (1951), and *Edge of the Sea* (1955) constituted a biography of the ocean that made her famous as a naturalist and science writer (Lear, 2000:1). Her best seller, *The Silent Spring* (1962), touched off an international controversy over the long-range effects of pesticides. By shocking the world with her presentation of the disasters brewing in the immediate future, she magnified the public's environmental awareness.

The youngest of three children, Rachel Louise Carson was born in Springdale, Pennsylvania, where she came to love the natural environment on her family's farm. In large measure, she owed her love of nature to her mother, a graduate of Washington Female Seminary, who "taught her as a tiny child joy in the out-of-doors and the lore of birds, insects, and residents of the streams and ponds" (Rothe, 1952:101). In later years the study of birds became a hobby. She became an associate member of the American Ornithologist's Union and a director of the Audubon Society of the District of Columbia.

Carson's writing career began at the early age of ten when she won an award for her contribution to *St. Nicholas* magazine. Intent on becoming a writer, she entered the Pennsylvania College for Women (now Chatham College) in Pittsburgh with a scholarship. She participated in a wide range of activities, including field hockey and basketball, but her interest in writing was redirected to science. "Biology," she told a friend, "has given me something to write about" (Strong, 1988:180).

Graduating magna cum laude with a degree in zoology in 1929, Carson taught part-time and entered Johns Hopkins University for postgraduate study, which led to her M.A. degree in 1932. Her plans to obtain a doctorate were never fulfilled due to family responsibilities. For a few years she taught zoology at the University of Maryland and continued her studies in the summer at the Marine Biological Laboratory in Woods Hole, Massachusetts (Matthiessen, 1999:1). There she first saw and became enamored with the mysteries of the sea. With the death of her ailing father in 1935 and her sister the following year, Carson's family responsibilities grew when she resolved to raise her two orphaned nieces. She elected not to marry, and continued her devotion to her family throughout her life. In later years she cared for her elderly mother and adopted her five-year-old great nephew after the death of a beloved niece.

To make ends meet, "Ray" Carson, as she was known to some of her friends, began writing articles on scientific topics for the *Baltimore Sunday Sun* and science radio scripts for the United States Bureau of Fisheries (later the Fish and Wildlife Service) in Washington, D.C. The later part-time position led to a full-time appointment as junior aquatic biologist in 1936. She wrote bulletins, leaflets, and other informative literature. One of her early government publications seemed so outstanding to her editor that he encouraged her to submit it to the *Atlantic Monthly*. Her first publication "Undersea" appeared in 1937. This article captured the attention of a publisher from Simon and Schuster, who asked her to write a full-length book concerning the sea. Her publication, along with one of her *Sun* features served as a starting point for her first and favorite book, *Under the Sea-Wind*. The book, subtitled "a naturalists picture of ocean life," was critically and scientifically praised, but sold only 1,400 copies in its first year (De Bruhl, 1981: 109).

As Carson continued to write articles, she rose within the ranks of the Fish and Wildlife Service to biologist, information specialist, and Editor-in-Chief in 1949. That year she was given a Eugene F. Saxton Memorial Fellowship, and in 1950 the George Westinghouse Foundation award for outstanding magazine writing in the field of science. She hired a literary agent for her second book that was serialized as "A Profile of the Sea" in the *New Yorker* before it was released in 1951. Entitled *The Sea Around Us,* the blockbuster went into a ninth printing, placed on the nonfiction best-seller lists throughout the country, was translated into more than 30 languages, and won the National Book Award. The reader is taken through successive periods of geological time and warned of the dangers of polluting the oceans with atomic wastes. In her chapter "The Long Snowfall," Carson shares her scientific insight and emotional sensitivity:

> Every part of earth or air or sea has an atmosphere peculiarly its own, a quality or characteristic that sets it apart from all others. When I think of the floor of the deep sea, the single, overwhelming fact that possesses my imagination is the accumulation of sediments. I see always the steady, unremitting, downward drift of materials from above, flake upon flake, layer upon layer—a drift that has continued for hundreds of millions of years, that will go on as long as there are seas and continents. For the sediments are the materials of the most stupendous "snowfall" the earth has ever seen...

Research for the book entailed learning deep-sea diving at shallow depths and included a ten-day voyage on a research ship. With little time to do her own creative work, however, her book had progressed slowly, taking three years. Everything changed after its success. A Guggenheim Fellowship allowed her the opportunity for a year's sabbatical to begin work on a third book. After reissue of her first book, it was an instant best seller, too. Royalties from both books gave her the economic independence to resign her position at the Fish and Wildlife Service to follow her dream. Preparation for *The Edge of the Sea,* which explored the border zone where sea meets land, included wading in icy tidal pools for so long that she sometimes became numb with cold and had to be carried out. By studying minute sea creatures under her binocular microscope, she felt a spiritual closeness to the individual creatures about whom she wrote. Her third book of the sea trilogy also became a best seller, but it was her fourth book, the landmark *Silent Spring,* that set into motion environmentalism, one of the great movements of the century (De Bruhl, 1981:109). Carson's grim warning was instrumental in bringing about awareness of the dangers of some pesticides and herbicides that could kill everyone and everything if humanity failed to check their use. Her text ended on the following note:

> The "control of nature" is a phrase conceived in arrogance, born of the Neanderthal age of biology and philosophy, when it was supposed that nature exists for the convenience of man. The concepts and practices of applied entomology for the most part date from that Stone Age of science. It is our alarming misfortune that so primitive a science has armed itself with the most modern and terrible weapons, and that in turning them against the insects it has also turned them against the earth.

Before the book's release, *Silent Spring* was serialized in the *New Yorker*. Bringing public attention to her book, opponents threatened lawsuits and called Carson an alarmist. Monsanto Chemical Company responded, for example, with a report to advise the public of the horrors of a pesticide-free world (De Bruhl, 1981:109). Carson realized the controversial nature of her topic, but she was rightly confident about her facts and knew that she could count on the support of leading scientists and conservation organizations (Matthiessen, 1999:4). "Who are we,"

Carson questioned, "to say that those who come after us may never see some of today's rare and endangered species?" (Carson, 1963:262). At about the same time, newspapers reported the death of five million fish on the lower Mississippi River, the worst of a series of incidents (Strong, 1988: 190) and the public outcry could not be ignored. President John F. Kennedy read the best-seller with its call to prove "our mastery, not of nature, but of ourselves" (Steinbauer, 1990:18) and then appointed a special presidential advisory committee to study the issue. The committee called for more research into the potential health hazard of pesticides, and warned against their indiscriminate use. Despite her failing health, Carson made specific recommendations at congressional hearings in 1963. Eventually many pesticides, including DDT, were banned, and others were brought under stricter controls.

After Carson's death by cancer, her books continued to reach new audiences. Carson would have preferred to be remembered for her books about the sea, where the grandeur of her style is visible (Graham, 1970:270). Her joy came from sharing the wonder and beauty of the living world with others. In her 1955 article "Help Your Child to Wonder," she even challenged her readers to do the same by encouraging children to keep alive their instinctive interests in what is "beautiful and awe-inspiring" (Strong, 1988:184). Reluctantly, her focus changed when her reverence for life called her to bring the message of modern crisis to public attention in *Silent Spring*. As she explained it, "What I discovered was that everything which meant most to me as a naturalist was being threatened, and that nothing I could do would be more important" (Brooks, 1972:233).

Embedded in all of Carson's writings was her belief that humans constituted only a portion of nature, and what differentiated them from the rest of nature was their ability to destroy it, in some cases irreversibly (Lear, 2000:1). Her numerous awards included her election to the American Academy of Arts and Science, while her unusual blend of science and art was acknowledged through the Burroughs Medal, an honor that associated her with immortals in nature such as Henry David Thoreau (Gartner, 1983:2). In 1973 she was elected to the Women's Hall of Fame, and at the end of the twentieth century she was listed by *Time Magazine* as one of the 100 most important Americans of the century.

THE PRACTITIONER PIONEERS

The mere description of nature and the advocacy to preserve it would not have saved natural areas if it were not for the efforts of the practitioners, those who worked in the parks and wilderness areas and struggled to conserve and preserve their qualities and make areas available to others and future generations. Among these leaders are Frederick Law Olmsted, Gifford Pinchot, Stephen Mather, and Aldo Leopold.

Frederick Law Olmsted (1822-1903)

In the early years of the nineteenth century, New York City had a number of pleasure gardens that gradually gave way to buildings. By 1855 there were no gardens left, and city residents began visiting cemeteries for their foliage, lawns, and park-like amenities (Olmsted & Kimball, 1970:21). Although other cities of America at that time may have had open space and/or small parks, it was the establishment of New York's Central Park under the watchful eye of its architect, Frederick Law Olmsted, that signaled the birth of city parks in the United States.

As complaints about insufficient open space in New York continued, the Common Council of the city acquired an 840-acre parcel of rocky swamp land just north of the city's boundaries. In 1857 a nonpartisan board was appointed to develop the park. A design competition was conducted in which Olmsted and British-born architect Calvert Vaux participated. Their design, nicknamed *Greensward,* was awarded top prize over more than 30 competitors in April 1858, a year after Olmsted was appointed superintendent of the yet-undesigned Central Park (Doell & Twardzik, 1979: 42).

Born in Hartford, Connecticut, Frederick Law Olmsted was placed in the care of a Congregational minister after his mother's death when he was six. His enrollment in a succession of schools was interspersed with long vacations that were taken in New York, New England, and Canada with his father, a wealthy merchant. After nearly being blinded by sumac poisoning at age 15, his plans for college were abandoned. A favorite activity during his convalescence was drawing plans for hypothetical cities and towns. It may have been his upbringing and tendency to ramble in the New England countryside that contributed to his interest in extending the natural environment into urban life-style (Havard, 1989: 29). Nevertheless, before embarking on a career as a landscape architect, the profession that he created, he shipped out for China as an apprentice seaman in 1843 and also tried his hands at farming, writing, and other occupations.

Settling on a farm financed by Olmsted's father in Staten Island in 1848, Olmsted practiced landscape gardening and improved the grounds to such an extent that his neighbors would often seek his advice. He chose to interrupt rural life in 1850 to take an extensive trip to Europe, where the English landscape and city parks in Liverpool and London made a lasting impression on him. When he returned he wrote *Walks and Talks of an American Farmer in England*, and was soon embarking on a career as a writer. Almost immediately, Olmsted gained literary success (Strong, 1988:18). Among the most influential books that he produced were *Journey In the Backcountry* (1860) and *The Cotton Kingdom* (1861), both published by Mason brothers of New York. His writing was based on his dispatches as a *New York Times* correspondent in the pre-Civil War South. He also helped launch *The Nation*, the respected liberal journal still in circulation today. In 1855 he became partner in a New York publishing firm, and for a time edited *Putnam's Monthly Magazine*. When his firm went bankrupt two years later, he needed

capital, but, in his absence, the condition of the farm had become run down.

Olmsted's second career as environmental planner and designer began with his appointment in 1857, at the age of 35, as the superintendent of Central Park. He had to be politically astute to get such an appointment at a time when New York City was having many political battles over the potential park development. The state legislature passed an act for "the Regulation and Governance of Central Park in the City of New York." The act was a reaction to the lack of progress in developing the park coupled with the corruption and inefficiency of the politicians in charge (Jubenville, 1976:31). The idea for the park had dated back to at least 1844, when poet William Cullen Bryant made the proposal.

Central Park, Olmsted's first and most famous work, is so natural today that it is hard to believe that it emerged as a direct result of two men's ingenuity. Their design suggested that the development of the park revolve around a number of concepts that are still used in the planning of outdoor recreation areas. The two planners felt that a park is a single, coordinated work of art that should be framed upon a single, noble motive. The park should allow for some relief from the confinement of urban life. Yet uses of the park are not necessarily compatible, and accordingly different areas of the park should be spatially separated to reduce conflict and confusion. Moreover, the primary purpose of the park is to provide the best practicable means of healthful recreation for the inhabitants of all classes. Olmsted wanted to provide the lower classes with "a specimen of God's handiwork that shall be to them, inexpensively, what a month or two in the White Mountains, or the Adirondacks is. . . to those in easier circumstances" (Olmsted, Jr. & Kimball, 1970:46).

When the Civil War broke out in 1861, the United States Sanitary Commission, which became the American Red Cross, asked Olmsted to serve as its general secretary. In that capacity he was charged with providing troops with medical and sanitary supplies. Two years later he was offered the position of general manager of the Mariposa Company, a gold mining company near the Yosemite in California. The more lucrative position helped him pay his debt and support his wife and her three children; he had married his brother's widow. A year later Olmsted became Commissioner of Yosemite and Mariposa Big Tree Grove. In a report, he set forth justification and philosophic base for setting aside future parks the first statement of its kind in the United States and recommended that they be treated as museums of natural history. Although he listed reasons to establish Yosemite as a park, his report went unnoticed and even disappeared, perhaps because there was such competition for state funds (Strong, 1988:23-24). During his stay there, he was asked to provide a plan for the campus of the New University of California at Berkeley and the Golden Gate Park in San Francisco.

Olmsted returned to the East Coast in 1865, where he completed Central Park and undertook a number of landscaping projects, among which were Prospect Park in Brooklyn, Fairmont in Philadelphia, and Lincoln Park in Chicago. One of Olmsted's innovative concepts was the idea of a string of green spaces around a city to bring recreation areas close to every citizen. In 1888, Olmsted and Charles Eliot introduced this concept in Boston. The park was named the "Emerald Necklace." The idea was adopted by many cities.

The success of Central Park set off a mania for park building, and Olmsted's trademark sprouted up in the Midwest as well, in Belle Isle Park in Detroit, Cherokee Park in Louisville, and Lake Park in Milwaukee (Havard, 1989:32). His idea of a commuter village, a suburb of an urban center, such as Riverside is to Chicago, is still regarded as model for suburban design.

Among many of Olmsted's contributions aimed at underscoring the natural environment in the lives of those who live surrounded by buildings were landscape plans for numerous campuses and private estates. The Amherst, Trinity, West Point, George Washington, and Stanford campuses have his stamp. Biltmore, the estate of George Vanderbilt in Asheville, North Carolina, was designed by Olmsted, and later proclaimed by the nation's first chief of the forest service Gifford Pinchot as the "nest egg for practical Forestry in the United States" (Stevenson, 1977:404). He helped plan Boston's Arnold Arboretum, which served as a forest laboratory. In 1874 Olmsted was selected to improve the grounds of the Capitol in Washington, D.C. He played a major role in petitioning the United States and Canadian governments to protect Niagara Falls from waterpower development, and helped to establish the Adirondacks as a state forest preserve.

As an advocate of comprehensive city planning, Olmsted urged that a city plan "would make provisions for physical and mental health, safety and transportation needs in commercial and residential district, proper housing and recreation" (Fisher, 1986:2). Although Olmsted recognized the importance of outdoor recreation and sightseeing for health, vigor, and social transformation, we must point out that he had no patience with requests for organized recreation. "He saw his parks as places for walking, riding and relaxing in a naturalistic retreat from the harshness of the city" (Knudson, 1984:164). This attitude may have caused the friction that led to the rise of the playground and recreation movement of Joseph Lee, Jane Addams, and Luther Gulick, which will be discussed later. Today the park and recreation movements have come together to form a union, where the legacy of the nation's foremost park maker endures.

Following Olmsted's retirement in 1895, his son Frederick Law Olmsted, Jr., took over the leadership of his father's firm along with his stepbrother John Charles. The Olmsted Brothers' firm continued to carry on the work of Frederick Law Olmsted, employing nearly 60 staff at its peak in the early 1930s. Olmsted, Jr., who founded the first formal training program in landscape architecture at Harvard University in 1900, maintained a lifelong commitment to conservation, contributing the guiding language in legislation establishing the National Park Service in 1916. John Charles became the first president of the American Society of Landscape Architects in 1899 and led the office in comprehensive planning for metropolitan open spaces and park systems (National Park Service, 1998:2-3).

Gifford Pinchot (1865-1946)

America's first professionally trained forester, Gifford Pinchot, could have lived a life of luxury and ease. Instead he chose to travel wilderness trails and camp the wooded country, rising to national prominence as a conservationist and politician, who fought for wiser use of natural resources. Pinchot, born to wealth and social prominence at his family's summer home in Simsbury, Connecticut, was raised in New York City and at his family's wooded estate in Pennsylvania. Aware of his father's concern for the dwindling state of the nation's forests, he was quick to notice the more impressive European management of forests when he vacationed abroad with his family. Because no American university offered a course of instruction in forestry, he arranged his course of study at Yale. After graduation, he studied European forests while doing postgraduate work at the French National Forestry School at Nancy. Upon his return to the United States he began to explore the nation, observing the relationship of people and forests. He noted that forests were facing a desperate and losing struggle to loggers. Trees were vanishing along the eastern seaboard; also the hardwood forests of the South and the pine forests of the Midwest had been decimated. Recognizing that it was only a matter of time before timberlands in the West would disappear, Pinchot advocated the regulation of the commercial use of public and private forests. This included selective cutting, planning for future growth and the establishment of fire prevention measures. If properly managed, he was convinced that sustained yield was possible if it could be shown to be both practical and profitable. Pinchot expressed his sentiments at a later date:

> When I came home [from France] not a single acre of Government, State, or private timberland was under systematic forest management anywhere on the most richly timbered of all continents. ... When the Gay Nineties began, the common word for forests was "inexhaustible." To waste timber was a virtue and not a crime. There would always be plenty of timber. ...The lumbermen. . . regarded forest devastation as normal and second growth as a delusion of fools. ... And as for sustained yield, no such idea had ever entered their heads. The few friends of the forest were spoken of, when they were spoken of at all, as impractical theorists, fanatics, or "denudatics," more or less touched in the head. What talk there was about forest protection was no more to the average American than the buzzing of a mosquito, and just about as irritating (Williams, 2000:14-15).

Pinchot applied principles of scientific forestry in the private North Carolina forest of George W. Vanderbilt in North Carolina. Here Frederick Law Olmstead initiated the principle of selective logging, where young trees are given the opportunity to mature, and some mature trees are protected so that they may seed. After achieving a reasonable amount of success, Pinchot prepared an exhibit for the Chicago World's Fair in 1893 with an accompanying pamphlet, *Biltmore Forest*, the first of his many publications. Shortly thereafter, he became a consultant forester in New York City, made surveys of the forest lands of New Jersey, and drew plans for two private tracts in the Adirondacks. Greatly impacting Pinchot's career was the Congressional passage in 1891 of a bill providing that forest reserves could be set aside as government land through a presidential proclamation. Many of these reserved lands were eventually to come under his supervision.

In 1896 Pinchot was appointed to the National Forest Commission of the National Academy of Science, whose chairman supported U.S. Army protection to defend the reserves from poachers. Pinchot, the commission's secretary, voiced his objectives, which favored regulated use through a forest service whose members had received scientific training. Since he was the first American to make forestry a profession, Pinchot presumably saw himself in a leading position (Fox, 1981:110-113). In the end, the National Forest Commission's study helped bring about authorization for commercial use of these reserves through passage of the Forest Management Act of 1897 (see Chapter 7).

After serving as "special forest agent" for the secretary of interior, Pinchot was named chief of the small Federal Division of Forestry with the Agriculture Department in 1898, a departmental shift that Pinchot had supported since the later department employed professional foresters. Establishing a decentralized organization with built-in flexibility, he immediately began to establish his concepts of scientific forestry. His loyal, dedicated, and competent employees offered advice to some of the nation's largest lumber companies. Gradually they took on more responsibilities toward the management of the forest reserves, which remained with the Interior Department in the General Land Office. By 1901 his division had become the Bureau of Forestry. With the firm support and backing of President Theodore Roosevelt, Pinchot campaigned for Congress to transfer the forest reserves to the Department of Agriculture. Backing the transfer bill were stockmen, lumbermen, and others, who preferred the advantages of Pinchot's promise of long-term protection through controlled use to the potential prohibition of commercial use that might result from the formation of parks and game reserves with the Department of Interior (Strong, 1988:70-71).

In 1905, passage of the Transfer Act gave the Bureau, which was renamed the Forest Service, control of the national forest reserves. During Pinchot's administration, the national forests increased from 60 "forest reserves" covering 56 million acres in 1905 to 150 "national forests" covering 172 million acres in 1910 (Williams, 2000:14). He controlled their use, instituted a system of permits and fees, and regulated their harvest—it was not

until after World War II that large-scale logging and other controversial procedures, such as clear-cutting took place (Strong, 1988:72). Pinchot also arranged for the creation of an official badge for the forest rangers, encouraged uniform standards, and a high level of competency. He composed the principles upon which the Forest Service was to administer its new responsibilities:

> In the administration of the forest reserves it must be clearly borne in mind that all land is to be devoted to its most productive use for the permanent good of the whole people and not for the temporary benefit of individuals or companies. All the resources of the forest reserves are for use, and this use must be brought about in a thoroughly prompt and business-like manner, under such restrictions only as will insure the permanence of these resources (Cameron, 1928:239).

Pinchot believed in the public control of natural resources to ensure the rational, scientific use of the land to maximize its benefits for the greatest number of people. Opponents of the Pinchot-Roosevelt conservation program did not believe in the expansion of government control. Still others wished to exploit the nation's resources. With President Theodore Roosevelt's help, Pinchot organized a White House Conference on the Conservation of Natural Resources to which all the nation's governors and other leading figures were invited. Additionally the National Conservation Commission, chaired by Pinchot, was organized to make an inventory of the country's resources and their date of probable exhaustion. Once Roosevelt left office, however, the conservation movement declined. Pinchot's conservation policies went under the direct attack of the new secretary of interior, Richard A. Ballinger. Ballinger's appointment, by President William H. Taft, ended the interdepartmental cooperative agreements that had taken place between the Forest Service and interior when James R. Garfield (son of the former president) served as secretary of the interior in the Roosevelt administration.

The eventual struggle between Ballinger and Pinchot led to a split in the Taft administration. In 1910 Taft felt forced to dismiss Pinchot from government service after his public criticism of the President's decision to support Ballinger.

Application of Pinchot's *conservation* policy—using the land and its resources "for the benefit of many, and not merely for the profit of a few," caused the loss of the support of the preservationist wing of the conservationists. With his policy in mind, Pinchot consistently chose the wise use of resources over proposals to use the land for parks (Strong, 1988:73). In the Hetch Hetchy debate, for example (see Chapter 7), John Muir and the preservationists supported protection of the Hetch Hetchy Valley in Yosemite National Park for its beauty, while Pinchot supported San Francisco's request to acquire the area as a reservoir. Pinchot's view was brought before Congressional hearings in 1913. When asked if he knew of John Muir and his criticism of the bill, he replied:

> Yes, sir; I know him very well. He is an old and a very good friend of mine. ... When I became Forester and denied the right to exclude sheep and cows from the Sierras, Mr. Muir thought I had made a great mistake, because I allowed the use by an acquired right of a large number of people to interfere with what would have been the utmost beauty of the forest. In this case, I think he has unduly given away to beauty as against use (Nash, 1970:88).

Still interested in national politics, Pinchot made his first of several unsuccessful attempts for the Senate in 1914, running as a Progressive. That same year he married Cornelia Bryce at age 49. They had a son, Gifford Bryce Pinchot. She used her boundless energy to help with the campaigning, addressed housewives demanding the vote, and eventually sought election herself. In 1920, Pinchot was appointed Commissioner of Forestry by the governor of Pennsylvania, and in 1922 he was elected governor. Barred from succeeding himself, he tried again for the Senate

as a Republican candidate before being elected to a second term as governor in 1930. During his last year in office, he gave one last try for the United States Senate, but failed to gain the assistance of Republicans due to his support of Democrat Franklin D. Roosevelt's economic recovery programs. At age 72 he made a bid for nomination for governor once again, but the Republican votes overwhelmingly defeated him. Pinchot suffered a major heart attack in 1939, but he filled his remaining years by writing a book about his life as a forester, giving advice to the President, and devising a fishing kit that was used in lifeboats during World War II (Pennsylvania Historical and Museum Commission, 2001:2-4). Pinchot died of leukemia at age 81.

Throughout his years, Pinchot was a leader in matters involving conservation. In 1909 he founded the National Conservation Association and directed it from 1910 until it dissolved in 1923. He was involved in the passage of the Weeks Act in 1911, which provided for the expansion of forest reserves by purchase. A founder of the Society of American Foresters, he served as its president from 1900-1908 and 1910-1911. He continued his interest in forestry by serving as a nonresident lecturer and professor at the Yale School of Forestry, established through a lectureship grant awarded by his father. He wrote *The Fight for Conservation* in 1910, and his autobiography, *Breaking New Ground*, was published posthumously in 1947 (Penick, 1974:665).

Gifford Pinchot, the utilitarian champion, viewed conservation as a demand for the welfare of the present generation first, and future generations later. Eventually this view gave way. Men of the Forest Service, such as Aldo Leopold, shifted from a dominance of nature, in the Pinchot tradition, to a more cooperative harmony with nature. As such, the foundation was laid for stronger recreation and wilderness values. Pinchot's legacy remained, however, molding Forest Service culture and values of conservation leadership, public service, responsiveness, integrity, a strong land ethic, and professionalism characterized by people who know their jobs and do them well. These values are the bedrock on which the Forest Service stands (see the chapter on Federal Resources).

Stephen Mather (1867-1930)

Stephen Mather was a staunch conservationist, and he was among the first to urge the United States Congress to set aside areas that are of scenic, historic, and scientific significance. Born in San Francisco, California, he developed at an early age a great affection for the natural beauty of the great Sierras. In 1887 Mather graduated from the University of California, Berkeley, and moved to the East Coast to work as a reporter for the *New York Sun* for five years. After he married Jane Floy he decided to pursue a career as his father had in the borax mining business, where he became an executive with a passion for advertising. In this capacity he helped to create the celebrated trade slogan "20 Mule Team Borax." A lucrative partnership developed with a friend followed in 1903. The 11-year association at the Thorkildsen-Mather Borax Company not only made Mather a millionaire, it provided the committed conservationist with time to do volunteer work and enjoy hiking and mountaineering.

As a member of the Sierra Club, Mather took trips to the Sierra Nevada, where he met John Muir, who urged him to take a stand to protect the region against destructive activities such as logging and mining. While visiting the Yosemite and Sequoia National Parks, Mather became aware of private landholding in scenic areas, cattle grazing in the national parks, and poor roads and trails (Strong, 1988:113). Concerned about the deteriorating condition of the national parks, Mather wrote to this effect to his acquaintance Frank Lane, the secretary of the interior. Lane simply invited him "to come to Washington and do something about it." Enticed out of retirement, Mather showed up in 1915 ready to go to work. Mather was made assistant to the secretary. Until his appointment, there had been no one person

to take on the direction of the 13 national parks and 18 national monuments. In fact, their management, which came under the auspices of the Department of the Interior at the time of his arrival, was accomplished by a loose organizational coalition of the Departments of Interior, War, and Agriculture (Simpson, 1989:95). Moreover, the pool from which park superintendents were selected was political rather than professional in nature. Mather realized that the system needed a vast overhaul, which he set forth to accomplish. The plan was to tackle the problem on five fronts (Shankland, 1970:56).

1. Get Congress interested enough in the national parks (a) to make vast increases in their appropriations and (b) to authorize a bureau of national parks.
2. Authorize a bureau and start it functioning.
3. Get the public excited about the national parks.
4. Make park travel easier by promoting wholesale improvements in hotels, camps, and other concessions and in roads and transportation facilities both inside the national parks and outside.
5. Sell national park integrity to the point where Congress would
(a) Add to the system all appropriate sites possible, (b) keep out inappropriate sites, (c) keep the established sites safe from invasion, and
(d) Purge the established sites of private holdings. (Shankland, 1970:56)

The first task was not an easy one, since previous attempts to get the United States Congress to establish a federal bureau had failed, beginning with a bill drafted by J. Horace McFarland and Frederick Law Olmsted, Jr. in 1910. Seeing the difficult road ahead, Lane helped by appointing a young lawyer from California, Horace Albright, to assist him. Mather contributed to the cause by reaching into his own pockets to create the position of publicity chief, which he offered to Robert Sterling Yard, a friend from the *New York Sun*. Yard served in this position, and then chief, from 1915 to 1919. During his first year Yard prepared *The National Parks Portfolio* for distribution to 270,000 opinion makers throughout the country, helped to generate numerous articles about the national parks, and personally wrote pamphlets and articles designed to capture the attention of the public (Albright, 1990:17). To convince Congress to support a bureau of national parks, Mather invited influential persons, including newspaper publishers and editors, railroad executives, and influential Congressmen to tour Sequoia National Park at his expense. As could be expected, primary opposition came from the Forest Service. With many of the parks next to national forests, Forest Service administrators had hoped that the national parks would be transferred to the Department of Agriculture. On the other hand, the 1913 loss of Hetch Hetchy caused many conservationists to support the development of a bureau that could provide protection for the parks.

Mather's public relations campaign was a success. Congress appropriated the majority of the money needed to purchase Giant Forest within Sequoia National Park and the National Geographic Society donated the remainder needed. Public awareness increased as articles in prestigious magazines such as *National Geographic* and *Saturday Evening Post* as well as in prominent newspapers exulted America's natural beauty and supported the need for its preservation. In the meantime, Mather, too, visited most of the parks, gathering information about basic visitor needs.

In August of 1916, President Woodrow Wilson signed the bill to establish the National Park Service that became Public Law 64-235. For 15 years Mather ran the national park service as its first director, and Albright, who succeeded him as director in 1929, became his assistant. Major achievements soon followed. In 1916 Lassen Volcanic National Park (in Califor-

nia) and Hawaii National Park (now called Haleakala) were added to the system. Mount McKinley (now Denali) National Park was added in 1917. Attendance at all of the parks increased at a rapid rate, as did the demand for material about the parks. Nonetheless, Mather was always under constant pressure from critics. He suffered a breakdown. During an 18-month rest, Albright took over. Returning with new zeal, Mather worked to open the parks to recreational activities, joined Albright in his fight to ward off commercial pressures, and Mather opposed proposals for waterpower development in Yellowstone National Park (Strong, 1988:118-119). In his director's report, Mather made the following plea:

> Is there not some place in this great nation of ours where lakes can be preserved in their natural state; where we and all generations to follow us can enjoy the beauty and charm of mountain waters in the midst of primeval forests? The country is large enough to spare a few such lakes and beauty spots. The nation has wisely set apart a few national parks where a state of nature is to be preserved. If the lakes and forest of these parks cannot be spared from the hand of commercialization, what hope can we entertain for the preservation of any scenic features of the mountains in the interest of posterity? (Mather, 1919:963)

Once the park service was on solid ground, Mather took a few months off after a friend died and to recuperate from his latest round of battles. His next goal was to increase the Service's holdings to include "scenery of supreme and distinctive quality or some natural features so extraordinary or unique as to be of national interest and importance" (Lane, 1918:112-113). After the number of national parks and monuments nearly doubled, Mather decided to concentrate on extending some of their boundaries. Since extensions often involved expanding into the national forests, the rivalry between the two agencies openly grew. Although the Forest Service responded by preserving some of their prized scenic areas, most were eventually lost to the National Park Service. Mather also set up a commission to study potential parks in the east, supported the Save-the-Redwoods League to save the coastal redwoods of California, and championed the development of state parks throughout the nation by organizing a convention on state parks at Des Moines, Iowa in 1921 (Strong, 1988: 122-126).

In an effort to make all of the national parks and monuments accessible to the majority of Americans, Mather continued to invite Congressional representatives and their families to personally visit these outstanding lands. While there, they were also driven on the poor roads. When appropriations for roads more than doubled, Mather stressed the importance of building roads through a portion of the park's most representative sections, but maintained that the remainder of the park should remain as natural as possible. To arrange for visitor needs, Mather recommended that one qualified operator hold a license for the concessions in order to eliminate potential for commercialization and waste. This would also enable the government to approve rates and standards of service (Strong, 1988:122-129). While there were those who opposed this system of regulated monopoly, others protested any form of improvements in the parks. Mather's greatest clash, however, was with corrupt politicians who pushed for franchises for friends. Mather fought back and won.

Stephen Mather, who accepted the invitation to come to Washington, did do something about the conditions of the nation's fledgling national parks and monuments. During his administration, he publicized the value of preserving the nation's heritage, designed policies that guide the public's use of scenic and historic resources, cultivated an exceptional personnel organization, launched campfire programs with park rangers, promoted museums and other means of interpretation, improved public access and use, blocked private enterprise from actions that would destroy a park's scenic beauty, arranged for large donations, and won the cooperation of Congress and big business. The national park system, thus became a model for other countries. Although he planned to stay in his position longer, Mather left the service after he suffered a massive stroke. His life is summarized on bronze markers through many parks which read:

> He laid the foundation of the National Park Service, defining and establishing the policies under which its areas shall be developed and conserved, unimpaired for future generations. There will never come an end to the good he has done . . .

Aldo Leopold (1887-1948)

Prominent wildlife ecologist, uncommon conservationist, and environmental philosopher Aldo Leopold was born the eldest of four children in Burlington, Iowa. This Mississippi River community afforded him the opportunity to become acquainted with wildlife at a young age. He recognized the steady decline of the wood duck population and the forest lands. His father, Carl Leopold, who owned a thriving desk factory, enjoyed the outdoors and nature. Setting an example of sportsmanship for the younger Leopold, he refused to hunt waterfowl during the nesting season long before such practices had been enacted by federal law. While in high school, Leopold kept a journal of his observations of nature, the beginnings of his prolific writings. Expected to take over the family business, he instead entered Yale University's Sheffield's Scientific School, where he received his B.S. in 1908. The following year he entered the Yale School of Forestry, founded by a grant from James Pinchot, and received his Master of Forestry degree. After graduation he was employed as a forest assistant on the Apache National Forest in Arizona in the Arizona Territory, just four years after the Forest Service was established. By 1911, Leopold was promoted to deputy forest supervisor, and a year later, supervisor of the Carson National Forest in the New Mexico Territory, where he became aware that the country was losing its wilderness (Wilderness Society, 1998:1). He married Estella Bergere from Santa Fe, with whom he had five children. Starker, Luna, Nina, Carl, and Estella all built their own careers as conservationists and scientists.

Leopold's career was placed on hold for almost 17 months when he suffered from a near-fatal attack of acute nephritis, probably as a result of over-exposure while camping during an assignment. During his convalescence he read widely including, most likely, the writings of Thoreau (Rogers & Ford, 1989:187). Returning to the service in 1914 he was assigned to the Office of Grazing at district headquarters in Albuquerque, where he became interested in the new science of ecology and began his life's work on wildlife management issues, including game refuges, law enforcement, and predator control (Forest Service, 2000:62). While working on recreation, fish, and game, Leopold recommended that game refuges be established within the district, and he prepared the Forest Service's first game and fish handbook. He founded a number of big game protective associations in New Mexico and Arizona, edited a quarterly newspaper of the New Mexico Game Protective Association called *The Pine Cone*, and received the W. T. Hornaday's Permanent Wildlife Protection Fund's Gold Medal for his work in the field. Although Leopold was once an advocate of the elimination of predators, including wolves and mountain lions, in order to preserve game species such as deer, he changed his opinion, advocating ecological balance. Years later in his essay, "Thinking Like a Mountain," he shared a story about his earlier encounter with a dying old wolf, explaining, "I thought that because fewer wolves meant more deer, that no wolves would mean hunters' paradise. But after seeing the green fire die, I sensed that neither the wolf nor the mountain agreed with such a view" (Gibbons, 1991:690).

In 1918 Leopold took a leave of absence from the Forest Service to become Secretary of the Albuquerque Chamber of Commerce. Leopold was supportive of Congressional action, which allowed national forest lands to be used for recreational as well as commercial purposes. With the United States' entry into World War I, the Forest Service was obligated to shift priorities from recreational development to a more utilitarian management of forest resources. Upon his return the next year as Assistant District Forester for Operations in the southwestern Region, he became concerned about the rapid pace of road expansion after the war and began to call for the protection of wilderness lands within the national forests as places of preservation and human activity. In 1921, he wrote his most significant article, "The Wilderness and its Place in Forest Recreational Policy," which was published in the *Journal of Forestry*. Through his efforts, the 500,000-acre Gila Wilderness Area in New Mexico became the first administrative wilderness designated for recreation in 1924. Camping and backpacking were permissible activities in the wilderness area, but tourist campgrounds were not to be provided. This novel plan was articulated 40 years later at the national level in the Wilderness Act, thereby making Leopold a "Pioneer of Wilderness" (Rogers & Ford, 1989:187-188). Leopold believed that wilderness preservation symbolized self-restraint in the developing society; served as a reminder of our pioneer legacy, and provided an undisturbed ecosystem for environmental study (Nash, 1974:48).

In 1924 Leopold moved to Madison, Wisconsin, to become the Assistant, then Associate Director of the Forest Products Laboratory of the Forest Service. Continuing his efforts toward wilderness preservation, he wrote a 1925 article entitled "Wilderness as a Form of Land Use," which developed the notion that Americans no longer needed to conquer the wilderness, but that they needed to set aside large portions of it for posterity. As a speaker at the second National Conference on Outdoor Recreation in 1926, he called wilderness a fundamental recreation resource, and urged the development of national wilderness preservation policy. William B. Greeley, U.S. Forest Service Chief, endorsed his idea, and an inventory of roadless land areas in the United States was conducted and reported at the Third National Conference on Outdoor Recreation in 1928. By 1929 the pathfinding L-20 Regulations directed the Forest Service districts to preserve undeveloped land; thus began the movement to establish "primitive areas" within national forests (Rogers & Ford, 1989:188-189).

Leopold resigned from the Forest Service in 1928 to design a new profession in game management, which he modeled on the profession of forestry. His game survey of nine Midwestern states was funded by the Sporting Arms and Ammunition Manufacturers' Institute. These surveys were summarized in his 1931 *Report on a Game Survey of the North Central States,* one of the first intensive studies of game population ever undertaken in the United States. He also helped develop the country's first game management policy for the American Game Protective Association and was appointed to President Franklin D. Roosevelt's Committee on Wildlife Restoration. As one of the country's finest authorities on native game, Leopold became known as the "Father of Game Management" and more recently the "Father of Wildlife Ecology." His landmark book *Game Management* (1933) clarified the fundamental skills and techniques for managing and restoring wildlife populations. By weaving forestry, agriculture, biology, zoology, ecology, education, and communication, he had created a new science and defined the new profession (Aldo Leopold Nature Center, 2001:1). Soon after publication, Leopold accepted an appointment to a new chair in the Department of Agricultural Economics at the University of Wisconsin. When the university created the Department of Wildlife Management in 1939, Leopold became the first person in the nation to chair the new science, holding this position until his death. Although Leopold spent the next several decades with wildlife management issues, his interests expanded to the field of ecology, where he is most revered today (Forest Service, 2000:63-64).

Leopold's concepts, based on the emerging science of systems ecology, synthesized the most progressive knowledge of population dynamics, food chains, and habitat protection (Nash, 1974:483). He noted that "we stand guard over works of art, but species representing the work of aeons are stolen from under our noses" (Gibbons, 1991: 690-91). Basic to his beliefs was the idea that the environment is not a commodity for humans to control but a community to which they belong. This innovative idea stimulated the development of Leopold's most important concept, "the land ethic," which he wrote of in his most widely read book, *A Sand County Almanac:*

> A land ethic, then, reflects the existence of an ecological conscience, and this in turn reflects a conviction of individual responsibility for the health of the land. Health is the capacity of the land for self-renewal. Conservation is our effort to understand and preserve this capacity. . . . It is inconceivable to me that an ethical relation to land can exist without love, respect, and admiration for land, and a high regard for its value. By value, I of course mean something far broader than mere economic value; I mean value in the philosophical sense. Perhaps the most serious obstacle impeding the evolution of a land ethic is the fact that our educational and economic system is headed away from, rather than toward, an intense consciousness of land. . . .In short, land is something he has "outgrown" (Leopold, 1966:236).

Although he had no religious affiliation of his own, many consider Leopold's "land ethic" a spiritual act of consequence to the future of life on earth (Nash, 1974: 484). He rationalized that we develop a revolutionary appreciation for land by entering it. For land brings the human race to it as a responsible member of that land community, not as its conqueror. Although published after his death, *A Sand County Almanac (1949)* contains ecological essays that Leopold began before World War II. It shares a lifetime of his observations of nature and the development of his ideas. His work, which has been compared to that of Henry David Thoreau and John Muir, is regarded as a classic in environmental literature and a bible for the environmental movement. Many of his observations and essays were written at his vacation home, fondly known as "The Shack." When the Leopold family purchased a worn-out farm on the Wisconsin River in an area known as the sand counties near Baraboo in 1935, they rebuilt the only standing structure on the property, an old chicken coop, turning it into a cabin. Today it is still called " The Shack" and he would be proud to see the forest and prairie that surround it. True to his creed, Leopold and his family participated in the land's restoration by planting prairie and thousands of trees on the property. They also revitalized a low area into a wetland that attracts waterfowl. According to Leopold, "We abuse land when we regard it as a commodity belonging to us. When we see land as a community to which we belong, we may begin to use it with love and respect" (Hirsh, 1971:150).

During Leopold's last vacation at "The Shack," smoke was spotted across the swamp on a neighbor's farm. Gathering his family, he handed out buckets and brooms, and went with them to put out the fire, but in the process he died of a heart attack at age 61. Before his death, Leopold had been active in a number of conservation endeavors, which included: member of the council of the Society of American Foresters (1927-1931); elected fellow 1946; director of the National Audubon Society; vice-president of the American Forestry Association; founder of the Wilderness Society in 1935 with Robert Marshall, Benton MacKaye, Harvey Broome, Barnard Frank, Harold Anderson, Ernest Oberholtzer, and Sterling Yard; president of the Wilderness Society in 1939; president of the Ecological Society of America (1947); and member of the Wisconsin Conservation Commission from 1943 until his death (Nash, 1974:484). Additionally Leopold traveled to Germany to study forestry and wildlife management in the fall of 1935 when he received the Carl Schurz fellowship, and he took the first of two pack trips along the Rio Gavilan in Chihuahua, Mexico in 1936. *Round River, from the Journal of Aldo Leopold* (1953) was, like *A Sand County Almanac*, edited by his daughter, Luna B. Leopold, and published posthumously. Today the Aldo Leopold Foundation holds the rights to all of his unpublished material and those works published by nonextant publications at the University of Wisconsin Archives.

SUMMARY

This chapter dealt with the visionaries and practitioner pioneers who foresaw the need for preservation of areas, establishment of programs, and development of concepts that enhance the pursuit of leisure in natural resources. The transcendentalists, Ralph Waldo Emerson and Henry David Thoreau, venerated nature and called on citizens of this country and the world to respect and preserve it. The depth of their commitment is only overshadowed by the depth of the meaning behind their words. Both men were among the literary giants of the 19th century.

The scientist-naturalists, John Audubon, John Muir, and Rachel Carson, observed nature and recorded their observations, which were eventually shared with millions of people. Wilderness to them was a place of awe and worship. Their life work spearheaded a preservation movement that gained momentum in the mid 1900s and is in the mainstream of society's activity today.

The pioneer practitioners of Frederick Law Olmsted, Gifford Pinchot, Stephen Mather, and Aldo Leopold put into practice the concepts gained from the transcendentalists and scientist-naturalists. They laid the foundations for our nation's fledgling institutions that manage our recreational resources and they helped to shape the roles of the park rangers and foresters who manage the natural resources for multiple use, limited use, and the betterment of the ecosystem. Frederick Law Olmsted is called the father of the American park: Gifford Pinchot was the pioneer of American forests; Stephen Mather was the first director of the National Park Service, and Aldo Leopold was a promoter of wilderness areas and a founder of the Wilderness Society.

REFERENCES

Albright, J. (1990). Robert Sterling Yard In W. Sontag (Ed.), *National Park Service: The first 75 years*. Fort Washington, PA: Eastern National Park & Monument Association.

Aldo Leopold Nature Center. (2001). *Who was Aldo Leopold?* [On-line]. Available: http://www.naturenet.com/alnc/aldo.html.

Atkinson, B., (Ed.). (1950). *The selected writings of Ralph Waldo Emerson*. New York: Modern

Audubon, J. J. (1960). *Audubon and his journals*, Vol.1, II. New York: Diver Publications.

BCD. (1998). Henry David Thoreau. [CD-ROM]. *Encyclopedia Britannica*, 1-4, file://C:\Program%20Files\Britannica\BCE\Cache_5_ArticleRil.htm.

Benet, L. (1966). *Famous English and American essayists*. New York: Dodd, Mead.

Bolton, S. (1954). *Famous American authors*. New York: Thomas Y. Crowell.

Brooks, A., (Ed.). (1950). *The complete essays and other writings of Ralph Waldo Emerson*. New York: Random House.

Brooks, P. (1972). *The house of life: Rachel Carson at work*. Boston: Houghton Mifflin.

Cameron, J. (1928). *The development of forest control in the United States*. Baltimore: Johns Hopkins University Press.

Carson, R. (1963, September/October). Rachel Carson answers her critics. *Audubon, 65-66*, 262.

De Bruhl, M. (1981). Carson. In *Dictionary of American biology, supplement seven*, (pp. 1961-65). New York: Charles Scribner's Sons.

Doell, C., & L. Twardzik. (1979). *Elements of park and recreation administration*. Minneapolis, MN: Burgess.

Downing, L. (1992). *John Muir and the United States National Park System*. [On-line]. Available: ww.sierraclub.org/john_muir_exhibit/life/muir_and_nps_downing_1992.html.

Elman, R. (1977). *First in the field*. New York: Mason/Chartu.

Fisher, C. (1949). *The life of Audubon*. New York: Harper and Brothers.

Fisher, I. D. (1986). *Frederick Law Olmsted and the city planning movement in the United States*. Ann Arbor, MI: UMI Research Press.

Ford, P. (1989). John Muir. In H. Ibrahim (Ed.), *Pioneers in leisure*. Reston, VA: American Alliance for Health, Physical Education, Recreation and Dance (AAHPERD).

Fox, S. R. (*1981*). *John Muir and his legacy: The American conservation movement*. Boston: Little, Brown.

Gartner, C. (1983). *Rachel Carson*. New York: Frederick Ungar.

Gibbons, B. (1981, November). Aldo Leopold: A durable scale of values. *National Geographic, 160*(5), 682-708.

Gilbert, A. (1914). *More than conquerors*. New York: Century.

Graham, Jr., F. (1970). *Since silent spring*. Boston: Houghton Mifflin.

Grossman, A., & Beardwood, V. (1961). *Trails of his own*. New York: Longmans, Green.

Harding, W. (1954). *Thoreau: A century of criticism*. Dallas, TX: Southern Methodist University Press.

Havard, R. (1989). Frederick Law Olmsted. In H. Ibrahim (Ed.), *Pioneers in leisure and recreation*. Reston, VA: AAHPERD.

Hirsh, C. S. (1971). *Guardians of tomorrow*. New York: Viking.

Jubenville, A. (1976). *Outdoor recreation planning*. Philadelphia: W. B. Saunders.

Lane, F. (1918). *Report of the Secretary of Interior*, 65th Congress, 3rd session, H.Doc.1455.

Lear, L. (2000). *Rachel Louise Carson*. [On-line]. Available: http://www.rachelcarson.org/index.cfm?fuseaction=bio

Knudson, D. (1984). *Outdoor recreation*. New York: Macmillan.

Leopold, A. (1966). *A Sand County almanac*. New York: Oxford University Press.

Leshuk, D. (1988). *John Muir's Wisconsin days*. [On-line]. Available: http://www.sierraclub.org/john_muir_exhibit/life/muir_wisconsin_dave_leshuk.html.

Mather, S. (1919). Report of the Director of the National Park Service. In *Reports of the*

Department of the Interior, 66th Congress 2nd session, H.Doc. 409.

Matthiessen, P. (1999, June 14). *Rachel Carson*. [On-line]. Available: www.time.com/time/time100/scientist/profile/carson.html.

Muir, J. (1977). *The mountains of California*. Berkeley, CA: Ten Speed Press. Reissue.

Muir, J. (1975). *The story of my boyhood and youth*. Dunwoody, GA: Norman S. Berg. Reissue.

M.V.D. (1931). Emerson. In *Dictionary of American Bibliography*, Vol. VI. New York: Charles Scribner's Sons.

Nash, R. (1970). *The call of the wild (1900-1916)*. New York: George Braziller.

Nash, R. (1974). Aldo Leopold. In *Dictionary of American Biography*. Supplement Four, (pp. 146-50). New York: Charles Scribner's Sons.

National Audubon Society. (2001). John James Audubon 1785-1851. [On-line]. Available: http//www.jjaudubon.com/bio/chronos.html.

National Park Service. (1998). Olmsted and sons: the Olmsted office, 1-4. [On-line]. Available: http://www.nps.gov/frla/background.htm.

Olmsted, Jr., F., & Kimball, T. (Eds.). (1970). *Frederick Law Olmsted, landscape architect, 1822-1903*. New York: Benjamin Blorn.

Penick, Jr., J. (1974). Gifford Pinchot. In *Dictionary of American Biography*. Supplement Four, 1946. New York: Charles Scribner's Sons.

Pennsylvania Historical and Museum Commission (2001). Gifford Pinchot, 1-4. [On-line]. Available: http://www.dep.state.pa.us/dep/PA_Env-Her/pinchot_bio.htm.

Rogers, S. E., & Ford, P. (1989). Aldo Leopold. In H. Ibrahim (Ed.), *Pioneers in leisure and recreation*. Reston, VA: AAHPERD.

Ronald, A. (1987). *Words from the wild*. San Francisco: Sierra Club Books.

Rothe, A., (Ed.). (1952). *Current Biography: Who's new and why, 1951*. New York: H. W. Wilson.

R.W.A., & H.S.C. (1936). Thoreau. In *Dictionary of American Bibliography*, Vol. XVIII. New York: Charles Scribner's Sons.

Schildgen, B. (2001, November/December). Deconstructing Thoreau. *Sierra 86*(6), 74.

Shankland, R. (1970). *Steven Mather of the national parks*, 3rd ed. New York: ALfred A. Knopf.

Simpson, R. (1989). "Stephen T. Mather" in *Pioneers in leisure and recreation*, H. Ibrahim, (ed.). Reston, VA: AAHPERD.

Stevenson, E. (1977). *Park maker: A life of Frederick Law Olmsted*. New York: Macmillan.

Stone, D. (1988). *Dreamers and defenders American conservationists*. University of Nebraska Press.

Ryan, P. (1990). "John Muir" in *National Park Service: The first 75 years*, W. Sontag, (Ed.). Fort Washington, PA: Eastern National Park & Monument Association.

Teale, E. (1962). *The thoughts of Thoreau*. New York: Dodd, Mead.

Teale, F. (1954). *The wilderness world of John Muir*. Boston: Houghton Mifflin.

Thoreau, H. (1965). *The Maine Woods*. West Raven, CT: College and University Press. Reprint.

Vickery, J. (1989). "Wilderness Visions." *Backpacker* 17(5):45.

W.F.B. (1934). "John Muir" in *Dictionary of American Bibliography*, Vol. XIII. New York: Charles Scribner's Sons.

White, G. (1996). "John Muir: The Wilderness Journeys," 1-7, http://www.sierraclub.org/john_muir_exhibit/life/wilderness_journeys_white.html.

Wilkins, T. (1995). *John Muir: Apostle of nature*. Norman and London: University of Oklahoma Press.

Williams, G. (2000). *The USDA Forest Service–The first century*. Washington, D.C.:FS-650 (July).

Wolf, W. (1974). *Thoreau: Mystic, prophet, ecologist*.

Wolfe, L. (1945). *Son of the wilderness: The life of John Muir*. Madison: The University of Wisconsin Press.

4 PSYCHOLOGY AND THE NATURAL ENVIRONMENT

This chapter concerns itself with the psychology of the outdoor experience. A short presentation of the field of psychology will be given, followed by a presentation of the different attempts to explain the outdoor experience in psychological terms. Attempts at analyzing leisure activities as a unit have not been very fruitful in producing a unified psychology of leisure. Ingham (1986:276) suggested that these attempts can be classified into two approaches: the experiential approach, which emphasizes the subjective qualities of the leisure experience, relying extensively on self-reporting with little attempt at discovering the underlying physiological bases that accompany these experiences, and a second approach that includes the reported motivation, satisfaction, and attribute of the leisure experience. While it seems that the two schools do not see eye to eye, since few mutual citations appear in their research, they both tend to agree that perceived freedom (from obligation) and intrinsic motivation (an activity for its own sake) are two concepts to which they can subscribe.

LEISURE AS A STATE OF MIND

The difficulty in viewing leisure as a state of mind only lies in the fact that leisure is a complex phenomenon. Its physiological, social, and psychological dimensions usually overlap. Analyzing the psychological side of the leisure experience is of interest to a small number of psychologists, who suggested a number of criteria for a bona fide leisure experience to occur.

Perceived Freedom

To John Neulinger, at least early in his career, the primary psychological factor in a leisure experience is perceived freedom. This is "a state in which the person feels that what he is doing, he is doing by choice and because he wants to do it" (1974:15). What is relevant is that the person perceives the activity as being freely chosen. Neulinger later added two more criteria: motivation for the leisure activity and the quality of its outcome. According to Kelly, these two criteria are attitudinal, criteria which "can be found in almost any context since there is no necessary condition for the perception outside the individual" (1987:26). A recent study showed that when adolescents engaged in activities because they wanted to, they reported lower levels of boredom and higher levels of intrinsic motivation (Caldwell et al, 1999).

The concept of freedom in leisure research has been criticized in that it does not differentiate between freedom from (stress) and freedom to (choose an activity). Nonetheless, this concept is still in use in defining leisure behavior (Mannell & Kleiber, 1999).

Autotelic Activities

These are activities that are meaningful in, and by, themselves. "Does greater freedom always lead to greater leisure?" asked Mannell and Bradley (1986). In their study of freedom and leisure, they found that externally oriented subjects were less absorbed in their leisure experience than the internally oriented subjects. Their findings add support to the contention that it is perceived freedom that is critical in determining the experience of leisure.

Perception continues to be of importance in the work of Mihalyi Csikszentmihalyi (1975). To him, the individual's perception of the activity is what matters, not the mere perception of freedom. If the participant perceives the activity as too difficult to handle, anxiety will occur. On the other hand, if the activity is perceived as too easy, boredom will result. He labeled the optimum condition for a meaningful experience of activity as "flow."

Beneficial Outcome

The work of B.L. Driver, H. E. A. Tinsley, and their associates concentrated on studying the benefits derived from leisure experiences. B.L. Driver employed a series of scales to measure the outcomes of the recreational use of natural resources (1976). Thirty-nine psychological benefits representing 19 domains were identified, and the Recreation Experience Preference (REP) scales were constructed to measure these benefits. According to Driver's model, a person will partake of a leisure activity because of his or her expectations for a positively valued benefit.

> Driver and Brown (1978) later developed a system that would assist managers of leisure delivery systems to use the information gained from REP scales which they entitled the Recreation Opportunity Spectrum (ROS). The system presents the leisure environment as a spectrum of opportunity available to the individual. It identifies six levels of "naturalness" : primitive, semi primitive non-motorized, semi primitive motorized, roaded natural, rural, and urban. For

> ROS, the more primitive the setting, the more one can experience solitude, tranquility, self-reliance, and closeness to nature.

There will be more discussion of the psychological benefits of outdoor experience later in this chapter. Let us first examine the question of whether certain traits in some individuals make them inclined to partake of leisure experience.

TRAITS AND THE LEISURE EXPERIENCE

Personality traits can be looked upon as continuous dimensions on which individual differences can be observed. Thus, different leisure preferences may be arranged quantitatively or qualitatively. Traits are dispositions that may determine leisure behavior. Perhaps the most intriguing trait pertaining to outdoor recreation is the one labeled type T personality, belonging to the thrill seekers, risk takers, and adventurers who seek excitement and stimulation, giving activity providers great worry and undue headaches.

Although personality may cause or direct leisure behavior and experience, that relationship is rather complex (Mannell & Kleiber, 1999). Nonetheless, it is important to look into the traits that may affect leisure choice.

Leisure and the Type T Personality

According to Farley (1986), the type T personality is on one end of a continuum. At the opposite end of that continuum is the type t personality (with a lowercase "t"), belonging to those who cling to certainty and predictability. Most people fall in between these two extremes. One with a type T personality has a low physiological arousability and therefore seeks excitement. Humans normally seek to adjust to some middle ground between high and low arousals. Some are born with unusually low arousability and are not very responsive to mental or physical stimuli, and these are big T persons who may seek highly stimulating experiences and environments. The precise biological bases for

Personality traits seem to influence the choice of the recreational activity that people engage in most frequently. The Chesapeake and Ohio Canal National Historical Park follows the route of the 184-mile canal along the Potomac River. At Great Falls in Maryland, a number of activities are available to suit individual tastes from a peaceful day of fishing to an adventurous day of whitewater kayaking in the falls. Other activities include hiking, bicycling, horseback riding, rock climbing, nature photography, ranger-led programs, and visitations to historic sites.

their low arousability is not yet known. Coupled with biological differences are personality traits that set big T persons apart from others: they tend to be more creative, more extroverted, and more experimental, and they tend to take more risks. Activity providers will find more men and younger persons in this category. They are the ballooners, mountain climbers, and skydivers. The number of women in this category is increasing (Mills, 1986).

The Explorers Club, perhaps the most prestigious organization for adventurers in the world, which in the recent past was for males only, had 85 women among its 3,000 members in the 1990s. Among the risk activities partaken by women are crossing the Australian outback alone on a camel for five months covering 1,700 miles, ascending Ana Purna's 26,000 feet, and crossing Papua New Guinea alone on foot. Why did Jan Reynolds climb up to 25,000 feet to ski off peak Mustagata in western China? She answers: "The deep, smooth satisfaction I felt after I skied off Mustagata, under the golden, fading light of day was something that I will feel very seldom, if ever again, and that I will treasure like a precious jewel" (Mills, 1986:27).

Leisure and Personality Traits

In studying personality, theorists describe it as being composed of trait dimensions along a series of continua. These traits affect behavior, including leisure choices. Driver and Knopf (1977) used the Personality Research Form (PRF) to investigate the traits of 50 recreationists and arrived at the following conclusions:

1. Personality traits probably influence the choice of the recreational activity in which a person engages the most frequently.
2. Selected personality variables are significantly related to the amount of participation in a preferred activity once the choice has been made.
3. Personality traits do influence how important different types of desired consequences (or experiences) are to a recreationist when he or she decides to engage in preferred activities.

A criticism of the dependence on traits to try to understand leisure behavior is based on the exclusion of the role of the environment, both physical and social. A relatively new interest in environmental psychology helps in discovering the role it plays in leisure behavior.

ENVIRONMENT AND THE LEISURE EXPERIENCE

What role does the environment, particularly the natural environment, play in the motivation for, attitudes toward, and satisfaction with a leisure experience? Stokols and Altman (1987), two experts in environmental psychology, suggested that the emphasis in psychological research in the past concentrated on personal traits and interaction as seen in Table 4.1. The study of trait looks for universal laws, and the study of interaction focuses on the relationships among the elements.

Table 4.1 deals with the units of analysis used in arriving at conclusions concerning the motivation for, and the satisfaction with, certain behaviors. For our purposes, neither the trait nor the interactional approach produces a theoretical framework that is useful for the understanding of leisure behavior. We agree with Stokols and Altman (1987:36-37) that in examining the transactional approach, a better understanding of the role of the environment in human behavior will occur. Needless to say, such an approach is also relevant to the understanding of the leisure experience in a natural setting, which is the focus of this volume.

Attempts at finding answers to the question posed earlier on the role that the environment plays in the motivation for, attitudes towards, and the satisfaction with certain experiences, including leisure experiences, were made by a new type of psychologists. According to Williams (1986), a shift in the approach of social psychology from examining the person independent of his or her setting to examining the person within his or her setting took place in the late 1960s. Research conducted on the relationship between the individual and the setting can be roughly divided into three perspectives. The first approach, called experimental aesthetics, addresses the meaning of the setting in the person's experience. The second approach, environmental cognition, addresses the meaning of the setting in the experience, which is a reflection of one's perception of the setting. The third approach, called behavioral ecology, concentrates on directly observable behavioral patterns in the natural setting. Williams summarized the findings of each approach as follows:

Experimental Aesthetics

Research in this area focuses on structural or organizational qualities of the natural environment, for example, how manicured is the park? An aesthetic experience takes place following an affective event that is based on a certain level of arousal. This level is dependent on the structural or organizational qualities mentioned. Physiological arousal is experienced as a euphoric feeling and is seen as a major source of intrinsic motivation (Ellis, 1973). Yet arousal alone is not a sufficient condition for a leisure experience to take place—arousal could occur at work, for example. And, in fact, too much arousal, even in leisure activity, may end the perception of the activity as leisure. An activity that started as leisure may become too structured.

Environmental Cognition

According to Williams (1986:MIA) the emphasis here is on the perception of the environment, which is looked upon as a source of information rather than a source of stimulation. Interpreting the attributes of a natural setting could give clues as to the recreationally significant conditions and outcomes, for example, a fully packed slope will provide for an exhilarating skiing experience. Since human beings tend to categorize and label their experiences, accumulation of categories and labels could be useful, particularly to the manager of a leisure delivery system. Tversky and Hemenway (1983) applied this technique to natural environments: they identified their attributes and asked the subjects to identify the activities that were appropriate to each category, a process that could prove helpful to planners and managers, as will be presented under a subsequent section on the experience of nature.

Behavioral Ecology

This approach is concerned with how people experience and behave in everyday settings, including natural settings and not in research-contrived settings. Settings become the basic units that are used in analyzing behavior within a given space and for a specific time span; for example, studying behavior within a park at a particular season takes into consideration not only the physical attributes of the setting but also the psychological and social dimensions of behavior in the recreation place. This approach could prove helpful to managers and providers of leisure experiences including experiences in natural settings.

THE EXPERIENCE OF NATURE

Rachel and Stephen Kaplan (1989:ix) tried to answer a number of questions on the effect of the natural environment on human behavior:

1. Is the effect of nature on humans as powerful as it intuitively seems to be?
2. What lies behind the power of environments that not only attracts the appreciation of individuals but also makes many of them able to restore healthy and effective functioning?
3. Are some natural patterns, such as meadows, more effective than others, such as lakes?

Using the findings of research conducted in the area of environmental psychology, these authors came to a number of conclusions on the experience of nature. To them, humans, who are very sensitive to the spatial property of the environment, tend to categorize environments on the basis of their perception. This process produces a number of coherent perceptual categories. For example, research shows that wide-open, undifferentiated vistas as well as dense, impenetrable forests fail to provide information about one's whereabouts. These two settings tend to fall within a distinct category. Scenes that convey a sense of orderliness, such as manicured settings, are a second category, and a third category includes forests that are transparent, allowing sunlight to filter down, providing information on both accessibility and direction. These last two categories are preferred, which means that to attract the most people, a natural setting must include informational patterns that are readily interpretable. These informational patterns are, in many instances, provided by nature itself, and not necessarily by humans, as seen in the case of the transparent forest.

Natural Setting and Information Rate

Mehrebian and Russell (1974:84) suggested that since an outdoor natural setting is characterized by having a smaller density and slower pace of change than does an artificially created setting whether outdoor or indoors, a natural setting has a lower information rate, which is preferred by many recreationists. The concept of information rate can be explained by comparing two paintings, one containing two colors, the other eight colors, which means that the latter has four times as much "information" to deal with than the former. But the idea behind information rate is much more complicated and requires the use of mathematical formulas that are beyond the scope of this volume. Suffice it to say that the number of colors in the above examples is not the only variable to be considered in calculating the information rate. The space that each color covers and its location on the painting are taken into consideration as well.

According to Mehrebian and Russell, the acceleration of information input triggers the General Adaptation Syndrome suggested by Selye (1956). The syndrome begins with a burdensome physiological arousal and a concomitant feeling of displeasure. A high rate of information input takes place in crowded, condensed areas. As

Table 4.1 General Comparison of Trait, Interactional, Organismic, and Transactional World Views

SELECTED GOALS AND PHILOSOPHY OF SCIENCE

	Unit of Analysis	Time and Change	Causation	Observers	Other
Trait	Persons, psychological qualities of persons	Usually assume stability: change infrequent in present operation: change often occurs according to preestablished teleological mechanisms and developmental stages.	Emphasizes *material causes*, i.e., cause internal to phenomena.	Observers are separate, objective, and detached from phenomena: equivalent observations by different observers.	Focus on trait and seek universal laws of psychological functioning according to few principles associated with person qualities: study prediction and manifestation of trait in various psychological domains.
Interactional	Psychological qualities of person and social or physical environment underlying entities, with interaction between parts.	Change results from interaction of separate person and environment times occurs in accord with underlying regulatory mechanisms, e.g., homeostasis; time and change not intrinsic to phenomena.	Emphasizes *efficient causes*, i.e., antecedent consequent relations, causation.	Observers are separate, objective, and detached from phenomena; equivalent observations by different observers.	Focus on elements and relations between elements seek laws of relations between variables and parts of system: understand system by prediction and control and by cumulating additive information about relations between elements.
Organismic	Holistic entities composed of separate person and environment components, elements or parts whose relations and interactions yield qualities of the whole that are "more than the sum of the parts."	Change results from interaction of person and environment entities. Change usually occurs in accord with underlying regulatory mechanisms, e.g., homeostasis and long range directional teleological mechanisms, i.e., ideal developmental states. Change irrelevant once ideal state is reached, assumes that system stability is goal.	Emphasizes *final causes*, i.e., teleology, "pull" toward ideal state.	Observers are separate, objective, and detached from phenomena; equivalent observations by different observers.	Focus on principles that govern the whole, emphasize unity of knowledge, principles of holistic systems and hierarchy of subsystems; identify principles and laws of whole system.

continued

Transactional	Holistic entities composed of "aspects," not separate parts or elements; aspects are mutually defining: temporal qualities are intrinsic features of wholes.	Stability/change are intrinsic and defining features of psychological phenomena; change occurs continuously; directions of change emergent and not preestablished.	Emphasizes *formal causes,* i.e., description and understanding of patterns, shapes and form of phenomena.	Relative: Observers are aspects of phenomena; observers in different "locations" (physical and psychological) yield different information about phenomena.	Focus on event, i.e., confluence people, space, and time; describe and understand patterning and forms of events; openness in seeking general principles, but primary interest in accounting for event; pragmatic application of principles and laws as appropriate to situations; openness to emergent explanation principles; prediction acceptable if not necessary.

Source: D. Stokols and I. Altman, *Handbook of Environmental Psychology* (New York: John Wiley and Sons, 1987), 75. (Reprinted with permission.)

a result, "understandably, those residing in congested urban areas express unrelenting desires to visit simple and rural settings such as national parks" (Mehrebian & Russell, 1974:205). These two authors concluded that the relationship between internal behavioral patterns and external rhythms suggests a mechanism that directly relates arousal to information rate from the environment. It is not surprising, therefore, that the tempo of work, and even recreation, in an urban setting far exceeds that in a natural setting.

Preference for Natural Settings

Kaplan and Kaplan (1989:49) suggest that in the context of natural settings, those with human intrusions are less preferred than those where nature dominates. In the meantime, in very open vistas as well as in blocked areas, where it is difficult to anticipate what might happen, preference tends to be very low. In other words, humans respond negatively to both a high rate of information and to a paucity of information. This suggests that preference for a setting is related to how effectively a person can perceive himself or herself functioning in it. Humans prefer a setting where they feel safe, comfortable, and competent. Nonetheless, a natural setting could post an enticing challenge to some persons or to others under their charge who may have low arousability. A challenge

of nature may help some people to achieve optimal arousability (see the section on leisure and the type T personality).

Wilderness as a Challenge

In the past, the wilderness posed a challenge to human beings in their quest for survival. Although survival in the wilderness is rarely a concern in modern life, programs in wilderness survival abound and are used to experience self-discovery and enhance self-concept. In the 1980s there were over 300 wilderness programs in the world, many of which were directed toward special populations such as juvenile delinquents, the handicapped, and psychiatric patients. These programs are conducted for young people, adults, and seniors (Burton, 1981). Outward Bound was established by Kurt Hahn and is considered a prototype wilderness challenge program (Ewert, 1989). The first Outward Bound school started in Wales in 1941 to train merchant marines to withstand the challenges they had to face during World War II. The school was later moved to the United States. Burton listed five features of Outward Bound and similar programs:

1. A contrasting or novel physical environment.
2. A challenging set of problem-solving tasks.
3. A duration of at least seven days.

Table 4.2 Outdoor Challenge Participants

Year	No. groups	Boys	Girls	Adults	Total
1972	2	10			10
1973	2	12	8		20
1974	1	8			8
1975	3	13	6	4	23
1976	3	6	12	8	26
1977	2	6	3	3	12
1978	3	6	7	6	19
1979	3	5	3	3	11
1980	6	11	11	13	35
1981	2		3	9	12
Total	27	77	53	46	176

Source: R. Kaplan and S. Kaplan, *The Experience of Nature* (Cambridge: Cambridge University Press, 1989), 124. (Reprinted with permission.)

4. A leader or instructor.
5. A group of at least four participants.

In the outdoor challenge programs, conducted by the U.S. Forest Service's North Central Forest Experimental Station in Michigan's Upper Peninsula, the offering remained constant for a ten-year period. Table 4.2 shows the types and numbers of participants. Most of the features in the program remained constant over the ten-year period. The practice hike on the first evening led to instruction in map reading and compass orientation. The participants went through dense, trackless forest for the first few days. A 48-hour solo hike followed, which ended with a hike on one's own back to base camp to continue the program with others. Although the program lasted for two weeks in its first eight years, it was reduced to nine days in the last two years. The research tools used to evaluate the program remained the same: questionnaires were filled out on the first day and at various times, including the end of the program, and participants kept journals to record their feelings and reactions.

A number of pertinent questions were raised by Kaplan and Kaplan (1989:147): Does it require a wilderness setting to experience self-discovery and enhance self-concept? Does it take two weeks to achieve such gains? Are there short cuts to achieve a sense of tranquility and a feeling of oneness with nature?

Kaplan and Kaplan stated that Thoreau wrote of nature as a source of spiritual renewal and inspiration. A surprising outcome of wilderness research that they reviewed has been the remarkable depth of spiritual impact wilderness experiences have on those who participate in them. Yet the participants spent much less time in the wilderness and were engaged in less overtly cerebral activities than those of Thoreau. His quest for tranquility, peace, and silence was called a quest for serenity by Kaplan and Kaplan. In addition, the researchers seem to find two more quests occurring among the participants, oneness and integration.

Kaplan and Kaplan concluded that they had not anticipated this research program would provide them with an education in the ways of human nature. They felt they had been introduced to some human concerns that are bound to broaden the conception of human motivation and priorities.

What is intriguing about the aforementioned results is that they correspond with what Aristotle suggested in the remote past—that the greatest of leisure experience is contemplation, which he placed at the top of the hierarchy of leisure experiences (see Figure 1.1). Human life has become so complicated that contemplation is rarely a priority in human affairs. Understanding the nature of human motivation as it relates to human needs may shed more light on the nature of the leisure experience.

MOTIVATION, HUMAN NEEDS AND LEISURE

Among the many attempts to understand human behavior, including leisure behavior in the natural setting, is the attempt to answer the question, "What motivates a person to partake of a certain activity?" The question of motivation has been a major part of research in psychology from the beginning. Researchers concentrated their efforts on finding a single factor that is responsible for human behavior. The terms instinct and drive were used to describe this single factor.

Early Motivational Theories

The term instinct was used to describe a variety of human behaviors in the pre-World War I era. In his classical textbook *The Principles of Psychology*, William James defined instinct as the capability to act so as to bring about a certain event. Human beings possess many instincts, among which is the one (or ones) that motivate(s) us to play, recreate, and participate in leisure activity. The question became, which instinct? Although the scholars who attempted to answer this question at that time agreed that humans are instinctually motivated to play and recreate, they did not agree on the nature of the instinct. Accordingly, four classical theories were forwarded, which could lead to contradictory outcomes given the same circumstances (Levy, 1979:155). The surplus energy theory, which explains play as based on leftover energy, contradicts the relaxation theory and the teleological theory, which explain leisure behavior in terms of the future, and all three contradict the recapitulation theory, which explains leisure behavior in terms of our past. Although these theories have been, in general, discarded by the leisure scholars, they served as precursors to some of the recent interpretations that there is a biological basis for play and recreation (Eisen, 1988; Marano, 1999).

The concept of drive was adopted by psychologists after World War I and was used to explain human behavior as attempts to reduce certain needs. An essential group of needs were termed primary needs, which were deemed necessary for survival. Human beings attempt to reduce the need for food, warmth, exertion, sex, and security and accordingly achieve homeostasis, a state of physiologic equilibrium. Another group of needs were called secondary needs, which stem from the circumstances that surround our attempts to satisfy the primary needs. Among these needs are achievement, affiliation, creativity, curiosity, gregariousness, risk, self-abasement, and self-assertion. Later the terms basic needs and acquired needs were used to describe primary and secondary needs, respectively. A working session on needs and leisure held at the University of Illinois some years ago, generated the following list of 17 needs or groups of needs deemed important to leisure behavior:

1. Enjoying nature, escaping civilization
2. Escape from routine and responsibility
3. Physical exercise
4. Creativity
5. Relaxation self-improvement, ability

6. Social contact
7. Meeting new people
8. Contact with prospective mates
9. Family contact
10. Recognition status
11. Social power
12. Altruism (helping others)
13. Stimulus seeking
14. Self-actualization (feedback, self-improvement, ability utilization)
15. Challenge, achievement, competition
16. Killing time, avoiding boredom
17. Intellectual aestheticism

Crandall suggested that behavior, including leisure behavior, is caused by the interaction of the person and the situation (1980:51). Levy advocated that behavior is a function of the interaction of needs (of persons) and pressure (from the environment) (1979:159). This interactive model was used to identify a number of environmental contexts. In the area of leisure behavior, the person-environment interactive model was used to explain the need for a leisure experience. Levy (1977) reported that the need for relaxation is one of the leading motives for engaging in leisure behavior, a position which supported Dumazedier's claim to the same (1967).

A few years later, Ruskin and Shamir (1984) identified relaxation as a key motivation in leisure behavior. No research was conducted since then and in fact recently, an author lamented the fact that relaxation is neglected in leisure research (Kleiber, 2000). On the other hand, human needs are much more complicated than simple responses to primary and secondary drives, as shown in the following study. London et al. (1977) found that the respondents in their study viewed leisure activities in terms of three need dimensions: liking, feedback, and positive interpersonal involvement. In order to develop a psychologically meaningful categorization of leisure activities, the authors took three elements into account simultaneously: the activities, the needs they satisfy, and individual differences in perceiving the

Table 4.3 Core Matrix Based on Rotated Factors

NEEDS FACTORS

Individual Factor	Activities Factors	Feedback	Liking	Positive Interpersonal Involvement
I	Sports	60.1	45.5	9.9
	Cultural-Passive	−53.2	58.0	−16.4
	Productive-Intellectual	59.9	38.3	−34.5
II	Sports	−17.1	37.0	−35.4
	Cultural-Passive	−94.3	25.3	−66.1
	Productive-Intellectual	−8.1	8.9	−86.4
III	Sports	77.2	65.8	64.0
	Cultural-Passive	−47.7	40.6	−14.9
	Productive-Intellectual	61.3	29.4	−10.9

Source: M. London et al., "The Psychological Structure of Leisure Activities, Needs, People," *Journal of Leisure Research* (National Recreation and Park Association, 1977):260. (Reprinted with permission.)

activity. Factor analyses were applied, and the findings seem to replicate activity dimensions found in previous studies. These activity dimensions as well as need dimensions are shown in Table 4.3. While leisure activity in a natural setting is not listed in Table 4.3, the data in the table show that a leisure activity may fulfill a multitude of needs: feedback, liking, and positive interpersonal involvement. Tinsley and Kass (1978) found their results to be in substantial agreement with previous studies. Needs such as catharsis, independence, advancement, getting along with others, reward, understanding, activity, ability, utilization, exhibition, and sex appear to be mostly leisure activity specific.

Need, as a concept, became central to the attempts to give psychological meaning to leisure behavior. But what is a leisure need? While most of the studies cited here treated it as being stable, Iso-Ahola and Allen (1982:142) suggested that the need for leisure is not stable but is always changing. They refer to a leisure need as a perceived reason for participating in a variety of activities. One of the assumptions in their approach to the leisure need involves change across situations under which needs change from before to after participation. After testing this hypothesis they concluded that leisure needs seem to

be sensitive to the influence of the leisure experience itself. Does that mean that the need to participate in leisure activity is changing? Or is the way that it is fulfilled changing? For example, the need to survive motivates humans to eat. Varieties in foods have nothing to do with the need to survive, but food does. On that very basic level, survival is supreme, whether we like the food or not. Whether the eating companions were stimulating or not, humans will have to eat to survive. Is (are) the leisure need(s) that powerful? The answer may lie in the hierarchy of needs. In lieu of need, the term expectation has been explored by other leisure scholars on the assumption that the participant in a leisure pursuit is goal oriented, knowledgeable, and select the activity that suits him or her (Mannell & Kleiber, 1999). Nonetheless, a visit to Maslow's hierarchy of needs is appropriate at this point.

The Hierarchy of Human Needs

Although the idea of placing human needs in a hierarchy is credited to Maslow (1968), the concept was forwarded almost five centuries ago by a medieval Arab scholar. In a hierarchical model, Ibn Khaldun places bodily appetite at the bottom level progressing to the desires for security, companionship, and superiority and on to

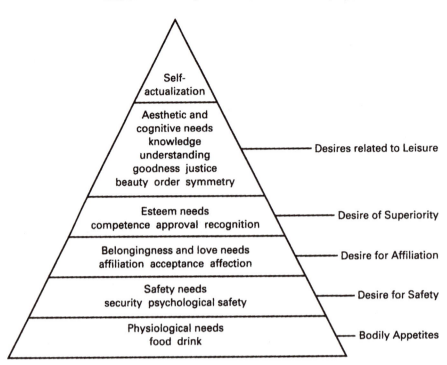

Maslow's Hierarchy of Needs   Ibn Khaldun's Desires

Self-actualization

Aesthetic and cognitive needs
knowledge
understanding
goodness justice
beauty order symmetry

— Desires related to Leisure

Esteem needs
competence approval recognition

— Desire of Superiority

Belongingness and love needs
affiliation acceptance affection

— Desire for Affiliation

Safety needs
security psychological safety

— Desire for Safety

Physiological needs
food drink

— Bodily Appetites

Figure 4.1 Representation of Ibn Khaldun's list of human desires versus Maslow's hierarchy of needs.

the final desire for leisure (Ibrahim, 1981). It is interesting to note that the original conceptualization of Maslow included a need (desire) for leisure also, as shown in Figure 4.1.

Levy presented the hierarchical order of Maslow's modified five prepotent need sets in Figure 4.2. While the historian Ibn Khaldun never indicated the outcome of fulfilling these desires, the psychologist Maslow promised self-actualization as the outcome of fulfilling the needs in his hierarchy.

To Maslow, self-actualization is a positive ideal of mental health. Could leisure experience, particularly in a natural setting, help in achieving such an ideal? (Scott, 1974). Young and Crandall (1984) tested such a claim by comparing wilderness users to nonusers in their self-actualization scores. Using Shostrom's Person Orientation Inventory (1974), which is the most validated measure of self-actualiza-

tion as defined by Maslow, the authors concluded that while wilderness activities may help some individuals self-actualize, the relationship between self-actualization and wilderness use is very weak. In 1991, Csikszentmihalyi and Kleiber reported that there seems to be a link between leisure pursuit, in general, and self-actualization (1991).

SATISFACTION, ATTITUDES, AND THE LEISURE EXPERIENCE

If the need for a leisure experience is satisfactorily met, does satisfaction then become the causative factor in further participation in the same leisure experience? Does this lead to a positive attitude toward the leisure experience?

Satisfaction and Leisure
The National Academy of Science Report (1969) suggested that in order to under-

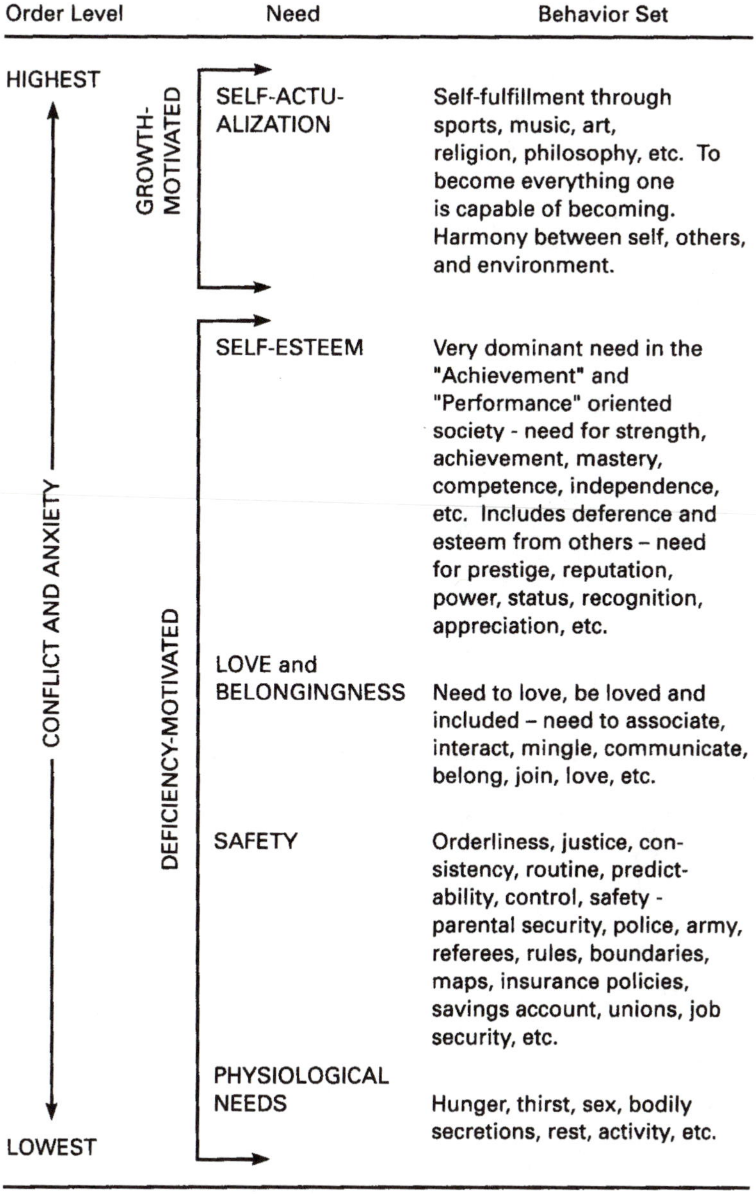

Order Level	Need	Behavior Set

HIGHEST

GROWTH-MOTIVATED

SELF-ACTU-ALIZATION

Self-fulfillment through sports, music, art, religion, philosophy, etc. To become everything one is capable of becoming. Harmony between self, others, and environment.

SELF-ESTEEM

Very dominant need in the "Achievement" and "Performance" oriented society - need for strength, achievement, mastery, competence, independence, etc. Includes deference and esteem from others – need for prestige, reputation, power, status, recognition, appreciation, etc.

DEFICIENCY-MOTIVATED

LOVE and BELONGINGNESS

Need to love, be loved and included – need to associate, interact, mingle, communicate, belong, join, love, etc.

SAFETY

Orderliness, justice, consistency, routine, predictability, control, safety - parental security, police, army, referees, rules, boundaries, maps, insurance policies, savings account, unions, job security, etc.

PHYSIOLOGICAL NEEDS

Hunger, thirst, sex, bodily secretions, rest, activity, etc.

LOWEST

CONFLICT AND ANXIETY

Figure 4.2 A schematic representation of Maslow's hierarchy of human needs.

stand recreation better, research should be directed at the analysis of satisfactions sought in it. Hawes (1979) sought to study satisfactions derived from participation in leisure activity in an attempt to steer away from the traditional head count. His nationwide exploratory study utilized 50 selected leisure pursuits along with 12 "satisfaction" statements. A sample of 603 females and 512 males was used for analysis. Of interest is Hawes's finding that individuals can relate their participation in outdoor, active, group-oriented pursuits more readily to satisfactions than they can participation in indoor, passive, primarily individual pursuits.

According to Ingham (1986), leisure satisfaction is very much linked to motivation. He quoted Calder and Shaw stating that "satisfaction derives from an activity which is perceived as intrinsically motivated because of a person's need to feel a sense of personal causation in his or her action" (1975:599). This brings us back to the notion of perceived freedom as being crucial to a bona fide leisure experience. Graef et al. (1983) found that intrinsically motivated activities, be they leisure activities or otherwise, lead to a state of happiness. Their study supports the proposal that satisfaction with an activity depends on perceived intrinsic motivation, which relies on a freedom of choice.

Recently, studies showed that satisfaction increases with better performance and familiarity with the setting (Hultsman, 1998). Another study shows that leisure satisfaction has inverse relationship with burnout (Stanton-Rich & Iso-Ahola, 1998). Still another study showed that satisfaction with life is influenced indirectly by satisfaction with leisure activities (Zamorron, 2001). Studies in leisure satisfaction continue despite the warning that the measurement of satisfaction in leisure pursuit is inadequate because satisfaction is relative, too broad, and a multi-dimensional concept (Manning, 1999 p.14-15).

Attitudes Toward Leisure

A concept that is much related to, and in fact to some extent dependent on, satisfaction is attitude, which is defined as a learned predisposition to respond in a constantly favorable or unfavorable manner to a given object (Crandall, 1979). Implicit in this definition is the fact that attitudes can predict behavior. This requires that attitudes be measured. Attempts at measuring attitudes toward leisure activities are found in Burdge (1961), Neulinger (1974), and Crandall and Slivken (1979). Not only have applications of the scales constructed by these scholars been very limited, but the one constructed by Burdge has deteriorated considerably over time, as per the author himself (Yoesting & Burdge, 1976). Neulinger (1974) suggested that leisure attitudes manifest themselves clearly in cultural

settings, a point that will be covered in a different section of this volume.

Studies in leisure attitudes could be useful for managers and providers of leisure programs, as shown by Wohlwill and Heft (1977). In comparing attitudes toward development and facilities in two contrasting natural recreation areas, the authors suggested that one-time study would not suffice in providing information on leisure preference. A feedback model was suggested, the basis of which is the interaction of three separable factors: objectives of the agency, attitude of visitors (to the natural areas), and the impact of visitations.

Another use of attitudinal studies is the effect of leisure participation on the attitude toward the environment. Jackson (1986) found that participants in "appreciative" activities (for example, cross-country skiing and hiking) hold more pro-environmental attitudes than participants in "consumptive" activities (for example, snowmobiling and trail biking). He also found that participation in outdoor pursuits is strongly related to attitudes toward those specific aspects of the environment necessary in pursuing the activities than to general issues of environmental concerns. A recent study showed that outdoor recreational participation is positively associated with pro-environmental behavior (Theodori et al, 1998).

PSYCHOLOGICAL BENEFITS OF LEISURE EXPERIENCE

Societies sanction activities that are deemed beneficial to the membership collectively and individually. Leisure activities provide many sorts of benefits. Some are economic, others are social, and many are psychological. Tinsley (1986) lists the psychological benefits derived from leisure experiences as measured by the Recreation Experience Preference scale as follows:

- Achievement
- Leadership/autonomy
- Risk-taking

- Successful use of equipment
- Family togetherness
- Social contact
- Meeting/observing new people
- Learning/discovery
- Relationships with nature
- Reflection on personal values
- Creativity
- Nostalgia
- Exercise/physical fitness
- Physical rest
- Escape personal and social pressures
- Escape physical pressure
- Security
- Escape family
- Enjoyment of temperature

Earlier, Tensley and his associates (1977) identified 44 psychological benefits derived from leisure experiences. Utilizing the Leisure Activities Questionnaire (LAQ), information from over 4000 respondents participating in 82 activities produced the following two lists:

Leisure Activity Specific Benefits:

These are benefits that can be gained to a significantly greater degree through participation in some leisure activities than by participation in other leisure activities.

Ability	Cooperation	Security
Utilization	Creativity	Self-esteem
Achievement	Dominance	Sentience
Activity	Exhibition	Sex
Advancement	Independence	Social Service
Affiliation	Nurturance	Social Status
Aggression	Play	Supervision
Authority	Responsibility	Understanding
Catharsis	Reward	Variety
Compensation		

Leisure Activity General Benefits

These are benefits that are gained to approximately the same degree from leisure activities.

Abasement	Justice	Self-control
Autonomy	Moral value	Succorance
Counteraction	Order	Task

Deference	Recognition	Generalization
Harm	Rejection	Tolerance
Avoidance	Relaxation	

The authors derived the following psychological benefit factors that can be used in distinguishing among leisure activities:

Self-expression
Companionship
Compensation
Security
Service
Intellectual aestheticism
Solitude

Psychological Benefits of Outdoor Experience

So far what has been listed refers to leisure experiences in general, be they active, passive, indoor, or outdoor. Does the leisure experience that takes place outdoors have its own characteristic benefits? Brown (1981) identified a number of highly valued experiences gained during outdoor recreational activities which came from many sources, covering research conducted in many sections of the United States, as follows:

Relationship with nature
Escape from physical pressures
Escape from social pressures
Achievement/challenge
Autonomy/independence/freedom
Reflection on personal values
Recollection/nostalgia
Risk-taking/action/excitement
Meeting/observing other people
Use and care of equipment
Exercise/physical fitness
Being with one's recreation group
Learning/exploration
Family togetherness
Privacy
Security
Physical rest

As can be clearly seen, relationship with nature was one of the most valued experiences in a natural setting, along with being with one's recreation group, a topic to be discussed in the next chapter.

Despite the tremendous desirability of an outdoor recreation experience, there are reasons why many individuals may not participate. Barriers to participation in outdoor experience can be psychological. Examples are the different types of phobias. These exaggerated fears may include fear of dogs, snakes, insects, and other animals, which could render an outing miserable. A social phobia triggered when one is exposed to possible scrutiny by others would render group camping difficult. Other barriers are cultural, which fall within the parameters of the next chapter.

SUMMARY

This chapter discusses the psychological elements of an outdoor experience. As defined, leisure is predicated as a state of mind, which by its nature impacts one's psychological orientation. Yet there are personal traits that may affect one's involvement in a leisure experience. Additionally, the external environment plays a decisive role in the enjoyment of such an experience. For instance, humans prefer places where they feel safe and comfortable and where they believe they can function effectively.

When the leisure experience takes place in the out-of-doors, a new set of elements is taken into consideration. In general, the average natural setting with a lower information rate, that is, with a low number of stimuli, has relatively limited appeal to humans. Sometimes a natural setting has too few stimuli, as in a barren area, which may lead to boredom. On the other hand, too many stimuli may lead to anxiety. Thus humans seek natural areas with optimum stimuli.

What motivates a person to participate in an outdoor activity in the first place is discussed in relationship to the prevailing theories of motivation. The psychological benefits from such participation as reported in the literature are presented. While fulfilling primary needs may serve to reduce physiological disequilibrium, secondary needs may include the need for achievement, affiliation, curiosity, self-assertion, and the like. Leisure pursuits provide opportunities to fulfill these needs.

REFERENCES

Brown, P. (1981). Psychological benefits of outdoor recreation. In J. Kelly (Ed.), *Social benefits of outdoor recreation.* Champaign, IL: University of Illinois.

Burdge, R. J. (1961). *The development of a leisure orientation scale.* Unpublished thesis. Columbus, OH: Ohio State University.

Calder, B. J., & Shaw, B. M. (1975). Self-perception of extrinsic motivation. *Journal of Personality and Social Psychology, 31*, 599-605.

Caldwell, L. L., et al. (1999). Why Are you bored? An examination of psychological and social control causes of boredom among adolescents." *Journal of Leisure Research, 31*(2), 130.

Crandall, R. (1979). Attitudes toward leisure. In H. Ibrahim & R. Crandall (Ed.), *Leisure: A psychological approach.* Los Alamitos, CA: Hwong Publishing.

Crandall, R. (1980). Motivations for leisure. *Journal of Leisure Research, 12*, 45-54.

Crandall, R., & Slivken, K. (1979). Leisure attitudes and their measurement. In S. Iso-Ahola (Ed.). *Social psychological perspectives on leisure and recreation.* Springfield, IL: C. Thomas.

Csikszentmihalyi, M. (1975). *Beyond boredom and anxiety.* San Francisco: Jossey-Bass.

Csikszentmihalyi, M., & Kleiber, D. A. (1991). Leisure and self-actualization. In B. L. Drivers (Ed.), *Benefits of leisure.* State College, PA: Venture Publishing.

Driver, B. L., & Tinsley, H., et al. (1976). Quantification of outdoor recreationists' preferences In B. Vander Smissen (Ed.), *Research, camping and environmental education.* University Park, PA: Pennsylvania State University. HPER Series No. 11.

Driver, B. L., & Knopf, R. C. (1977). Personality: Outdoor recreation and expected consequences. *Environment and Behavior, 9*, 169.

Driver, B. L., & Brown, P. (1978). *The opportunity spectrum concept and behavioral information in outdoor recreation resource supply inventories.* Fort Collins. CO: Rocky Mountain Experiment Station of the U.S. Forest Service.

Dumazedier, J. (1967). *Toward a society of leisure.* New York: Free Press

Eisen, G. (1988). Theories of play. In G. Gerson et al. (Eds.), *Understanding leisure.* Dubuque, IA: Kendall and Hunt.

Ellis, M. (1973). *Why people play.* Englewood Cliffs, NJ: Prentice-Hall.

Ewert, A. (1989). Kurt Hahn. In H. Ibrahim (Ed.), *Pioneers in leisure and recreation.* Reston, VA: AAHPERD.

Farley, F. (1986, May). The big tin personality. *Psychology Today,* 44-50.

Graef, R., Csikszentmihalyi, M., & Gianimo, S. J. (1983). Measuring intrinsic motivation in everyday life. *Leisure Studies, 2,* 155-68.

Hawes, D. K. (1979). Satisfaction derived from leisure pursuits: An exploratory nationwide survey. *Journal of Leisure Research, 10,* 247-64.

Hultsman, W. (1998). The multiday, competitive leisure event: Examining satisfaction over time. *Journal of Leisure Research, 30,* 472-486.

Ibrahim, H. (1988). Leisure, idleness and Ibn Khaldun. *Leisure Studies, 7,* 51-58.

Ingham, R. (1986). Psychological contribution to the study of leisure. *Leisure Studies* 5, 255-79.

Iso-Ahola, S.C., & Allen, J. (1982). The dynamics of leisure motivation: The effect outcome on leisure needs. *Research Quarterly for Exercise and Sport, 53,* 141-49.

Jackson, E. (1986). Outdoor recreation participation and attitudes toward the environment. *Leisure Studies, 5,* 1-23.

Kaplan, R., & Kaplan, S. (1989). *The experience of nature: A psychological perspective.* Cambridge: Cambridge University Press.

Kelly, J. (1987). *Freedom to be: A new sociology of leisure.* New York: Macmillan.

Kleiber, D. A. (2000). The neglect of relaxation. *Journal of Leisure Research, 32*(1), 82.

Levy, J. (1977, October). *Leisure module: A multidimensional approach to the study of leisure behavior.* Paper presented at the Symposium on Leisure Research, Congress of the National Recreation and Park Association, Las Vegas; NV.

Levy, J. (1979). Motivation for leisure: An interactionist approach. In H. Ibrahim and R.

Crandall (Eds.), Leisure: A psychological approach. Los Alamitos, CA: Hwong Publishing.

London, M., R. Crandall, & Fitzgibbons, D. (1977). The psychological structure of leisure activities, needs, people. *Journal of Leisure Research, 9,* 252-63.

Mannell, R., & Bradley, W. (1986). Does greater freedom always lead to a greater leisure? *Journal of Leisure Research, 12,* 215-30.

Mannell, R., & Kleiber, D. A. (1999). *A social psychology of leisure.* State College , PA, Venture Publishing.

Marano, H. E. (1999). The power of play. *Psychology Today,* 32:36

Maslow, A. (1968). *Toward a psychology of being.* Princeton, NJ: Van Nostrand.

Mehrebian, A., & Russell, J. (1974). *An approach to environmental psychology.* Cambridge, MA: MIT Press.

Mills, J. (1986, March). Living on the edge, *Women's Sports and Fitness,* 24.

National Academy of Science. (1969). *A program for outdoor recreation research.* Washington, D.C.: National Academy of Science.

Neulinger, J. (1974). *The psychology of leisure.* Springfield, IL: C. C. Thomas.

Ruskin, H., & Shamir, B. (1984). Motivation as a factor affecting males' participation in physical activity during leisure time. *Society and Leisure, 7,* 141-61.

Scott, N. (1974). Toward a psychology of wilderness experience. *Natural Resource Journal, 14,* 231-37.

Selye, H. (1956). *The stress of life.* New York: McGraw-Hill.

Shostrom, E. (1974). *Manual for the personality orientation inventory.* San Diego, CA: Educational and Industrial Testing Service.

Statton-Rich, H. M., & Iso Ahola, S. E. (1998). Burnout and leisure. *Journal of Applied Social Psychology, 28*(21), 1931.

Stokols, D., & Altman, L. (1987). *Handbook of environmental psychology.* New York: John Wiley and Sons.

Theodori, G. L., Luloff, A. E., & Wilitis, F. K. (1998). The Association of Outdoor Recreation and Environmental Concern. *Sociology, 63*(1), 94.

Tinsley, H. (1986). Motivations to participate in recreation: Their identification and measurements. In *The President's commission Americans outdoors: A literature review.* Washington, D.C.: U.S. Government Printing Office.

Tinsley., H., Barrett, T. C., & Kass, R. A. (1977). Leisure activities and need satisfaction. *Journal of Leisure Research, 9,* 110-120.

Tinsley, H., & Kass, R. A. (1978). Leisure activities and need satisfaction: A replication and extension. *Journal of Leisure Research, 10,* 191-202.

Tversky, B., & Hemenway , K. (1983). Categories of environmental scenes. *Cognitive Psychology, 15,*23-42.

Williams, D. (1986). Psychological perspectives on the environment. Experience relationship: implications for recreation resources management. In *The President's Commission on American Outdoors: A Literature Review.* Washington, D.C.: U.S. Government Printing Office.

Wohlwill, J. F., & Heft, H. (1977). A comparative study of user attitudes towards development and facilities in two contrasting natural recreation areas. *Journal of Leisure Research, 9,* 264-80.

Yoesting, D. R., & Burdge, R. J. (1976). Utility of a leisure orientation scale. *Iowa State Journal of Research, 50,* 345-56.

Young, R., & Crandall, R. (1984). Wilderness use and self-actualization. *Journal of Leisure Research, 16,* 49.

Zamarron, M. D. (2001). The contribution of socio-demographic and psychological factors to life satisfaction. *Ageing and Society,* 21, 25.

5

THE SOCIAL ASPECT OF OUTDOOR EXPERIENCES

The last chapter concentrated on the individual as an individual, on his or her traits, needs, attitudes, and satisfactions as they relate to leisure pursuits, with an emphasis on outdoor experiences This chapter will look at the individual as a member of a society and as a member of its subgroups. The roles of culture and subculture are probed as they pertain to leisure behavior. These considerations are important to both managers and recreation participants.

THE NATURE OF HUMAN SOCIETY

As a system, the human society is composed of different structures and performs certain functions. Regardless of their historical time or geographical locations, all human societies are, to a great extent, similar when it comes to social structures and social functions. Following are the basic social institutions of society.

The Family

The family could be nuclear, referring to a male, a female, and their offspring, or extended to include blood and marriage relatives. The impact of the family on the life of both young and old cannot be denied, perhaps because the family is involved in many social, psychological and economical functions as follows:

1. Sexual satisfaction
2. Reproduction
3. Socialization
4. Psychological sustenance
5. Economic support

The role of the family on leisure behavior in general and on outdoor recreation, in particular, along with the impact of leisure on the family members will be elaborated on later.

Religion

Religion is the second most important major social institution in almost all human societies. Durkheim (1915), suggested that religion is the outcome of the collectivity of ritual. As indicated, rituals played and still play a very important role in the lives of individuals and societies. One view is that ritual was and is the cement that holds the society together. Such is the Durkheimian view, which was challenged by Victor Turner (1982), who believes that in addition to its role in maintaining the social order, the ritual was the locus for rudimentary forms of leisure pursuits.

An important function of religion is that it determines that which is sacred and that which is profane. In other words, religion determines, to a great extent, what is acceptable and unacceptable human behavior. The role of religion, then, is very important in leisure pursuits. An example comes to us from colonial America, when the Puritans and Quakers prohibited horse racing and frowned on mixed dancing.

Political Institutions

The political structure of any society revolves around the source of power and its allocation. The organization of political power can produce, or may fail to produce, the following:

1. Internal peace
2. External protection and expansion
3. National, regional and local policies
4. Interest alignment
5. Distribution of wealth
6. Protection of the environment

The significant roles played by the federal, state, and local governments as it applies to these six areas will be discussed in details in chapters 7, 8 and 9 respectively.

The Economic System

In economic systems we see an evolution from the very simple systems of barter to the complex system of the stock market, long-term financing, and multinational corporations. One way of looking at the level of economic sophistication of a given society or region is through a tripartite classification based on the location of the bulk of the labor force, as follows:

1. Primary economy: agriculture and extractive business dominate
2. Secondary economy: industry and manufacturing dominate
3. Tertiary economy: most of the labor force in services and trade

The American society has reached a tertiary economy in that most of its labor force is in services and trade. In the leisure sector of the economy, this means an increasing number of workers and professionals are seen in the leisure delivery systems, be they public or private. Chapter six is devoted to the relationship between leisure pursuits in general, and outdoor recreational activities, in particular, and

the status of the American economy, nationally, regionally and locally.

Technology

Technology is both a social and a material institution. It refers to the organization, dissipation, and utilization of knowledge in the service of societal goals. Social technology includes formal and informal education, the media, and voluntary education. Material technology, on the other hand, includes science and industry. Leisure scholars agree that the technological-industrial advances of the last two centuries helped in the increase of free time, an important ingredient for leisure pursuits. It is becoming evidently clear that some people who are living in this age of technology are paying a heavy toll in that technology did not make their life easier, just busier (*Newsweek,* 1995). On the other hand, some scholars believe that we are witnessing a convergence between leisure and technology (Hill & McLean, 1999).

Besides the five social institutions of the family, religion, government, the economy, and technology, secondary institutions such as play and work groups play important roles in our lives. Accordingly, a number of social processes help the individual learn the roles he or she is supposed to play in these institutions. Foremost among these social processes is socialization.

SOCIALIZATION AND LEISURE BEHAVIOR

A human being is born socially neutral. Socialization is a process through which the culture of the community and/or society is instilled in the individual. This process, which begins at birth and continues throughout life, helps the individual to correctly play his or her assigned roles in the society. Playing the role, as expected by the social groups with which the individual interacts, not only gives the needed admission to these groups, but also serves as the threshold to self-esteem. Humans play many roles in their lifetime, among which are leisure roles. Leisure roles include, but are not limited to, being a player on a sports team, an actor in a school play, or a member of the church choir.

The Age of Socialization into Leisure

As previously stated, socialization is a continual process, yet social scientists agree that there is a certain age when socialization is so powerful that the activity partaken could become a life-long practice. There are a number of studies that focused on the age of socialization into outdoor recreational activities. Bevins et al. (1968) found that childhood participation in hunting and fishing was highly correlated with adulthood participation in the same activities. Hendee (1969) found that 70 percent of the adult participants in wilderness camping had taken their first camping trip before the age of 15. Bradshaw and Jackson (1979) investigated socialization into leisure activities in general, and concluded such socialization takes place before age 13. Yoestng and Burkhead (1973) found that individuals who were active in outdoor recreation continued to be active in outdoor life during their adult years, and that the opposite was true, inactive children continued being inactive in these activities as adults. Their findings do not support Kelly's study that humans could be socialized into new activities in adulthood (1983). Yet, it is possible that the inactive persons were not exposed to outdoor recreational pursuits. Had they been, they may have become active in them.

On the other hand, it seems that elementary and junior high school students pass through an "extracurricular career" that begins with recreational ambience progressing from competitive to elite activities as they grow older. Their leisure pursuits become less spontaneous and more rationalized. This may be the means of socializing them into the corporate world of the American culture (Adler & Adler, 1994).

Agents for Socialization into Leisure

The family seems to be the most influential agent of socialization into leisure generally, and also into outdoor recreational activities. Kelly (1974) found that of the 744 activities reported in his study, 63 percent began with the family, most of which were either sports or outdoor recreational activities.

The school is considered by many as another socializing agent for leisure. Yet there is a paucity of studies on the role of the school as a socializing agent into outdoor recreational pursuits. As early as 1936, Neumeyer and Neumeyer suggested that in preparation for leisure, the school should include in its curriculum nature studies and activities for the exploration of the out-of-doors. Many of the school districts in the United States provide for some form of outdoor experiences, but the impact of these offerings has not been investigated. One of the early studies conducted in the United States showed that the less educated go more often to parks, but how much they appreciate nature is not known (White, 1955). Also, do the less educated go to the park because it is the only leisure outlet available, compared with the theatre, the movies, and the zoo, where the middle and upper classes tend to go more often because they can afford them?

A few empirical studies have been conducted on the role of youth-serving agencies (YMCA, Boy Scouts, Campfire Girls, and the like) in experiences in the outdoors. Kleiber and Rickards (1981) suggested that the outdoor experiences provided by these agencies serve as a theatre. Experiences in that theatre, according to Shepar (1977), enhance the process of gathering and consolidating a range of skills at the end of childhood in preparation for the emancipation from the parental home. Outdoor activities also serve to prepare the young for initiation into puberty.

Places of worship, whether they are churches, synagogues, temples or mosques, have been providing outdoor recreational activities for many years for both youth and adults, yet there is hardly any empirical study on their role in enhancing, or reducing, the leisure experience in natural settings. According to MacLean et al. (1985:262), outdoor experiences are so valued by the sponsors that they assume part of the expense and provide volunteer counselors. A recent trend in the provision of these activities is to organize family camping.

Private and publicly sponsored camps are also agencies for outdoor experiences. The private camp may be operated by a nonprofit organization such as the YMCA or for profit by an entrepreneur. In the second case, only the well-to-do can afford to attend. Public recreation and park agencies also conduct both day and resident camps for the young. While day camps are found in almost every region of the United States, resident camps operated by public agencies are found mainly in the West. Here too, there is little empirical research conducted on the role of day or resident camps in the socialization into outdoor leisure experiences or the benefits derived from such experiences.

Leisure as a Socializing Agent

Csikszentmihalyi (1981) advocated that socialization into leisure, or more precisely into expressive activities, is important because these activities could serve as the criteria by which instrumental activities are evaluated. In general, an instrumental activity is one in which the end product is supreme (fishing commercially for the purpose of selling the fish) as opposed to an expressive activity in which the process is more important (fishing for sport). Although most leisure pursuits are to some extent expressive, Csikszentmihalyi's notion does not pertain solely to leisure activities. Work could be expressive to some. His point, though, is that expressive activities are used in the growing years as criteria by which other activities are evaluated.

Humans are socialized into a number of leisure roles in their lives. They might move from being young athletes to adult poker players to senior RV campers. In the process they become acquainted with the requirements for playing any of these roles. In the evolution of societies, leisure roles were not crucial to the society's welfare or to its members' survival. These roles are becoming increasingly important to the members of industrial/bureaucratic societies. According to Kelly, (1983:115), leisure may be found to be central rather than residual in some phases of life, mainly in the growing years and in retirement. Two spheres that affect human behavior are leisure behavior in primary and secondary groups, as discussed in the following sections.

PRIMARY GROUPS AND LEISURE PURSUITS

Human dependency on others, which is witnessed from birth, tends to continue throughout life. Dependency is greater in the early years of life and remains at a high rate during childhood. Having the longest childhood among animals, including primates, makes humans more dependent on others for a longer period than are other animals. Humans are by necessity social, and they enter a greater number of social circles of different sizes and importance in their life course. The smallest of these circles consists of only two persons, called a dyad. Other circles include primary face-to-face groups such as family and peers and secondary groups such as schoolmates, neighbors, and coworkers. Dyads, primary groups, and secondary groups are all socializing agents as well as providers of outdoor recreational opportunities.

Dyads and Outdoor Pursuits

Perhaps the first dyadic relationships to occur are mother-infant, father-infant, and two-sibling dyads. It was Eric Erikson who brought to our attention the importance of the mother-infant dyad in the particular relationship of ritualization (1977). Manning pioneered a theoretic study on backpacking and the basic needs of infants that included information on how to plan for toddlers and how to make hiking acceptable to children (1975).

Another form of dyadic relationship begins at the late teens and early adulthood, partnership that can lead to sexual intimacy, which could be enhanced through leisure pursuits. It is no wonder that commercial advertisements use outdoor and leisure scenes intimating closeness between lovers. While empirical studies on

Parents of the very youngest children are the most likely to report involvement in outdoor recreation as a family. These two dads expose their children to a fun day of activity at Kings Mountain National Military Park in South Carolina. Mom goes backpacking with her baby on the Appalachian Trail at Grafton Notch in Bethel Maine.

the role outdoor pursuits in the lives of couples are lacking, studies of the role of organized sport in the lives of couples exist (Eitzen & Sage, 1989:83-93). In either case, it is expected that the couples' participation in these pursuits may increase marriage stability and reduce gender inequality (Fong & Zhang, 2000).

Other than sexual dyads, dyadic friendship also exists in the form of two-person long-term relationships. The role that leisure pursuits, including outdoor experiences, play in dyadic relationships is still under investigation. Although a few studies have been conducted, a recent one showed that individual leisure satisfaction is not necessarily reflected on the dyadic relationship (Berg et al, 2001). These findings support the findings of a previous study (Fink, 1995).

The role of leisure pursuits in enhancing, or destroying, dyadic relationship, be they romantic or friendship, remains to be investigated. This does not mean that small primacy groups such as family or peer do not play a role in these relationships.

The Family and Outdoor Pursuits

Despite the changes that have taken place in the family structure, its main function as the dominant socializing agent in human societies remains the same. This, despite the encroachment of school, church, and peers on this particular function, let alone the most recent assault by the powerful medium of television. The family provides both the physical setting and the social setting for leisure activities. Glyptis and Chambers (1982) reported that not only is most free time spent at home, but

Peers and Outdoor Pursuits

[In thousands (13,890 represents 13,890,000), except percent. For spring 1998. Based on sample and subject to sampling error; see source]

Activity	Participated in the last 12 months		Two or more times a week		Once a week		Two to three times a month		Once a month or less	
	Number	Percent	Number	Percent	Number	Percent	Number	Percent	Number	Percent
Attend auto shows	13,890	7.1	¹340	0.2	313	0.2	411	0.2	8,275	4.2
Adult education courses	16,006	8.2	3,259	1.7	3,238	1.7	662	0.3	5,958	3.1
Attend horse races	5,951	3.0	¹188	0.1	369	0.2	¹418	0.2	3,749	1.9
Attend music performances	42,946	22.0	853	0.4	1,108	0.6	2,616	1.3	31,025	15.9
Attend dance performances	11,862	6.1	¹185	0.1	552	0.3	644	0.3	7,705	4.0
Backgammon	6,277	3.2	654	0.3	547	0.3	1,077	0.6	2,913	1.5
Baking	40,751	20.9	9,358	4.8	6,477	3.3	9,383	4.8	9,815	5.0
Barbecuing	64,130	32.9	10,827	5.5	11,149	5.7	14,863	7.6	16,430	8.4
Go to bars/night clubs	39,095	20.0	4,372	2.2	5,829	3.0	6,666	3.4	16,756	8.6
Go to beach	48,363	24.8	3,048	1.6	2,362	1.2	5,013	2.6	28,730	14.7
Billiards/pool	22,183	11.4	2,158	1.1	2,272	1.2	2,745	1.4	10,539	5.4
Birdwatching	10,044	5.1	4,506	2.3	951	0.5	1,082	0.6	1,815	0.9
Board games	28,196	14.4	2,488	1.3	2,840	1.5	5,684	2.9	12,958	6.6
Chess	8,677	4.4	780	0.4	865	0.4	1,288	0.7	3,758	1.9
Cooking for fun	36,305	18.6	11,997	6.1	6,597	3.4	5,536	2.8	6,513	3.3
Concerts on radio	10,660	5.5	2,523	1.3	1,103	0.6	1,389	0.7	2,74⁶	1.4
Crossword puzzles	32,058	16.4	14,166	7.3	4,783	2.5	2,568	1.3	5,206	2.7
Dance/go dancing	25,306	13.0	1,963	1.0	3,163	1.6	3,469	1.8	12,021	6.2
Dining out	95,221	48.8	20,155	10.3	21,962	11.3	20,690	10.6	19,023	9.8
Electronic games (not TV)	16,626	8.5	4,934	2.5	2,038	1.0	2,443	1.3	4,150	2.2
Entertain friends or relatives at home	84,886	43.5	10,011	5.1	11,412	5.8	18,663	9.6	32,828	16.8
Fly kites	7,154	3.7	¹121	0.1	¹308	0.2	¹383	0.2	4,756	2.4
Furniture refinishing	9,137	4.7	¹291	0.1	¹212	0.1	412	0.2	6,505	3.3
Go to live theater	28,213	14.5	¹222	0.1	620	0.3	1,397	0.7	20,229	10.3
Model making	4,374	2.2	364	0.2	477	0.2	444	0.2	2,206	1.1
Go to museums	29,632	15.2	500	0.3	575	0.3	701	0.4	22,157	11.3
Painting, drawing	12,544	6.4	2,783	1.4	1,123	0.6	1,829	0.9	4,278	2.2
Photography	21,150	10.8	2,045	1.0	2,185	1.1	3,966	2.0	9,439	4.8
Picnic	30,731	15.7	557	0.3	824	0.4	2,354	1.2	19,484	10.0
Play bingo	12,014	6.2	1,482	0.8	2,037	1.0	959	0.5	5,026	2.6
Play cards	55,661	28.5	8,044	4.1	7,963	4.1	8,957	4.6	21,475	11.0
Play musical instrument	14,814	7.6	6,062	3.1	1,928	1.0	1,577	0.8	3,419	1.8
Reading books	78,581	40.3	45,009	23.1	7,195	3.7	6,286	3.2	9,316	4.8
Word games	15,507	7.9	4,593	2.4	2,106	1.1	1,996	1.0	3,790	2.0
Trivia games	14,196	7.3	1,731	0.9	1,491	0.8	2,056	1.1	6,180	3.2
Video games	24,227	12.4	8,630	4.4	2,510	1.3	2,799	1.4	5,730	2.9
Woodworking	12,026	6.2	2,771	1.4	1,170	0.6	1,821	0.9	4,491	2.3
Zoo attendance	26,583	13.6	¹90	(Z)	¹299	0.2	482	0.2	20,491	10.5

Z Less than .05 percent.   ¹ Figure does not meet standards of reliability or precision.

Source: Mediamark Research, Inc., New York, NY, *Top-line Reports* (copyright). Internet site <http://www.mediamark.com/mri/docs/TopLineReports.html> (accessed 23 March 2000).

the home is a physical source for many leisure pursuits, providing space and equipment. The backyard as a space for outdoor pursuits has not been thoroughly studied, but it is evident that many pursuits take place there. Suffice it to say that barbecuing is one of the most participated in outdoor activities in this country (see Table 5.1).

According to Orthner (1976), leisure, in general, contributes to marital cohesion. In an earlier study, West and Merriam (1970) found that outdoor recreational activities lead to family cohesiveness. According to Kelly (1981:47), the critical variable for the building of family cohesion is the nature of the integration. He suggested that the work of B.L. Driver indicates that the perceived benefits of outdoor experience include two elements for effective interaction: is the strengthening of significant relationships and the enjoyment of companionship.

Where the family as unit is concerned, leisure experience, including outdoor

These members of an outrigger club function together as a team and socialize during race events.

pursuits, support key needs over the life cycle. These key needs include attachment, bonding, identification, interaction, stress management and social support (Orthner et al, 1994).

Peers and Outdoor Pursuits

According to Cheek (1981:49), leisure literature, both professional and investigatory, describes outdoor recreational activities as taking place in a group of around four persons. And although escaping urban pressure is an important motivational factor in participating in a wilderness experience, hardly anyone does it alone. The solitude sought is usually a communal, not a solo, solitude. Based on the findings of the research conducted in the 1960s and 1970s, Cheek concluded that it is either kinship or friendship that is the basis of the social group in an outdoor leisure pursuit. Earlier, Cheek and Burch (1976) reported that members of an outdoor

leisure pursuit group tend to remain physically together and to share decision-making, two elements that add to cohesion and intimacy.

Cheek also suggested that outdoor pursuits offer a unique opportunity for a human being to behave as a human being, a condition denied him or her in the too-rational industrial society. He asked;

> When may humans exalt their natures in addition or perhaps in contrast to their exactedness? . . . Only under very limited conditions; for limited periods of time; and with very few others of their kind. Outdoor recreation activities appear to offer the unique combination of these conditions in modern industrial societies (Cheek 1981:51).

To Cheek the most important use of outdoor settings is the all too infrequently recognized function—to feel and exchange indications of special caring and liking.

Recently, Edwards underscored that the need for more contact with peers can be provided in the recreational opportunities for middle school children and young adults (2001).

LEISURE AND SECONDARY GROUPS

Other than the primary groups where frequent face-to-face interaction takes place, secondary groups play important roles as agents for leisure. Among secondary groups are schoolmates, youth groups, and adult groups.

Outdoor Pursuits with Schoolmates

It seems the first programs that provided outdoor experience through the school were made possible by the Kellogg Foundation of Battle Creek, Michigan, in the early 1930s (Smith et al., 1970). The Clear Lake Camp and its staff were made available to three Michigan schools. Students from grades 4 through 12 went to the camp for a period of two weeks. The program was enhanced when an act was passed by the Michigan legislature in 1945, which enabled school districts to acquire camps and operate them as a part of the regular educational and recreational programs of the schools.

According to Burrus-Bammel and Bammel (1990), there is sufficient evidence to conclude that outdoor/environmental education programs have the potential to produce benefits for both the participants and society. And although results of specific program evaluation have very little generalizability, the results have a remarkable consistency of demonstrative positive change. Malsam and Nelson (1984) reported an increase in the trust and respect for teachers, leaders, and other students after a four-day residential program for sixth graders. According to Burrus-Bammel and Bammel (1990), programs do not have to be of long duration in order to promote lasting effects.

Outdoor Pursuits with Youth Groups

Youth groups include members of youth-serving organizations, young church members, and members of youth clubs. The idea of organizing activities for the young under the tutelage of adults is an old idea which emanated, most probably, from the need to socialize them in a manner acceptable to the elders. Neumeyer and Neumeyer (1936) wrote of Junglingsverein, a club of young unmarried men in Bremen, Germany in 1709. By 1863, when George Williams organized his first YMCA in London, England, many of these Junglingsverein existed (1949:328). The YMCA and YWCA were urban youth centers concentrating on serving youth and saving them from urban decay.

According to Turner (1985:29), YMCA camping experience could go as far back as 1867, but actual records show that the Brooklyn's YMCA took 30 boys on a trip described as camping out in 1881. In April 1884 the first encampment took place by Orange Lake, New Jersey, when YMCA boys went boating and fishing there. Bible study took one to two hours each day. A year later, some YMCA boys went to an encampment by Lake Champlain, New York, under the leadership of Sumner Dudley, after whose death it was named Dudley Camp. In 1908 the camp was moved to Westport, New York. Today there are 275 YMCA resident camps encompassing approximately 100,000 acres. In addition, the YMCAs administer close to 1,300 day camps reaching approximately 1.5 million young people annually (1985:36).

The youth group that conducted its activity in natural settings from its inception was the paramilitary Boy Scouts, initiated by Lord Robert Stephenson Smyth Baden-Powell in London in 1908 at the heel of the British defeat in the Boer War in South Africa. His idea was to utilize the outdoors in developing physical fitness, self-reliance, and patriotism. According to Rosenthal (1986:162), the notion of the scout as a serviceable citizen trained to follow orders in wartime is at the heart of scouting. Yet Baden-Powell tried from the very beginning to define the movement as anti-militaristic (Rosenthal, 1986:190). In fact Baden-Powell was much influenced by Ernest Thompson Seton, one of the great artist/naturalists of this century. Seton founded the Woodcraft Movement after his immigration to America in the 1880s. Rosenthal states, "For Seton, the natural wisdom of the woods was the highest available to man: individuals had to learn to trust their instincts and open themselves to the prompting of nature in order to achieve their full realization as human beings" (1986:65). Today the scout movement, for both boys and girls, has touched the lives of many young Americans. The numbers speak for themselves, as shown in Table 5.2.

According to Butler (1961:7), Dr. Luther Gulick and his wife, who were instrumental in establishing the Boy Scout movement in America in 1910, became interested in having a similar movement for girls. Moreover, the Gulicks were convinced that the scouts' educational curriculum at the time was inadequate: "The solution was the establishment of the private camp which could teach all the topics the directors felt might be missing in the stringent but stagnating curricula of the day" (Ford, 1989:87). The Gulicks encouraged William Chauncy Langdon, a poet and a consultant on pageantry, to organize an outing experience for a dozen girls from Thetford, Vermont. The girls were called Camp Fire Girls, and they were set up in three ranks of achievement—Wood Gatherers, Fire Makers, and Torch Bearers—ranks that are still in use today. The philosophy of Ernest Thompson Seton was more influential in this movement than in the Scout movement. The Woodcraft Ranger approach, teaching youngsters to use their hands as rangers do, with its strong American motif, Indian Lore, is very clear in the Camp Fire Girls. Now, after admitting boys, the organization is called simply Camp Fire.

From a single club in Hartford, Connecticut, in 1860 the Boys' Club grew to a nationwide organization with over one million boys in more than 700 clubs across the United States. The club is designed to serve boys of urban centers. A similar movement for girls started in 1945. Both Boys' Clubs and Girls' Clubs offer outdoor experiences for their members whenever possible (MacLean et al., 1985).

Table 5.2 Boy Scouts and Girl Scouts, Membership and Units: 1960 to 1985 (in thousands)

[In thousands (6,287 represents 6,287,000). Boy Scouts as of Dec. 31; Girl Scouts as of Sept. 30. Includes Puerto Rico and outlying areas.]

Item	1970	1975	1980	1985	1990	1994	1995	1996	1997	1998	1999
BOY SCOUTS OF AMERICA											
Membership	6,287	5,316	4,318	4,845	5,448	5,378	5,457	5,629	5,835	5,049	6,248
Boys	4,683	3,933	3,207	3,755	4,293	4,188	4,256	4,399	4,574	4,756	4,956
Adults	1,604	1,385	1,110	1,090	1,155	1,190	1,201	1,230	1,262	1,293	1,292
Total units (packs, troops, posts, groups)	157	150	129	134	130	129	132	135	139	142	145
GIRL SCOUTS OF THE U.S.A.											
Membership	3,922	3,234	2,784	2,802	3,269	3,363	3,318	3,390	3,525	3,567	3,630
Girls	3,248	2,723	2,250	2,172	2,480	2,561	2,534	2,584	2,671	2,708	2,749
Adults	674	511	534	630	788	802	784	807	855	858	881
Total units (troops, groups)	164	159	154	166	202	218	215	219	223	226	230

Source: Boy Scouts of America, National Council, Irving, TX, *Annual Report*; and Girl Scouts of the United States of America, New York, NY, *Annual Report*.

Outdoor Pursuits with Adult Groups

For the lack of a better word, the term adult group is used to include the stable membership of voluntary associations, the makeshift groups that form around an outdoor experience, and workplace-centered groups. Voluntary associations include both instrumental and expressive groups. The instrumental associations usually revolve around professions and occupations and are concerned with specific outcomes for their members, usually of extrinsic value, such as wage increases and fringe benefits. Sometimes they also offer the membership some leisure and expressive activities. On the other hand, expressive voluntary associations revolve around activities that are of intrinsic value. The following are some of the expressive associations that deal with nature: American Camping Association, American Youth Hostels, National Audubon Society, Save-the-Redwood League, and the Sierra Club.

DEMOGRAPHIC CORRELATES OF OUTDOOR PURSUITS

The demographic factors that have an affect-effect relationship to leisure behavior include age, life course, gender, occupation, residence, and ethnicity. Although these factors provide a moderate basis for outdoor recreation participation (Manning 1985), nonetheless they should be presented and discussed.

Leisure Pursuits and Age

Play is witnessed among the upper orders of the class mammal of the animal kingdom. Play activities of young humans seem to go through stages that are universal despite differences in race, ethnicity, or cultural background. These activities are usually very simple and become increasingly complex as the society itself becomes more complex. Play may seem to be so natural that learning to play seems unnecessary, but learning to play helps one appreciate the intrinsic values of

certain activities which may reflect on instrumental activities (activities that may lack the element of play) (Csikszentmihalyi, 1981).

Leisure education is a recently coined term that describes the acquisition of skills for the enjoyment of leisure activities both now and in the future. Leisure counseling, also a recently coined term, is used to describe the process used by a professional to help a person choose and become involved in a leisure pursuit. While a young age is ideal for the acquisition of a desire for lifelong leisure pursuit (Bevins et al., 1968; Hendee, 1969; Bradshaw & Jackson, 1979), leisure counseling would be useful to the adult who needs help in selecting a meaningful leisure pursuit.

Leisure Pursuits and Life Course

As life progresses, we assume new roles, including leisure roles. Also, some roles are given up, sometimes by choice and sometimes not by choice. Examples of the taking on and abandoning of leisure roles are provided in Snyder and Spreitzer (1978:57-62). Young men and women were found to assess their own competence as athletes, and if they believed that their competencies were below group expectations, they tended to withdraw from the leisure activity. Kelly (183:50) suggested that participants in leisure pursuits evaluate not only their satisfaction with the activity but also its long-term benefits. Accordingly, they form attitudes, either negative or positive, toward the activity. This process of evaluation goes on throughout the course of life.

As life progresses, new leisure roles should be taken on and old ones abandoned. Examples of leisure roles in different phases of life are given in Bammel and Burrus-Bammel (1981), Kelly (1983), and Gerson et al. (1988) and are summarized and shown in Table 5.3. A study conducted some years ago showed that the level of leisure pursuits decline with age, but it is not clear if the decline is in all three levels, amusive, recreative or contemplative (Gordon et al., 1976).

Table 5.3 Leisure Pursuits and Age Groups

Kelly	Bammel and Burrus-Bammel	Gerson et al.
I. *Preparation Period*: (Birth to early 20s) Play in childhood varies with age and sex and is a means of interaction and a way of self-discovery.	*Teens*: Active participation in vigorous form of recreation activity both outdoors and indoors. *Twenties*: Active participation, especially in outdoor activities. Wilderness backpacking, canoeing, etc.	*Birth-2*: Individual play, expanding horizon, becoming aware of environment. *2-3*: Beginning of imitative and creative play. *3-4*: Parallel and symbolic play, social play, begin aquatics. *5-7*: Large muscle development. Family activities important. *8-9*: Greater desire to participate and to succeed. *9-12*: Team sport. Sexual differences in play.
II. *Establishment Period* (Mid 20s to mid 40s) Leisure roles complement family and community roles. Investment in leisure pursuits increases after children are grown.	*Thirties*: Less active and less frequent participation in outdoor recreation. Camping replaces backpacking. *Forties*: Less active participation, more spectating. Car or van camping replaces tent camping. *Fifties*: Greater emphasis on spectating for the great majority. For a minority, renewed attempt at physical conditioning. Bowling.	*13-18*: Group influence, instant gratification, need to accept socially acceptable activities. *19-22 (Identity)*: Testing intimate relationships. Test self through high-risk activities. *23-30 (Intimacy)*: Peak of physical prowess. Active in sports and high-risk activities. *30-38 (Establishment)*: Activities of couples, social and community services. Children may be used as prestige symbols.
III. *Culmination Period*: (Mid 40s on) More choices in leisure pursuit are seen. Reestablishment of marital dyad occurs.	*Sixties*: Spectating and decrease in physical character of activities. Gardening. *Seventies*: Some new sport activities may begin with retirement. Golf, swimming, shuffleboard, etc.	*38-55 (Adjustment)*: Less physical activity. Participation more spontaneous. Preference in smaller and family groups. *55-65 (Mellow)*: Enjoyment of cultural and creative activities. Expansion to large groups for entertainment. *65+ (Seniors)*: Physical fitness paramount. Preference for activity with same age group.

Leisure Pursuits and Gender

Although the gap separating the two sexes has been narrowed somewhat in recent times, studies show that they still play differently. DiPietro (1981) reported on his experiments when three young girls and three young boys, age four and-half years, were compared as they organized themselves to play together. The boys' play was rougher and more aggressive. Does this mean that society still expects boys to be more aggressive? Or indeed is there a biological difference in the type of play imprinted in the brain of the human male as opposed to the imprint in the brain of the female? In their study of 75 adolescents, Csikszentmihalyi and Larson (1984) found that the males spent over six hours a week on sports while the females spent half that time on sports. Also, the girls spent 31 percent of their waking hours on the arts (music, painting, drawing) while the boys spent half that much time on these activities. Is the difference in interests biologically based? Or is it a product of cultural orientation? Society and societal values seem to play an important part in determining interests, at least when it comes to considering the time freed from familial and civic obligation, as shown in the next study. Jackson and Henderson suggested that constraints to leisure participation among women are functions of cultural interpretation and not merely biological tendency (1995).

According to Bialeschki and Henderson (1986), despite the emancipation of the American woman and her entry into the work world, she is still expected to keep family and home together. In cross-cultural studies, men were found to have more time for leisure in Egypt (Ibrahim et al., 1981), Israel (Shamir & Ruskin, 1983), the USSR (Moskoff, 1984), Norway (Fasting & Sisjord, 185), and Canada (Shaw, 1985). How the imbalance of leisure time between genders is reflected in outdoor pursuits has not been empirically investigated. Are there more men recreating outdoors than women? In 1983 Kelly stated that while gender differences in the type of leisure activities pursued are negligible, women tend not to participate in hunting and drinking. Still women's participation is lower in many of the vigorous activities (Jacob, 2000).

Leisure Pursuits and Occupation

Among the early studies conducted on the relationship between occupation and leisure is Clarke's (1956). He used five levels of occupational groupings: professional, managerial, clerical, skilled, and unskilled workers. Members of the top occupations tend to go to theaters, concerts, lectures, and art galleries and to read, study, and play bridge more often than do members of other occupations. Greater attendance at sports events and commercial recreation is witnessed among members of the middle occupations. Members of the blue-collar occupations tend to attend bars and watch television more often than do the members of the higher occupations. Burdge (1969) used the same classification of occupations and concluded that members of higher occupations seem to participate in greater variety of leisure pursuits, including more participation in outdoor recreational pursuits. Bultena and Field (1978)

found occupations to be significantly related to participation in outdoor activity, supporting Burdge's conclusion that persons occupying higher-paying positions tend to participate in more leisure pursuits, including outdoor ones.

Roberts (1970:28-29) suggested that occupations affect leisure pursuits and are affected by them as follows:

1. Manual occupations demand a great deal of time and energy, leaving manual laborers unable to cultivate active leisure pursuits.
2. Manual occupations are physically arduous and therefore may result in a need to spend leisure simply relaxing or recuperating.
3. Less financially well off persons do not have substantial incomes to invest in leisure interests outside the home and do not have discretionary money to spare for club subscriptions, recreational equipment, and the like.
4. White-collar families have a greater opportunity to travel abroad, and this exposure may stimulate other leisure interests. Certain leisure activities appear to trigger participating in others.
5. Education awakens white-collar people to leisure interests found outside the sphere of the manual worker.
6. A white-collar worker's job may create more opportunities for one to acquire skills that can be exploited during leisure time.
7. Leisure habits emerge as status attitudes generated at work spill over into and influence people's leisure lives.

Tied somewhat to one's occupation is one's income, which affects affordability of certain leisure pursuits. Data from the United Media study (1983) show that households where income is $40,000 or more have 70 percent book readers, 29 percent other material readers, and only 1 percent non-readers in comparison to 35 percent book readers, 54 percent other material readers, and 11 percent non-readers in homes with incomes of $11,000 or less. Is income a factor in the selection of outdoor pursuits? According to Burdge (1969), the more expensive outdoor activities seem to appeal to the person in the higher levels of occupation with higher incomes. A quarter of century later this assertion was supported by Walker and Kiecolt who found that wilderness use is dominated by highly educated professionals (1995).

Leisure Pursuits and Residence

To what extent does the rural-urban dichotomy affect one's leisure pursuit? A study by Knopp (1972) showed that the urban male is more inclined to seek solitude and exercise than is his rural counterpart. Bammel and Burrus-Bammel, (1981) stated that urban residents tend to watch TV, go to the movies, and enjoy swimming more often than do rural dwellers who appreciate the amenities provided in a natural setting, such as solitude and sentience. Rural dweller also like to hunt. Allen et al. (1987:33) surveyed rural households to determine their satisfaction with their leisure activities. Their neutral responses led the authors to conclude that rural residents may be seeking more leisure opportunities than the ones provided in nearby areas. Their conclusion confirms Foret's conclusions drawn when she investigated the relationship between life satisfaction and leisure activities of rural and urban residents. Her data show that age and residence caused no significant differences in leisure satisfaction. However, urban dwellers were more recreationally active than were rural residents (1985). In 1963, Sessoms reviewed most of the studies on age, residence, and occupation conducted up until 1963, which had to do with demographic characteristics and concluded the following:

1. Active participation in outdoor pursuits declines with age.

2. Greater participation is witnessed with higher income.
3. Varied participation increases with higher occupational prestige.
4. More participation is observed among urban residents.
5. Less participation is seen by families with small children.

According to Manning (1985:17), research conducted on the demographic correlates since 1963 has tended to corroborate Sessoms' findings. The studies cited by Manning show near uniformity in who is using the outdoor recreation resources: younger persons of higher socioeconomic status. This does not mean persons from a particular social class. In fact, the whole concept of social class is being replaced by another concept: life-style.

Leisure and Ethnicity

Ethnicity refers to one's ancestral identity, which involves one's total heritage such as values and customs; taste and ritual; as well as some physical features. In the pluralistic American society, a number of ethnic groups, blacks, Latinos, Asians and others are important parts of the American mosaic. In early 1960s The Outdoor Recreation Resources Review Committee reported a significant difference in the outdoor pursuits between whites and America's minority population. The Committee's assertion was confirmed by the many studies conducted so far (Manning, 1999) (See Table 5.4).

Ethnic groups should be encouraged to participate in outdoor pursuits but not necessarily to be assimilated into the main culture. Ethnic identity should be maintained, although assimilation in the main culture has its advantages as shown in these two studies. It seems that inter-ethnic contacts increase similarity in leisure pursuits between blacks and whites (Floyd & Shinew, 1999). Also bicultural Hispanic groups place greater importance on family-related recreation benefits compared to the least assimilated Hispanics (Shaull & Gramann, 2001). The number

Table 5.4 Participation in Various Leisure Activities: 1997

[In percent, except as indicated (195.6 represents 195,600,000). Covers activities engaged in at least once in the prior 12 months. See headnote, Table 440. See also Table 441]

Item	Adult population (mil.)	Attendance at—			Participation in—				
		Movies	Sports events	Amusement park	Exercise program	Playing sports	Charity work	Home improvement/ repair	Computer hobbies
Total............	195.6	66	41	57	76	45	43	66	40
Sex: Male.............	94.2	66	49	58	75	56	40	71	44
Female..............	101.4	65	34	57	77	35	46	61	37
Race: Hispanic	19.1	59	35	66	69	35	31	61	25
White..............	146.1	68	44	56	78	48	45	70	43
African American........	22.1	60	35	55	74	34	44	51	37
American Indian	3.0	65	34	59	83	49	34	58	37
Asian	5.3	76	29	58	70	48	41	58	62
Age: 18 to 24 years old.....	23.7	88	51	76	85	67	35	57	68
25 to 34 years old......	40.1	79	51	70	82	63	41	63	51
35 to 44 years old.......	45.3	73	46	68	79	52	50	76	47
45 to 54 years old.......	33.7	65	42	53	77	40	46	75	40
55 to 64 years old......	20.9	46	33	40	69	19	44	71	23
65 to 74 years old......	19.6	38	21	29	65	23	40	55	11
75 years old and over	12.3	20	16	18	56	13	40	44	7
Education: Grade school	13.7	14	13	34	46	13	20	40	1
Some high school.......	26.9	52	25	54	66	30	31	59	19
High school graduate.....	62.0	62	38	58	74	41	36	65	35
Some college..........	50.3	78	48	64	81	54	50	71	52
College graduate	25.2	82	59	61	87	61	55	76	63
Graduate school........	17.4	81	55	53	88	57	67	73	59
Income: $10,000 or less	15.0	37	15	39	55	19	32	42	19
$10,001 to $20,000......	26.5	46	26	51	69	27	34	53	22
$20,001 to $30,000......	29.4	56	28	55	72	40	37	61	30
$30,001 to $40,000......	32.1	71	42	64	77	46	47	68	40
$40,001 to $50,000......	25.9	73	51	67	80	51	42	75	47
$50,001 to $75,000......	35.0	82	54	65	86	60	50	80	54
$75,001 to $100,000......	16.2	81	66	64	86	61	51	79	64
Over $100,000	15.5	87	65	56	90	66	59	81	69

Source: U.S. National Endowment for the Arts, *1997 Survey of Public Participation in the Arts*, Research Division Report No. 39, December 1998.

of persons with Asian heritage is increasing in the United Sates. Although many forms of traditional activities are practiced by this population depending on the country of origin, it seems that the assimilation of youth with these backgrounds in the main culture is meeting some difficulties (Tirone & Pedlar, 1997).

LEISURE PURSUITS AND LIFE-STYLE

It seems that the combined effect of all the demographic variables listed above: age, life course, education, occupation, residence, and ethnicity produce a certain lifestyle. According to Bradshaw (1978:2) lifestyle refers to "the generalized ways people

act and consume, that is somewhat more fine grained than subcultures—but more general than specific groups or experiences." Gattas et al. (1986) believe that to ask what one does in one's free time is not as important as asking with whom one spends one's free time. They believed leisure research should focus on groups and not activities. An elaborate study of life-styles in America was conducted by Mitchell (1983). Through a survey of 800 questions, 1,600 persons over 18 years of age, living in the contiguous 48 states, were divided into four comprehensive groups and subdivided into nine life-styles as follows:

Need-Driven Groups

Survivor Life-style
Terrible poverty marks these six million survivors of whom only 22 percent made over $5,000 in 1979. Their daily activities are heavily influenced by their high age, low education, and limited resources. They are absent from pursuits requiring a high level of physical energy such as active, and even spectator, sports. They score high on watching television and cigarette smoking.

Sustainer Life-style
Angry and combative, sustainers have not given up hope. Living on the edge of poverty with an income of about $11,000 in 1979, the 11 million sustainers are heavily eschewed to machine, manual, and service occupations. Sustainers attend horse racing more than any other group, watch nature on TV, like to go fishing, read tabloids, and see a lot of X-rated movies.

Outer-Directed Groups

Belonger Life-style
Generally regarded as middle-class America for whom soap opera and romance magazines were created to fill their emotional needs, belongers watch their spending and are not given to faddish activities. These 57 million Americans have a deep-seeded desire to fit in rather than stand out. They prefer home and family activities and such pursuits as gardening, baking, and watching television.

Emulator Life-style
The emulators are intensely striving people seeking to be like the achievers (see item 5). Despite their young age, a median of 27 years, they had an average income of over $18,000 in 1979. Their activities show they are second in conformity to belongers and tied with achievers. The 16 million emulators like bowling and pool, visit night clubs and arcades, and eat at fast food establishments.

Achiever Life-style
These are the driving and the driven people of the American system. Most of the 37 million persons in this group are the professionals such as teachers, lawyers, and physicians. They score high in such activities as playing golf, attending cultural events, drinking cocktails, traveling for pleasure, and reading magazines and newspapers.

Inner-Directed Groups

I-am-me Life-style
A shift from an outer to an inner focus of attention brings a discovery of new interests that redirect life goals. Here, active sports participation, artistic work, and readership of specialized magazines is distinctive. I-am-mes, eight million of them, have the highest of ownership of recreational gear such as backpacking, exercising, and bicycling equipment.

Experiential Life-style
The experiential, 11 million in total, seek direct and vivid experiences. They are well educated with good earning power (over $25,000 in 1979). They love swimming, racquet sports and snow skiing. They engage in yoga and eat health food. They attend lots of movies and like to entertain. They drive European cars and own racing bicycles and backpacking equipment.

Societally Conscious Life-style
Feeling that they have attained positions of affluence, hence no longer feeling the need for self-display, members of this group of 14 million engage in healthful outdoor sports such as bicycling, jogging, swimming, and sailing as well as chess. They, like the achievers, watch many sports programs on television.

Table 5.5 Federal and State Prisoners by Sex: 1980 to1997

[Based on U.S. Census Bureau estimated resident population, as of **December 31.** Includes all persons under jurisdiction of Federal and state authorities rather than those in the custody of such authorities. Represents inmates sentenced to maximum term of more than a year]

Year	Total	Rate [1]	State	Male	Female	Year	Total	Rate [1]	State	Male	Female
1980 . . .	315,974	139	295,363	303,643	12,331	1989 . . .	680,907	276	633,739	643,643	37,264
1981 . . .	353,167	154	331,504	338,940	14,227	1990 . . .	739,980	297	689,577	699,416	40,564
1982 . . .	394,374	171	371,864	378,045	16,329	1991 . . .	789,610	313	732,914	745,808	43,802
1983 . . .	419,820	179	393,015	402,391	17,429	1992 . . .	846,277	332	780,571	799,776	46,501
1984 . . .	443,398	188	415,796	424,193	19,205	1993 . . .	932,074	359	857,675	878,037	54,037
1985 . . .	480,568	202	447,873	458,972	21,296	1994 . . .	1,016,691	389	936,896	956,566	60,125
1986 . . .	522,084	217	485,553	497,540	24,544	1995 . . .	1,085,022	411	1,001,359	1,021,059	63,963
1987 . . .	560,812	231	521,289	533,990	26,822	1996 . . .	1,137,722	427	1,048,907	1,068,123	69,599
1988 . . .	603,732	247	560,994	573,587	30,145	1997 . . .	1,194,581	444	1,099,594	1,120,787	73,794

[1] Rate per 100,000 estimated population.

Source: U.S. Bureau of Justice Statistics, *Prisoners in State and Federal Institutions on December 31,* annual.

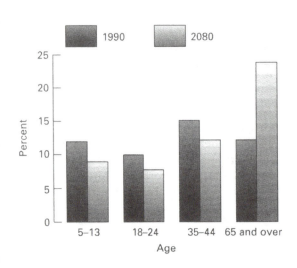

Figure 5.1 Percent distribution of the population by age.

Combined Outer- and Inner Directed Groups

Integrated Life-style

The author estimated that over three million persons had reached maturity, balance and a sense of what is fitting, the prime characteristics of the integrated life-style. Since only 33 persons (two percent of the sample) were identified in this group, the author declined to generalize. Another reason is that the integrateds are highly diverse, subtle in their response, and complex in their outlook. All of these make generalization difficult.

OUTDOOR PURSUITS AND SPECIAL POPULATIONS

Kennedy et al. (1987) state that there are many shortcomings in the labeling of the members of special populations, yet labels must be used to emphasize their special needs. Special populations refer to groups of individuals with special needs that should be attended to by specially trained

Table 5.6 Children and Youth With Disabilities Served by Selected Programs: 1990 to 1999

[For school year ending in year shown (4,210.8 represents 4,210,800). Excludes outlying areas. Through 1994, for persons age 6 to 21 years old served under IDEA (Individuals with Disabilities Act) Part B and Chapter 1 of ESEA (Elementary and Secondary Education Act), SOP (State Operated Programs); beginning 1995, IDEA, Part B only]

Item	1990	1993	1994	1995	1996	1997	1998	1999
All conditions (1,000)	4,210.8	4,586.2	4,730.4	4,859.1	5,028.7	5,177.6	5,338.7	5,486.8
PERCENT DISTRIBUTION								
Specific learning disabilities.	48.6	51.3	50.9	51.2	51.3	51.2	51.0	50.8
Speech or language impairments	23.1	21.7	21.4	20.9	20.3	20.1	19.8	19.5
Mental retardation	13.0	11.3	11.3	11.4	11.3	11.2	11.0	10.9
Serious emotional disturbance	9.0	8.7	8.7	8.8	8.7	8.6	8.5	8.4
Hearing impairments	1.3	1.3	1.3	1.3	1.3	1.3	1.3	1.3
Orthopedic impairments	1.1	1.1	1.2	1.2	1.2	1.3	1.3	1.3
Other health impairments	1.2	1.4	1.7	2.2	2.6	3.1	3.6	4.0
Visually impaired.	0.5	0.5	0.5	0.5	0.5	0.5	0.5	0.5
Multiple disabilities.	2.0	2.2	2.3	1.8	1.8	1.9	2.0	1.9
Deaf/blind	(Z)	(Z)	(Z)	(Z)	(Z)	(Z)	(Z)	(Z)
Autism.	(NA)	0.3	0.4	0.5	0.6	0.7	0.8	1.0
Traumatic brain injury.	(NA)	0.1	0.1	0.1	0.2	0.2	0.2	0.2
Developmental delay	(NA)	(NA)	(NA)	(NA)	(NA)	(NA)	0.1	0.2

NA Not available.   Z less than .05 percent.

Source: U.S. Department of Education, Office of Special Education Programs, Data Analysis System (DANS).

and qualified personnel. Examples of special populations are the physically handicapped, the mentally retarded, and the mentally ill. Select information is needed on the conditions of each group so that special programs may be provided for them in the outdoors. While the data on their conditions are readily available, data on the numbers of the members in each special population are not available. O'Morrow (1980:9) gave the following reasons for the difficulties in gathering such data. First, the line of demarcation between members of special populations and others is not very clear and cannot be agreed upon by the people concerned. Second, definitions change from time to time and from place to place. This is particularly true in legislative enactments. Third, since there are no central agencies, governmental or otherwise, a uniform reporting procedure is

lacking. Fourth, reporting varies so much that even within one region, classification is difficult. Accordingly it is difficult to estimate how many persons are in each category. Perhaps the most reliable source would be the Statistical Abstracts of the United States, 2001. Tables 5.5 and 5.6 show some of the figures on some special populations.

The data available show that there were over four million persons under the age of 22 who were in need of special education. In addition, there are two more special populations that need special attention, the poor and the elderly. Figure 5.1 shows that in 1990, 12 percent of Americans or some 30 million people were 65 years of age or over. The poor are estimated to be about 32 million people. Although there is much overlap between all these groups, nonetheless there is a need to serve the impaired, handicapped, destitute, aged, and outdoor experiences prove to be a very useful tool.

The Mentally Challenged and Outdoor Experiences

The mentally retarded suffer from a number of impairments in cultural conformity, interpersonal relations, and responsiveness as well as in motor skills and speech skills. Sometimes the mentally retarded suffer from auditory and visual limitations. It is estimated that there are about six million such persons in the United States, most of whom are mild cases (educable), followed by moderate cases (trainable), and only five percent severe and profound cases (custodial) as shown in Table 5.5. Studies show that outdoor experiences for the special populations are quite useful and beneficial. Table 5.7 lists these benefits. In addition to camping, Kenedy et al. (1987:19) state that through activities such as rock climbing, white-water rafting, spelunking, and backpacking the retarded are faced with personal challenges as they are involved in interpersonal interaction and small group cooperation.

The Physically Challenged and Outdoor Experiences

It is estimated that over six million Americans have some limitation that could prevent them from participating in regular recreation programs. Many of these people's limitations are not profound, but facilitation to their participation must be provided. These cases include the orthopedically impaired, the cerebral palsied, the blind, the deaf, and persons suffering from muscular dystrophy, multiple sclerosis, and cardiac malfunction. Many of these patients show interest in leisure pursuits, including outdoor ones, yet their therapists who are aware of their interests utilize a limited percentage of them (Pati et al., 1999). Depending on the case, the outdoor experience should be modified accordingly. Kennedy et al. (1987:142) suggested the following guidelines:

1. Change as little as necessary. For example, try to keep the structure of the activity as close as possible to the existing activity. It is better to undermodify so as to challenge the individual and to provide normalized experiences.

2. Where possible, involve the person in the selection and activity modification process. Many times the user is a good source of information. Trails for the physically challenged are based on this phenomenon. All of the modifications have historically needed the approval of the participants.

3. There may be elements of competition to consider when working with groups of children and adults. For instance, in ski competitions, past performance, age and sex of the participant are usually taken into consideration when pitting one person against another.

4. Try to offer activities that are characteristic of those individuals who are in the mainstream of society. Offer to persons with disabilities the same leisure opportunities that exist in society. The normalization principle should be emphasized, and the idea of inventing activities should be deemphasized.

5. Where possible, activities should have common denominators, especially if they are modified. For example, in ski competitions everyone follows the same rules. The physical impairment and the fact that everyone follows the same rules are the common denominators for equality in participation.

6. In many instances the person with a disability is cast in a role of spectator. The authors of this volume strongly feel that individual

Table 5.7 Benefits for Handicapped: A Codified Statement

Primary Benefits	Functional Benefits
Attitudes	**Educational**
independence/self-confidence	learning opportunities
motivation	learn new skills and activities
self-awareness	opportunity for success
heightened morale	improved verbalization
improved behavior	higher academic achievement
improved discipline	creativity
improved cooperation	**Physical**
respect for others	activities of daily living
Social	increased opportunity for participation
socialization/informal group participation	improved coordination and physical fitness
group identity	**Vocational**
relationships with adults of a nonprofessional nature	organizing own activities
get along with others	camping as possible future employment
opportunity for sharing	initiating own activities
Environmental	**Recreational**
expanded environment	activities
heightened community interest/ awareness	fun
opportunity for normal experiences	education for leisure
adapt to community	
adapt to family	

Source: C. C. Hansen, "Content Analysis of Current Literature on Camping for Handicapped Children" in *Training Needs and Strategies in Camping for the Handicapped* by Nesbitt et al. (Eugene, OR: University of Oregon Press, 1972), 34–35. (Reprinted with permission.)

should be provided opportunities to participate in, and in some cases be "nudged" into, participant-based activities.

7. Although the authors do not devalue cooperative and other noncompetitive leisure experiences, the person who is disabled should have ample opportunities to participate in equitable competitive situations.

8. Start at the level where the participants are currently functioning. This does not mean starting at the lowest level.

9. Individuals should be given opportunities for free choice.

This may enhance the feeling of control and reduce feelings of "learned helplessness."

The Socially Deviant and Outdoor Experiences

While sociologists look at deviancy as the outcome of cultural and environmental factors, psychologists tend to view it as the result of some personality disorganization. Whatever the case, the two million or so individuals who are in the correctional system may benefit from recreational experiences in natural settings. In some instances the experience is used as a form of rehabilitation, as is the case with the deep-sea diving program in the men's colony in Chino, California. If these men were Type T personalities, risk-takers, such a program would provide the challenge they need. In other cases, the activity is deemed somewhat preventive, as with provisions of outdoor experiences in the Outward Bound program for the juvenile delinquent. Here the activity is thought to keep the person from deteriorating into further deviancy.

The Elderly and Outdoor Experiences

As shown earlier in the section on leisure pursuits and life course, the interests of the elderly will change due to a number of factors. According to Burdman (1986), the reduction in the number of muscular and nerve cells is accompanied by a loss of elasticity. Also the person suffers from less efficiency in all body systems. The outcome is an increase in ailments such as cardiovascular, respiratory, and musculoskeletal problems, diabetes mellitus, and hypothermia. Moreover the elderly could suffer from some psychological problems such as depression, dementia, and alcoholism. Recreation programs including outdoor experiences have proven beneficial. For instance, Owens (1982) found that satisfaction with leisure contributed significantly to life satisfaction of the 205 elders he studied.

According to Leitner and Leitner (1985:16), the leisure patterns of the elderly, although diverse, are dominated by television viewing and reading. A possible reason for this could be their physical limitations. This may add to the feeling of loneliness as shown by the studies of Creecy, Wright, and Berg (1982). On the other hand, popular outdoor activities, which include gardening and camping may decrease loneliness through socialization (McAvoy, 1982, Leitner & Leitner, 1985).

SUMMARY

In this chapter on the social aspects of outdoor experiences, the roles played by the socializing agents were taken into consideration. The family is one of the most important in that respect, as is religion. Both agents could determine what is acceptable,

and what is not, as a recreational activity. While there are enough empirical studies on the role that the family plays in this regard, there is a paucity of empirical evidence on the role of religion. Still, it is clear from the study of rituals that some elements of leisure pursuits may have evolved thereof. For example, Shrove Tuesday activities in Chester, England, were the starting point for soccer, which has evolved into the world's most poplar sport.

Three other social institutions affect leisure behavior, namely the political structure, the economic system, and the technological level of the society at hand. The political structure controls leisure offerings through legislation on the local, state, or federal levels. Details on these three levels will be given in Chapters 7, 8, and 9. In the next chapter, the relationship between the economic structure and leisure is presented. Technology is presented here as divided into two aspects, material and social technology. Material technology refers to scientific advances as well as industrialization. Their impact on outdoor pursuits is exemplified in the increasing number of snowmobiles in North America. Social technology refers to education and the mass media. The introduction of nature documentaries on television has helped to make people aware of the importance of conservation.

Other than primary and secondary groups, demographic factors such as age, gender, occupation, residence, and ethnicity have been studied by various researchers. The results of these studies are presented in this chapter. For instance, early socialization into outdoor pursuits has been shown to be desirable. Also, it has been found that men seem to have more free time than women, and that the higher-paying one's occupation is, the greater the participation in outdoor pursuits. Rural dwellers seem to enjoy more nature activities than do urban dwellers.

The relationship between life-style and leisure pursuits is another important area of study. Life-style refers to the unique combination of age, educational attainment, and income that results in a certain way of living. Life-style is reflected in outdoor pursuits in the choice of activities. For example, professionals might travel for pleasure, while semi-skilled workers might instead tend to go fishing. The role that recreational activities play in the lives of special populations is presented here also. It seems that outdoor recreational activities help the mentally retarded person's self-awareness, the physically challenged person's self-confidence, and the social deviant's self-expression.

REFERENCES

Abbcott, C. M. (1998). Thoreau's "Walden," *The Explicator, 56*(2), 74.

Adler, P. A., & Adler, A. (1999). Social reproduction and the corporate other: The institutionalization of after school activities. *The Sociological Quarterly, 35*(2), 309.

Allen, L., (1987, April). The role of leisure: Satisfaction in rural communities. *Leisure Today,*5-8.

Bammel, G., & Burrus-Bammel, L. (1981). *Human behavior and leisure*. Dubuque, IA: Wm. C. Brown.

Berg, E. C., et al. (2000). Dyadic exploration of the relationship of leisure satisfaction, leisure time and gender to relationship satisfaction. *Leisure Sciences, 23,* 35.

Bevins, M., Bond, R., Concorn, T., McIntosh, K., & McNeil, R. (1968). Characteristics of hunters and fishermen in six northeastern states. *Vermont Agriculture Experimental Station Bulletin 565*.

Bialeschki, M., & Henderson, K. (1986). Leisure in the common world of women. *Leisure Studies, 53,* 299-308.

Bradshaw, R., & Jackson, J. (1979). Socialization for leisure. In H. Ibrahim & R Crandall (Eds.) Leisure: A Psychological Approach. Los Alamitos, CA: Hwong.

Bradshaw, T. K. (1978). *Lifestyle in the advanced industrial societies*. Berkeley, CA: Institute of Governmental Studies, University of California.

Bultena, G., & Field, D. (1978). Visitors to national parks: Test of the elitism argument. *Leisure Sciences, 1*(4).

Burdge, R. J. (1969). Levels of occupational prestige and leisure activity. *Journal of Leisure Research, 1*(3), 202-24.

Burdmen, G. M. (1986). *Healthful aging*. Englewood Cliffs, NJ: Prentice-Hall.

Burrus-Bammel, L., & Bammel, G. (1990, April). Outdoor/environmental education: An overview for the wise use of leisure." *Leisure Today*, 17-22.

Butler, G. (1961). *Introduction to community recreation*. New York: Macmillan.

Cheek, N., & Burch, W. (1976). *The social organization of leisure in human society*. New York: Harper and Row.

Cheek, N. (1981). Social cohesion and outdoor recreation. In J. Kelly (Ed.), *Social benefits of outdoor recreation*. Champaign, Il: Leisure Behavior Laboratory, University of Illinois.

Clarke, A. C. (1956). The use of leisure and its relation to levels of occupational prestige. *American Sociological Review, 21*, 301-7.

Creecy, R. F., Wright, R., & Berg, W. E. (1982). Correlates of loneliness among the black elderly. *Activities Adaptation and Aging, 3*(2), 9-16.

Csikszentmihalyi, M. (1981, December). Leisure and socialization. *Social Forces, 60*, 2.

Csikszentmialyi, M., & Larson, R. (1984). *Being adolescent*. New York: Basic Books.

DiPietro, J. (1981). Rough and tumble play: A function of gender. *Developmental Psychology, 12*, 50-58.

Durkheim, E. (1915). *The elementary forms of religious life*. London: George Allen and Unwin.

Edwards, C. P. (2001). Worlds of experience after school. *Human Development, 44*, 59.

Eitzen, D. S., & Sage, G. (1989). *Sociology of North American sport*. Dubuque, IA: Wm. C. Brown.

Erikson, E. (1977). *Toys and reason: Stages in the ritualization of experience*. New York: Norton.

Fasting, K., & Sisjord, M. K. (1985). Gender roles and barriers to participation in sport. *Sociology of Sport Journal, 2*(4), 345 -51.

Fink, B., & Wild, K. (1995). Similarities in leisure interests: Effect of selection and socialization on friendships. *Journal of Social Psychology, 135*, 471.

Floyd, M. R., & Shinew, K. J. (1999). Convergence and divergence toward an interracial contact hypothesis." *Journal of Leisure Research, 3*(4), 359.

Fong, Y., & Zhang. J. (2001). The identification of unobservable independent and spousal leisure. *Journal of Political Economy, 109*, 19.

Ford, P. (1989). Luther Gulick. In H. Ibrahim (Ed.), Pioneers in leisure and recreation. Reston, VA: AAHPERD.

Foret, C. M. (1985). *Life satisfaction and leisure satisfaction among young-old and old-old adults with rural and urban residence.* Unpublished Ph.D. dissertation. Denton, TX: Texas Women's University.

Gattas, J. T., et al. (1986). Leisure and lifestyle: Towards a research agenda. *Society and Leisure, 9*(2), 524-37.

Gerson, G., et al. (1988). *Understanding leisure: An interdisciplinary approach.* Dubuque, IA: Kendall/Hunt.

Glyptis, S., & Chambers, D. (1982). No place like home. *Leisure Studies, 1*, 247-62.

Gordon, C, Gaitz, C. M., & Scott, J. (1976). Leisure and life. In R. Binstock & E. Shamas (Eds.), *Handbook of aging and social science.* New York: Van Nostrand Reinhold Company.

Hendee, J. (1969). Rural-urban differences reflected in outdoor recreation participation. *Journal of Leisure Research, 1*, 33-41.

Hill, J., & McLean, D. (1999) Introduction: Defining our perspective of the future. *JOPERD, 70*, 21.

Ibrahim, H., et al. (1981). Leisure behavior among contemporary Egyptians. *Journal of Leisure Research, 13*, 89-104.

Jackson. E., & Henderson, K. (1995). Gender-based analysis of leisure constraints. *Leisure Sciences, 17*, 31.

Kelly, J. (1974). Socialization toward leisure: A developmental approach. *Journal of Leisure Research, 6*, 181-93.

Kelly, J. (1981). Family benefit from outdoor recreation. In J. Kelly (Ed.), *The social benefits of outdoor recreation.* Champaign, IL: Leisure Behavior Laboratory, University of Illinois.

Kelly, J. (1983). *Leisure identities and interaction.* London: George Allen and Unwin.

Kennedy, D., Austin, D., & Smith, R. (1987). *Special recreation: Opportunities for persons with disabilities.* Philadelphia: Saunders.

Kleiber, D., & Rickards, W. (1981). Outdoor recreation and child development. In J. Kelly (Ed.), *Social benefits of outdoor recreation.* Champaign, IL: Leisure Behavior Laboratory. University of Illinois.

Knopp, T. (1972). Environmental determinants of recreation behavior. *Journal of Leisure Behavior, 4*, 129-38.

Leitner, M., & Leitner, S. (1985). *Leisure in later life.* New York: Hawthorn Press.

Maclean, J., Peterson, J., & Martin, W. D. (1985). *Recreation and leisure: The changing scene.* New York: Macmillan.

Malsam, M., & Nelson, L. (1984). Integrating curriculum objectives. *Journal of Physical Education, Recreation, and Dance, 55*(7), 52-54.

Manning, H. (1975). *Backpacking: One step at a time.* New York: Vintage Books.

Manning, R. (1985). *Studies in outdoor recreation: Search and research for satisfaction.* Corvallis, OR: Oregon State University Press.

Mayhew, L. (1971). *Society: Institutions and activity.* Glenview, IL: Scott, Foresmn and Company.

McAvoy, L. H. (1982). The leisure preference problems and needs of the elderly. *Journal of Gerontology, 11*(I), 40-47.

Mitchell, A. (1983). *The nine American lifestyles: Who we are and where we're going.* New York: Macmillan.

Moskoff, W. (1984). *Labor and leisure in the Soviet Union.* New York: St. Martin's Press.

Neumeyer, M., & Neumeyer, E. (1936 and 1949). *Leisure and recreation.* New York: A. S. Bames.

Newsweek (1995, March). *Breaking Point, 6*, 56.

O'Morrow, G. (1980). *Therapeutic recreation: A helping profession.* Reston, VA: Reston Publishing.

Orthner, D. (1976). Patterns of leisure and marital interaction. *Journal of Leisure Research, 8*, 98-116.

Orthner, D., Barnett, L., & Ancinin, J. (1994). Leisure and family over the life cycle. In L. L'Abate (Ed.), *Handbook of developmental psychology and psychotherapy*. New York: John Wiley.

Owens, D. J. (1982). *The relationship of frequency and types of activity to life satisfaction in elderly deaf people*. Doctoral dissertation, New York University. Dissertation Abstracts International 42:311A.

Roberts, K. (1970). *Leisure*. London: Longman.

Rosenthal, M. (1986). *The character factory: Baden-Powell's Boy Scouts and the imperative of the empire*. New York: Pantheon Books.

Sessoms, H. D. (1963, October). An analysis of selected variables affecting outdoor recreation patterns. *Social Forces, 42*, 112-15.

Shamir, B., & Ruskin, H. (1983). Sex differences in recreational sport behavior and attitudes: A study of married couples in Israel. *Leisure Studies, 2*(3), 253-68.

Shaull, S. L., & Gramann, J. H. (2001). The effect of cultural assimilation on the importance of family related and nature related recreation among Hispanic Americans. *Journal of Leisure Research, 30*(1), 47.

Shaw, S. (1985). Gender and leisure: Inequality in the distribution of leisure Time. *Journal of Leisure Research, 17*(4), 266-82.

Shepard, P. (1977). Place and human development. In *Children, nature and the urban environment*. U.S. Forest Service General Technical Report. Washington, D.C.: U.S. Government Printing Office.

Smith, J., Carlson, R., Donaldson, G., & Masters, H. (1970). *Outdoor education*. Englewood Cliffs, NJ: Prentice-Hall.

Snyder, E., & Spreitzer, E. (1978). *Social aspects of sport*. Englewood Cliffs, NJ: Prentice-Hall.

Tirone, S., & Pedlar, A. (1997). Assimilation and conflict: Leisure experiences in the lives of South Asian adolescents in Canada. NRPA Leisure Research Symposium.

Turner, V. (1985). *100 years of YMCA camping*. Chicago, IL: YMCA of the USA.

United Media Enterprises. (1983). *Where does the time go*? New York: Newspaper Enterprise Association.

U.S. Bureau of the Census. (1987). *Statistical abstracts of the United States*. Washington, D.C.: U.S. Government Printing Office.

U.S. Bureau of the Census. (1989). *Statistical abstracts of the United States*. Washington, D.C.: U.S. Government Printing Office.

Walker, G. J., & Kiecolt, K. I. (1995). Social class and wilderness use. *Leisure Sciences 17*: 295.

West, P., & Merriam, L. (1970). Outdoor recreation and family cohesiveness. *Journal of Leisure Research, 2*, 251-59.

White, C. (1955). Social class differences in the uses of leisure. *American Journal of Sociology, 61*, 145-50.

Yoesting, D., & Burkhead, D. (1973). Significance of childhood recreation experience on adult leisure behavior. *Journal of Leisure Research, 5*, 25-36.

6 THE ECONOMICS OF OUTDOOR PURSUITS

Why is it that in a society with such a capitalistic orientation, many American politicians and naturalists argue for the preservation of large chunks of government land for outdoor enjoyment? Why do they also fight for the provision of programs and activities on those lands? Perhaps because some of them feel that Americans should be rewarded for their hard work. Work is necessary, because although unpleasant, it is important to life. Leisure, on the other hand, is not only pleasant, it could be meaningful (Marano,1999). Meaningful activities are those with which a person can easily identify. Some claim that leisure in a natural setting is more than pleasant and meaningful, it is important to human welfare and could be therapeutic, if not euphoric (Esteve, et al., 1999).

Many believe the claim that leisure is beneficial to human welfare is exaggerated (Olson, 1961), yet the provisions for outdoor experiences continue to exist even though the number of those who participate in genuine outdoor pursuits may seem too small to warrant the expense of maintaining vast outdoor recreation opportunities (Simmons, 1975:5). The support for providing areas and allocating funds for programs to be conducted in these areas will not subside. Perhaps because outdoor pursuits have become an integral part of the total leisure scene in the countries of the Western world, particularly the United States and Canada. In fact, natural areas and related programs are provided in many Third World countries such as Egypt and India, not necessarily for the citizens but for badly needed hard currency coming from foreign tourists (Ibrahim, 1991: 95,100). In other words, leisure has become a source of income for the producers of its goods and services as well as a source of pleasure and meaningfulness for the ones who consume these goods and services. How did this come about, in a country that was not long ago straddled with a puritanical ideology so ingrained that at the time of the writing of the Constitution a proposal was forwarded to include in its articles a prohibition against horse racing, gambling, and all extravagance (Dulles, 1965:65)? A presentation on the nature of the economic system and the changes that have taken place will shed some light on this development.

THE NATURE OF THE ECONOMIC SYSTEM

The work of Rostow (1960) shows that there are certain requirements that have to be met and certain steps to be taken before leisure spending can become an important ingredient in society's economic system. In essence, the society should be at the stage of high consumption (see Figure 6.1), that is, when most of its citizens could become high consumers of goods and services

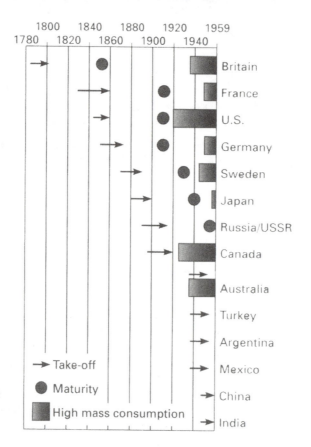

Figure 6.1 Five Stages of Economic Growth

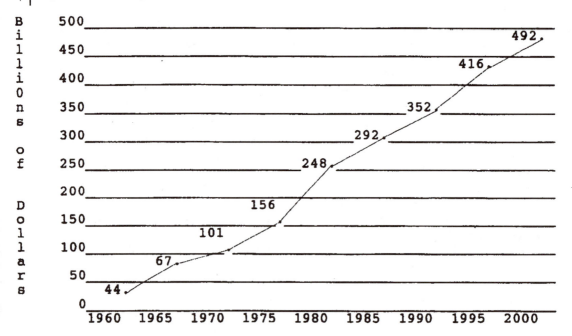

Source: Bureau of the Census, Statistical Abstracts of the United States, many editions.

Figure 6.2 Spending trends for leisure in the United States 1960-2000

[In billions of dollars (284.9 represents $284,900,000,000), except porcent. Roprosents markol value of purchases of goods and services by individuals and nonprofit institutions]

Type of product or service	1990	1993	1994	1995	1996	1997	1998
Total recreation expenditures	284.9	340.1	368.7	401.6	429.6	457.8	494.7
Percent of total personal consumption [1]	7.4	7.6	7.8	8.1	8.2	8.3	8.5
Books and maps	16.2	18.8	20.8	23.1	24.9	26.6	27.8
Magazines, newspapers, and sheet music	21.6	23.1	24.9	26.2	27.6	29.5	31.9
Nondurable toys and sport supplies	32.8	39.5	43.4	47.2	50.6	53.7	57.7
Wheel goods, sports and photographic equipment [2]	29.7	32.5	35.2	38.5	40.5	43.2	47.1
Video and audio products, computer equipment, and musical instruments	52.9	62.6	71.0	77.0	80.0	84.0	92.6
Video and audio goods, including and musical instruments	43.9	48.1	53.0	55.9	56.4	57.8	62.2
Computers, peripherals, and software	8.9	14.5	18.0	21.0	23.6	26.2	30.4
Radio and television repair.	3.7	3.3	3.3	3.6	3.7	3.9	3.9
Flowers, seeds, and potted plants	10.9	12.5	13.2	13.8	14.9	15.6	16.5
Admissions to specified spectator amusements	14.8	17.5	18.2	19.2	20.7	22.2	23.8
Motion picture theaters	5.1	5.0	5.2	5.5	5.8	6.4	6.8
Legitimate theaters and opera, and entertainments of nonprofit institutions [3]	5.2	6.8	7.2	7.6	8.0	8.7	9.4
Spectator sports [4]	4.5	5.7	5.8	6.1	6.9	7.1	7.6
Clubs and fratornal organizations except Insurance [5]	8.7	11.1	11.8	12.7	14.0	14.4	14.9
Commercial participant amusements [6]	24.6	34.0	38.6	43.9	48.3	52.3	56.2
Pari-mutuel net receipts.	3.5	3.3	3.4	3.5	3.5	3.6	3.7
Other [7]	65.4	81.9	84.7	93.1	100.8	109.0	118.6

[2] Includes boats and pleasure aircraft. [3] Except athletic. [4] Consists of admissions to professional and amateur athletic events and to racetracks, including horse, dog, and auto. [5] Consists of dues and fees excluding insurance premiums. [6] Consists of billiard parlors; bowling alleys; dancing, riding, shooting, skating, and swimming places; amusement devices and parks; golf courses; sightseeing buses and guides; private flying operations; casino gambling; and other commercial participant amusements. [7] Consists of net receipts of lotteries and expenditures for purchases of pets and pet care services, cable TV, film processing, photographic studios, sporting and recreation camps, video cassette rentals, and recreational services, not elsewhere classified.

Source: U.S. Bureau of Economic Analysis, *The National Income and Product Accounts of the United States, 1929-94*, Vol.1, and *Survey of Current Business*, June 2000.

including leisure goods and services. At an earlier stage of economic development, it is possible that only a few privileged citizens become high consumers. These were the members of the leisure class of past eras (Veblen, 1953). Today most of us are members of that leisure class; most of us are high consumers.

Figure 6.1 shows that in the 1920s the American economy entered the high mass consumption phase, which includes leisure spending. The figures for such spending are shown in Table 6.1.

Figure 6.2 shows spending trends for leisure in the United States for 1962-1982. The amounts in Figure 6.2 do not include government spending, nor do they include the spending of some private and public agencies on recreation.

According to the data presented in Table 6.1 and Figures 6.1 and 6.2, two-thirds of the American economic output consists of goods and services to be consumed by individuals, households and groups, a good share of which are included under leisure spending. In 1962 leisure spending was about $48 billion, and in a quarter of a century the figure jumped to almost $320 billion. Today it stands at a little less than $500 billion. What made leisure such a potent force in the American economy? MacLean et al. state that the following three important factors are responsible for making leisure play a leading role in the economy of this society (1985:58-60):

1. **Productivity:** The productivity of a given market today is eight times what it was 140 years ago. The gross national product (GNP), which is the total market value of goods and services, has increased at an average rate of three percent per year for many years. Also, the labor force has grown steadily in the past few years. Increased productivity means that more goods and services are provided to be consumed. This requires a concomitant increase in income.

2. **Increased Income:** A substantial increase in income above and beyond what is needed to purchase essential goods and services becomes necessary for the consumption of "the nonessentials," that is, leisure services and equipment, whether provided by the private or public sector. This increase is called discretionary income. An increase in productivity and a viable discretionary income might not, in themselves, have led to the increase in leisure pursuits that has been witnessed in the last few decades in the United States. Another ingredient was at work, an increase in free time.

3. **Increased Free Time:** In order for leisure to become an important facet of a society it was crucial to have time freed from familial, civil, and work obligations—time in which a person could partake of an activity for its own sake, for its intrinsic value. Societal values play important roles in how one perceives time as being free from all obligations, and a study of the value system in American society is necessary. The American value system has gone through drastic changes since the early settlement of the country. There were attempts to include in the U.S. Constitution provisions that prohibit gambling, horse racing, and the like. Today some of these activities are sponsored by government agencies. Also, Americans have witnessed a change in their attitude toward work. Changes in work time are shown in Figure 6.3. The drop in work time from 50+ hours per week to 30+ hours per week in 100 years allowed for an increase in free time to about 32 hours per week (Jensen, 1985 and the United Media Enterprises, 1983). Jensen's figures are based on a summary of previous time-budget studies, and the United Media Enterprises work is based on interviews of 1,024 persons from the general public, 101 newspaper editors, 105 cable television directors, and 116 network television news directors.

In addition to increased productivity, increased income, and increased free time, the high level of mobility of Americans played an important role in the phenomenal increase in leisure pursuits in this country. The automobile, which facilitated business and trade, became an important element in leisure pursuits as well. It provided access to the vast recreational resources in this country. More recently, the new American invention, the RV, began taking people of all ages into areas that had been inaccessible to anyone a genera-

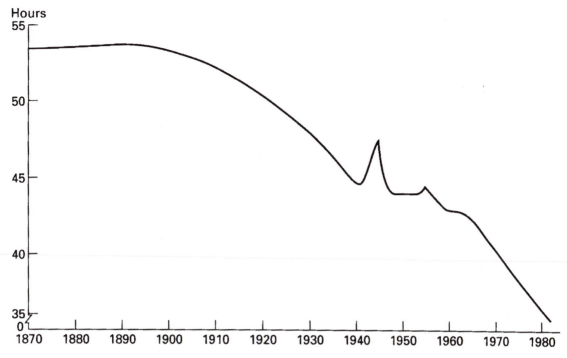

Source: Bosserman, P. "The Evolution of and Trends in Work and Non-Work Time in the United States Society (1920-1970)," Society and Leisure 7(1):94. (Reprinted with permission.) Modified to 1983.

Figure 6.3 Average weekly hours per worker, U.S., 1869-1983. Other studies do not agree with Jensen's and United Media's research that work hours declined in the 1970s.

tion ago. There, they found another American invention, the campground, which has evolved in a short time into a very convenient recreational facility provided with such amenities as flush toilets and hot showers. The convenience of the campground is surpassed only by the convenience of the RV, which has been recently described as the great indoors in the great outdoors.

While these four variables, productivity, discretionary income, discretionary time, and mobility, are still affecting leisure behavior in the United States and other industrial societies, the rate of population growth, which at one point was instrumental in increased demand for leisure services, leveled off a few years ago. In fact, both discretionary income and discretionary time are leveling off also (see Table

6.1). In addition, the rate of increase in productivity is not as high as it used to be a decade or two ago.

Nonetheless, spending on leisure goods such as pleasure boats, RVs, snowmobiles, athletic equipment, and sportswear continued to climb in the last few years, as shown in Tables 6.1 and 6.2.

Recreation Expenditure

The exact expenditures on leisure pursuits either by individuals or by agencies are hard to obtain. This may be due to the lack of precise definition of what a leisure pursuit is. How can pleasure travel be separated from business travel? Another factor is the overlap in the categorization of leisure spending. Should vacationing in a recreational vehicle be classified as travel or outdoor recreation? Nonetheless, estimates show that spending on leisure pursuits, in total, has steadily increased over the years. *U.S. News and World Report,* which monitored spending for many years, estimated leisure spending by individuals, households, and groups at $50 billion in 1965, which rose to $300 billion in the late 1980s (Ibrahim, 1991:175). Today it is estimated to be close to $500 billion (See table 6.1).   MacLean et al. (1985:62-67) classified leisure spending in five categories:

1. **Recreation Supplies and Equipment:** This category includes durable items such as recreational vehicles and motorcycles; televisions, radios, and tape recorders; camping and sports equipment; musical instruments and art supplies; and garden supplies.

2. **Travel and Vacation Businesses:** With the marked improvement in transportation, travel and vacationing have become very large businesses in this country. Although ownership of a second home (for vacations) is not as prevalent as it used to be, the concept of timeshare purchase of vacation accommodation is gaining ground. Many states, such as Florida, are becoming dependent on travel as their most important source of income. Also many countries today are becoming dependent on tourism, for example Egypt, Greece, and Mexico.

3. **Sport and Outdoor Recreation:** Next to travel and vacationing, outdoor recreation and sports account for the largest expenditure on leisure activities. Sports have been an important part of the leisure scene in America for many years. In addition, the recent increased interest in wellness and fitness has added to the expenditure in this category. A

quarter of a century ago, the Bureau of Outdoor Recreation predicted a 141 percent increase in outdoor pursuits from the year 1965 to the year 2000. And it is estimated that millions of Americans flock to water resources, mountains, and deserts to pursue their leisure activities. Total communities around these areas have been established, and their economy depends entirely on the sport aficionado and outdoor enthusiast.

4. **Cultural Activities:** This category includes music, drama, dance, arts and crafts, books and other publications, and museums. Not only are televisions, radios, cassettes, and digital recordings selling in record numbers, but attendance at musical and dramatic plays has also increased. Even in the area where growth was once slow, as in opera and symphony performances, attendance is increasing. Expenditure on arts and crafts supplies has also increased. The same is witnessed in books and other publications. Also, attendance at museums has increased significantly in the last few years.

5. **Home Expenditure:** As previously stated, the home is the most important center for leisure activity. Not only are most homes equipped with a backyard, but some are also equipped with a recreation room, a hot tub, and a swimming pool. Home expenditures on leisure include playground equipment, hobby shops, and entertainment equipment, including computerized games. Away from home, family spending on leisure includes going to movies, amusement parks, and theme restaurants.

Table 6.2 Sporting Good Sales by Product Category: 1990 to 1999

[In millions of dollars (50,725 represents $50,725,000,000), except percent. Based on a sample survey of consumer purchases of 80,000 households, (100,000 beginning 1995), except recreational transport, which was provided by industry associations. Excludes Alaska and Hawaii. Minus sign (-) indicates decrease]

Selected product category	1990	1992	1993	1994	1995	1996	1997	1998	1999, proj.
Sales, all products	**50,725**	**49,633**	**51,900**	**56,162**	**59,794**	**62,818**	**67,333**	**68,680**	**71,300**
Annual percent change	-0.4	-0.3	4.6	8.2	6.5	5.1	7.2	2.0	3.8
Percent of retail sales	2.7	2.5	2.5	2.5	2.5	2.5	2.6	2.5	2.4
Athletic and sport clothing [2]	10,130	8,990	9,096	9,521	10,311	11,127	12,035	12,637	13,390
Athletic and sport footwear [2]	11,654	11,733	11,084	11,120	11,415	12,815	13,319	13,020	13,211
Walking shoes	2,950	2,688	2,673	2,543	2,841	3,079	3,236	3,192	3,204
Gym shoes, sneakers	2,536	2,397	2,016	1,869	1,741	1,996	1,980	2,010	2,050
Jogging and running shoes	1,110	1,232	1,231	1,069	1,043	1,132	1,482	1,469	1,587
Tennis shoes	740	748	599	556	480	541	545	515	499
Aerobic shoes	611	590	500	356	372	401	380	334	307
Basketball shoes	918	984	874	867	999	1,192	1,134	1,000	1,003
Cross training shoes	679	799	877	1,101	1,191	1,417	1,450	1,402	1,486
Golf shoes	228	260	275	238	225	231	239	220	225
Athletic and sport equipment [2]	14,439	15,369	16,651	17,966	18,809	18,988	19,033	18,605	19,212
Archery	265	300	285	300	287	276	270	261	259
Baseball and softball	217	256	323	295	251	277	290	303	321
Camping	1,072	903	906	1,017	1,205	1,127	1,153	1,204	1,240
Exercise equipment	1,824	2,078	2,602	2,781	2,960	3,232	2,968	2,850	3,078
Firearms and hunting	2,202	2,533	2,722	3,523	3,003	2,521	2,562	2,200	2,310
Fishing tackle	1,910	1,906	1,952	1,951	2,010	1,970	1,891	1,903	1,905
Golf	2,514	2,606	2,723	2,747	3,194	3,560	3,703	3,641	3,714
In-line skating and wheel sports	150	268	377	545	646	590	562	515	504
Optics	438	465	493	503	655	673	690	710	739
Pool/billiards	192	238	313	313	304	271	242	251	259
Skiing, alpine	475	521	569	609	562	707	723	718	739
Skin diving and scuba	294	297	315	322	328	340	332	345	356
Tennis	333	310	327	313	297	296	319	313	319
Recreational transport	14,502	13,541	15,069	17,555	19,259	19,888	22,946	24,418	25,487
Pleasure boats	7,644	5,765	6,246	7,679	9,064	9,399	10,208	10,140	10,444
Recreational vehicles	4,113	4,412	4,775	5,690	5,895	6,327	6,904	8,364	9,078
Bicycles and supplies	2,423	2,973	3,534	3,470	3,390	3,187	4,860	4,957	5,007
Snowmobiles	322	391	515	715	910	974	975	957	958

[1] Represents change from immediate prior year.   [2] Includes other products not shown separately.

Source: National Sporting Goods Association, Mt. Prospect, IL, *The Sporting Goods Market in 1999*; and prior issues (copyright).

The expenditures on travel, vacationing, and outdoor recreation are important facts of our economy. Clearly, as seen in Tables 6.1 and 6.2 and as suggested by many authors (MacLean et al., 1985, Jensen, 1985, & Knudson 1984), these are the largest expenditures on leisure pursuits. They are supplemented by government expenditures in the provision of outdoor recreation areas, as discussed next.

Government Expenditure

All three levels of government—local, state, and federal—are involved directly in outdoor recreation. Their major contribution is in the provision of areas such as parks and forests, and they also provide programs in many of these areas. It is difficult to find out how much the government spends on recreation because, in many instances, these expenditures are not listed under a separate category. Nonetheless, Jensen (1985:72-74) tried to elucidate the government's involvement in outdoor recreation as follows:

Federal Government Expenditure

Two federal departments are directly involved in the outdoor pursuits of Americans as they take place on federal lands: the Department of Agriculture through the management of national forests and the Department of the Interior through the management of national parks spend large sums on maintaining these areas. Moreover, other federal agencies provide recreation for millions of Americans on their lands. Clearly it is hard to estimate the federal government's expenditure on outdoor recreation. In Chapter 7 the role of the federal government in outdoor recreation will be discussed.

State Expenditure

The 50 states spend close to $1 billion in financing outdoor recreation. Most of this money is raised through taxes. Sometimes a certain tax is specified for recreation expenditure, such as the cigarette tax in Texas. Another source of income to be used for recreation purposes is licensing fees, for example, fees for hunting and fishing licenses. State bond elections have been used very successfully in park development and natural resources expansion. User fees are also required in many locations.

Local Government Expenditure

While Jensen (1985:74) suggests that local governments spend, on the average, 2.3 percent of their income on recreational facilities and programs, MacLean et al. suggest 3.7 percent (1985:82). The total amount spent by local governments could reach $2 billion. Chapter 9 is devoted to local government and outdoor recreation.

Other Expenditures

Other than leisure pursuit expenditures by individuals, households, and governments, there are expenditures by both public and private agencies that should be included in the estimates of the total expenditure picture. For instance, the camps of the different youth service organizations are an example of nonprofit organizations spending on leisure pursuits and a school camp is an example of what a public agency spends on leisure pursuits.

Spending on, and for, leisure pursuits is only half of the total picture, the other half being the incomes accrued from these activities. These incomes have strong impact on the economy of the nation, a region, and/or a state.

NATIONAL ECONOMIC IMPACT

It is estimated that private recreation business provides nearly seven percent of the total employment in the United States (Walsh, 1986:1). When the number of those employed in the recreation services provided by the public sector is added to the above, the impact of leisure spending on the American economy becomes clearer. In addition, foreign tourists account for four percent of the total exports of American goods and services, which helps in addressing the problem of trade deficit in the U.S. economy.

Demand and Supply

Knudson (1984:10) suggested that the outdoor recreation system could be looked upon as composed of four elements that correspond to four economic parallels, as follows:

Visitors and their characteristics ➡	Demand
Recreational resources ➡	Supply
Plans and policies ➡	Pricing
Tools for implementation ➡	Management

These four economic parallels affect outdoor pursuits as follows: In the American economic system, the concepts of demand and supply are used to determine economic policy. Demand is based on the ability and willingness of consumers to buy specific quantities of goods and services at a given time (Kelly, 1985:38). To what extent is the American consumer able and willing to buy goods and services pertaining to outdoor pursuits? It is clear that he or she has the purchasing power, as depicted in a discretionary income of about 6.9 percent to do so. She or he is willing, as a consequence of value inculcation and life-style, to pursue leisure activities. What comes next is the matter of supply. According to Kelly (1985:3), there are two types of supply mechanisms in the leisure business. The first is direct supply, which includes the manufacturing, wholesaling, and retailing of equipment and apparel, as well as the provision of services. In direct supply, the supplier deals directly with the consumer. In the second type of supply, some suppliers deal indirectly with the consumer, such as the writers who write the books we read in our leisure time, or the actor in the movies we watch. Other suppliers, the service providers, deal with our leisure experiences directly, such as the ones from whom we rent our fishing boat, or the ones who fix and maintain our recreation vehicle.

Clawson and Knetsch (1966) pioneered a study of demand in outdoor recreation in America. They used a single exploratory variable, the average direct cost of auto operation times the distance, as a proxy for the price the consumer is willing to pay for an outdoor leisure experience. Over the years researchers agreed that other nonprice variables are an important determinant in the demand for recreation goods and leisure services. Walsh (1986:157) lists them as follows:

1. Socioeconomic characteristics of the consumer.
2. Attractiveness and quality of the recreation site.
3. Availability of substitute service.
4. Travel time.
5. Congestion or crowding.
6. Taste and preference of the consumer.

The supply side of the demand-supply continuum in outdoor recreation includes the recreation resources that are available to the consumer. Clawson and Knetsch (1966) suggested the following simple

classification of these resources, which is still in use:

User-Oriented Areas

The primary consideration is easy accessibility for the recreation consumer. Most local public and private facilities would fall into this category.

Intermediate Areas

The resource partially dictates the accessibility into these areas. Most regional and state-run facilities would fall into this category.

Resource-Oriented Areas

The resource determines to a great extent the accessibility of the area to the consumer. National parks, forests, and wildlife refuges would fall into this category.

PRICING AND MANAGING

It is hard to determine the price that a leisure consumer should pay for the use of a government-run recreation facility, due to the absence of competitive markets. Walsh states that "as a result, the efficient operation of recreation programs by public agency is likely to depend on the ability of managers to adopt the correct least-cost price policy" (1986:503). Accordingly, the user fee should be set at the intersection of the demand curve with the marginal cost and average cost curve. The demand curve shows how the quantity demanded of some recreation activity during a specific period will change as its price changes. Average cost includes the cost of investment plus the cost of operation. When and if the demand is equal to the supply, marginal cost will equal average cost. If the demand exceeds the supply, marginal cost will increase and profits will result. If the supply exceeds the demand, marginal cost will decrease and subsidy will be needed. It is clear how difficult it is to set user fees for a government-run recreation facility. Suffice it to say that one of the most difficult decisions to make concerning fees, as based on the above formula, is the cost of investment: what is the monetary value

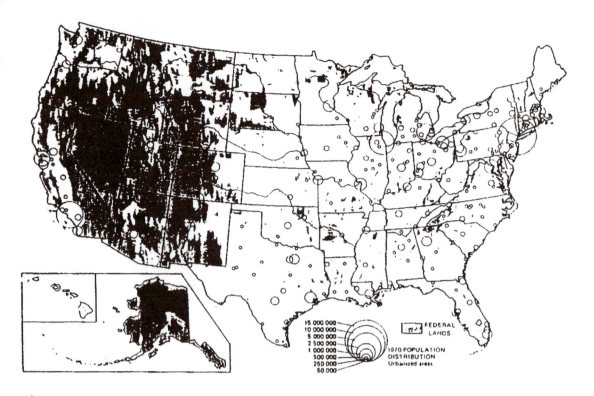

Figure 6.4 Distribution of public land to population in the United States.

of a national park or a national forest? Adding to the difficulty is the inverse relationship between the demand for outdoor recreation and the supply of natural resources, as shown in Figure 6.4. The supply of these resources is abundant in areas that are located far from population concentration where the demand is great.

The problem of the inverse relationship between location of public lands and population centers was recognized in the report of the Outdoor Recreation Resources Review Commission (ORRRC) in 1962. It was recommended in that report that the individual states develop comprehensive plans detailing their outdoor recreation supply and demand and providing recommendations for improvement of the situation. The plan was to be repeated every five years. A nationwide plan for outdoor recreation was prepared by the Bureau of Outdoor Recreation in 1973. Another plan was issued in 1979. Further details are provided in Chapter 7.

Another factor that plays an important role in the economic aspects of an outdoor experience is management. Knudson (1984:18) suggested that a large number of conceptual, biological, legal, and organizational skills are needed to effectively manage these areas and the programs provided in them. Successful programs are an economic asset to their sponsoring agency. If success in management of outdoor recreational resources is to be attained, it must be preceded by an attempt to improve management.

The Economic Benefits of Outdoor Recreation

Outdoor recreation programs along with their facilities and lands, being a service to the public, may appear to involve expenditures only. In fact, there are economic benefits to the general public, which is the actual owner of the lands involved. Peterson and Brown (1986:Vii) suggested that economic benefits are generally defined relative to two basic economic

Table 6.3 Expenditures for Wildlife Related Rereation Activities: 1996

[See headnote, Table 428. (37,797 represents $37,797,000,000)]

Type of expenditure	Fishing			Hunting			Wildlife watching		
	Expen-ditures (mil. dol.)	Spenders		Expen-ditures (mil. dol.)	Spenders		Expen-ditures (mil. dol.)	Spenders	
		Number (1,000)	Percent of anglers		Number (1,000)	Percent of hunters		Number (1,000)	Percent of watchers
Total [1]	37,797	34,002	96	20,613	13,769	99	29,228	52,729	84
Food and lodging	5,990	28,452	81	2,512	11,073	79	5,352	17,922	76
Food	4,256	28,267	80	2,078	11,060	79	3,447	17,761	75
Lodging.	1,734	8,020	23	434	1,909	14	1,905	6,783	29
Transportation	3,730	28,741	82	1,780	12,022	86	2,943	20,260	86
Public.	559	1,780	5	145	479	3	811	2,229	9
Private	3,171	28,382	81	1,634	11,926	85	2,132	19,863	84
Other trip-related costs	5,661	28,398	81	864	4,378	31	1,150	9,340	39
Sport specific equipment [2] . . .	5,309	24,726	70	5,519	11,278	81	8,230	47,355	75
Auxiliary equipment [3]	1,037	6,006	17	1,233	5,730	41	858	4,763	8
Special equipment [4]	12,828	3,599	10	4,521	805	6	7,564	1,094	2
Other expenditures [5].	3,242	24,944	71	4,185	12,471	89	3,132	23,827	40

[1] Total not adjusted for multiple responses or nonresponse. [2] Items owned primarily for each specific activity, such as rods and reels for fishing and guns and rifles for hunting. [3] Equipment such as camping gear owned for wildlife-associated recreation. [4] "Big ticket" equipment such as campers and boats owned for wildlife-associated recreation. [5] Books, magazines, membership dues and contributions, land leasing and ownership, licenses, and plantings.

Source of Tables 428 and 429: U.S. Fish and Wildlife Service, *1996 National Survey of Fishing, Hunting, and Wildlife Associated Recreation.*

objectives. First, efficiency is seen when the monetary value of the benefits exceeds the monetary value of the costs. Second, equity is seen when the distribution of purchasing power among individual citizens is fair. There are many concerns related to efficiency and equity. Granted, the interest on the national level is in seeing that growth in national assets occurs and that the wealth of Americans improves, "however, our national concern in the international scene is not so much for efficiency at a world scale as it is for a favorable national balance of payment" (Peterson & Brown, 1986:V13). The same may be applied to state and local governments, where each jurisdiction tries to become internally efficient by maximizing internal net gain within their own boundaries.

Another important concern, expressed by Walsh and Loomis (1986, V37), is how much should government spend on outdoor recreation projects? Will these projects contribute to national economic development (NED)? The NED objective is to increase the value of the output of goods and services. The contribution of outdoor recreation to NED is defined in terms of the net willingness of the consumers to pay for the goods and services. Payments are done in the form of taxes to be approved by the citizens and in fees to be paid by the recreationists. It is only recently that economists began to estimate the contribution of outdoor recreation to NED. Walsh and Loomis (1986:V40) provided us with an estimate based on the direct consumption benefits of on-site leisure activities and the indirect consumption of the flow of information about these activities and sites and the preservation and protection of the sites. The authors offered information shown in Tables 6.3, 6.4, and 6.5 to illustrate the contribution of outdoor recreation to national economic development.

Table 6.4 Participants in Wildlife-Related Recreation Activities: 1996

[In thousands (39,694 represents 39,694,000). For persons 16 years old and over engaging in activity at least once in 1996. Based on survey and subject to sampling error; see source for details]

Participant	Number	Days of participation	Trips	Participant	Number	Days of participation
Total sportsmen [1]	39,694	882,569	729,495	Wildlife watchers [1]	62,868	(X)
Total anglers	35,246	625,893	506,557	Nonresidential [2]	23,652	313,790
Freshwater	29,734	515,115	420,010	Observe wildlife	22,878	278,683
Excluding Great Lakes . .	28,921	485,474	402,814	Photograph wildlife . . .	12,038	79,342
Great Lakes	2,039	20,095	17,195	Feed wildlife.	9,976	89,606
Saltwater.	9,438	103,034	86,547			
				Residential [3]	60,751	(X)
Total hunters	13,975	256,676	222,938	Observe wildlife	44,063	(X)
Big game	11,288	153,784	113,971	Photograph wildlife . .	16,021	(X)
Small game	6,945	75,117	63,744	Feed wild birds [4]	54,122	(X)
Migratory birds	3,073	26,501	22,509	Visit public parks. . . .	11,011	(X)
Other animals	1,521	24,522	22,714	Maintain plantings or natural areas	13,401	(X)

X Not applicable.   [1] Detail does not add to total due to multiple responses and nonresponse.   [2] Persons taking a trip of at least 1 mile for activity.   [3] Activity within 1 mile of home.   [4] Or other wildlife.

Table 6.5 Trend in Recreation Visitation on Federal Lands

Agency	1950[a]	1960[a]	1980	1984	1987	1993
			Millions of Visitor Days			
Forest Service	16.4	55.5	234.9	227.5	238.4	287.7
Corps of Engineers	9.6	63.6	160.5	137.7	148.6	192.2
National Park Service	19.6	43.7	86.8	103.3	114.7	115.8
Bureau of Land Management	n.d.	n.d.	5.7	17.4	43.1	46.9
Tennessee Valley Authority	9.9	25.4	7.2	6.6	6.5	11.4
Bureau of Reclamation	3.9	14.5	33.9	23.5	31.7	22.4
Fish and Wildlife Service	3.2	6.4	1.4	4.7	5.9	17.7[a]

[a] Estimated from recreation visits; n.d. = no data.

Source: Years 1950–1984: Walsh, 1986; years 1987–1993: U.S. Department of the Interior, 1993, p. 22.

Table 6.3 summarizes the contribution of park and recreation programs to NED; Table 6.4 shows the range of participants in wildlife related recreation activities, most of which occur on Federal Land and Table 6.5 shows the phenomenal increase in the visits to these lands.

THE ECONOMICS OF TOURISM

Included in the economics of outdoor recreational activities is the economics of tourism. Granted, some tourists may not engage in outdoor pursuits, but since most do, the impact of this fast-growing leisure pursuit should be included in our discussion.

Tourism has become a strong economic institution of global significance. An island resort on Cozumel Island in Mexico attracts SCUBA divers who can take a break to visit ancient Mayan ruins.

Jafari (1983:3) estimated that tourism has become a strong economic institution of global significance. He estimated that it comprises about $700 billion, or six percent of the world gross national product (GNP). According to Lemer and Abbott (1982:2), between 1975 and 1980, international travel increased by 75 percent, at an average of a 15 percent increase per year. Yet international business did not increase by an equivalent amount during that period. In fact, that period witnessed an increase in vacation days globally.

The United States' share in this bonanza is quite sizeable. Hunt estimates that this country received 20.8 million tourists in 1984, or 6.9 percent of total international arrival, and captured 11.4 percent of international receipts (1986:V-60). Most of these tourists came from Canada, Mexico, Japan, and Great Britain. These foreign tourists spent less money here than did American tourists visiting other lands. In other words, international tourism is not economically beneficial to the national economy. Most of the American tourists go to Canada and Mexico (58 percent), followed by Europe. Maybe the

U.S. government should have an office to promote tourism to the United States, as many countries do. In fact, some Canadian provinces have offices abroad to promote tourism to their particular region of Canada. Most of the efforts of state tourism officers in the United States are directed to attract tourists from within the country. Their efforts are indeed successful.

Of the total travel expenditure of $234 billion spent by Americans in 1984, $217 billion, or 92.7 percent, were spent on domestic travel (Hunt, 1986:V-61). Nine out of ten of the trips taken by Americans are for pleasure. Three-fifths of these trips are long-term vacations, and two-fifths are weekend trips. The economic impact of pleasure travel is sizeable, accounting for seven percent of the American GNP. Travel generates 4.7 million jobs, with a payroll of $50.9 billion and tax revenues of $13.6, $8.9, and $2.7 billion for federal, state, and local treasuries, respectively.

Within the United States, the inter-state promotion of tourism is faring rather well. According to Spandoni (1986:1), state campaign budgets totaled about $82.8 million dollars for 1985, an increase of about 11.8 percent from the previous year. In the same year, 554.4 million trips were taken within the United States, about 30.2 million more than the previous year. Air travel dominates travel in the United States, but other modes are being used. The sale of recreational vehicles peaked at 540,000 in 1972, leveled off, dropped to 200,000 in the early 1980s, and saw an increase to 300,000 in 1985.

Studies show that Americans travel to national forests and parks and to national, state, and local recreational areas to pursue a number of outdoor pursuits. As shown earlier, walking for pleasure is the most participated in leisure activity, followed by swimming, visiting zoos, picnicking, driving for pleasure, and sightseeing. Researchers are finding out that leisure pursuits are an essential part of tourism. Vacationers select a destination where they can participate in certain activities, and not just a particular destination (Epperson, 1983:31). According to Rubenstein (1980), who surveyed 11,000 persons as to their reasons for taking a vacation, rest and relaxation topped the list (63 percent), followed by escaping routine (52 percent), visiting friends and relatives (45 percent), renewal (45 percent), and exploring new places (35 percent).

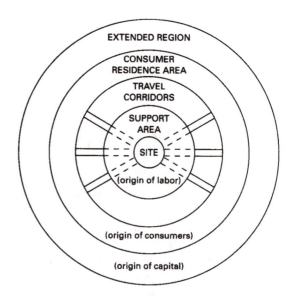

Source: Stevens, B., and A. Z. Rose. (1985). "Regional Input-Output Methods for Tourism Impact Analysis." Assessing the Economic Impacts of Recreation and Tourism. D. Propst, ed. USDA Forest Service, Southeastern Forest Experiment Station, Asheville, NC.

Figure 6.5 Regions impacted by recreation

REGIONAL AND LOCAL ECONOMIC IMPACTS

This section deals with the economic activities generated in a region or locality by the recreational use of natural resources within its boundaries. Many regions, states, and local communities establish their own economic development projects. Although an outdoor recreation project may look economically beneficial, Millard and Fischer (1979) suggested that the planners take into consideration the loss of the natural resource to activities other than recreation, the increase in medical and other assistance to non-local tourists, and the increase in local prices due to the willingness of the tourists to overpay.

According to Alward (1986), the economic effects of investing in recreational development projects are divided into two categories. The first category includes the direct impact of transactions intimately related to the project or activities. The second category encompasses the chain of consequences that result from the direct effect. These secondary economic impacts go beyond the recreation site. For example, recreationists visit motels and restaurants on their way to and from recreation sites, and gas stations supply the recreationists with fuel to make the trip. While most, if not all, of the direct economic impacts will take place at or close to the recreation site, the indirect impacts may be felt far from the site due to the predominance of interregional trade links.

Spatially, Stevens and Rose (1985) propose a hierarchical conceptualization of the impacted region, as shown in Figure 6.5. In the figure, the smallest spatial unit is the recreation site. Most of the direct economic impact of recreation activities occurs in the second unit, the support area. This area encompasses the retail outlets where the recreationists buy services and goods. A third area includes the travel corridors where there are impacts on transportation, food, and lodging services. The fourth area includes the residences of the recreationists along with the businesses that will provide them with the goods needed for the activities—the recreational clothing, equipment, and supplies. The fifth and final area extends beyond the fourth into the rest of the United States and possibly the world where most, if not all, of the clothing, equipment, and supplies purchased in the fourth area may have been manufactured.

It is clear how complicated the economic impacts of outdoor recreation are, and how difficult it is to assess them. The task is easier when the recreation site is small, serving a small circle of recreationists. But when the recreation site is large, the analysis of its economic impact becomes more difficult. The situation is complicated once the site becomes nationally and internationally renowned, as is true of some of the national parks. For example, tourists from abroad may have purchased their camping equipment outside the United States.

Empirical Findings

The National Environmental Policy Act (NEPA) requires under certain circumstances that project plans include information on social and economic effects. Environmental impact studies have yielded important information on the economic impact in the vicinity of a large recreation site. Large in this case means that the construction of the site would have an environmental impact. If there are no such impacts, information on the economic and social impact would be lacking, since the construction will have no significant effect on the quality of the environment. According to Walsh (1986:375), these studies include the estimated changes in direct and indirect output of each industry and

business, income and employment, population shifts, and tax revenue and expenditure for social services in the region. Also included are the effects on environmental quality such as air and water pollution. The studies also show the distribution of economic gains and losses of industry and businesses resulting from the construction of the recreation site.

Walsh stated that studies of regional economic impacts have tended to emphasize gains and have failed to count losses, particularly of secondary nature. He reviewed Millard and Fischer (1979), which was previously cited, and showed the following:

1. Development of a recreation site usually means that the natural resource cannot be used for other purposes.
2. An increase in local services will occur to provide for the influx of tourists and recreationists.
3. The site will be overutilized during the season and underutilized otherwise.
4. Higher prices may result as the influx of out-of-towners increases, who are willing to pay more for goods and services.
5. Congestion may result on roads and in the local businesses, which may alter the locals' lifestyle.
6. It is possible that the average resident, who is not employed in an industry or business having to do with the recreation site, will be the one affected negatively by the change.

The Multiplier Effect

According to Knudson (1984:79), the money that stays in a community or region increases the spending ability of those who receive the wages and profits. The multiplier effect is a term used to indicate that the effect of one dollar spent at one point will be more than merely one dollar. In a small region, one dollar spent may produce the effect of $1.53. And if the whole nation is considered, each dollar spent in a national park considered with the multiplier effect would reach $3.02. But one dollar spent in a small community does not remain within its boundaries, since a good portion of it will be spent on supplies and goods imported to the region.

The economic impact of large recreation sites is both considerable and far-reaching, as shown in the case of Olympic National Park (Knudson, 1984:79). Visitors to the park spent $21.8 million, of which $18.3 million were spent in the state of Washington, and only $8 million were spent on the Olympic Peninsula, where the park is located. The $21.8 million spent had a multiplier effect of $66 million across the United States.

Walsh (1986:378) suggested that a formula be used to assess the multiplier effect of a recreation site. The multiplier for a recreation business is equal to one divided by the inverse value added, as expressed in percentage of direct sales:

Multiplier = 1/1-Value Added (in percent)

Value added is defined as the proportion of total sales taking place in the region. The more business in the region, the higher the multiplier. For instance, if 40 percent of the sales took place in the region, then the multiplier is expressed as 1/ (1-.40) or 1.67. But if regional sales were 50 percent, the multiplier would be 1/(1-.50)= 2.0 and at 60 percent the multiplier would be 1/(1-.60)= 2.5. Needless to say, if no sales took place in the region the multiplier will be 1/ (1-0) = 1, or no multiplier at all.

Walsh (1986:380) summarized the results of several regional economic impact studies, as shown in Table 6.6. The multipliers for these recreational activities across the United States varied from 1.46 to 2.60, with an average of 2.00. The main reason for the variation in the multiplier's effect is attributed to the size of the area from which the participants are drawn. Also the type of services and industries located in the region as related to the activities provided in the recreation site will affect the size of the multiplier.

OUTDOOR RESOURCES AND TAXATION

Land is a good source of income to the government if it is privately owned and taxed. Once private land is acquired by a government agency, taxes are lost. Knudson (1984) believes that the reduction in government income in such cases is negligible when the piece of land is small and the acquisition is gradual. Moreover, fees, licensing, and sales tax on the site, once developed, usually compensate for the lost property tax. He cited Rosner's study (1977) in northwestern Wisconsin, which reported that public land acquisition by the National Park Service and Wisconsin companies, the Department of Natural Resource (over 17,000 acres) did not affect the local tax rate for the following reasons:

1. The county tax loss represented less than one percent of the valuation in the two counties that were affected.
2. An increase in school aid offset lost school revenue.
3. Shared state taxes as well as tax credits compensated for other local losses in revenue.

COMMERCIAL/PRIVATE OUTDOOR RECREATION

Commercial/private outdoor recreation enterprises vary in size from a small pond opened for fishing on weekends to Disneyland and Disney World. Bullaro and Edginton (1986:70) estimate that the share of the outdoor recreation system, both private and public, would be $83 billion of the $300 billion in leisure spending in this country. There are over 130,000 private suppliers of outdoor recreation services and businesses in the United States. The economic impact of these enterprises will vary according to the size, type, and orientation of each.

Knudson cites the economic impact of Disney World as including the construction of close to 20,000 hotel/motel rooms along the interstate highway leading to the site,

Table 6.6 Regional Output of Sales Multipliers for Expenditures on Recreation Goods and Services, United States

Regions	Sources	Types of Recreation Development	Output of Sales Multipliers
Teton County, Wyoming	Rajender et al.	Tourism	1.46
Southwest Counties, Wyoming	Kite and Schultz	Fishing, Flaming Gorge Reservoir	2.07
Sullivan County, Pennsylvania	Gamble	Summer homes	1.60
Itasca County, Minnesota	Hughes	Summer resorts	2.23
Ely County, Minnesota	Lichty and Steinnes	Boundary Waters Canoe Area, tourism	2.23
Wadsworth County, Wisconsin	Kalter and Lord	Tourism	1.87
Baldwin County, Alabama	Main	Tourism	2.58
Montana	Haroldon	Winter resorts	2.40
Grand County, Colorado	Rhody and Lovegrove	Hunting and fishing	2.00
Colorado Counties	McKean and Nobe	Hunting and fishing resident and nonresident	1.75 2.60
Yaquina Bay, Oregon	Stoevener et al.	Fishing	2.06
United States	National Marine Fisheries Service	Saltwater fishing	1.90

Source: R. Walsh *Recreation Economic Decisions* State College, PA: Venture Publishing, 1986, 380. (Reprinted with permission.)

which displaced orange groves. Also, commercial campgrounds are located within easy driving distance, and another theme park, Sea World, is close by (1984:84). Negative impacts include serious water pollution problems, congested traffic, and high prices for local residents. The Disney Corporation tried to benefit from its experience in Disneyland in Anaheim, California, where the site was smaller and control over adjacent land was difficult. For Disney World, the corporation acquired a much larger parcel, with the intention of controlling the area surrounding the site. It was successful in preserving many species of birds, mammals, and plants. Nonetheless, the control could not be exerted over the hotels, motels, restaurants, and campgrounds built outside Disney's 27,000-acre property, a sign of overcommercialization.

The problem of overcommercialization is greater in the case of Niagara Falls, where commercial enterprises grew on both sides of the river, as soon as the area gained fame and tourists began to visit the falls in the early 1900s. Both the Province of Ontario and New York State tried certain controls that proved difficult to implement. According to Knudson (1984:86), the honky-tonk atmosphere still prevails there as well as in the Great Smokey Mountains National Park, Gettysburg National Military Park, and the Rocky Mountain National Park. While the multiplier effect is at work in these areas, Knudson decries the lack of quality and appropriateness of some of these commercial enterprises.

CAREERS IN OUTDOOR RECREATION

It has only been recently that most people work and play indoors. In the past most human endeavors took place outdoors. Working outdoors is not a new thing. Today, many people long for an outdoor career where there is plenty of fresh air and natural light.

Outdoor careers are found in many fields other than outdoor recreation, such as agriculture, anthropology, archeology, botany, conservation, and construction. Careers in engineering, geology, marine biology, meteorology, mining, seamanship, and surveying can also be outdoor careers. This section will be limited to presenting some of the career possibilities in outdoor recreation.

Foresters

Foresters manage and protect forests. They also estimate the potential growth of areas under their jurisdiction. Jobs are available in local, state, and the federal government as well as in private companies. The duties of the forester vary significantly from wildlife protection to providing information to the public. A bachelor's degree in forestry is a minimum educational requirement for an entry-level job in forestry.

Forestry Technicians

Foresters are supported in their work by forestry technicians, who usually have one or two years of college education. Forestry technicians may take part in the maintenance of recreation areas in forests, as well as inspect trees for disease and engage in fire fighting and flood control.

Game Wardens

Game wardens are the professionals charged with the protection of natural wildlife resources. State conservation departments as well as federal agencies employ most game wardens. A college degree plus some experience in outdoor life is required.

Naturalists

Naturalists are the interpreters of nature in outdoor recreation sites. Skill in oral communication is needed, as well as a college degree. Jobs are found in the federal and state governments and also with private companies that outfit recreationists for outdoor experiences into remote areas

such as the Everglades. Knowledge and skill in the use of equipment needed for the outings are desirable.

Nature Photographers

Most nature photographers are free-lancers who work in harsh and sometimes hazardous environments in pursuit of unique photographs of animals, plants, or nature scenes. Other than technical training, certain personal traits are required for success in this field, including dedication, patience, and perseverance.

Park Rangers

Park rangers, particularly the ones at small parks, are jacks- and jills-of-all-trades. Their work varies from recreation planning to park administration. A park ranger supervises aides, gives out information, serves as an interpreter of nature, and checks on public safety. He or she may act as a police officer in many instances.

Range Managers

Range managers are professionals charged with the management and protection of range resources in determining the degree of their multiple use: grazing, lumber cutting, fishing, hunting, and other outdoor recreational activities. Most range managers are employed in federal and state government agencies.

Recreation Specialists

National parks and forests as well as state and local parks need the services of recreation specialists in planning and executing different outdoor recreational activities, which may be of a general nature or highly specialized.

The following are some of the highly specialized careers in outdoor recreation:

1. **Deep-Sea Sport-Fishing Guide:** These guides organize excursions for sport fishing at offshore locations. Knowledge and experience in deep-sea sport fishing are needed in this job, as well as the ability to operate a boat. A license from

This back-country guide in Wyoming takes time out to check his GPS for directions.

the U.S. Coast Guard is required. The license is obtained by taking a test.

2. **Hang Glider Instructor:** Needless to say, a special skill and lengthy prior experience are needed for this career. Since this activity is relatively new, there are not that many career opportunities.

3. **Hunting and Fishing Guide:** Knowledge of the fish and game habitats and hunting and fishing techniques in the region is needed by a successful guide. This means that substantial experience in fishing and/or hunting in the particular territory are needed before embarking on this career.

4. **Scuba Diving Instructor:** The recent growth in recreational diving has led to the increased demand for scuba diving instructors. Certification is needed for such a job, and it is offered through professional organizations.

5. **Ski Instructor:** Skiing is also a growing recreational activity, and the need for ski instructors is increasing. While there is certification for one to become a ski instructor, some ski areas conduct their own clinics for the purpose of preparing instructors.

6. **White-Water Rafting Guide:** These are the professionals who take parties through rapids, over falls, and around boulders. They use large rubber rafts, rowing through churning white water. Substantial experience in white-water rafting is needed.

7. **Back-Country Adventure Guide:** These individuals generally operate adventure tours through scenic areas. An intimate knowledge of special sites ranging from native petroglyphs to spectacular waterfalls is necessary. Frequently transportation via four-wheel drive vehicles, horses, or mules is provided, so training in these specialized areas is needed

as well. Most guides are self-employed or work for a small outfitter, although there are outfitters that are growing rapidly into bigger organizations due to the popularity of the adventures.

The National Association of State Park Directors published a list of salaries for five levels of personnel who work in state parks across the United States. This list is shown in Table 6.7.

Table 6.7 Salaries of Personnel in State Natural Resources

| | Field Unit Employee | | Field Unit Manager | | Field Supervisor | |
State	Minimum	Maximum	Minimum	Maximum	Minimum	Maximum
Alabama	$15,400	$21,226	$29,263	$44,366	-	-
Alaska	$33,156	$45,456	$38,076	$52,116	$50,208	$68,124
Arizona	$17,405	$42,127	$27,901	$59,445	$37,206	$64,682
Arkansas	$20,466	$39,750	$24,931	$48,086	$32,093	$61,777
California	$30,218	$43,268	$39,486	$66,016	$54,720	$80,394
Colorado	$26,100	$52,068	$39,396	$60,288	$52,788	$89,052
Connecticut	$26,129	$41,622	$42,645	$73,725	$60,913	$82,930
Delaware	$21,903	$32,855	$37,638	$56,456	$43,093	$64,639
Florida	$16,800	$38,270	$25,677	$56,254	$39,529	$80,625
Georgia	$14,088	$41,196	$27,978	$60,204	$47,286	$80,196
Hawaii	$21,588	$23,388	$23,388	$27,270	$37,924	$48,380
Idaho	$26,957	$39,645	$31,824	$55,661	$47,923	$70,491
Illinois	$21,948	$41,148	$27,684	$70,608	$44,848	$104,532
Indiana	$13,754	$40,000	$22,022	$65,000	$35,334	$53,872
Iowa	$27,944	$34,501	$36,165	$47,767	$45,043	$57,002
Kansas	$25,600	$35,900	$29,100	$41,900	$36,100	$51,900
Kentucky	$10,044	$51,048	$24,084	$75,336	$35,592	$77,952
Louisiana	$9,816*	$22,992	$28,164	$39,504	$28,980	$35,216
Maine	$14,456	$26,395	$19,656	$33,030	$35,131	$49,025
Maryland	$30,991	$49,384	$46,339	$70,893	$54,313	$76,339
Massachusetts	$21,151	$27,374	$25,854	$46,956	$41,837	$65,884
Michigan	$24,704	$39,166	$36,887	$55,714	$30,263	$55,714
Minnesota	$22,526	$30,368	$33,095	$66,482	$48,191	$69,322
Mississippi	$11,891	$24,330	$21,554	$38,711	$31,823	$47,352
Missouri	$18,336	$42,888	$32,196	$47,652	$26,520	$57,912
Montana	$28,827	$33,844	$31,520	$37,065	$41,585	$49,156
Nebraska	$22,410	$32,449	$29,926	$43,402	-	-
Nevada	$28,314	$45,395	$33,482	$49,613	$38,071	$56,798
New Hampshire	$14,810	$16,661	$18,949	$22,152	$28,434	$33,613
New Jersey	$17,848	$61,376	$34,776	$66,447	$58,581	$82,076
New Mexico	$25,045	$37,567	$29,449	$44,171	$34,016	$51,022
New York	$21,000	$31,000	$39,000	$64,000	$75,000	$95,800
North Carolina	$17,196	$44,890	$25,343	$51,436	$35,519	$56,340
North Dakota	$18,000	$35,880	$25,908	$43,188	-	-
Ohio	$25,002	$33,488	$32,323	$64,979	-	-
Oklahoma	$14,616	$29,378	$28,931	$44,670	$49,762	$49,762
Oregon	$20,808	$34,272	$33,252	$54,288	$46,836	$69,300
Pennsylvania	$18,269	$45,069	$26,210	$67,013	$50,328	$76,499
Rhode Island	$22,422	$23,213	$27,589	$30,862	$38,301	$43,088
South Carolina	$12,028	$38,552	$23,445	$57,081	$37,539	$69,450
South Dakota	$23,233	$34,840	$28,412	$42,640	$35,360	$53,040
Tennessee	$21,096	$33,216	$22,908	$46,608	-	-
Texas	$13,176	$29,868	$27,323	$41,859	$64,138	$64,138
Utah	$24,400	$38,800	$30,300	$59,700	$39,700	$63,000
Vermont	$17,056	$24,553	$27,040	$42,744	$34,028	$54,038
Virignia	$23,675	$36,986	$33,611	$52,787	$36,962	$57,706
Washington	$16,908	$55,212	$32,112	$58,032	$48,792	$62,460
West Virginia	$10,008	$34,440	$19,764	$42,204	$29,712	$48,336
Wisconsin	$19,012	$35,876	$31,464	$59,202	$45,609	$80,020
Wyoming	$14,460	$35,436	$16,152	$46,956	$33,624	$62,208
AVERAGE	$20,473	$36,573	$29,604	$51,851	$42,212	$63,804

*Part-time Salary. Not included in the Average

Table 6.7 Salaries of Personnel in State Natural Resources (continued)

Per Annum Salary Range

State	Operations Chief		Director	
	Minimum	Maximum	Minimum	Maximum
Alabama	$39,229	$59,753	$58,295	$88,819
Alaska	$61,380	$83,988	$73,008	$100,176
Arizona	$40,731	$77,120	$61,965	$105,000
Arkansas	$34,160	$65,780	$75,737	$75,737
California	$92,520	$107,166	$112,559	$112,559
Colorado	$58,489	$89,052	$74,698	$112,053
Connecticut	-	-	$80,947	$103,834
Delaware	$56,486	$84,728	$79,225	$118,837
Florida	$53,081	$107,983	$47,452	$96,499
Georgia	$57,030	$96,804	$62,628	$117,462
Hawaii	$50,450	$70,125	$60,125	$72,500
Idaho	$51,590	$75,908	$64,584	$94,973
Illinois	$44,848	$104,532	$44,848	$104,532
Indiana	$38,168	$59,358	$47,814	$74,802
Iowa	$59,691	$75,498	$68,753	$86,928
Kansas	$41,000	$55,900	$51,100	$65,900
Kentucky	$47,388	$79,956	$70,000	$85,000
Louisiana	$33,180	$51,768	$61,200	$61,200
Maine	-	-	$50,000	$75,305
Maryland	$58,452	$82,222	$68,210	$88,130
Massachusetts	$41,837	$65,884	$50,908	$73,364
Michigan	$49,091	$68,258	$71,623	$95,307
Minnesota	$49,966	$71,744	$61,760	$85,712
Mississippi	$38,523	$57,391	$55,992	$83,584
Missouri	$66,648	$66,648	$83,256	$83,256
Montana	$41,585	$49,156	$50,140	$59,466
Nebraska	$42,974	$62,312	$53,386	$77,410
Nevada	$47,458	$65,141	$67,822	$67,882
New Hampshire	$34,593	$41,243	$42,806	$54,615
New Jersey	$71,208	$99,774	$82,490	$115,506
New Mexico	$37,785	$56,676	$45,626	$68,430
New York	$80,000	$107,000	$127,000	$127,000
North Carolina	$42,594	$67,806	$48,812	$77,978
North Dakota	$35,088	$58,488	$55,000	$75,000
Ohio	$51,675	$67,164	$61,872	$90,645
Oklahoma	$87,999	$87,999	$57,107	$57,107
Oregon	$51,720	$76,356	$62,820	$92,832
Pennsylvania	$50,328	$76,499	$65,565	$95,081
Rhode Island	$39,732	$44,706	$53,804	$61,024
South Carolina	$39,014	$69,450	$49,649	$84,504
South Dakota	$44,220	$66,352	$58,697	$88,067
Tennessee	$27,072	$55,572	$45,168	$72,384
Texas	$67,956	$70,905	$82,585	$82,585
Utah	$44,300	$70,200	$59,700	$92,100
Vermont	$38,459	$61,131	$46,426	$74,069
Virignia	$48,827	$75,387	$52,757	$82,412
Washington	$52,536	$67,272	-	$100,786
West Virginia	$34,032	$55,344	$41,712	$67,812
Wisconsin	$45,609	$80,020	$54,188	$95,078
Wyoming	$38,700	$71,952	$54,000	$87,000
AVERAGE	$49,154	$72,114	$62,364	$86,165

Table 6.7 Salaries of Personnel in State Natural Resources (continued)

			Per Annum Salary Range			
	Rangers		Maintenance Workers		Interpreters/Naturalists	
State	Minimum	Maximum	Minimum	Maximum	Minimum	Maximum
Alabama	$17,345	$24,526	$15,400	$21,226	$17,004	$24,045
Alaska	$33,156	$52,116	$26,890	$42,725	-	-
Arizona	$21,422	$42,127	$17,405	$42,127	$17,405	$42,127
Arkansas	$20,466	$39,750	$17,081	$32,919	$20,466	$39,750
California	$30,218	$43,268	$31,117	$36,816	$33,173	$43,118
Colorado	$26,100	$52,068	$30,876	$57,408	$26,100	$63,288
Connecticut	$46,889	$61,357	$26,129	$40,727	$35,527	$48,019
Delaware	$24,902	$38,902	$19,135	$37,621	$28,713	$43,069
Florida	$20,549	$30,938	$17,472	$32,568	$24,436	$38,270
Georgia	$19,062	$37,524	$14,088	$41,196	$19,062	$37,524
Hawaii	-	-	$19,008	$33,672	$24,744	$32,544
Idaho	$26,957	$39,645	$23,982	$35,277	$29,328	$43,139
Illinois	$25,044	$35,244	$21,948	$33,552	$27,420	$45,780
Indiana	$15,678	$42,250	$16,978	$30,758	$16,666	$37,336
Iowa	$33,999	$43,042	$23,196	$30,069	$31,428	$38,563
Kansas	$25,600	$35,900	$21,100	$31,900	-	-
Kentucky	$14,796	$28,452	$12,228	$23,532	$17,964	$38,100
Louisiana	$14,736	$38,164	$9,816	$22,992	$15,768	$24,600
Maine	$18,158	$23,732	$14,456	$26,395	$21,465	$28,745
Maryland	$34,386	$51,023	$16,002	$45,102	$28,350	$42,233
Massachusetts	$25,854	$33,017	$21,051	$27,374	$21,051	$25,548
Michigan	$24,684	$39,166	$24,704	$39,166	$30,988	$46,365
Minnesota	$23,114	$31,842	$21,570	$28,766	$29,107	$51,657
Mississippi	$16,128	$26,689	$13,707	$24,330	$15,000	$20,930
Missouri	$29,172	$47,652	$18,336	$43,764	$18,684	$40,296
Montana	$26,397	$30,935	$19,945	$33,844	$17,164	$19,945
Nebraska	$22,410	$32,449	$16,783	$24,335	-	-
Nevada	$28,314	$45,395	$28,314	$45,395	$32,092	$45,395
New Hampshire	$17,596	$35,214	$14,206	$23,213	$16,474	$20,613
New Jersey	$32,706	$61,376	$22,874	$52,475	$30,326	$63,342
New Mexico	$19,227	$28,839	$20,302	$30,471	$27,940	$41,912
New York	$21,000	$70,000	$29,500	$50,000	$30,500	$49,000
North Carolina	$20,752	$37,427	$17,196	$44,890	$28,729	$44,890
North Dakota	$21,528	$35,880	$19,788	$32,976	$21,528	$35,880
Ohio	$28,766	$35,402	$25,002	$33,488	$25,387	$28,686
Oklahoma	$21,047	$29,378	$16,641	$31,445	$22,717	$26,706
Oregon	$24,732	$31,248	$18,384	$24,732	$24,732	$31,248
Pennsylvania	$24,369	$48,676	$18,269	$45,069	$23,218	$51,443
Rhode Island	$4,592[a]	-	$5,000[a]	-	$5,008[a]	-
South Carolina	$18,524	$38,552	$12,028	$38,552	$20,838	$38,552
South Dakota	$23,233	$34,840	$18,033	$27,060	$23,233	$34,840
Tennessee	$21,096	$33,216	$13,176	$29,832	$21,096	$33,216
Texas	$17,532	$31,068	$13,176	$19,392	$23,232	$29,868
Utah	$24,400	$38,800	$25,200	$34,800	$25,800	$38,800
Vermont	$24,585	$45,702	$24,169	$38,251	$17,056	$18,249
Virginia	$25,881	$40,406	$19,811	$30,929	$23,675	$36,986
Washington	$23,760	$58,032	$16,908	$40,004	$21,144	$47,616
West Virginia	$18,468	$30,072	$10,008	$30,072	$18,468	$30,072
Wisconsin	$22,967	$35,876	$19,012	$29,264	$27,761	$45,408
Wyoming	$18,720	$46,956	$14,460	$27,748	$18,720	$35,436
AVERAGE	$23,676	$39,461	$19,324	$34,290	$23,732	$37,895

[a]Part-time Salary. Not included in the Average

SUMMARY

This chapter deals with the economics of outdoor pursuits and begins with a question: "Why does the national policy of a capitalistic-oriented society include the preservation of a large part of public lands for outdoor pursuits?" Moreover, the policy calls for the provision of costly programs and facilities to be provided on these lands. Despite the appearance of these provisions and activities as being mere expenditures, the fact is that outdoor pursuits represent an important part of national, regional, and state economies.

A delicate balance between consumption and production takes place as the economic system evolves. Personal expenditure on leisure pursuits is calculated in the total economic picture, which reached $48 billion in 1962. In a quarter of a century the figure jumped to $320 billion, making leisure a potent force in the American economy. Productivity, increased income, increased free time, and mobility are suggested as the reasons for making leisure play a leading role in the economy. Americans are spending good sums of money on recreation supplies and equipment, travel and vacations, sports and outdoor pursuits, cultural activities, and home entertainment.

It is hard to estimate the exact amounts of governmental expenditure on the provision of areas, facilities, and programs in recreation. It is also hard to estimate the expenditure of non-profit organizations on similar activities. But expenditure is only half of the picture of the relationship between leisure and the economy. The other half is the economic impact of such expenditure. The economy of the outdoor recreation system revolves around four elements: demands of the recreationists, supply of natural resources and programs, plans and policies concerning the use of these resources and programs, and the management and implementation of these plans and policies.

The economic impact of leisure is exemplified in the tourism business. It is estimated that tourism now represents six percent of the world gross national product (GNP). The United States' share is quite sizeable. Regional and local economic impacts are felt in that if one dollar is spent locally, its impact is felt regionally and even nationally. Yet there are some negative impacts from the use of an indoor recreational site which include overuse during the season, higher prices for locals, and congestion on roads and in local businesses.

The expansion in the provision of outdoor recreational pursuits has helped in the creating of new specialties, some of which require rigorous and professional training. The career possibilities in outdoor recreation include, but are not limited to, foresters, forestry technicians, game wardens, naturalists, nature photographers, park rangers, range managers, and recreational specialists.

REFERENCES

Alward, G. (1986). *Local and regional economic impacts of outdoor recreation development.* In The President's Commission of Americans Outdoors in a literature review. Washington, D.C.: U.S. Government Printing Office.

Bullaro, J., & Edginton, C. (1986). *Commercial leisure services.* New York: Macmillan.

Clawson, M., & Knetsch, J. (1966). *Economics of outdoor recreation.* Baltimore: Johns Hopkins University Press.

Dulles, F. R. (1965). *A history of recreation.* New York: Appleton-Century-Croft.

Epperson, A. (1983, April). Why people travel. *Leisure Today,* 31.

Esteve, R., et al. (1999). Grasping the meaning of leisure: Developing a self-report measurement tool. *Leisure Studies,* 18(2), 79.

Hunt, J. D. (1986). *Tourist expenditure in the United States.* In The President's Commission on Americans Outdoors, literature review. Washington, D.C.: U.S. Government Printing Office.

Ibrahim, H. (1991). *Leisure and society: A comparative approach.* Dubuque, IA: Wm. C. Brown.

Jafari, J. (1983, April). Tourism Today. *Leisure Today,* 3-5.

Jensen, C. (1985). *Outdoor recreation in America.* Minneapolis, MN: Burgess.

Kelly, J. (1985). *Recreation business.* New York: Macmillan.

Kelly, J. (1987). *Freedom to be: A new sociology of leisure.* New York: Macmillan.

Knudson, D. (1984). *Outdoor recreation.* New York: Macmillan.

Lerner, E., & Abbott, C. B. (1982). *The Way To Go.* New York: Warner Books.

MacLean, J., Peterson, J., & Martin, D. (1985). *Leisure and recreation: The changing scene.* New York: Macmillan.

Millard, F., & Fischer, D. (1979). The local economic impact of outdoor recreation facilities. In C. Van Doren et al., (Eds.), *Land and leisure: Concepts and methods in outdoor recreation.* Chicago, IL: Maaroufa Press.

National Association of State Park Directors. (1999). Annual information exchange. Tallahassee, FL: NASPD.

Olson, S. (1961). The spiritual aspects of wilderness. In D. Brower (Ed.), *Wilderness: America's living heritage.* San Francisco, CA: Sierra Club.

Peterson, G., & Brown, T. (1986). *The economic benefits of outdoor recreation.* In The President's Commission on Americans Outdoors, literature review. Washington, D.C.: U.S. Government Printing Office.

Rosner, M. (1977). *Impact upon local property taxes of acquisitions within the St. Croix River State Forest in Burnett and Polk Counties.* Madison, WI: Department of Natural Resources, Technical Bulletin No. 101.

Rostow, E. (1960). *The stages of economic growth.* Cambridge, MA: Harvard University Press.

Rubenstein, C. (1980, March). Vacations. *Psychology Today*, 62-67.

Simmons, I. G. (1975). *Rural recreation in the industrial world.* New York: John Wiley.

Spandoni, M. (1986, July). Special report: Travel and tourism. *Advertising Age*, 14, 6.

Stevens, B., & Rose, A. Z. (1985). Regional input-output methods for tourism impact analysis. In D. Propst (Ed.), *Assessing the economic impacts of recreation and tourism.* Asheville, NC: USDA Forest Service, Southeastern Forest Experiment Station.

United Media Enterprises. (1983). *Where does the time go?* New York: Newspaper Enterprises Association.

Veblen, T. (1953). *The theory of leisure class.* New York: New American Library.

Walsh, R. (1986). *Recreation economic decision: Comparing benefits and costs.* State College, PA: Venture Publishing.

Walsh, R., & Loomis, J. (1986). *The contribution of recreation to national economic development.* In The President's Commission on Americans Outdoors. literature review. Washington, D.C.: U.S. Government Printing Office

—Part Two—

Outdoor Resources

This part consists of five chapters that examine the locations of outdoor recreational areas. Chapters Seven, Eight and Nine cover the recreational areas and facilities owned and operated by the federal, state and local government in the United States. Chapter Ten is devoted to looking into the contributions of commercial enterprises and private individuals to outdoor pursuits. Chapter Eleven presents the outdoor recreational opportunities in other countries. Considerable attention is given to Canada in this chapter. Available information was instrumental in the selection of the five countries that are included in Chapter Eleven.

7 | FEDERAL RESOURCES AND RECREATION

The United States is recognized as a global leader in conservation legislation (Meier, 1997:35) and has assembled a world-class system of public outdoor recreation lands, beginning with the protection of Yosemite Valley in the 1860s and Yellowstone, the first national park, in 1872. The system has been carved mostly from the old "public domain," the unregulated expanses of Western open space acquired by the United States through treaty, purchase, and the forcible eviction of earlier inhabitants. By the late nineteenth century, private enterprises had come to regard the public domain as common property and spoils for the bold. They had profitably stripped its timber, mined its substrates for minerals, and diverted and dammed its rivers, often leaving behind a burned, scarred, and eroded landscape. Though the public owned the resources, the exploiters paid little or no fee for the booty. Prodded by some foresighted Americans, Congress acted, albeit in piecemeal fashion, to limit the abuse and future exploitation. Thus were born the first national park (1872), the first national wildlife refuge (1903), the first national monuments (1906), and the National Park System (1916), all managed by the Department of the Interior. Congress "withdrew" these lands from the public domain, and preserved them because they exhibited special values. Most of the remaining public domain, still vast, stayed with the Department of the Interior under what is now the Bureau of Land Management. The extent of federal public domain today is shown in Figure 7.1.

In addition, Congress created the Forest Service in 1905 and endowed it by transferring 85 million acres to the Department of Agriculture for forest management. The National Forest System embodies the Forest Service's tradition of regarding timber as a crop, to be harvested according to the principle of sustainability, that is, to cut and grow wood at a rate that can be sustained over the long term. This principal has evolved to include the sustainability of the ecosystem of the forest. At the federal level, the Forest Service and the National Park Service represent two types of agencies. The latter agency practices preservation, and the former practices multiple use, where the primary challenge is to balance economic use and conservation. Figure 7.2 illustrates the diverse uses of forest and rangeland resources.

Multiple-use management takes advantage of the resource's ability to provide a bundle of uses and benefits from the same land. The Forest Service, for example, has a special legislative mandate to implement multiple-use management on National Forest Systems by administering the national forests for outdoor recreation,

Federal Lands in the United States

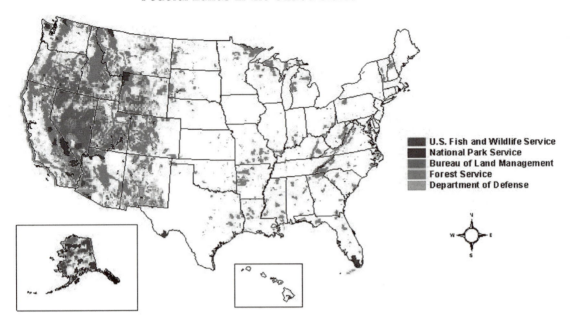

U.S. Fish and Wildlife Service
National Park Service
Bureau of Land Management
Forest Service
Department of Defense

Figure 7.1 Federal Lands in the United States.

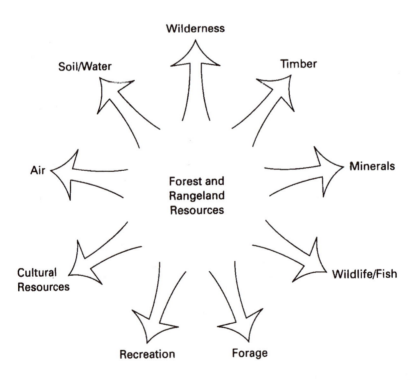

Figure 7.2 Multiple-use management provides the opportunity to simultaneously produce a number of resource benefits from the same parcel of land. Source: The Forest Service, U.S. Department of Agriculture, *Program for Forest and Rangeland Resources: A Long-Term Strategic Plan.* (U.S. Government Printing Office, 1990),1-3.

range, timber, watershed and wildlife and fish. Other multiple-use agencies include the Bureau of Land Management, Bureau of Reclamation, Army Corps of Engineers, Tennessee Valley Authority, and National Marine Fisheries Service.

The National Park Service (NPS) represents the single-use, or restricted use, concept. The 1916 Organic Act that established the agency (Mackintosh, 1990:16) directed the Park Service, in managing the parks, to conserve the scenery and the natural and historic objects and the wildlife therein and to provide for the enjoyment of the same in such manner and by such means as will leave them unimpaired for the enjoyment of future generations. The resources do not exist to be exploited for profit such as by harvesting or milling; but since the resources are protected for the enjoyment of the people, recreation is permitted as long as the activity is not destructive to the unique values of the park unit. Another single-use agency is the U.S. Fish and Wildlife Service. Wild and scenic rivers and wilderness areas are also managed under the single-use philosophy. From the purist sense, any recreation use on wilderness lands is disruptive to the wild ecological system. Therefore decisions involving recreational use on these lands are critical (Jensen, 1985:328-29).

The distinction between various agencies' land management philosophies is narrowing, and this trend is expected to continue. For instance, traditionally hunting has not been permitted in national parks, but is permitted on designated areas of the BLM lands and the national forests. Today, hunting occurs in the national reserves administered by the NPS. Despite the differences in land management philosophy, recreation usage is a major concern of each federal agency that has federal lands under management. Figure 7.3 shows the proportion of federal lands managed by the various federal land management agencies.

These two philosophies, single use and multiple use, led to a split between two early outdoor leaders, John Muir and Gifford Pinchot (refer to Chapter 3 for their biographies), who were once allies in the crusade to redeem the public domain from uncontrolled exploitation. Their differences surfaced over the Hetch Hetchy Valley controversy in which the proponents of multiple use won the right to create a water reservoir by inundating a spectacularly beautiful valley next to the Yosemite Valley, both contained within Yosemite National Park. This reservoir would serve the water needs of the growing city of San Francisco. Pinchot, the spokesperson for the emerging doctrine of conservation, argued for damming the Hetch Hetchy. He believed that the strict preservation creed of the park bureau supporters unnecessarily limited the utilization of the nation's resources. As such he believed that the preservation of the Yosemite Valley in its pristine state met the needs of the park, and that a more practical use of the neighboring valley allowed for multiple use of this land. To him, this arrangement permitted both aesthetic and economic uses.

An outraged Muir, a major proponent of the preservationists, claimed that the argument of the dam builders was a devise for destruction. He believed that the entire park should be preserved in its natural state, including both spectacular valleys. In his preservationist outlook, there was no room for compromise. This dispute was closely followed by the San Francisco media, and because of this, a schism between the conservationists and preservationists was in full view of the public. A closer look at the differing philosophies is possible by profiling the agencies that practice them.

U.S.D.A. FOREST SERVICE

The National Forest System contains approximately 192 million acres of public land dispersed throughout 44 states, Puerto Rico, and the Virgin Islands (see Figure 7.4). This expanse constitutes 8.5 percent of the total land area in the United States and about 30% of the federal land holdings. Roughly 18 percent of the national forest land comprise 400 congressionally designated wilderness areas that

Who manages the federal lands?

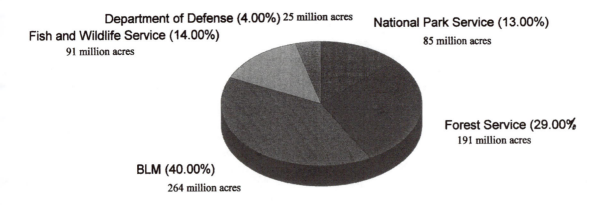

Department of Defense (4.00%) 25 million acres

Fish and Wildlife Service (14.00%)
91 million acres

National Park Service (13.00%)
85 million acres

Forest Service (29.00%)
191 million acres

BLM (40.00%)
264 million acres

Figure 7.3 Who manages the federal lands?

span more than 35 million acres. These wilderness areas offer some of the country's most spectacular scenery and a more primitive recreational experience. The overall national forest system includes 155 national forests and 20 national grasslands administered by more than 600 district ranger offices in nine regions. It is believed that more outdoor recreation takes place on these national forests lands than on any other public lands. Thirty-one national recreation areas, national scenic areas or national monuments and 277,000 national heritage sites are significant Forest Service attractions. To cross the lands, there are more than 7,700 miles of scenic byways and 133,000 miles of trails including portions of six national scenic trails, 11 national historic trails, and more than 400 national recreation trails. More than 4,000 miles of rivers are managed as wild and scenic rivers. In cooperation with the private sector, the national forests have more than 40 percent of the nation's downhill skiing, as well as sites for 480 lodges or resorts, and more than 15,000 summer homes. There are at least 10,000

recreational sites including 4,300 campgrounds, 1,400 picnic grounds, and 50 major visitor centers. To manage all of these assets, the Forest Service has a dedicated workforce of approximately 32,000 employees (FS, 2000:3) and many more volunteers.

History of the National Forests

The Creative Act of March 3, 1891 authorized the president to establish forest reserves from forest and rangelands in the public domain. The impetus for the establishment of these reserves came from recreation and conservation groups who believed strongly that forested areas should be placed under official governmental protection (Tweed, 1980:iii). By 1897 the Organic Administration Act was passed, which, however, provided for the right of entry to persons for prospecting, locating, and developing mineral resources, and for the use of water and timber resources found on forest reserves. On February 1, 1905, President Theodore Roosevelt signed the Transfer Act, which transferred the nation's forest reserves

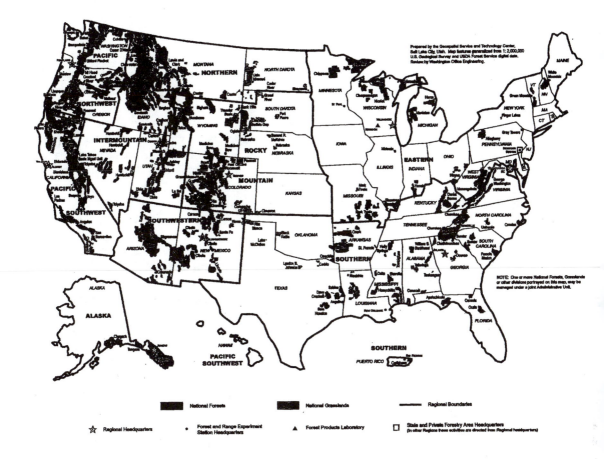

Figure 7.4 Forest Service lands in the United States. Source: The Forest Service, U.S. Department of Agriculture, The First Century (U.S. Government Printing Office, 2000), 143.

A national forest *visit* is:

The entry of one person to a national forest to participate in recreation activities for an unspecified period of time. A national forest visit can be composed of multiple site visits.

A national forest *site visit* is:

The entry of one person to a national forest site or area to participate in recreation activities for an unspecified period of time.

Nationally, during calendar year 2000 there were 209 million national forest visits plus or minus 36 million visits (17% error rate) at the 80% confidence level. On the average, each national forest visitor went to 1.2 recreation sites, thus producing 257million national forest site visits. Additionally, another 258 million people viewed national forest scenery (labeled Viewing Corridors) from non-Forest Service managed roads and waterways (FS, 2001:1).

from the Department of the Interior to the Department of Agriculture. That same day, Secretary of Agriculture James Wilson endorsed Gifford Pinchot's conservation philosophy establishing that the forests were to be utilized and not merely reserved. The forest reserves, later renamed the national forests, were to be managed for the greatest good for the greatest number of people on a long-term basis. Local questions were to be decided by local officials, a philosophy that has made the Forest Service one of the most decentralized and responsive agencies in the federal government.

Recreational Development

Recreational use of forest lands grew slowly at first, then more rapidly as automobiles became numerous and roads penetrated into previously remote and inaccessible areas. Increased prosperity and more free time encouraged recreational improvements. The first official report recognizing the prominence of recreational use in the national forests was made in the U.S. Department of Agriculture's 1919 edition of the annual *Report of the Forester*. William C. Tweed (1980:1-26) researched early recreation use in the national forests up to World War II and found that recreation was one of the major activities on the forests with the granting of temporary leases for summer cottages and camp sites. Thousands of recreation permits were issued in 1913 for pleasure resorts and boat-houses, and there were over one million day visitors, 231,000 campers, hunters, anglers, boaters, swimmers, and climbers, and 191,000 guests at houses, hotels, and sanitariums. Early budget limitations and priorities precluded recreation spending by the federal government, so to a large extent these visitors depended upon privately owned facilities for their basic needs. Forest rangers cleared inflammable material from around heavily used camp spots and built crude rock fireplaces, erected toilets, dug garbage pits, and developed sources of water supply.

The initial areas of concentration of summer visitors were in the Angeles National Forest of southern California, the Oregon (later renamed Mt. Hood) National Forest in northern Oregon, and the Pike and San Isabel National Forests of central Colorado, all in mountains areas near cities (Tweed, 1980:1-26). Holders of summer-home permits often formed cooperative associations to provide common facilities and services. In 1915, forester Henry Graves recommended to the secretary of Agriculture that the Columbia Gorge Park be developed in the Oregon National Forest. This became the first time that the Forest Service dedicated an extended area for purely recreational use, prohibiting timber sales and the distribution of permits for home sites. Soon the Eagle Creek Campground and Eagle Creek Trail were developed by the Forest Service, and by 1919 the North Pacific District created a recreation office.

It may have been that a broader interest in recreation resulted from the constant creation of national parks out of national forests. Mt. Rainier National Park was created from part of the Mt. Rainier Forest Reserve in 1899, Crater Lake National Park from part of the Cascade Forest Reserve in 1902, Glacier National Park from part of the Blackfoot National Forest in 1910, Rocky Mountain National Park from parts of the Arapaho and Colorado National Forests in 1915, and Lassen Volcanic National Park from part of the Lassen National Forest in 1916. More transfers followed.

Pinchot and his division, the Bureau of Forestry (later renamed the Forest Service), campaigned to assume the administration of the national parks. But by 1910 another campaign developed to create a separate Bureau of National Parks within the Department of the Interior. Supporters of the park bureau concept, such as John Muir and Robert Underwood Johnson, based their rejection of possible Forest Service management largely on fears of Pinchot's controversial support of the Hetch Hetchy reservoir project within Yosemite National Park. Pinchot and his successor, Henry Graves, viewed strict preservation by supporters of the park bureau to be unnecessarily limiting and wasteful of the nation's resources. It is probably safe to assume that at least a portion of the Forest Service's recreation interest in the second decade resulted from the Forest Service's hope of preventing the creation of (or limiting the growth of) a parks bureau that would have as a major purpose the development of recreation facilities.

Because of the role of landscape architects in the development of the nation's urban parks, various landscape architects looked upon themselves as the logical people to develop professionally planned recreation facilities in the national forests and parks. As early as 1910, proposals for a parks bureau included a role in the new agency for landscape architects. And by 1916 it became apparent to the Forest Service that if it were to compete successfully with the newly created National Park Service, it ultimately would have to develop professionally planned recreation facilities. Early in 1917 the service employed Frank A. Waugh, professor of landscape architecture at Massachusetts Agricultural College in Amherst, to prepare a national study of recreation uses of the national forests. In his report Waugh suggested that certain parts of the forest be developed as scenic reservations, allowing no use that would significantly detract from the inherent recreation values. He discussed briefly the recreation potential of the national monuments, then under Forest Service control, explaining their status as scenic or scientific preserves. Waugh argued that recreation must be considered one of the major uses of the national forests, equal in importance to timber harvesting, watershed protection, and grazing. It was his belief that nearly all national forest lands had potential for public recreational use. Under these circumstances he felt that it would be impossible for one agency to manage all of the recreational development while another looked after other resource management problems. Either the Forest Service and the National Park Service would have to merge, or each would have to develop its own recreation program. To him

the latter was preferable. His report concluded that there was a need for the Forest Service to hire professional personnel for its recreation program.

World War I to the Great Depression

As soon as World War I ended, the Forest Service hired landscape engineer Arthur H. Carhart to work in the Rocky Mountain District. At the same time the North Pacific District made forester Fred Cleator its recreation specialist. Carhart designed a foot trail for tourist use on Pikes Peak. Since Congress had appropriated no funds for recreation, the Commerce Club of Pueblo (Colorado) raised money and cooperated with the city to erect a few shelters, toilets, and fire-places in Squirrel Creek Canyon, 30 miles from town. It was Carhart's belief that recreation planning for the national forests would inevitably have to pass beyond the construction of single campgrounds to comprehensive general planning. By late 1919 he began work on such a plan for the San Isabel National Forest.

Financially backed by the San Isabel Public Recreation Association, Carhart's plans for an extensive system of campgrounds, picnic grounds, roads, and trails were implemented. This collaboration served as a model for other communities that continued until the Great Depression. Similar cooperation eventually produced a significant number of national forest recreation areas at a time when the Forest Service chose not to, or could not, expend much of its regular appropriation on such work. Carhart also helped to develop the idea of wilderness, or limited recreational development, in certain superb natural environments. One result was a landmark policy statement on wilderness from Secretary of Agriculture William M. Jardine in 1926, which pledged 1,000 square miles of wilderness in the Superior National Forest, the forerunner of the Boundary Waters Canoe Area.

Convinced that important progress had occurred, Carhart asked Chief Forester William B. Greeley to seek $50,000 for recreation work in the national forests for

1922. The request was made, but the money was not approved. Carhart made a similar request for funding for 1923. Again funding was denied, and instead Congress reluctantly provided $10,000 for simple facilities required by recreationists for fire and sanitary protection. Carhart responded with his resignation, which vacated the single position in the Forest Service dedicated wholly to recreation. The Forest Service generally held that the recreational role of the national forest was to provide space for recreation. Publicly financed recreation facilities in these forest areas remained limited in number and simple in nature.

For nearly a decade after Carhart's resignation, two groups, foresters and collaborators, handled all Forest Service recreation problems. Most of the responsibility fell to the foresters, who assumed responsibility for the design, construction, and administration of recreation sites. In the meantime, H. R. Francis of New York State College of Forestry at Syracuse University developed a general course for forestry students in the basic concepts and requirements of forest recreation. Whether academically trained in recreation work or not, foresters carried out the Forest Service recreation program. It was these foresters who received the first congressional appropriations for recreational development beyond fire prevention and sanitary facilities. As campgrounds improved, recreational use rose by 38 percent in the mid 1920s. A few positions specializing in recreation work began to develop as the Forest Service found itself year after year settling deeper into the recreation business. But just as it became apparent that the hiring of technically trained personnel in recreation was necessary, the Great Depression forced Congress to cut rather than increase recreational spending.

The Great Depression through World War II
A policy statement in the 1930s reaffirmed that the responsibility for recreational planning still rested entirely on regional foresters and forest supervisors. A cautious, conservative site development policy continued. This policy fit the budget and goals of the Hoover administration. This modest level of national forest recreation development escalated, however, with the election of President Franklin Delano Roosevelt in 1933. A decade of frenzied activity followed that was checked only by World War II. During the height of the New Deal, the Forest Service received recreation funds and support far beyond its wildest dreams. These changes in the magnitude and scope of the Forest Service recreation program resulted in inevitable changes in its recreation policy. To cope with the severe national economic crisis, authorization and funds for public works in forest, water, and soil conservation were provided. With Executive Order 6101, Roosevelt created the Emergency Conservation Work (ECW) program to carry out specified activities. The Civilian Conservation Corps (CCC) was viewed by FDR as primarily a forestry organization dedicated to fighting fires, planting trees, thinning timber stands, and stopping soil erosion and floods. But the field personnel of the state and federal agencies soon realized that CCC labor might also be directed toward the construction of forest improvements— particularly roads, trails, buildings, and recreation sites. Through its provisions for public works spending, the National Industrial Recovery Act of June 16, 1933, provided yet another opportunity for Forest Service recreation facilities to be built. Permanent recreation improvements were encouraged and erected from coast to coast. The level of development of some of the more popular national forest areas in the Northwest even surpassed that of the national parks of the region. Public Works Administration (PWA) funds were made available for the building of the beautiful Timberline Lodge on Mt. Hood, which became known as one of the wonders of the Northwest. By 1935 it became apparent that a central office for recreation was needed to oversee recreation planning and development in the National Forest System. Ernest E. Walker, a trained landscape architect, was hired for the Washington office. In 1937 the Recreation and Lands Division received a chief, Robert Marshall.

A forester and wilderness enthusiast, Robert Marshall had previously served as the chief forester for the Indian Service, U.S. Department of the Interior. Marshall had a strong and long-lasting influence on Forest Service recreation policy and development, despite the fact that his career was cut short by an early death after only 30 months in office. He worked tirelessly to establish a secure position for recreation on an equal footing with other more dominant phases of national forest management such as timber and range use. An ardent outdoorsman, indefatigable hiker, and persistent advocate of wilderness and primitive areas, he was a strong advocate for adequate camping, outing, scenic, and other recreation areas. He had written the recreation section of the National Plan for American Forestry in 1933. Independently wealthy, he helped to found and endow the Wilderness Society. Under his direction, the service built a number of camps, along with substantial facilities designed primarily for the use of low-income adults, 4-H clubs, and similar youth groups. Downhill skiing areas began to appear as interest increased. Expansion of facilities had become impressive, and by 1939 the Forest Service's first book on recreation, *Forest Outings*, appeared, and recreation had been established as a major priority of the Forest Service.

The 1940s brought a decline of the CCC recreation projects and employment of technical personnel. Entry of the United States into World War II in December 1941 caused national defense to take priority. Later rebuilding of a recreational staff would take many years, although work continued on individual family camping and picnic units. Never again, however, did the Forest Service look at recreation as a mere designation of a few roadside camping areas with tables and privies. National forest recreation had become a valued part of life for millions of Americans (Tweed, 1980:1-26).

Post World War II: the 1950s and 1960s

In 1954, the agency became responsible for nearly four million acres of Land Utilization Project holdings. These grazing lands

were relinquished or were abandoned farms acquired by the federal government during the Depression years of the 1930s. In the 1960s these would become the first of the national grasslands. By 1957 *Operation Outdoors* commenced to improve and replace the aging CCC-built forest service structures and to expand the recreation facilities to meet the increased demand for recreation. As this five-year program drew to a close, the Accelerated Public Works program of 1963 and 1964 employed more that 9,000 men to make improvements that included picnic grounds, trails, lookout towers and other facilities on more than 100 forests. Another new work program, Job Corps, began in 1964 and utilized unemployed youth in forest service work including recreation activities. (Williams, 2000:100-107).

In the meantime, the Multiple Use-Sustained Yield Act of 1960 supplemented the purpose for which the national forests were established to include outdoor recreation, watershed, range, timber, and wildlife and fish purposes. Meeting increased demands for recreational opportunities became a major aim of forest land managers. Because each acre of the National Forest System has recreation potential, it was routinely mandated that recreation be considered when planning or executing resources management programs. Containing some of the nation's greatest assets, almost all National Forest System lands became available for outdoor recreation.

The culmination of decades of work on the part of several forest service employees and other leaders resulted in the establishment of the National Wilderness Preservation System in 1964. Overnight the Forest Service wilderness became a part of the new system, as did the Wild and Scenic Rivers in 1968 when that legislation passed.

Closing Decades of the 20th Century

In 1974 Congress enacted the Forest and Rangeland Renewable Resources Planning Act (RPA), which directed the Secretary of Agriculture to periodically assess the nation's forest and rangeland resources and to regularly submit recommended long-range Forest Service programs. The first program recommended an increase in the supply of outdoor recreation opportunities and services. The new programs would emphasize dispersed recreation, that is, forest and rangeland-oriented recreation that makes use of sites other than ones already designed for concentrated recreational use.

In 1987 a new plan, the National Recreation Strategy Project, was developed. The plan called for a strategy to manage recreation on national forest lands within the context of multiple-use management, and for the development of several marketing plans that focus on customer satisfaction (Forest Service, 1988:3). The importance of meeting the needs of urban populations through recreational opportunities in nearby national forests began to be emphasized. The strategy allowed the service the flexibility to reach its outdoor recreation potential without dictating policy. It encouraged creative and imaginative thinking, increased opportunities for professionals in recreation, built on cost-sharing programs, and promoted interpretation and environmental education as an important part of outdoor recreation.

Partly as a result of the National Recreation Strategy Project, the Forest Service in the 1990s developed partnerships with local, county, state, and federal government, private interest groups, senior citizen groups, disabled youth groups, correction facility inmates, high schools, colleges, universities, utility companies, recreation industry corporations, timber operators, interpretive associations, and private businesses. These projects provided barrier-free access to recreation facilities, improved hiking trails, rehabilitated and modernized campgrounds, interpretive signing, summer youth employment in recreation site operation and maintenance, vegetation management for scenic resources, development of the 1988 Forest Service Scenic Byways program for vehicular recreation, renovation of historical buildings for interpretation, and the

initiatives promoting river safety. Innovations included partnerships with private cruise lines in Alaska that paid Forest Service interpreters. In the eastern United States a partnership between the Forest Service, the National Park Service, the Appalachian Trail Conference, and others helped make the Appalachian National Scenic Trail world renowned.

Recent Trends

The Forest Service (2000:iv) indicated an important shift in focus when the central mission in managing the national forests and grasslands moved away from producing timber, range, and other outputs to restoring and maintaining healthy, resilient ecosystems. While *sustainability* has been the essence of Forest Service land and natural resource management from the very beginnings of the National Forest System (NFS), *sustainability* came to mean sustaining ecosystem health as well as multiple products and uses. The strategic plan now focuses on outcomes or long-term results, such as the health of the land, the quality of water, and customer satisfaction. These strategic goals are responsive to their mission: to sustain the health, diversity, and productivity of the Nation's forests and grasslands to meet the needs of present and future generations. The four goals of the plan collectively provide purpose and context for future management actions and investments, as well as a set of milestones for evaluating progress toward the goals.

The Forest Service's Recreation Agenda (2000: 1) provides guidance for the activities it undertakes to meet the recreation, heritage, and wilderness-related goals and objectives in the Strategic Plan. The five key focus areas are:

1. Improve the settings for outdoor recreation.
2. Improve visitor satisfaction with facilities and services.
3. Improve educational opportunities for the public about the values of conservation, land stewardship, and responsible recreation.

Aspen, balsam, birch, maple, oak, and pine present a profusion of fall color along the Ice Age National Scenic Trail in the Chequamegon National Forest in Wisconsin.

Where do Americans say they visit the outdoors?

NPS	46
USFWS	27
USDAFS	23
Tribal Lands	9
Army Corps	8
BLM	8
TVA	4

% who have personally used public lands managed by each agency in the last 12 months.

Source: Roper Starch (2000) Outdoor Recreation in America 1999:

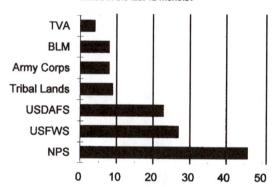

What lands do Americans say they have visited in the last 12 months?

Figure 7.5 What lands do Americans say they visit? Source: Design by Jane Lammers from data derived from Roper Starch *Outdoor Recreation in America 1999: The Family and the Environment*, 2000.

4. Strengthen relationships with private entities and volunteer-based nonprofit organizations.
5. Establish professionally managed partnerships and intergovernmental cooperative efforts.

The recreational use of forests and grasslands has been increasing for decades, and is expected to continue to increase. Almost 95 percent of the U. S. population 16 years old and older participate in some form of outdoor recreation, and one of every seven Americans lives within a two-hour drive of a national forest. The most popular outdoor recreation activities (measured in number of days) are walking, non-consumptive wildlife activities, biking, sight-seeing, non-pool swimming, fishing, family gathering, and picnicking. The five fastest-growing outdoor recreation activities (measured in number of days) through the year 2050 are projected to be visiting historic places, downhill skiing, snowmobiling, sight-seeing, and participating in non-consumptive wildlife activity (FS, 2000: 1).

The NFS contains the greatest diversity of wildlife, fish, and plant species of any single land ownership in the country. With goals to maintain ecosystem diversity, the service responds to recreational and commercial uses of fish and wildlife. Fish

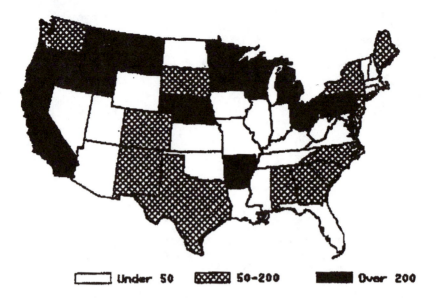

Source: National Park Service. Division of Park Planning and Special Studies. River mileage classifications for components of the National Wild and Scenic Rivers System. November 1996.

Figure 7.6a Miles of National Wild and Scenic Rivers by State, 1996.

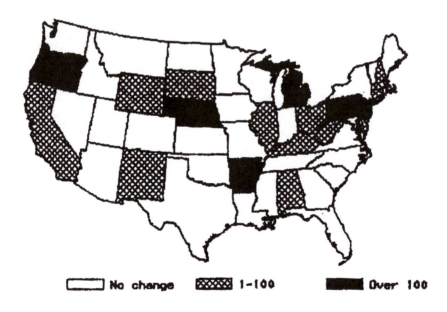

Source: National Park Service. Division of Park Planning and Special Studies. River mileage classifications for components of the National Wild and Scenic Rivers System. November 1996.

Figure 7.6b Miles of National Wild and Scenic Rivers Added between 1987 and 1996, by State
More National Wild and Scenic River (WSR) miles are managed by the Forest Service (40%) than any other agency. Next is the NPS with 23% and BLM with 19%. The FWS, state agencies, the Corps of Engineers, and two Indian tribes also manage WSRs.

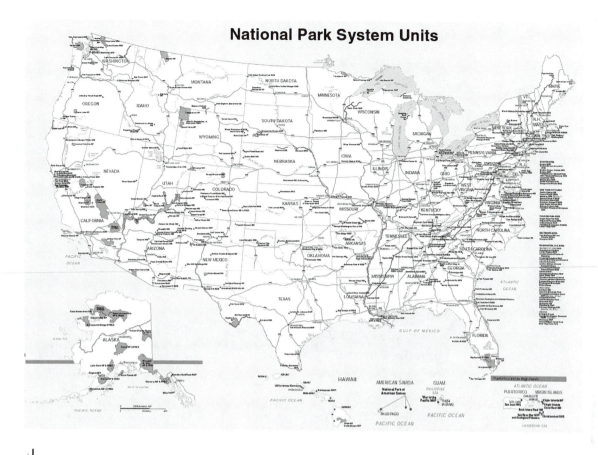

Figure 7.7 The National Park System. Source: www.nps.gov/htdocs3/hfc/carto/npsmap.html

and wildlife resources of the NFS provided over 41 million user days of recreation for anglers, hunters, and non-consumptive fish and wildlife users representing about 17 percent of all recreation in national forests. Figure 7.5 indicates the high level of frequency of fish and wildlife, national forest, as well as national park annual visits reported. Forest land recreational development has continued to expand in scope and significance, showing no sign of diminishing in our time.

NATIONAL PARK SERVICE

National Park Service (NPS) holdings constitute about 13% of the federal land holdings, or 84 million acres of land, in 49 states, the District of Columbia, American Samoa, Guam, Puerto Rico, Saipan, and the Virgin Islands (as shown in Figure 7.7) and are referred to as the National Park System. A national park is of such national significance as to justify special recognition and protection, and it takes an act of Congress to create it. Additionally the president has authority, under the Antiquities Act of 1906, to proclaim national monuments on lands already under federal jurisdiction. This distinction has been given to great natural reservations, historic military fortifications, prehistoric ruins, fossil sites, and to the Statue of Liberty. Most but not all national monuments are managed by the NPS. The secretary of the interior is usually asked by Congress for recommendations on proposed additions to the system. The secretary is counseled by the National Park System Advisory Board, which is composed of private citizens who

Table 7.1 Statistical Summary of the National Park System

Classification	Number
National Battlefields	11
National Battlefield Parks	3
National Battlefield Site	1
National Military Parks	9
National Historical Parks	39
National Historic Sites	76
International Historic Sites	1
National Lakeshores	4
National Memorials	28
National Monuments	72
National Parks	55
National Parkways	4
National Preserves	16
National Reserves	2
National Recreation Area	19
National Rivers	6
National Wild and Scenic Rivers and Riverways	9
National Scenic Trails	3
National Seashores	10
Units Without Designation	11
Totals	**379**

Source: U.S. Department of the Interior, National Parks: Index 2000 (Washington, D.C., U.S. Government Printing Office, 2000), 13.

offer advice on possible additions to the system and policies for its management.

Areas added to the National Park System may be of exceptional historical, cultural, or natural value. Areas set aside due to their natural values are expanses or features of land or water of great scenic and scientific quality and are usually designated as national parks, monuments, preserves, seashores, lakeshores, riverways, or trails. Such areas contain one or more distinctive attributes such as forest, grassland, tundra, desert, estuary, or river systems; or they may contain "windows" on the past for a view of geological history; or they may have imposing landforms such as mountains, mesas, thermal areas, and caverns. They may also be habitats of abundant or rare wildlife and plant-life. Components, individually known as *units*, of the National Park System are listed in Table 7.1.

Writer Freeman Tilden, recognized in 1954 by Director Conrad L. Wirth of the National Park Service for his perceptive and spiritual interpretation of the scenic and scientific areas of the system, penned:

> The national parks are not merely places of physical recreation. If finer and more recreative recreation can be found anywhere in the world, the spots have not yet been revealed. But the word recreation covers a host of activities, and many of them can be had in municipal, state or other areas, in the national forests, and in Lake Mead, Millerton, Coulee Dam. . . . I cannot understand why anyone should travel long distances to the national parks for physical recreation as such, but if they represent a special dividend, deriving from a larger appreciation a higher use, then visiting them becomes a most desirable thing (Tilden, 1959:14).

National Park History

After America won its independence from Britain, the country had few unique sites of natural beauty that had been recognized as recreation areas, the most prominent of which, Niagara Falls, had been exploited commercially to its detriment. During the western expansion, the giant sierra redwood trees of California were rediscovered in Yosemite Valley. The magnificence of the Yosemite Valley displaced all claims that the European countryside was more scenic. America finally had a claim to antiquity; the huge trees had been growing before the time of Christ, and they certainly made up for America's lack of old European castles in the countryside. By 1864 the nation moved to preserve and showcase their

Independence Hall in Philadelphia was constructed between 1732 and 1756 and is part of Independence Hall National Historical Park in Philadelphia.

greatness, and the nation's greatness too, when the U.S. government ceded lands in Yosemite Valley to the state of California to protect the magnificent Sequoia trees. Specifically, in the conditions of acceptance, the federal government stated the retention of the land was for "public use, resort, and recreation" and the lands were to be held "inalienable for all time" (Runte, 1987:29-30).

Later, in 1872, Yellowstone National Park was established. For these lands no state government existed to which the parklands could be entrusted, therefore, Yellowstone remained in the custody of the Department of the Interior as a national park (Mackintosh, 1990:6). This was the first time the term national park appeared, although the earlier Yosemite protection had embodied the concept. Even earlier, the artist George Catlin is credited with

Visitors climb a ladder to one of the well-preserved cliff dwellings at Mesa Verde National Park in southwestern Colorado.

articulating the need for a wildland park for the nation. In 1832, after traveling through Sioux Indian lands and foreseeing their eventual destruction, he proposed that a park be established to preserve the Sioux culture and the bison on which they were so dependent (Wellman, 1987:51-52). Catlin's vision never fully materialized, though, and even after Yellowstone was created, it was almost two decades later before another national park was set aside. At the urging of John Muir and Robert Underwood Johnson, Congress passed bills in 1890 providing for the protection of additional lands that would become Sequoia, General Grant, and Yosemite National Parks. Soon after, Mount Rainier National Park and Crater Lake National Park were added.

During these early years a policy had evolved in Congress that only "worthless" lands could be set aside as national parks. This meant that it was necessary to first demonstrate there was no possibility of economic viability before Congress would act to set land aside. Therefore, repeatedly in congressional hearings, exhaustive lists of the unsuitability of the land for development and profit, save for scenic beauty, were presented (Runte, 1987:30).

In 1891 the passage of the Forest Reserve Act gave the president unilateral authority to proclaim forest reservations, which provided a means to avoid the lengthy congressional "worthlessness" debates. Within two years' time, President Benjamin Harrison proclaimed 13 million acres in the West as forest reserves. These holdings were increased to 46 million acres by presidents Grover Cleveland and William McKinley. During the administration of President Theodore Roosevelt, the naturalist and conservationist more than tripled the forest lands to nearly 130 million acres, and many of the subsequently named national parks were carved from these holdings. Roosevelt also made expansive use of the Antiquities Act of 1906, which empowers the president to preserve "objects of historic or scientific interest" as national monuments if the land is already under the jurisdiction of the federal government. Until then, national parks had only been established to preserve scenic wonders; Roosevelt interpreted "scientific" to mean of geological significance as well, and as such he designated Devil's Tower, a basalt monolith rising 865 feet in the air in Wyoming, the first scientific national monument. Petrified Forest, Montezuma Castle, El Morro, other Indian cliff dwellings, and Lassen Peak soon followed as national monuments. All of the monuments were relatively modest in size until 800,000 acres were set aside around the Grand Canyon and 600,000 acres around Mount Olympus as national monuments (Runte, 1987:65-81). Before Roosevelt left office, he used the Antiquities Act to proclaim a total of 18 national monuments (Mackintosh, 1990: 9).

During this period it was still important that the lands be considered useless or worthless for economic gain in order to be set aside, and they needed to meet the criterion that the lands be of unique scenic beauty for designation as a national park. A dismal failure of conservation was a result of this narrow policy. Next to Yosemite Valley lay Hetch Hetchy Valley which was, to some, just as beautiful and magnificent as Yosemite. However, since there were two valleys right next to each other, Hetch Hetchy was not deemed unique, and it was this absence of singularity that permitted its demise. Together with the establishment of its economic worth as a water reservoir, its park status was stripped. At the close of the long and bitter struggle by preservationists to save the area, San Francisco won the right to flood the valley to create a reservoir for the city. The painful loss of Hetch Hetchy Valley in 1913 was blamed in part on the dispersed nature of federal land management. With the spotlight on the need to unify the management and protection of the parks, the Organic Act of 1916 was passed creating the National Park Service. No longer would the management of the parks, monuments, and forests be distributed among numerous government agencies with no one agency clearly the protector of the parks.

Stephen Mather, a skilled promoter and eventually the first director of the NPS (see Chapter 3, Visionaries and Pioneers), appealed to the utilitarian conservatives in Congress in his cause to establish a bureau to protect the parks. He demonstrated that the parks, too, had economic worth measured in tourism dollars when he vigorously promoted the "See America First" campaign, designed to keep tourists in the United States rather than going abroad. Economic mandates were heard in Congress again, and the valuable asset of the national parks was recognized and protected by the 1916 act (Runte, 1987: 51, 81,95). More than 120 nations have followed the United States' lead in creating the world's first National Park Service (Craig, 1991:41).

The preservationists' idea of protecting and preserving parklands through annexation of areas within the park ecosystem did not take hold for years. The authorization of Everglades National Park in 1934 was a clear public pledge in this direction of preservation. For the first time, flora and fauna in a fragile ecosystem were protected, although, sadly, the boundaries of the park were not large enough to protect against the damage from residues of farming and urban populations. The increasingly high cost of setting aside land for national parks was evident, too, as private holdings were allowed to stand and dot the otherwise public parklands. In that same year, Great Smoky Mountain National Park was authorized, and Shenandoah National Park had joined the system a year earlier, both largely possible due to donations from private citizens, including $3 million from John D. Rockefeller, Jr.

Earlier, Rockefeller had also acquired approximately 35,000 acres near Jackson Hole, Wyoming, to supplement the expansion of Yellowstone National Park and to thwart the blight of gas stations and tourist traps in the area. Although the purchase was completed by 1929, Congress did not expand the park status for another 20 years. Instead, in 1929 they authorized Grand Teton National Park, which comprised only mountaintops that were clearly economically insignificant. Congress viewed the Jackson Hole Valley area connecting Grand Teton to Yellowstone as too valuable to be set aside despite the fact that the land would be donated. In essence, Congress continued to ignore the preservation of wildlife that wintered in this lower elevation area and were therefore open game during hunting season. Once again, the need to protect the entire ecosystem was overlooked. Finally, in 1950, Congress annexed a large segment of the valley to Grand Teton National Park, after appeasing hunters with a proposal to omit from the park a strip of forestland between Grand Teton and Yellowstone.

Throughout the 1930s, the depression-era Civilian Conservation Corps (CCC) completed conservation, rehabilitation, and construction projects in federal and state parklands that continue to provide value today. At the program's peak in 1935, there were 600 CCC camps with 118 in federal parklands and 482 in state parks. The park service oversaw the program that had 6,000 professional supervisors and 120,000 enrollees that came from the ranks of the unemployed (Mackintosh, 1990: 36). Other labor-intensive projects that were added to the national park system in the 1930s were the Blue Ridge Parkway, the Natchez Trace Parkway, and the recreational resources surrounding the Hoover Dam reservoir, later named Lake Mead.

World War II brought park development to a halt and decreased park use. Afterward visitation catapulted from six million in 1942, to 33 million in 1950, to 72 million in 1960. This rapid increase demanded the rehabilitation of existing infrastructure and the construction of more. By 1960, the park service had developed 56 visitor centers with interpretive exhibits and audiovisual programs, with many more to follow. The National Historic Preservation Act of 1966 expanded the historical interpretation role of the NPS with the maintenance of the National Register of Historic Places. Listed properties were afforded various forms of assistance to encourage historic preservation (Mackintosh, 1990: 51).

Ecosystem management did not take a lead in park service activities until the 1960s. In 1963, a team of distinguished scientists chaired by A. Starker Leopold wrote in *Wildlife Management in the National Parks*, "The major policy change that we would recommend to the National Park Service, is that it recognize the enormous complexity of ecologic communities. ..." (Runte, 1987:198). Although the Save the Redwoods movement had begun as early as 1892 and major groves had been set aside as state parks and Muir Woods National Monument, the movement's goal to protect the redwoods' coastal ecosystem from the lumberman's axe was not achieved until the late 1960s. Finally, the Redwood National Park was designated, and three state parks were adjoined through the federal purchase of contiguous private lands. A painful catalyst for designation was the neighboring lumbering activity that toppled more than 300 huge redwoods (Runte, 1987:138-54). The Land and Water Conservation Fund of 1965 (see Chapter 12, Management Policies) provided the majority of funds to acquire additional parklands from revenues from off-shore drilling leases for oil and gas, admissions and user fees at federal recreational sites, surplus-land sales, and excise taxes on motorboat fuel (Jensen, 1985:187; & Knudson, 1984:368).

With Alaska achieving statehood in 1959, it offered the last frontier in which complete ecological preserves could be set aside as national parks, wilderness areas, and wildlife refuges. This fertile setting created a long, controversial debate that culminated in President Jimmy Carter and Secretary of the Interior Cecil D. Andrus taking action to force Congress to finally protect more than 100 million acres, or 28 percent of the state. *The Alaska National Interests Lands Conservation Act of 1980* more than doubled the acreage of national parklands (see Figure 7.8), by setting aside 43.6 million acres for new national parklands, as well as 53.8 million acres for wildlife refuges, and 1.2 million acres for the National Wild and Scenic Rivers System. Even with the vast amount of land

protected, preservationists gradually learned that ecosystems had been severed by economic interests. For instance, significant expanses of land were protected as "preserves" that permitted hunting, fishing, and mining. These designations were a compromise struck to accommodate the economic interests of tourism and mining (Runte, 1987:236-58).

The 1980s were a time of reassessment and expansion of urban parklands. A 1988 study, The National Park System Plan, concluded that 69 percent of all national parks needed their boundaries expanded in order for the National Park System to preserve them for future generations (Craig, 1991:42). Much of this expansion became necessary because ecosystems were not well understood at the time the parks were established.

Not Only Parks and Monuments

The park service's role in historical interpretation was greatly expanded in the 1930s with the transfer of the War Department's historical parks, monuments, and battlefield sites, and the transfer of the national capital parks, including the Jefferson Memorial and the Washington Monument. Together, more than 50 historical areas in the East rounded out the park system that had previously been heavily weighted in the western states, rendering the system national in scope (Mackintosh, 1990: 34). Many other nontraditional national areas were established in the 1960s and 1970s, including Cape Cod National Seashore, Indiana Dunes National Lakeshore, and Gateway National Recreation Area on the outskirts of New York. Many of these acquisitions were funded by the Land and Water Conservation Fund (discussed in Chapter 12, Management Policies). The Wild and Scenic Rivers System was established with 1968 legislation, and passage of the National Trails System Act of 1968 created the National Trails System. The passage of the National Parks and Recreation Act of 1978 provided for a host of even more new and expanded park areas, including Santa Monica Mountains National Recreation

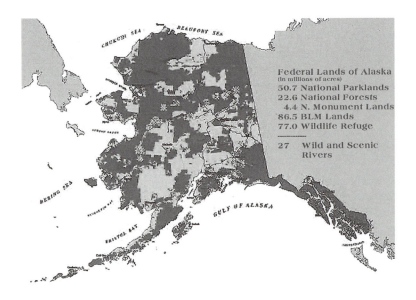

Figure 7.8 Federal Lands in Alaska.

Area near Los Angeles and New River Gorge National River in western Virginia. In all, 15 units were added to the National Park System by the 1978 act.

Recreational Opportunities and Park Nomenclature

The National Park Service offers some of the world's greatest camping areas, backcountry camping, camping modifications for handicapped persons, especially those in wheelchairs or those who have difficulty walking, and concessions for tourists. Park diversity impacts the recreational opportunities available, and a wide range of special activities from horseback riding to canoeing to studying wildlife is available for visitors. Most park rangers conduct interpretive programs and evening programs around the campfire. To understand the opportunities one must understand park nomenclature. In recent years Congress and the National Park Service have attempted to simplify the nomenclature and to establish basic criteria for use of the different official titles. Brief definitions of the most common titles as described by the National Park Service (2000:8-9) follow:

National Park

Generally a national park contains a variety of resources and encompasses large land or water areas to help provide adequate protection of the resources. For example, Hawaii's Haleakala National Park preserves the outstanding features of Haleakala Crater on that island of Maui and protects the unique and fragile ecosystems of the Kipahulu Valley.

National Monument

A national monument is intended to preserve at least one nationally significant resource. It is usually smaller than a national park and lacks its diversity of attractions. For example, New York's Fort Stanwix National Monument is a complete reconstruction of the fort where the Americans withstood British invasion and the site of the treaty with the Iroquois. There are also national monuments that are managed by other federal agencies, including 15 administered by the Bureau of Land Management.

National Preserves

The category of national preserve is established primarily for the protection of

Historic reenactments occur at many of the national battlefield and military parks, such as Antietam National Battlefield in Maryland and Vicksburg National Military Park in Mississippi.

Petrified Forest National Park in Arizona was first protected as a National Monument in 1906.

Pecos National Historical Park in New Mexico protects two Spanish missions and the ruins of the ancient pueblo of Pecos, a landmark along the Santa Fe Trail.

Ruins of a large pueblo of the Salado Indians who flourished in the Verde Valley between A.D. 1100 and 1450 can be seen at Tuzigoot National Monument near Clarksdale, Arizona.

The dome-shaped cliffs white-cap rock along the Freemont River accounts for the name of Capitol Reef National Park in Utah.

certain resources. Activities such as hunting and fishing or the extraction of mineral; and fuels may be permitted if they do not jeopardize the natural values of a site. In 1974 Big Cypress and Big Thicket were authorized as the first national preserves. Big Cypress National Preserves (Florida) adjoins the Everglades National Park, providing a freshwater supply crucial to the park's development. Big Thicket National Preserve (Texas) offers an excellent opportunity to study and research a great number of plant and animal species in this "biological crossroad of North America" (National Park Service, 2000:82).

National Lakeshore and National Seashore

Preserving shoreline areas and offshore islands, the national lakeshore and national seashore focus on the preservation of natural values while at the same time providing water-oriented recreation. Although national lakeshores can be established on the shore of any natural freshwater lake, the existing four are all located on the shores of the Great Lakes. Sleeping Bear Dunes National Lakeshore and Indiana Dunes are both on Lake Michigan, and Pictured Rocks and Apostle Islands are both on Lake Superior. The ten national seashores are on the Atlantic, Gulf, and Pacific coasts. They include Assateague Island (Maryland and Virginia), Canaveral (Florida), Cape Cod (Massachusetts), Cape Lookout and Cape Hatteras (North Carolina), Cumberland Island (Georgia), Fire Island (New York), Gulf Islands (Mississippi), Padre Island (Texas) and Point Reyes (California).

National River and Wild and Scenic Riverway

These designations preserve ribbons of land bordering on free-flowing streams that have not been dammed, channelized, or otherwise altered by humans. Besides preserving rivers in their natural state, these areas provide opportunities for outdoor activities such as hiking, canoeing, and hunting. The Merced River (California), Alatna Wild River (Alaska), and

Delaware National Scenic River (Pennsylvania) are examples of rivers preserved in these categories.

National Scenic Trails

These trails are generally long-distance footpaths winding through extended corridors of natural beauty. The Appalachian National Scenic Trail, for example, follows the Appalachian Mountains from Mount Katahdin, Maine to Springer Mountain in Georgia for approximately 2,000 miles. The Pacific Crest National Scenic Trail stretches along the mountain crests from the Canadian border in Washington state to the Mexican border in California. The National Trails System (described later in this chapter), of which the National Scenic Trails are a part, is administered by the National Park Service. The NPS coordinates with the Forest Service who manages several of the individual national scenic trails, and encourages other public and private agencies to develop, maintain, and protect trails; expand and designate trails; and, where feasible, cooperate with and support the efforts of the trails community nationwide. The Continental Divide, Florida, Ice Age, Natchez Trace, North Country, and Potomac Heritage are additional national scenic trails (Cordes, 2001: 3).

National Historic Trails

These trails recognize past routes of exploration and migration and of freedom-seeking and military actions. They preserve stories of our country's past. Not necessarily continuous, they identify historic routes (often paralleled by marked driving routes), remains, and artifacts that together tell the story of past adventures and conflicts. They invite today's adventurer back into time and into an environment that was experienced by earlier inhabitants, explorers, pioneers, entrepreneurs, and freedom fighters. The stories of the Oregon, California, and Mormon Pioneer Trails; the El Camino Real, the Ala Kahakai, and the Santa Fe Trail; the Lewis and Clark and the Juan Bautista de Anza expeditions; the Overmountain revolutionary war campaign; the Pony Express; the Trail of Tears; the flight of the Nez Perce; the Iditarod race for gold and the Selma-to-Montgomery voting rights march have all captured the American spirit and have kept alive our rich—and, at times, tragic national heritage. While the National Park Service oversees the entire set of national trails, the Bureau of Land Management has more miles of national historic trails on its lands than any federal agency (Cordes, 1999:3).

National Historic Site

These sites preserve places and commemorate persons, events, and activities important in the nation's history. They range from archeological sites associated with prehistoric Indian civilizations to sites related to the lives of modern Americans. Historical areas are customarily preserved or restored to reflect their appearance during the period of their greatest historical significance. A wide variety of titles—national military park, national battlefield park, national battlefield site, and national battlefield—have been used for areas associated "with American military history." But other areas such as national monuments and national historic parks may include features associated with military history. National historic parks are commonly areas of greater physical extent and complexity than national historic sites. The lone international historic site, International Peace Garden (North Dakota and Manitoba), refers to a site relevant to both U.S. and Canadian history.

National Memorial

The title national memorial is most often used for areas that are primarily commemorative. But they need not be sites or structures historically associated with their subjects. For example, the home of Abraham Lincoln (Illinois) is a national historic site, but the Lincoln Memorial (in Washington, D.C.) is a national memorial. Several other areas administered by the National Capital Region whose titles do not include the words national memorial, such as the Washington Monument (Washington, D.C.) are, nevertheless, classified as national memorials.

National Recreation Area

Originally, national recreation areas such as Coulee Dam National Recreation Area (Washington) were units surrounding reservoirs impounded by dams built by other federal agencies. The National Park Service manages many of these areas under cooperative agreements. The concept of recreational areas has grown to encompass other lands and waters set aside for recreational use by acts of Congress and now includes major areas in urban centers such as Gateway National Recreation Area (New York) and Santa Monica Mountains National Recreation Area (California). There are also national recreation areas outside the National Park System that are administered by the U.S. Forest Service. For example, the latter two units of the Whiskeytown-Shasta-Trinity National Recreation Area are administered by the Forest Service.

National Parkway

National parkways encompass ribbons of land flanking roadways and offer an opportunity for leisurely driving through areas of scenic interest. They are not designed for high-speed travel. Besides the areas set aside as parkways, other units of the National Park System include parkways within their boundaries. The Blue Ridge Parkway (North Carolina and Virginia), for example, is a 470-mile parkway that follows the crest of the Blue Ridge Mountains. A portion of the Blue Ridge Parkway and all of the Natchez Trace Parkway have been designated All American Roads by the National Scenic Byway Program of the Department of Transportation.

National Wilderness Area

Congress designated national wilderness areas (discussed later in this chapter) in many units of the National Park System as well as within units managed by other federal agencies. This designation does not remove wilderness lands from the parks, but it does ensure that they will be managed to retain the "primeval character and influence, without permanent improvements or human habitation..." (National Park Service, 2000:8).

Performing Arts

Two areas of the National Park System have been set aside primarily as sites for the performing arts. These are Wolf Trap Farm Park for the Performing Arts (Virginia), America's first such national park, and the John F. Kennedy Center for the Performing Arts (Washington, D.C.). Two historical areas, Ford's Theater National Historic Site (Washington, D.C.) and Chamizal National Memorial (Texas), also provide facilities for the performing arts.

National Capital Parks

Parks in the nation's capital are administered by the National Park Service under the Reorganization Act of 1933, which was the first major expansion of the park service holdings. Most parklands in the capital are included in the federal holdings, although the District of Columbia also operates parks, playgrounds, and recreational facilities. The National Park Service also administers several units in Maryland, Virginia, and West Virginia.

Affiliated Areas

Besides the National Park System, the Wild and Scenic Rivers System, and the National Trails System, there are areas known as affiliated areas. These are areas that are neither federally owned nor directly administered by the NPS but that utilize NPS assistance. They comprise a variety of locations in the United States and Canada that preserve significant properties outside the National Park System, such as the David Berger National Memorial in Ohio. The memorial honors the memory of the eleven Israeli athletes who were assassinated at the 1972 Olympic Games in Munich. Some affiliated areas have been recognized by acts of Congress, others have been designated national

historic sites by the secretary of the interior under authority of the Historic Sites Act of 1935. All draw on technical or financial aid from the NPS.

National Heritage Areas

National Heritage Areas are a dynamic young segment of NPS-affiliated areas. These are regions in which entire communities live and work, and in which residents, businesses, and local governments have come together to conserve special landscapes and their own heritage. Through a number of independent authorities, Congress has established 15 National Heritage Areas. In these areas the National Park Service does not acquire new land. Conservation, interpretation and other activities are managed in partnerships among federal, state, and local governments and private nonprofit organization. The NPS plays the role of the catalyst by providing technical assistance and financial assistance for a limited period. The visitor who explores a National Heritage Area will gain insight into how a particular part of the American experience came to be. For example, West Virginia's National Coal Heritage Area is a rich cultural geography that has been influenced over the last 125 years by the role of coal extraction. The Coal Heritage National Scenic Byway is a convenient route of exploration of this fascinating national heritage area that impacted America's development in profound ways.

The National Park Service in the Twenty-First Century

In the twenty-first century the National Park System Advisory Board (2001:3) recommends that the National Park Service address these challenges:

- Embrace its mission, as educator, to become a more significant part of America's educational system by providing formal and informal programs for students and learners of all ages inside and outside park boundaries.

- Encourage the study of the American past, developing programs based on current scholarship, linking specific places to the narrative of our history, and encouraging a public exploration and discussion of the American experience.
- Adopt the conservation of biodiversity as a core principle in carrying out its preservation mandate and participate in efforts to protect marine as well as terrestrial resources.
- Advance the principles of sustainability, while first practicing what is preached.
- Actively acknowledge the connections between native cultures and the parks, and assure that no relevant chapter in the American heritage experience remains unopened.
- Encourage collaboration among park and recreation systems at every level—federal, regional, state, local—in order to help build an outdoor recreation network accessible to all Americans.
- Improve the Service's institutional capacity by developing new organizational talents and abilities and a workforce that reflects America's diversity.

NATIONAL WILDERNESS PRESERVATION SYSTEM

Wilderness is a place where the imprint of humans is substantially unnoticed, and where natural processes are the primary influences and human activity is limited to primitive recreation and minimum tools. Change will occur primarily through natural disturbance and minimum human influence. And those who do experience wild places, go there without intention to disturb or destroy natural processes. The passage of the Wilderness Act in 1964 formalized the nation's desire to protect its wilderness resource restricting grazing,

mining, timber cutting and mechanized vehicles in these areas. These lands are protected and valued for their ecological, historical, scientific and experiential resources. The law protects these values for future generations (Wilderness, 2001:1). Wilderness is defined by the act as areas that:

- Are affected primarily by the forces of nature, where humans are visitors.
- Possess outstanding opportunities for solitude or primitive and unconfined types of recreation.
- Are undeveloped, federally owned, and generally over 5,000 acres in size.
- Are protected and managed so as to allow natural ecological processes to operate freely.
- May contain ecological, geological, scenic, or historic value.

Wilderness History

The early national parks were intended to provide an outdoor experience in relative comfort. Visitors enjoyed transportation by train or carriage, and plush resorts awaited them after a day's sojourn in the spectacular scenery. But there was a growing issue between recreationists who wanted comfort and facilities and those who wished to rough it in a wilderness environment. The current federal concept of wilderness—land left essentially wild and free from human impact originated with the Forest Service (Cordell et al., 1990:4). In the 1920s the Forest Service's Aldo Leopold, Arthur Carhart, and others advocated the preservation of large areas in an undisturbed state. In 1921, Leopold (see Chapter 3, Visionaries and Pioneers), defined wilderness as "a continuous stretch of country preserved in its natural state, open to lawful hunting and fishing, big enough to absorb a two-week's pack trip, and kept devoid of roads, artificial trails, cottages, or other works of man" (Wellman, 1987:132). According to Wellman (1987:132-34), Leopold advocated that for a minority of people, preservation of wilderness would be the greatest priority, and that these views should be represented when possible. His proposal in 1921 for a wilderness area in New Mexico's Gila National Forest, backed by local hunters, won support the following year, and in 1924 the area was designated the Gila Roadless Area. The nation's first wilderness preserve consisted of approximately 500,000 acres. Soon five other roadless areas were established within the National Forest System, and several more were under consideration. In the meantime, Arthur Carhart was also making progress toward establishing a roadless area in the Superior National Forest in Minnesota. His proposal for a lakeland wilderness area was approved by the secretary of agriculture in 1923. Supported by later legislation, his plan provided the foundation for the million-acre Boundary Waters Canoe Area Wilderness (Wellman, 1987:133). Soon the National Park Service had to respond to the pressures of preservationists. Scientific research parks were established, one of the earliest being a 4,480-acre "primitive" area in Yosemite National Park.

Responding to this National Park Service challenge and to Leopold and others within the Forest Service, the Forest Service developed the "L-20" regulations of 1929, which directed national forest staffs to protect "primitive" undeveloped lands. This represented one of the first attempts to establish wilderness as a general classification of land use with specific management guidelines. Under these regulations, some 63 primitive areas encompassing nearly 8.5 million acres were established. But protection was tenuous, boundaries could be changed by administrative order, and many wilderness areas contained state or private lands that were subject to development. Wilderness advocates, especially Robert Marshall, then chief of the Forest Service's Recreation and Lands Division, pressed for far stronger measures. The result was the "U-Regulations" of 1939, which established three land categories: U-1 "wilderness" (areas of more than 100,000 acres to be left undeveloped), U-2 "wild" (5,000-100,000 acres to be managed as

wilderness), and U-3 "recreation" (roadless areas where timber harvest and some other development were permitted) (Cordell et al., 1990:4).

Following World War II, wilderness proponents, led by Howard Zahnisher of the Wilderness Society, pressed for congressional action to provide greater protection. With impetus provided by the Outdoor Recreation Resources Review Commission (ORRRC), the Wilderness Act became law in 1964 (P.L. 8-577; see Chapter 15, Outdoor Recreational Activities). Passage of the act created the National Wilderness Preservation System (NWPS), which required affirmative action by Congress on each addition to the wilderness system. It shifted the process of wilderness designation from the Forest Service to Congress.

Marshall's 1939 definition became the basis for the legislative definition of wilderness, and his equal emphasis on human use and preservation of the primitive environment carried through to current wilderness management guidelines. The Wilderness Act applied to the national forests, national parks, and national wildlife refuges. Its early effects were felt mainly by the Forest Service, which already possessed large areas of protected wilderness (Cordell et al., 1990:4). The National Park Service had utilized a zoning system to protect wilderness values in undeveloped areas more than a half mile from roads. The Fish and Wildlife Service had not managed any area specifically for wilderness purposes (although today they manage significant portions of the wilderness expanse), because manipulation of habitat to enhance wildlife values often resulted in substantial modification of areas, thereby conflicting with wilderness values. Nevertheless, once charged with wilderness responsibilities, Congress designated Great Swamp Wildlife Refuge in New Jersey as the first refuge to be admitted to the National Wilderness Preservation System (Hendee et al., 1978:67). Lands managed by the Bureau of Land Management were not subject to the Wilderness Act until passage of the Federal Land Policy and Management Act of 1976.

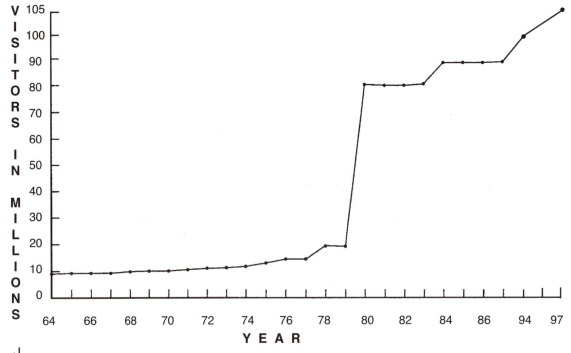

Figure 7.9 National Wilderness Preservation System growth.

National Park System
38.5 million acres of wilderness

System totals 80 million acres

National Wildlife Refuge System
19.3 million acres of wilderness

System totals 90 million acres

National Forest System
32.4 million acres of wilderness

System totals 191 million acres

Bureau of Land Management Lands
0.5 million acres of wilderness

System totals 250 million acres*

*BLM holdings after settlement of state and native claims under the Statehood Act of 1958 and the Alaska Native Claims Settlement Act of 1971.

Figure 7.10 Who manages the wilderness?

The Wilderness Act accorded statutory protection specifically to lands that met the wilderness definition: an area where the earth and its community of life are untrammeled by humans, where humans themselves are visitors who do not remain. It was the Wilderness Act that did much to alter the concept of wilderness from that of a residual land resource or even useless land to that of a primary resource central to national recreation policy. Prior to the act's passage, the first wilderness bill was introduced in Congress by Senator Hubert H. Humphrey in 1956. Subsequently, 64 additional wilderness bills were introduced and considered by Congress before passage (Browning et al., 1988:1). After President Lyndon B. Johnson signed the Wilderness Act of 1964, nine million acres were immediately designated as national wilderness, but it was not until 1970 and then 1976 and 1978 that other significant lands were set aside.

The nearly 650-unit National Wilderness Preservation System spans nearly 105 million acres and is considered by many the best of America's public land heritage. The lands are managed proportionately by the National Park Service (42%), the Forest Service (33%), the Fish and Wildlife Service (20%), and the Bureau of Land Management (5%) (Wilderness, 2001: 1). These wilderness areas stand as living testimony to the wisdom and foresight of Congress and the American people to preserve the lands in their natural state for the enjoyment of future generations. Accordingly, wilderness areas are protected from development—the construction of roads, dams, or other permanent structures, timber cutting, the operation of motorized vehicles and equipment, and, since 1984, new mining claims and mineral leasing. Figure 7.9 shows the growth of national wilderness and figure 7.10 shows the present holdings.

High-Priority Issues for Wilderness Preservation

High-priority issues for wilderness preservation include (Cordell et al., 1990:6):

Allocation

The appropriate criteria or agenda that determines the final size and composition of the NWPS is much debated. Aside from the obvious recreational demand, advocates of increasing the NWPS point to the need to protect representative ecosystems and areas to monitor environmental changes, among other reasons. Those who argue against enlarging the NWPS are concerned that wilderness restrictions on water use, grazing, mining, and energy extraction do not contribute to the national economic growth.

Nontraditional wilderness

A related issue is whether the NWPS should be expanded to include aquatic and underground wilderness units. In addition to amending the Wilderness Act, Congress would need to resolve a number of potential problems, including determining surface rights.

Wilderness degradation

The qualities important to a wilderness area are vulnerable. Even the Wilderness Act itself sets up a tension between human use and preservation of wilderness character. Some wilderness areas are heavily used for recreation, resulting in soil erosion, plant loss, water pollution, disruption of wildlife, and loss of opportunities for solitude. Wilderness areas are also threatened from outside influences including aircraft overflights, air pollution, and the invasion of exotic plant species (see Chapter 16, The Environment). Furthermore, wilderness areas may be threatened from such global influences as ozone depletion, acid precipitation, and deforestation.

International cooperation

The National Wilderness Preservation System is unique in the world in terms of its purpose and scope. With appropriate international cooperation, it could serve as a component of a larger global system of wild areas for resource protection.

Management coordination and consistency

According to the Wilderness Act, wilderness is a supplemental purpose in forests, parks, wildlife refuges, and public lands. Because each agency has a somewhat different mission, the management of wilderness areas is not entirely coordinated or consistent.

Funding and training

The designation of a wilderness area by law does not ensure the preservation of an area in its original condition. Inadequately trained wilderness managers and understaffed and poorly funded wilderness management programs seriously hamper the mandated responsibility to preserve wilderness character.

Education

Wilderness managers alone cannot prevent the degradation of the wilderness resource.

The public must also understand wilderness values and how to use wilderness with respect and restraint, so the wilderness does not lose its character. The development of effective educational and interpretive techniques and material to teach low-impact use skills to the public is a continual challenge (see Chapter 15, Outdoor Recreational Activities).

Wild and Scenic Rivers System

The Wild and Scenic Rivers Act of 1968 provided for the establishment of a system of rivers to be preserved as free-flowing streams accessible for public use and enjoyment. According to the National Park Service (2000:108), components of the system, or portions of component rivers, may be designated as wild, scenic, or recreational rivers. Rivers are classified according to the natural qualities they possess and the evidence as viewed from the river of human presence in the area. Rivers have been classified as wild, scenic, or recreational on the basis of the following traits:

- *Wild rivers* display little evidence of human presence in the area. These rivers are free of impoundments (dams), and are generally inaccessible except by trail.
- *Scenic rivers* have relatively primitive shorelines and are largely undeveloped, but they are accessible in places by road.
- *Recreational rivers* have more development, are accessible by road or railroad, and may have been dammed.

Federally managed components of the system are designated by act of Congress. Usually Congress first requires, by law, a detailed study to determine the qualification of a river area for the system and then makes the decision. Rivers administered by federal land managers are units of their respective systems as well. For instance those rivers administered by the National Park Service are units of the National Park System, and those administered by the U.S. Fish and Wildlife Service are components of the National Wildlife Refuge System.

State rivers and streams may become units of the Wild and Scenic Rivers System when established under state laws and developed with river management plans acceptable to the secretary of the interior. Once a river area is designated a component of the Wild and Scenic Rivers System, the objective of the managing agency—local, state, or federal—is to preserve or enhance those qualities which qualified the river for inclusion within the system. Recreational use must be compatible with preservation. Wild and Scenic River designation provides the following important protections (Hendee et al., 1978:129):

- It provides complete protection against dam construction and other water development projects.
- It prohibits construction of power transmission lines.
- It permits administering agencies to condemn private land, if less than 50 percent of the entire river area is owned by federal, state, or local government. However, land within a city, village, or borough cannot be condemned if valid zoning ordinances protecting the river areas are in effect.
- It calls for complete withdrawal from mineral entry of lands within 1/4 of a mile of the bank of any river designated for management under the "wild" category.

Passage of the Wild and Scenic Rivers Act established an important milestone in the conservation of our nation's great natural resources. It recognized the value of rivers and their environs as an outstanding natural feature that must be preserved for future generations to enjoy. The search continues for outstanding rivers that should be included in this prestigious system now containing at least 96 rivers. Figures 7.6a and 7.6b, shown earlier, display the distribution and growth of the system in the continental United States.

The National Trails System

The National Trail System Act of 1968 calls for establishing trails in both urban and rural settings for persons of all ages, interests, skills, and physical abilities. The act established four classes of trails: congressionally designated long-distance national scenic trails, national historic trails, side or connecting trails, and national recreation trails (Cordes, 2001:3). The act promotes public access to, enjoyment of, and appreciation for those trails. The law designated the Appalachian National Scenic Trail and the Pacific Crest National Scenic Trail as the first long-distance trails winding through some of the most striking natural beauty in the country. To date eight national scenic trails and 14 national historic trails have been designated (see Table 7.2). Other potential routes are under study to determine whether they are suitable for designation as units of the system.

National recreation trails are managed by public or private agencies and are designated by the secretary of the interior, or, if they are within national forests, by the secretary of agriculture. A national recreation trail must be fully developed and ready to be used at the time of designation. This is certified by the administering agency that also must assure that the trail will be open for public use for at least 10 years following designation. National Recreation Trails are jointly administered by the National Park Service and USDA Forest Service, with support from the Bureau of Land Management, U.S. Fish and Wildlife Service, U.S. Army Corps of Engineers, Federal Highway Administration, American Recreation Coalition, Rails-to-Trails Conservancy, American Trails, American Hiking Society, and the National Association of State Trail Administrators.

More than 800 national recreation trails have been designated throughout the country and are located in every state, the District of Columbia, and Puerto Rico. They range in length from 1/4 mile to 485 miles, and together boast a total of nearly 9,000 miles. The majority of the trails are on federal lands, with at least 80 on state property, 30 on private lands; 150 considered local trails, and 12 under joint sponsorship. In 1990, the National Trails Agenda Project created a task force of 15 trails leaders led by the American Hiking Society. Their *Trails for All Americans Report* called for a vast, interconnecting network of trails across the country (NPS et al, 2001:2). To celebrate the Millennium, Secretary of Transportation Rodney Slater and Senator (then First Lady) Hillary Rodham Clinton designated a set of spectacular Millennium Trails to spark the further development of this vision of a national network of trails accessible by all Americans (Cordes and Lammers, 2002:231). Inspired by this effort, a cooperative group of public and private organizations has undertaken the revitalization of the National Recreation Trails program, and a searchable database is now available at *www.americantrails.org/nationalrecreationtrails*. Successful establishment of new trails has resulted in the designation of old aqueducts, abandoned railroads corridors, canal towpaths, and old logging trails for public use. Numerous trail users benefit from the designations including hikers, backpackers, horseback riders, bicyclists, motorcyclists, ski tourers, snowshoers, snowmobilers, all-terrain-vehicle riders, joggers, and mountain bikers. Because trails are utilized by diverse groups, the potential for conflict exists. Managers have attempted to designate trails for specific use in order to minimize conflicts, for instance designations may separate motorized users from hikers.

Trail use is on the increase, and resources are attempting to catch up with the demand. The task of building national trails is a difficult one, since they typically cross private and government land, with the latter managed by various federal and state agencies. Many trails are severely threatened by forces like urban sprawl, air pollution, or conflicts with other trail users. In a massive volunteer effort, hundreds of dynamic trail clubs and organizations comprised of dedicated volunteers work hard to address these threats, and to build

Table 7.2 National Trails System.

America's National Scenic Trails:

Trail Name	Authorized Mileage	Administering Agency	States
Appalachian	2,144	NPS	CT, GA, MD, MA, ME, NH, NJ, NJ, NY, NC, PA, TN, VT, VA, WV
Continental Divide	3,200	USFS	CO, ID, MT, NM, WY.
Florida	1,300	USFS	FL.
Ice Age	1,000	NPS	WI.
Natchez Trace	694	NPS	AL, MS, TN.
North Country	4,300	NPS	MI, MN, NY, ND, OH, PA, WI.
Pacific Crest	2,638	USFS	CA, OR, WA.
Potomac	704	NPS	MD, PA, VA, and District of Columbia.

America's National Historic Trails:

Trail Name	Authorized Mileage	Administering Agency	States
Ala Kahakai	175	NPS	Hawaii
California	5,665	NPS	CA, CO, ID, IA, KS, MO NE, NV, OR, UT, WY.
El Camino Real	404	BLM/NPS	NM, TX
Iditarod	2,450	BLM	AK.
Juan Bautista de Anza	1,200	NPS	AZ, CA.
Lewis and Clark	3,700	NPS	ID, IA, IL, KS, MO, MT, NE, ND, OR, SD, WA.
Mormon Pioneer	1,300	NPS	IL, IO, NE, UT, WY.
Nez Perce	1,170	NPS	ID, MT, OR, WY.
Oregon	2,170	NPS	ID, KS, MO, NE, OR, WA.
Overmountain Victory	300	NPS	NC, SC, TN, VA.
Pony Express	1,966	NPS	CA, CO, KS, MO, NE, NV, UT, WY.
Santa Fe	1,203	NPS	CO, KS, MO, NM, OK.
Selma to Montgomery	53	NPS	AL.
Trail of Tears	2,219	NPS	AL, AR, GA, IL, KY, MO, NC, OK, TN.

Reprinted with permission from the author Kathleen Cordes:
America's National Scenic Trails Norman:University of Oklahoma Press, p. 7, 2001.

and maintain trails. American Trails, Rails-to-Trails Conservancy, and America Hiking Society are leading the way. The latter's national web directory of internships and volunteer opportunities, *Helping Out in the Outdoors*, lists one-week to one-year volunteer positions. The most successful individual trail organization to date is the Appalachian Trail Conference comprised of 31 volunteer trail clubs. Through a public-private partnership, the ATC manages the day-to-day operations of the Appalachian National Scenic Trail known throughout the world.

U.S. FISH AND WILDLIFE SERVICE

The U.S. Fish and Wildlife Service is the principal agency through which the federal government carries out its responsibilities to conserve, protect, and enhance the nation's fish and wildlife and their habitats for the continuing benefit of people. The service's major responsibilities are for migratory birds, endangered species, certain marine mammals, and freshwater and anadromous fisheries.

The service's origins date back to 1871 when Congress established the U.S. Fish Commission to study the decrease of the nation's food fishes and recommend ways to reverse the decline. Created as an independent agency, it was placed under the Department of Commerce in 1903 and renamed the Bureau of Fisheries. Meanwhile, in 1885, Congress created an Office of Economic Ornithology in the Department of Agriculture. The office studied the food habits and migratory patterns of birds, especially the ones that have an effect on agriculture. This office gradually grew in responsibilities and was renamed the Bureau of Biological Survey in 1905. In addition to studying the abundance, distribution, and habitats of birds and mammals, the survey managed the nation's first wildlife refuges, controlled predators, enforced wildlife laws, and conserved dwindling populations of heron, egrets, and other waterfowl and migratory birds.

The Bureau of Fisheries and Bureau of Biological Survey were transferred to the Department of the Interior in 1939. One year later, in 1940, they were combined and named the Fish and Wildlife Service. Further reorganization came in 1956 when the Fish and Wildlife Act created the U.S. Fish and Wildlife Service and established within the agency two separate bureaus—Commercial Fisheries, and Sport Fisheries and Wildlife. The Bureau of Commercial Fisheries was transferred to the Department of Commerce in 1970 and is now known as the National Marine Fisheries Service (described later in this chapter). The Bureau of Sport Fisheries and Wildlife remained in the Department of the Interior. In 1974, the "Bureau" was dropped and the agency was called simply the U.S. Fish and Wildlife Service. Today the service employs approximately 7,500 people at facilities across the country, including a headquarters office in Washington, D.C., seven regional offices including one for research, and over 700 field units. Among these are national wildlife refuges and fish hatcheries, research laboratories, field offices, and law enforcement agents.

The Fish and Wildlife Service leads the federal effort to protect and restore animals and plants that are in danger of extinction both in the United States and worldwide. It maintains major research laboratories and field stations, as well as cooperative research units at universities across the country. It provides biological advice to other agencies and members of the public concerning the conservation of habitat that may be affected by development activities. For instance, service biologists developed many of the captive breeding techniques that have benefitted such rare species as whooping cranes, California condors and black-footed ferrets. Rachel Carson (see Chapter 3, Visionaries and Pioneers), once a service employee, awakened the American public in her book *Silent Spring* to threats to fish and wildlife from highly toxic and long-lasting pesticides such as DDT. The service is making major efforts to restore nationally significant fisheries, depleted by overfishing, pollution, or other habitat damage. The service is responsible for the conservation of over 800 species of migratory birds, regulates hunting of bird populations, and acquires and manages many national wildlife refuges to provide secure habitats for migratory birds.

The National Wildlife Refuge System

The National Wildlife Refuge System is a network of federal lands and waters managed specifically for wildlife. Vitally important, refuges provide habitat for approximately 60 endangered species and hundreds of species of birds, mammals, reptiles, amphibians, fish, and plants. More than 530 refuges and 3,000 waterfowl production areas are located on 15% of all federal lands—more than 93 million acres of land and water—in all 50 states and five trust territories. Units of the system stretch across the continent from the north shore of Alaska to the Florida keys and beyond to islands in the Caribbean and South Pacific. These units range in size from Minnesota's tiny Mille Lacs, less than an acre in size, to Alaska's 20-million acre Arctic National Wildlife Refuge, the crown jewel of wild America (see Figure 7.11). Approximately 7,500 employees manage the vast refuge system and about 36,000 volunteers provide valuable assistance.

At the turn of the century, ladies' fashions contributed to the need for establishment of the first refuges. Herons and egrets were being killed in large numbers for their plumes, used for hats. Other human and natural calamities also contributed to the need to establish refuges. In 1903, President Theodore Roosevelt signed an executive order protecting the herons, egrets, and other birds on Florida's Pelican Island, making it the first national wildlife refuge. During

---

Federal Aid and International Programs

Two laws administered by the Fish and Wildlife Service—the Federal Aid in Wildlife Restoration Act of 1937 and the Federal Aid in Sport Fisheries Restoration Act of 1950—have created some of the most successful programs in the history of fish and wildlife conservation. Known as Pittman-Robertson (wildlife) and Dingell-Johnson (fish) after their congressional sponsors, these programs provide hundreds of millions in federal grant money to support specific projects carried out by state fish and wildlife agencies. The money comes from federal excise taxes on sporting arms and ammunition, archery equipment, and sport fishing tackle. In 1984 the sport fisheries restoration legislation was supplemented by new provisions known as the Wallop-Breaux amendments. These provisions increased revenue for sport fish restoration by extending the excise tax to previously untaxed items of sporting equipment, and by channeling into fisheries restoration a portion of the existing federal tax on motorboat fuels and import duties on fishing tackle and pleasure boats. Funds are used to acquire land for wildlife habitat and for fishing and recreation, for research to provide access to hunting, to develop fishing and boating areas, to manage and maintain fish and wildlife habitats, and to carry out hunter safety training and aquatic education.

Cooperating with other countries on wildlife research and management programs, the Fish and Wildlife Service also has a variety of international responsibilities under some 40 treaties, statutes, and agreements. When requested, it offers technical assistance to foreign countries. Additionally it seeks to stem the global loss of wetlands and establish guidelines for wise use of wetlands through the international wetlands convention.

| **Figure 7.11** The National Wildlife Refuge System.

his tenure as president, Roosevelt designated 66 other properties as national wildlife reservations, laying the foundation of the present-day refuge system. The first refuges established for big-game animals are Oklahoma's Wichita Mountains Wildlife Refuge in 1905, the National Bison Range in Montana in 1908, and Wyoming's National Elk Refuge in 1912.

Initial passage of the Migratory Bird Treaty Act of 1918 was a landmark in wildlife conservation legislation and provides for the regulation of migratory bird hunting. Later, as the wheat fields of North America dried up and blew away in the 1930s, so did many of the wetlands necessary for the breeding of migratory waterfowl. In response, President Franklin Roosevelt appointed a special committee to discover a means to conserve migratory waterfowl. Headed by Thomas Beck, editor of *Collier's* magazine, the committee eventually included Aldo Leopold and Jay Norwood "Ding" Darling. With surprising swiftness in March 1934, Roosevelt signed the Migratory Bird

Hunting Stamp Act of 1934, and the first duck stamps, designed by Darling (see figure 7.12), were sold for $1. Meanwhile, thousands of depression-era workers from the Civilian Conservation Corps and Works Progress Administration improved habitat and built the infrastructure of over 50 national wildlife refuges and fish hatcheries (Madison, 2001:1).

The passage of numerous laws have had a powerful influence on the development and management of the system. Significant legislation included the Federal Aid in Wildlife Restoration Act of 1937 (commonly referred to as the Pittman-Robertson Act), the Fish and Wildlife Coordination Act of 1946, Federal Aid in Sport Fish Restoration Act of 1950 (commonly referred to as the Dingell-Johnson Act), the Fish and Wildlife Act of 1956, the Duck Stamp Act of 1958, the Refuge Recreation Act of 1962, the National Wildlife Refuge System Administration Act of 1964, The Land and Water Conservation Act of 1964, The Wilderness Act of 1964, the National Wildlife Refuge System Act of

Figure 7.12 The first duck stamp, 1934. Credit: Brush and ink drawing of mallards by Jay N. Ding" Darling.

1966, the Endangered Species Act of 1967 and 1973, the Alaska National Interest Lands Conservation Act of 1980, the National Wildlife Refuge System Improvement Act of 1997, and the National Wildlife Refuge System Centennial Act of 2000 (FWS. 2000: 1-2).

Today the refuge system is a unique collection of diverse areas administered by the U.S. Fish and Wildlife Service. Many refuges are located along the major north-south flyways, providing feeding and resting areas for the great semiannual migrations of ducks, geese, and other birds. Other areas serve as sanctuaries for endangered or unusual species. For example, the Aransas Refuge in Texas is the winter home of the whooping crane, and the Hawaiian Islands Refuge provides the only habitat for a number of endangered species including the Hawaiian monk seal and green sea turtle.

Archeological artifacts and areas of historical significance located on refuge lands are preserved along with wildlife habitat. DeSoto Refuge in Iowa, for instance, maintains an exhibit and collection of items reclaimed from the historic steamship Bertrand, which sank in the Missouri River in 1865.

Recreation

National wildlife refuges offer a wide variety of recreational opportunities. An estimated 35 million people visit these lands annually. Although public uses are regulated so they do not interfere with the wildlife purposes of the refuge, many activities are available. Recreational uses may include wildlife observation, photography, nature study, hiking, boating, hunting, and fishing. Some refuges provide visitor centers, special study areas, environmental education programs, interpretive trails and drives, wildlife observation towers, photographic blinds, and other public facilities. Activities vary with each refuge and may depend on the season of the year. Visitors are advised to check with refuge personnel prior to a visit to determine which activities are allowed and what regulations apply toward the consideration of the wildlife. Every visit to a refuge is different, and each person has an individual experience.

The prevailing refuge management philosophy for many years was a commitment to anonymity, the belief being that the fewer who knew about refuges, the better. People have discovered that refuges are natural treasures (see Chapter 13, Outdoor Recreational Activities), and the U.S. Fish and Wildlife Service is meeting the challenge of tourists by providing extensive outdoor experiences while protecting the wildlife for which the refuges were created. The Center for Wildlife Information suggests etiquette for viewing and photographing wildlife to avoid stressing the animals or birds. Their guidelines include observation from a distance through binoculars, spotting scopes, and telephoto lenses; allow wildlife

> Wild beasts and birds are by right not the property merely of the people who are alive today, but the property of unknown generations, whose belongings we have no right to squander.
>
> Theodore Roosevelt

to keep the visitor in view; do not follow or chase wildlife; and wildlife should be viewed for a limited time. Viewing early or late in the day provides optimum viewing opportunities.

OTHER FEDERAL AGENCIES

Other federal agencies, because of the vast resources they manage, have a significant impact on outdoor recreation. These include the Bureau of Land Management, which has taken on an increasingly dynamic role in recreation, the Bureau of Indian Affairs, the U.S. Army Corps of Engineers, the Bureau of Reclamation, the Tennessee Valley Authority, and the National Oceanic and Atmospheric Administration.

The Bureau of Land Management

The Bureau of Land Management (BLM) is responsible for managing 264 million acres of the nation's public lands and about 300 million additional acres of subsurface mineral resources in a combination of ways that best serves the needs of the American people (see Figure 7.13). These are lands that remain of the nation's once vast land holdings—the public domain had once included nearly two billion acres of land. In the course of the country's national expansion and development, public lands were sold or deeded by the federal government to the states and their counties and municipalities, to educational institutions, to private citizens, and to industries. Other lands were set aside as national parks and monuments, forests, wildlife refuges, and military installations. The public lands managed by the BLM are located primarily in 12 states in the west including Alaska. They comprise about one-eighth of our nation's land area, and about 42% of federal land holdings. These public lands are a vast storehouse of fossil fuels, other important minerals, and timber. Livestock forage on millions of acres, and the lands support hundreds of thousands of pronghorn antelope, deer, elk, and caribou, millions of smaller creatures, and about 50,000 wild horses and burros.

Management is based on the principles of multiple use and sustained yield, com-

bining uses and balancing needs of future generations for renewable and nonrenewable resources. These resources include recreation, range, timber, minerals, watershed, fish and wildlife, and wilderness. Most of the BLM's 8,700 employees and 17,000 volunteers work in field offices in the western United States, although the headquarters is in Washington, D.C. There are 12 state offices, 58 district offices, and 140 resource area offices. Diverse skills and talents are required for positions such as recreation specialists, foresters, range conservationists, wildlife biologists, archeologists, surveyors, and engineers. Two threats facing the land holdings are widespread noxious weeds that have taken hold and the prevalence of abandoned land mine shafts that are hazardous to visitors.

History of the BLM

The BLM's roots go back to the Land Ordinance of 1785 and the Northwest Ordinance of 1787. These laws provided for the survey and settlement of the lands that the original 13 colonies ceded to the federal government after the War of Independence. As additional lands were acquired by the United States from Spain, France, and other countries, Congress directed that they be explored, surveyed, and made available for settlement. In 1812, Congress established the General Land Office in the Department of the Treasury to oversee the disposition of these Federal lands. As the 19th century progressed and the Nation's land base expanded further west, Congress encouraged the settlement of the land by enacting a wide variety of laws, including the Homesteading Laws and the Mining Law of 1872. These statutes served one of the major policy goals of the young country—settlement of the Western territories. With the exception of the Mining Law of 1872 and the Desert Land Act of 1877, all have since been repealed or superseded by other statutes (BLM, 2001:2).

The late 19th century marked a shift in federal land management priorities with the creation of the first national parks, forests, and wildlife refuges. By withdraw-

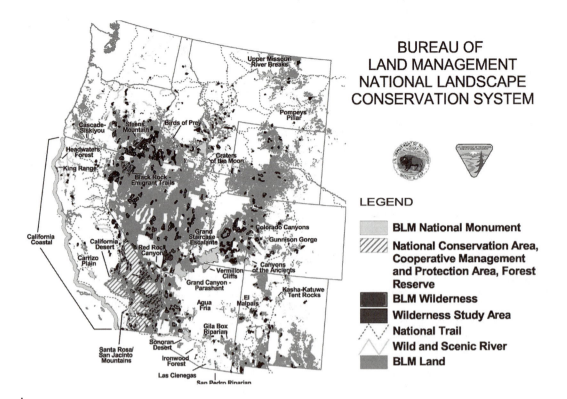

BUREAU OF LAND MANAGEMENT NATIONAL LANDSCAPE CONSERVATION SYSTEM

LEGEND

- BLM National Monument
- National Conservation Area, Cooperative Management and Protection Area, Forest Reserve
- BLM Wilderness
- Wilderness Study Area
- National Trail
- Wild and Scenic River
- BLM Land

Figure 7.13 BLM's National Conservation System. Source: Bureau of Land Management, Department of the *Interior www.blm.gov/nlcs/map.htm,* July 17, 2001.

ing these lands from settlement, Congress signaled a shift in the policy goals served by the public lands. Instead of using them to promote settlement, Congress recognized that they should be held in public ownership because of their other resource values In the early 20th century, Congress took additional steps toward recognizing the value of the assets on public lands and directed the Executive Branch to manage activities on the remaining public lands. The Mineral Leasing Act of 1920 allowed leasing, exploration, and production of selected commodities such as coal, oil, gas, and sodium to take place on public lands. The Taylor Grazing Act of 1934 established the U.S. Grazing Service to manage the public rangelands. And the Oregon and California (O&C) Act of August 28, 1937, required sustained yield management of the timberlands in western Oregon. In 1946, the Grazing Service was merged with

the General Land Office to form the Bureau of Land Management within the Department of the Interior. When the BLM was initially created, there were over 2,000 unrelated and often conflicting laws for managing the public lands (BLM, 2001: 2).

The BLM had no unified legislative mandate until Congress enacted the Federal Land Policy Management Act of 1976 (FLPMA). In it, Congress recognized the value of the remaining public lands by declaring that these lands would remain in public ownership, and it established a coherent legislative mandate for managing the public lands, making the BLM a true multiple-use agency.

Recreation

As the new millennium unfolded, the BLM took a bold step to raise the profile of recreation on their lands by establishing the National Landscape Conservation

System (NLCS). The system holds some of the nation's most remarkable and rugged landscapes including the agency's 15 National Monuments that include the impressive Grand Staircase Escalante and the Grand Canyon Parashant. Included, too, are the 13 congressionally designated National Conservation Areas including California's vast 9.5 million-acre California Desert and Nevada's 1.2 million-acre Black Rock Desert-High Rock Canyon Emigrant Trails. The latter, established in 2000, protects wagon ruts, historic inscriptions, and a wilderness landscape that is largely unchanged from when pioneers moved westward in the 1800s. Other lands of the NLCS include the Headwaters Forest Reserve in California—a stand of old-growth redwoods and surrounding lands totaling 7,400 acres, 148 wilderness areas, 600 wilderness study areas, 2,000 miles of 35 wild and scenic rivers, 3600 miles of nine national historic trails, 640 miles of national scenic trails, and other areas designated for important scientific and ecological characteristics.

Offering a greater diversity of outdoor recreation opportunities than national parks and national forests, the BLM accommodates about 54 million recreation visits each year. Visitors engage in recreational activities that include camping, hiking, hunting, fishing, boating, skiing, hang gliding, mountain biking, off-road travel, cave exploration, rock-hounding, watching wildlife, birding, visiting natural and cultural heritage sites, and enjoying solitude. The BLM administers more than 470 developed recreation sites that offer 200,000 miles of fishable streams that have trout, salmon, and other sport fish. They also have 2.2 million acres of lakes and reservoirs, 6,600 miles of floatable rivers, and more than 500 boating access points, 69 national back country byways and 300 watchable wildlife sites, as well as thousands of miles of multiple-use trails used by motorcyclists, hikers, equestrians, and mountain bikers. (BLM, 2001:1-7).

The Bureau of Indian Affairs

The mission of the Bureau of Indian Affairs (BIA) is to enhance the quality of life, to promote economic opportunity, and to carry out the responsibility to protect and improve the trust assets of American Indians, Indian tribes and Alaska Natives. BIA accomplishes this through the delivery of quality services, maintaining government-to-government relationships within the spirit of Indian self-determination. BIA is the principal agent of the United States in carrying on the government-to-government relationship that exists between the United States and federally recognized Indian tribes.

One of the principal programs of the BIA is administering and managing some 56 million acres of land held in trust by the United States for Indians. The program is designed to assist tribes with the protection and development of forest, water, mineral, and energy resources. While the BIA is headquartered in Washington, D.C., most of its employees work in 12 area offices, 84 agencies, and 180 schools throughout the country. More than 80 percent of the employees are Native Americans. To Native Americans their land provides a cultural, religious, and economic subsistence base.

Recreation

The substantial land and water resource base is utilized by both Indians and non-Indians for outdoor recreation. These areas constitute an additional wilderness resource for the country, and contain habitat that is critical to the recovery of a number of species that are listed as threatened or

The desert at Monument Valley National Tribal Park is a beautiful, but fragile ecosystem.

endangered, from fish and birds to big game. Not so many years ago, remote reservations were generally inaccessible to the public, but today, they are open to visitors and offer numerous recreational facilities. Because of their economic potential, the Bureau of Indian Affairs has supported commercial recreational developments with financial and administrative assistance. Tourism efforts have promoted job opportunities on reservations with Indians operating facilities, supervising campgrounds, and working as rangers similar to rangers in the national parks and forests.

Many reservations have spectacular scenery, and most offer hiking opportunities and hunting and fishing facilities. Others offer horseback riding, boating, and skiing. Major reservations conduct tours to archeological sites and areas of scenic interest. Powwows, dance ceremonials, crafts sales, casinos and museums also attract many visitors. The most successful developments are those of the White Mountain Apaches of Arizona, the Mescalero Apaches of New Mexico, and the Confederated Warm Springs Tribes of Oregon. Navajo Tribal Park in Monument Valley of Arizona and Utah abounds with ancient ruins and spectacular vistas. A corps of Navajo rangers runs the park and offer interpretive services. According to the United States Commission on Civil Rights (1973:1), a state cannot enforce its game and fish laws within the boundaries of an Indian reservation; therefore, permission to hunt or fish on reservations must be received from the tribe. When visiting reservations, visitors are guests in a place where cultural attitudes, social customs, and often language, can be distinctive. Entry fees may be required for parks, and permits are required for backcountry travel. A fee or permit may also be required for photography, and it is polite to request permission to photograph individuals. Photography of restricted areas or events is not generally allowed, and special permission is needed to observe private or sacred dances.

National Reservoir Areas

More recreationists visit large flood control reservoirs than national parks, and many believe these areas receive more individual visits than national forests (Knudson, 1984:281-82). With 68,000 dams in the United States, there are abundant water-related recreational opportunities. In general, reservoirs are popular recreation sites for fishing, boating, water-skiing, swimming, camping, picnicking, hiking, sight-seeing, and a variety of other activities. Large dams built under the direction of the U.S. Army Corps of Engineers, the Bureau of Reclamation, and the Tennessee Valley Authority offer recreational attractions. These agencies, however, had few official responsibilities for recreational planning and management before 1962, when John F. Kennedy approved Senate Document 97, which specified the need for outdoor recreation and fish and wildlife enhancement in planning for water projects. With the passage of the Federal Water Projects Recreation Act of 1965, procedures for developing multipurpose water resource projects were established, and plans for recreation use were required. The act provided that:

- Recreation, fish, and wildlife enhancement be considered a purpose of federal water resource projects, though not to exceed 50 percent of the benefits or costs of such multipurpose projects.
- Recreation possibilities be considered for existent and planned federal, state, and local public developments.
- Recreation, fish, and wildlife enhancement features must be administered by nonfederal administration.

The benefits of recreation bolstered the justification of new projects, but a provision requiring state and local cooperation gave veto power to these groups which, on occasion, stopped projects. Implementation of the act, however, clearly made the federal government the nation's largest provider of inland water-related opportunities. Conversely, while these projects created new water-related recreational opportunities, previous recreational opportunities were impaired due to the destruction of excellent trout streams, scenic canyons, and archeological remains. Public concern for natural diversity has caused public resistance to many new dam projects and the dismantling of existing dams where feasible.

U.S. Army Corps of Engineers

The U.S. Army Corps of Engineers, housed in the Department of Defense, traces its origins to the American Revolution. On June 16, 1775, when the Continental Congress established the army, it provided for a chief engineer to direct fortifications for the Battle of Bunker Hill. By 1802 the Corps of Engineers was made permanent, and the U.S. Military Academy was established at West Point, New York, under the chief of army engineers as the only engineering college in the nation. The corps has maintained a tradition of responding to the nation's military and civil engineering needs. In earlier times, those needs included coastal fortifications and lighthouses, surveying and pathfinding on the frontier, construction of public buildings, clearing of river channels, and operation of such early national parks as Yellowstone and Yosemite.

Today the Corps (2001:1-7) is engaged in complex military facilities, flood control, comprehensive water resources management, fish and wildlife conservation, recreation resources, environmental restoration, management of toxic wastes, energy resources, and the space program. They maintain more than 12,000 miles (19,200 km) of inland waterways and operate 235 locks. These waterways—a system of rivers, lakes and coastal bays improved for commercial and recreational transportation—carry about 1/6 of the nation's inter-city freight. The Corps also maintains 600 smaller harbors and 300 commercial harbors, through which pass two billion tons of cargo a year.

The corps employs 48,000 military and civilian members and more than 1,000 architect engineer and construction firms. It has a network of eight divisions and 41 subordinate districts, eight major laboratories and research centers, and hundreds of offices at projects throughout the country. Legislation passed in 1990 established environmental protection as one of the primary missions of water resources projects—along with navigation and flood control. In one of the largest restoration projects ever attempted, the Corps and the National Park Service are cooperating on restoring the hydrologic regime for the Everglades in Florida, with funds provided by both agencies.

Recreational Development

The army engineers, as explorers and cartographers for pioneers, were among the first to advocate protection of natural resources, according to Turhollow (n.d.: II-18). Among the first to explore the Yellowstone area, they urged that it be set aside and protected. Eventually the roads they designed, built, and maintained opened the spectacular area to the public. Army engineers along with the U.S. Geological Survey also explored and mapped the Yosemite Valley. After John Muir and other conservationists persuaded Congress in 1890 to declare it a national park under joint control of California and the federal government, the army was asked by the Department of the Interior to take administrative charge of the park until 1911. Besides policing the park, army engineers also laid out trails, produced a map for tourists, and preserved the fauna and flora from destruction by tourists and private owners of land in the park. Army engineer Hiram M. Chitenden, who had helped preserve Yellowstone and published the first book-length study of that area, *Yellowstone National Park*, was selected to oversee the new park. Based on recommendations from Chitenden's commission, the park boundary was established to include 1,200 square miles that became the Yosemite National Park that we know today.

Originally the work of a privately funded organization to honor the memory of the first president, in 1876 Congress assigned the corps the task of reengineering the Washington Monument after technical problems and bankruptcy caused a half-finished eyesore to stand for almost 30 years. The corps, after 12 years of construction, completed the monument with a lightning rod placed on top made of a strange new metal for that time called aluminum. The monument, as part of the National Park System, is the tallest load-bearing masonry structure in the world.

The Federal Water Project Recreation Act of 1965 requires that the planning of all projects by the corps give consideration to the inclusion of facilities for swimming, boating, fishing, camping, and sightseeing wherever appropriate. In developing plans for recreational facilities, the corps seeks the cooperation of all federal and state agencies concerned. In addition, the Corps bears responsibility for the environmental protection of the sources for various recreational activities. The Corps manages 2,500 recreation sites at 456 lakes and reservoirs, and leases and additional 1,800 sites to state, local, and private recreation groups. Corps-operated visitor centers, campgrounds, picnic areas, boat ramps and hiking facilities are available at most projects, and cooperative arrangements exist with many state parks. Fishing, hunting, summer vacation activities, and winter sport activities, such as cross-country skiing, are popular. The Corps estimates that 25 million Americans (one in ten) visit a Corps project at least once a year, and more than 70,000 volunteers assist the Corps in recreation and natural resources management. Since the vast majority of the recreation areas are located next to water, the Corps, in partnership with other agencies, is active in the National Water Safety Program that provides materials to teach and promote water safety.

Bureau of Reclamation

The Bureau of Reclamation (BuREC) is housed in the Department of the Interior, and is best known for the 600 dams, canals, and power plants constructed in the western 17 states. The two most notable projects are the Grand Coulee Dam on the Columbia River and Hoover Dam on the Colorado River. These huge projects and their forerunners made a significant impact on settlement in the West. Chartered in 1902, Reclamation's name comes from its original mission to reclaim the arid lands of the western United States for farming by providing a secure, year-round supply of water for irrigation. Impetus for the great dams came from farmers and townspeople who repaid the costs of construction many times over through production of food, fiber, jobs, energy, and other investments that contributed to America's prosperity.

As the West grew and water resource needs increased, Reclamation's mission expanded as well. In addition to irrigation, its responsibilities include hydroelectric power generation, management of municipal and industrial water supplies, river regulation and flood control, development and management of outdoor recreation, enhancement of fish and wildlife habitats, and research. Headquarters is in Washington, D.C., with seven regional offices located throughout the United States.

Recreational Development

The Bureau of Reclamation (2001: 1-7) provides more than 80 million visitors a year with exciting water-based recreation at more than 300 reservoirs in the 17 western states. Nearly 200 of these recreation areas are managed by non-federal governmental entities, such as state and county parks. Many are managed by other Federal agencies, like the National Park Service and the USDA Forest Service. There are eight National Recreation Areas including Lake Mead and Grand Coulee.

Partnerships have also been developed with organizations such as the Bass Anglers Sportsman's Society, Trout Unlimited, and America Outdoors to sponsor fishing and outdoor events in cooperation with local businesses and community groups. In addition, there are over 200 concession operations that offer facilities and services such as marinas, camp-grounds, swimming beaches, equestrian centers, and golf courses. Fishing and boating are the most popular activities, accounting for more than 27 million user days on about 1.7 million surface acres of water. Many of the facilities are accessible to the disabled.

Reclamation offers guided tours at some of its major structures, such as Hoover Dam near Las Vegas, Nevada, and Grand Coulee Dam near Spokane, Washington. The visitor center at Hoover Dam accommodates more than 1.5 million people a year to tour the dam and the powerplant.

The Tennessee Valley Authority (TVA)

The Tennessee Valley Authority (TVA) is a government-owned corporation created by an act passed May 18, 1933. In the depths of the Great Depression, President Franklin Roosevelt asked Congress to create "a corporation clothed with the power of government but possessed of the flexibility and initiative of a private enter-prise." Today, the TVA is America's largest public power company with 11 fossil plants, 29 hydroelectric dams, three nuclear plants, and four combustion-turbine plants. A system of dams built by the TVA on the Tennessee River and its larger tributaries provides flood regulation and maintains a continuous nine-foot-draft channel for navigation for the length of the main-stream of the 650-mile Tennessee River. The dams harness the power of the rivers to produce electricity and provide other benefits, including potential for outdoor recreation (Henderson, 1991:715).

The TVA conducts a unified program of resource development for growth in the Tennessee Valley region. Technical assis-tance is available in industrial development, regional waste management, trail manage-ment, tourism promotion, community preparedness, and vanpool organization. In cooperation with other agencies, the TVA conducts research and development pro-grams in forestry, fish and game, watershed protection, health services related to the operation, and economic development of Tennessee Valley communities.

Recreational Development

From its beginning, the TVA has worked to encourage development of a wide variety of outdoor recreation facilities in the valley, particularly on TVA lakes and shorelines. To secure the involvement of those most affected, their recreation policy is struc-tured to stimulate, support, and comple-ment the actions of concerned agencies and individuals. This policy includes identifica-tion of recreation resources for develop-ment by other public agencies and private investors, technical assistance to achieve this development, and the provision of basic facilities to assure safe access to the lakes and to protect the shoreline.

Since 1969 the TVA has provided basic recreation improvements including picnic facilities, boat-launching ramps, access roads, and sanitary facilities along many of its reservoir shorelines. By 1978, use of these facilities grew to such an extent that a new policy for facility management was needed. The new policy maintained TVA's long-standing recreational goals—to provide a quality outdoor experience, to encourage state and local government agencies to develop parks and other recre-ation facilities wherever feasible, and to assist in the growth and development of quality private recreational opportunities in the valley. Implementation of specific plans for facilities on reservoir properties began in 1979. They designated certain areas for specific uses such as day use or overnight camping for which a modest fee is charged, and began employing onsite resident caretakers.

One of the most effective ways the TVA supports its recreation commitment is to make suitable portions of its shoreline lands available to others for development. Land and land rights have been trans-ferred or conveyed for a nominal consider-ation to federal, state, and local govern-mental agencies for the development of public parks and access areas. Lands have been leased, licensed, and sold to quasi-public groups and organizations for group camps. With the increased popularity of canoeing, river fishing, hiking, and biking, the TVA is working with various groups to promote protection of streams while providing for their use. Concentrating its trail development on agency lands near population centers and developed recreation clusters, the TVA plans are carried out on a regional basis to assure that trail development meets the larger goals of state and national programs. In addition to these activities on reservoir lands, the TVA has provided a wide range of technical assistance to others to help them improve their own recreational programs.

Large tracts of reservoir shoreline have been set aside for wildlife management, hunting areas, wildlife refuges, and duck and geese feeding areas that are managed by state fish and game agencies and the U.S. Fish and Wildlife Service. Also, over 100,000 acres of reservoir lands have been transferred to the National Park Service and the U.S. D.A. Forest Service, which administer them as natural forest lands.

National Oceanic and Atmospheric Administration

Title III of the Marine Protection, Research and Sanctuaries Act of 1972 authorized the secretary of commerce to designate discrete marine areas of special national significance as national marine sanctuaries to provide comprehensive, protective management of their conservation, recreational, ecological, historical, research, educational, or aesthetic value. The marine sanctuary program is administered by the National Oceanic and Atmospheric Administration (NOAA), an agency of the United States Department of Commerce, through the Sanctuaries and Reserves Division of the Office of Ocean and Coastal Resource Management. Two years after the Act was passed, the nation's first marine sanctuary was designated to preserve the wreckage of the *USS Monitor*, a Civil War ironclad, resting in 240 feet of water off North Carolina, 16 miles off the coast of North Carolina.

Twelve additional marine sanctuaries (as shown in figure 7.14) have been added since the first that encompass deep ocean gardens, nearshore coral reefs, whale migration corridors, deep sea canyons, and even underwater archeological sites. They range in size from one-quarter square mile in Fagatele Bay, American Samoa to over 5,300 square miles in Monterey Bay, California, one of the largest marine protected areas in the world. Together these sanctuaries protect nearly 18,000 square miles of ocean waters and habitats, an area nearly the size of Vermont and New Hampshire combined. While some activities are regulated or prohibited in sanctuaries to protect resources, multiple uses such as recreation, commercial fishing, and shipping, are encouraged in certain areas. Research, educational, and outreach activities are other major components in each sanctuary's program of resource protection (NOAA, 2001:1)

In the Atlantic Ocean, Gray's Reef, Stellwagen Bank, and the Florida Keys National Marine Sanctuaries protect delicate coral reefs and rich fishing grounds, loggerhead turtles and right whales. The Flower Garden Banks is a coral oasis in a sea of oil rigs in the Gulf of Mexico. Thunder Bay, in Michigan, is the first named in the Great Lakes region, and offers a wealth of historic shipwrecks preserved in the cold waters of Lake Huron. On the Pacific Ocean, Cordell Bank, Monterey Bay, Gulf of the Farallones, Olympic Coast, and Washington State National Marine Sanctuaries contribute a rich diversity of marine ecosystems to the system. In the Hawaiian Islands, a sanctuary protects the Humpback Whales along with important breeding grounds of these vulnerable cetaceans. And the marine sanctuary farthest from the U.S. mainland is Fagatale Bay, American Samoa in a fringing coral reef nestled within an eroded volcanic crater (NOAA, 2001:1).

These national marine sanctuaries are the aquatic counterpart of our national parks—the unique areas are meant to be managed for the long-term benefit and enjoyment of the public. Specifically, resources are to be protected, the public is to be given a better awareness of the marine environment, and scientific research and ecological monitoring are to be encouraged. Some traditional commercial

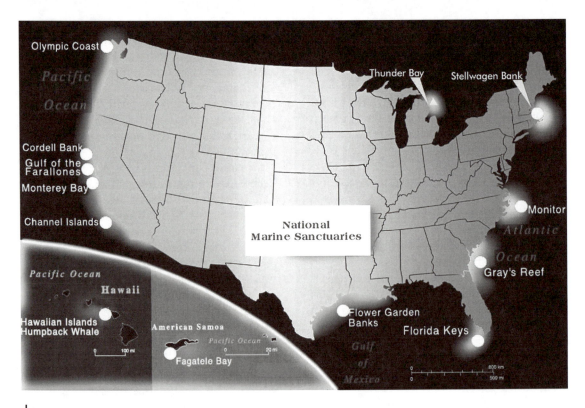

Figure 7.14 The National Marine Sanctuary System. Source: Adapted from National Oceanic and Atmospheric Administration *(www.sanctuaries.nos.noaa.gov)*, 2001.

activities, which are mostly banned in national parks, are allowed in national marine sanctuaries as long as they do not undermine the fundamental health and integrity of the area (NOAA, 2001:1).

For instance, integrity of the ecosystem was of major concern when the Florida Keys National Marine Sanctuary was designated. Encompassing approximately 2,600 square nautical miles, it extends 220 miles in a northeast to southwest arc between the southern tip of Key Biscayne, to beyond, but not including, the Dry Tortugas Islands. This immense sanctuary was established to stem mounting threats to the health and ecological future of the coral reef ecosystem. Major issues facing the sanctuary include declines in healthy corals brought on by an increase in coral disease and coral bleaching, invasion of algae in seagrass beds and coral reefs, overfishing, reduced freshwater inflow from Florida Bay, and damage to coral from

careless boaters, snorkelers, divers and occasional large ship groundings (NOAA, 2001:1). Threats to the coral reef are discussed in Chapter 16, The Environment.

The National Marine Fisheries Service

The National Marine Fisheries Service (NMFS), is the federal service that manages the sea's living resources between three and 200 miles off the U.S. coast. Organized in 1970, the NMFS is composed of headquarters offices, five regional offices, and four regional fisheries. It administers federal regulations designed to assure that fishing practices remain within sound biological and economic limitations and that U.S. commercial and recreational anglers have the opportunity to harvest resources within these limitations. The service regulates foreign fishing in the U.S. Exclusive Economic Zone (EEZ). It also protects marine habitats and marine animals such as the great whales, porpoises, and sea turtles. The NMFS shares with the U.S. Fish and Wildlife Service the administration of the Marine Mammal Protection Act, which protects marine mammals. In addition the NMFS collects data on commercial and recreational catch. In the Marine Recreational Fisheries Statistics —Executive Order 12962,—President Clinton required federal agencies, in cooperation with States and Tribes, to work together to improve the quantity, function, sustainable productivity, and distribution of U.S. aquatic resources for increased recreational fishing opportunities.

Recreational Development

The NMFS (2000:1) Office of Intergovernmental and Recreational Fisheries is committed to the promotion of increased opportunities for marine recreational fishing. They also provide a forum at the national level for interaction with the marine recreational fishing community and other agencies involved in marine recreational fisheries issues, working to provide for increased marine recreational fishing opportunities. Recognizing that fishery resources and aquatic ecosystems are integral components of the country's heritage and play an important role in the nation's social, cultural, and economic well-being (DOI, 1996: 27978), NMFS is increasingly engaged in the rebuild and conservation of marine fishery resources and habitats.

Since 1979 NMFS has conducted the annual Marine Recreational Fisheries Statistics Survey to provide a reliable database for estimating the impact of recreational fishing on marine resources. This impact can be quite large for many recreationally fished species. In 1997, anglers took nearly 68 million marine fishing trips to the Atlantic, Gulf, and Pacific coasts, and the estimated marine recreational finfish catch was 366 million fish, more than 50% of which was released alive. Some of these fisheries with high sport harvest include bluefish, red drum, striped bass, Spanish mackerel, spotted seatrout, summer flounder, and winter flounder. The research center reviews, evaluates, and, as needed, upgrades its stock assessment capabilities to ensure that assessments for species of recreational importance, and for forage species upon which these fish depend, are provided.

Developed in cooperation with a wide range of constituent groups, NMFS (2000:1) *"Code of Angling Ethics"*, was published in the Federal Register. The development of the angling code represents just one of the steps taken by the NMFS to foster sound resource management attitudes and actions among recreationists.

Public/Private Federal Programs

Two public/private partnership arrangements, Scenic Byways and Watchable Wildlife, have emerged as major trends in outdoor recreation. Although driving for pleasure and watching wildlife both have long traditions in America, these two formal federal programs to designate national level opportunities took hold in the 1990s (Betz, English & Cordell, 1999:94).

Scenic Byways

The U.S. Department of Transportation Federal Highway Administration manages the 82-unit National Scenic Byways Program. This program is the result of the Intermodal Surface Transportation Efficiency Act of 1991 referred to as ISTEA. The legislation charged the secretary of transportation with developing criteria for designations of roads that have outstanding scenic, historic, recreational, cultural, natural, and/or archaeological qualities as either "National Scenic Byways" or "All American Roads." To be designated a national scenic byway, a road must meet the criteria for at least one of the six intrinsic qualities. Examples of national scenic byways are the Merritt Parkway in Connecticut, the Coal Heritage Trail in West Virginia, the Gold Belt Tour in Colorado, and the Outback Scenic Byway and the McKenzie Pass-Santiam Pass in Oregon. All American Roads must meet the criteria for multiple intrinsic qualities and these routes are destinations unto them-

Passing through Yosemite National Park, the Tioga Road/Big Oak Flat Road, designated an All-American Road by the secretary of the Department of Transportation, offers one of the most spectacular passages over the Sierra Nevada.

selves that attract national and international visitors. Examples of All American Roads are the Big Sur in California, the Blue Ridge Parkway in North Carolina, the Historic Columbia River Highway in Oregon, and the San Juan Skyway in Colorado.

The Department of Transportation nomination process allows state designated byways and federal agency byways to be nominated for the National Scenic Byway program, and participation in the program is purely voluntary. As a result, several of the national scenic byways and All American Roads are also roads that have been designated by the Department of Agriculture Forest Service's 133-unit National Forest Scenic Byway Program that began in 1988. West Virginia's Highland Scenic Byway, South Dakota's Peter Norbeck Scenic Byway and Colorado's Grand Mesa Scenic and Historic Byway have this dual

designation as national scenic byways and Forest Service scenic byways. The Forest Service emphasis is on showcasing roads with outstanding scenic vistas. National Scenic byways may also be a part of the Bureau of Land Management's 64-unit Back Country Byways Program that started in 1989. The goal of this program is to provide visitors with the opportunity to explore some of the BLM's less accessible unique and scenic lands. Most of the National Scenic Byways and All American Roads hold dual status as a State Scenic Byway. There are 35 states plus the District of Columbia that have Scenic Byway Programs (Tannen, 1999:92).

Watchable Wildlife

The Watchable Wildlife program provides a framework for federal, state, and private conservation groups to coordinate their numerous wildlife-viewing programs. In

1990 a formal Memorandum of Understanding (MOU) was signed by the federal participants at the time, including the Bureau of Land Management, the Fish and Wildlife Service, and the USDA Forest Service. A wide variety of facilities and activities fall under the umbrella of the program: observing wildlife of all kinds including fish, birds, and animals; viewing insects and flowers; general nature study; butterfly gardens; visitor center interpretive displays; aquariums; and fish hatcheries (Anderson, 1999:99).

The Forest Service started its own wildlife-watching program in 1988 and has been the driving force behind the development of the national collaborative effort. Current federal participants are the BLM, Bureau of Reclamation, Department of the Air Force, Department of the Navy, National Park Service, Forest Service and the Fish and Wildlife Service. Conservation groups include the American Birding Association, Defender of Wildlife, Ducks Unlimited, Humane Society, International Association of Fish and Wildlife Agencies, National Fish and Wildlife Foundation, Izaak Walton League of America, and Wildlife Forever. They work together as a coalition to meet the high level of keen interest in wildlife-associated recreation. There is now a network of viewing sites, a uniform viewing site signing system, a series of 34 viewing guide books, and a public awareness and support program. The binocular logo designates nearby wildlife viewing areas on federal highway signs across the country (Anderson, 1999:98-99).

SUMMARY

The U.S. government plays a crucial role in outdoor recreation in America and still holds one-third of the land in this country, that is, in excess of 700 million acres of a total two billion acres. Two of the federal agencies, the United States Forest Service and the National Park Service, that provide numerous resources and varied programs for the nature aficionado are presented in detail. The historical development of these agencies and the extent of their offerings are covered. Attention is given to the provision of wilderness areas on federal land. The idea of preserving areas in their pristine condition has been gaining support, and a number of federal acts were passed underscoring the importance of these areas to the American people. Accordingly a number of systems are now provided for the enjoyment of the recreationist, for example, the Wild and Scenic Rivers System and the National Trails System. Numerous federal agencies are involved in the offerings of outdoor pursuits. Among these are the Bureau of Land Management, which offers the recently named National Conservation Lands System, the U.S. Fish and Wildlife Service, the U.S. Army Corps of Engineers, the Bureau of Land Reclamation, the Tennessee Valley Authority, the National Oceanic and Atmospheric Administration with its national marine sanctuary program, and the National Marine Fisheries Service. Two public/private partnerships are presented: The Department of Transportation administered National Scenic Byway Program and the Forest Service-led Watchable Wildlife Program.

REFERENCES

Anderson, K. (1999). Watchable wildlife. In H. K. Cordell, *Outdoor recreation in American life: A national assessment of demand and supply trends*. Champaign, IL: Sagamore Publishing, Inc.

Betz, C., English, D., & Cordell, H. K. (1999). Outdoor recreation resources. In H. K. Cordell, *Outdoor recreation in American life: A national assessment of demand and supply trends*. Champaign, IL: Sagamore Publishing, Inc.

Browning, J., Hendee, J., & Roggenbuck, J. (1988). *Wilderness laws: Milestones and management direction in wilderness legislation, 1964-1987*. Bulletin No. 5. Moscow, ID: University of Idaho.

Bureau of Land Management. (2001). *Facts and history of the BLM.* [On-line]. Available: http://www.blm.gov/nhp/facts

Bureau of Indian Affairs, U.S. Department of the Interior. (1987): *American Indians today.* Washington, D.C.: U.S. Government Printing Office.

Bureau of Reclamation. (2001). *Recreation.* [On-line]. Available: http://www.usbr.gov/main/programs/ recreation.html

Coral Reef Coalition (No Date) *Inside the new Florida Keys National Marine Sanctuary.*

Cordell, H. K. (1999). *Outdoor recreation in American life: A national assessment of demand and supply trends.* Champaign, IL: Sagamore Publishing, Inc.

Cordell, H., Bergstrom, J., Hartmenn, L., & English, D. (1990). *An analysis of the outdoor recreation and wilderness situation in the United States: 1989-2040.* Fort Collins, CO: United States Department of Agriculture Forest Service General Technical Report RM-189.

Cordes, K., & J. Lammers. (photography) (1999). *America's national historic trails.* Norman: University of Oklahoma Press.

Cordes, K., & J. Lammers. (photography) (2001). *America's national scenic trails.* Norman: University of Oklahoma Press.

Cordes, K., & Lammers, J. (2002). America's Millenium Trails Pathways for the 21st Century. Reston: AALR/AAPHERD.

Craig, B. (1991, May/June). Diamonds and rust. *National Parks, 65*(6).

Department of the Interior. (1996, June). Notice of policy for conserving species listed or proposed for listing under the Endangered Species Act while providing and enhancing recreational fisheries opportunities. *The Federal Register, 61*(107), 27978.

Fish and Wildlife Service. (2000). *America's national wildlife refuge system: A century of conservation.* U.S. Department of the Interior.

Forest Service, U.S. Department of Agriculture. (2001). *National forest visitor use monitoring project national and regional project results May 2001.* [On-line]. Available: http://www.fs.fed.us/recreation/recuse/reports/year1/National_Report_Yr1.html

Forest Service, U.S. Department of Agriculture. (2000). *Draft USDA Forest Service strategic plan.* Washington, D.C.: U.S. Government Printing Office.

Forest Service, U.S. Department of Agriculture. (2000). *The recreation agenda.* Washington, D.C.: U.S. Government Printing Office, FS-691.

Forest Service, U.S. Department of Agriculture. (1988*). The national forests: America's great outdoors national recreation strategy.* Washington, D.C.: U.S. Government Printing Office.

Forest Service, U.S. Department of Agriculture. (1990). *Report of the Forest Service fiscal year 1989.* Washington, D.C.: U.S. Government Printing Office.

Harvey, T., & Henley, S. (1989). *The status of trails in national forests, national parks, and Bureau of Land Management areas.* Washington, D.C.: The American Hiking Society.

Hendee, J., Stankey, G., & Lucas, R. (1978). *Wilderness management.* Forest Service, U.S. Department of Agriculture. Washington, D.C.: U.S. Government Printing Office.

Henderson, G. (Ed.). (1991). *"TVA" in The U.S. Government manual (1990-1991).* Tanham, MD: Beman Press.

Jensen, C. (1985). *Outdoor recreation in America.* Minneapolis, MN: Burgess.

Knudson. D. (1984). *Outdoor recreation.* New York: Macmillan.

Mackintosh, B. (Sontag, B. Ed.). (1990). Parks and people*: Preserving our past for the future National Park Service the first 75 years.* Fort Washington, PA: Eastern National Park & Monument Association.

Madison, M. (2001). *At the forefront of conservation: A history of the U.S. Fish and Wildlife Service in conserving our nations resources.* U.S. Fish and Wildlife Service, [On-line]. Available: http://training.fws.gov/history/

Meier, J. (1997, October). Protecting our public estate. *JOPERD, 68*(8), 35-38.

National Marine Fisheries Service. (2000, July). *Recreational Fisheries.* [On-line]. Available: http://www.nmfs.noaa.gov/irf/ethics.html,www.st.nmfs.gov/st1/recreational/executive_order.html

National Oceanic and Atmospheric Administration. (2001). *The national marine sanctuaries.* [On-line]. Available: http://www.sanctuaries.nos.noaa.gov/

National Park Service, U.S. Department of the Interior. (2000). *The National Parks: Index 1999.* Washington, D.C.: U.S. Government Printing Office.

National Park System Advisory Board. (2001). *Rethinking the National Parks for the 21st century.* [On-line]. Available: http://www.nps.gov/policy/report.htm

National Park Service et al. (2001). *National recreation trails caring for America's community of trails.* [On-line]. Available: http://www.americantrails.org/nationalrecreationtrails

Ridenour, J. (1991, May/June). Building on a legacy. *National Parks, 65(5-6).*

Runte, A. (1987). *National parks: The American experience.* Lincoln, NE: University of Nebraska Press.

Tannen, J. W. (1999). Scenic byways. In H. K. Cordel *(Ed.), Outdoor recreation in American life: A National assessment of demand and supply trends.* Champaign, IL: Sagamore Publishing, Inc.

Tennessee Valley Authority. (1984). *Recreation on TVA lakes.* Knoxville, TN.

Tilden, F. (1959). *The national parks: What they mean to me.* New York: Alfred A. Knopf.

Turhollow, A. (undated*). Do you know?* Los Angeles: U.S. Army Corp of Engineers.

Tweed, W. (1980). *Recreation site planning and improvement in national forests 1891-1942.* U.S. Department of Agriculture. Washington, D.C.: U.S. Government Printing Office.

U.S. Army Corps of Engineers. (2001). *Services for the public,* September 12, 2001. [On-line]. Available: http://www.usace.army.mil/public.html#Civil

United States Commission on Civil Rights. (1973, March). *Staff memorandum: Constitutional States of American Indians.* Washington, D.C..

Wellman, J. (1987). *Midland recreation policy.* New York: John Wiley and Sons.

Wilderness. (2001). *Land management agencies.* November 6, 2001, [On-line]. Available: http://www.wilderness.net

8 STATE RESOURCES AND RECREATION

Prior to the establishment of the United States of America, the Massachusetts Bay Colony set aside 90,000 acres for fishing and fowling. The *Great Ponds Act* of 1641 protected about 2,000 sites of freshwater bodies, each 10 acres or more in size. The hunting and fishing that took place at these ponds were for survival, not recreational, purposes. Nonetheless, the Great Ponds Act could be looked upon as the genesis of state involvement in preserving natural resources (Foss, 1968:223).

After independence and the establishment of the United States, the federal government in 1832 granted the territorial governor of the Arkansas Territory the right to hold the Arkansas Hot Springs and Washita River Salt Springs from private ownership. The governor had the right to lease these areas, which were considered valuable because of their healing power (Fazio, 1979:214). Arkansas Hot Springs was taken back by the federal government and made into a national park in 1921 in a manner similar to what happened to the Yosemite Valley, which was granted to California in 1864 but was taken back to eventually become the nation's second national park in 1875. These actions by the states and the federal government were not intended to enhance recreational opportunities, but rather to preserve some of the nation's natural resources.

Fazio (1979:214) credits the state of New York with the earliest significant, lasting contributions to state action concerning recreational resources. Its action came as a response to the deplorable conditions and uncontrollable commercial development of the areas surrounding Niagara Falls, which led Frederick Olmsted to decry the loss of beauty around the falls. In 1885 the U.S. Congress placed these areas under the care of the state of New York as the New York State Reservation of Niagara. Conditions at Niagara may have improved slightly after that. According to Knudson (1984:86), "It was difficult to see the falls because of all the hucksters and makeshift commercial shops that lined the sides of the scenic wonder."

At the time Niagara was put under its care, New York was considering the creation of another open-space area, the Adirondack Wilderness. A total of 715,000 acres of lakes and mountains were dedicated as the state's "Forest Preserve." Although it was the fear of water shortage that prompted the action initially, Nash (1967:118) argues that recreational rationale had finally achieved legal recognition when the Adirondack and Catskill regions became "forever wild" as stipulated in the New York state constitution.

State park legislation increased at the turn of the century. Minnesota developed Itasca State Park when it received a federal grant to protect the headwaters of the Mississippi River. Illinois initiated the nation's first state agency for state parks in 1903. Its first park was Fort Massac, which led to the establishment of the state's park system.

Stephen Mather, director of the National Park Service since 1916, became interested in helping states develop their own systems of parks. He organized the first National Conference on State Parks in Des Moines, Iowa, in 1921. At that time only 19 states had state park systems or similar arrangements, such as state forests and preserves. The National Conference on State Parks became a permanent organization known today as the National Society for Park Resources, an affiliate of the National Recreation and Park Association.

The Depression years brought about greater cooperation between the states and the federal government. The Park, Parkway and Recreational Area Study Act of 1936 produced numerous inventories, which were developed by NPS personnel on states' situations. The states became aware of their needs for natural resources. Two more acts helped the states acquire more natural resources, the Surplus Property Act of 1944 and the Recreation and Public Purposes Act of 1954. And with the passage of the Land and Water Conservation Act of 1965, the states were able not only to acquire lands but also to receive technical assistance in expanding their natural resources.

In general, state-run recreational areas have become important features in outdoor recreation. Studies that were conducted over the past three decades show that these areas make significant contributions to the local economies. This despite the fact that visitor days are much fewer than the ones at national areas (Donnelly, et al., 1998).

THE STATE AND OUTDOOR RECREATION

The Tenth Amendment to the Constitution of the United States (also known as "the states' rights"), which passed in 1923, clarified the role of the state vis-à-vis the role of the federal government in providing services to its residents. The amendment specifies that "the powers not delegated to the United States by the Constitution, not prohibited by it to the states, are reserved to the states respectively, or to the people." The Tenth Amendment became the authority by which state governments began to provide services that had been provided by private agencies. The earlier services included education, health, and welfare. Eventually recreation became a recognized function of state government.

In the Third Nationwide Outdoor Recreation Plan (Heritage, 1979:74-75), the state is described as having several unique powers that give it a dominant role in providing recreation service, as follows:

1. The state has a repository of police powers for land use control, which is the basic tool for land preservation or designation for recreation.
2. The state can finance recreation through bond issues, special taxes, and fees. It is also responsible for the administration of the monies allocated to local authorities for recreation through the Land and Water Conservation Fund. The enactment of these funds requires a Statewide Comprehensive Outdoor Recreation Plan (SCORP), which makes it clear that the state could play an important role in outdoor recreation.

According to the Plan (Heritage, 1979) public visitations to outdoor recreation areas managed by the state increased drastically from the 1960s to the 1970s. From the inception of the Land and Water Conservation Fund in 1965 until the year 1978, close to $2 billion have been given, on a matching basis, to state and local governments. This means that close to $3.9 billion were spent in 14 years to enhance outdoor recreation opportunities on state and local natural resources. About 1.77 million acres of new recreation land were acquired nationwide during this time.

During the period from 1965 to 1978, approximately 22,000 different recreation units were assisted through the Land and Water Conservation Fund. The units ranged from small neighborhood parks to large regional or state recreation areas. Local projects utilized 58 percent of funding and accounted for 16,779 projects and 312,000 acres. The states utilized the remaining 42 percent of funding and accounted for 5,272 projects and 1.46 million acres. The states provided guidance and technical assistance to the local authorities in their quest for enhancing recreation services.

Today the states own millions of acres of land and water that are used, or have the potential to be used, for outdoor recreation. Table 8.1 shows the classification of state lands.

According to the Heritage Conservation and Recreation Service, the 13 western states have the most state-owned acreage, and the 12 southern states the least, as shown in Table 8.2. Alaska and California have the most acreage in state parks, Washington and Minnesota in state forests, and Mississippi and Pennsylvania in state fish and wildlife areas.

Table 8.1 State Land Classification

MSE Classification	Acreage *
Parks	7,989,950
Recreation Areas	1,420,014
Forests	1,343,812
Natural Areas	1,270,247
Fish and Wildlife Areas	161,479
Historic Sites	84,325
Education Areas	31,218
Scientific Areas	10,160
Misc.	495,989
Total	12,807,194

*Does not include unclassified lands.
Source: National Association of State Park Directors. **The 2001 Annual Information Exchange**, Tucson, AZ: NASPD.

Table 8.2 State-Owned Land Distribution by Region

Region	Total State-Owned Land (Acres)	Percent of State-Owned Land	Percent of U.S. Population in Region
West	51,225,102	65%	17%
North Central	12,492,490	16%	28%
Northeast	9,524,583	12%	24%
South	4,595,583	6%	31%

Source: Heritage Conservation and Recreation Service, *The Third Nationwide Outdoor Recreation Plan* (Washington, D.C.: U.S. Government Printing Office, 1979), 75.

Baxter State Park in Maine presents a tranquil view of Katahdin from the banks of Daicey Pond. The mountain, named by the Penobscot Indians, is the crown jewel of the park and the northern terminus of the Appalachian Trail.

State Functions and Recreation

Today most of the 50 states see recreation as an important service to be provided for their residents. Although there is no universal agreement as to what constitutes a good package in leisure and recreation services to be offered, facilitated, or enhanced by the state government, the following eight functions are considered sufficient by MacLean et al. (1985:104-106):

1. **Enactment of Permissive Legislation** Permissive legislation refers to state laws that allow local public bodies to finance and operate services. Certain qualification of personnel involved in the service may be required. Education, health, welfare, as well as recreation are enacted by local authorities according to permissive legislation. The first enabling act in

recreation was passed in 1919 in New Jersey. Today all states have such acts.

2. **Service to Local Recreation Authorities** Many states have established offices or departments of recreation, one function of which is to assist the local authority in providing adequate service to the local residents. Assistance could come in many ways, among which are studying needs, providing information, conducting programs, conducting in-service training, developing standards, allocating grants-in-aid, and coordinating and monitoring federally funded programs.

3. **Provision of Areas, Facilities, and Programs** Although the acreage of the lands provided for recreation by

the state is dwarfed by the acreage of the lands provided by the federal government, the state lands' proximity to population centers makes them more accessible. The total acreage of state lands available for recreation is approximately six percent of the amount of federal lands available for the same purpose. On state lands the states have developed roads, trails, swimming pools, beaches, picnic grounds, playgrounds, and campgrounds. In addition, recreation is offered in state-run institutions such as hospitals, prisons, colleges, and universities.

4. **Management of Plants and Wildlife** The propagation, distribution, and protection of living plant or animal, fall under the joint concern of the state and federal governments. The latter is concerned with wildlife that crosses state and international boundaries, such as migratory birds. Within its boundaries, each state manages plants and wildlife through a number of activities such as reforestation; protection of rare trees, plants, flowers, and endangered species; setting aside of reserves; improvement of wildlife habitat; and regulation of hunting and fishing.

5. **Research and Education** Most of the above functions require the backing of research. In many instances, research units are established within the concerned department. Social research is conducted in relationship to the use and the need for areas, facilities, and programs. Scientific research is conducted in relationship to the management of plants and wildlife. Recreation education is provided by the state in a

number of ways: education that prepares a recreation professional is offered through the state colleges and universities; recreation education for the layperson is offered through publications, films, videos, exhibits, and lectures; and in media education that could be provided by the state department of parks and recreation directly or through assistance given by the state to local recreation authorities.

6. **Promotion of Tourism** Tourism has become a leading business for some states, which, along with many other states, are waging campaigns to attract tourists. Special efforts are exerted to provide the tourist with the necessary conveniences in improved roads, adequate accommodations, and necessary services.

7. **Standards and Regulations** The state endeavors to protect both the recreationists and the resource through standards and regulations. The recreationist is protected through safety and health standards and regulations that are observed in beaches, camps, resorts, restaurants, and swimming pools. The resource is protected through inspection, licenses, and permits.

8. **Cooperation with Federal Agencies** As previously stated, there are a number of federal laws pertaining to recreation in the natural environment that have some bearing on state and local offerings either directly or indirectly. Cooperation with federal agencies, as has been shown, enables all fifty states to expand their recreation resources, facilities, and programs. Moreover, since most states have counterparts to federal agencies,

it makes sense that agencies of the same orientation should cooperate and coordinate their efforts in achieving what seems to be similar goals. For instance, the National Park Service and the state park department, also the U.S. Forest Service and the state forestry service, should enhance their offerings through cooperation and coordination.

State Recreation Services

The states have become increasingly involved in providing recreation services. Although the structures through which these recreational services are provided may vary, the services themselves are similar.

State Recreation Commissions/Boards

Thirty-four of the 50 United States have commissions or boards to monitor and promote the recreation offering by the state.

State Department of Parks and Recreation

Not all states will have a department entitled as such, but all have an agency that serves as a liaison for recreation. This service is required in the administration of the Land and Water Conservation Act funds provided by the 1965 act, which led to the next service.

State Outdoor Recreation Plan

In order to become eligible for federal money from Land and Water Conservation Act the state is required to designate an agency to handle the funds, to prepare an outdoor recreation plan, and to develop a procedure for raising matching funds required of the local community, This requirement led to an increase in the number of park and recreation commissions/boards on both the local and state levels. It also made each state take a serious look at its natural resources.

State Recreation Resources

Most of state recreation lands, whether they are forests or parks, were originally acquired as gifts, tax-delinquent lands, original holdings since colonial time, or federal land turned over to the states. As the demand for recreation increased after World War II, states began to purchase lands using bonds or earmarked taxes. While the bonds were the main sources for acquiring lands, special taxes on cigarettes and gasoline were also used for that purpose.

Some federal laws made acquisition of recreation lands easier on most states by applying the concept of matching funds. The first of these laws was the Pittman-Robertson Act of 1937, which allowed federal funds to be used in wildlife management. In 1950, the Dingell-Johnson Act was used to improve fisheries. But it was the Land and Water Conservation Act of 1965 that allowed for matching funds to be used for the acquisition of lands for recreation and as open space.

Today state resources that can be used for outdoor recreation are classified into many categories, such as, parks, recreation areas, forests, natural areas, fish and wildlife areas, historic sites, educational areas, scientific areas, and others. Table 8.1 shows the acreage of state lands, including land that are used for recreation.

STATE PARKS

The impetus for establishing state parks which resulted in the First National Conference in Des Moines, Iowa, in 1921 was provided by the desire of members of the federal government to get the states to develop their own systems. The two criteria for park site selection suggested then by Richard Leiber, a leader in that movement, were scenic value and/or historical significance. Yet the state park was, in fact, dedicated to the public for the intelligent use of its leisure time (Knudson, 1984:197).

Today all 50 states have some form of state park, although the parks vary in number, size, and administrative affiliation. They range in type from highly developed, with lodges and marinas, to completely primitive, without roads or signs. The numbers and sizes of parks are so disproportionately distributed that 53 percent of state park lands are in only three states: Alaska, California, and New York. New York's Adirondack State Park is the largest state park in the United States with its six million acres. Most state parks are of medium size and are close enough to population centers for the citizens' enjoyment of outdoor activities such as boating, camping, and hiking along with the organized activities of golf and tennis. While New York has the largest acreage of state parks, located mainly in the Adirondacks, California has over one million acres of state park land and Alaska has a little less than one million acres.

The organizational structures under which these parks are administered vary according to each state's administrative setup. While the State Park Department oversees the state parks in Arizona, Georgia, Idaho, and Kentucky, the Department of Conservation oversees them in Alabama, Illinois, Iowa, and New York. The Department of Natural Resources manages the state parks in Alaska, California, Hawaii, Indiana, Michigan, and Utah. In Arkansas and South Carolina state parks are charged to the Tourism Division. In some states, the state parks are administered by the highway department.

STATE FORESTS

Of the 50 states, only four do not have state forests: Kansas, Nebraska, Oklahoma, and Texas (Knudson, 1984:192). According to Jensen (1985:125), state forests are better developed in the eastern, southern, and mid-western states where the forests are of high quality. The forests in the plains states and western states are of poor quality and are less developed.

When state forests were acquired, the major thrust was to protect the land from erosion, to develop areas for timber, and to provide experimental and demonstration areas. Recreation as such was not considered until after World War II. Today out-door recreation is an acceptable activity in most state forests. Although many specific areas have been designated for recreation, attempts are made to keep these areas as primitive as possible while still providing comfortable accommodations and, in many instances, interpretive service.

The activities that take place in state forests typically include, but are not limited to, boating, camping, fishing, horseback riding, hunting, nature study, and picnicking. Campsites, with or without modern conveniences, are provided in many of the nation's state forests.

NATURE PRESERVES

Among the many nonprofit organizations that promote the enjoyment of the aesthetic aspects of outdoor recreation (such as the National Wildlife Federation, the National Park and Conservation Association, the Izaak Walton League, the Audubon Society, and the Sierra Club), the Nature Conservancy is unique in that it directs its efforts to acquiring and preserving land. The Conservancy buys endangered natural areas and turns them over to other agencies for protection and management. Its Heritage Program is conducted in cooperation with state governments in identifying, locating, and inventorying natural areas, endangered species, and unusual physical phenomena, which could become the basis for acquisition.

Many states have followed the concept of preserving lands that have outstanding natural significance. According to Knudson (1984:195), Illinois' efforts in this direction started as early as 1858. Cook County, Illinois, has more dedicated natural areas—areas to be preserved for posterity—than any other county in the state. They are not all administered by one agency; some are still held privately or run by industry.

FISH AND WILDLIFE AREAS

Each of the 50 states has a department charged with the management of fish and

Table 8.3 Total Acreage of Outdoor Resources in the Fifty States

State	Number	Total Area Number Operating	Acreage	State	Number	Total Area Number Operating	Acreage
Alabama	24	24	49,710	Montana	365	365	64,916
Alaska	139	136	3,291,209	Nebraska	85	84	133,044
Arizona	30	28	58,528	Nevada	24	24	132,885
Arkansas	51	49	50,945	New Hampshire	84	84	74,471
California	266	266	1,412,825	New Jersey	115	115	345,425
Colorado	126	104	347,176	New Mexico	31	31	90,693
Connecticut	130	130	182,993	New York	661	238	1,015,911
Delaware	25	23	21,142	North Carolina	57	38	159,028
Florida	148	148	547,020	North Dakota	31	28	20,046
Georgia	66	62	75,712	Ohio	73	73	205,047
Hawaii	62	59	26,689	Oklahoma	51	51	71,586
Idaho	28	26	43,456	Oregon	230	179	94,869
Illinois	308	308	304,879	Pennsylvania	118	111	288,486
Indiana	33	32	178,315	Rhode Island	74	62	8,748
Iowa	174	174	63,171	South Carolina	55	52	80,459
Kansas	24	24	32,300	South Dakota	94	94	97,637
Kentucky	49	49	43,508	Tennessee	54	54	141,247
Louisiana	56	33	36,099	Texas	123	118	631,018
Maine	126	96	94,970	Utah	54	53	113,592
Maryland	74	61	258,621	Vermont	66	54	84,007
Massachusetts	236	210	288,801	Virginia	70	70	72,998
Michigan	99	96	351,223	Washington	255	125	258,502
Minnesota	81	78	255,793	West Virginia	47	47	195,565
Mississippi	28	28	24,287	Wisconsin	65	58	129,353
Missouri	81	77	137,120	Wyoming	36	35	121,170
Total			8,176,492				4,630,703

| Grand Total | | | | | | | 12,807,195 |

Source: National Association of State Park Directors. Annual Exchange Information (Tucson, AZ, 2001).

wildlife or a division in an agency for the same purpose. The responsibilities of such a department or agency are to propagate fish and wildlife, to distribute game animals, game birds, and game fish, and to manage fisheries and refuges. In the areas administered by such a department or agency, fishing, hunting, and trapping take place according to the state laws and regulation and with the licensing obtained from the department or agency.

According to Knudson (1984:196), wildlife management by regulation began during the colonial period. In fact, bounty was imposed on some wildlife. By the mid 1800s the concept of seasons was used to protect big game animals as land clearing and wetland drainage were threatening many habitats. Still, human population expansion continued to threaten many wildlife species. It was not until the opening years of the twentieth century that recreational hunters and fishermen set aside refuges and preserves for exotic and threatened species.

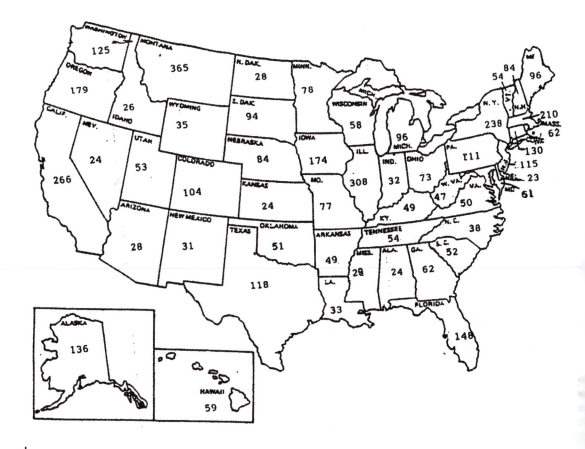

Figure 8.1 Operational recreational areas in the 50 states.

Despite, or maybe because of, the primitive nature of wildlife and fish areas, recreation has become popular there. While fishing and hunting are on top of the list of activities that take place in wildlife and fish areas, other outdoor recreation activities are observed there also; in fact, camping, hiking, nature study, and picnicking are more popular because their seasons are longer when compared to the fishing and hunting seasons. Interpretive services are also provided in many of these areas along with facilities for observation of wildlife.

REGIONAL DIFFERENCES

The National Association of State Park Directors publishes an Annual Information Exchange, the latest of which was published in March of 2001. The data collected by the Association detailing the total acreage of outdoor resources in each of the fifty states is shown in Table 8.3. According to Chubb and Chubb (1981), there are regional differences not only in the number of units but also in their characteristics. The Pacific Region of the United States (Alaska, California, Hawaii, Oregon, and Washington) is the leading region, accounting for approximately 20 percent of the total state park acreage. The Middle Atlantic Region, another leading region, accounts for 11 percent of the total state park acreage. That region includes New York, Pennsylvania, and Rhode Island. The South Central Region (Arkansas, Louisiana, Oklahoma, and Texas) has the least acreage in state parks, approximately 2.5 percent of the national total.

The degree of development varies from state to state and park to park, as do the types of activities that take place in each park. Some parks adhere to the original

Table 8.4 Parks Share of State Expenditures.

State	Total State Expenditures	Share of State Budget State Park Operating Budget	% of state budget
Alabama	7,365,418,835	29,868,208	0.41%
Alaska	3,593,500,000	5,333,179	0.15%
Arizona	14,205,636,100	15,754,037	0.11%
Arkansas	9,156,700,000	28,313,209	0.31%
California	31,258,532,000	232,978,000	0.75%
Colorado	11,119,128,930	21,166,283	0.19%
Connecticut	11,619,000,000	11,523,000	0.10%
Delaware	2,736,700,500	19,259,122	0.70%
Florida	50,053,100,000	63,197,806	0.13%
Georgia	13,291,103,880	47,268,910	0.36%
Hawaii	6,399,441,267	6,786,678	0.11%
Idaho	3,401,918,000	8,261,139	0.24%
Illinois	45,718,506,700	44,626,200	0.10%
Indiana	15,793,851,999	40,889,680	0.26%
Iowa	4,391,000,000	10,548,000	0.24%
Kansas	9,545,900,000	7,208,525	0.08%
Kentucky	13,918,692,491	75,712,755	0.54%
Louisiana	13,932,202,998	15,047,370	0.11%
Maine	2,316,629,198	6,724,035	0.24%
Maryland	18,772,654,516	35,673,815	0.19%
Massachusetts	19,963,655,760	32,068,230	0.16%
Michigan	25,638,598,326	51,187,945	0.20%
Minnesota	19,044,000,000	24,763,000	0.13%
Mississippi	2,956,162,418	18,747,581	0.63%
Missouri	16,247,673,866	31,657,988	0.19%
Montana	2,800,000,000	5,822,947	0.21%
Nebraska	4,500,000,000	18,081,216	0.40%
Nevada	1,570,379,711	7,956,039	0.51%
New Hampshire	2,724,342,544	7,489,150	0.27%
New Jersey	19,514,382,000	34,650,000	0.18%
New Mexico	7,800,000,000	15,740,700	0.20%
New York	72,656,000,000	141,431,700	0.19%
North Carolina	24,290,400,000	22,635,280	0.09%
North Dakota	2,163,190,606	2,319,182	0.11%
Ohio	38,736,405,256	65,892,085	0.17%
Oklahoma	20,010,523,487	43,830,890	0.22%
Oregon	14,196,864,000	35,124,582	0.25%
Pennsylvania	38,500,000,000	67,097,000	0.17%
Rhode Island	4,276,346,624	4,572,539	0.11%
South Carolina	13,004,130,657	25,796,749	0.20%
South Dakota	1,742,645,524	9,990,040	0.57%
Tennessee	16,568,164,800	51,415,600	0.31%
Texas	49,234,957,845	50,382,272	0.10%
Utah	3,057,761,400	22,295,800	0.73%
Vermont	2,226,000,000	5,492,581	0.25%
Virignia	21,398,967,256	15,569,099	0.07%
Washington	17,500,000,000	38,071,116	0.22%
West Virginia	7,478,000,000	29,537,017	0.39%
Wisconsin	20,200,000,000	17,396,684	0.09%
Wyoming	1,620,810,363	4,785,585	0.30%
TOTAL	780,749,512,659	$1,627,940,548	-
AVERAGE	-	-	0.26%

concept of a state park as suggested by Richard Leiber, a leading authority on state parks, in 1928:

> A typical portion of the state's original domain; tract of adequate size, preserved in primeval, unspoilt, "unimproved," or "beautified" condition. It is a physical expression of life, liberty, and the pursuit of happiness. A state park must have either scenic or historic value or both, and is dedicated to the public for the intelligent use of its leisure time (Michaud 1966:561).

The early state parks were oriented toward providing for contemplative leisure. The features that were commonly protected or displayed were waterfalls, river gorges, picturesque coastlines, beautiful lakes, cave systems, mountain peaks, mature forests, undisturbed swamps, paleontological sites, geologic phenomena, and important historic sites (Chubb & Chubb, 1981:468). As the demand for recreative leisure increased, so did the types of facilities to accommodate their users: picnickers, beach users, horseback riders, and winter sport enthusiasts. Lodges were provided in the early era when there was both a lack of commercial accommodations outside parks and when reaching many parks required a long trek by automobile traveling slowly on undeveloped roads.

Recently attempts have been made to classify state parks according to use. The idea is to limit the use of the term "state park" to rustic areas as the original concept indicated and to give names such as "state recreation area" to spots where there is more active participation in various outdoor sports than in actual contemplation of rustic nature. Today there are over 4,500 recreational areas run by the fifty states (see Figure 8.1).

Spending on state parks varies from state to state, as shown in Table 8.4, which shows that California spends .75 % of its budget on state parks, followed by Utah .73%, and Delaware .70%.

California and Outdoor Recreation: A Case Study

Article I, Declaration of Rights, Section I of the Constitution of the State of California (1849) reads as follows:

> All men are by nature free and independent, and have certain inalienable rights, among which are those of enjoying and defending life and liberty; acquiring, possessing, and protecting property and pursuing and obtaining safety and happiness.

Pursuit of happiness through leisure and recreation started with the first settlers in California and became part of the state and local government beginning at the turn of the 20th century. Although the federal government gave Yosemite to California in 1864, it was eventually taken back to become the second national park after Yellowstone, so the California state park system actually began with the creation of the Redwood Park at Big Basin in 1902. In 1909 California passed the Park and Playground Act, the purpose of which was to enable local authorities to establish such facilities. But it was not until 1939 that the state park system was formalized with the establishment of the State Park Commission (State of California Recreation Commission 1950:111).

In 1961, Edmund G. Brown, governor of California, adopted a recreation policy for the state of California. At the time of the adoption of the policy, the California Department of Natural Resources had four divisions, one of which was called the Division of Beaches and Parks. The division was to be administered by a chief, appointed by the director (of the Department of Natural Resources) upon nomination by the State Park Commission.

The State Park Commission was established in 1947 and consisted of five members appointed by the governor with the advice and consent of the state senate. Members are selected because of their interest in park and conservation matters and serve for terms of four years.

The Department of Natural Resources, through the State Park Commission, has control of the California Park System. The commission is to administer, protect, and develop the system for the use and enjoyment of the public. In its annual report to the governor, it should gather, digest, and summarize information concerning the state park system, including suggesting means for conserving, developing, and utilizing the scenic and recreational resources of the state. The commission is authorized to receive and accept in the name of the people of California any gift to be added or used in connection with the state park system. The commission, whenever in its judgment it is practicable to do so, shall collect fees, rentals, and other return for the use of parks. The state of California created in its treasury a state park fund to be used for improvement and maintenance of the state parks.

California Recreation Policy

The California Public Resources Code (Section 540b, 1977 and 1981) states that the commission (now called the California Park and Recreation Commission)

> . . . shall formulate, in cooperation with other agencies, interested organizations and citizens, and shall recommend to the Director (of the Department of Parks and Recreation) a comprehensive recreational policy for the State of California.

The policy statement of 1974 was reviewed and another statement was approved by the commission and issued on July 15, 1981, which indicated the general, scope and direction for all recreation and recreation-related programs and actions undertaken or funded by the state. It gives clear indication of the objectives desired for federal and local agencies, as well as for private sector activities in the recreation field. This policy has been put into effect through a planning process, as indicated in the following section.

California Recreation Planning Program

California's statewide recreation planning program calls for a continuous process of identifying, analyzing, and solving the problems of providing recreation opportunities for the state's citizens and visitors. Under direction of the California Department of Parks and Recreation, the planning program provides leadership, policy guidance, program direction, and information to public and private recreation suppliers. This effort helps suppliers offer the facilities and programs best suited to the needs and desires of recreationists.

The major objectives of this program are as follows:

- To identify, on a statewide basis, the recreation needs of Californians.
- To examine critical recreation problems related to providing needed recreation opportunities.
- To provide a policy and program framework in which the various public and private recreation suppliers can work together to meet the public's recreation needs.
- To have government agencies and the private sector work together to devise solutions, mobilize resources, and resolve conflicts related to recreation matters.
- To maintain California's eligibility to receive money from the federal Land and Water Conservation Fund.

In both its concept and execution, this approach to statewide recreation planning is new in California and the nation. This program is innovative in its orientation toward future trends, its emphasis on process and continuity, its wide variety of activities and products, its overall unity, and its process of making state agencies accountable for following the plan.

The state of California, in order to receive federal grants, must publish a recreation plan every five years. The purposes of this document are to periodically examine the current recreation environment in California; to evaluate existing programs and planning materials; to rethink current state recreation policy and objectives; and to recommend or direct relevant public and private recreation involvement in the subsequent five-year planning period.

At any given time, the California Outdoor Recreation Plan is the summary of all current materials and efforts. The Outdoor Recreation Plan does not specify programs as such. The California Recreation Action Program Reports, when approved by the governor, direct recreation efforts of all state agencies and regulate their relationships with other suppliers of recreational opportunities from the private sector.

Today the California Parks and Recreation Department is changed with following:

Park Units	266
Acres	1.4 million
Visitors	80 million
Employees	2,500
Picnic Sites	11,000
Campsites	15,000
Miles of Coastline	280
Miles of Lake and River Frontage	630
Miles of Trails	3,000
Historic, Archaeological, and Archival Artifacts	2.8 million
Historic Buildings	1,500

Leisure Pursuits of Californians

Over a decade ago, the Department of Parks and Recreation conducted a survey of 2,140 randomly selected California residents. The survey showed that Californians devote more than a billion participation days per year to the pursuit of outdoor recreation. A participation day reflects the engagement of one person in a recreation activity for any amount of time on any one day. The average household in California for purposes of statistics consists of 2.4 persons. The survey contained 38 recreation pursuits, as shown in Table 8.5.

The California Department of Parks and Recreation interpretation is that the activities in which the highest percentages of California's population participated were among the simplest and least expensive. Examples are walking, picnicking, and beach activities. These same activities have also been consistently identified as most popular since such research began in the early 1960s.

Water activities seem to play an important role in California. More than two-thirds of all Californians engage in beach activities, and more than half go swimming each year. More than 20 percent of all household activities are directly related to water and beaches. The less popular activities among Californians tend to require expensive and specialized equipment, a high degree of skill or proficiency, or physical prowess. These activities involve smaller numbers of people who participate more frequently in them. For example, soccer players constitute only about 7.4 percent of the population, with a very high degree of participation.

At the turn of the century, the Department of Park and Recreation revealed that over 80 million day visits took place between July 2000 and June 2001 in the following percentages (Planning Division 2001).

- Free day Use
  - In vehicle   35.20%
  - Non-vehicle   28.80%
  - In groups   1.90%
- Pay Day Use
  - In vehicle   22.60%
  - Non-vehicle   2.20%
  - In-groups   .38%
- Overnight Camping
  - In sites   7.70%
  - Other areas   .26%
  - In groups   .53%
- Boat Launched   .40%

                          99.97%

Table 8.5 Outdoor Activity Participation (1987 Survey)

	Percent of Total Population Participating	Average Days Per Participant	Total Estimated Household Participation Days (Millions)
Walking	76.6	52.2 Days	149.6
Driving for pleasure	75.5	33.4	81.8
Visiting museums, zoos, etc.	72.0	10.1	31.7
Beach activities	67.9	24.5	69.0
Picnicking-developed sites	64.4	14.4	31.6
Use of open turf areas	64.4	28.1	69.1
Swimming-lakes, rivers, ocean	59.0	18.8	42.6
Attending sports events	50.4	16.2	28.1
Attending cultural events	49.7	7.9	15.1
Birdwatching, nature study	47.4	23.4	31.5
Camping-developed sites	46.1	12.5	18.3
Trail hiking/mountain climbing	37.7	10.0	14.8
Freshwater fishing	36.3	19.5	19.5
Play equipment/tot lots	34.0	24.7	35.1
Swimming pools	31.1	31.5	33.3
Softball, baseball	25.6	21.0	19.2
Sledding, snow play, ice skating	25.0	7.6	5.4
Camping-primitive/backpacking	24.9	10.4	8.2
Bicycling	23.0	32.9	46.0
Power boating	19.8	16.6	9.7
Saltwater fishing	18.5	13.7	9.6
Tennis	17.6	21.4	18.2
Downhill skiing	17.5	8.4	4.9
Golf	16.4	30.7	16.8
Kayaking, rowboating, etc.	15.7	7.2	4.1
Water skiing	14.6	12.0	5.6
Four-wheel driving	14.3	23.1	8.3
Target shooting	14.0	9.4	4.2
Off-road vehicles	13.0	22.4	9.6
Jogging/running	12.6	58.3	55.1
Horseback riding	12.5	16.3	6.1
Hunting	12.2	15.0	3.9
Basketball	11.5	23.1	10.3
Sailing, windsurfing	10.3	11.5	4.2
Cross-country skiing	9.5	6.3	2.2
Football	9.1	15.8	6.0
Soccer	7.4	43.8	9.5
Surfing	4.1	25.7	5.5

Source: *California Outdoor Recreation Plan* (Sacramento, CA: Department of Parks and Recreation, 1988), 25.

The above statistics show that the highest use is free day areas followed by payday use, overnight camping and boat launching.

Providers of State Recreation

A number of state agencies play one or more roles in the provision of outdoor recreation opportunities, as described in the following paragraphs.

Department of Parks and Recreation

This department manages four distinct programs, as follow:

1. As shown previously, *the California State Park System* includes 266 units totaling 1,412,825 acres. Recreation facilities provided at these units include over 12,000 campsites and almost 11,000 picnic sites, as well as 57 boat ramps, over 2,300 boat slips, and over 3,000 miles of trails. Many of the units offer interpretive programs and facilities including visitor centers, museums, and interpretive panels and displays. There are more than 1,500 historic structures within the units of the State Park System. A series of subunits within the system offers increased protection to designated areas. Currently, there are ten cultural preserves, 33 natural preserves, and seven state wildernesses.

Over 80 million visits are made to the State Park System each year. Day-use visitation to the system has continued to increase. The number of visitors seems to increase as the population increases around the state's major population centers along the Pacific coast. The problem with expanding facilities to serve the increased number of visitors is that it not only costs more to buy near-urban land, but it is also more expensive to operate recreation facilities near such areas.

An important factor in the state's growing and changing population is the large increases in Hispanic and Asian people immigrating to California. These groups have different recreation preferences and habits than those of the Anglo clientele of the past. Both groups tend to prefer family-oriented facilities, activities, and programs. These demographic changes are forcing the State Park System to reevaluate its program and rethink its role as a recreation provider.

2. *The Off-Highway Motor Vehicle Recreation* (OHMVR) Program has been established by law as a separate program entity within the Department of Parks and Recreation. A seven-member OHMVR Commission, with three members appointed by the governor and two members each appointed by the Senate Rules Committee and the Speaker of the Assembly, oversees the program. A deputy director manages the program with a staff of about 70 full-time and 40 part-time employees. The program includes two major components:

- The state OHMVR system
- Assistance to other agencies for OHMVR facilities

The law establishing the state's OHMVR program expired January 1, 1988. New legislation passed in the 1987 session of the legislature that extended the program again. The legislation mandates that 33 percent of the program's budget be allocated to pay for conservation and law enforcement measures. This provision is designed to assure a solid resource management program that includes law enforcement and wildlife enhancement. The OHMVR system includes seven state vehicular recreation areas (SVRAs) covering approximately 40,000 acres serving about a million and a half visitors each year. There is a growing demand due to the strong attraction of backcountry off-roading for people who feel constrained by their urban existence, and also due to the limitations being placed on this type of recreational use in many open-space areas in the state. In addition to the visitors to the state areas, over four and a half million off-highway visitor-days of use are estimated to take place at federal and local off-road facilities each year.

3. *The Historic Preservation Program* helps to ensure that examples of California's diverse cultural heritage are preserved. The program's scope includes preserving historic buildings, archeological sites, artifacts, records, and traditions. Many of these historic materials are an integral part of many types of outdoor recreation, offering scenery for many urban residents, and providing backdrops for outdoor recreation such as picnicking, playing ball, sunbathing, photography, painting, and nature study. Visiting museums and historic sites are popular outdoor recreation activities for which there is a great deal of public support.

The program has two major components, federal historic preservation in California and state financial assistance for historic preservation. Under the federal program, the department identifies historic properties, places outstanding examples on the National Register, and takes further action to help preserve many of them. This may include granting of federal monies for restoration or rehabilitation. State financial assistance has been provided by the 1984 State Park Bond Act, which included $10 million for this purpose. Also, $4 million was appropriated in 1987 to assist major historic preservation projects. Park bond issues that passed later provided $20 million for historic preservation projects.

4. *Financial Assistance to Local Park and Recreation Agencies* as well as a limited amount of technical advice and consultation have been available through the Department of Parks and Recreation. Most of the money has come from state general obligation bonds approved at periodic intervals by the California voters. Also a small amount of money is made available from the federal Land and Water Conservation Fund. This money is administered by the department under the supervision of the National Park Service, which dictates firm guidelines on how these funds can be distributed and used. The money is used for acquisition of park properties and development of new facilities, but not for park operation and maintenance. In recent years, the lack of such money has served to restrain enthusiasm for grants acquisition and development. This factor could become critical in the coming years. In addition to the Land and Water Conservation Fund money, which has been reduced to only $2.5 million in 1986-87, most local grant funds come from the following state bond acts:

a. The California Park and Recreational Facilities Act of 1984.
b. The Community Parklands Act of 1986.

The Department of Boating and Waterways

This department has the responsibility for developing and improving boating facilities throughout the state. This is accomplished through loans to various agencies and jurisdictions for small-craft harbors and marinas, as well as by providing launching-facility grants and capital outlay investment in boating facilities at State Park System units and facilities.

The department's annual financial assistance for boating facilities amounts to more than $25 million. The department also promotes boating safety and conducts beach erosion control efforts in cooperation with federal and local agencies.

The department is concerned that the demand for additional boating facilities is out-stripping the supply. This problem is aggravated by a growing inability or unwillingness of many client agencies to assume responsibility for the operation of more facilities. Many existing facilities are not being kept in proper condition for the intensive use they receive.

The Department of Fish and Game

This department manages the state's game and non-game species for scientific, economic, as well as recreational purposes. It owns about 350,000 acres of land and water, most of which offers opportunities for a wide variety of wildlife-associated recreation activities such as hunting and fishing. Recently, the numbers of hunters and anglers have declined, with a significant increase in more non-consumptive wildlife recreation such as bird watching, nature photography, sketching, and painting. To offset the drop in hunting and fishing license fees and to help cover the cost of maintaining the facilities needed for the non-hunting and non-fishing activities, the department is charging a fee at some of its wildlife areas for these activities.

Department of Water Resources

This agency manages California's vast complex of dams, aqueducts, pumping plants, and other appurtenant structures that store and transport water. Although

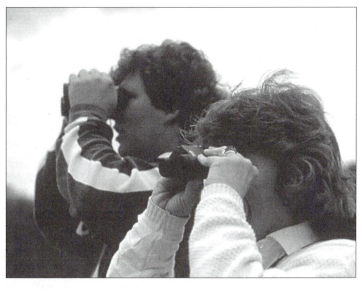

While the number of hunters and anglers have declined, birdwatching, wildlife viewing, and other non-consumptive wildlife recreation has increased.

these facilities are designed primarily to generate power and deliver water to contracting agricultural, industrial, and residential users, they have great recreation potential. Unfortunately the department is experiencing a problem of meeting public expectations for recreation and an inability of other public agencies to supply funds for this purpose. Also, the department is having problems with water quality at some reservoirs as a result of the poor hygienic practices of recreationists. Growing liability problems are reflected in an increasing number of lawsuits brought by people who claim they've been injured while recreating at water project facilities. Large awards have been made to claimants in many cases, which forced the department to close some of its sites to recreationists.

Department of Forestry and Fire Protection

This department's primary responsibility is to provide fire protection and watershed management services for private and state-owned forests, deserts, and grasslands. The department is finding that operating its recreational offerings is a growing problem because of drug and alcohol abuse, vandal-

ism, theft, and the presence of an increasing number of homeless people. Also, off-highway vehicle operators tear up the terrain, contributing to higher patrol and training costs. In addition, the department finds that many recreationists fail to understand that their behavior leads to a less than pristine appearance of the forests. Accordingly the department is experiencing increasing costs in operating its recreation sites.

Coastal Commission

This regulatory agency for California's coastal resources is concerned with the provision of access to recreational opportunities, protection of the marine environment, promotion of land use policies, and regulation of various types of development. The commission does not operate any recreation lands or facilities; it depends entirely on other agencies to assume this responsibility. Tighter operating budgets for those agencies, stricter staffing limitations, expenditure ceilings, and liability concerns are hampering the commission's mission.

State Coastal Conservancy

Under its Public Access Program, the conservancy grants awards to public agencies or nonprofit organizations to provide coastal accessways, acquire land for public access to significant coastline resources, and accept dedication of lands to provide public access to recreation and resource areas.

The conservancy is authorized to receive sites for parks, recreation, fish and wildlife habitat, historical preservation, or scientific study. It can acquire excess lands, open-space lands, and areas needed to undertake enhancement. The conservancy does not manage or operate lands on a long-term basis. It turns over its properties to cities, counties, state or federal agencies, or nonprofit organizations for operational responsibility.

The conservancy has a role in effecting urban waterfront restoration and in providing funding for parks, open space, coastal access, and other public areas and facilities. It plans and coordinates federal surplus land sales in the coastal zone.

Wildlife Conservation Board

The Wildlife Conservation Board acquires property to preserve or restore wildlife habitat, and it develops or improves facilities for wildlife-associated recreation on land owned by itself and local government agencies. These facilities may include fishing piers and floats, boat ramps, jetty access walkways, lake or reservoir improvements, boardwalks, nature trails, and interpretive areas. These projects are generally undertaken in coordination with local agencies, which operate and maintain the facilities for public use.

The board has acquired or developed 467 state and local units. Each unit offers some type of wildlife-associated recreation. The lands acquired or dedicated to this purpose by the board comprise most of the 350,000 acres owned by the Department of Fish and Game. These lands are managed by the department, either directly or by agreement with local agencies.

As project operators, local agencies are being allowed to impose user fees or to develop revenue-generating related facilities, such as campgrounds, at their cost, to help offset operation and maintenance costs. The board is aware of the public pressure for more urban and suburban recreation opportunities, as well as the emerging interest in barrier-free design for disabled accessibility wherever possible.

Tahoe Conservancy

The conservancy was established to implement the $85 million Lake Tahoe Acquisition Bond Act through land acquisition, land management, resource protection, and public access and recreation. At present, the conservancy is managing 2,900 acres at Lake Tahoe, focusing on erosion control in the lake basin. Grants are provided to local jurisdictions to provide lake access and recreation opportunities, and to state and federal agencies for wildlife management. The overriding concern for the conservancy is the deterioration of the quality of Lake Tahoe's water.

Santa Monica Mountains Conservancy

This agency implements the Santa Monica Mountains Comprehensive Plan by acquiring, restoring, and consolidating land in the Santa Monica Mountains Zone for park, recreation, or conservation purposes. To accomplish this, the conservancy acquires property to protect the natural environment, manages the lands on an interim basis, and works with established land management agencies to take over these lands. Its acquisition program is focused on the most critical open space and recreation land in the area. In addition, the conservancy is providing grants to local agencies for acquisition and development of their own park and recreation lands.

The conservancy has identified a number of concerns. Primary among them is the need to link existing park units through development of a trail system. The State Department of Parks and Recreation owns 35,000 acres and the National Park Service owns about 15,000 acres, while the conservancy itself owns 10,000 acres. These lands need to be tied together. Other concerns include the increasing use of trails, the need for additional camping facilities, and the need to improve public access to the land already in public ownership.

SUMMARY

This chapter is concerned with the development and role of state government in outdoor recreation areas and offerings. While the initial involvement was through the development of parks, other functions, such as coastal conservation and desert preservation, were added over the years. In addition, state structures dealing with recreation directly were established in many states. As the recreation services increased, areas that are owned and run by the state came into being. Today there is hardly a state in the Union that does not have a state park, a state forest, or a historical monument.

A number of federal acts that were passed during the last four decades increased the pressure on the states to develop comprehensive outdoor recreation plans. A plan is required if the state is to receive federal funds. Typically the plan covers the state policy on recreation and describes the issues the state faces where recreation is concerned.

There are regional differences in what the states offer in the way of outdoor recreation. An example of state offerings is given with a case study of California, along with an examination of the state's role in regional and local recreational offerings. The study of what Californians like to do plays an important role in developing comprehensive plans for the state.

REFERENCES

Chubb, M., & Chubb, C. (1981). *One third of our time? An introduction to recreation behavior and resources.* New York: John Wiley and Sons.

Department of Parks and Recreation. (1981). *Recreation in California: Issues and actions: 1981-1985.* Sacramento, CA: Department of Parks and Recreation.

Department of Parks and Recreation. (1988). *California outdoor plan—1988.* Sacramento, CA: Department of Parks and Recreation.

Donnelly, M.P., et al. (1998). Economic impacts of State Parks: Effect of park visitation, park facilities, and county economic diversity. *Journal of Park and Recreation Administration, 18*(3), 57-72.

Fazio, J. (1979). Parks and other recreational resources, In H. Ibrahim and J. Shivers (Eds.), *Leisure: Emergence and expansion.* Los Alamitos, CA: Hwong Publishing.

Foss, P. (1968). *Recreation: Conservation in the United States: A documentary history.* New York: Chelsea House.

Jensen, C. (1985). *Outdoor recreation in America.* Minneapolis, MN: Burgess Press.

Knudson, D. (1984). *Outdoor recreation.* New York: Macmillan.

Heritage Conservation and Recreation Service. (1979). *The third nationwide outdoor recreation plan.* Washington, D.C.: U.S. Government Printing Office.

MacLean, J., Peterson, J., & Martin, W. (1985). *Recreation and leisure: The changing scene.* New York: MacMillan.

Michaud, H. (1966). State parks. In A. Lindsey (Ed.), *Natural features of Indiana.* Indianapolis, IN: Indiana Academy of Science.

Nash, R. (1967). *Wilderness and the American mind.* New Haven, CT: Yale University Press.

National Association of State Park Directors. (2001). *Annual information exchange.* Tucson, AZ: Division of State Parks.

Planning Division (2001). *Planning milestones: California State Park system.* Sacramento, CA: Department of Park and Recreation.

State of California Recreation Commission. (1950). *Recreation in California.* Sacramento, CA: State of California Recreation Commission.

9 LOCAL RESOURCES AND RECREATION

In colonial America, the dominance of puritan values kept recreational activities from being a local concern. Localities were settlements built on land that was granted to homogeneous groups who agreed to participate in their community affairs, which were handled in town meetings. As communities increased in size, a committee was selected to run the affairs of each community. Recreation was not a concern then, but open space was.

The town common played an important role in providing public open space. The earliest common was established in Boston in 1634. William Penn decreed a 10-acre common in the center of Philadelphia in 1682. Another common of Philadelphia's size was provided in Savannah, Georgia, in 1733. Earlier, in the area settled by Spain in the New World, it was required that the new cities include a plaza or a city square, as was the case in Saint Augustine, Florida.

It is questionable whether recreational activity motivated the establishment of these open spaces. According to Fazio (1979:207), most of the commons then were meant to be meeting lots, used as an equivalent to a church, except in open air. And according to Knudson (1984:149), a common served many other purposes, including being a cow pasture, a military training field, and a public hanging post where pirates, witches, and Quakers met their earthly end. Also the commons served as America's version of Hyde Park, London, for public speakers and their hecklers. The commons later became the open space for parades and celebrations, the place for music and sport, and the spot for strolling and picnicking.

The Boston Public Garden was founded in 1832 across the street from Boston Commons; it included the first botanical garden in America. Arnold Arboretum was established there in 1876. Boston also saw the first children's sand garden, which was promoted by Dr. Maria Zakzrewska. A large sand pile was placed in the yard of the Children's Mission on Parmenter Street, where 15 children spent three days a week for six weeks during July and August of 1883. In 1887, paid matrons were hired to observe the children; a supervisor was hired in 1893 and organized play was introduced. Funds for operating the playground were provided by the Massachusetts Emergency and Hygiene Association. In 1899, the City Council allocated $3,000 toward meeting the playground operating costs.

The concept of urban parks was promoted by Charles Elliot and Frederick Law Olmsted (Knudson. 1984:149). The first planned park, New York's Central Park, was authorized in 1833 by the City of New York, and it took many years to complete. The park set the standard for municipal

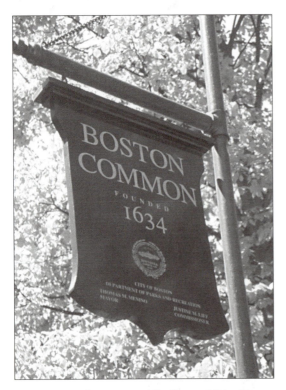

The Boston Common, originally established in 1634 for common use as a cow pasture and training field, is the oldest public park in the country.

parks in the United States. In 1888 Boston set aside a string of green spaces on the city outskirts, which were nicknamed the "Emerald Necklace." According to Haines (1977:139), William Cullen Bryan began to emphasize the need for a park in New York City in 1836. In fact there was an earlier complaint by a citizen to the city's mayor in 1783 about the lack of a "proper spot where the inhabitants (of New York) could enjoy the benefits of exercise necessary for health and amusement" (Foss, 1968:304). The city acquired 740 acres of swamps and brambles for open spaces. But Frederick Law Olmsted advocated that human existence would be more bearable if parks rather than swamps and brambles were provided. He believed that parks are facsimiles of rural landscapes, which provide tranquility and rest to the mind (Cans, 1974:16). His adoption of the natural style in this urban park served as the model for America's city parks in the

future. According to Fazio (1979:208), parkland development follows certain steps, as shown in Figure 9.1.

Many city parks were built in the second half of the nineteenth century, except for during the Civil War years. While the first three decades of the twentieth century saw some growth in state and national natural resources, the Depression years led to a phenomenal growth in urban parks. Many of the anti-Depression public works programs provided by the federal government proved to be very beneficial to city parks.

According to Caro (1974), in 1932 New York City had about 13,000 acres of parkland and 119 playgrounds. By 1939, 20,000 acres were added to the city parks, along with 233 new playgrounds and 10 new swimming pools. Despite the growth, many of the city's poorer areas did not benefit from it.

After World War II, a number of federal acts helped in the development of urban open space and recreational resources. Notably, the Land and Water Conservation Fund Act of 1963 led to considerable growth in urban and suburban parks.

LOCAL GOVERNMENT STRUCTURE

All states empower their local governments to provide services to their citizens. The states do so through enabling legislation or by allowing the local governments to use their charters and special laws. An enabling law is an act by the state legislature that allows the local government to do the following (Moiseichik & Bodey, 2000):

1. Authorization for local government to exercise certain powers.
2. Authorization for local government to establish a board or agency to administer the powers granted.
3. Authorization of powers given under specific limits or under certain conditions.
4. Provision for joint exercise of power by two or more local, political jurisdictions to

Utilization → Awareness of the need for open space → Action to convert land or preserve remaining land → Planning and development → Protection from inroads → Management problems

Figure 9.1 Stages of park development.

establish and deliver park
and recreation services.

5. Provision for financing the
powers granted, usually including authorization to appropriate
money from the general fund to
operate a park and recreation
agency, to accept monetary gifts
or other donations, and to
establish a user fee system.

MacLean et al. (1985:82) suggest that
state enabling acts include the following:

1. A method of establishing the
managing authority and board.
2. A listing of powers of the
administrative authority and
executive.
3. A description of fiscal procedures to be followed, including
how money can be obtained,
accounted for, and spent.
4. Cooperative agreements among
existing government agencies.
5. Guidelines for qualification and
selection of personnel.

Enabling acts allow the local government to provide services to its constituency.
Structurally, there are three types of local
governments in the United States—county,
city, and district. Following are county and
city government, special district is presented later.

County Government

There are 3,043 counties in the United
States, varying in number from three

counties in Rhode Island and Hawaii to 234
counties in Texas. Technically there are no
counties in Louisiana, where the term
"parish" is used instead, or in Alaska,
where the term "borough" is used.

There are three basic forms of county
government: 1.) The Commission form of
government began in Pennsylvania in
1724 and spread widely; it is the most
dominant form today. The governing body
is elected specifically for the purpose and
fulfills both the executive and legislative
functions in county government. The
commissioners (called supervisors in some
states, including California and Iowa),
serve in a commission that is usually
composed of three to five members; 2.) The
supervisor form, another type of county
government, evolved in New York and
differs from the commission in that the
governing body is made up of persons who
were first elected as township supervisors.
There the typical size of the governing
body is about 20 supervisors; and 3.) The
executive form in county government
revolves around a county manager who
reports to a county board, which serves as
the policy-making body.

Most American county governments
superimpose a number of special boards or
commissions for special purposes among
which are park, recreation, and leisure
services.

City Government

It is estimated that there are over 18,000
municipalities in the United States, varying in the number of residents from less

than a hundred to several million. There are basically three types of government in American cities: 1) The mayor-council type of government is the oldest and most common. Usually voters at large vote for the mayor and voters by wards vote for the council; 2) The commission form of government allows the commissioners to perform both legislative and executive functions. Each commissioner will oversee a department or more. Voters at large vote for the board of commissioners; and 3) The council-manager type of government gives the legislative power to the council and the executive power to the manager.

FUNCTIONS OF LOCAL BOARDS/COMMISSIONS

A local board or commission typically performs the following functions:

1. *Approves the acts of the department under its jurisdiction.* As the governing board responsible for the results of the work of the department, the board/commission receives work reports through the superintendent and records its approval of them.

2. *Acts as a court of final appeal.* Any disagreement arising among employees or between the public and employees, if not satisfactorily resolved by the superintendent, may be considered by the commission, whose decisions are final.

3. *Advises the superintendent on problems of administration.* All superintendents need advice in the performance of their managerial duties and in carrying out the policies set by the commission. The advice of the commission should not be interpreted as instructions or regulations unless given such force by action of the commission as a whole.

4. *Interprets the department and the general operation of the system to the public.* The commission fulfills this responsibility by published actions, by public discussion and address, and by planned use of available means of public communication. The members of the commission often symbolize the aims and objectives of the department, for the character of the department is reflected in the members, who are appointed commissioners, no less than by the employees.

5. *Represents the general public.* Commissioners should conduct meetings that are open to the public and should permit individuals or delegations to address them on pertinent subjects. Most frequently the matter brought before a commission in this way is such that an immediate answer is not always possible or expedient. Often the petitioner is not in agreement with the commission. It should be remembered that the prerogative of the petitioner is only to state views and not to participate in the action. The responsibility for the action, if any is taken, rests with the commission, which after giving a respectful hearing to the petitioner, makes its own decision based on the facts involved. The decision need not be made at the time the matter is brought before the commission; the subject may be taken under advisement and a decision announced in due course.

6. *Represents the department at official occasions.* Commissioners often act as spokespersons for the department at public ceremonies, public hearings on problems concerning the department, and conferences on recreational programs, policies, or other relevant issues.

7. *Negotiates advantages for the department.* Because of their individual and collective pres-

tige, commissioners are often in a better position than the superintendent or others to negotiate advantages for the department with the local governing authority, other public officials, and the general public. Among these advantages might be an adequate budget for departmental operations. The layperson who does not derive pecuniary gain from the appropriation for the department is usually more effective than a salaried employee in such negotiations.

8. *Appoints standing and ad hoc committees.* When the work of the department becomes extensive, the commission may appoint a special committee, usually consisting of only one person. A standing committee makes it convenient to assign to a commissioner, for further investigation and consideration, any matter on which the commission may not be ready to act. Committees will not have administrative powers in the matters referred to them. No committee or individual member has any authority except by referral to and through the entire body.

9. *Separates managerial from policy-making activities.* Execution of policy is delegated to the superintendent and the employed staff. Although there is no lack of interest in all phases of departmental operations by commission members, creation of an administrative department to handle such matters provides for a sharp delineation between formulation and administration of policy.

LOCAL GOVERNMENT AND LEISURE SERVICES

Leisure services, which include the provisions for outdoor recreation opportunities, were not among the services provided by local governments initially. The dominant puritanical outlook of colonial America viewed play as sinful. The puritans adopted a harsh work ethic emphasizing the virtue of simplicity of living and industry in working. To create God's kingdom on earth, they believed recreation was to be negated. The councils or commissions that were set up to run local affairs had nothing to do with the establishment of facilities or the provision of programs in recreation. Eventually the local government became involved in the provision of open space and the building of parks, but it was voluntary associations that became concerned with the provision of recreation, particularly for the young.

Some years after the Boston experiment of the Sand Garden of 1883, Chicago Hull House became involved in the creation of a children's playground in 1892. Hull House, which began as a center for improvement of the conditions of slum dwellers, became involved in recreation. More playgrounds sprang up in the east and midwest. The Playground Association of America was formed by concerned citizens such as Jane Addams, Henry Curtis, and Luther Gulick. The association's magazine, *Playground*, voiced their concern over the lack of recreational opportunities for the young. With the change of its name, the Playground and Recreation Association of America in 1911 was voicing concern over recreation for everyone. This voluntary association was named the National Recreation Association in 1926. In 1963 the name was changed to the National Recreation and Park Association. The word "park" signaled an emphasis on the role that the outdoors played in American recreation as well as in the work of this voluntary association.

It was not until the early 1900s that local governments began to show interest in providing local leisure services. Butler

(1940:407) suggested that municipal recreation started in large metropolitan areas with the provision of children's playgrounds. This took place before local governments were empowered by the states to do so through enabling legislation. General welfare laws and/or police powers in state constitutions or local charters were used as bases for the provision of these early recreation services.

As suggested by Rainwater (1922:192), the playground movement, which started as a philanthropic deed, went through the following nine distinct transitions from its inception in the 1880s until the end of World War 1:

1. The limited provisions of activities to little children expanded to all ages.
2. The summer-only programs expanded to year-long programs.
3. The offerings expanded to include indoor activities, instead of outdoor activities only.
4. The program expanded to rural areas, rather than existing merely in congested urban centers.
5. The support shifted from philanthropic groups to total community support.
6. Play became organized instead of being free, with schedules provided for activities.
7. The projects became rather complex and varied.
8. The philosophy shifted to include varied activities, and not just the provision of facilities.
9. Community and group activities were considered before individual interests.

These transitions are witnessed in seven distinct stages through which the playground movement evolved, accompanied by the expansion in the number of local parks (Rainwater, 1922:60):

1. The sand garden, 1883-1895
2. The model playground, 1895-1900
3. The small park, 1900-1903
4. The recreation center, 1905-1912
5. Civic art and welfare, 1912-1915
6. Neighborhood organization, 1915-1918
7. Community service, 1918-1922

Hjelte (1940:16) suggested that between 1922 and 1940, five additional transitions took place:

1. The play movement became a recreation movement.
2. The movement became more than just municipal; it became a state and national movement.
3. The program became integrated with public education curriculum and systems.
4. The organization expanded into rural as well as urban areas.
5. The organization eventually came under the public sector in place of the previously subsidized quasi-public control.

The new social conscience of the 1930s helped to increase understanding of the need for the provision of municipal recreation assisted by the much welcomed role of the federal government in alleviating the scourge of the Depression. To combat the rampaging unemployment at that time, federal projects were organized, among which were the building of many local parks under the auspices of the Works Projects Administration.

Originally these local parks were organized under a department, which became responsible for the acquisition, development, and maintenance of parks and outdoor resources. Eventually another function, that is, recreation, evolved to provide various activities initially for children and later for adults. In many instances, a separate department for recreation was established; otherwise, parks and recreation went hand in hand. Today, more than two-thirds of the local governments have a combined department of parks and recreation (see Figures 9.2, 9.3, and 9.4).

A study conducted by the National Recreation and Park Association in cooperation with the International City Management Association showed that nine out of ten local governments in the United States have a year-round, full-time park and recreation agency to fulfill the following functions (Heritage Conservation and Recreation Service, 1979: 76):

- Planning, acquiring, developing, and maintaining parkland and recreation areas and facilities.
- Providing services for groups and individuals with special leisure service needs.
- Providing education for attainment of specific leisure skills.
- Sponsoring special community events and celebrations.

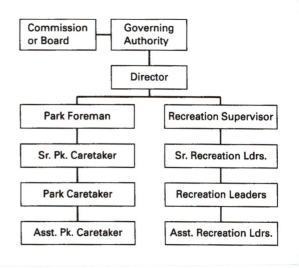

Figure 9.2 Small city park and recreation structure.

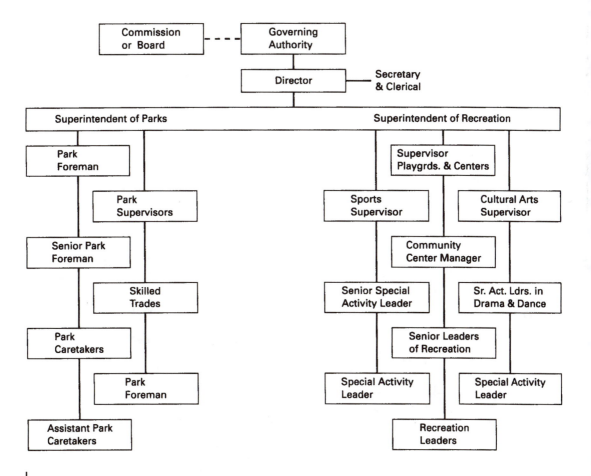

Figure 9.3 Medium-size city (over 50,000) park and recreation structure.

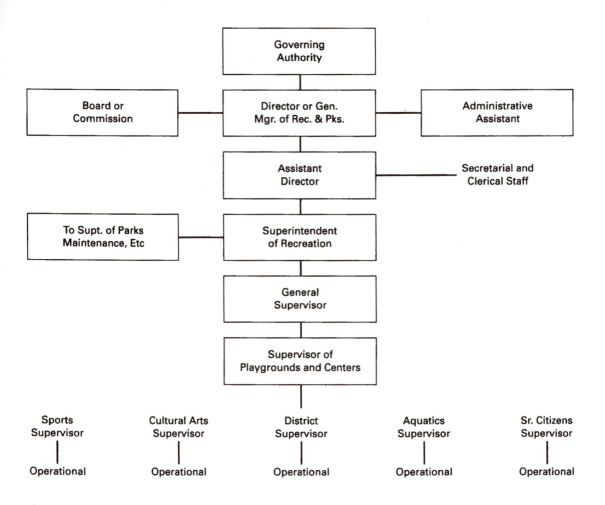

Figure 9.4 Large city (over 100,000) park and recreation structure.

- Sponsoring social, cultural, and athletic programs on a continuing basis.

The structure of the agency providing leisure services may vary greatly according to the size of the population (see Figures 9.2, 9.3, and 9.4).

Special Districts

In some states, enabling laws allow for the formation of a special district that allows two or more municipalities to establish a joint park and recreation service. While there are numerous metropolitan districts of this sort, there are rural ones as well. The board controlling some of these park and recreation districts is elected directly by the constituents.

Recreation through School Districts

In many instances, local recreation offerings are provided through the education board. According to Hjelte and Shivers (1972: 122), this is neither the major administrative organization for park and recreation services, nor the most desirable one, since it tends to exclude, necessarily by design, the adult population.

Recreation through a Single Local Agency

Ibrahim et al. (1987:77-79) listed the advantages and disadvantages of combining parks and recreation under one local agency as follows:

I. Combined Recreation and Parks Department

Advantages:

1. Consolidation of all related activities under one municipal department.
2. Development of a comprehensive and diversified program of both passive and leadership-oriented activities.
3. Reduction of dual development of facilities and areas.
4. Central control.
5. Flexibility of budget.
6. Even distribution of workload.
7. Improved communication.
8. Better understanding by public.
9. Elimination of duplication of efforts.
10. Scope of leisure philosophy not splintered within a personal framework.

Disadvantages:

1. Park or recreation developments might be seriously subordinated to opposite ideology, depending on interest or background of administrator.
2. School facilities are not automatically utilized.

II. Separate Recreation Department

Advantages:

1. Selection of recreation specialists as staff members.
2. Orientation toward activity; planning of facilities accordingly.
3. Assurance that a recreation board can coordinate efforts on recreation.
4. Recreation budgets specifically set aside for that purpose and not sacrificed for other services.
5. Broad perspective for providing programs and services.
6. Easier placement of responsibility for success or failure of recreation administration.
7. Emphasis on studying recreational needs and interests of a community.
8. Effective recreation service rendered.

Disadvantages:

1. Overlapping and duplication of effort.
2. Public confusion over responsibility.
3. Duplication impedes planning.
4. Overlapping with schools.
5. Additional administrative machinery needs.
6. Difficulty in defining recreation role and jurisdiction.
7. Recreation cannot work in a vacuum, cuts across the work of other departments.
8. Facilities used are under control of a second agency.
9. Lack of coordination between parks and programs.

III. Separate Park Department

Advantages:

1. Development and maintenance of park facilities under own auspices.
2. Experience in dealing with large numbers of patrons.
3. Large budgets usually allocated.
4. Park board is less likely to be politically influenced.
5. Parks lend prestige to recreation.
6. Trained staff in horticulture, construction, and maintenance of parks.

Disadvantages:

1. Major attention on physical properties and natural resources.
2. Buildings needed for recreation are in the jurisdiction of park departments, which means that the parks department may refuse to allow certain activities in the park.
3. Boards burdened with property problems.

4. Attitude of park authorities toward recreation is conservative and hesitant.
5. Recreation is of secondary importance.
6. Lack of motivation to insist on high-quality recreation leadership.
7. Great difficulty in securing school buildings.
8. Budget cuts affect recreation more than park services.

A study was conducted in 1976 by the National Recreation and Parks Association on the degree of involvement of cities with populations of 10,000 or more in municipal recreation. The study showed that of the responding cities, 66 percent provided leisure services under a combined park and recreation department, 96 percent cooperated with local school systems in providing recreation opportunity, and 88 percent provided full-time, year-round programs.

FINANCING LOCAL RECREATION

The principal sources of funds for the cooperation of local services, which are different from capital development funds, are as follows:

1. **Appropriation from general fund.** The monies collected for local services are to be appropriated as needed by the government body, be it the city council or the county board of supervisors. These are usually tax monies collected for services such as police, fire, and public works. In most cases, the park and recreation board or commission reviews the needs, as presented by the head or heads of the departments concerned. The request for funds is then sent to the city council or board of supervisors for approval.
2. **Special Recreation Tax.** Some states authorize the levying of a tax for a special purpose such as recreation. In this case the money is, by law, allocated for that very purpose and only that purpose. This provides a form of stability from year to year, and the advisory body does not have to sell its program to the city council or board of supervisors year after year. It also provides the local park and recreation boards with some independence. This special tax is usually expressed in so many cents of the valuation of the local community to be served. For instance, if the amount needed to administer a program is $200,000 and fees and charges will bring in $80,000, the amount to be levied would be $200,000-$80,000=$120,000. And if the total valuation of the community equals $60,000,000, the special tax rate would be $120,000/60,000,000=$.20 per $100 assessed valuation. This means that the owner of a property worth $100,000 in that community will pay $200 a year to support the local recreation program.
3. **Fees And Charges.** Park and recreation departments used to attempt to provide their programs at either low cost or no cost at all. The budget crisis has altered the situation recently, and more and more departments are increasing their fees and charges. An alternative would be that fees and charges be a percentage of total expenses. Fees and charges for use of recreation areas, including outdoor recreation facilities, fall in one of six categories: entrance fees are charged for large areas such as zoos and botanical gardens; admission fees are charged for entry into a building having a program or event; rental fees are used for the

exclusive use of a facility; user fees are charged for participation in an activity; permit fees are for the privilege of participation; special service fees are applied for specific uses. Higher fees could be charged nonresidents. Fees and charges must be approved by the local legislative authority (Seller & Gladwell, 1999:604).

4. **Other Sources.** Beginning in the mid 1960s many municipal recreation and park departments began calling on major companies for more significant forms of help. Among the types of help are outright gifts, sponsorship of programs and events, adoption of a facility or area, and provision of technical assistance. To stimulate giving this type of assistance, some park and recreation departments have developed gift catalogs which itemize and illustrate the specific needs of the department. Among the plans that enhance outdoor recreation is the adopt-a-park idea. Usually the adoption is for a specified period of time, such as three years. Friends of the park is another idea that revolves around forming a tax-exempt organization for the purpose of maintaining and improving the facility.

SOURCES FOR CAPITAL DEVELOPMENT

The adding of facilities and areas may come from funds raised for this particular purpose and could include the following:

1. **Bond Issues.** The money accrued from a bond, which is to be paid along with interest in the future, is to be used for building costly projects that the current budget could otherwise not afford. Although a bond is a liability, it is a reasonable means for expansion of areas

and facilities. General obligation bonds are paid off by additional assessments on property. Revenue bonds are paid off by the revenues accrued from the use of a facility or area built by bond monies.

2. **Federal Funds.** Federal acts in the 1960s and 1970s such as the Land and Water Conservation Fund assisted many localities in acquiring and developing open space and outdoor recreation areas. Community development block grants were used in 7.7 percent of local recreation facilities and programs. General revenue-sharing (GRS) grants provided millions of dollars to local recreation, which ranked fifth among all local government expenditures of GRS funds. Unfortunately federal funds were drastically reduced in the 1980s. A direct mail survey was conducted by the California Department of Parks and Recreation in 1997 to obtain basic information about the status of local recreation services. When the respondents were asked to list the most critical issues facing their agency during the coming five years (1988-1993), they responded as follows:

Issue	Percentage
Declining public funds	100
Increasing insurance	48
Development of new parks	40
Deterioration of existing parks	35
Provision of special recreation	31

3. **Donations and Gifts.** Decreasing federal funding led local park and recreation agencies to seek donations and gifts as means of capital development. Among the examples given by the Heritage Conservation and Recreation Service (1979:14-15), some took place

Boardwalks over marshy wetlands are creating parks out of previously inaccessible areas and are within easy access of many large cities.

before the burgeoning federal deficit became public. For instance, Catalina Island Company donated a 41,000-acre open space to Los Angeles County, the Irvine Company gave two acres and a yacht club structure to the city of Irvine, California, for a youth center, and the Janss Corporation donated a golf course to the city of Conejo, California.

4. **Special Assessment**. This is the least used, and least recommended, method in financing capital development for park and recreation services. The assessment is to be paid by those who use the facility or area among the property owners in the community. If the facility or area is needed in a well-to-do neighborhood, the residents might be persuaded to vote for the special assessment, but in a poor area, even if the residents are persuaded to support a special assessment, it might represent a hardship for many of them. Accordingly this method is not used by many agencies (MacLean et al., 1985:85).

EXAMPLES OF LOCAL OFFERINGS

Recreational offerings in Los Angeles County California, and Tacoma, Washington, are examined as examples of what a county or city can provide.

Los Angeles County

Los Angeles has the largest county government in the United States. A board of five supervisors serves both the legislative and executive functions. It is the governing body for the benefit of the citizens of the unincorporated county area. It enacts ordinances and establishes rules for the

Miramar Lake, a reservoir for the city of San Diego, has a five-mile path around its perimeter which is frequented by nearby city dwellers.

administration of the county's departments and special districts. The board is assisted by the chief administrative officer, who is responsible for making recommendations concerning procedures and actions (see Figure 9.5).

Los Angeles County, as a subdivision of the State of California, is charged with the responsibility of providing services to all its citizens, if such services are not provided by the municipalities in which they live. There are 83 cities in the county, whose residents totaled over seven million in 1988. Along with the one million residents of the unincorporated area, Los Angeles County population reached over eight million in 1988. The county's largest city, the city of Los Angeles, had 3,311,544 residents in 1988, and the smallest city, Vernon, accounted for 92 residents in the same year.

The 1989-1990 Los Angeles County budget totaled over $9 billion. Of that

amount, 74 percent was earmarked for mandated and/or special projects such as health and welfare services, roads, and flood control. Law enforcement used six percent of the budget, as did parks and recreation. Figure 9.6 shows revenues and expenditures of the Los Angeles County budget.

The Los Angeles County Department of Parks and Recreation seeks to meet the needs of the eight million people who live in the county. The prime responsibility of the department is to serve the one million residents of unincorporated areas. To do so, it operates a network of major regional parks to provide specialized outdoor recreation for county residents. County parkland totals about 72,000 acres. While this may seem to be adequate acreage per capita (10 acres per 1,000 residents), most of this land, 41,000 acres, is on Santa Catalina Island, which is 27 miles offshore. The county provides over 130 miles of

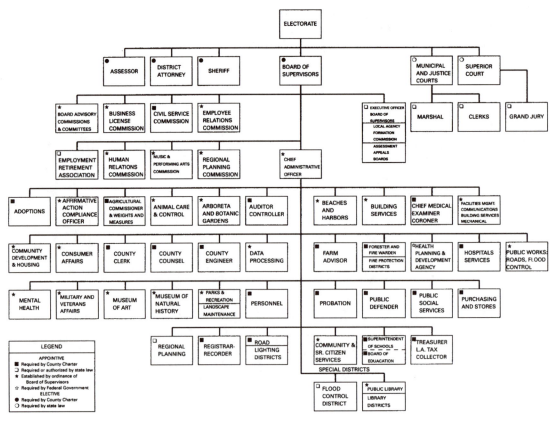

Source: L.A. County Board of Supervisors, County of Los Angeles Department of Parks and Recreation Guide (1990).

Figure 9.5 Los Angeles County government organization

hiking trails and 76 miles of beaches (administered by the Department of Beaches). The Department of Parks and Recreation administers five nature study centers that provide interpretive programs. Each of these centers is located in a natural wild area.

There are 35 regional parks and recreation areas run by the county. Santa Catalina Island has the largest acreage of unspoiled land for backpacking, hiking, and camping. Peck Road Water Conservation Park, one of the smallest regional parks in Los Angeles County, has an 80-acre lake that provides shoreline fishing in a flood control basin that was converted for outdoor recreation use.

There are 126 neighborhood and community parks administered by Los Angeles County. The county has turned over more than 50 parks to cities that are incorporated around these parks.

These neighborhood and community parks vary in size from .37 to 40 acres (Ibrahim, 1999).

Tacoma, Washington

With a population of 170,000, this city is expecting to reach 183,000 by the year 2000. It is located in Pierce County, which has a population of about 673,000. Three local government agencies are responsible for the majority of public park and recreation offerings, as follows:

1. **Metropolitan Park District**: The park and recreation facilities and programs for the city are primarily the responsibility of the Metropolitan Park District. The five board members are elected directly by the voters of the district. The board appoints the director, who is

THE COUNTY BUDGET

**Revenue Sources
1989–90**

TOTAL: $9,182,800,000

**Expenditures
1989–90**

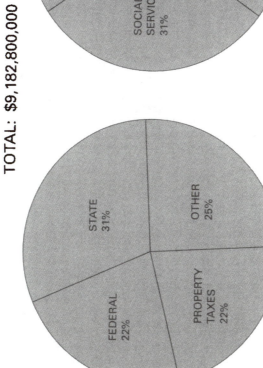

Other Sources: Contract Cities, Sales Tax, Courts, Vehicle License Fees, Forfeiture, Deed-Transfers, Parking/Traffic Violations, Public Health Licenses.

Source: L.A. County Board of Supervisors, County of Los Angeles Department of Parks and Recreation Guide (1990).

Figure 9.6 Los Angeles County revenues and expenditure, 1989-1990

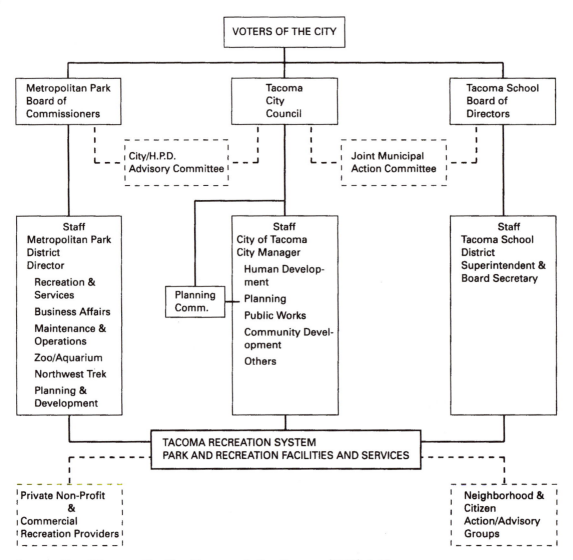

Source: City of Tacoma, Five-Year Recovery Action Program (1982), 1-10.

Figure 9.7 Tacoma recreation system.

responsible for the development and maintenance of the district's parks and recreation facilities and programs. As a separate governmental agency, the Metropolitan Park District has taxing authority for special levies and bonds.

2. **City of Tacoma:** Since 1953, Tacoma has had a council-manager government. The council is directly elected by the voters of the city electoral districts with three at-large positions. These positions, as well as that of mayor, are part-time positions. The Tacoma City Council has the responsibility for establishing city policy, formulating annual budgets, appointing the city manager and director of public utilities, as well as appointing citizens to various citizens' boards and commissions. At least four major city departments are actively

engaged in planning, maintaining, and implementing recreation opportunities. City departments outside the public utilities department are the responsibility of the city manager.

3. **Tacoma School District:** The Tacoma School District has five board members elected by the district at large. The superintendent of schools, appointed by the board, is responsible for implementation of policies established by the board and for fulfilling criteria mandated by state education requirements. The Tacoma School District makes gymnasiums, athletic fields, and playgrounds available for public recreation purposes. District recreation facilities are the responsibility of the assistant superintendent for school facilities. The Tacoma Recreation System is comprised of three agencies of the public sector which individually and collectively provide recreational opportunities to the people of Tacoma. Although the Metropolitan Park District is charged with the primary responsibility of providing parks and recreational opportunities to the city's residents, the Tacoma School District as well as the City of Tacoma, through several departments, also contribute to the overall recreation system. In addition to the formal governmental structure, advisory committees such as the City/Metropolitan Park Board and the Joint Municipal Action Committee (composed of members of the Tacoma School Board and the Tacoma City Council) meet on matters of mutual interest.

Recreation and open space planning is a function of the Tacoma City Planning Department under the direction of the Tacoma Planning Commission and in close coordination with the Metropolitan Park District and the Tacoma School District. Implementation is primarily the responsibility of the Metropolitan Park District (See Figure 9.7).

Under the direction of the Metropolitan Park Board and the Tacoma Planning Commission, the respective staffs of the three agencies are preparing a Recreation and Open Space Facilities Plan. This plan will be a guide for the location, acquisition, development, and improvement of recreation and open space in Tacoma. Staffs of the Metropolitan Park District, the Tacoma School District, and the City of Tacoma work closely in planning programs and services to provide recreational opportunities to the people of Tacoma. This cooperative planning aims at providing efficient service and effectively using public dollars.

PROBLEMS IN LOCAL OFFERINGS

In studying the recreation resources, behaviors, and evaluations of people in the Detroit region, Marans and Fly (1981) compared those living in the inner city to those in its suburbs. Low levels of participation in leisure pursuits characterize residents of the city of Detroit, where only one in ten children play in the public park. Most of the children play in backyards or on sidewalks.

Although recreation resources are unevenly distributed in Detroit, favoring the suburban resident over the inner city resident, local parks are available to the city dweller. There is a park within a mile for eight out of ten households in the inner city. Yet their use is limited due to the same problems found in other inner cities: gangs, vandalism, alcoholism, stray dogs, and other unsafe conditions. Marans and Fly suggested that the municipal department of recreation consider the qualitative as well as the quantitative dimensions of recreation resources under its jurisdiction.

Lawrence (1984) compared public recreation opportunities in central Los

Angeles to the opportunities in its affluent suburbs and revealed a series of gaps, as follows:

1. The inner city community has less public recreation land than the suburban communities studied.
2. The suburban staff put in 39 percent more hours per week than did the inner city staff.
3. Community support was very limited in most inner city recreation areas, while the suburban areas enjoyed volunteer support.
4. Inner city areas seem to suffer from special problems of gangs and vandalism.

The author concluded that two distinct and separate systems of recreation offerings seem to be emerging in Los Angeles. She suggested that the commissioners and the Department of Parks and Recreation examine their policies, allocate more resources, and train personnel to reduce the gap between inner city and the suburbs in recreation offerings. She called on the department to involve the local community in its efforts by organizing advisory councils to help in planning strategies to meet local needs (Lawrence, 1984).

In the closing years of the 20th century, Davis wrote about his concern for social justice in that recreational planning and open space were pointedly ignored in the Greater Los Angeles Area (1994). His concern was supported by the findings of a study supported by the Environmental Protection Agency that revealed that a large segment of that area of 28 cities varied significantly in parkland and open space. Some parks in that segment of the Greater Los Angeles Area are .37 of an acre large. Granted the Area has a large park that includes a zoo and a museum, nonetheless, these small parks are located in the poor sections of the metropolis. The problem is compounded by the fact that these parks are located in highly densely populated section where the average household income is $19,195 (Ibrahim, 1999).

Even the closest national land that could provide some recreational opportunities, Angeles National Forest, is frequently closed due to crowding (Pacific Southwest Research Station, 2001). Moreover, as per Davis, the market driven urbanization has left very limited access to public beach frontage (Davis, 1994).

SUMMARY

The evolution of offerings in outdoor recreation at the local level, be it municipal or county, is traced from the mere provision of open space to the establishment of highly complex recreational organization. The leaders in this respect, Frederick Law Olmsted and Charles Elliot, were presented first along with the philosophy that guided them in designing parks that represented the American way of life.

Local government structures, as they relate to the establishment of natural resources and the provision of outdoor programs, were investigated. So was the role of citizens in overseeing the services provided to the local citizens. Sources for the financing of areas, facilities, and programs were enumerated. Sources for operations include appropriations for the general fund, special recreation taxes, fees and charges, as well as gifts and development, which include, but are not limited to, bond issues, federal funds, donations, and special assessment.

Two examples of local offerings in outdoor recreation were cited. The offerings of the county of Los Angeles, California, as well as the city of Tacoma, Washington, were given. Some of the problems facing local authorities where public recreation is concerned include low level of participation, uneven distribution of resources, and unsafe conditions in the recreation place. Suggestions for improvement of leisure services offerings were given.

REFERENCES

Butler, G. (1940). *Introduction to community recreation.* New York: McGraw Hill.

Caro, R. (1974). *The power broker.* New York Vintage Press.

City of Tacoma. (1982). *Five-year recover action plan.* Tacoma, WA: City of Tacoma.

County of Los Angeles. (1990). *Los Angeles County Almanac: A guide to government.* County of Los Angeles.

Davis, M. (1994). *How Eden was lost.* Unpublished Paper.

Davis, M. (1998). Cited in book Review: *Ecology of fear: Los Angeles and the imagination of disaster.* New York: Henry Holt (published in *New York Times,* August 21).

Fazio, J. (1979). Parks and other recreation resources. In H. Ibrahim, & J. Shivers (Eds.), *Leisure: Emergence and expansion.* Los Alamitos, CA: Hwong Publishing.

Foss, P. (1968). *Recreation: Conservation in the United States, a documentary history.* New York: Chelsea House.

Gans, H. (1974). Outdoor recreation and mental health. In D. Fischer, T. Lewis, & G. Priddle (Eds.), *Land and leisure: Concepts and methods in outdoor recreation.* Chicago: Maaroufa Press.

Haines, A. (1977). *The Yellowstone story.* Yellowstone, WY: Yellowstone Library and Museum Association.

Heritage Conservation and Recreation Service. (1979). *Fundraising handbook.* U.S. Department of the Interior. Washington, D.C.: U.S Government Printing Office.

Hjelte, G. (1940). *The administration of public recreation.* New York: Macmillan.

Hjelte, G., & Shivers, J. (1972). *Public administration of recreational services.* Philadelphia: Lea and Febiger.

Ibrahim, H. (1999). *Environmental justice: The Whittier College study of parkland and open space.* Santa Clara, California: CPRS Research Session.

Ibrahim, H., Banes, R., & Gerson, G. (1987). *Effective park and recreation boards and commissions.* Reston, VA: AAHPERD.

Knudson, D. (1984). *Outdoor recreation.* New York: Macmillan.

Kraus, R. (2000). *Leisure in a changing America: Trends and issues for the 21st century.* Boston: Allyn and Bacon.

Kraus, R., & Curtis, J. (1982). *Creative management in recreation and parks.* St. Louis, MO: C. V. Mosley.

Lawrence, D. (1984). *The recreation gap.* Los Angeles: University of Southern California.

MacLean, J., Peterson, P., & Martin, W. (1985). *Recreation and leisure: The changing scene.* New York: Macmillan.

Marans, R., & Fly, J. (1999). *Recreation and the quality of urban life.* Ann Arbor, MI: Institute of Urban Research, University of Michigan.

Rainwater, C. (1922). *The play movement in the United States.* Chicago: University of Chicago.

10 OTHER OUTDOOR RECREATION RESOURCES

The natural resources that are discussed in the previous three chapters are owned by governmental agencies. Here we discuss the non-governmental lands and resources available for outdoor recreation. Private rural lands make up over 60 percent of the land base of the 48 contiguous states– approximately 1.28 billion acres. In the East, private land is an extremely important potential resource. Unlike public lands there is limited information known about the availability of these lands for use by recreationists (Cordell, 1999:34).

Private resources are classified in this chapter into five categories:

1. Personal resources that include second homes, cottages, RVs and trailers, time-share facilities, houseboats, and hunting facilities.
2. Private organization resources such as social and athletic clubs, hiking and mountaineering groups, and travel associations.
3. Semi-public organization resources such as youth organizations and preservation associations.
4. Industrial and business resources available to employees or communities.
5. Commercial recreation resources such as amusement parks, campgrounds, marinas, farms, ranches and resorts.

PERSONAL RESOURCES

Personal resources that allow for outdoor recreation opportunities include one's primary residence as well the ownership of other facilities such as vacation homes, campers, houseboats, and land.

Primary Residence Resources

American residences are equipped for the most part with a backyard or balcony which provides a facility for outdoor recreational activities including wildlife watching, outdoor games, and family barbecues on summer evenings. Many children have their first outdoor recreation experience in their backyards and the U.S. Department of Interior (1997:5) reports that 60.8 million wildlife-watchers participate in wildlife-watching activities that include observing, feeding, or photographing at their home or within a mile of it. In residences that lack backyards, many have balconies and flat roofs that function as resources for outdoor recreation activities, including wild-life watching, star-gazing, gardening, and eating outside. Another important home facility for outdoor recreation is the family swimming pool and/or spa. Entirely new resort and retirement communities have primary residences that are used year-round as a base for outdoor recreation activities.

Second Home Resources

The idea of having a vacation home, which was limited to the very rich in earlier times, gained popularity in Great Britain during the Victorian era (Ibrahim, 1991:234). In the United States, the Forest Service began as early as 1915 to lease summer home sites. Although this practice is now de-emphasized, it became a big business in the 1960s when real estate companies offered millions of acres of forest land and/or waterfront land, most by mail or telephone to customers who sometimes acquired the land without even seeing it. Beginning in the late 1960s, many ski resorts developed new mountain villages adjacent to ski areas that are visited year-round and offer second homes and timeshare arrangements. Resort real estate development is an integral part of most ski area businesses (BBC Research, 1999: III-16).

About five to six million American families own a second home for seasonal or occasional use. Fourteen percent are cottages or cabins that are not suitable for year-round use, and approximately 15 percent are either cooperatives or condominiums. Only about eight percent of these second homes are utilized by the owners as rentals (U.S. Census, 2000:1). Locations of these second homes vary greatly. Originally, when the British middle class began to imitate the wealthy stratum, second homes were places in the country away from the crowded English industrial cities of late 1800s. These were retreats for the well off to enjoy open space, socialize with friends, or work on a hobby. In the United States more than half (54%) of the owners report that the area surrounding their second home is either open space, park, woods, farm, or ranch (U.S. Census, 2000:1).

Mountain second homes are often either located at all-season ski resorts or are cabins that are used primarily during the hunting season and are located away from lakes or rivers. Fishing, hiking, biking, snowmobiling, and ski-oriented activities could take place while vacationing at a mountain second home. Water-oriented second homes are prevalent, with nearly 40 percent located very close to a body of water and with 21 percent actually waterfront property (U.S. Census, 2000:1). Most of these homes are modest structures that are extensively used in summer months along the Atlantic, Pacific, and Great Lakes shorelines. Naturally aquatic recreation activities are dominant along these shorelines. Desert second homes are used in the winter months by owners whose primary homes are in areas with cold climates. These homes are located in the southwestern United States.

Outright ownership of a second home proved to be a difficult undertaking for many people, and the alternative to individual or family ownership of a second home involves property sharing. This is an arrangement that allows the family to enjoy the full benefits of a personal second home without having to carry the whole financial burden. When a second home is owned by two or more individuals or families, a shared whole ownership is in practice. Time-sharing is another concept for second homes, which is practiced in two ways. In the membership plan, the developers continue to own the property and give the person and/or the family the right to use it for a specific period of time. In the interval-ownership plan, the buyer receives the title to the property for a particular period.

Other Personal Resources

Some people in North America use houseboats as second homes. Houseboats are generally less expensive than many traditional second homes. In addition, they can be moved from one location to another. Scarcity of berths and high docking and berthing fees are making this alternative increasingly difficult, with more people choosing to rent houseboats at the lake visited. Recreational vehicles referred to as *RVs* and recreational trailers referred to at times as *fifth-wheels* are also used as second homes. Also, one in ten Americans own a sport utility vehicle (SUV) that offer advantages when camping and exploring the outdoors. Although they are also used for routine transportation, more than one-third of SUV owners cite recreational use as very important in their decision to buy their SUV (Roper, 2001:26).

Privately Owned Lands

Another resource that is used for outdoor pursuits is private land. Farms, ranches, woodlands, ponds, and laneways can be used for hunting, fishing, swimming, boating, horseback riding, snowmobiling, cross-country skiing, observing wildlife, or simply walking. The National Private Forest Land Study of 1994 estimated that there are a total of 9.9 million owners of 393.5 million acres of privately owned forest. The study found that many types of recreational activities occur on private land, with hunting, fishing, hiking, and camping among the most popular. Seventy percent of landowners across the U.S. said they engaged in recreational activities on their own land and only 50 percent said they allowed access to others outside their own family (Teasley et al, 1999:214). One-third of the rural landowners said portions of their lands were completely closed to others and only 15 percent allowed access to outside people, with the largest percentage of owners allowing access to only family, friends, and other people they knew personally. The "completely closed" category showed a significant decrease from ten years earlier when 25 percent of respondents allowed access to outside people. This decrease may be due to the concern with liability that is always an issue with landowners (Teasley et al, 1999:214-215).

Providing a slightly different view, the 1992 National Resource Inventory estimated that of the 1.3 billion acres of nonfederal forests and agricultural lands in the United States (excluding Alaska) approximately 181 million acres are nonindustrial private lands available for others to recreate on, with most, or 72%, open to the general public. The remainder are leased to either individuals or groups. The South, with about 64.2 million acres either open or leased, has over one-third of

the U.S. private land that is available to others for recreation with the Rocky Mountain Region at 56.3 million acres, the second most available (Betz, English & Cordel,l 1999:144).

Private lands are used for hunting by 11.4 million of the 14 million hunters, and the Department of Interior reports that there are 362.4 million acres of private land owned or leased primarily for hunting by 1.6 million hunters. Nearly 900,000 anglers own or lease 17.7 million acres for fishing in the United States (Department of the Interior, et al, 1997:85), and people also purchase or lease land primarily for wildlife watching. It is estimated that 571,000 people hold 38.6 million acres for this purpose (Department of the Interior, et al, 1997:83, 96). Outdoor recreation activities considered to have the best potential for future use of private land include hunting, fishing, wildlife observation, and hiking (Teasley et al, 1999:216).

PRIVATE ORGANIZATION RESOURCES

Humans tend to organize themselves into groups to fulfill specific functions. Private organizations are witnessed in almost all human societies and should be distinguished from semipublic organizations. Membership in private organizations is usually more restricted than is membership in semipublic organizations. Private organizations can generally be divided into two groups. The first—*instrumental organizations*—emphasize the achievement of certain goals. Examples of instrumental associations are professional organizations and labor unions. In contrast, the emphasis of the second group—*expressive organizations*—is associational and interactional. Examples are social, sport, and hobby clubs. The concept may have started with Saint Andrew's Golf Club in Scotland in the 1500s, but the idea did not reach North America until 1888 when Brookline Country Club was established near Boston (Dulles, 1965:242).

Sport and Athletic Clubs

Like social clubs that cater to all kinds of expressive activities, sport and athletic clubs vary in size from small, loosely organized teams that do not own facilities to the powerful, sometimes elitist, country clubs with their expansive grounds and facilities. The most frequently found types of sport/athletic clubs in Canada and the United States cater mostly to those who play golf, tennis, and racquetball. In the United States there are 3,212 golf courses and country clubs exempt from federal income taxes and another 8,546 golf courses and country clubs in the United States considered commercial enterprises. The annual revenues and receipts of these clubs are more than $5.6 and $7.9 billion respectively (U.S. Census, 2001:8-9). Although a current study is not available, in the past there have been at least 40 private ski clubs that not only own the slopes and the lifts, but are also equipped with a clubhouse with all the needed amenities (Chubb & Chubb, 1981:339). Skating and curling clubs are found in Canada, and tennis and soccer clubs are found in the United States as well.

Sportspersons Clubs

In the United States there are nearly 40 million sportspersons, of which 14 million are hunters and 35-plus million are anglers (U.S. Department of the Interior et. al., 1997:4). Many of these participants belong to sportspersons clubs, usually oriented around fishing, hunting, and shooting. The size and structure of these clubs vary significantly. Some clubs are formed by middle-income individuals who acquire a few acres of land with a potential for outdoor activities. The more affluent outdoor aficionados purchase or lease prime areas and sometimes employ a warden to manage the fish or game. There are also a number of private rifle and skeet shooting clubs where demonstrations and competitions are held. The National Private Forest Land Study estimated that 7.76 million acres of forestland are owned by recreation/sport clubs or associations (Betz, English & Cordell, 1999:144).

Boat and Yacht Clubs

Boat and yacht clubs purchase or lease waterfront property, the development of which varies according to the financial resources of the club members. The basic service provided is the mooring and/or storing of vessels. Services may expand to include a clubhouse, an extensive marina, and a restaurant. Today there were 4,217 commercial marinas in the United States with annual receipts of $2.5 billion (U.S. Census, 2001:8). It is unclear how many of these marinas have any facilities associated with clubs, or how many of the 16.6 million boat owners (U.S. Census, 2000:261) belong to a boating club, but their sheer numbers provide us with an idea of the impact this activity has on society.

Hiking and Mountaineering Clubs

Although most hiking takes place on publicly owned land in the United States and Canada, shelters and lodges are provided on leased and owned land by hiking and mountaineering clubs. Thirty-one such clubs, organized into the Appalachian Trail Conference, provide shelters along the 2,100-mile Appalachian Trail from Georgia to Maine (Cordes, 2001:20). The Appalachian Mountain Club (AMC) of Boston, the biggest and oldest affiliate of the Appalachian Trail Conference, offers to the public eight huts and a lodge that are situated about a day's hike apart in the White Mountains region of New Hampshire. AMC's Pinkham Notch Lodge has an impressive visitor center tailored for hikers and also manages the historic Bascom Lodge along the Appalachian Trail in Massachusetts. Similarly, the Adirondack Mountain Club owns and operates two lodges in the Adirondack Mountains, and the Alpine Club of Canada owns and operates similar facilities in Alberta and British Columbia.

The Sierra Club operates several rustic alpine lodges and huts in California. These facilities give members and potential members the opportunity to explore and enjoy wild areas and encourage a commitment to wilderness preservation. For instance, at the Clair Tappaan Lodge, constructed in 1934 and located at Donner Pass, there is no membership requirement and activities include hiking, swimming, fishing, road/mountain biking, rock climbing, cross-country skiing, and photography. There are regional and local clubs around the country that have facilities for members and, in some cases, the public. In the shadow of Mount Washington and the Presidential Range in New Hampshire is the Jackson Ski Touring Foundation, a nonprofit membership organization, chartered to maintain trails in and about the village of Jackson. They provide a lodge from which to base activities and rentals for winter recreation and educational opportunities such as cross-country skiing and snowshoeing. And they maintain more than 100 miles of the area's trail system.

SEMIPUBLIC ORGANIZATION RESOURCES

Semipublic organizations are those that depend on public donations and/or government grants. Although the line of demarcation is blurred between purely private organizations and semipublic ones, the latter are open to public scrutiny more than are the former, since they receive and accept public funds. Today in the United States there are numerous entities that are exempt from federal income tax that provide recreational resources to the public. For instance, there are 276 exempt nature parks and other similar institutions, 269 exempt zoos and botanical gardens, 814 exempt historical sites that by their nature have land resources available to the public. Together these public/semipublic entities have combined revenues of $1.75 billion. There are another 4,679 fitness and recreational sports centers that are exempt with $670 million in revenue, and another 3,434 exempt museums with $4.5 billion in revenue (U.S. Census, 2001:9). In this section two types of semipublic organization are presented: youth-serving organizations and preservation organizations.

Youth-Serving Organizations

Some youth-serving organizations own or lease outdoor recreation resources; others are not owners but are involved in outdoor recreational activities. Many of the summer camps do not actually own the land on which the camps reside. Instead they have long-term contracts to build and operate facilities on Forest Service or other public lands. Together, non-profits including youth agencies and religious organizations have 6,200 camps, with approximately 65 percent of these resident camps. Not all of these camps are for children; adults, families and seniors attend as well and some are specialized programs such as for youth at risk, persons with disabilities, and campers with cancer. To give an idea of the impact these camps have, they employ 500,000 adults as counselors, leaders, and program directors, and many others for support services. Where feasible, many camp facilities are undergoing conversions to all-season use in order to accommodate year-round schools. Some camp facilities are available for rent by other groups that wish to hold a group camp experience, a conference, or a retreat. The American Camping Association publishes *A Guide to ACA-Accredited Camps* that lists programs for potential campers and for those seeking summer employment opportunities (Coutellier, 1999:154-155). Several of the youth organizations, such as the Boy Scouts and the Girl Scouts, are discussed in more detail in this section.

Boy Scouts

The Boy Scouts were organized in England in 1908 by Lord Baden-Powell who, during the Boer War, had seen the English soldiers in need of outdoor survival skills. He set about to help boys secure this essential training. William D. Boyce, a Chicago publisher, and other enthusiastic supporters organized the Boy Scouts of America (BSA) in 1910. The movement has spread throughout the world, with an international structure representing about 145 countries with headquarters in Switzerland. The BSA has 4.5 million members, one-third of whom are adult leaders. Since its inception, the BSA's membership has included more than 110 million persons.

Scouting is open to boys of all religions and races, and troops are sponsored by religious, educational, civic, fraternal, business, and labor organizations; governmental bodies; corporations; professional associations; and citizens' groups. The purpose of the overall Boy Scouts of America is to provide an educational program for boys and young adults to build character, to train in the responsibilities of participating citizenship, and to develop personal fitness. Various scouting programs are available depending on age, such as the Cub Scouts and the Boy Scouts. Boy Scouting, for boys 11 through 17, utilizes a vigorous outdoor program and peer group leadership with the counsel of an adult scoutmaster, and is designed to take place outdoors. It is in the outdoor setting that scouts share responsibilities and learn to live with one another. And it is in the outdoors that the skills and activities practiced at troop meetings come alive with purpose. Being close to nature helps Boy Scouts gain an appreciation for the beauty of the world. The outdoors is the laboratory in which Boy Scouts learn ecology and practice conservation of nature's resources.

Most of the 124,000 Scout troops in the United States have access to one or more of the 600 Scout camps operated by the 400-plus local Scout councils, plus the national office has three national high-adventure areas. The Northern Tier National High Adventure Program offers wilderness canoe expeditions and cold-weather camping in Minnesota and Canada; the Florida National High Adventure Sea Base offers aquatics programs in the Florida Keys; and Philmont Scout Ranch offers backpacking treks in the rugged high country of northern New Mexico. The Philmont Scout Ranch is on 137,000 acres and is well equipped for outdoor pursuits in hiking, camping, and wilderness survival. Volunteer leaders may attend the Philmont Training Center each summer for a week-long training conference.

Girl Scout/Girl Guide

The Girl Scout/Girl Guide movement started in Great Britain by Lord Robert Baden-Powell and his sister, Lady Agnes Baden-Powell, in 1909. With 10 million girls and adult members worldwide, there are 140 countries today with their own Scouting association for girls. These organizations form the World Association of Girl Guides and Girl Scouts and maintain world centers in Switzerland, England, Mexico, and India. The centers offer Girl Scouts and Girl Guides opportunities to meet members of Scouting movements in other countries. In the United States, the first Girl Scout troop was formed in 1912 in Savannah, Georgia, by Juliette Gordon Low, who organized the troop in her hometown. She had been active in the Girl Guide movement in England and in Scotland, and she patterned the American troops accordingly. Today, there are 3.7 million Girl Scouts with nearly one million of these adult members, and 233,000 Scout troops and groups. The Girl Scout movement provides girls with opportunities to develop their potential to make new friends, to take active leadership roles in their communities, and to learn outdoor survival skills at the many camp facilities. More than 50 million women in the United States have been members of the Scouts.

The Girl Scout movement has day-camp and resident-camp properties that are shared by troops for their outdoor programs and by leaders for training sessions. There are larger national centers in Wyoming, New York, Maryland, and Georgia. The Girl Scout National Center West in Wyoming provides a wide variety of outdoor-living opportunities for older Scouts. The Rockwood Girl Scout National Center in Potomac, Maryland, is a year-round 93-acre facility that serves as a hostel for Girl Scouts from the United States and other nations. The center is also used for a variety of programs concerning nature conservation.

YMCA

The Young Men's Christian Association (YMCA) began with George Williams in London, England, in 1844 for the purpose of instilling Christian morals among youth. The first American YMCA was formed in Boston in 1851. Today the National Council of the Young Men's Christian Association of the United States is headquartered in Chicago and has about 2,400 member associations serving more than 17.9 million men, women, and children of all faiths, races, ages and incomes, including nine million children. After World War II women and girls were admitted as members and today comprise half of the membership. Forty-four YMCAs in 39 cities across the United States operate 12,000 low-cost rooms to encourage less affluent travelers to visit the United States. World-wide there are 30 million members in more than 120 countries with facilities that include thousands of swimming pools, gymnasia, hostels, and cafeterias.

American YMCAs operate more than 400 resident camps and more than 1,200 day camps. Their day and overnight resident camps provide the opportunity to have fun and learn how to make new friends, build new skills and grow in self-reliance. Many Y camps use a natural setting to teach youth about the wonders of the world around them and how they can take good care of it. In the Y- Indian Guide programs, a parent and child meet with other parent and children teams in a small group called a tribe. Tribes get together for tribal meetings and participate in fun and educational outside activities. The Y is well known for its swimming facilities and staff that offer instruction in swimming and SCUBA. In fact, the history of national dive training in the United States began with the development of the YMCA SCUBA Program based on the principles of the YMCA triangle: the Spirit, the Mind and the Body.

YWCA

The Young Women's Christian Association (YWCA) began in London, England, in 1855 to meet the needs of working women. By 1894 a worldwide YWCA was in the making, with 83 nations represented in its membership. Now the YWCA operates facilities, many including lodging, in more than 100 countries. In the United States, Boston was the first association to use YWCA in its name in 1859, although the YWCA of New York City formed its association a year earlier, in 1858. The YWCA pioneered in the task of working against racial discrimination toward full integration, fighting obvious segregation practices and exposing hidden patterns of discrimination in legislation, institutions and systems. Although there is some emphasis on outdoor pursuits, the program revolves around the development of personal physical fitness and health, values, political skills, employment opportunities, social justice, and providing day care services. Recreation classes in their facilities generally include music, arts and crafts, dramatics, tennis, swimming, archery, aerobics, volleyball, and bowling.

4-H

The Smith-Lever Act of 1914 provided for cooperative extension work in agriculture and home economics, and it included boys' and girls' 4-H Clubs. The 4-H still stands for Head, Heart, Hands, and Health and is symbolized by the four-leaf clover. The 4-H idea has spread to more than 80 countries. Through the International Four-H Youth Exchange, young Americans visit other countries and young foreigners may live and work with American families for months at a time. In the United States, 4-H has 6.8 million members from 3,067 counties, with 143,000 clubs and special-interest groups guided by more than 600,000 adult and teenage leaders. Only 10 percent of the members live on farms; 32 percent live in towns with less than 10,000 in population and in open country, and the remainder live in larger towns, suburbs, and cities. Youth participate in more than 110 4-H program areas, including community service, environmental education, earth sciences, healthy life-style education, plants and animals, leadership, and science. More than 300,000 youth attend nearly 10,000 youth camping programs at 4-H facilities each year. There are 45 million adults in the United States who have been members of 4-H.

Camp Fire

Although the name may indicate an exclusively outdoor orientation, the Camp Fire organization serves youth in a variety of ways including camp facilities. The organization was started as the Camp Fire Girls by Luther and Charlotte Gulick in 1910. In 1975 admission of boys to this once all-girls organization led to a change in the name. Today Camp Fire is a national organization with 650,000 members, 54% of which are girls. Its purpose is to provide a program of informal education and opportunities for youth to realize their potential to function effectively as caring, self-directed individuals, and leaders for tomorrow. The organization also seeks to improve conditions in society that affect youth. This non-profit agency for youth ages through 21 is open to all without regard to race, creed, ethnic origin, sex, or income level. The entire family is engaged in many of the organization's activities.

Boys & Girls Club

The Boys & Girls Club of America has more than 2,800 neighborhood-based facilities that serve some 3.3 million young people annually, primarily from disadvantaged circumstances. Known as "The Positive Place for Kids," Clubs provide guidance-oriented programs on a daily basis for children 6-18 years old, conducted by a full-time professional staff. Key programs emphasize character and leadership development, the environment, educational enhancement, career preparation, health and life skills, the arts, sports, fitness and recreation, and they offer day and overnight camping experiences. National headquarters are located in Atlanta. The Boys and Girls Club movement originated in 1860 when three women in Hartford, Connecticut, invited a group of street boys into their home for tea and cake, and from this the movement took off.

The emphasis in the program for boys and girls is on the enhancement of the youngsters' lifestyle.

Preservation Organizations

Although the main objectives of preservation organizations is the preservation of natural areas and historical sites, numerous outdoor pursuits can take place on their premises. Not all organizations concerned with preservation own the property to be preserved; many of these organizations work to encourage other organizations, agencies, and individuals to preserve property for future generations. Some land and conservation easements donated by companies, corporations, or individuals save income tax, capital gains tax, or estate tax. Following are just a few of the nonprofit organizations that deal with preservation and outdoor pursuits.

The Nature Conservancy

The Nature Conservancy (TNC) is the largest preservation organization in the United States with more than one million members, 2,800 employees, and 60,000 volunteers. Its mission is to preserve the plants, animals and natural communities that represent the diversity of life on Earth by protecting the lands and waters they need to survive. Since 1951, the Conservancy has protected more than 92 million acres of land and water around the world, including 12 million acres in the United States. It owns more than 1,400 preserves in the country—the largest private system of nature sanctuaries in the world, and other tracts of land referred to as managed area with about half open to the public. The land is either purchased, donated, or acquired because it is ecologically significant, and many times the land acquired by the conservancy is turned over to governmental agencies to manage. Among the most popular recreational areas of the conservancy are the Virginia Coast Reserve and California's Santa Cruz Island. The Virginia Coast Reserve consists of 13 barrier islands which, along with their tidal pools, amount to 35,000 acres.

California's Santa Cruz Island, with an interpretive center, overnight accommodations, hiking expeditions, and boating trips, has 55,000 acres which are home to many rare and endangered species. A growing number of Nature Conservancy programs and projects offer overnight accommodations and their international ecotourism program strives to enhance biodiversity conservation and sustainable community development through partnerships in such countries as Ecuador and Belize. The Nature Conservancy (2001:4) has more than 100 current preservation deals in process.

National Audubon Society

Founded in 1905 throughout the Americas, the National Audubon Society conserves and restores natural ecosystems for the benefit of humanity and the Earth's biological diversity. The 600,000-member organization is supported by more than 500 chapters that seek the protection of wildlife populations, particularly birds. Their more than 100 wildlife sanctuaries vary in size from 12 to 26,800 acres and may be open to the public or require permission well in advance of a visit. For instance, the 5,400-acre Francis Beidler Forest Sanctuary northwest of Charleston, South Carolina, with a visitor center and on-site manager, is the largest known tract of virgin tupelo/bald cypress left in the world. This sanctuary is dwarfed by the special-arrangement-only 26,800-acre Rainey Wildlife Sanctuary that is a coastal marsh in Louisiana. Audubon has six national outdoor education centers, the 192-acre Aulwood Audubon Center and Farm outside of Dayton, Ohio, with a hardwood forest, meadow, farmland, sugarbrush, a stream, bog, and ponds is just one of them. Their three summer ecology camps in Maine, Connecticut, and Wyoming, offer intense natural history sessions for adults, while the Audubon Expedition Institute offers travel-study programs. The permanent staff at some of the sanctuaries serve as interpreters of wildlife and conduct hikes through the refuges (see Chapter 14, Education and the Outdoors).

The Sierra Club

The Sierra Club strives to preserve irreplaceable wildlands, save endangered and threatened wildlife, and protect the fragile environment through congressional lobbying and grassroots action on environmental issues. While they do own several lodges mentioned earlier, their focus on preservation activities does not emphasize ownership of lands. Their 700,000-member organization's mission statement is to:

- Explore, enjoy, and protect the wild places of the earth.
- Practice and promote the responsible use of the earth's ecosystems and resources.
- Educate and enlist humanity to protect and restore the quality of the natural and human environment.
- Use all lawful means to carry out these objectives.

Most Sierra Club chapter-sponsored outings across the nation have no membership requirement and may be day hikes, peak scrambles, bird-watching trips, conservation-oriented walks into the remaining natural areas of a major urban region.

National Trust for Historic Preservation

The National Trust for Historic Preservation, with more than one quarter of a million members, encourages and assists agencies, organizations, and individuals to undertake historic preservation. The Trust owns and operates 21 historic sites that serve more than 800,000 visitors annually and has an Associate Sites Program that is a national network of historic places grouped by theme and region. Working with the National Park Service, the National Trust for Historic Preservation serves as the principal partner for planning and implementing *Save America's Treasures*, a national effort to protect America's threatened cultural treasures, including significant documents, works of art, maps, journals, and historic structures that document and illuminate the history and culture of the United States.

Rails-to-Trails Conservancy

Rails-to-Trails Conservancy (RTC) is involved in the development and protection of greenways in the United States. Founded in 1986, their mission is to protect America's railroad corridors, which are being abandoned at the rate of about 2,000 miles per year. The creation of rail-trails is primarily a result of the efforts of local trail enthusiasts—including citizens, politicians, and business leaders who see the potential to convert a rail corridor and seize the opportunity. RTC strengthens this process by providing technical, legal, and policy assistance to local trail development groups. More than 10,000 miles of rail corridor has been converted to rail-trails so far and this trend shows no signs of slowing down with more than 18,000 miles of additional rail-trail projects underway. RTC does not actually own any of the rail-trails (Morris, 1999:140).

RARE

RARE Center for Tropical Conservation is a U.S.-based international nonprofit organization based in Arlington, Virginia, that has been active in 30 countries in Latin America, the Caribbean, and the Pacific since 1973. RARE Center's mission is to protect wildlands of globally significant biological diversity by empowering local people to benefit from their preservation. Just north of Guatemala on the southern Pacific coast of Mexico, alliance members funds and technical assistance to create a nature trail for birdwatching. The trail contains breaks in the thick vegetation where birds can be seen, and a birdwatching tower allows visitors a view above the forest canopy.

Land Trust Alliance

Based in Washington, D.C. and founded in 1982, the Land Trust Alliance (2001:1) is the leader of local and regional land trusts. Together, the more than 1,200 trusts protect a variety of land types including wetlands, river corridors, watersheds/water quality, farmland, and ranchland that total more than 6.4 million acres of open space. The Alliance provides resources and training at the grassroots level to help trusts protect important open spaces. California, New York and Montana lead the nation in the amount of acreage protected by this group.

Trust for Public Lands

Since 1972, the Trust for Public Lands (TPL) has helped protect more 1.4 million acres in 45 states in 2,200 park and open space projects. The areas range from expansive recreation areas to historic homesteads and small city parks. TPL's Conservation Finance Program works with community groups, elected officials, and public agencies to help design and pass conservation funding measures. For the November 2000 elections, their Conservation Finance Program assisted 54 local and state ballot efforts nationwide generating $3.3 billion to protect parks and open space.

Other Organizations

There are numerous other organizations that are involved in nature preservation including American Land Conservation, The Conservation Fund, Brooks Bird Club, Bass Anglers Society, Sport Fishing Institute, the Garden Club of America, and others.

INDUSTRIAL AND BUSINESS RESOURCES

In this section, we discuss the provision of recreation resources by industry and business.

Employee Recreation

Provision of recreational opportunities by industry and business for their employees began at the heel of the advent of industrialization in the mid 1800s. Peacedale Manufacturing Company of Rhode Island is credited with providing library resources and singing classes as early as 1854. Other companies followed suit when the Pullman Company, the National Cash Register Company, and the Metropolitan Life Insurance Company provided recreation centers and golf courses and organized picnics and outings for their employees.

Today thousands of companies sponsor recreational activities for their employees from modest walking clubs to large onsite facilities.

A 1913 survey by the U.S. Bureau of Labor Statistics shows that more than 50 percent of the 51 companies surveyed offered some form of employee recreation. In 1918 San Francisco established the first citywide industrial recreation association. A significant increase in this sort of offering was witnessed in the late 1930s, when the international recreation department was established by the United Auto Workers. In 1941 the National Industrial Recreation Association was created.

Cummins Engine Company of Columbus, Indiana, has received national recognition for their employee recreation program started more than 30 years ago. The 345-acre Ceraland Park, owned and operated by the Cummins Employees Recreation Association, a nonprofit association, has wooded parkland with several large picnic shelters, lakefront log cabins, a large group campground with 56 stoned campsites, 265 individual campsites, a camp store, and an archery and rifle range. Groups, guests of employees, Good Sam and FMCA RV-club members are also welcome to rent the campsites for a limited number of days. The boat dock and aquatic center on 11-acre Lake Lucille has paddle boats, canoes, and rowboats available for rent at nominal fees.

Industrial Land and Outdoor Recreation

Industrial land provided a significant portion of outdoor recreational opportunities in the United States in the past, when 72 percent of corporate land was open for some form of recreation. Forty-four percent of the land was open to the general public for recreation use without permission. Most of the 68 million acres used for that purpose were in the southern states (Cordell et al., 1979:38-83).

There are motivating factors behind the involvement of profit-oriented corporations in sponsoring outdoor pursuits, but profit does not seem to be the dominant factor, although there are indications this may be on the rise.

Some companies open their land to recreationists because it was always open before the land was acquired. The company may feel that the best public relations can occur if the land is left open for recreation use. On the other hand, the opening of private land to public use may lead to difficulties, one of which is the cost of operation. In order to provide adequate service, the operating company may find it necessary to provide facilities, collect trash, control fire hazards, and build roads, among other things.

Another problem the company may face is legal liability. Innovative legal agreements have been drafted that ease this concern, as in the Hatfield-McCoy trails network in West Virginia. And states wanting private land to be open to public use in some form passed legislation that shield landowners from liability in certain situations. All 50 states have recreation user statutes to limit liability of landowners for injuries occurring to recreation visitors while on their land. Although the degree of immunity varies, the statutes are consistent in shielding the landowner who does not charge entry fees. Charging an entry fee typically negates the protection (Douglass, 1999:15; Voth & Wright, 1995:113-119).

Four types of industries offer significant lands that are either utilized in outdoor pursuits or have potential for such use (Knudson, 1984:136):

1. ***Wood-Using Industries.***
   Weyerhaeuser Corporation was the first of the large wood-using companies to start a tree farm in 1941. Since 1975, portions of its lands have been open to the public for a nominal fee as recreation resources. For instance, the Snoqualmie and White River Forest Areas in Washington state are open for fishing or just a break from the crowds. Access Permits are available from a variety of vendors and are sold on an annual basis. Activities provided on Weyerhaeuser lands are cross-country skiing, hiking, orienteering, biking, hunting, horseback riding, berry picking, and wildlife tracking. Weyerhaeuser hires professional staff to protect and manage wildlife and to supervise and conduct activities on its natural resources.

2. ***Utility Companies.*** Electric power derived from hydroelectric plants is monitored by the Federal Energy Regulatory Commission. Among the commission's requirements is the development of recreational opportunities and utilization of each plant's reservoir as a recreation site. In California, the Pacific Gas and Electric Company (PGE), derives most of its electric power from hydroelectric plants in California mountains an owns 160,000 acres of prime watershed land in the Sierra Nevada, Cascade and Coast ranges. Systems of dams built by PG&E store this water in reservoirs resulting in 130 lakes operated by PG&E that help sustain river flows during dry summer months. These lakes also store large volumes of water during heavy spring runoffs, thus diminishing the threat of floods. Large lakes such as Almanor, Spaulding, Silver and Britton are man-made lakes used for hydroelectric power and recreation. Most of the lakes offer fishing, swimming and boating. Additionally, since power company profits are limited by California laws, excess income goes to recreation and park projects.

3. ***Other Manufacturing Companies.*** Included among these companies are steel and mining companies. In southern West Virginia, private companies in the coal mining region teamed with federal trail experts to develop the innovative Hatfield-McCoy Recreation Area that opened in the fall of 2000 with over 300 miles of multiple-use trails. The innovative Hatfield-McCoy, selected as one of the 16 National Millennium Trails, will eventually consist of more than 2,000 miles of trail in West Virginia and Kentucky.

4. ***Land-Holding Companies.*** Many companies have donated land as public preserves managed by nonprofit preservation organizations such as The Nature Conservancy. Others, like the Louisiana Land and Title Company, open their own recreational resources to the public.

Private operators provide opportunities for thrill-seekers to bungee jump in many parts of the United States.

COMMERCIAL ENTERPRISES

In the past 20 years, the number of commercial facilities and leisure service providers that provide recreational opportunities has burgeoned, with many of these enterprises combining private resources and operations with public land and water resources. Overall in the United States the Census Bureau (2001:8) reports that there are 16,604 commercial fitness and recreational sports centers with $7.9 billion in receipts; and other commercial enterprises including 4,217 marinas, 8,546 golf courses, and 379 ski facilities with combined receipts of $12.5 billion. Lodging operators have still more resources used for outdoor recreation.

Commercial enterprises having to do with outdoor pursuits come in many types, sizes, and orientations. There are small outfitters that have boathouses, rafts, vehicles, and even planes and lodges available for outdoor recreation adventures. Sky Trekking Alaska, for example, with a lodge and several small planes, offers custom small group adventures in the Alaskan outback to ice-fish, mush, snowshoe, hike, wildlife watch, salmon-fish, and photograph. Some larger companies such as Mountain Travel Sobek, Backroads, Backcountry, and GORP provide substantial resources that enable thousands to bike, hike, paddle, climb, snorkel, fish, hunt, cave, camp, wildlife watch, ski, snowboard, and outdoor drive. Many outfitters, lodges, and other commercial enterprises link together along National Scenic Byways to provide world-class outdoor adventures that combine private and public resources. Others, such as ARAMARK Sports and Entertainment, operate resorts at several national and state parks. One of ARAMARK's 14 locations, Lake Powell Resorts and Marinas in Glen Canyon National Recreation Area, has four marinas; several lodges; RV hookups; tour boats; and rental houseboats, power boats, kayaks, and canoes.

The following section provides a closer look at commercial enterprises that offer camping facilities, ski areas, resorts, amusement parks, and guest ranches.

Camp Facilities and Commercial Campgrounds

The American Camping Association is the accrediting body for the camp profession and accredits both the nonprofit and the for-profit resident and day camp facilities. Traditionally these facilities enroll campers during the summer months for a period that ranges from several days, a week, a month, or even the entire summer. Of the estimated 8,500 American camps, 2,300 are privately owned by independent for-profit operators that either own or lease their camp facilities (Coutellier, 1999:154). Private camp operations may be found in rural, suburban or urban communities; and operate on several thousand back country acres or in city parks. Year-round use of private camp facilities is growing.

Another type of camp facility is the commercial campground that offers campsites for rent, lease, or sale. Directories published by *Woodall's* and *Trailer Life* list nearly 15,000 campgrounds nationwide, of which only 4,000 are public campgrounds (Betz, English & Cordell, 1999:144). The rest are campgrounds operated by commercial enterprises. Estimates indicate that there are at least 814,000 private individual campsites available with 480,000 of these offering full hookups for RVs. About 58 percent of the campgrounds are open year round and 61 percent lease sites to campers on an annual basis (McEwen, 1999:151). Many commercial campgrounds have elaborate facilities such as swimming pools, tennis courts, and cable tv/phone hookups. A small number of campgrounds

The first KOA Kampground was founded in Billings, Montana, in 1962 to serve travelers headed to and from the Seattle World's Fair. Travelers could rent a space for the night or other short-term period to park their trailer or pitch their tent. As the franchise grew, the potential franchise owner of a KOA campground purchased the use of the KOA name and its services, and received a guarantee of a certain territory in which there would be no other KOAs.

are rustic and provide traditional outdoor pursuits such as hiking and nature walks. A smaller number provide roadside overnight camping with hardly any promise for outdoor pursuits. Horseshoe continues to be the most popular recreational facility at private campgrounds with 64% of them offering it (McEwen, 1999: 152).

Campground associations have been formed in many states and provinces to promote business, affect governmental decisions, and provide the needed information and education for members and others. On the national level the Association of RV Parks & Campgrounds (ARVC), a trade association with 3,700 members, represents the commercial RV park and campground industry throughout the United States and has certification programs for operators.

Campgrounds operate as businesses open for use by the general public such as Kampgrounds of America (KOA; see box), as condominium-style campgrounds, or as membership campgrounds. The condominium-style campground entails one of two approaches. The individual camper owns a specific lot located in the campground. This site can be rented out when the owner chooses, or the person can own an undivided interest in the entire property. Examples of condominium-style campgrounds are Bryn Mawr Camp Resorts and Yogi Bear Jellystone Parks. Membership campgrounds require a membership to use sites at a network of campgrounds and sometimes offer a time-sharing arrangement at other campgrounds. Such an arrangement allows the member to use other sites at affiliated campgrounds across the United States and Canada. For example, Camp Coast to Coast coordinates visits among 150 campgrounds in North America. Good Sam Parks offers another type of campground arrangement. The sites are not owned by the Good Sam Club, but rather are independently owned campgrounds that receive a stamp of approval from the million-member RV club.

The development of KOA-type franchises, condominium-style campgrounds, and membership-style campgrounds expanded in the 1980s along with other full-hookup campgrounds. Together this group increased from 285,532 in 1977 to 483,672 by 1987. Since that time this category has leveled off (McEwen, 1999:153)

Although public campgrounds tripled their capacity of improved sites over the past two decades and some offer advanced reservations, many travelers find commercial campgrounds more desirable because of the following features (Chubb & Chubb, 1981:387; McEwen, 1999:92):

- Acceptance of advance reservations, thus making it possible to plan an itinerary that includes a series of popular destinations without a concern about campsite availability.
- Availability of more amenities, such as electric, water, and sewer hookups; paved camping spaces; bathhouse and laundromat facilities; recreation halls; and well-lit, patrolled campsite areas.
- A policy of remaining open in the off-season, thus making it possible for people to camp while enjoying such activities as snowmobiling, ice fishing, hunting, and cross-country skiing.
- Provision by some campsites of fully equipped tents or RVs so that campers traveling by air and others not wishing to bring their own equipment may still enjoy the advantages of camping. This also allows noncampers to try camping and see how they enjoy the experience before investing in equipment of their own.

Ski Areas

Lift-served skiing originated over 50 years ago in North America, and the number of facilities grew slowly until the 1960s when skiing exploded in popularity. According to the National Ski Areas Association there

Table 10.1 Characteristics of U.S. Ski Regions.

Characteristics	The East	The Midwest	The Rocky Mountains	The Far West
Range	Northern Georgia and western North Carolina to Maine.	Michigan, Wisconsin, Minnesota, parts of Illinois, Ohio, and Indiana.	Mountain areas of New Mexico, Colorado, Utah, Idaho, and Montana.	Pacific coast mountain areas of California, Oregon, Washington, and Alaska. Similar to Rocky Mountains region.
Elevation (above sea level)	Modest; 460–1400 meters (1500–4500 ft.).	Minor; glacier-produced hills reach 490 meters (1600 ft.) at most.	High; between 1500–3300 meters (5000–11,000 ft.); some resorts at 2400 meters (8000 ft.).	
Skiing opportunities	Enormous variety; some of the most interesting and stimulating skiing; most trails are carved through forests and are narrower than elsewhere; good cross-country skiing opportunities.	Less variety; ideal learner and intermediate slopes; runs are often cut through woods; lacks rugged terrain; drops 60–180 meters (200–600 ft) at most; excellent slalom course and ski jump facilities; competitions numerous; exceptional cross-country skiing.	Best skiing for expert skiers; some runs are through forest; many open slopes are 300 feet or more in width; satisfying long runs; greatest vertical drop in United States; status-skiing opportunities; some gentle slopes permit use by less than expert skiers.	Exceptional bowl and panoramic skiing; excellent opportunities for learners as well as experts; sheer scale of High Sierra skiing unsurpassed; some ski areas are close to urban centers in Northwest.
Major resort areas	Intensive development along mountainous spine of Vermont; most challenging areas are in New Hampshire; one big mountain (Whiteface) is in New York along with 100 smaller areas; Sugarloaf area in Maine is well known and impressive; several popular resorts in Pennsylvania.	Clusters of centers ideal for learners around Detroit, Chicago, Milwaukee, Minneapolis–St. Paul metropolitan area; chain of resorts bordering Great Lakes from Lutsen, Minnesota, across Wisconsin to Boyne City, Michigan; Boyne Country ski development is leader in Midwest—first in world to install a quadruple chairlift.	Contains nation's most prestigious resorts (Colorado in particular); even small resorts match largest resorts elsewhere in skiable area but not necessarily in facilities; subregional differences not substantial, but southern resorts have drier powder snow, whereas northern areas have greater snow depths.	Two concentrations in southern California—areas within 160 km (100 miles) of Los Angeles and the High Sierra resorts of Lake Tahoe region; prime ski area in northern California is Mt. Shasta; three areas on flanks of Mt. Hood near Portland, Oregon; three areas in Snoqualmie Pass near Seattle, WA; more than 30 areas in Oregon and Washington designed primarily as day areas.
Advantages or disadvantages	Closest to heaviest concentrations of potential skiers; most areas readily accessible by car; best areas seriously overcrowded at times; many areas have distinctive atmospheres and many loyal users.	Many resorts within a 1- or 2-hour drive of large urban centers; midwestern skiers known for their enthusiasm and dedication; excellent ski services and instruction opportunities.	Many resorts not readily accessible; cost and altitude problems for non-Westerners; some of the most beautiful settings in the world; great diversity of winter sports and après-ski opportunities.	Access often difficult in Sierra Nevadas; evening and weekend opportunities excellent in some areas; best areas are away from usual vacation routes; some cost and altitude problems for skiers from the East; exotic settings available on highest slopes.

continued

Table 10.1 Characteristics of U.S. Ski Regions. (continued)

Length of season	Usually 3 or 4 months; extended and made more reliable by heavy use of snow-making equipment; occasional mild winter can be disastrous, especially in the South.	Similar to the East but colder temperatures an asset; adequate skiing almost a certainty throughout season where snow-making equipment is used.	Longer season than East or Midwest; depends on latitude and elevation.	Longest season; year-round skiing possible in some high northern locations.
Skiing conditions	Winds occasionally strong.	Often extremely cold temperatures, sometimes accompanied by strong winds.	Most comfortable climatic conditions; mostly skiing below timberline, which provides wind-protected trails; more sunny days than other regions.	Threat of storms; risk of being snowed in.
Snow and trail conditions	Unpredictable; extreme cold periods alternate with devastating thaws; snow on trails often packed hard because of heavy use.	Heavy snowfalls supplemented by use of snow-making equipment; has most uniform conditions of all regions.	Large quantities of snow in average season; dry-air conditions produce snow that rarely packs into hard snow or ice; best consistency in world—better even than in European Alps; danger of avalanches; problems with whiteouts and flat light.	Heavy snowfalls—often too much; reaches depths of 5 m (15 ft) in Sierra Nevadas in average season; snow very persistent—comes early and stays late; unfortunately often damp, sometimes wet conditions.
Examples of major resort developments	Stowe, Vt., considered to be the ski capital of the East; steep, narrow trails provide challenge; 660 m (2150 ft) vertical drop; 58 different lodge facilities.	Boyne Country, Michigan, largest privately owned ski development in U.S.; foremost complex in the Midwest; best racing slopes in region; 190 m vertical drop; can accommodate 1500 people in deluxe lodge, inn, and villa facilities.	Aspen, Co., considered by many to be the ski capital of the world; includes 4 huge mountain slopes; one just for beginners; 1160 m vertical drop; 95 places to stay, providing 1608 rooms and 1469 condominium facilities.	Heavenly Valley, California-Nevada border, largest ski area in the world; 5200 hectares (20 sq. miles) of lift-served terrain; 1100-1200 m (3600-4000 ft) vertical drop; 24 places to stay.

Source: M. Chubb, and H. Chubb, *One Third of Our Time: An Introduction to Recreation Resources and Behavior* (New York: Wiley, 1981), 391–92. Reprinted with permission.

A Few of the World-Class Ski Resort Areas in the United States

Alta, Utah. Alta is for famous for deep powder, spectacular runs, serious skiers, steep ungroomed chutes, on and off the trail map, and classic ski lodges. There are good beginner slopes too, but over the years Alta has attracted and produced elite skiers. Alta is in the same canyon as Snowbird and about 35 miles from Salt Lake City, Utah.

Aspen, Colorado. Aspen has four mountains—Ajax, Buttermilk, Highlands and Snowmass that offer diverse good skiing, with few rivals in the Rockies. Outdoor activities of all kinds abound year-round. Denver is the major city nearby.

Breckenridge, Colorado. Breckenridge is about 100 miles from Denver. Its four mountains are quite different and offer terrain for all grades of skier and outdoor enthusiasts. Imperial Bowl is the highest in-bounds skiing in the USA at slightly less than 13,000 ft.

Crested Butte, Colorado. Crested Butte is a paradox: it is small yet marketed internationally, and has some of the gentlest and most challenging skiing in the Rockies. Its fame comes from its extreme skiing and for offering one of the biggest programs for disabled skiers in the country.

Heavenly, California. Heavenly is intersected by the California-Nevada border where the views from the top are startlingly different: Lake Tahoe on the California side and the Nevada Desert on the other. With good intermediate skiing and hiking and biking trails, two-thirds of the area's 150 miles of trails have snow-making.

Jackson Hole, Wyoming. Jackson Hole ski resort at Teton Village is mainly for intermediates and experts. It has a reputation as one of the best ski areas in the United States. It is not only the dynamic skiing or the vertical drop—the biggest in the U.S., but the mix of slopes and scenery including the Teton mountain range, wildlife, wild-west atmosphere, and the wilderness of Yellowstone National Park.

Mammoth, California. Mammoth is 300 miles from Los Angeles and one of the biggest ski resorts stretching seven miles from end to end. Located on an ancient volcano, it is in a remote and wild part of the Eastern Sierras not far from Yosemite National Park. Mammoth has dramatic scenery of its own, especially the jagged, toothy Minarets.

Park City, Utah. Park City, open since 1963, is known for world-renowned skiing and legendary dry powder. There are three large ski resort with areas for snowboarding, cross-country, and the full gamut of winter and summer sports. Park City hosted the Olympics in 2002.

Snowbird, Utah. Snowbird has excellent snow, challenging bowls, one of the widest intermediate trails in the country; a large, fast cablecar, and scenery: Snowbird's most challenging in-bounds skiing is in its steep-sided bowls where chutes serve as launching pads for those who like the "free-fall" dimension of skiing. It is 30 miles from Salt Lake City international airport.

Squaw Valley, California. Squaw Valley is the most challenging of the 15 ski areas scattered around the shores of Lake Tahoe. Squaw's six mountains encompass every type of terrain: from moguls on a steep face to beginners slopes. Squaw has "radical" skiing off the Pallisades and 33 lifts.

Sun Valley, Idaho. Sun Valley was built in 1936 by Averell Harriman, president of the Union Pacific Railway, but only after a long search to find a resort that would attract passengers during the lean winter months. Mount Baldy is a mountain with a steep pitch and more than half a dozen bowls and 78 ski runs, many for intermediate cruising runs. Summertime has biking, hiking, skating, walking, horseback riding, and llama treks.

Taos, New Mexico. Taos ski area is known for light, dry powder and steep, deep and high- adventure, ungroomed runs with some still requiring an initial hike of an hour. Ernie

Blake, a German-born Swiss who worked as an interrogator for Allied Intelligence, invented this ski area in New Mexico's Sangre de Cristo mountains that has an exotic mixture of cultural influences from European to Pueblo Indian.

Telluride, Colorado. Telluride, with year-round sports, is famously steep in places and located in a box canyon in a remote corner of southwest Colorado, amidst the San Juan Mountains. The sophisticated cult ski resort, is right next a National Historic District, the 19th century silver mining town that has an old main street dominated by the New Sheridan Hotel. There are black diamond trails, cruising, and some easy skiing.

Vail/Beaver Creek, Colorado. Vail has some of the best back bowls in North America with more than two-thirds of the 110 runs graded beginner or intermediate. Built in the early 1960s in the image of a Tyrolean/Bavarian hybrid, the resort has a cosmopolitan atmosphere, cross-country ski trails, and off-season activities such as rafting and mountain biking.

Source: Modified and adapted from Media Odyssey, Inc. "Ski the World: The Best Resorts in the World" http://www.wu-wien.ac.at/usr/h94/h9450102/skiing.html 2001.

Commercial ski resorts supply a variety of services, programs, and facilities for ski-related activities and for hikers, mountain bikers and less active guests (Chubb & Chubb, 1981: 380;BBC Research 1999:III14). Some of these facilities include:

- Lighted slopes and trails (especially at resorts close to metropolitan areas) to extend the skiing day and accommodate all-season visitors.

- Reasonably priced equipment rentals and ski, snowboarder, and climbing schools with ample beginners' facilities to attract new participants.

- Rope tows, chairlifts, gondolas, and trams to transport skiers, snowboarders, climbers, hikers, and other outdoor enthusiasts rapidly and effortlessly to the skiing and recreation areas.

- Snow-cat or helicopter transportation and guide services to make backcountry areas accessible.

- Iceskating rinks, snow tubes, toboggan runs, sleigh rides, heated swimming pools, and multi-use trails to provide other outdoor activities and to attract nonskiers.

- Indoor swimming pools and tennis courts to attract nonskiers and skiers, most of whom swim and about 65 percent of whom play tennis.

- Apres-ski programs, including movies, live entertainment, and parties involving the use of resort-provided lounges, gamerooms, restaurants, bars, and nightclubs.

---

are 521 operating ski areas in the United States. Many are owned by about 20 large corporations (BBC Research, 1999:III-3, 10). This trend toward consolidation has taken place over the past decade. Two enterprises, the American Ski Company and the former owners of Vail Associates have purchased numerous ski resorts around the country (Gardner, 1999:158). Although many ski areas are developed and managed by large corporations, most are located on national forest land.

About 50 to 55 million skier visits are recorded at American resorts each year

(USDA Forest Service, 2001: 3-299, 3-302) with snowboarders accounting for 20 percent of the total skiers. In recent years participation in skiing and ski-related activities stabilized although the mix of activities and the concentration of visitors at destination resorts continues to shift. Today's areas have a variety of snow activities that use snowboards, fat skis, snowbikes, skwals, luge, as well as traditional skis. At least 50 of the ski areas in the United States and Canada are regarded as world-renowned resorts, including Aspen in Colorado, Snowbird in Utah, and Whistler in British Columbia. The Forest Service guides the establishment of new areas, as well as the development and operation of the areas located within its jurisdiction. For example, the number of skiers on a slope, in a given day, is controlled. Construction of ski trails is also controlled in order to reduce land disturbance. Material in Table 10.1 and the boxes provide additional information about ski areas in the United States.

Other Resorts

Ski-oriented multi-season resorts are a type of resort facility that have become quite elaborate, with most open year-round. They double as ski resorts in the winter season and destinations for outdoor recreation enthusiasts of all types during other seasons offering hiking, mountain-biking, climbing, horseback riding, canoeing, kayaking, rafting, bird watching, wildlife viewing, and fishing. For instance, the ski resort of Alta, Utah has world-class fly-fishing and wildflower viewing, and is a popular family reunion destination; Telluride is a skiing, snowboarding, and mountain-biking mecca; and Park City and most other mountain resorts have year-round outdoor adventures. Some double as beauty and health resorts, but many health resorts do not have anything to do with winter ski activities. There are also strictly warm-weather resorts with water-oriented outdoor facilities that range from simple to luxurious, and sport resorts that focus on instruction and practice facilities. Lodging facilities and resorts at the national and state parks are frequently operated by commercial enterprises such as AMFAC and TW Services, and are usually oriented around use of the park and participation in outdoor activities.

Health and beauty resorts are more prevalent in Europe than in North America and are found around the Czech Republic's Karlsbad, France's Vichy, and Germany's Bad Pyrmont. The emphasis in Europe is on mineral water therapy that probably dates back to the Romans. Mineral hot springs have been meccas in the United States, too, with Hot Springs, Arkansas, developing facilities for tourists, and benefitting from federal protection as early as 1832. During the roaring 1920s, ornate spas were built there along Bathhouse Row. Not all health spas are oriented around mineral springs though. Rancho La Puerta, founded in 1940 in a broad valley just across from the United States border in Tecate, Baja California, Mexico, is considered one of the original North American health spas to emphasize mind, body, and spirit. At their facility they have created a 3,000-acre nature preserve that extends to the foot of 3,885-foot Mt. Kuchumaa. They have daily hiking and fitness programs, lectures, healthy meals, as well as traditional spa activities such as facials, massages, and manicures. This model is followed by many of the health spas across the country.

Warm-weather active resorts exploded onto the scene in the 1950s with Club Mediterranean. War-weary Europeans needed a vacation, and an Olympic water polo champion from Belgium named Gerard Blitz organized a beach holiday for a few hundred of his friends in Majorca, Spain. The program was simple: sun and fun on the shores of the Mediterranean, activities, sports, and relaxation in a setting of natural beauty. With more than one million members today, the club operates 80 resort villages in 30 countries from North America to Asia. Most of these resorts are beach oriented, and 30 are ski-oriented villages in the mountains. Couples, families, older individuals, as well as singles use these resorts. Many other sun resorts followed suit with active vacation facilities in relaxing locations, mostly near beaches.

With a private mile-long fishing pond, Tim Pond Camps in Maine is the oldest set of sporting camps in New England, hosting guests since the mid-1800s. At most sport resorts, water sports are by far the most popular activities, with fishing, boating, rafting, and water skiing taking place. Many resorts provide outdoor pursuits such as horseback riding, hiking, birding, and wildlife viewing. In the past century, sport resorts have expanded rapidly, particularly those that emphasize tennis and golf. For example North Carolina's Pinehurst Club has a 200-mile trail for horseback riding. In addition, it has very attractive features such as a health spa, a trap-and-skeet shooting facility, and a lake for boating. In a much more rustic approach, the privately run San Juan Hut Systems operates six wooden huts along a 206-mile mountain bike route from Telluride, Colorado, to Moab, Utah, that crosses four national forests including alpine tundra of the San Juan Mountains to the desert canyon country of Utah. The Seaway Trail along New York's St. Lawrence Seaway and the Oregon Coast National Scenic Byways have networks of resorts and outfitters located along their respective shorelines that work together with public officials to link substantial private resources for the benefit of outdoor recreationists. Sailors, water skiers, hanggliders, sailboarders, kayakers, and beachcombers all benefit as do persons embarking on fishing, scuba, rafting, and hiking expeditions.

Theme and Amusement Parks

A small, private park, Jones Wood, provided entertainment on Manhattan Island as early as 1850. But it was the building of Coney Island on the southwestern end of Long Island, New York, that may have signaled the birth of amusement parks in America. The idea was copied from the world-famous Luna Park in Paris.

Today there are 450 amusement theme parks, 157 water theme parks, 117 zoos, 78 historical sites, and 166 nature parks considered commercial enterprises in the United States. The annual receipts of these parks is more than 7.4 billion (U.S. Census, 2001:7). Parks vary from small ones where rides, games, and shows are all together, to medium-size parks. Designated by the UNESCO as an International Biosphere Reserve, Grandfather Mountain is a medium-size private park with nature exhibits and 13 miles of alpine trails on the highest peak in the Blue Ridge near Boone, North Carolina. Huge theme parks such as Seaworld and Disneyland's California Adventure Park draw millions of visitors annually. Some major theme parks are developed on large parcels of land with enough open space and natural features to contribute to a genuine outdoor experience.

Guest Ranches and Vacation Farms

Guest ranches known to some as dude ranches are working ranches and farms that acquire additional income by opening them to guests. Accommodating guests often becomes the main source of income, with livestock and the production of crops as secondary interests (Jensen, 1985:253). Most of these ranches are 1,000 acres or more but some are quite small. In Cedersedge, Colorado, along the Grand Mesa National Scenic Byway, the ten-acre Cedar's Edge Llama Bed and Breakfast has interaction with llamas, llama care, and llama breeding. At most guest ranches, such as Arizona's 2,000-acre Flying E Ranch in Wickenburg, horseback riding is the main outdoor activity. Since most of these ranches are in the west, the life-style is western. In the Midwest many small farmers have opened their farms for outdoor pursuits, particularly for fishing, as a means of augmenting their income. Hunting is also allowed for a seasonal or daily fee on farms with pastures and woodlands. Some farms are providing swimming pools and golf courses.

Summary

Private outdoor recreation resources could come from personal, nonprofit, semipublic, industrial, and business resources. Their offerings not only supplement public offerings, but could serve as models in a number of cases. While the personal resources may include residences, second homes, boats, RVs, and the like private organizations include social, sport, and hiking clubs, boat and yacht clubs, as well as nature clubs. Semipublic organizations such as the YMCA and the Girl Scouts, and preservation organizations such as The Nature Conservancy and Audubon Society offer members many outdoor pursuits. In the meantime, a number of industries are seeking to provide their employees and local communities with these opportunities. Commercial enterprises have been in the business of providing outdoor recreation facilities and activities for many years. Campgrounds and ski areas resorts accommodate many a recreationist. Other resorts, theme parks, and guest ranches have played important roles in providing outdoor opportunities for young and mature alike.

REFERENCES

BBC Research. (1999). New England Winter Recreation Industry and Market Analysis Final Report Prepared for The U.S. Department of Agriculture Forest Service August 20, 1999.

Betz, C., English, D., & Cordell, H. K. (Eds.), (1999). Outdoor recreation resources. In *Outdoor recreation in American life: A national assessment of demand and supply trends.* Champaign, IL: Sagamore Publishing, Inc.

Chubb, M., & Chubb, H. (1981). *One third of our time: An introduction to recreation behavior and resources.* New York: Wiley and Sons.

Cordell, H. K. (1999). *Outdoor recreation in American life: A national assessment of demand and supply trends.* Champaign, IL: Sagamore Publishing, Inc.

Cordell, H., Legg, H., & McLellan, R. (1979). The private outdoor estate. *The third nationwide outdoor recreation plan.* Washington, D.C.: U.S. Government Printing Office.

Cordes, K., & Lammers, J. (photographer). (2001). *America's National Scenic Trails.* Norman, OK: University of Oklahoma Press.

Coutellier, C. (1999). Organized camps in the United States In H. K. Cordell *(Ed.), Outdoor recreation in American life: A national assessment of demand and supply trends.* Champaign, IL: Sagamore Publishing, Inc.

Douglass, R. W. (1999). History of outdoor recreation and nature-based tourism in the United States. In H. K. Cordell *(Ed.), Outdoor recreation in American life: A national assessment of demand and supply Trends.* Champaign, IL: Sagamore Publishing, Inc.

Dulles, F. (1965). *A history of recreation* (2nd ed.). New York: Appleton-Century-Crofts.

Gardner, S. (1999). Downhill ski area trends in the United States. In H. K. Cordell *(Ed.), Outdoor Recreation in American Life: A national assessment of demand and supply trends.* Champaign, IL: Sagamore Publishing, Inc.

Ibrahim, H. (1991). *Leisure and society: A comparative approach.* Dubuque, IA: Wm C. Brown.

Jensen, C. (1985). *Outdoor recreation in America.* Minneapolis, MN: Burgess Publishing.

Knudson, D. (1984). *Outdoor recreation.* New York: Macmillan.

Land Trust Alliance. (2001, September). *National land trust census.* [On-line]. Available: http://www.lta.org/newsroom/census2000.htm

McEwen, D. (1999). Campgrounds. In H. K. Cordell (Ed.), *Outdoor recreation in American life: A national assessment of demand and supply trends.* Champaign, IL: Sagamore Publishing, Inc.

Morris, H. (1999). Rails-to-Trails. In H. K. Cordell (Ed.), *Outdoor recreation in American life: A national assessment of demand and supply trends.* Champaign, IL: Sagamore Publishing, Inc.

Roper Starch. (2001). *Outdoor recreation in America 1999: The family and the environment* (A report prepared for the Recreation Roundtable Washington, D.C.)

Teasley, R., Bergstrom, J., Cordell, H. K., Zarnoch, S., & Gentle, G. (1999). Private lands and outdoor recreation in the United States " In H. K. Cordell *(Ed.), Outdoor recreation in American life: A national assessment of demand and supply trends.* Champaign, IL: Sagamore Publishing, Inc.

The Nature Conservancy. (2001). *The annual report for fiscal year 2000.* [On-line]. Available: http://nature.org/aboutus/annual/art2273.html

U.S. Census Bureau. (2001). *1997 Economic census arts, entertainment, and recreation subject series.* Washington, D.C.: U.S. Department of Commerce.

U.S. Census Bureau. (2000). *Statistical abstracts of the United States: 2000* (120th Edition). Washington, D.C.: U.S. Government Printing Office.

USDA Forest Service. (2001). *White river national forest land and resource management plan ski-based resorts draft environmental impact statement.*

U.S. Department of the Interior, Fish and Wildlife Service and U.S. Department of Commerce, Bureau of the Census. (1997). *1996 National survey of fishing, hunting, and wildlife-associated recreation* FHW/96 Nat.

11 OUTDOOR RECREATION IN OTHER COUNTRIES

Many countries showed interest in providing natural resources for the enjoyment of their citizens at about the same time that the United States did. Two such countries are Canada and Australia, and their park systems are addressed in this chapter. The development of their outdoor pursuits differs from development in the European countries included in this chapter. Additionally, the system that prevailed in the USSR before its dissolution is discussed, since it followed economic, political, and social systems that were in contrast with the ones espoused by the United States, Canada, Australia, Great Britain, or France. The impact on recreation from the political upheavals of the early 1990s in the former USSR and Eastern Europe will be interesting to follow in the political entities that have emerged. The strong trend to establish national parks and preserves in many Third World countries is explored in the last pages of this chapter.

OUTDOOR RECREATION IN CANADA

Canada is a vast country that extends from the Atlantic Ocean to the Pacific Ocean and from the Arctic to the northern border of the United States. Located so far north, Canada has harsh winters in addition to its diverse topographic features, which include the maritime provinces of Newfoundland, Prince Edward Island, New Brunswick, and Nova Scotia, followed by the densely forested regions of Quebec and Ontario that eventually turn into fertile lowlands. As one continues westward, one finds an industrial region, followed by the Canadian shield, a central depression of hard, old rocks. The vast prairie region of southern Manitoba, Saskatchewan, and Alberta is followed by the mountain and forests of British Columbia. North of this expansive land is the Arctic region, where most of the Eskimos live. The native Indians live across the southern tier, a strip of land 250 miles wide, north of the midwestern United States. The two European communities that settled in Canada—the French and the English—live in different areas across Canada.

It is assumed that the ancestors of both the Eskimos and Indians came by the northwestern route across the Bering Strait. Despite the hazards of life in the Arctic region, the Eskimos subsisted on whatever they were able to extract from their harsh surroundings. Eventually they established a life-style, which was somewhat playful (Blanchard & Cheska, 1983:142). Most of their playful activities were related to survival techniques. According to Johnson (1979:338), "most, if not all, Eskimo activities that might have had an impact on leisure in general, and outdoor recreation in particular, disappeared with the advent of the white people."

But this was not the case with the Native Indians. While many of the Indians' activities that had some bearing on outdoor recreation disappeared, some activities were adopted by the Europeans. An example would be *Baggataway*, which was practiced by the Algonquin and Iroquois people. *Baggataway* was a military scrimmage, infused with a religious ceremony designed to obtain the blessings of the gods, who would grant health and fertility on the victorious team. *Baggataway's* new name, lacrosse, was given to it by the French settlers, because the implement used in the activity had a curved, netted neck, which resembles a bishop's crosier (crooked staff). But the Native Indian implement that was adopted by European settlers that had a real impact on outdoor recreation in Canada (and elsewhere) in later years was the canoe. According to Johnson (1979:337), 14 percent of all Canadians participate in the outdoor recreational activity of canoeing.

The first Europeans to settle in Canada around the mid 1500s were French adventurers who landed on the shores of Nova Scotia and Newfoundland. Some settlers followed the St. Lawrence River to the location of today's Montreal and on today's site of Quebec. The settlers sold knives and hatchets to the natives and began the fur trade. The country of New France was founded in 1627, and it became engaged in a war with the Iroquois tribe a decade later. A quarter of a century after that, New France was in war with England. Although there were periods of peace between New France and England, the struggle continued. By 1763 most of Canada became a British dominion. Nonetheless, there are still two European communities in Canada, English and French.

French Canada

According to Johnson (1979:342-45), the Catholic Church played a decisive role in the lives of early French Canadians. Strict puritanical behavior was expected of every French Canadian, with gambling and dancing prohibited. Another important factor that affected recreational activities was the climate. Long winters required that the settler be physically fit in order to survive. Accordingly, the French Canadians developed proficiencies in outdoor activities, which served as the nucleus of their recreational activities later. They became skillful at canoeing, hunting, and snowshoeing. During the severe Canadian winter they participated in races on the snow and frozen rivers. One of their favorite races was in the horse-drawn carriole (sleigh). Summer, on the other hand, was the time for hard work on the land.

After the building of a few French settlements in New France, three distinct life-styles evolved. The affluent, earlier settlers lived in the larger population centers and imitated the French aristocracy. Douville and Casanova (1967:193) suggest that during their lavish ceremonies and elaborate banquets, one could easily have imagined oneself breathing the atmosphere of Versailles rather than the air of Quebec.

The more typical French Canadian lived in the outlying settlements and depended on kin and neighbors to extract a livelihood. Life in the linear villages along the St. Lawrence had none of the pomp of life in the larger settlements. The inhabitants lived according to what the church and the seigneur allowed or disallowed. Recreational activities revolved around their close-knit communities.

A third type of a French Canadian was the *Coureur de Bois*, the lover of nature, who imitated the ways of the natives. These people not only abandoned European values, they adopted the habits, customs, and recreational activities of the native people. They lived in the wilderness and removed themselves from the moral dictates of the settled French and their authority.

English Canada

The same hard conditions faced English Canadians, and the settlers had to rely on communal activities to get certain tasks done. This cooperative spirit led to the rise of the bee, a group working together to harvest, raise a barn, and the like. Eventually the bee included a social element in which the host supplied food, drink, and amusement. The drink was usually whiskey, and the amusement included a hoe-down and contests. The bee was a way of accomplishing a communal task eventually died out when the play element dominated the work element.

English villages of Canada began to provide for recreational outlets through the inn and the tavern, which were patterned after the English pub. Traveler and resident alike began to participate in the infamous blood sports, which were also seen in Great Britain, bear and bull baiting, and dog and cock fighting.

Imitation of the British extended to the upper class of English Canada. In their attempts to emulate the English aristocracy of the old country, the life-style of the wealthy in the New World was filled with organized and informal outdoor activities. They became "fond of horse racing, and field sports, fishing and sailing in the summer, and skating and caroling in winter . . ." (Guillet, 1933:323).

According to Baker (1982:160), curling was introduced to Canada by Scottish immigrants as early as 1807. An annual festivity was held called bonspiels, which featured the sliding of a round, flattened stone on a frozen lake. In the meantime ice hockey was being practiced by the English troops stationed in Kingston in 1855. A few years earlier, in 1842, some of the English settlers began to compete with the natives in their *Baggataway*. Soon a set of rules and standards for fields and equipment were drawn, and the game was renamed lacrosse by the Europeans.

Settlement of western and northern Canada by Europeans was very slow. Once it started, a true mix of people came to live in compact communities, each having its own traditions, amusements, and recreational activities. In the North particularly, communities were far apart.

At the end of the seven-year war in Europe in the 1750s, most of Canada was ceded to Great Britain. Quebec was to retain a French civil law to protect the position of the Catholic Church. A hundred years later, the Dominion of Canada came into being on July 1, 1867. At that time, the early dominance of garrison towns came to an end and the strong class distinction in both French and English Canada began to break down. Canada was turning into a modern industrial society. Canadians began to seek other forms of recreational activities, especially the mechanized forms of bicycling and motoring. The negative reaction of the conservative to such activities was swift, and the federal government's Lord's Day Act of 1906 was meant to keep the purity of the Sabbath. But in contrast, some civic-minded organizations were aware of the need for, and the value of, leisure pursuits particularly among the young.

Canadians had at that time a reasonable acreage of dedicated open space, but it was not necessarily play space. In fact, as early as 1859, the Toronto City Council had regarded park "breathing spaces where citizens might stroll, drive or sit to enjoy the open air" (McFarland, 1970:14). Other cities had their designated open spaces. In a manner not dissimilar to what occcured in its neighboring country, the United States, three levels of government became involved in outdoor recreation in Canada, as described in the following sections.

Role of the Federal Government

Prior to the 1900s, the role of the federal government in outdoor pursuits was limited to the provision of open space. In the meantime some cities were involved in providing open space. A century later, as will be shown, many federal agencies have direct impact on the recreational activities of Canadians, and some agencies have indirect influences.

One of the federal agencies that has a direct impact on leisure pursuits in Canada is the Ministry of National Health, which oversees fitness and amateur sports. One of the ministry's two departments has a direct impact on leisure pursuits, and it is called Recreation Canada. The other section, Sport Canada, promotes national and international competition in the country.

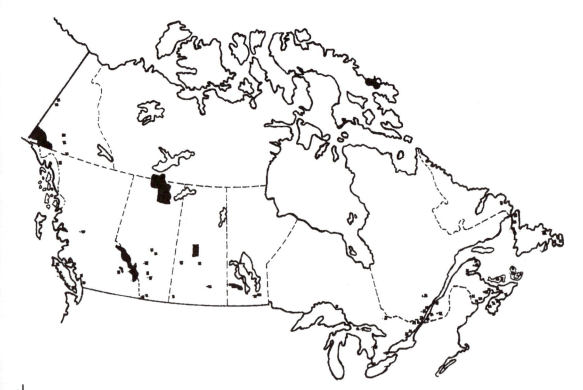

Figure 11.1 National Parks of Canada.

100% = 3.6 million person-trips

Western Region

Prairie Region

Ontario Region

Quebec Region

Atlantic Region

84%

9%

7%

3%

17%

Figure 11.2 Visitation to National Parks by Parks Canada Regions, 1994.

The Angel Wing Glacier found on Mount Edith Cavell in Alberta, Canada, is one of many protected by national parks in Canada.

Recreation Canada is decentralized in that it provides funds and offers assistance to organizations in the provinces. Demonstration projects are given wherever needed, and attention is directed to the recreation needs of special populations. Recreation Canada encourages businesses and industries to provide all forms of recreation, including outdoor pursuits, for their employees.

Environment Canada-Parks, an agency of the Ministry of Indian and Northern Affairs, also has a direct impact on outdoor recreation. Environment Canada-Parks has three branches, the National Parks Branch, the National Historic Parks and Sites Branch, and the Policy and Research Branch. The first branch oversees Canada's 28 national parks (see Figure 11.1), which cover 30,000 square miles or close to 32 million acres, making Canada's national parks one of the largest park systems in the world. These are areas that have significant scenic, geological, geographical, and biological elements that are to be preserved for future generations. There are five huge national parks in Canada, which amount to 82 percent of the total acreage of Canada's national park system: Wood Buffalo, Kluane, Jasper, Glacier, and Banff, totaling over 26 million acres. Small units constitute the remaining six million acres in the system. According to Chubb and Chubb (1981:324), these smaller units have been established primarily because of their historical significance. There are over 75 such sites that are operated like parks.

Almost half of Canada's national parks are located in the prairie provinces of Alberta, Manitoba, and Saskatchewan. Twenty percent of park lands are in the far west in British Columbia and the Yukon Territory, and 20 percent more are in the Northwest Territory. The four Atlantic provinces of New Brunswick, Newfoundland, Nova Scotia, and Prince Edward

Niagara Falls ranks as a natural wonder of the world. On March 30, 1885, the Ontario legislature passed the Niagara Falls Park Act establishing Ontario's first Provincial Parkland. The Queen Victoria Niagara Falls Park Act in 1887 officially established the Niagara Parks Commission, and in May of 1888, the park was officially opened to the public.

Island contain 3.2 percent of Canada's national parks, leaving populated Ontario and Quebec with a mere two percent of the system's land (Chubb & Chubb, 1981:326). Fortunately these two provinces are able to compensate for the lack of federal recreation resources because of the nature of the role of the provinces.

Role of Provincial Government

There are ten provinces in Canada, and each has its own government. Ten percent of Canadians, or 2.3 million people, live in the four Atlantic provinces, New Brunswick, Newfoundland, Nova Scotia, and Prince Edward Island. Further west, 23 percent of Canadians live in Quebec and 30 percent live in Ontario. The prairie provinces west of Ontario have a population that lives in a wedge that broadens westward. This means that most of

Canada's national parks are in the least populated areas. This makes the role of the provincial government, particularly in the East, an important one when it comes to outdoor recreation offerings.

Unlike the situation in each state in the United States, the provincial government is less dependent on the federal government where land and/or open space are concerned. Unsettled public lands in Canada, known as the Crown lands, are under the control of the provinces. Individual U.S. states do not control public land, and their involvement in outdoor recreation has been somewhat limited by this factor. In Canada the provinces have found that it is easy, politically and financially, to allocate large pieces of land as parks and forests. Following are examples of provincial outdoor resources in Canada.

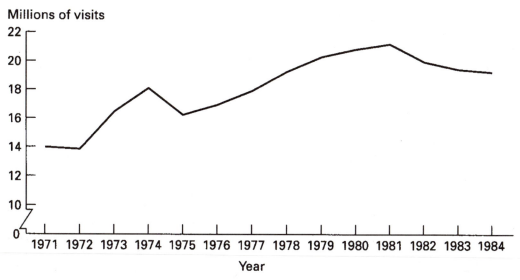

Figure 11.3 National park attendance, Canada, 1971-1984.

Ontario

Queen Victoria Park in Ontario is part of the Niagara Parks System, which extends for 32 miles between Lake Erie and Lake Ontario. This is a chain of parks along the Niagara River with views over Niagara Falls and adjacent natural vistas. The facilities in the chain include picnic areas, playing fields, horticulture displays, and amphitheaters.

The Ontario park system originated with a single park in 1893, Algonquin Provincial Park. Other parks were added during the next half-century until the Provincial Parks Act of 1934 officially made Ontario's system the largest provincial park system in Canada. The system totals nearly 10 million acres with an annual attendance of over 11 million visitors, of which one-fourth are for overnight camping (Ibrahim, 1991:136). The system consists of 130 units that include 20,000 campsites, 73 miles of beaches, 3000 miles of canoe routes, and 1,000 miles of trails. Ontario Parks, which constitutes five percent of the province's land, is administered by the Ministry of Natural Resources, which controls all open space in Ontario, a 230-million acre estate. Most of Ontario's parks are either surrounded by or are adjacent to Crown lands, which makes it very easy to expand the system.

The Ministry of Natural Resources of Ontario uses a five-class system of parks, as follows:

1. Primitive parks, which are large undeveloped areas.
2. Nature reserves, which feature distinctive land forms or ecosystems.
3. Natural environment parks, which have outstanding recreational landscapes.
4. Recreation parks, which offer a wide range of activities.
5. Wild rivers, which are undeveloped rivers.

The Ministry of Natural Resources of Ontario also administers the province's forests. Chubb and Chubb estimate that 73 million recreation occasions take place in these forests each year (1981:301). Visits to vacation cottages represent 33 percent of these occasions, camping represents 21 percent, fishing 13 percent, swimming eight percent, boating six percent, hiking six percent, snowmobiling six percent, hunting four percent, and canoeing two percent.

British Columbia

This province's park system began with the Stratcona Park on Vancouver Island in

1911. Today the park system is administered by the Park Branch of the province's Department of Recreation and Conservation. The park acreage is close to 8.5 million acres, with one park, Tweedsmuir, representing seven percent of the total. Tweedsmuir is Canada's largest provincial park and is dominated by spectacular Rainbow Mountain (Knudson, 1984:203). The British Columbia Park Act classifies its parks into the following six groups:

Class A:	Preserves offering outstanding features.
Class B:	Parks providing public outdoor recreation opportunities.
Class C:	Locally controlled parks.
Class D:	Public recreation areas.
Class E:	Wilderness conservancy.
Class F:	Nature conservancy.

While class A parks are the most numerous, comprising two-thirds of the system, class B parks are fewer yet larger in size. The locally controlled parks in British Columbia are smaller in size (Chubb & Chubb, 1981:493).

Saskatchewan

The Saskatchewan Department of Culture and Youth provides grants of 13 to 30 percent of cost to municipalities to help in the development of recreational facilities and programs. Fieldhouses and community centers as well as skating and curling rinks have been developed under this program in this prairie province. The department also encourages heritage and historic conservation and interpretation. Some of these activities have direct bearing on the pursuit of outdoor activities (Ibrahim, 1991, 157).

Quebec

According to Knudson (1984:202), the Quebec provincial park system is larger than the entire national park complex, having 32,000 square miles of parks. Most of Quebec parks are in the Laurentian Mountains and contain hundreds of lakes, many miles of fishing streams, elaborate skiing facilities, and numerous holiday resorts. Quebec still owns huge areas classified as Crown lands which are adjacent to, or surrounding, its provincial parks.

Role of Municipalities

Local self-government was slow in developing in Canada due to the dominance of the provincial government, particularly in New Brunswick, Nova Scotia, Quebec, and Ontario. Nonetheless, the establishment of municipal parks began in earnest with the beginning of the settlements. For instance, as early as 1763, Halifax Commons was granted to the city. Montreal had its first public square in 1821, and Hamilton built its Gore Park in 1832. As the provinces began to enact enabling laws empowering their municipalities to build parks, set procedures for acquisition of land, and establish standards for the management of natural resources, Montreal established its Mount Royal Park in 1860. Twenty years later, Vancouver built Stanley, London-Victoria, and Saint John-Rockwood parks.

According to McFarland (1970:37), the Canadian citizenry became aware in the late 1800s of the importance of recreation in their life-style and the role that natural resources could play in the pursuits of outdoor activities. Voices were raised proclaiming the importance of providing recreational opportunities, particularly in urban slums where poor families lived as early as the 1860s. A resolution passed by the National Council of Women spoke to this very point.

In a manner not dissimilar to what happened in the United States, concern among social reformers led to the formation of a playground association in 1914. This led to the establishment of municipal park boards in the large cities of the eastern provinces. Another development by civic-minded individuals in the prairie and western provinces led to the establishment of community leagues that promoted playgrounds and parks alongside community centers and swimming pools. The

Lindblad Special Expeditions cruise the western coast of British Columbia with kayaks aboard so that passengers can paddle the tranquil waters of Princess Louisa Marine Park for a closer look at waterfalls, seabirds, and tidal life found in Princess Louisa Inlet.

Bicyclists tour the eastern coast of Nova Scotia, where they are rewarded with nautical scenes like this one in Peggy's Cove.

Table 11.1 Percentage of Canadians 18 Years and Over Participating in Selected Recreation Activities.

Activity	1967	1969	1972	1976
Tent camping	13	12	19	19
Trailer camping	6	6	10	12
Camping with pick-up truck	—	2	4	9
Swimming (non-pool)	—	—	—	42
Canoeing	5	8	10	14
Bicycling	—	13	19	28
Walking or hiking	13	37	38	54
Wilderness tripping	—	—	—	17
Cross-country skiing	—	—	2	10
Driving for pleasure	—	67	63	66
Sightseeing from vehicle	—	—	37	49
Picnicking	40	54	52	57
Canal use				
Commercial boat	—	—	2	5
Private boat	—	—	6	9
Non-boating	—	—	8	12
Visiting historic sites	16	37	35	43
Visiting national parks (during past 12 months)	13	—	22	29

Source: R. Johnson, "Leisure in Canada" in *Leisure: Emergence and Expansion*, H. Ibrahim and J. Shivers, editors (Los Alamitos, CA, 1979), 350. (Reprinted with permission from Hwong Publishing.)

community league is a merger of more than one civic organization, each of which is concerned with the development of the local community (Kraus, 1984:127).

Outdoor Pursuits of Canadians

Canada is well endowed in natural resources, and its citizens enjoy outdoor recreational activities. The data in Table 11.1 show that driving for pleasure was the most pursued outdoor activity for the period studied, 1967-1976. Picnicking and hiking followed, and hiking showed an increase from 13 percent participation by persons over 18 years of age in 1967 to 54 percent by 1976. Visiting historical sites increased 400 percent in the same nine-year period. Attendance at national parks continued to increase into the mid 1980s, as shown in Figure 11.3. Visitations

to national parks by regions in 1984 are shown in Figure 11.2. The figure shows that the western region is the most popular (64 percent), followed by the Ontario region (seven percent) and the Quebec region (three percent). Longitudinal surveys show stability in leisure participation among Canadians. Walking as exercise comes first, followed by gardening or swimming, and/or bicycling (Zuzanek, 1996).

While it is hard to define what percentage of tourism actually involves outdoor activities, tourism to and from Canada is on the increase. Many U.S. citizens take trips to Canada for the enjoyment of its natural resources as well as other attractions. Canada accounts for the second-largest share of Americans traveling abroad, with 18 percent in 1986 in comparison to 22 percent of Americans traveling to Mexico and eight percent to Great Britain. Tourism in Canada is an important economic factor in the reduction of deficits in travel accounts. Statistics Canada (2000: vii) shows that 40.4 million trips were taken by Canadians abroad and 40.5 million trips by Americans and others were made to Canada. A trip of 24 hours or more conforms to the international definition that is used in tourism statistics.

OUTDOOR RECREATION IN GREAT BRITAIN

The leisure pursuits of Britons originated in two sources. The first is the rituals and traditions inherited from the Saxons and the Normans. The other source is the life-style of British nobility. Strutt (1970) wrote of the great parades of the Saxons and the tournaments of the Normans. His work was first published in 1801 and points out that in the pre-Reformation days, feasts and frolics were associated with religious events. Some of the activities of the commoners, which were needed for survival, became pastimes of the rich. Hunting is a good example: the masses were allowed to hunt for rabbit and vermin, but the wealthy were allowed the prizes such as fox and bear. Despite their attempts to protect their vast estates from the encroachment of the commoners, members of the aristocracy were eventually forced to share their game with the masses.

The commoners in Britain were by no means serfs, like the poor people on the continent. They were free men and women, although poor. They had a reasonable sense of freedom from the dominance of an elite class, which may have been a factor in the growth of what is now called blood sports such as cockthrowing, which consisted of throwing missiles at a tethered cock until it died. Soccer was actually a battle of 1,000 villagers pitted against another 1,000 from another village. The melee took place on Shrove Tuesday, supposedly a religious holy day.

The commoners' activities led to severe criticism by the clergy, who failed to cause reform in the Britons' leisure behavior at that time. It was the Industrial Revolution that eventually led to change. Emphasis on production ended the riotous and cruel blood sport of the country-side, since most of the men were lured to the city in search of their fortunes. The Industrial Revolution created many changes, including a drastic reduction in the number of holy days, thus days off.

In the nineteenth century, a revolution took place in the leisure habits in Great Britain. A clear distinction between work and leisure became obvious, as free time was regularized into weekly and annual blocks. Discussions on the need for constructive use of free time took place and involved not only men of the cloth, but also social reformers.

Changes were also taking place in the social structure of the British populations. A middle class was on the rise, a class that was bent on imitating the aristocracy, which traditionally lived in the country and enjoyed open space. Rich gentlemen started what Lowerson and Myerscough call "Consumer Town" resorts, which led to the popularization of seaside holidays for the middle class. A train excursion was organized on Easter day of 1844 that took the passengers from London to the seaside resort of Brighton. It created great popular excitement (1977:32). Seaside trips, which began in the 1840s (see Figure 11.4), have become a national institution—75 percent of British vacations are spent this way. "In fact, the traditional and ritualistic aspects of the trip appear to be an essential ingredient for most of the participants," write Chubb and Chubb (1981:129).

Interest in sport also grew in the Victorian era, when it was believed that sport was the best method of converting people from destructive leisure habits such as drinking and gambling. Alcoholic consumption continued to go hand in hand with sport, however, as had happened in the previous century. The public house, or pub was the center of the social lives of the poor people provided amusement, warmth, and lavatories. Some pubs became the "easies," the precursors of the music hall.

Punting along the Cam River in Cambridge, England, is a favorite outdoor pastime of students at the university.

Backpacking in England along the Cotswold Way is a favorite activity. This 97.5-mile trail follows the top of a steep escarpment and has beautiful views.

NORTH EASTERN RAILWAY

NIDDERDALE FEAST.

CHEAP EXCURSION TO THE SEA-SIDE.

On **TUESDAY**, Sept. 20th, 1870,

A SPECIAL TRAIN will leave PATELEY BRIDGE, and Stations as under, for

SCARBRO

LEAVE	A.M.
Pateley Bridge	6 0
Dacre Banks :-	6 8
Darley	6 12
Birstwith	6 17
Hampsthwaite	6 21
Ripley	6 30
Starbeck	6 40
Knaresbro'	6 50

FARE THERE AND BACK.
COVERED CARRIAGES.

3s.

Children under Twelve Years of Age, Half-fare.

The Return Train will leave Scarbro' at 5.30 p.m. same day.

NO LUGGAGE ALLOWED.

☞ The Tickets are only available for Scarbro' in going, and for the Stations at which they were issued on return.

As only a limited number of Carriages can be allotted to this Train, the following Regulations will be strictly observed, in order, as far as possible, to secure the comfort of the public, and to avoid delay :- The number of Tickets supplied for Issue will only be equal to the amount of Carriage accommodation, and no persons except holders of Tickets for this Train will be permitted to travel by it, and any person attempting to travel without a Ticket will be charged the full ordinary fare both ways. The Tickets are at the Stations ready for issue; and persons who intend to travel by this Train must apply early enough to enable the Station Clerks to procure any additional Tickets that may be required.

YORK, August, 1870.   **W. O'BRIEN, General Manager.**

EDWARD BAINES AND SONS, GENERAL PRINTERS, LEEDS.

Figure 11.4 North Eastern Railway excursion handbill, 1870.

Outdoor Pursuits

Despite the sudden expansion in leisure pursuit of Britons at the beginning of the twentieth century, outdoor activities were not dominant among activities pursued. Like other European countries, and unlike Canada or the United States, Great Britain was unable to establish publicly owned parks. Its first national park was established in 1930. In fact the parks shown in Figure 11.5 are still predominantly private-owned. The first attempt at providing outdoor recreation through legislation took place in 1844 when a bill was introduced in Parliament to permit public access to open land. During World War II a similar bill was introduced, but it was not until 1949 that the National Parks and Access to the Countryside Act was passed. A National Parks Commission was set up under the Ministry of Housing and Local Government and was charged with the duty of "...

exercising the function conferred on them by the following provisions of this Act: a) for the preservation and enhancement of natural beauty in England and Wales, and particularly in the areas designated under the Act as National Parks or as Areas of Outstanding Natural Beauty; b) for encouraging the provision or improvement, for person; resorting to National Parks, of facilities for the enjoyment of the opportunities for open air recreation and study of nature afforded thereby..." (Section 1, National Parks and Access to the Countryside Act, 1949).

According to Chubb and Chubb (1981:527), national parks represent one-tenth of the land in England and Wales. Most of them are more or less pastures, which were originally hardwood forests. Within these areas are state forests designated for outdoor activities such as pleasure driving, walking, picnicking, fishing, camping, and orienteering. The National Parks Commission's name has changed to Countryside Commission, but it still performs the same functions (See figures 11.6 and 11.7).

Three surveys were conducted by the government's Office of Population Census and Surveys, in 1973, 1977, and 1980, which included queries about leisure activities. The General Household Survey (GHS) was administered on 20,000 persons aged 16 and over. Veal (1984) analyzed the data and concluded that walking for pleasure is dominant in outdoor pursuits, and that darts and snooker/billiards, the usual English pub pastimes, are dominant among indoor activities. Tourism is also very popular among Britons; the data of the GHS reveal that 17 percent of the sample visited historical buildings in the four weeks before the interview took place. Tourism would be the second-most popular out-of-the-home or out-of-the-park activity after walking for pleasure (17 percent and 21 percent, respectively). A more recent review of leisure participation in Great Britain reveals a stability in the aforementioned pursuit (Gratton, 1996).

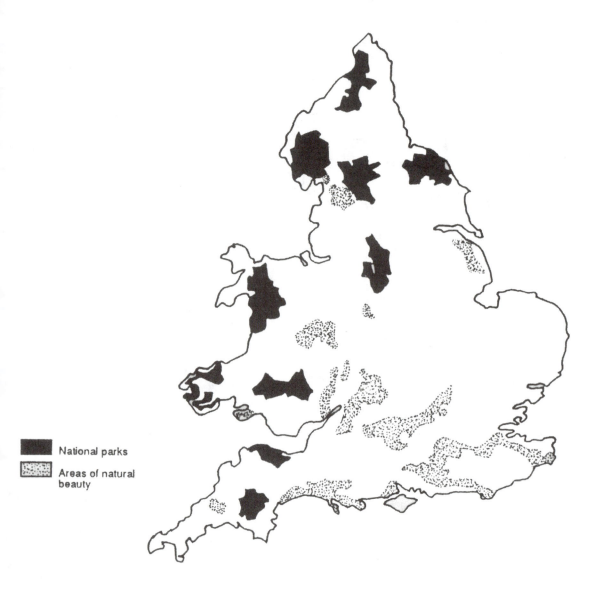

Figure 11.5 National resources in England and Wales.

National parks

Areas of natural beauty

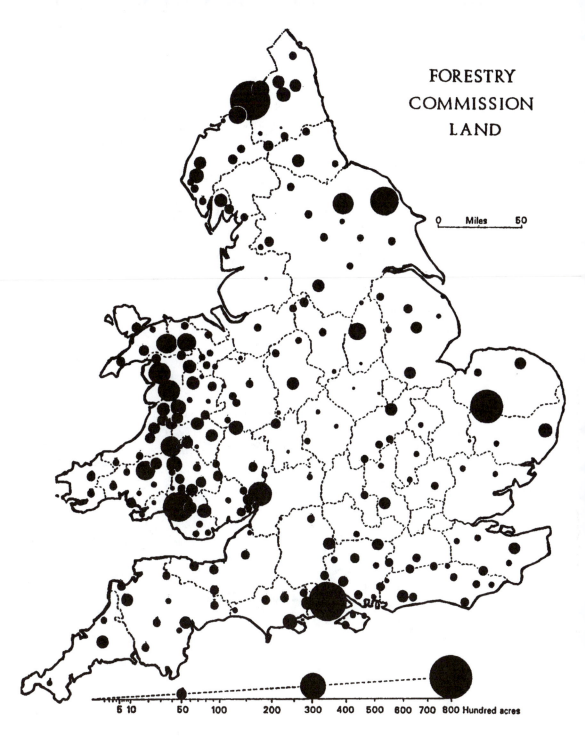

FORESTRY
COMMISSION
LAND

0   Miles   50

5   10   50   100   200   300   400   500   600   700   800 Hundred acres

Figure 11.6 Forestry Commision land.

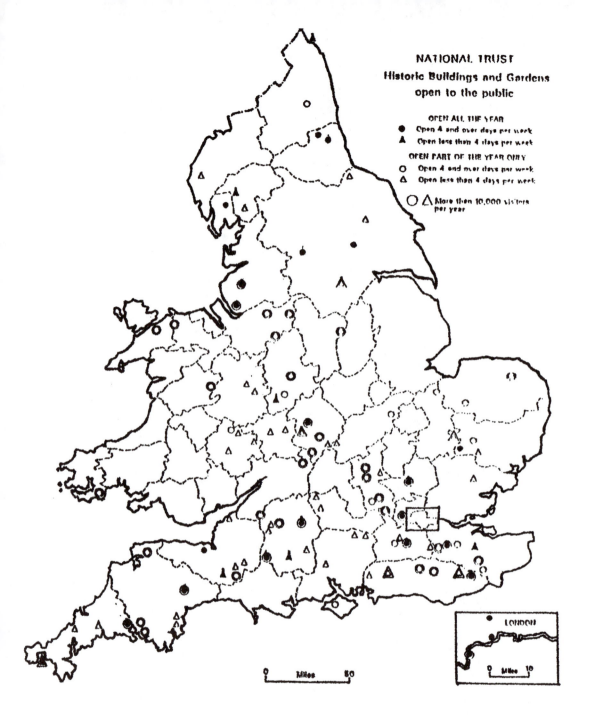

Figure 11.7 Properties owned by the National Trust.

Outdoor Recreation in France

Although the concept of a public garden may be traced back to Mesopotamia's Hanging Gardens of Babylon, Rome added to the concept a millennium later by providing gardens around villas. The Persians developed the concept of *paradeisos*, from which the word paradise was derived. The Greeks added a term to describe the concept of open space, *agora*, but it was the Normans who provided the park, the unruffled hunting estate which remained out-of-bounds to the commoners until recently. While the concept of a "natural" park developed in the British Isles, the preference was for a manicured garden on the continent, particularly in the estates of the French aristocracy.

Although the French aristocracy may be credited with the development of manicured gardens such as the Tuileries and Versailles, it was the Italian aristocracy that first opened up its private estates for the commoners to enjoy. The French aristocracy built grounds for themselves that are characterized by topiary work, aviaries, and fish ponds. Grand mansions were built for the owners' enjoyment. For instance, in Versailles, the terrace of the main building was adorned with ornamental basins, statues, and vases. The garden included a grand canal 200 feet wide and a mile long, complete with gondolas. The artificial lake was filled with water fowl and was connected to a waterfall.

Initially these pleasure gardens were limited to the aristocracy, which eventually succumbed to public pressure and opened the gardens to the public. Later, open space along the ramparts of the Seine in Paris was provided for Parisian citizens. Today the French people enjoy these resources for their outdoor pursuits.

France, and Great Britain were the first countries to legislate a 40-hour work week and a two-week paid vacation. Today France is allowing for a five-week vacation. Samuel shows that leisure participation in France follows a stable pattern (1996). Watching television dominates the leisure scene there, followed by reading and visiting friends. Visiting a castle or historic monument comes next.

Among the many leisure pursuits that the French enjoy is traveling. It is reported that 77 percent of Paris residents take a vacation; 45 percent of vacationers choose to visit the country-side, 23 percent the sea, and 13 percent the mountains. The remaining 13 percent stay at home for lack of means (Ibrahim, 1991:142). The study conducted by Szalai et al. (1972) shows the French sample spending 9.9 percent of its free time in outdoor activities compared to 16 percent for the American sample and 13.3 percent for the Russian sample.

Outdoor Recreation in the CIS

The USSR, until recently a group of republics ruled by traditional communism, is undergoing rapid political change. Today 11 of the original 15 republics are struggling to remain together as the Commonwealth of Independent States (CIS). Outdoor recreational programs will probably reflect the impact of these political upheavals to some extent. To understand the full ramifications of these changes, it is necessary to look at outdoor recreation as it existed at the time the USSR was composed of 15 republics ruled by communism.

Under communism, the former USSR treated leisure pursuits as important elements in increasing the productivity of labor, and the control over free time was greater than what was seen under other systems. Treated from an economic point of view, free time was used for the regeneration of the labor force. In a study of the recreational geography of the USSR that was translated to English, the original editors emphasized the role of health resorts in maintaining or increasing the productivity of the labor force (Preobrazhensky & Krivosheyev, 1982).

The authors divided the country into five recreational zones based on the density of the recreational offerings and facilities (see Figure 11.8). These five zones were in turn divided into 20 regions. The recreational facilities range from a very high concentration (Zone 1), to high concentra-

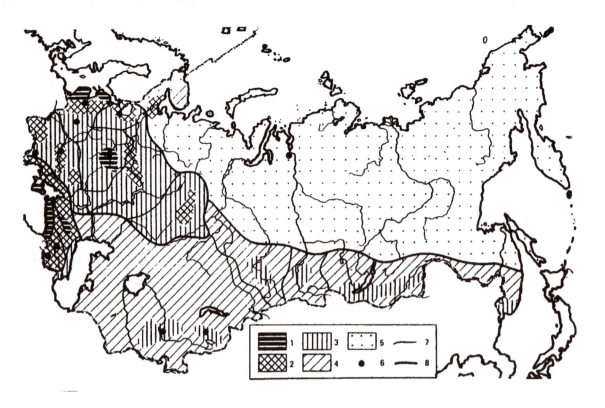

Figure 11.8 Recreational zoning of the CIS (Commonwealth of Independent States). Regions and localizations with the density of institutions: 1—very high; 2—high; 3—average; 4—low; 5—very low; 6—excursion centers; 7—boundaries of recreational regions; 8—boundaries of recreational zones.

tion (Zone 2), to average concentration (Zone 3), to low concentration (Zone 4). Zone 5 has hardly any facilities at all.

The classification of land under communism did not include land for recreation. Nature preserves, as a class, were strictly scientific research areas sometimes used for recreation. A new addition to these areas, Moose Island National Park, is now 15 years old. According to Gorokhov and Vishneveskaya (1988) the founding of Moose Island National Park coincided with the beginning of *perestroika* and *glasnost*. Although there were attempts to make Moose Island a national park as early as 1912, World War I wrecked the plan. It is by no means the only national park in the USSR: the first one was established in Estonia in 1971 and is called Lahemaa National Park. The exciting thing about Moose Island is its proximity to Moscow, a city of 10 million people.

Outdoor Pursuits

The average workweek decreased gradually in the former Soviet Union, from 58.3 hours before World War II to 47.8 hours in 1955 to 41.8 hours in 1965, to 39.4 hours in 1990 (Ibrahim, 1991:113). But the great gain was in the two-day weekend. Time budget studies showed that the average Soviet citizen spent more time on the same leisure activities he or she enjoyed before the advent of the two-day weekend: they watched more television, read more books and magazines, and went to the movies more frequently. Weekends away from home were limited by the lack of accommodations, the availability of which was controlled by the government. This limited availability persisted despite the fact that not only weekend time but vacation time also increased in the Soviet Union (Table 11.2).

Table 11.2 Relative importance of several nonwork-time activities in large cities in European parts of the USSR, various years (hours per week)

	1923–24	1936	1963	1965–68	1967–70
1. Housework and work in the private plot (excluding the care of children)	35.0	24.0	21.2	19.5	18.5
2. Daily cultural life					
(a) leisure, including	6.7	5.5	12.4	16.0	17.3
Reading books and magazines	2.1	1.0	2.3	2.1	3.3
Reading newspapers	2.9	1.8	1.4	1.6	2.5
TV and radio	-	1.0	5.1	6.2	7.5
Movies, theater and other public performances	0.6	0.7	0.9	1.3	1.3
(b) studying		.0	.6	.0	.3
(c) amateur talent activities and other kinds of nonprofessional creative works	1.1	-	0.1	0.8	0.4
3. Physical culture (i.e., education), sports, hunting and fishing, going to the country	0.2	0.3	0.7	0.7	1.6
4. Meeting with friends, guests, and dances	6.2	7.6	5.8	5.2	5.8
5. Occupied with children	5.6	4.3	3.0	5.0	3.1
Caring for children	5.0	-	1.9	2.9	1.5
Upbringing of children	0.6	-	1.1	3.0	1.6

Source: W. Moskoff, *Labour and Leisure in the Soviet Union* (New York: St. Martin's Press, 1984), 83. (Reprinted with permission.)

Although vacations were eliminated altogether during World War II, the policy of giving a two-week vacation after six months of employment was resumed after the war. In 1955 a one-month minimum vacation was granted to workers aged 16-18. The two-week vacation for older workers was increased to three weeks. Scientific researchers and educators have up to 48 days of vacation.

Vacations can be spent in a state-run facility or a rented *dacha*, or country cottage. To do the former, the worker must be a member of a group granted permission to use the state-run facility. These are houses of rest, sanitoria, or pensions. Workers on vacation are allowed into houses of rest. Pensions are, to some extent, similar to the houses of rest with a little more freedom on the part of the resident. A sanatorium is used for workers referred by medical professionals who need treatment and therapy.

Dachas were important in citizen life and will probably continue to be popular in the new system. Their popularity stems from the fact that they allow an extended family to stay together. Although few of them exist, the demand for the *Dachas* is so strong that private ownership was allowed under the previous strict socialist's period. There are also individual enterprises that own and operate some of the *Dachas*.

Changes in the leisure patterns of citizen over the years are shown in Table 11.3. Outdoor sports such as hunting, fishing, and hiking increased eightfold from the 1940s to the 1970s. Table 11.3 shows that tourism moved from the 14th rank of recreational activities in 1940 to the second position among the same sixteen activities in 1970.

Preobrazhensky and Krivosheyev (1982:208) recognized the dilemma of the Soviet citizen when it came to recreational

Table 11.3 Sixteen recreational activities by order of number of participants, selected years between 1940 and 1970, in the USSR.

Sport	1940	1945	1955	1960	1965	1970
1. Athletics	3	3	1	1	1	1
2. Tourism	14	18	14	11	4	2
3. Volleyball	5	6	2	3	2	3
4. Skiing	2	1	3	2	3	4
5. Pistol shooting	6	7	5	6	5	5
6. Football	7	9	7	8	7	6
7. Basketball	11	12	9	7	8	7
8. Chess	1	2	4	4	6	8
9. Draughts	–	4	6	5	9	9
10. Fishing	–	–	–	–	–	10
11. Table tennis	–	–	12	10	10	11
12. Shooting	–	–	–	–	–	12
13. Swimming	8	8	11	13	11	13
14. Cycling	9	10	10	12	12	14
15. Gymnastics	4	8	8	9	13	15
16. Speed skating	10	13	13	14	14	16

Source: J. Riordan, "Leisure, the State and the Individual in the USSR," *Leisure Studies* 1(1):89. Reprinted with permission.

offerings. The authors point out the discrepancy between the changing patterns of recreational activities and existing facilities. For instance, hiking and mountaineering were becoming the most popular recreational activities in the USSR, yet there were not enough facilities for the recreationists. The need for more natural resources is evident in the poll that was cited by these two authors. Persons between the ages of 16 and 60 indicated that they prefer to spend their vacations in forests (35 percent), by a river or lake (30 percent), by the sea (28 percent), in the mountains (five percent), or near a mineral spring (two percent). On the other hand, Shaw (1980) believes that as long as there is central control of land and means of production, easy solutions to problems and/or good planning in recreation will not be found. Riordan (1982:74) believes that the Soviet leaders had opted for the following, which was a hindrance to any in provement on the leisure scene:

1. The organization of working people in their leisure time to the maximum possible extent within the framework of a tidy hierarchical and functional structure.

2. The cultivation of competitive activities, as in sports (a leisure-time analog of the competition between people at work designed to raise work tempos), and material rewards for victors, which more effectively improve people's readiness for work and pre-train soldiers for the Soviet nation state.

3. Using leisure, specifically, as a means of obtaining a fit, obedient, and disciplined work force needed for achieving economic and military strength and efficiency, in particular, in order to:

a. Raise physical and social health standards, the latter meaning to simply educate people in the virtues of bodily hygiene, regular exercise, and sound nutrition, but also combat unhealthy, deviant, antisocial (and therefore anti-Soviet) behavior: drunkenness, delinquency, prostitution, "sexual perversions," even religiosity and intellectual dissidence.

b. Develop general physical dexterity motor skills, and other physical qualities useful for "labor and defense."

c. Socialize the population into the establishment system of values such as loyalty, conformity, team spirit, cooperation, and discipline. Encourage a population in transition from a rural to an urban way of life to identify with wider communities, such as the work place, the neighborhood, the town district, the region, the republic, and, ultimately, the whole country.

By associating leisure activities or organizations with the work place, the Party leadership and its agencies were able to better supervise, control, and "rationalize" the leisure time activities of employees.

The policies stated do not correspond to the Western view of leisure. Whether there will be any change with glasnost, perestroika, and the fundamental political and economic changes that have occurred will be an interesting area of study. The scattered studies conducted after the drastic change that took place there show a decline in leisure participation. For instance, the clubs that were previously organized along ideologically collective lines are now managed along private lines and are frequented by the new Russians for their stylish relaxation amidst lavish surroundings (Azhgikhina & Sirtcliffe, 2000). In the meantime the low salary of the common Russian is forcing him or her to take a second job, leaving no free time. Younger Russians complain about their intensive work, which does not allow free time, but also is overtaxing their health (Nazarova, 2000).

OUTDOOR RECREATION IN AUSTRALIA

Some Australian writers claim that the concept of a national park was realized in Australia first. They say that Yellowstone, which is claimed to be the first national park ever, did not receive the official name of National Park until 1890. By that time the Royal National Park at Port Hacking, Australia, had already been set aside in 1881 for "the purpose of a National Park" during a citizen and parliamentary campaign for better recreation provision (Mosley, 1978:27).

The demand for such natural areas began with hiking groups in Sydney just before the turn of the twentieth century. The idea of hiking and walking clubs grew very quickly. The idea was to protect the wilderness from the incursions of the motor car and the motorist. When Aldo Leopold pressed for wilderness areas within the U.S. National Forest, the concept had already been adopted by the conservationists of New South Wales. The National Park and Primitive Areas Council was formed in 1932, and it proposed a two-pronged approach: open areas for tourists and limited-access primitive areas. Things worked well until the mid-1940s, when a rift formed between the naturalists and recreationists on the percentage of land to be preserved and closed to recreation. The naturalists were successful in passing a legislative provision for a state system of floral reserves in 1948. In 1967 another bill, the National Park and Wildlife Act, provided for nature preserves within national parks. In 1973, the Common Wealth National Parks and Wildlife Conservation Act provided for the declaration of the whole or part of a national park as a wilderness zone. Mosley (1978:32) states that the wilderness reserve movement in Australia developed as a result of local needs, "but owes something to an awareness of the success of this method in the U.S.A."

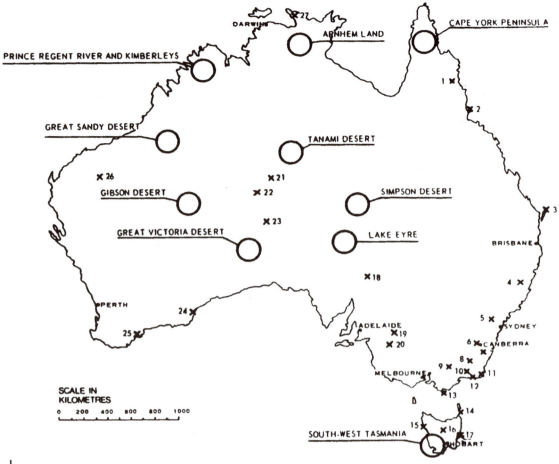

Figure 11.9 Australian outback.

A Sample of Leisure Pursuits

A study of the recreational use of the Baw Baw Alpine Reserve was conducted in 1997. Baw Baw is a natural preserve that is widely used by different interest groups (see Figure 11.10). It is about 20,000 acres in size and is about 100 miles east of Melbourne. Two questionnaires were mailed to a stratified sample of Victorian households, and 1,400 were received back. The questionnaires explored the respondents' attitudes towards, and perceptions of, wilderness areas; and sought details of recreational patterns and preferences along with personal data.

Table 11.4 summarizes the findings of these studies. Bushwalking (hiking) is practiced by 70 percent of all recreationist, regardless of their reasons for being at the reserve and is followed in popularity by sight-seeing (38 percent) and downhill skiing (43 percent). Activities participated in by fewer recreationists include fishing (six percent), tent camping (seven percent), ski orienteering (seven percent), and driving a 4WD vehicle (seven percent). Bushwalking is also listed as the second-most-preferred activity by those visitors whose main reasons for coming to the reserve were sight-seeing, skiing, and motoring. Figure 11.10 shows that the greatest number of visitors (16,000 a year) came for snow sight-seeing, followed by mountain ranges sight-seeing and downhill skiing (4,500) and bush camping (3,000). Only 300 visits a year were paid to the

BAW BAW ALPINE RESERVE
PRESENT ACCESS AND USAGE PATTERNS OF VISITORS.

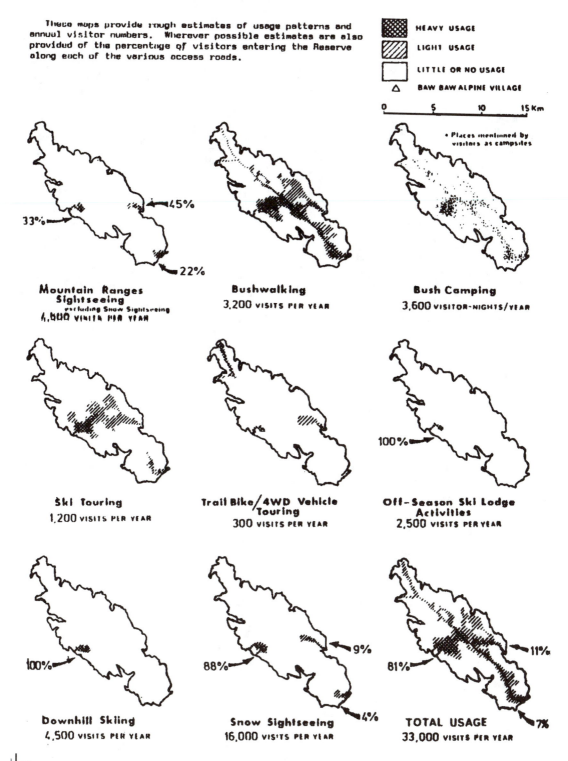

These maps provide rough estimates of usage patterns and annual visitor numbers. Wherever possible estimates are also provided of the percentage of visitors entering the Reserve along each of the various access roads.

HEAVY USAGE

LIGHT USAGE

LITTLE OR NO USAGE

△ BAW BAW ALPINE VILLAGE

0   5   10   15 Km

• Places mentioned by visitors as campsites

Mountain Ranges Sightseeing excluding Snow Sightseeing
6,800 VISITS PER YEAR

Bushwalking
3,200 VISITS PER YEAR

Bush Camping
3,600 VISITOR-NIGHTS/YEAR

Ski Touring
1,200 VISITS PER YEAR

Trail Bike/4WD Vehicle Touring
300 VISITS PER YEAR

Off-Season Ski Lodge Activities
2,500 VISITS PER YEAR

Downhill Skiing
4,500 VISITS PER YEAR

Snow Sightseeing
16,000 VISITS PER YEAR

TOTAL USAGE
33,000 VISITS PER YEAR

Figure 11.10 Patterns and volumes of recreational use of the Baw Baw Alpine Reserve.

National park systems help to protect the natural treasures of South America and present ecotourism opportunities.

Angel Falls, in Venezuela's Parque National Canaima, is the highest waterfall in the world at around 3,000 feet.

reserve with motoring on a bike or in a 4WD vehicle in mind.

A few years earlier, the Australian Labor government created the Ministry of Tourism and Recreation in accord with the following general principles underlying the National Recreation Program:

1. That prime emphasis be placed upon the enrichment and advancement of recreational participation at the local community level.
2. That the entire population, whether rich or poor, young or old, physically adept or inept, be encouraged to participate in some form of constructive, regular recreational activity.
3. That recreation programs be coordinated with all types of associated agencies in the community.

4. That recreation be recognized as an essential part of life in this age and in the future, and that citizens be educated to cope with the subsequent changes in their life pattern.

Unfortunately the ministry was short-lived. The Cabinet decided to eliminate such a federal office, but the Australian love for outdoor pursuits continues.

Although Australia is blessed with a moderate climate and despite its endowment with adequate natural resources, outdoor recreational activities do not dominate leisure participation there (Darcey & Veal, 1996). As is the case with many other nations, watching television is number-one leisure pursuit followed by listening to the radio and visiting with friends. Walking for pleasure was practiced by only 26.6% of the sample in The *National Recreation Participation Survey*

Table 11.4 Activities Suited to the Reserve: Visitor Preference Profiles.

5 Most Preferred Activities in Reserve Include . . .	All visitors	Mountain Ranges Sightseers	Snow Sightseers	Trail Bike/4WD Vehicle Enthusiasts	Bushwalkers	Downhill Skiers	Ski Tourers	Conservation Group Members
Bushwalking	70	84	66	56	100	54	80	94
Sightseeing	58	82	75	41	44	19	12	31
Downhill skiing	43	17	31	25	21	100	41	15
Barbeques and/or Picnics	34	44	47	28	25	7	8	12
Frolicking in snow	32	23	44	40	23	16	11	12
Ski touring	29	6	20	8	24	57	85	37
Climbing mountains	28	44	26	23	47	14	32	57
Photography	27	27	25	23	31	33	18	42
Tobogganing	26	17	34	35	17	19	4	9
Nature Study	22	31	21	7	30	16	19	51
Camping in open	20	37	14	31	45	6	34	50
Staying overnight in Village	20	10	12	13	9	50	18	6
Socializing in Village	19	9	14	10	8	43	19	9
Driving for pleasure	13	19	15	11	9	6	4	4
Riding on chairlift	12	10	15	18	7	10	6	2
Trail bike riding	10	15	12	71	10	1	3	2
Horseback Riding	9	9	11	20	7	4	4	4
Camping in huts	8	10	10	18	11	0	6	12
Riding in 4WD vehicles	7	9	10	41	6	1	4	4
Ski orienteering	7	1	6	3	3	11	32	9
Camping in snow	7	3	6	9	16	3	30	28
Fishing	6	11	6	23	11	1	1	4

Source: F. Mosley, editor, *Australia's Wilderness* (Hathorn, Victoria, Australia: Australian Conservation Foundation, 1978), 40. (Reprinted with permission.)

(NRPS) in 1994. NRPS is conducted on behalf of Australia's Federal Government by a market research company.

OUTDOOR RESOURCES AND THE THIRD WORLD

In countries outside the Western and Eastern blocs, the tendency to preserve natural resources for either conservation and/or recreation is catching on (National Geographic Society, 1989).

Many African countries have taken the necessary steps to establish national parks and conservation areas. Tanzania, for example, has set aside the Ngorongoro Crater conservation area, which borders Serengeti National Park. Tanzania has also acted to preserve another national treasure by creating Kilimanjaro National Park. Kenya decided to create a national reserve on Masai-Mara land, at the northern tip of the Serengeti ecosystem. Botswana's Chobe National Park is only one of its many

Native hammocks are available for overnight stays in the jungle regions of the Amazonas.

national parks. In North Africa, Algeria devoted a forest of dry rock as Tassili-n-Ajjer National Park and Egypt decided to protect its Red Sea reef as Ras Mohamed Natural Preserve.

In Asia, China dedicated large areas of primitive forests, hillsides of flowers, and hundreds of lakes as Jiuzhaigou National Park. Nepal gave the mountain whose peak touches the sky national park status as Sagarmatha National Park. Taal Volcano Island in the Philippines was dedicated as a national park, as was Bromo-Tenger-Semeru in Indonesia. Ranthambhore National Park in India is where the almost—extinct tiger now roams.

The lguazu National Park of Argentina is adjacent to the lguazu National Park of Brazil. The world's widest waterfall is found here, surrounded by many miles of subtropical rain forest. Venezuela's Angel Falls, the highest waterfall in the world, is protected in Canaima National Park. In Guatemala, pre-Columbian pyramids in a sea of green are protected as Tikal National Park. Ecuador preserved the famed Galapagos, the natural laboratory of evolution, as a national park; and near the southern reaches of the Andes, Chile created the Torres del Paine National Park. Peru, on the other hand, selected Manu Biosphere as a natural preserve where previously jaguars were hunted almost to extinction.

These are but a sample of the international trends to preserve and protect natural resources for everyone's enjoyment.

SUMMARY

While the United States may be a leader in providing outdoor resources to its citizens for their leisure pursuits, other countries are interested in doing the same. Canada has been a pioneer as well in many respects. It also has a three-tier government structure—local, provincial, and federal—

and all three levels of government are involved in providing facilities and programs in outdoor recreation. In Europe, Great Britain was able to convert a number of privately owned lands into public use. France's contribution was in opening the manicured gardens of the past aristocracy to the public.

Outdoor offerings in the former Soviet Union suffered from too many bureaucratic obstacles. There is hope that fresh ideas and modified policies will prevail in the new federation of republics.

The wilderness movement in Australia traced to the beginning of the 20th century, along with a description of the conflicts that ensued between naturalists and recreationists. Specific uses by each recreationist group are discussed.

Also presented are some of the national parks and natural preserves that are now seen Africa, Asia, and Latin America as evidence of an international trend to provide outdoor opportunities for everyone.

REFERENCES

Azhgikhina, N., & Sutcliffe, B. M. (2000). Russian club life. *Studies in the Twentieth Century Literature, 24*, 169.

Baker, W. (1982). *Sports in the western world.* Totowa, NJ: Rowan and Littlefield.

Blanchard, K., & Cheska, A. (1985). *The anthropology of sport: An introduction.* South Hadley, MA: Bergin and Garvey.

Chubb, M., & Chubb, H. (1981). *One third of our time: Introduction to leisure behavior and resources.* New York: Wiley and Sons.

Darcy, S., & Veal, A. J. (1996). Australia. In G. Cushman et at., (Eds.), *World leisure participation: Free time in the global village.* Oxon, UK: CABI

Douville, R., & Casanova, J. (1967). *Daily life in early Canada.* New York: MacMillan.

Gorokhov, V., & Vishneveskaya, S. (1988). The Soviet experiment, creating a national park in the midst of Moscow. *National Parks* (Nov/Dec): I6-17.

Gratton, C. (1996). Great Britain. In G Cushman et al., (Eds.), *World leisure participation: Free time in the global village.* Oxon, UK: CABI

Guillet, E. (1933*). Early life in Upper Canada.* Toronto: University of Toronto Press.

Ibrahim, H. (1991). *Leisure and society: A comparative approach.* Dubuque, IA: W Brown.

Johnson, R. (1979). Leisure in Canada. In H. Ibrahim, & J. Shivers, (Eds.), *Leisure: Emergence and expansion.* Los Alamitos, C.A.: Hwong Publishing,

Knudson, D. (1984). *Outdoor recreation.* New York: Macmillan.

Kraus, R. (1984). *Recreation and leisure in modern society.* Glenview, IL: Scott, Foresman.

Lowerson, J., & Myerscough, J. (1977). *Time to spare in Victorian England.* Hassocks, Sussex: Harvester Press.

McFarland, E. (1970). *The development of public recreation in Canada.* Ottawa: Canadian Parks and Recreation Association.

Moskoff, W. (1984). *Labour and leisure in the Soviet Union.* New York: Saint Martin's Press.

Mosley, F. (Editor). (1978). *Australia's wilderness.* Hathorn, Victoria, Australia: Australian Conservation Foundation.

National Geographic Society. (1989). *Nature's wonderlands: National parks of the world.* Washington D.C.: National Geographic Society.

Nazarova, I. (2000). Self-rated health and occupational conditions in Russia. *Social Science and Medicine, 51*(9), 1375.

Preobrazhensky, V., & Krivosheyev, V. (Eds.). (1982). *Recreational geography in the USSR.* Moscow: Progress Publishers.

Riordan, J. (1982). Leisure, the state and the individual in the USSR. *Leisure Studies, 1*, 65-79.

Samuel, N. (1996). France. In G. Cushman et al., (Eds.), *World leisure participation: Free time in the global village.* Oxon, UK:CABI

Shaw, D. (1980). Achievements and Problems in Soviet Recreational Planning. In J. Brine (Ed.), *Home, school and leisure in the Soviet Union.* London: Allen & Unwin.

Statistics Canada. (1986). *Tourism and recreation.* Ottawa: Ministry of Supplies and Services.

Strutt, J. (1970). *The sports and pastimes of the people of England.* New York: Angustus Kelly.

Szalai, A. (Ed.). (1972). *The use of time: Daily activities of urban and suburban population in twelve countries.* The Hague, Netherlands: Mouton.

Veal, A. (1984). Leisure in England and Wales: A research note. *Leisure Studies, 2*(2), 221-29.

Zuzanek, J. (1996). Canada. In G. Cushman et al., (Eds.), *World leisure participation: Free time in the global village.* Oxon, UK: CABI

—Part Three—

Management, Education, and Participation

In this last section of this volume, the chapters that are included are the ones dealing with the policies, procedures, and problems in the management of outdoor recreational resources. Chapter twelve presents the policies in the management of these resources. Management procedures such as charging fees, carrying capacity, and visitor management are discussed in Chapter Thirteen. Education of the participants and the training of outdoor recreational personnel are discussed in Chapter Fourteen. Chapter Fifteen describes some of the activities that could be pursued out of doors which, without prudent use, may lead to problems. In order to reduce overuse and or abuse of the limited natural resources where outdoor recreational activities take place, Chapter Sixteen presents the problems that may arise and how to avoid adding to them by the carelessness of some recreationists.

12 MANAGEMENT POLICIES IN OUTDOOR RECREATION

C an Americans continue to pursue their outdoor recreational activities without destroying America's natural resources? According to Cole (1986:M-1), recreation impact increases as one moves from the urban and developed end of the recreational opportunity spectrum toward its primitive and wild end. Washburne and Cole (1983) reported that vegetation impacts are a problem in 71 percent of wilderness areas, and soil impacts are a problem in 61 percent of them. A discussion on the policies toward American natural resources will provide the needed background for understanding current strategies that are intended to keep natural resources available for recreational use for many years to come.

There are two management policies that govern the natural areas used for recreation in this country. The first policy is based on the preservation principle, which is followed in most of America's federal parks and is followed somewhat in state and local parks. The second policy, which is based on the multiple-use principle, is followed in federal, state, and private forests.

PRESERVATION POLICY

The legislation that established the first national park, Yellowstone, is important in that it provided the basis for the concept

that federal land would be dedicated and set apart as a public park or pleasuring ground for the benefit and enjoyment of the people (Frakt & Rankin, 1982:17). The park was established by an act of Congress in 1872. By the turn of the century, four more national parks had been established. The executive branch of the federal government had the authority to reserve land from the public domain and preserve it in its current status. Prior to 1910, this authority was exercised repeatedly for purposes which included the establishment of wildlife reserves. Other purposes include the establishment of Indian and military reservations, reservation of timberland, and withdrawal of land from its current use pending classification. In 1906 the Antiquity Act was passed, which authorized the president of the United States to reserve lands with scientific beauty and scientific importance. In 1916 Congress established the National Park Service. The act creating this agency specified its purpose as follows:

> To conserve the scenery and the natural and historic objects and the wildlife therein and to provide for the enjoyment of the same in such manner and by such means as will leave them unimpaired for the enjoyment of future generations. (Everhart, 1972).

Absolute preservation dictates no human use, but even then there is no way to preserve a landscape, since natural processes bring about change. In Bryce Canyon National Park, it is erosion that has formed the innumerable highly colored pinnacles, walls, and spires that visitors come to see. Essentially managers identify aspects of the biophysical and social environments that are important and can be monitored for change as recreational use proceeds.

According to Nash (1978:13), the passage of the National Park Service Act did not change the original concept of public enjoyment. It is clear in hindsight that pleasure-seeking people could (and did) impair nature despite the legislative stipulation that the parks' scenery and wildlife should be left "unimpaired." Nash writes of how Stephen Mather, the first director of the National Park Service, was instructed by his boss, the secretary of the interior, in a letter dated May 13, 1918, to let the public enjoy the parks in the manner that best satisfied the individual taste. In other words, no attempts were made then to define what kind of enjoyment is appropriate in a natural setting.

Nash believes that the concept of preservation was set aside at that time,

and efforts were directed toward having the National Park Service stand on its own feet in its early years. A circus image of parks was generated, with drive-through sequoias, soap-sudded geysers, bear feedings, and caged wildlife as the techniques used to attract visitors. The firefall replaced the chicken fall in Yosemite where a giant wood fire on top of Glacier Point, 3,000 feet above the valley floor, was pushed over the cliff as music was played. This activity was not questioned until the late 1960s.

The results of these amusing activities were on the minds of those who legislated the Everglades National Park in 1934. Their bill specified that no development of the project or plan for the entertainment of visitors should be undertaken that would interfere with preservation of natural conditions (1978:31-32). Nash cites the work of two persons, George Wright and Lowell Sumner of the National Park Service, who brought the agency's attention to the need for preservation. Sumner urged the establishment of a recreation saturation point or a carrying capacity, which he defined as the maximum degree of the highest type of recreational use which a wilderness can receive, consistent with its long-term preservation (1978:33).

The Division of Forestry of the Department of Agriculture became the U.S. Forest Service in the early years of the 20th century. Soon thereafter, recreation was added as one of the multiple uses of the national forests. Preservation was not a priority, and roads and structures grew all over national forests. Two foresters, Arthur Carhart and Aldo Leopold, were instrumental in setting aside large blocks of acreage, which became the United States', and perhaps the world's, first designated wilderness (see Chapter 7, Federal Resources). Preservation of these wilderness areas revolved around limiting the modes of travel permitted in them, but not the number of visitors to them. Later preservation was underscored with the establishment of research reserves, which included virgin forests of scientific importance. Today these are called experimental stations.

Another pioneer in the preservation of wilderness areas was Robert Marshall who, as director of the Forestry Division of the U.S. Office of Indian Affairs, crusaded the curtailment of road building in primitive areas. Both he and Aldo Leopold were instrumental in forming the Wilderness Society, whose effort was directed toward keeping adverse effects out. The Wilderness Society intervenes directly with government officials to halt projects that may threaten wilderness. The society has found it necessary to go to court for this very purpose.

Preservation through management became the focus of attention of the Sierra Club in the late 1930s. Proposals were numerous, including the curtailing of

buildings and use of trails, certification of outdoorsmen, and limits on overnight camping. The Sierra Club sponsored the High Sierra Wilderness Conference in 1949, which grew to today's Biennial Wilderness Conference. The idea of a National Wilderness Preservation System did not materialize until 1964 with the passage of the Wilderness Act. But this took hard work on the part of the preservationsts fighting those who wanted to dam wild rivers and exploit the wilderness.

The Wilderness Act (Public Law 88-577) directed the secretaries of Agriculture and the Interior to review lands within their jurisdictions, that is, national forests and national parks, respectively, and to recommend their suitability as wilderness areas. Currently, close to 90 million acres are so classified and are the basis of the primitive areas within national forests and the roadless areas of national parks. According to Nash (1978:39), while the earlier legislation emphasized pleasuring and enjoyment, this time the law specified that the protected land was to be enjoyed *as wilderness*.

The Wilderness Act defines wilderness as an area where the earth and its community of life are untrammeled (uninterrupted) by humans and where each person is a visitor who does not remain. If wilderness is not managed according to this definition, the alternatives are either to prohibit all use of wilderness areas or to permit an open-door policy that will eventually lead to the destruction of wilderness areas.

In 1975 the Eastern Wilderness Act allowed select Forest Service areas east of the 100th meridian to be included as wilderness areas although they did not meet the criterion of being free from human influence. They were to be allowed to revert to their natural condition. A few years later, a large section in Alaska was added to the system.

By the mid-1980s the National Wilderness Preservation System consisted of 445 areas totaling about 89 million acres, most of which are in Alaska. This is expected to increase as stipulated in the Federal Land

Table 12.1 Participants in Wildlife Related Activities: 1996

[In thousands (39,694 represents 39,694,000). For persons 16 years old and over engaging in activity at least once in 1996. Based on survey and subject to sampling error, see source for details]

Participant	Number	Days of Participation	Trips	Participant	Number	Days of Participation
Total Sportsmen[1]	39,694	882,569	729,495	Wildlife watchers	62,868	(X)
Total anglers	35,246	625,893	506,557	Nonresidential[2]	23,652	313,790
Freshwater	29,734	515,115	420,010	Observe wildlife	22,878	278,683
Excluding Great						
Lakes	28,921	485,474	402,814	Photograph wildlife	12,038	79,342
Great Lakes	2,039	20,095	17,195	Feed wildlife	9,976	89,606
Saltwater	9,438	103,034	86,547			
				Residential[3]	60,751	(X)
Total hunters	13,975	256,676	222,938	Observe wildlife	44,063	(X)
Big game	11,288	153,784	113,971	Photograph wildlife	16,021	(X)
Small game	6,945	75,117	63,744	Feed wild birds[4]	54,122	(X)
Migratory birds	3,073	26,501	22,509	Visit public parks	11,011	(X)
Other animals	1,521	24,522	22,714	Maintain plantings or natural areas	13,401	(X)

X Not applicable. [1]Detail does not add to total due to multiple responses and nonresponse. [2]Persons taking a trip of al least 1 mile for activity. [3]Activity within 1 mile of home. [4]Or other wildlife.

Policy and Management Act of 1976, under which the Bureau of Land Management must submit areas in its jurisdiction as wilderness candidates. According to the National Park Service (1993), by the early 1990s the United States had set aside approximately 8% of its land under this policy. These lands will help in sustaining natural sources and biological diversity.

When it comes to participation in Wildlife areas, Table 12.1 shows that fishing in freshwater comes first, followed by observing wildlife, hunting, feeding wildlife, and photographing wildlife.

According to Knudson (1984:434-37), nine states have wilderness policies and two have legislation that meets the same standards of federal wilderness: California has two areas totaling 97,000 acres, and New York has 16 areas totaling about one million acres.

Principles of Wilderness Management

Hendee et al. (1978:137-48) suggested the following 11 principles for wilderness management:

1. Wilderness is one extreme of the outdoor opportunity spectrum. Recreationists in America have a wide choice in a continuum of settings ranging from the paved to primeval. Recreational demands that are inconsistent with the intended character of wilderness can be met elsewhere. And there is (are) plenty of elsewhere(s).

2. Management of wilderness areas may be viewed in relationship to the management of adjacent lands. This principle is also based on the outdoor opportunity spectrum. Heavy recreational use in the area adjacent to wilderness is bound to affect the wilderness area. The creation of a buffer zone between the two areas to absorb the impact may be a good solution, as would be the creation of zones for different uses.

3. Wilderness is a distinct, composite resource with inseparable

parts. This principle necessitates that wilderness be managed in toto, with no separate managements, one for vegetation, another for wildlife, and a third for recreation. Here the focus is on the protection of the naturalness of relationships between the wilderness ecosystem parts.

4. The purpose of wilderness is to produce human value and benefits. Wilderness is set aside not for its flora and fauna, but for the people. Recreational, therapeutic, and scientific benefits are to be derived from wilderness. (This view, known as the anthropocentric position, takes the "use and enjoyment" phrase in the Wilderness Act literally. The other view, the biocentric position, calls for the natural ecological process to operate as freely as possible, which eliminates humans from wilderness).

5. Wilderness preservation requires management of human use and its impact. Recreational use of wilderness area has the greatest impact if contrasted to scientific use. Accordingly, it is the management of recreationists that is becoming crucial.

6. Wilderness management should be guided by objectives set forth in area management plans. Without such a plan, management will be uncoordinated, even counterproductive (Wilderness plans will be discussed later).

7. Wilderness preservation requires carrying capacity constraints. The level of tolerance a wilderness area can sustain before unacceptable impact occurs must be specified (Carrying Capacity will be discussed later).

8. Wilderness management should strive to reduce the physical and social-psychological impacts of use. This principle calls for selective restrictions focusing on certain impacts. Kind, timing, and location of use could be regulated. For instance, the number of persons in a camping party, the length of a hike, and the use of fire should be regulated.

9. Only minimum regulation necessary to achieve wilderness management objectives should be applied. In order that the recreationist may benefit from leisure experience, restrictions should be at a minimum so that the salient characteristics of such an experience (freedom, spontaneity, etc.) may be felt.

10. The management of individual areas should be governed by a concept of nondegradation. This idea calls for not only the maintenance of the present environmental levels, but also restoration from below-minimum levels. In other words, the management should strive to elevate some conditions to at least a minimum level.

11. Wilderness-dependent activities should be favored. From scientific study to leisure pursuits, wilderness should provide the place for some of these activities, but not necessarily all of them. Laboratories are places of scientific study and pools are places for swimming; accordingly, only the activities that require and depend on wilderness should be allowed there.

MULTIPLE-USE POLICY

The multiple-use policy is applicable in most national forests, the lands administered by the Bureau of Land Management, and most state forests. Many activities are allowed under this concept, including grazing, timber cutting, and of course recreation. The concept was reaffirmed in the Multiple-Use Sustained-Yield Act of 1960, Public Law 86-517. Congress emphasized that the national forests are established and shall be administered for outdoor recreation, range, timber, watershed, and wildlife purposes.

Multiple-use means that the management of all renewable surface resources are directed to meet the multiple needs of the American people. Sustained yield means the achievement and maintenance in perpetuity of a high-level output of these renewable resources. According to Knudson, the concept of multiple-use is a slippery one, and it is difficult to define to the satisfaction of each group that uses the land (1984:473). The concept applies to the two largest land management agencies in the United States: the Bureau of Land Management and the U.S. Forest Service. In application, certain areas of these two agencies may be administered under a single-use concept, but they should fit within the broad concept of multiple-use within the agency. For example a campground would be restricted to recreational use and a watershed to wildlife protection, and both would fit under the multiple-use concept.

The lands under the jurisdiction of the Bureau of Land Management are managed under multiple-use as described in Public Law 94-579, the Federal Land Policy and Management Act. The act was passed in 1976, 16 years after the Multiple-Use Sustained-Yield Act of 1960, which regulated the use of national forests. The language of the 1976 act is similar to the language of the 1960 act in that it is stipulated that the lands under the jurisdiction of BLM should be managed according to the multiple-use and sustained-yield principles. The 1976 act required that certain areas of BLM lands that are qualified as wilderness areas be included under the National Wilderness Preservation System. BLM was given 15 years (until 1991) to review its potential wilderness candidates. Although multiple-use seems to be a sound policy, its application is met with difficulties. At the core of these difficulties is the fact that different groups view America's natural resources differently. For instance, Knudson (1984:474) gave the following five views of the American forest:

American Indians (19th Century and before)

The forest was home, and nature was a force that could be used but not dominated. Small areas could be used up, but there was always more.

Pilgrims and Pioneers

The forest was a wilderness and the home of a hostile enemy, but it produced food, shelter, and export capital. Though the forest was a necessity, it was believed that the forest must be reduced by a substantial amount.

Lumbermen (at the turn of the century)

The forest was a timber mine, a resource. (The forest was not yet treated as a renewable source).

Foresters

The forest is a renewable resource. It must be protected and nurtured; the timber harvest must be rationalized.

Recreationists

The forest is a service environment. Romantic and esthetic aspects predominate.

It is clear that these interests are in many instances incompatible and the management of lands designated for multiple-use should carry the burden of upholding the law. Philosophically and legally, the multiple-use concept centers on the greatest total benefit over a long period of time. This makes the task of the contemporary manager very difficult indeed, particularly that the demand for visitations on federal land has increased dramatically in the last few years (see Table 12.2).

Table 12.2 shows that visitations to federal lands increased dramatically in the second half of the 20th century. The data

Table 12.2 Trend in Recreation Visitation on Federal Lands

Agency	1950*	1960	1980	1984	1987	1993
			Millions of Visitor Days			
Forest Service	16.4	55.5	234.9	227.5	238.4	287.7
Corps of Engineers	9.6	63.6	160.5	137.7	148.6	192.2
National Park Service	19.6	43.7	86.8	103.3	114.7	115.8
Bureau of Land Management	n.d.	n.d.	5.7	17.4	43.1	46.9
Tennessee Valley Authority	9.9	25.4	7.2	6.6	6.5	11.4
Bureau of Reclamation	3.9	14.5	33.9	23.5	31.7	22.4
Fish and Wildlife Service	3.2	6.4	1.4	4.7	5.9	17.7*

*Estimated from recreation visits; n.d. = no data.

show that in 1993 about 700 million visitor days were paid to federal land as follows:

National Forests	41.6%
Corps of Engineer Areas	27.6%
National Parks	16.9%
BLM areas	6.8%
Bureaus of Reclamation land	3.1%
Fish & Wildlife areas	2.5%
Tennessee Valley Authority	1.5%

CLASSIFICATION OF RECREATION RESOURCES

The total area of the United States is 3.62 million square miles, 98 percent of which is land and two percent inland water. These are the two basic recreation resources.

Land Resources

Of the 2.2 billion acres of land in the United States, 58 percent is privately owned, 34 percent is owned by the federal government, five percent by the states, two percent by Indians (reservations), and one percent by local government. There are many ways of classifying recreation sources on these lands, among them Clawson and Knetsch (1966) classification which follows:

User-oriented areas are located and designed with the access and use by the visitor as the principal but not the only consideration. This classification includes most city and county recreation areas and many commercial areas.

Intermediate areas are located and planned to meet the needs of users, but in areas dictated partially by the resource. These areas are managed with resource maintenance and used as balancing considerations; they include most state parks, forests, and reservoir projects, many fish and wildlife areas, and some commercial recreation areas.

Resource-oriented areas are located and planned with the resource base as the key criterion, with recreation use coming a result of the resource. The large areas of national forests, most national wildlife refuges, national parks, national resource lands, and some large state properties fall into this category, as do forest industry lands.

Knudson (1984:299) suggested a method of classification based on identifying the source of the recreation resource. He suggested methods of classification, as follows:

1. *Ownership or jurisdiction classes*
   This approach was used in Section Two of this book relating recreation offerings to firms, individuals, or public agencies that own and manage them. This system does much to describe in a few words the

Different groups have differing views regarding America's natural resources. Sometimes these interests are incompatible.

goals and policies affecting the property.

2. *Designation classes*

Properties called parks, forests, wildlife areas, nature preserves, memorials, recreation areas parkways, trails, or scenic rivers, lakes, parkways, trails, or scenic rivers, lakes, or reservoirs. There are specific facility designations, such as wilderness, golf course, country club, arboretum, ski area, and camp that help define the character and features of the area. The most commonly understood classes are combinations of the jurisdiction and facility designation, quickly describing the resource to people who have any familiarity with the resource system.

3. *Service area classification*

For people concerned primarily with planning, this classification approach defines the parks and open spaces by size and service areas of public facilities, regardless of the agency managing them. This system is used to define the character of supply and point out the kinds of resources most needed. Variations of this approach have been used for years by the National Recreation and Park Association. A number of states and cities have adopted similar categories, referring to facilities in terms of whether they serve a neighborhood, community, or region (See Chapter on Local Offerings).

4. *Orientation classification*
   This classification was described earlier. It defines management and policy purposes in rough groupings as to whether they are user-oriented, intermediate, or resource-oriented. This merely identifies management emphasis. It is most valuable in explaining the policies of an agency to interested visitors or in interagency discussions of proper roles for various resources.
5. *Resource classification*
   Within a property, the land base can be classified into various resources related to its purpose and intensity of development.

Six classes of resources were proposed by the Outdoor Recreation Resources Review Commission (ORRRC). This commission was established by the president of the United States in 1958. Its report in 1962 suggested the following classes of outdoor recreation resources:

I. **High-Density Recreation Areas**: Intensively developed and managed for mass use.
   - *Facilities:* Heavy investment concentrated in relatively small areas, many facilities usually present.
   - *Use:* Exclusively for recreating: heavy peak load pressures (e.g., weekends).
   - *Land Use:* Often competes with residential construction and commercial uses, due to location near urban centers.
   - *Examples:* Beaches, boardwalks, swimming pools, highly developed trailer camps, some mass-use picnic/game areas.

II. **General Outdoor Recreation Areas**: Areas subject to substantial development for specific recreation uses.
   - *Facilities:* Many, but usually fewer than in high-density recreation areas—always some human-built facilities.
   - *Use:* Accommodates the major share of all outdoor recreation day, weekend, and vacation use. Use is concentrated, but not as much as in category I. Zoning may be needed.
   - *Land Use:* Competes with a wide variety of uses, due to locations in both urban and rural settings.
   - *Examples:* Campsites, picnic areas, ski areas, resorts, coastal areas, hunting preserves.

III. **Natural Environment Areas**: Areas suitable for recreation in natural environments, intermediate between categories II and IV.
   - *Facilities:* Few and simple; user enjoys resources "as is" in an environment where humans fend largely for themselves; management emphasis is on the natural rather than the human-made. Access roads, trails, primitive camping areas, and safety and fire provisions are present.
   - *Use:* Generally dispersed, not concentrated; hunting, birding, fishing, canoeing, rustic camping, sight-seeing, snowmobiling, or ORV use (family style).
   - *Land Use:* Often multiple-use lands; largest class in acreage.
   - *Examples:* Most national forest and BLM lands, buffers in national parks. Most of state and county forests, most fish and wildlife areas, most reservoirs.

IV. **Unique Natural Areas**: Areas of outstanding scenic splendor, natural wonder, or scientific importance.

- *Facilities:* Few—acceptable only if they enhance protection of the natural feature.
- *Use:* Limited to observation and study in many cases. Management focuses on preservation of feature, not public demand.
- *Land Use:* Areas often small, special; incompatible uses excluded.
- *Examples:* Old Faithful geyser, Old Man of the Mountain, Bristlecone Pine area of Inyo National Forest, nature preserves.

V. **Primitive Areas**: Undisturbed roadless areas in a natural wild condition.
- *Facilities:* None except trails, no structures, no machines.
- *Use:* Goal is to provide solitude from evidence of civilization; commercial uses prohibited except guide service. Use may be restricted in order to:
  a) Provide opportunity for solitude by user, and
  b) Preserve primitive conditions.
- *Land Use:* Competes with several other wildland uses—timber production, grazing, power dam construction, and mining. These uses and roads are generally excluded from primitive areas. (For reasons found acceptable by Congress, mining and grazing have been allowed to continue temporarily in some areas.)
- *Examples:* Gila Wilderness Area; most of Rocky Mountain National Park; portions of Porcupine Mountain State Park, Michigan; Quetico-Superior Boundary Waters Canoe Area, Minnesota-Ontario; Wood Buffalo National Park, Alberta.

VI. **Historic and Cultural Sites**: Sites of major historic or cultural significance, local, regional, or national.
- Facilities: Emphasis is on restoration and preservation of the historic features; facilities usually relate to protection of features during visitor use and interpretation of the historical significance, providing suitable access.
- *Use:* Varies considerably, depending upon type and fragility of features; always appropriate to the historic feature. Overuse is prevented, not accommodated.
- *Land Use:* Exclusively for appreciation of history and culture and associated recreation values of the site.
- *Examples:* Mt. Vernon, Russell Cave (Ala.), Tippecanoe Battlefield.

Land Mass

Jensen classifies the land mass in the United States into four categories: forest lands, grasslands, deserts, and tundra. The features and resources of each are varied, as described in the following paragraphs (1985).

Forest Lands

America was covered with forests initially, but consumptive use of timber over the past two centuries has reduced the area of forest to only one-third of the nation. Today there are 748 million acres of forest land, most of which (420 million acres) are privately owned. The U.S. Forest Service controls 187 million acres, the National Park Service 30 million acres, and state and local agencies 38 million acres. Forests vary in terrain, elevation, and type of trees that they support. Forests are a good source for many types of outdoor recreation.

Grasslands

The grasslands that supported grazing animals in the past have become America's food basket in the last two centuries. Attempts are now being made to recover as much of America's grasslands as possible for scenic, scientific, and recreational purposes. Heavy vegetation around water resources have high recreation potential. A Great Plains Grass lands National Park has been proposed.

Deserts

Lands receiving less than 10 inches of annual precipitation are generally classified as desert. These range from sand dunes and dry lake beds to plateaus, mountains, and canyons. Despite the prevailing concept that deserts are inhospitable, they have become a significant source for outdoor recreation. Traditional outdoor pursuits have been augmented with newer ones: parachuting, sand sailing, and hang gliding. The Bureau of Land Management controls most of the U.S. desert lands that have recreational potential.

Tundra

This natural ecosystem around the arctic and alpine zones stretches across the northern section of the continent, with Alaska accounting for most of it. Smaller regions of tundra are found in the Rocky Mountains, the Sierra Nevada, and the Cascades. Tundra lacks trees but contains grasses, hedges, herbs, and shrubs. Its harsh winter makes recreation pursuits rather limited. In addition, its vegetation is too delicate to allow for mass leisure pursuits. The Bureau of Land Management and the National Park Service own most of the lands that are classified as tundra in the United States.

Water Resources

Water resources that are utilized for recreation can be classified into rivers, wetlands, shorelines, lakes, and reservoirs.

Rivers

Although most American rivers are found in segments of 25 miles (40 kilometers) or less, these rivers have served as transportation routes with adjacent trails. There an approximately 3.25 million miles (5.24 million kilometers) of rivers in the United States, some of which are free-flowing through natural settings. Accordingly, rivers provide unique opportunities for a variety of leisure pursuits. Among these are swimming, boating, and fishing as well as rafting, kayaking, and canoeing.

Wetlands

This term describes marshes, swamps, bogs, wet meadows, and shallow ponds. It is estimated that there are 75 million acres of wetlands in the United States today. Examples of wetlands are the Everglades, Hackensack Meadowlands, the Great Dismal Swamp and the Okefenokee Swamp. The recreational opportunities provided in wetlands include fishing, hunting, trapping, bird watching, hiking, canoeing, and photography.

Shorelines

The coastlines around and within the United States total around 100,000 miles, or 161,000 kilometers. Most of the American coastline is developed; 70 percent of the continental U.S. coastline is privately owned. The federal government controls 11 percent of the coastline, state and local governments control 19 percent. This does not mean that the 30 percent of coastline controlled by government is available for public recreation. Topographically, only 10 percent of American coastline, or only 10,000 miles, is available for public recreation, including aquatic activities such as swimming, boating, sailing, fishing, and diving. Also camping, hiking, and picnicking take place along the coast.

Lakes

There are close to 100,000 natural lakes in the United States, varying in size from a prairie pond to the expansive Great Lakes. The leisure pursuits on these lakes vary from swimming and fishing to sailing, boating, and water skiing. Also at the shores of these lakes, recreationists camp, hike, picnic, jog, walk, and watch birds. The surface acreage of fresh water available for recreation is about 22 million acres, comprised of both natural lakes and human-made reservoirs.

Reservoirs

There are close to 50,000 reservoirs in this country, which have been constructed by government agencies and private individuals for the purpose of flood control, generating electricity, or providing water for irrigation. Most of these reservoirs are small, some are medium size, and a few are large. The medium ones were built with the help of the Soil Conservation Service or the Fish and Wildlife Service. The larger ones were built under the direction of the Bureau of Land Management, the U.S. Army Corps of Engineers, or the Tennessee Valley Authority.

PLANNING FOR OUTDOOR RECREATION

Planning takes into consideration the general purpose related to the kind of service being offered or suggested. In the case of outdoor recreation, the objective is to provide constructive leisure pursuits in a safe, natural environment. The work of the scholars who were concerned with leisure in the early years of the twentieth century set the tone for such an objective. The formation of the Playground Association of America was in conjunction with advocacy. Local, state, and federal agencies as well as private organization began programs in fulfillment of this objective. As industrialization, automation, and urbanization increased, so did the demand for organized leisure pursuits, including outdoor recreation experiences.

By the middle of the twentieth century, public interest in recreation was heightened when the demand for expanded facilities led to a crisis in outdoor recreation. According to La Page (1988:127), that crisis was responded to by massive state and federal reinvestment in our public outdoor recreation estate. The response included numerous state bond issues, the Forest Service's Operation Outdoor and the National Park Service's Mission 66. Most important was President Eisenhower's decision to appoint the Outdoor Recreation Resources Review Commission (ORRRC). It became clear from analyzing past offerings and considering present programs that planning is important for the future of outdoor recreation.

Planning Procedure

Planning should be based on the policies, regulations, and plans of the agency or agencies involved. In addition the public should be involved in the planning procedure. Jensen (1985:311) suggested the following six methods of public involvement:

1. Public meetings where people have a chance to hear proposals and voice their support or resistance.
2. Coverage in the news media. This exposes ideas and alternatives to the public and stimulates involvement.
3. The appointment of advisory committees to represent the public.
4. Public surveys or polls to provide information for the planning process.
5. Agency sensitivity to views of members of the public.
6. Presentations at the meetings of service clubs, political groups, and auxiliary organizations.

Stages in the Planning Procedures: After forming the advisory board, the following steps should be taken:

1. The city council and/or the board should determine the guiding principles for designing the facility, i.e., relation to the master plan, current and future needs, and realistic cost.
2. Services of a consultant may prove to be very beneficial. Qualifications of the consultant are of prime importance.

3. Data on enrollment trends, demographic changes, and new standards should be included.
4. Survey existing facilities as to size, features, conditions, and current standards. These data should be compared to currently acceptable practices.
5. Calculate the cost of the facility. The input by the consultant is useful at this point or a visit to a nearby facility may help this endeavor.
6. Prepare document that describes the steps taken and includes the data collected. The document should be widely distributed and feedback required.

There are four levels of recreation plans in the United States today:

1. Nationwide plans
2. State comprehensive plans
3. Local (city, district or county) plans
4. Project or site plans

Regardless of the level of the plan, Jensen (1985:304) suggested that the following 12 principles be observed:

1. Park and recreation areas should provide opportunities for all persons regardless of race, creed, age, gender, or economic status.
2. To meet the needs in a particular geographic area, consideration should be made of all the resources available, including lakes and streams, woodlands, marshes, mountains, historical and archeological sites, areas of scenic value, and areas of special interest.
3. Multiple-use can often add to the total use of an area; therefore, multiple-use should be considered, even though it is not always accepted.
4. Early acquisition of land based on a comprehensive recreation plan is essential. Unless sites are acquired well in advance of

demand, land costs often become prohibitive.
5. Timely evaluation should be made of present recreational needs and future trends to accurately project for the future.
6. Insofar as possible, recreation areas and facilities should be properly distributed in accordance with the population, so that all of the people have approximately equal availability of recreational opportunities.
7. The design of individual park and recreation sites should be as flexible as possible to accommodate changing patterns of recreation in the given area.
8. Barriers should be avoided whenever possible to provide for easy access to recreation areas by the elderly, the handicapped, and others with mobility restrictions.
9. There should be citizen involvement in planning whenever possible, because this results in good ideas and added enthusiasm toward using the areas once they are developed.
10. Responsibilities should be defined and agreed upon by the various governmental and private agencies so that the duplication of areas, facilities, and services will be avoided and so the public will receive the best return possible on the dollars spent.
11. Park and recreation lands should be protected in perpetuity against encroachment and non-recreation purposes. These areas should not be considered the path of least resistance for highways, public utilities, and buildings.
12. The plan for a particular recreation area or the plan for a system of areas and facilities should be carefully integrated with the total master plan for

the particular agency or area. Park and recreation planning is not an isolated function. It should be integrated with the total plan.

NATIONAL OUTDOOR RECREATION PLANS

There were unsuccessful attempts to develop some comprehensive national plans for outdoor recreation after World War I. President Calvin Coolidge called a National Conference on Outdoor Recreation in 1924 where 128 public and private agencies were represented. The final report, which appeared in the Senate document number 158 of May 1928, made recommendations for future outdoor recreation pursuits. But the recommendations were set aside with the coming of the Great Depression. With the establishment of the Works Progress Administration to ward off unemployment at that time, many facilities and programs were built on federal, state, and local lands. Nash (1978:36) believes that because of lack of planning, roads were built in wild places in national parks and forests by thousands of job-hungry men. Federal care threatened to divide and conquer the last really large wilderness areas in the country.

After World War II, different federal agencies responded to the increasing demands for outdoor recreation pursuits by developing their own individual plans such as Mission 66 of the National Park Service and Operation Outdoor of the U.S. Forest Service. The first comprehensive planning effort on a national level was done by the Outdoor Recreation Resources Review Commission in the 1960s.

Outdoor Recreation Resources Review Commission

Upon the suggestion of President Eisenhower, Congress established the Outdoor Recreation Resources Review Commission, known as ORRRC, in 1958. Eight members of Congress and seven private citizens were appointed by the president of the United States to serve on the commission, chaired by Lawrence Rockefeller. The commission was charged to survey the outdoor recreation needs of the American people for the following four decades and to recommend a plan of action to meet those needs.

The commission surveyed America's stock of outdoor recreation areas, both actual and potential, and conducted interviews, giving questionnaires to a cross section of the American public in an attempt to discern recreational needs and demands on the natural resources. ORRRC's recommendations were included in its final report to Congress in 1961; the report included 27 volumes, each written on a separate topic.

The ORRRC report defined a policy framework, which divided the responsibilities for outdoor recreation in the United States along the following lines:

1. Local and state governments are to take the basic responsibility for supplying recreational opportunities.
2. The federal government is to preserve areas of national significance.
3. The federal government is to offer financial and technical assistance, provide leadership in getting all states to supply increased opportunities, and manage existing federal lands for broad recreation benefits.
4. Individual and private efforts are expected to continue providing places and activities, equipment, services, and other products, and to lead preservation of land through nonprofit groups.

The commission recognized that demand will exceed supply in outdoor recreation opportunities in the following years unless certain actions were taken immediately. The problem was compounded by the fact that the extant facilities for outdoor recreation were not only overtaxed, but also antiquated. According to Knudson (1984:329), ORRRC's recommendations have been implemented to a remarkable degree. Most important was the establishment of the Bureau of Outdoor Recreation, which provided a federal focus on national outdoor recreation planning, including the 1973 and 1979 nationwide outdoor recreation plans. The bureau changed its name to the Heritage Conservation and Recreation Service in 1978 and was discontinued in 1981.

Other outcomes of the commission's recommendations include the following:

1 Expansion of the National Park System.
2 Establishment of the National Wilderness System.
3 Inauguration of the Land and Conservation Fund Program.
4 Establishment of the Wild and Scenic Rivers System.
5 Establishment of the National Trail System.
6 Authorization of state and local land acquisition programs

Public Land Law Review Commission Report (1970)

Congress decided in 1964 that there was a need for a bipartisan commission to review the nation's land use, laws, and policies. The Public Land Law Review Commission (PLLRC) was to report to Congress the status of land use, the problems associated with such use, and the changes needed for more effective use. Its report of 1970 contained 452 recommendations based on the input of hundreds of economists, planners, and managers. The recommendations related to the recreational use of land were commensurate with ORRRC recommendations, as follows:

- *Role of the federal government*: The federal government should be responsible for the preservation of scenic areas, natural wonders, primitive areas, and historic sites of national significance; for cooperation with the states through technical and financial assistance; for the promotion of interstate arrange-

ments, and for management of federal lands for the broadest recreation benefit consistent with other essential uses.
- *Role of state governments*: The states should play a pivotal role in making outdoor recreation opportunities available by effecting the acquisition of land; by developing sites; and by providing and maintaining facilities of state or regional significance; by providing assistance to local governments; and by providing leadership and planning.
- *Role of local governments*: Local governments should expand their efforts to provide outdoor recreation opportunities, with particular emphasis upon securing open space and developing recreation areas in and around metropolitan and other urban areas.
- *Role of the private sector*: Individual initiative and private enterprise should continue to be the most important force in outdoor recreation, providing many various opportunities for a vast number of people, as well as the goods and services used by people in their recreation activities. Government should encourage the work of nonprofit groups wherever possible. It should also stimulate desirable commercial development, which can be particularly effective in providing facilities and services where demand is sufficient to return a profit.

Other recommendations of the PLLRC included the following:

1. Emphasis on the preservation concept for the public land under the jurisdiction of the National Park Service.
2. Continuation of the multiple-use policy of the public lands under

the jurisdiction of the Forest Service and the Bureau of Land Management with recreation as a primary use.

3. Purchase of private lands that could provide for right-of-way corridors or access to otherwise inaccessible recreation areas.
4. Expansion of the National Park System, wilderness areas, seashores, and the Wild and Scenic Rivers System.
5. Improvement in the land classification and acquisition program as related to recreation with the use of advanced methods of financing acquisition and allocating funds for development.

Despite its significance to outdoor recreation, the report of the PLLRC has not received much attention because the commission chair, Wayne Aspinell, was not reelected and because there was no single program for implementation (Knudson, 1984:332). Nonetheless, the report raised a number of national and regional issues pertaining to recreation policy and planning in the United States.

Nationwide Outdoor Recreation Plan of 1973

Public Law 88-29, known as the Organic Act, required that the secretary of the Interior should:

> … formulate and maintain a comprehensive nationwide outdoor recreation plan, taking into consideration the plans of the various Federal agencies, States, and their political subdivisions. The plan shall set forth the needs and demands of the public for outdoor recreation and the current and foreseeable availability in the future of outdoor recreation resources to meet those needs. The plan shall identify critical outdoor recreation problems, recommend solutions, and recommend desirable actions to be taken at each level of government and by private interest.
>
> (Jensen & Thorstenson, 1977:247).

In 1973 the Bureau of Outdoor Recreation of the Department of the Interior published a national plan entitled *Outdoor Recreation: A Legacy for America*. It was a policy document on the roles of the three levels of government. According to Knudson (1984:332-33), a draft of the plan was presented to President Richard Nixon earlier with a strong urban emphasis and a multi-billion dollar price tag. The plan was printed for the record by the Senate Interior Committee under the title "The Recreation Imperative." It recommended that 30 percent of the Land and Water Conservation Fund go to urban centers and that grants should be allowed for operational expenses such as implementing recreational programs. This nationwide recreation plan was based on surveys of over 4,000 persons across the country. The data showed that participation in leisure pursuits had increased sharply since the previous ORRRC study. In the meantime, recreation resources did not increase at the same rate. The report called for quick action on part of all three levels of government and the private sector to aid in increasing resources. The report also pointed to the increasing problem of pollution of America's natural resources that provide for recreational outlets. Carrying capacity determinants were suggested as an important managerial tool to reduce abuse.

According to Jensen (1985:316-17), the 1973 plan specified the following functions for the federal government:

1. Complete a program of identification, selection, and planning for acquisition of those superlative areas needed to round out the federal recreation estate.
2. Continue to use the Land and Water Conservation Fund to acquire needed federal recreation lands and assist the states in doing the same.
3. Open to the public directly or through state and local entities those underused portions of federal properties or facilities having public recreation values,

when such lands are not available for transfer.

4. Accelerate evaluations of proposed trails, wild and scenic rivers, wilderness areas, wetlands, and historical properties to ensure that those unique lands are preserved by federal, state, or local governments or private interests for the benefit of the public; and accelerate the evaluation of federal land holdings to determine if beaches, shorelines, islands, and natural areas can be made available for increased public recreation use.

Further, the plan stated that to improve the management and administration of recreation resources and programs, the federal government will:

1. Accelerate the identification and no-cost transfer of surplus and underused real property to state and local governments for parks and other recreation sites.

2. When the land is not available for transfer, and direct federal management is not necessary or desirable, take necessary steps to transfer management responsibility for existing recreational units to state and local governments.

3. Promote recreation developments on or near federal lands on the basis of regional land-use plans. Whenever possible, private investment should be used for the provision of these services.

4. Undertake preparation of recreation land-use plans for all management units and coordinate such planning with all interested federal, state, and local government agencies and private entities.

Nationwide Outdoor Recreation Plan of 1979

The Nationwide Outdoor Recreation Plan of 1979 was quite different from the plan of 1973 in that it was developed from a series of task force reports on specific issues, which were reviewed by the public and revised accordingly. It also included surveys on recreation preference and participation. The report followed two major themes—an assessment of outdoor recreation and a suggested action program (Jensen, 1985:317).

Assessment of Outdoor Recreation

The assessment provides a summary of trends, needs, and opportunities along with benefits accrued from participation in recreation activities. Included were the demographic variables affecting participation and agencies providing facilities and programs, along with a description of problems facing recreation.

Action Program

A program of action was suggested to revolve around nine issues of national significance:

1. *Federal land acquisition.*
   a. A new and more effective planning and decision-making process will be instituted to identify and select lands eligible for the federal portion of the Land and Water Conservation Fund.
   b. A policy will be developed defining the federal role in protection and acquisition of land for conservation of natural, cultural, and recreational resources. This policy will encourage alternatives to outright acquisition.
2. *Wild, scenic, and recreational rivers.*
   a. New guidelines will be developed to shorten the time required to study potential wild, scenic, and recreational rivers.

b. Federal agencies will develop guidelines to avoid adverse effects on potential wild and scenic rivers identified in the nationwide rivers inventory.

c. Federal land-managing agencies will assess the potential of rivers identified in the nationwide inventory located in their lands and take steps to designate or manage these rivers as components of the National Wild and Scenic Rivers System.

d. Administration of the Clean Water Act and the Wild and Scenic Rivers Act will be better coordinated to ensure that investments made to clean up rivers and waterways provide maximum public recreation benefits.

3. *National trails and trail systems.*
   a. The Forest Service will establish 145 additional national recreation trails in the National Forest System.
   b. Federal land-managing agencies will establish goals for creating additional national recreation trails on public lands other than national forests.
   c. The Department of the Interior will accelerate its efforts to encourage state, local, and private land managers to submit applications for new national recreation trails.
   d. A grass-roots effort will be undertaken across the country to assess national trail needs. This assessment will be made by representatives of state, local, and private trail interests in cooperation with federal agencies.

e. States, localities, and private landholders will be more actively encouraged to develop trails on their lands and to participate with federal agencies and trail users in creating national trails system to meet public needs.

f. The accomplishments of the "rail-to-trails" program of the Railroad Revitalization and Regulatory Reform Act will be evaluated and further recommendations made to eliminate outstanding problems.

g. State and local governments will be encouraged to develop appropriate types of bike-ways using existing federal programs.

4. *Water Resources.*
   a. Federal water quality grants will more closely examined to determine the degree to which they include recreation considerations.
   b. Nonstructural alternatives to flood control, including the preservation of open space for recreation, will be evaluated for their applicability in flood-prone communities.
   c. Actions will be taken to ensure that urban waterfront revitalization projects include considerations for recreation and public access.

5. *Energy Conservation.*
   a. A program of energy conservation will be developed for all recreation lands, facilities, and programs, and guidelines will be issued for all federal recreation grant programs to state and local governments.

6. *Environmental education.*
   a. Guidelines will be prepared for all Department of the Interior agencies and coordinated with other federal agencies.

Table 12.3 Source: National Park Service *The Vail Agenda* (Washignton, D.C.: U.S. Government Printing Office, 1991), pp.3, 123-124.

Six Strategic NPS Objectives

1. *Resource Stewardship and Protection.* The primary responsibility of the National Park Service must be the protection of park resources.

2. *Access and Enjoyment.* Each park unit should be managed to provide the nation's diverse public with access to, and recreational and educational enjoyment of the lessons contained in that unit, while maintaining unimpaired those unique attributes that are its contribution to the national park system.

3. *Education and Interpretation.* It should be the responsibility of the National Park Service to interpret and convey each park unit's and the park system's contributions to the nation's values, character, and experience.

4. *Proactive Leadership.* The National Park Service must be a leader in local, national, and international park affairs, actively pursuing the mission of the national park system and assisting others in managing their park resources and values.

5. *Science and Research.* The National Park Service must engage in a sustained and integrated program of natural, cultural, and social science resource management and research aimed at acquiring and using the information needed to manage and protect park resources.

6. *Professional.* The National Park Service must create and maintain a highly professional organization and work force.

7. *The handicapped.*
   a. The Department of the Interior will provide improved access to recreation facilities.
   b. The Department of the Interior will establish procedures to involve disabled citizens in the development of recreation policy and programs.
8. *The private sector.*
   a. The feasibility of cooperative agreements between the private sector and public recreation agencies will be explored as an alternative method of improving public recreation opportunities, and appropriate demonstrations will be undertaken.
9. *Research.*
   a. A comprehensive national recreation research agenda will be prepared.

In order to ensure continuous planning, a division for this purpose was established in the National Park Service. Its mission is:

1. To define and monitor the annual action programs.
2. To update the five-year assessment.
3. To conduct nationwide recreation surveys and coordinate more specialized federal surveys.
4. To compile and update a national research agenda for recreation.
5. To promote long-range planning for the future of recreation in America.

The National Park Service initiated an intensive review of its responsibilities and future plans and presented the findings in a symposium entitled *Our National Parks: Challenges and Strategies for the 21st Century*. The symposium ended by creating a vision composed of six strategic objectives as listed in Table 12.3.

State Outdoor Recreation Plans

The role of the state in outdoor recreation activities was detailed in Chapter 8. In this chapter the discussion is limited to the states' plans for outdoor recreation pursuits. Prior to the passage of the Land and Water Conservation Fund Act in 1965, individual states had no incentive to prepare an outdoor recreation plan. With the passage of the Land and Water Conservation Fund Act, an incentive was provided. For a state to receive financial assistance from the fund, it must have a current plan that spells out the ways in which it, the state, will help satisfy the recreational needs of its residents. A new plan must be prepared every five years. From 1965 to 1980, every state in the Union prepared a comprehensive outdoor recreation plan that was renewed every five years as required. Many states stopped the practice of developing a new plan every five years when the Bureau of Outdoor Recreation (Heritage Conservation and Recreation Service) was eliminated.

The state is empowered through the United States Constitution to assume the responsibility for services that were not specified as federal government responsibility. Recreation is one of these responsibilities, and the planning for it was encouraged by the Land and Water Conservation Fund Act. The typical state outdoor recreation plan revolves around three areas: demand, supply, and future projection. Problems and issues are addressed in some plans. The department charges with overseeing state parks and recreation offerings is usually the department responsible for developing the state's outdoor recreation plan and the coordination of its implementation with the agencies of the federal government and within the state's political subdivisions such as counties and cities.

The guidelines require that, in preparing the plan, citizen input must be considered. The state must seek the views of both public officials and interested citizens. Public meetings are encouraged. The following information is required the plan:

1. A brief description of factors such as climate, topography, wildlife, history, populations, and urbanization that influence outdoor recreation in state.
2. A list of the federal and state agencies that are responsible for creating, administering, and financially assisting publicly owned recreation areas.
3. An inventory of recreation areas that are publicly or privately owned, summarized by region or county, and a list of historic sites.
4. An estimate of the number of people who participate in each of several recreational activities, now and in the future, and an estimate of the frequency with which they participate.
5. A statement of recreation needs that will be met by the state, county, and local governments.
6. A statement of recreation needs of special populations, such as the elderly, the handicapped, and the poor.

7. A description of actions proposed for the next five years to provide more outdoor recreation opportunities, such as proposals for acquisition and development, legislation, financial and technical assistance, and research.

Chapter eight provides the special case of the State of California and its planning milestone for parks in the 21st Century.

LOCAL OUTDOOR RECREATION PLAN

The local outdoor recreation plan addresses the demand and supply of local recreation opportunities and a prediction of future demands and the suggested answers to these demands. The same information that is to be included in a state plan should be included in a local plan, except that it would be limited to the locality. Most local governments, whether county, city, or township, have planning departments that can help provide some of the needed information. Sometimes the planning department prepares the whole document, if the department charged with parks and recreation would prefer not to prepare it because they lack staff. In other instances consultants are hired to prepare the local outdoor recreation plan.

According to Jensen, while there is no single best method of developing a plan, planners generally agree that the procedure can be divided into the following three major phases (1985:330):

1. Collection of data about history and present status.
2. Projection of future park and recreation needs.
3. Formulation of realistic proposals for both near and long-term future.

In implementing the plan, cooperation of public agencies and private citizens must be secured. Input of all concerned must be sought during the different phases of preparing the document. Also, adequate financial support needed for implementation must be secured in advance. To be effective, the implementation of the plan must proceed according to an approved timetable.

Knudson (1984:334) stated that time frames of five to 20 years are commonly used in the preparation of local outdoor recreation plans. While five years is adequate, 20 years seem to be a long time. Many changes, both demographic and spatial, take place in a span of 20 years. Not only would young adults become middle-aged persons in two decades, but also many new residents could move into the community, altering it considerably in less than a 20-year period. The altering of open space must be taken into consideration.

Project Plans

On the macro level, nationwide plans for outdoor recreation were discussed, and on the intermediate level, statewide and local plans were presented. On the micro level, the level of a single project, whether campground, waterfront, or ski resort, public or private, certain steps should be observed.

First, a master plan should be prepared that includes a description of the need for the development of the site based on demographics and predicted participatory figures. An inventory of existing (even if limited) resources would support the need for the proposed site. Also data on the physical characteristics of the site will be needed. How the site will be managed, in general terms, should be included. An important part of the master plan of a site is the preparation and submission of an environmental impact statement. The statement should be submitted, in conjunction with requirements of the Land and Water Conservation Fund Act, to the liaison office in each state.

It is imperative that the public become involved, not only because it is required in the case of public projects, but also because the public is, after all, the consumers to be served by the project. Market researchers for private enterprises conduct surveys to find out interest and preference of consumers. Such a process lacks interactive debate, which is explicitly required in public projects.

While each public agency dealing with projects for outdoor recreation may have its own way of developing a project, Jensen (1985:322) and Knudson (1984:339) suggested that the approach used by the Forest Service might serve as a model. The approach entails four major steps, as follows:

1. *Drafting of a detailed site map*, including:
   - Land lines and boundaries as well as ownership.
   - A permanently established baseline and reference points.
   - The map scale (usually no smaller than 1:600).
   - Contour lines with an interval of one or two feet (0.3-0.6 m).
2. *A narrative report*, consisting of three main parts:
   - Analysis and discussion of the physical characteristics of the site as they may influence design and construction.
   - Analysis and discussion of the physical and aesthetic requirements of the use or uses and the desired level of experience of users.
   - Statement of design objectives—that which you intend to do with design to accommodate the desired uses within the capability of the site to withstand the use.
3. *A general development plan*, usually made by tracing the detailed site map and adding proposed improvements. It would contain the following:
   - An overall design scheme.
   - The type and placement of all facilities but not layout details.
   - Road plan.
   - Survey control baseline and description.
   - Map showing the site and surrounding area.
   - Orientation.
   - Legend.
   - Aerial photo coverage.
4. *A final construction plan*, which conveys instructions to the contractor and includes:
   - Road design.
   - Water and sewage system designs.
   - Grading plans, including all contour modifications.
   - Family unit layout and construction details.
   - Construction drawings of all facilities and structures.
   - Layout information for the location of all site improvements.
   - All necessary specifications.

SUMMARY

In order for the managers of outdoor recreational areas and programs to be able to not only equitably, but also wisely, provide adequate opportunities to all their recreationists, certain management policies should be followed. The two basic policies of preservation and multiple-use are detailed in this chapter.

The preservation policy, which seeks to set apart certain lands for the benefit of all, and applied in particular to wilderness areas, is discussed in light of some 11 principles. The multiple-use policy that allows for certain forms of exploitation of natural resources is applicable to the national forests and is met with difficulties, at the core of which is the fact that different users view American natural resources differently.

Outdoor recreation resources are classified into two basic categories, land and water, and both in turn are classified into smaller units such as forests, grasslands, deserts, and tundra; and rivers, wetlands, shorelines, lakes and reservoirs. The policies to be followed in the utilization of each are presented along with the process of planning.

National outdoor recreation plans, were required by law, and are shown in this chapter. Also presented are state comprehensive plans, which were prompted by the passage of a number of federal acts. State plans for outdoor recreation were conducted every five years. Local outdoor recreation plans address the demand and supply of local offerings. On a micro level, the plan for a single local project is detailed from the master plan to the environmental impact report.

REFERENCES

Brown, P., Driver, B., & McConnell, C. (1978). *The opportunity spectrum concept in outdoor recreation supply inventories: Background and application.* Proceedings of the Integrated Renewable Resource Inventories Workshop. USDA Forest Service General Technical Report RM-55, 73-84.

Clawson, M., & Knetsch, J. (1966). *Economics of outdoor recreation.* Baltimore: Johns Hopkins University Press.

Cole, D. (1986). Resource impact caused by recreation. In *The President's commission on Americans outdoors*, (Literature Review). Washington, D.C.: U.S. Government Printing Office.

Everhart, W. (1972). *The national park service.* New York: Praeger.

Frakt, A., & Rankin, J., (1982). *The law of parks, recreation resources and leisure services.* Salt Lake City, Ut: Brighton Publishing Co.

Hendee, J., Stankey, G., & Lucas, R. (1978). *Wilderness management.* Forest Service, U.S. Department of Agriculture. Washington D.C.: U.S. Government Printing Office.

Jensen, C., & Thorstenson, C., (1977). *Issues in outdoor recreation.* Minneapolis, MN: Burgess.

Jensen, C. (1985). *Outdoor recreation in America.* Minneapolis, MN: Burgess Publishing.

Knudson, D. (1984). *Outdoor recreation.* New York: Macmillan.

La Page, W. (1988). Recreation management: Physical resources and environment. In S. H. Smith (Ed.), *Leisure today: Selected readings*, Vol. IV. Reston, VA: AAHPERD.

Nash, R. (1978). Historical roots of wilderness management. In J. Hendee, G. Stankey, & R. Lucas, (Eds.). Wilderness Management. Forest Service, U.S. Department of Agriculture. Washington, D.C.: U.S. Government Printing Office.

National Park Service. (1993). *Biological diversity.* GPO. 342-398/600138. United States Government Printing Office.

National Park Service. (1991). *The Vail agenda.* Washington, D.C.: U.S. Government Printing Office, pp.3, 123-124

Outdoor Recreation Resources Review Commission. (1962). *Outdoor recreation for America.* Washington, D.C.: U.S. Government Printing Office.

Washburne, R., & Cole, D. (1983). *Problems and practices in wilderness management: A survey of managers.* Research Paper INT-304. Ogden, UT: Forest Service, U.S. Department of Agriculture.

13 MANAGEMENT PROCEDURES IN OUTDOOR RECREATION

Management is both a science and an art. It has become increasingly important in recent years as social organizations became more complex. Managers need experience in order to help an organization achieve its goals and run smoothly. The accumulation of ideas from early managers led to a body of knowledge that is supported by theories borrowed, sometimes, from other fields, including sociology, psychology, economics, and business administration. A growing number of managers are depending on scientific knowledge to make decisions, but these decisions should be tempered by personal judgment, intuition, and inspiration, making management an art as well as a science.

While the information in this chapter is drawn from past experiences and accumulated knowledge of the best possible procedures to follow in the management of outdoor recreation resources and activities, needless to say, managers must depend on their own best judgment to arrive at sound conclusions.

BASIC CONCEPTS OF MANAGEMENT

There are a number of fundamental concepts that should be kept in mind in the management of outdoor recreation resources and activities. The science and art of management were born out of the business and industrial sectors of the society and not from its service sector. While they are very useful ideas emanating from business and industry, outdoor recreation opportunities are, nonetheless, offered as a service to the individual citizen, and they should be kept this way. Accordingly, not all basic concepts in business and industrial management are applicable to the outdoor recreation sphere.

- Benefit-based Management:
  This approach has potential in outdoor recreation in that it allows the managers to measure and facilitate participation.
- Management by Objectives:
  Requires that the manager and her or his staff become involved in both the establishment and/or the crystallization of the agency's objectives.
- Strategy Management:
  This approach entails following a continual process to effectively relate the agency's objectives and resources to the available opportunities.
- The Planning, Program, Budgeting System (PPBS):
  Calls for the careful development of goals, evaluation of the program or programs intended to reach these goals, and the

establishment of a budget for that very purpose.

- The Program Evaluation Review Technique (PERT):
  Uses mathematical formulas and computer simulations to identify all key activities designed to achieve the stated goals of the agency. A flow sequence showing time, resources, and performance for each task.
- Conflict Resolution:
  Is no longer viewed as always harmful or counterproductive. Conflict, in fact, may be an important vehicle for change. It is its resolution that should be handled with utmost care.
- Decision-Making:
  Is probably the central activity of management, because its effectiveness is measured by the quality of its decisions.

CARRYING CAPACITY

One of the most important decisions to be made by the management of an outdoor recreation resource is the carrying capacity of the resource. The idea behind carrying capacity is that when the resource encounters heavy use, its capacity to sustain recreation without deterioration should be determined (Fogg, 1975:13). The idea can be traced back to the mid 1930s, but the interest in it peaked in the 1960s and 1970s, when the demand on the outdoor recreation resources increased dramatically. Fogg (1975:14) suggested that the design load of a resource is dependent on several factors, which should take carrying capacity into consideration. These factors include:

1. The general attractiveness of the area.
2. The site in relation to population distribution.
3. The economic level of the tributary population.

4. The degree of urbanization of the tributory population.
5. The influence of an area of similar characteristics.

Many studies have been conducted on carrying capacity and its application in outdoor recreation areas (Stankey & Manning, 1986:M-47). Some studies show that there are difficulties in adopting the concept, and other studies show difficulties in implementing it. Washburne and Cole (1983) found that managers of two-thirds of national wilderness areas believe that their use exceeds their capacity by far, and only one-half of these managers reported some progress in establishing carrying capacities.

According to Hendee et al. (1978:171), recreation resources are used by many different people, seeking many different, and sometimes conflicting, experiences. And if carrying capacity is designed to maintain the resources for as long as possible, research has shown that capacity is a function of more than simple numbers of users: intensity of use, habitat type, seasonality, and location play decisive roles in carrying capacity. Some researchers have criticized the term as inappropriate, inadequate and misleading for recreation resource management. Hendee et al. suggest that the emphasis should be on the intent behind the concept of carrying capacity. They suggested the follow four criteria for carrying capacity:

1. The determination of carrying capacity is ultimately a judgmental decision.
2. Carrying capacity decisions depend on clearly defined objectives.
3. The range of available alternative opportunities must be taken into consideration.
4. Carrying capacity is a probabilistic concept and not an absolute measure.

Knudson (1984:315) discussed the factors that affect carrying capacity and grouped them into three major types.

1. **Characteristics of the Resource Base**

   The geology and soil of the resource are important factors in determining carrying capacity. Good soil has high carrying capacity, which, in turn, is dependent on its drainage and depth. If the resource is dry enough to allow for reasonable use during the season, this will add to its capacity. Too dry or too muddy soil reduces the capacity. Texture of the soil, its depth, and the type of underlying rocks play important roles in determining these factors. Topography is an important factor in determining carrying capacity. While rough topography does not allow for many campsites, smooth topography does. Slopes facing north hold snow longer, providing longer skiing seasons but shorter seasons for picnicking and swimming. Different types of vegetation differ in their ability to withstand use. Also vegetation can be used to provide special benefits such as windbreaking along beaches, which may increase carrying capacity by extending the season. Climate is an important factor in determining the length of the season. Rainfall patterns, fog, and storms determine to a great extent the length of the season and the type of activities. The existence of water, or lack thereof, determines the type of use, thus the carrying capacity of the resource, for both people and wildlife.

2. **Characteristics of Management**

   The philosophy and laws that govern the agency in charge determine, to a great extent, the elements of the carrying capacity of the source. Examples of both the philosophy and laws are seen in the number of campsites per acre and in the size of the campsite itself, which translates into a certain carrying capacity. The design of the resource determines its carrying capacity. Paved roads encourage more traffic in comparison to gravel roads. The addition of a beach to a lake would, possibly, increase use.

3. **Characteristics of Users**

   Some users visit an outdoor recreation area for the enjoyment of nature, and others may visit to be with a group. For the first type of users, crowding would be more of a problem than for the second type. Some recreationists use large equipment such as boats in their outings, others are content with smaller equipment. Also the type of activity practiced while in an outdoor recreation setting is very much related to carrying capacity. For instance, still hunting allows more hunters in an area than stalk hunting.

Knudson concluded that increased use or congestion may lead to sociologic impairment of the recreation experience and/or ecologic deterioration of the recreation resource. He suggested the use of the limiting factor approach, creating a ceiling of carrying capacity, not necessarily permanently. The ceiling can be raised to the next limiting factor as needed. On the other hand, Graefe et al. (1987:78) suggested that carrying capacity can be utilized within the framework of the Recreational Opportunity Spectrum (ROS). The ROS combines spatial allocations with activities for the purpose of providing for a range of recreational opportunities. Carrying capacity is determined through the interaction of the physical, social, and managerial settings. Following are the factors affecting carrying capacity:

1. Land Type:
    a. Height
    b. Density
    c. Resiliency
    d. Productivity
    e. Geologic size
    f. Resistance to compaction
2. Vegetation:
    a. Height
    b. Density
    c. Resiliency
    d. Reproducibility
3. Social:
    a. Number of contacts with others
    b. Types of encounters
    c. Types of activities
4. Other:
    a. Access
    b. Length of season
    c. Patterns of use
    d. Occupancy length
    e. Attractiveness of site for specific activities

Must carrying capacity be described in terms of standards for acceptable conditions? Washburne (1982) compared two standard-based approaches to carrying capacity. The traditional approach uses numerical capacity as being necessary to keep the desired conditions. This approach fails to recognize type, distribution, as well as the setting of the activities. He suggested an alternative approach by rearranging the sequencing and priorities and by focusing greater attention on a monitoring program. Numerical capacities are still used but are placed in perspective. In essence his suggestion is very similar to Graefe et al. He proposed Visitor Impact Management, which takes into consideration five major areas when dealing with carrying capacity and visitor impacts:

1. Impact interrelationships
2. Use-impact relationships
3. Varying tolerance to impacts
4. Activity-specific influences
5. Site-specific influences

Research Findings

Stankey and Manning (1986:M-49) summarized research findings on carrying capacity according to the following three sets of factors.

Natural resource factors

There exists a curvilinear relationship between recreational use and the impact of such use. Most recreational use leads to impact, but additional use causes little additional impact. Also, secondary effects must be taken into consideration. It is rather difficult to determine the most appropriate indicator of the impact on a natural resource, since many ecological impacts are subject to some degree of management control. In the meantime, most of the research done focused on vegetation and soil. Studies on water, air quality, and wildlife should be encouraged.

Social factors

Managers should make a distinction between crowding and overuse. Presence of others may be a motivational factor in recreation participation. The central factor seems to be that when others are seen to be sharing the same experience, perception of crowding declines. Satisfaction with an outdoor recreational experience is a complex, multifaceted concept.

Managerial factors

Management can use the following four basic strategies to handle carrying capacity:

1. Reduce use through restrictions.
2. Accommodate more use by providing more opportunities.
3. Modify the character of use to reduce impact.
4. Harden the resource base to increase its resilience.

Direct management techniques to control carrying capacity focus on visitor behavior and limit choice by using permits and regulations. Indirect techniques attempt to influence visitor behavior. Stankey and Manning (1986:M-54) indicated that several important gaps exist in our understanding of how carrying capacity works. They suggested that there is a need for better understanding of the interrelationships between ecological and social factors in setting carrying capacities. Also needed is our understanding of the consequences, social and ecological, when such capacities are exceeded. An understanding of how effective, or ineffective, certain management action is at addressing carrying capacity would be useful. Finally, more knowledge is needed on what constitutes compatibility among different groups, a concept that could be useful in minimizing crowding and conflict.

Several frameworks for determining and applying carrying capacity to outdoor recreation were presented in the literature. These frameworks provide a rational, structured process for making carrying capacity decisions.

A recent comparative analysis of carrying capacity frameworks affirms that similarity of their underlying structures and suggests a number of related themes shared among these frameworks (Nilsen & Taylor, 1997).

1. Encouragement of interdisciplinary planning teams.
2. A primary focus on management of recreation-related impacts.
3. A need for sound natural and social science information.
4. Establishment of clear, measurable management objectives.
5. Definition of recreation opportunities as comprised of natural, social, and managerial conditions.
6. A linkage among recreation activities, settings, experiences, and benefits.
7. Recognition that relationships between recreation use and resulting environmental and social impacts can be complex.

ESTIMATING USE RATES

Data on the use rates of outdoor recreation resources are useful in many ways. They are useful in planning; facts are needed for the adequate preparation for future use of a park, a forest, or any outdoor recreation resource. Another reason for keeping data on the use rate of the resource is to trace the changes that are occurring in utilizing the resource. The data could also be used, when needed, in public relations endeavors, whether directed to laypersons or to officials. Accurate data are also used in conjunction with obtaining federal and state grants and subsidies. Such data undoubtedly have budgetary implications on the local level.

Units of measurement

The 1973 Nationwide Outdoor Recreation Plan required that each federal land-managing agency report annually to the Bureau of Outdoor Recreation, in accordance with the Land and Water Conservation Fund Act of 1965, as amended, on recreation use at each management unit, using the recreation visitor-hour as the standard unit of measure. When available and appropriate, agencies also should include recreation visit and activity-hour data. The definitions of these terms are as follows:

- A recreation visitor-hour is the presence for recreation purposes of one or more persons for continuous, intermittent, or simultaneous periods of time aggregating 60 minutes.
- A recreation activity-hour is a recreation visitor-hour attributable to a specific recreation activity.
- A recreation visit is the entry of any person into a site or area of land or water for recreation purposes.

States and localities have begun to use the same terms in preparing their reports on recreational management units.

Another unit of measurement that has come into use is "activity day" or "recreation day," which gives the average number of hours of participation per day in a given activity.

Other than by making an actual count, which is not feasible in many instances, and pure guess, which is not accurate, Jensen (1985:332) suggested the following methods for keeping track of the use of a natural resource:

1. **Estimates based on observation**.
   This method involves no counting or sampling. It is simply a manager's best judgment of the number of visits to a particular area during a specified time. Obviously with this method there is much room for error, and the errors tend to be on the high side.

2. **The sampling method**.
   This involves either direct counts of people or counts of a related element, such as number of cars. Generally, the larger the sample the more reliable the data. There is the problem of whether the sample is representative of the total population.

3. **The pure count method**.
   This is the most cumbersome, yet the most accurate method of counting either individuals or a related phenomenon such as cars, entry fees, user fees, number of boats, campsite occupancy, or one of a number of other related elements.

Over the next 50 years, the Forest Service expects demands to increase from 800 million to 1.2 billion visits to the national forests per year (Forest Service, 1998:53). Estimate rates depict current trends, and current trends help managers to project future use of resources. Non-consumptive and wildlife activities are expected to increase 61 percent nationally to 2050, while hunting will decline by 11 percent (Cordell et al., 1990, 334-335). Technological innovations may lead to jet-pack backcountry camping, jet snow skis, and night activity with special hovercraft. Cellular phones and geographic positioning systems (GPS) may improve safety and communications, but may add a sense of security leading to present complications, such as over confidence and increased risk-taking.

Characteristics of uses

The characteristic of those using natural resource areas are described in Chapter 5. When, how, and with whom the participant uses the resource will be described in this section. According to Hendee et al. (1978:291), most visits to natural resource areas are short. Day use seems to prevail in small and medium-size areas. Day use in national park backcountry and national forest wilderness and primitive areas was 41 percent of total use. Length of stay for overnight campers in these natural resources varied from 1.6 to 5.9 days. The authors believe that length of stay has been the same for a number of years and that increased travel costs could lead to fewer trips in the future.

The parties of wilderness visitors are generally small, from two to four persons (Hendee et al., 1978:296). Parties of over ten persons account for five percent of all groups in most areas. This may be due, in part, to managerial regulation to reduce the impact of large groups on the environment and on other visitors.

Summer seems to be the preferred season for engaging in recreational activities in natural settings. Hunting continues into the fall in many areas, and skiing is enjoyed in the winter. Only in the southern and southwestern United States, particularly in low elevation areas, would outdoor recreational activities continue in the winter and spring. Weekenders attend these activities more so than do day participants, even in the summer.

Most natural settings in the United States draw visitors from all over the nation. Nonetheless, it seems that close-by residents seem to dominate the scene. For instance, 92 percent of the Yosemite visits are made by Californians, and residents of the state of Washington account for 78 percent of visits to the national parks in that state (Hendee et al., 1978:299).

FINANCING OUTDOOR RECREATION

Although both the public and private sectors deal with outdoor recreation opportunities, the former has much more to do with it than the latter. In turn, the public sector should be treated as comprising three subsectors when the subject is outdoor recreational resources and activities; the municipal (city/county), state, and the federal subsectors. How do these sectors finance outdoor recreation?

1. **Taxes**. General taxes are the most common form of revenues for a local program. There is usually a property tax in which an assessment is provided for a given fiscal year. The monies collected are used to provide municipal services such as education, sanitation, police, streets, health, recreation, and other local services by either a city, a township, or a county government. Sometimes more than one public body are joined to provide a service. In that case one, two, or more public bodies are empowered to establish special districts, for example a park and recreation district, with special taxes collected for such purpose. Sometimes a small part of the general tax, expressed in mills, is collected. A mill is one thousandth of a dollar ($.001). *Millage taxes* are allocated in some localities for a certain program, for example, a park and recreation program. In other instances, *special assessment taxes* are collected from those who stand to benefit from the activity and not from others.

2. **Bonds**. Bonds are used to finance major capital developments such as the acquisition of land and the building of facilities. There are many forms of bonds. A *term bond* is paid in its entirety at the end of a given period of time, usually 10 to 30 years. A *callable bond* allows the agency to pay it off before the end of the term. A *serial bond* allows for a specific portion to be paid yearly. A *general-obligation bond* is paid from general tax revenue. An *assessment bond* is derived from special assessment on those who would benefit from the project. A *revenue bond* is paid off from the income derived from the facility that has been built.

3. **Fees and Charges**. In public recreation, in general, there are seven common types of fees and charges (Warren, 1986:F-5). All of these are applicable to areas used for outdoor recreation, be they local, state, or federal.
   a. *Entrance Fees*. These are charges for the entrance into large facilities such as zoos, botanical gardens, or game reserves.
   b. *Admission Fees*. These charges are collected for performances, exhibitions, museums, and the like.
   c. *Rental Fees*. These are charges for the use of a property that is not consumed and is to be returned, such as boats or motorcycles.
   d. *User Fees*. These charges are for participation in an activity usually done with others, such as skiing, swimming, or playing golf.
   e. *License and Permit Fees*. Certain activities are allowed upon the payment of these fees, for example, hunting, fishing, and camping.
   f. *Special-Service Fees*. These charges cover special and atypical events such as workshops, summer camp, and class instruction.
   g. *Sales Revenue*. These monies are obtained from the opera-

tion of concessions, restaurants, and stores.

The philosophic basis for, or against, charging for public recreation will be discussed later in this chapter.

4. **Government Grants**. Grants through the federal government and other governments have brought billions of dollars to public recreation agencies. Although these have been drastically reduced in recent years, these funds allowed for an unprecedented expansion in outdoor recreation opportunities in the recent past.

   a. *Land and Water Conservation Fund*. Administered by the National Park Service, this fund assisted municipalities and states in acquiring and developing open space. Each state must prepare a State Comprehensive Outdoor Recreation Plan (SCORP) listing existing resources and identifying its future needs.

   b. *Community development block grants*. In the 1970s substantial sums were used from these grants to enhance outdoor recreation facilities, particularly within urban settings.

   c. *Revenue-sharing grants*. With no strings attached, expenditure of monies from revenue-sharing grants on recreation ranked fifth among all local government expenditure, after police, fire, transportation, and general expenditures. Most of the expenditure went to operating expenses rather than capital development in recreation.

   d. *Labor Assistance Programs*. Foremost among these programs is CETA, the Comprehensive Employment and Training Act, which was designed to provide short-term employment and training for unskilled workers. Grant monies were used, instead, to support operations and maintenance in recreation as well as other municipal services. The Job Training Partnership Act (JTPA) has replaced CETA.

   e. *Urban Park and Recreation Recovery Program*. This relatively small program was designed to help distressed communities rehabilitate rundown recreation systems. Indoor and outdoor facilities were included in the rehabilitation program.

   There are grants, both federal and state, that can be used in outdoor recreation for both capital development and operating expenses. In Canada, the federal government provides considerable assistance to provinces and municipalities.

5. **Foundation Grants**. Due to a shortage of public monies from both federal and state sources, many local park and recreation departments are approaching foundations and private citizens for grants and gifts. According to Kraus and Curtis (1982:252), there are several types of foundations, as follows:

   a. Special-purpose foundations are created for the purpose of meeting a special need. Sometimes recreation and sport are listed among those needs.

   b. Company-sponsored foundations are created for the purpose of corporate giving. Although a separate entity, this type of foundation is controlled by the mother company.

   c. Community foundations are established to serve a particular community, be it spiritual or residential.

d. Family foundations are established by a person or a family for the purpose of reducing taxes.

Kraus and Curtis suggested the following strategy in approaching foundations for gifts or grants (1982:253):

a. Establish a foundations committee composed of capable, willing individuals.

b. Prepare a list of foundations that may be interested in recreation, particularly outdoor recreation.

c. Develop a proposal concept that may be used to sound out the foundation before beginning the next step.

d. Prepare a formal grant proposal, which should be brief and convincing.

e. Present the proposal to the foundation in a timely fashion according to their published schedule.

f. Follow up by requesting a meeting within two to three weeks.

Grantsmanship is a relatively new term that shows how important it is to skillfully present a case to donors. Kraus and Curtis (1982:254) suggested that in order to achieve maximum results in obtaining a grant, the following points should be observed:

1. Beat the crowd, develop contacts, know about new grants before they are fully announced.

2. Visit grant headquarters, meet the key people, and personalize your approach. Remember, they are bored by the mountains of paper that flood them.

3. Invite "them" to your city, and make the visit memorable;

have "them" visit all sites.

4. Contact local political party leaders for assistance; seek industry and business people with high contacts.

5. In your presentations, use films, displays, large sketches, and graphics.

6. At first refusal or resistance, question why and follow up; persist until successful.

7. If a grant is awarded, get full newspaper coverage.

FEES FOR OUTDOOR RECREATION

The types of fees charged for the use of outdoor resources were presented earlier. This section deals with the philosophy for or against charging for outdoor recreation. The use of fees and charges for outdoor recreation activities goes back to 1908, when Mount Rainier National Park instituted an automobile fee. Charges were levied in Central Park by its concessionaire. Fees were charged in Connecticut state parks 1933. Yet the practice was not widespread. With the decline of governmental support, the need for new sources of financing became evident. In 1996, the Federal Land Management agencies were allowed to conduct recreational fee demonstration programs, the purpose of which is to test new or increased fees. The U.S. General Accounting Office (GAO) reviewed the result of this experiment and concluded in 1998 that increased or new fees had no major adverse effect on visitation to the fee demonstration sites (U.S. GAO, 1998). This does not mean that the other methods of financing, described earlier, are to be abandoned or even reduced in importance. Taxes, bonds, and grants are, and will always be, very important sources of financing public recreation.

Arguments for and against Fees

There are numerous arguments against the collection of fees in public recreation, if it is to continue to be public recreation. The bases for both capital outlay and operational allocation should be taxes. The support for the stand against fee collection for recreation comes from the case of public education, where fees are not collected and everyone is admitted. The proponents argue that the same should be observed in recreation and at all levels of public enterprise, local, regional, state, and federal. Another objection to charging fees revolves around the fact that those who need recreation the most are generally the least able to pay. Recreation is a service that should be provided not only on the same basis as education, but also on the same bases as sanitation and police protection (Kraus & Curtis, 1982:230). To charge for recreation means double taxes, which is not acceptable.

On the other hand, those who advocate the collection of fees in recreation argue that the public tends to appreciate more those services for which it pays. Moreover, charging fees can be a useful guide in that it points out the desired program and/or facility, which could be helpful in further planning.

Two additional arguments for charging fees in outdoor recreation are: 1) fees help control access to the natural setting, and 2) fees help to expand and improve current offerings. In 1979, the Heritage Conservation and Recreation Service (HCRS), the successor to the Bureau of Outdoor Recreation (BOR), supported the collection of fees, suggesting that the American consumer is both willing and able to pay (1979:5).

As early as the 1960s Rodney (1964:256) suggested a series of useful guides in establishing and maintaining fees in public recreation, as follows:

1. All fees and charges for recreation services should be in conformity with the long-term program policy of the recreation system and should be consistent with the legal authorization governing such practices.
2. Fees and charges should be viewed as a supplemental source of recreation and park funds and not as the primary source.

Therefore, the value of any proposed activity or facility should be judged with respect to its meeting public needs rather than its income-producing potential.

3. All services entailing fees or charges should be periodically reviewed by the department, and those facilities or programs meeting general and basic community-recreation needs should not have fees imposed on them.
4. Sound business procedures and administrative controls should be used in the collection and disbursement of special revenues.
5. Policies regarding concession operations or the lease of departmental facilities should be determined as part of the general administrative responsibility with respect to fees and charges.
6. In general, recreation facilities, when not being used for departmental programs, should be made available free or at minimal cost to nonprofit and nonrestricted community organizations, particularly character-building organizations serving school-age children.

Kraus and Curtis (1982:232) suggested a number of techniques in minimizing the impact of increased fees, as follows:

1. **Public Relations**. Park and recreation facility users should be provided the courtesy of advance notice of fee changes, as well as an explanation of the need for the revenues collected and the basis for them.
2. **Gradual Increases**. Gradual increases, clearly tied to rising costs, may be more acceptable to the constituency than sudden or drastic fee increases.

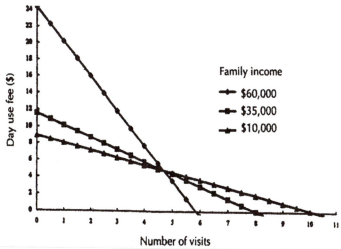

Source: Reiling, S., Cheng, H., Robinson, C., McCarville, R., and White,C. (1996). Potential equity effects of a new day use fee. **Proceedings of the 1995 Northeastern Recreation Research Symposium**. USDA Forest Service General Technical Report NE-218, 27-31.

Figure 13.1 Demand curves for day use recreation areas by income level.

3. **Fee-by-Fee Consideration**. Each type of activity or facility should be separately examined and an appropriate fee set, according to the level of demand, cost of the activity, types of fees asked at competing opportunities, possible cosponsorship of the activity, or similar factors. In some cases, activities or facilities that tend to yield a profit may be used to subsidize or partially subsidize the cost of others.

4. **Annual Passes**. Agencies may also provide frequent visitors to parks with the opportunity to purchase annual passes or other special privileges. The method may be used to increase both visitation volume and user identification with the recreation and park system; it is typically used for community swimming pools.

According to Manning (1999) the influence of fees on recreation use is dependent upon several factors, including:

1. The "elasticity of demand" for a park or recreation area. Elasticity refers to the slope of the demand curve that defines the relationship between price and quality consumed.

2. The significance of the recreation area. Parks of national significance are likely to have a relatively inelastic demand, suggesting that fees are not likely to be effective in limiting use.

3. The percentage of total cost represented by the fee. In cases where the fee charged represents a relatively high percentage of the total costs of visiting a recreation area, pricing is likely to be a more effective use-limiting approach.

4. The type of fee instituted. Pricing structure can be a potentially important element in determining the effectiveness of fees as management practice.

Research suggests that the acceptability of fees depends on several factors, including:

1. If revenue derived from fee programs is reinvested in facilities and services, then fees are often judged to be more acceptable by park visitors.
2. Public acceptance of new fees where none were charged before tends to be relatively low compared to increasing an existing fee.
3. Local visitors tend to be more resistant to new fees or increased fees than non-local visitors.
4. Visitors acceptance of fees is likely to be greater when information is provided on the cost of competing or substitute recreation opportunities.

One issue is that differential pricing may influence recreation use patterns. Another issue concerns the potential for pricing to discriminate against certain groups in society, particularly those with low incomes, as shown in Figure 13.1.

VISITOR MANAGEMENT

When a visitor arrives at an outdoor recreation site or area, a number of methods should be utilized to make his or her visit as pleasant as possible, while at the same time maintaining and preserving the natural setting on which the activity is taking place.

The Physical Aspects of Visitor Management

In addition to providing roads and trails, the agency should place signs wherever necessary. Signs are a major form of communication in outdoor recreation. Douglass (1975:313) suggested that they give directions, identify areas, give warning, supply information, and provide posting of agency regulations. He classified signs into the following four categories:

1. Administrative signs. These signs are used to identify boundaries, offices, and areas.

2. Directional signs. The internal direction sign is meant to inform pedestrians, while the external direction sign is for motorists.
3. Interpretive signs. These are designed to highlight the attraction, tell a brief history, or give some interpretation of the area.
4. Restrictive signs. These signs post regulations, control visitor movement, and remind visitors of their responsibilities.

Two other important physical aspects of visitor management are pedestrian and vehicular circulation. Both should be studied and developed according to the needs of the visitors as well as crowd control principles.

Information and Education

Roggenbuck and Ham (1986:M-59) conducted a review of literature on information-education programs in natural recreational settings and found them to be important components of management by both users and managers. These elements can be effective in solving certain management problems. They suggested that managers should endeavor to achieve the following:

- Develop an understanding of recreationists' characteristics, behavior, and informational needs so that programs can be designed to provide information that is important to managers.
- Develop cost-effective media presentations, both personal and nonpersonal, that are targeted at user groups whose wants are not being met or whose behavior is potentially problematic.
- Develop means to provide accurate information to recreationists early in the trip-planning process (computerized information systems seem to have potential).
- Assist in the benefit-cost analysis of information-education programs, especially with regard

Type of Management Indirect	Method	Specific Techniques
(Emphasis on influencing or modifying behavior. Individual retains freedom to choose. Control less complete; more variation in use possible.)	Physical Alterations	Improve, maintain, or neglect access roads. Improve, maintain, or neglect campsites. Make trails more or less difficult. Build trails or leave areas trailless. Improve fish or wildlife population or take no action (stock, or allow depletion or elimination).
	Information Dispersal	Advertise specific attributes of the wilderness. Identify range of recreation opportunities in surrounding area. Educate users to basic concepts of ecology and care of ecosystems. Advertise underused areas and general patterns of use.
	Eligibility Requirements	Charge constant entrance fee. Charge differential fees by trail zones, season, etc. Require proof of camping and ecological knowledge and/or skills.
Direct	Increased Enforcement	Impose fines. Increase surveillance of area.
(Emphasis on regulation of behavior. Individual choice restricted. High degree of control.)	Zoning	Separate incompatible uses (hiker-only zones in areas with horse use). Prohibit use at times of high damage potential (no horse use in high meadows until soil moisture declines, say July 1). Limit camping in some campsites to one night, or some other limit.
	Rationing Use Intensity	Rotate use (open or close access points, trails, campsites). Require reservations. Assign campsites and/or travel routes to each camper group. Limit usage via access point. Limit size of groups, number of horses. Limit camping to designated campsites only. Limit length of stay in area (max/min).
	Restriction on Activities	Restrict building campfires. Restrict horse use, hunting, or fishing.

Source: C. Gilbert, et al. "Toward A Model of Travel Behavior in the Boundary Waters Canoe Area," *Environment and Behavior.* 4:2(1972):131–57. (Reprinted with permission.)

A ranger at Fredericksburg and Sportsylvania National Military Park in Virginia identifies the four major battlefields and three historic structures where, during a two-year period, at least 100,000 soldiers were either killed or wounded.

to reducing physical impacts on recreation lands.

Hendee et al. (1978:323) noted that management actions are either direct or indirect. Direct action is authoritarian and allows little freedom of choice. Indirect action, which uses information and education, is more subtle and could be effective in modifying behavior. Ham (1984) found that campers' compliance with a park's efforts was related to the quality and clarity of instruction.

Instruction can be given via signs, in leaflets, or through personnel. Personnel-based technique can be costly (Martin & Taylor, 1981:104), and as a result some managers resort to the use of volunteers. Table 13.1 shows some of the direct and indirect management techniques used in wilderness areas.

Interpretive Service

According to Knudson (1984:396), there are three visitor-oriented objectives of interpretive service:

1. Tell the story of the recreational place.
2. Shape the visitor's experience.
3. Involve the participant in the activities of the place.

According to Jensen (1985:359), the application of the environment is another goal of interpretive service. The scope of the interpretation program includes nature hikes and tours led by trained interpreters. Sometimes self-guided activities are used on trails and in nature centers and demonstration areas.

Tilden (1962:67) suggested the following principles as the guidelines of nature interpretation:

1. Interpretation is revelation based upon information. Build a story into your presentation and incorporate the visitors into your stories. True interpretation deals not with parts but with the historical and spiritual whole.
2. Interpretation is art and can be taught. The story is art, not science. We are all poets and artists to some degree; images are adventures of the imagination. The interpreter must possess the skills of speaking and writing.
3. The chief aim is provocation, not instruction—to stimulate in the reader or hearer a hunger to widen his or her horizon of interests and knowledge. The national park or monument, the preserved battlefield, the historic restoration, and the nature center in a public recreation spot are all places where interpretation blooms and flourishes. First stimulate the visitor's interest, and then stimulate her or him to see and understand.
4. Interpretation should aim to present the whole to the whole person. Toward a perfect whole, the interpreter works for a complete experience, using all five senses. The visitor should leave with one or more pictures in mind.
5. Interpretation programs for children should use a different approach than those for adults. Children enjoy using superlatives, such as the largest this, the smallest that. They love to touch objects with their fingers and hands. Challenge their senses. The interpreter can help children relate to phenomena in terms they understand, without talking down to them.

Control of Undesirable Actions

Hendee et al. (1978:314) suggested that there are five undesirable actions, to which they suggested certain responses. The authors listed the following as categories of undesirable visitor behavior:

1. **Illegal Actions with Adverse Impacts**
   Examples are the illegal use of chain saws or motorbikes in wilderness. The manager should enforce the law in cases of illegal actions.
2. **Careless or Thoughtless Violations of Regulation with Adverse Impacts**
   Littering is an example, as are shortcutting a trail instead of walking on switchbacks, camping in closed areas, and building wood fires where they are not permitted. It is possible that informal education sessions could be useful in reducing careless and thoughtless behavior.
3. **Unskilled Actions with Adverse Impacts**
   Digging a drainage ditch around a tent is an example of an impact resulting from a lack of wilderness skills or knowledge. Perhaps a pre-activity session that is designed to go over basic skills for the activity would be in order. Also signs could be posted, both pictorial and with text, on how to pitch a tent.
4. **Uninformed Behavior which Intensifies Use Impacts**
   This is illustrated by large numbers of visitors who enter a wilderness at a few well-known access points during peak use periods when they might have dispersed themselves over a number of access points if they had been more informed about alternative places. Some form of educational sessions would be useful to combat this behavior.

Table 13.2 Backcountry Use for Nineteen California Wilderness Areas (Thousands of visitor-days)

Name	1976	1977	1978	1979	1980	1981	1982	1983	1984	1985	1986	Change Peak to 1986
Caribou	23.1	41.4	24.2	11.9	16.5	16.5	11.0	11.9	10.0	9.9	10.0	−76%
Cucamonga	17.5	8.9	50.1	24.0	48.9	14.3	14.2	26.1	36.3	39.9	3.46	−93%
Desolation	298.6	301.7	216.1	307.2	202.7	212.8	195.1	143.1	20.0	222.7	227.5	−26%
Dome Land	11.4	8.5	10.7	12.5	8.5	11.4	9.6	5.8	6.4	6.7	4.3	−66%
Emigrant Basin	156.1	244.3	207.1	209.2	258.0	257.8	195.4	117.5	216.9	62.4	59.9	−77%
Hoover	130.2	142.0	66.6	67.4	72.0	93.6	74.9	59.9	103.0	106.6	49.0	−66%
John Muir	812.9	903.2	848.2	827.4	688.5	791.6	602.2	358.8	449.9	397.5	451.9	−50%
Marble Mt.	92.6	91.7	87.7	89.4	90.8	68.3	58.8	48.4	60.1	64.1	67.5	−27%
Mokelumne	30.4	17.2	7.4	36.8	25.6	39.1	48.3	29.0	18.7	25.1	25.4	−48%
San Gabriel	34.9	41.9	46.4	73.5	53.3	33.3	33.6	28.8	28.8	26.7	23.5	−68%
San Gorgonio	253.8	246.8	273.7	260.1	280.2	299.2	317.3	239.3	191.7	190.3	190.6	−40%
San Jacinto	86.1	90.2	116.9	116.9	129.2	78.0	77.8	76.8	75.3	80.7	33.4	−74%
San Rafael	47.7	44.3	46.2	42.5	34.4	42.0	43.6	76.1	73.3	96.1	97.9	+64%
South Warner	29.8	11.4	14.2	14.3	21.5	12.1	13.0	14.4	14.7	14.9	15.3	−49%
Thous. Lakes	11.7	10.3	10.0	12.1	11.4	5.9	9.4	12.0	11.6	12.6	18.2	+36%
Yolla Bolly	24.7	23.3	20.2	42.1	44.9	31.8	36.4	33.8	36.5	29.6	33.4	−26%
Ventana	18.5	82.9	13.0	66.3	88.8	90.2	40.2	25.9	28.5	28.4	29.6	−67%
Golden Trout	—	—	—	72.7	114.1	122.5	104.6	92.6	97.5	104.7	69.6	−43%

Source: Forest Service, U.S. Department of Agriculture, *Use of National Forest Trails, National Wilderness Preservation System* (Washington, D.C.: U.S. Government Printing Office, 1988).

Another way to control access entries would be to close off that entry point with a physical barrier, posting signs (pictorial), and indicating the next entry point.

5. **Unavoidable Minimum Impacts**
   Examples are when visitors step on plants, when vegetation under a tent is damaged, and so on. The manager may have to revert to reduction in the use of the facility or area.

Litter control

Research shows that litter detracts seriously from the wilderness experience (Stankey, 1973, & Lee, 1975). The amount of litter that could be left by visitors might reach between 100 and 200 pounds for each visitor (Hendee et al., 1978:333). Fortunately the "incentive system of litter control" has proven to be very successful (Clark et al., 1972). This is the system in which the rangers contact families to solicit their children's help in keeping the natural area clean in return for rewards such as badges and presents. In the backcountry, where there are few children, an "appeal system" seems to be working in which the adult users are reminded to do their own litter pack-out.

The permit system

The use of mandatory permits to use special areas such as trails has the important benefit of providing communication between the user and the manager (see Figure 13.2). Information is provided that could improve the user's experience and reduce his or her impact on the area. According to Hendee et al. (1978:319), a self-issued permit could be used where the impacts are not high enough to require rationing.

WILDERNESS PERMIT
U.S. Department of Agriculture Forest Service

_____ Wilderness or Primitive Area

1 — 2

(Code)

When signed below, this Permit authorizes

_____

(Name)

_____

(Address)

_____

(City)   (State)

3 – 7

(Zip Code)

to visit this Wilderness or Primitive Area
and to build campfires in accordance with
applicable regulations.

from | 8 – 9 | 10 – 11 | to | 12 – 13 | 14 – 15 |

(Mo)   (Day)   (Mo)   (Day)

The number of people in the group will be . . . .

16 – 17

The number of pack or saddle stock used will be . . . .
(Enter "0" if no stock will be used)

18 – 19

The place of entry will be _____
(Location)

20 – 21

The trip will end _____
(Location)

22 – 23

I agree to abide by all laws, rules, and regulations which apply to this area, and to
follow the rules of behavior listed on, or attached to this permit. I will do my best
to see that everyone in my group does likewise.

_____   _____

(Date)   (Visitor's Signature)

_____   _____

(Date)   (Issuing Officer's Signature)

**The visitor must have this permit in his
possession during his visit to the Wilderness**

This section for optional use of issuing officer.
Planned travel route, duration, and location of camps.

Travel Zone (see map)	24 – 25	26 – 27	28 – 29	30 – 31	32 – 33	34 – 35	36 – 37	38 – 39	40 – 41	42 – 43
Nights of use by zone	44 – 45	46 – 47	48 – 49	50 – 51	52 – 53	54 – 55	56 – 57	58 – 59	60 – 61	62 – 63

Visitor receives white copy.
Send yellow copy to the Forest Service Regional Office in San Francisco.
Send pink copy to the Ranger District where the trip starts.

GPO 191 406   R5-2300-32 Rev. 3/72

Figure 13.2 The standard wilderness permit used in all National Forest wilderness and National Park
backcountry areas.

In a recent article, Pfister (1990:28) blamed the restrictive permit system on the sharp decline in the number of backcountry users of 19 California wilderness areas, as shown in Table 13.2.

Rationing of permits, suggested Pfister, could be the reason for the attitudinal change that has taken place among the enthusiastic backcountry backpackers who have adopted the concept of substitutability (Hendee & Burdge, 1974). They now freely shift among various choices in outdoor activities, as shown in some market surveys. Pfister suggests that management policies should attempt to:

1. Remove rationing techniques in areas of low participation.
2. Remove control over most areas except for those witnessing growth.
3. Devise new approaches to control use.

AREA MANAGEMENT: SPECIAL CASES

Outdoor recreation takes place in many locations, some of which have special characteristics that require special attention. Special management attention should be given to wilderness areas, rivers, and trails.

Wilderness Management

Wilderness in the United States is defined by the Wilderness Act of 1964 (Public Law 88-77). Wilderness is an area where human interference is kept at a minimum, yet recreation is practiced in it to a high degree. The act created the National Wilderness System, which contains 445 separate areas totaling close to 90 million acres, most of which are in Alaska and the West.

Patterns of use of these wilderness areas vary greatly, although day use seems to be the dominant pattern (Lucas & Krumpe, 1986:M-121). Hiking seems to be the most prevalent form of travel, followed by horseback riding and canoeing/boating. Along with hiking, fishing, photography, and nature study are also practiced in wilderness areas.

The Forest Service checks for permits in popular areas that are easily impacted by too many visitors.

Visitors to these areas seem to be young, well educated, and mostly males. Most come in pairs or small groups. Wilderness areas are visited mainly in the summer, although visits in the spring take place in the desert wilderness of the southwestern United States. Intensity of use varies significantly.

According to Lucas and Krumpe (1986:M-129), research has been conducted on the management of wilderness areas, yet a large gap in knowledge still exists. Further research is needed. Nonetheless, they proposed the following recommendations, which are consistent with the recommendations suggested in another study (Frome, 1985):

1. Reaffirm the goal of keeping wilderness distinctive. Preservation of natural processes and

conditions should be the overriding goal, along with provision of opportunities for a unique visitor experience dependent on natural conditions.

2. Complement wilderness with provision of a variety of high-quality semiprimitive recreation opportunities on undeveloped public lands outside wilderness areas. This will meet diverse public recreation needs and desires, and reduce pressures on wilderness areas for types of recreational use that would diminish their distinctive and special character.

3. Further apply and test the limits of an acceptable charge system as the most promising way of managing wilderness carrying capacity. (This idea was discussed in the section on carrying capacity.)

4. Emphasize the monitoring of wilderness use and conditions to provide a foundation for management.

5. Stress educational/informational approaches as a means of visitor management and as a means for minimizing regulations that tightly control visitor movement and behavior.

6. Increase trail maintenance to control environmental damage and meet visitor needs.

7. Relocate and redesign trail systems to reduce damage and provide better experiences for visitors.

8. Measure wilderness recreational use in comparable ways for all wildernesses; administered by the National Part Service, Forest Service, Fish and Wildlife Service, and Bureau of Land Management to provide comparisons and to identify trends.

River Recreation

River recreation has grown steadily over the past few years. There are close to three and a half million linear miles of rivers and streams in the United States. Some of these miles are fit for recreational settings, many of which have been protected as part of the Wild and Scenic Rivers System. According to Lime (1986: M-137), recreation associated with that system has become one of the fastest-expanding segments in Forest Service management. Lime painted a picture of the river recreationists as follows:

1. River recreationists vary widely in their activities, use patterns, motivation, and attitudes.

2. Socialization seems to be the most mentioned motivational factor behind choosing rivers as the loci for recreation.

3. Risk-taking seems to be a characteristic common to river recreationists.

4. River recreation seems to be a novice experience for many of those participating in it.

5. Group size of river recreationists seems to be considerably larger than for most other outdoor recreation activities in natural settings.

6. Most river recreationists are young, many below the age of 30.

7. River recreationists begin their activities at a later age than do most other recreationists, with the exception of tubers.

8. Participants in river recreation are predominantly white-collar workers with above average incomes.

Lime expects that the demand for river recreation in the future will produce a number of challenges that should be met. Not only will there be an increase in the demand for access to urban water resources, but there will also be an increase in recreational use of existing river riders. As the number of river recreation increases, so will the need for expansion in service, equipment, and related industries. Organizations and clubs are being formed to promote water-based recreation along with increase demand for these opportunities by minority women, and senior citizens. The manager of water-based resources should expect longer participation, demand for high-quality trips, and requests for handicapped access. Instruction in safety, good public relations, and high tech equipment will be in demand on water-based sources. Demand will continue for outfitters, boat liveries, and other commercial establishments along river corridors.

Recreation Trails

Hiking on trails in a natural setting gained popularity as a form of recreation in the early 1960s. In addition to hiking, trails provide other forms of recreation such as opportunities for nature study, photography, drawing and painting, and solitude. Trails can also serve as access to hunting, fishing, and camping. The passage of the National Trails System Act of 1968 (Public Law 90-543) provided the needed boost for these forms of recreation. The use of trails by recreationists more than doubled from 1969 to 1983. Although most of the increase took place in the 1970s with a leveling-off period in the 1980s, the 1990s may witness a substantial increase in trail recreation (Krumpe & Lucas, 1986:M-153).

Hiking, which takes place on the trail, is more or less a day use, and not much associated with overnight camping. The distances covered are modest. Hikers in wilderness areas desire solitude, low-level encounters, an unmodified natural setting. Other trail users desire other amenities, which create conflicts. Horseback riders, bicycle riders, and motorcycle riders do not use trails in wilderness areas, and their interests clash with the interests of others on non-wilderness trails. Similarly, cross-country skiers' interests clash with those of snowmobilers. Krumpe and Lucas (1986:M-155) suggested separation of trail users whenever possible.

The impact on trail use is seen in littering, horse manure, and deterioration of trails generally. Most of the trails in the United States were built 50 years ago for administrative purposes. Time and inadequate finances have contributed to the problem of trail deterioration. Rationing of users of trails has been suggested as a possible remedy. Other suggestions include a lottery system, a merit system, and trail fees. Limiting the number in a group entering a trail is another means of control.

According to Krumpe and Lucas (1986:M-159), research has concentrated on remote backcountry settings and little was done to investigate the use of trails located near metropolitan areas. The relationship between trail systems and the broader spectrum of recreation opportunities should also be explored. For instance, trail use has grown recently with the increased interest in wellness and fitness.

RISK MANAGEMENT: SPECIAL CASES

According to Hudson, Thompson, and Mack (1996), each year, over 200,000 children are injured on America's playgrounds, with the bulk of these accidents involving falls. Earlier the National Park System had 190 visitor fatalities and 2,483 visitor injuries as well as 1,505 injured employees in one year (Kraus & Curtis, 1982:286).

The following five guidelines can be used in accident reduction and risk management.

1. **Systematic Reporting and Record Keeping**. The agency should maintain an accurate picture of trends for possible future control.
2. **Facilities Inspection and Hazard Abatement**. Regular inspection should be made of all areas imposing special risks such as rockslide areas, sharp curves, thin-iced places, and similar hazards. Also all equipment should be regularly checked.
3. **Participant Safety Procedure**. All visitors should be made aware of the possible risk taken in some outdoor

recreational activities. Unsafe conduct and hazardous areas should be pointed out through bulletins, signs, and oral warnings.

4. **Staff Training**. Safety awareness and precautions should be made an important part of staff orientation and training. Members of the staff should take it upon themselves to make visitors aware of risky behavior and to firmly apply rules and regulations related to such behavior. Moreover, the staff should be licensed in First Aid.

5. **Emergency Procedures**. Emergency procedures should not only be established but also made known to all members of the staff. Regular patrols should be organized along with a speedy and effective means of communication with remote areas. Transportation should be available, and evacuation and escape routes should be delineated.

The process of law enforcement in a natural setting includes the following five steps, according to Harmon (1979):

1. To recruit and train competent personnel experienced in and responsible for various specialized duties.

2. To provide organization and training of personnel to deal with varied emergencies and challenges as they may occur, including ongoing in-service training in methods of law enforcement, First Aid, and similar functions.

3. To promote safe design and construction of facilities; while law enforcement personnel are not usually involved in this process, they can contribute helpful information at the planning stage to prevent problems that may occur later.

4. To provide a sound public relations and interpretative program, in order to give the visitor a high-quality experience in the natural environment, improve the public image of the park system, and familiarize visitors with the rationale underlying park regulations and ecologically sound use of the park setting.

5. To carry out fair and thorough enforcement of the rules, with emphasis on a positive and pleasant approach to the public, stressing education and helping to build positive attitudes, rather than a punitive or threatening approach.

LAW AND OUTDOOR RECREATION

The following legal terms are useful in our discussion of law and outdoor recreation:

Act of God. An unavoidable incident due to forces of nature that could not have been foreseen or prevented.

Assumption of risk. Participation or involvement in an activity or situation where an element of risk is inherent. Voluntary participation can be interpreted as an acceptance of risk. In outdoor recreation there is an element of reasonable risk that the participant assumes through his or her decision to participate.

Attractive nuisance. A facility, area, or situation that attracts participation and is hazardous. Examples are a footbridge in poor repair, a designated swimming area that is unsupervised or improperly regulated, or children's play equipment in poor repair. Whether a situation would be legally declared an attractive nuisance would be influenced by the laws of the particular state, the age and competence of the injured person, and the various circumstances surrounding the incident.

Civil law. Civil action implies a non-criminal infringement upon the rights of a person, agency, or corporation. Tort and contract disputes are examples of civil suits. Civil law is different from criminal law in that it regulates private, ordinary matters.

Common law. That body of governing principles and rules of action derived from past practices, customs, and traditions.

Contributory negligence. Where an individual's action was not the primary cause of negligence, but it was a contributing factor to the negligent act.

Equal protection of the law. The right of equal treatment by the law and the law enforcement agencies for all persons under similar circumstances.

Foreseeability. The degree to which danger may have been expected or an accident foreseen.

Immunity. Freedom or protection from legal action. Sovereign immunity refers to the protection of the government or the ruling body against possible suit or blame. It is based on the concept that "the king can do no wrong."

Injunction. A prohibitive ruling issued by a court directing a person or agency to refrain from performing a specific act.

Liability. Being responsible for a negligent act or other tort; having legal responsibility, which was not fulfilled and resulted in injury.

Liability insurance. Insurance policies that provide protection against financial loss from liability claims.

Mandatory legislation. Enacted legislation that must be observed. Its opposite is *permissive legislation.*

Negligent. Not exercising the proper care or following the procedures that a person of ordinary prudence would do under similar circumstances. It can take the form of either commission or omission of an act.

Permissive legislation. Legislation that legalizes an action but does not require or mandate it. Its opposite is *mandatory legislation.*

Proximate cause. The situation or factor that was the main cause of an injury or incident.

Prudent person. One who acts in a careful, discreet, and judicious manner in view of the particular circumstances.

Statutory law. Law that is made through legislative acts.

Tort. A civil wrong or injustice, independent of a contract, which produces an injury or damage to another person or to property.

Liability and Recreation Agencies

Not long ago liability was hardly a problem with which a recreation agency, public or private had to contend. Today the recreation provider and the equipment manufacturer are subject to the threats of a lawsuit. Previously the tradition of sovereign immunity protected public agencies, a right of government inherited from the British legal system where the King cannot be wrong. Today, the government and its agents are not so immune, and neither is the manufacturer. Attention must be given to acquiring safe equipment and to conducting safe recreation.

Tort Laws and Negligence

Civil wrongs that are not criminal in nature, such as trespassing, nuisance, defamation, and negligence, fall under tort laws. Most cases related to outdoor recreation come under negligence, which means that the person in charge failed to perform his or her responsibilities at the expected level of a prudent person under the same circumstances. Even if the acts of the person are not intentional, good intentions are not safeguards against prosecution. In the case of negligence, prosecution is done by the injured person and not by a law enforcement person. The prosecutor must show by a preponderance of evidence (over 50 percent) that the defendant was negligent.

According to Jensen (1985:343), for a person to be declared negligent, the following elements must exist:

1. The defendant must have a *duty toward the plaintiff*. Employees of recreation-sponsoring agencies clearly have certain duties toward participants. In most states a person does not have a legal duty toward a stranger even when the stranger is in dire need of help. To encourage aid when needed, some states have passed *Good Samaritan laws*, which provide legal protection for a person who tries to assist another person.
2. The plaintiff must have been harmed by the tort or wrong committed by the defendant. This could be in the form of property damage, personal injury, or damage to one's character or reputation.
3. The individual having *duty* must have breached that duty by an act of omission (*nonfeasance*). This means that a person who does nothing when something should have been done is often as liable as one who responds incorrectly.
4. The breach of duty mentioned in the previous item must have been directly related to the damage done to the plaintiff. In other words, the breach of duty was the proximate cause of the damage.

The situations that could lead to possible negligence include, but are not limited to, the following:

1. *Impudence*. (This is known as the reasonable-man test.) A duty of care is decided upon in court, which involves what a prudent individual should do to safeguard the persons under his or her care.
2. *Attractive nuisance*. This concept revolves around whether the facility or equipment therein are attractive, yet hazardous, unsecured, and/or unsupervised.
3. *Faulty equipment*. The malfunction of equipment or an instrument may lead to the injuring of a participant.

Visitors to outdoor recreation areas are subject to protection under tort law according to their status, which is decided upon by the courts. Knudson (1984:503) classified these visitors into three categories, as follows:

Trespassers

A trespasser is a person who enters the property of another without permission and not for the benefit of the property owner. The landowner has only minimal responsibility for the protection of the trespasser, taking due care to avoid injuring the person, if the trespasser's presence is known. The trespasser should be notified of dangers. Traps set for the trespasser or intentional shooting at the trespasser would make the landowner liable.

Licensees

A licensee is a person who enters a property with the consent, implied or stated, of the owners but not for the benefit of the owner. Examples of licensees are cross-country skiers who receive permission (no fee paid) to use company land or a farm, a person who asks permission to hunt pheasants in a cornfield, or a fisherman who is allowed to cross private land to reach a stream. The landowner is required to warn the licensee of hidden hazards (deep hole, snow-covered stumps, a violent bull) known to the owner, and the landowner is required to prevent willful harm to the licensee. Other than fulfilling those requirements, the owner has few responsibilities for injury to visitors. The landowner is not under obligation to inspect the premises for unknown dangers. The licensee cannot receive damages for injury to himself or herself, his or her vehicle, or equipment.

Invitees

The invitee class includes any visitor to a public park, forest, lake, refuge, or other recreation area, or a business visitor to a commercial recreation area, or any visitor to industrial or other land for the benefit of the landowner. If both the visitor and the landowner receive mutual benefit, the visitor is usually classified as an invitee. The owner has an obligation to keep the premises (that portion that is designated for recreation use) safe and to prevent injury to the visitor. This requires:

1. Warnings of danger to the visitor.
2. Regular inspection of the premises and facilities.
3. Removal of dangerous conditions or installation of safety measures where practicable.

Despite the vulnerable position of recreation agencies, recent lawsuits are showing that these agencies are winning. According to Rankin (1990), there are two fundamental explanations for this. First, managers of outdoor recreation resources are upgrading equipment and facilities to meet accepted safety standards. Second, agency defense in court revolves around a statutory scheme that relieves the agency of duty to protect the participant. The Federal Tort Claims Act and similar state statutes, which allowed public agencies and their employees to be sued, left several exceptions in the law, for example, policy-level immunity. Accordingly, when a lawsuit results from a questionable policy, the court will reinstate some immunity to insulate the agent from liability.

While the implied immunity applies mainly to public agencies, another method of defense is used by private, as well as public, recreation providers. A model statute was initiated in 1965 by the Council of State Governments entitled "Public recreation on private lands: limitations on liability." It became the basis for many state laws on this subject. If the owner allows for the recreational use of her or his land or facilities without charge, she or he owes no duty to keep the property safe or warn of dangerous conditions. But if fees are charged, or if the owner were to willfully and maliciously fail to warn against danger, then she or he is subject to a lawsuit.

Waivers/Release Agreements

There have been instances in which damage waivers were not upheld in court, but development in the past decade indicates differently (Rankin, 1990:9). As a general rule, waivers are held up by the court unless there is a statute to the contrary (e.g.) if the negligent act falls below the standard established by law, or if the case involves public interest. The decision as to what is of public interest is left up to the court. Also the court examines the language of the waiver to see that it is written in simple, clear, and unambiguous language understandable to lay persons.

Rankin (1990) reviewed a number of cases in risk recreation and suggested that although liability should be a concern of risk recreation providers, fear of unjust and excessive judgments by the courts is not justified. This claim is supported by the fact that in the case of Rubenstein v. United States (Kaiser, 1986:147), the court ruled in favor of the defendant (the United States). Burrell Rubenstein brought action against the United States under the Federal Torts Claim Act to recover for injuries that a client suffered from a bear attack while camping at Yellowstone National Park. The plaintiff was warned through a brochure and signs that bears were dangerous animals. It was difficult to envisage what additional measures could have been taken by the park authorities to ward off a possible attack by a bear. The plaintiff knew or should have known of the risk of an unprovoked attack.

But in another case, Niddangh v. United States (Kaiser, 1986:146), action was brought under the wrongful death statutes of the State of Wyoming. The plaintiff was acting on behalf of the estate of Stephan Athan who was killed by a falling tree at a campsite at Yellowstone National Park. Stephan Athan was an invitee to whom the United States owed the duty to keep the premise safe and to warn him of any danger. He was encouraged to enter the campground with a sense of assurance and did not assume the risk of camping. The United States was found negligent.

Robert Lee (1995) points out that almost all states have developed recreational-use statues intended to immunize property owners from liability when people enter their land for such activities as hunting or fishing and are injured or killed, or when their property is damaged or destroyed. Nonetheless, private landowners have no guarantee of safety from lawsuits in this regard.

Kozlowski (1982) points out that property owners or facility managers are not held liable for the criminal acts of others in such settings as multiuse trails or open playing field, however, they may have a duty to provide security. Similarly, they are likely to be held liable in the case of rapes or other criminal acts against youthful participants on field trips or outings.

Summary

This chapter provided an idea of how some management procedures can be utilized in outdoor recreation resources. The basic concepts in management such as Management by Objectives, Strategy Management, the PPB System, and PERT can be used in the management of outdoor recreation resources.

The management techniques that can be utilized in outdoor resources include the process to determine the carrying capacity of a facility, the process to estimate user rates, along with the units to be utilized to measure use.

Sources for financing outdoor recreation such as taxes, bonds, fees, and charges as well as grants were presented as the possible avenues of financing outdoor recreation. Arguments for and against charging fees for outdoor recreation pursuits on public lands were presented as well. While those who oppose fees use public education as their model, the proponents of fee argue that charging of fees will help center access to natural resources. Also, improvements could result from the use of fees for such a purpose.

Visitor management represents a problem for the manager of outdoor areas. Procedures for visitor control, which has some bearing on carrying capacity, were discussed, along with the need for management of special areas such as wilderness, rivers, and trails. Among the many techniques to be used in visitor management are improvement of the physical appearance of the natural resource, provision of adequate information and education systems, control of undesirable activities, litter control, and the permit system.

Since some outdoor pursuits present risk for many recreationists, a section on risk management was included along with the basic laws that govern liability. Two court cases on agency liability are described.

References

Clark, R., Hendee, J., & Burgess, R., (1972). The experimental control of littering. *Journal of Environmental Education, 4*(2), 22-28.

Cordell, H.K., Bergstrom, J. C., Hartmann, L.A., & English, B.K. (1990). *An analysis of the outdoor recreation and wilderness situation in the United States:1989-2040.* Forest Service RM-189 April, Washington, D.C.: U.S. Government Printing Office.

Douglass, R. (1975). *Forest recreation.* New York: Pergamon Press.

Fogg, G. (1975). *Park planning guidelines.* Alexandria, VA: National Recreation and Park Association.

Frakt, A. N. (1978, April). Adventure programming and legal liability. *Journal of Physical Education, Recreation and Dance, 49*, 25.

Frome, M. (1985). *Issues in wilderness management*. Boulder, CO: Westview Press.

Gilbert, C. et al. (1972). Toward a model of travel in the boundary water canoe area. *Environment and Behavior, 412*, 131-57.

Glover, J. (1979, March). MBO: A tool for leisure service management. *Parks and Recreatio, 26.*

Graefe, A., Kuss, F., & Vaske, J. (1987). *Recreation impacts and carrying capacity: A visitor impact management framework*. Washington, D.C.: National Parks and Conservation Association.

Ham, S. (1984). Communication and recycling in park campgrounds. *Journal of Environmental Education, 15*(2), 17-20.

Harmon, L. (1979, December). How to make park law enforcement work for you. *Parks and Recreation, 20.*

Hendee, J. C., & Burdge, R. J. (1974). The substitutability concept: Implication for recreation research and management. *Journal of Leisure Research* 157-63.

Hendee, J., Stankey, G., & Lucas, R. (1978). *Wilderness management*. U.S. Forest Service. Washington, D.C.: U.S. Government Printing Office.

Heritage Conservation and Recreation Service. (1979). *Fees and charges handbook*. Department of the Interior. Washington, D.C.: U.S. Government Printing Office.

Hines, T. (1968). *Budgeting for public parks and recreation*. Washington, D.C.: NRPA.

Hudson, S., Thompson, D., & Mack, M. (1996, April). America's playgrounds: Make them safe. *Parks and Recreation, 69.*

Jensen, C. (1985). *Outdoor recreation in America*. Minneapolis, MN: Burgess Publishing.

Kaiser, R. (1986). *Liability and law in recreation, parks, and sports*. Englewood Cliffs, NJ: Prentice-Hall.

Knudson, D. (1984). *Outdoor recreation*. New York: Macmillan.

Kozlowski, J. (1982, March). Validity of non-resident and other discriminatory regulations in municipal recreations. *Parks and Recreation,* 28-34.

Kraus, R., & Curtis, J. (1982). *Creative management in recreation and parks*. St. Louis, MO: Mosby.

Krumpe, E., & Lucas, R. (1986). Research on recreation trails and trail users. In *The President's commission on Americans outdoors, A literature review*. Washington, D.C.: U.S. Government Printing Office.

Lee, R. (1975). *The management of human component in the Yosemite National Park ecosystem*. Yosemite, CA: The Yosemite Institute.

Lee, R. (1995, Fall). Recreational use statues and private property in the 1900s. *Journal of park and Recreation Administration,* 71-83.

Lime, D. (1986). River recreation and natural resources management: A focus on river running and boating. In *The President's commission on Americans outdoors, A literature review*. Washington, D.C.: U.S. Government Printing Office.

Lucas, R., & Krumpe, E. (1986). Wilderness management. In *The President's commission on Americans outdoors, A literature review*. Washington, D.C.: U.S. Government Printing Office.

Martin, B. H., & Taylor, D. T. (1981). *Informing backcountry visitors: A catalog of techniques*. Gorham, NH: Appalachian Mountain Club.

Nilsen, P., & Tayler, G. (1997). *A comparative analysis of protected area planning and management frameworks. Proceedings-limits of acceptable change and related planning processes: Progress and future directions*. USDA Forest Service General Technical Report INT-371, 49-57.

Pfister, R. (1990, April). Participation and management policy: Backcountry recreationists' new preferences. *Leisure Today,* 28-31.

Rankin, J. (1990, April). The risk of risks: Program liability for injuries in high adventure activities. *Leisure Today,* 7-10.

Rodney, L. (1964). *Administration of public recreation*. New York: Ronald Press.

Roggenbuck, J., & Ham. S. (1986). Use of information and education in recreation management. In *The President's commission on Americans outdoors, A literature review*. Washington, D.C.: U.S. Government Printing Office.

Stankey, G. (1973). *Visitor perception of wilderness recreation carrying capacity*, INT-142. Ogden, UT: Ranger Experimental Station, U.S. Forest Service.

Stankey, G., & Manning, R. (1986). Carrying capacity of recreational settings. In *The President's commission on Americans outdoors, A literature review.* Washington, D.C.: U.S. Government Printing Office.

The United States General Accounting Office. (1998). *Recreation fees: Demonstrated fee program successful in raising revenues but could be improved.* Washington, D.C.

Tilden, F. (1962). *Interpreting our heritage.* Chapel Hill, NC: University of North Carolina Press.

Warren, R. (1986). Fees and charges. In *The President's commission on Americans outdoors, A literature review.* Washington, D.C.: U.S. Government Printing Office.

Washburne, R. (1982). Wilderness recreational carrying capacity: Are numbers necessary? *Journal of Forestry, 80*(I) 726-28.

Washburne, R., & Cole, D. (1983). *Problems and practices in wilderness Management: A Survey of Managers.* Research Paper, INTD-304. Intermountain forest and range experiment station. Washington, D.C.: U.S. Forest Service.

Zeigler, E., & Bowie, G. (1983). *Management competency development in sport and physical education.* Philadelphia, PA: Lea and Febiger.

14 | EDUCATION AND THE OUTDOORS

In some countries, including Canada, Australia, England, and Scotland, outdoor education means recreational activities such as hiking, camping, canoeing, and so forth. While many Americans also interpret it the same way, outdoor education is also a technique to encourage direct learning experiences that enrich the curriculum. Lloyd Burgess Sharp, an early leader in outdoor education, said, "In simple terms, outdoor education means all of that learning included in the curriculum in any subject matter area and at any grade level which can best be learned outside the classroom" (Rillo, 1985:7).

This statement suggests that outdoor education is not exclusionary. Rather, outdoor education is inclusive of many subject areas that deal directly with the natural environment and life situations outside of the classroom. Among the curricular areas often associated with outdoor education are language arts, social studies, physical education, mathematics, science, nature study, and music (Lappin, 2000:1). Outdoor education can take place in the schoolyard, on the playground, at a park, on a farm, at camping facilities, on a trail, or in the woods. School teachers, for example, can reorganize their classrooms so that they become places to organize, analyze, synthesize, and evaluate data that students have gathered from outside the school (Brown, 1998:200). An outdoor education experience can take place in minutes, overnight, or it may last for a week or more. Programs are sponsored through educational institutions, camps, recreation departments, or private entrepreneurs, and they may be directed toward curriculum, behavior, recreation, ecology, or wilderness survival. Instructors and leaders have a wide variety of professional backgrounds, ranging from recreation to biology. They tend to enjoy nature, outdoor recreation pursuits, or high-risk outdoor adventure activities. They often include those who enjoy teaching in a holistic manner, including the mental, physical, and social aspects of learning; those who incorporate the subject and the medium of the outdoors into their programs; and those who teach elementary school camping; and physical educators interested in lifelong fitness activities (Ford, 1989:30). As one outdoor physical education teacher put it, "If we want to keep our kids from staying inside and playing video games all year, we have to teach them how to play outside" (Rose, 2001:17)

The most common definition of outdoor education is "education *in*, *about*, and *for* the out-of-doors" (Coles, 2000:27). This simple definition, first coined by George Donaldson in 1950, uses three inseparable words to express the *place*, *topic*, and *purpose* of outdoor education. *In* tells us that outdoor education can take place in any outdoor setting that is conducive to direct experiences, allows contact with the topic, and permits participant interaction and socialization. *About* tells us that the topic includes the outdoors and all aspects related to the natural environment. While any subject may be taught, direct learning must take place through the outdoor experience. And although soil, water, animals, and plants make up the basic areas of study, the student may also learn and practice outdoor activities pursued during leisure time. *For* tells us that the purpose of outdoor education is related to developing knowledge, skills, and attitudes about the outdoor environment that will encourage protection and preservation. Programs that teach skills such as canoeing or rock climbing in the outdoors, for instance, have a responsibility to teach students something about the setting that is being used so that they will learn to appreciate it, care for it, and protect themselves from it (COE, 1989:31-32; Ford, 1989 4-8; Ford, 1987). The subject matter of outdoor education, then, represents a holistic approach to the study of the interrelationships of nature, humans, attitudes for caring about the environment, and skill development in using natural resources for survival as well as leisure pursuits. In the broadest terms, outdoor education is "the interrelationship of the human being and the natural resources upon which societies depend, with the goal of stewardship in mind" (Ford, 1989:7).

TERMINOLOGY

Another early leader in outdoor education, Julian Smith (1974:23-24), explained the desire of many who were involved in outdoor education to keep terminology simple. The definition of outdoor education becomes more difficult when it is associated with or used interchangeably with: environmental education, conservation education, camping education, outdoor recreation, adventure education, experiential education, environmental interpretation, resource-use education, nature education, nature recreation, and others. Smith (1974:24) said:

Whatever label is given to the outdoor "thing" there seems to be some common agreement that the vitalization of learning and the guarantee of a healthful, beautiful and permanent natural environment for today's and tomorrow's generations are goals which should be and can be realized. To achieve such high purposes, there is a great need for better communication, but with fewer words and more cooperative action by those who would be educational leaders in these times.

Learning definitions is necessary to continuing programs in outdoor education (Gilbert & Chase, 1988:26-28). Several definitions follow (COE 1989:32):

Environmental education refers to education about the total environment, including population growth, pollution, resource use and misuse, urban and rural planning, and modern technology with its demands on natural resources. Environmental education is all-encompassing, while outdoor education is seen by some to relate to natural resources and not to include the wide sense of the world environment. Many people, however, think of outdoor education in its broadest sense and prefer the term outdoor/environmental education.

Conservation education is the study of the wise use of natural resources. It tends to focus on animals, soil, water, and air as single topics in relation to their use for timber, agriculture, hunting, fishing, and human consumption. It is not usually concerned with preservation, recreation, or human relations and as such is more narrow than outdoor education. The use of this term has decreased since the 1960s.

Resident outdoor school is the process of taking children to a residential camp during school

Environmental interpretation is a term often associated with visitor centers administered by national park or forest service centers.

time for a period of usually three to five days to extend the curriculum through learning in the outdoors. This process was originally called camping education. It was later referred to as school camping, but these phrases were discontinued when parents and taxpayers believed they meant the same thing as summer camp, which seemed to be more recreational than educational.

Outdoor recreation refers to a broad spectrum of outdoor activities participated in during leisure time purely for pleasure or some other intrinsic value. Included are hiking, swimming, boating, winter sports, cycling, and camping. In many countries, and to some extent in the United States, these activities are called outdoor education, particularly if they are taught in the school as part of the curriculum.

Outdoor pursuits are generally non-mechanized, outdoor recreation activities done in areas remote from the amenities such as, emergency help and urban comforts. To many people, the terms outdoor recreation and outdoor pursuits are similar.

Adventure education refers to activities into which are purposely built elements perceived by the participants as being dangerous. The activities are not inherently dangerous as taught (under qualified instruction), but they appear to be so to the participant and thus they generate a sense of adventure. Adventure activities include such things as rope courses, white-water rafting, mountaineering, and rock climbing.

Experiential education refers to learning by doing or by experience. Many experiential education activities are synonymous with adventure activities and outdoor pursuits; however, experiential education can also mean any form of pragmatic educational experience. In many ways, outdoor education may be viewed as experiential, especially when learning takes place through outdoor experiences.

Environmental interpretation is a term usually associated with visitor centers administered by national park or forest service centers. The term refers to a technique used to help visitors understand the meanings of the phenomena on display, while simultaneously arousing curiosity for more information.

Nature education and nature recreation are learning or leisure activities related to natural resources. The terms were used from the 1920s to the 1950s, and the activities were not usually interrelated, nor did they focus on the overriding concerns of ecology and stewardship of the land. They were usually isolated, individual activities using natural resources for equipment and facilities, and involving knowledge of nature.

Organized camping consists of education/recreation activities led by trained leaders in an outdoor setting with emphasis on individual development and group living. The camp is a residential or day-use site operated by private individuals, youth agencies such as the Scouts, churches, or governmental agencies. Regardless of the programs offered, the age of the participants, or the duration of the program, the focus is on education, recreation, group activities, and individual adjustment in the out-of-doors. When

the program is sponsored by an educational agency, the program is usually referred to as the outdoor school or school camp.

HISTORY

The origin of outdoor education is difficult to trace. Some believe its beginnings go back as far as Socrates and Plato or to the dawn of humanity. Others attribute the beginnings to the "outing trips" of private schools in the 1800s such as those taken by students of the Round Hill School of Northampton, Massachusetts. Several trace outdoor education to British tented schools, founded prior to World War I and to German school country homes of the 1920s and early 1930s. Still others turn to the out-of-classroom activities in the Atlanta Public Schools of the 1920s and to summer recreation programs in California. But it is clear that industrialization of the early 1900s brought children from farms to crowded cities, and time and again participants in physical activities became spectators with physical health problems. An era in which tuberculosis frequently claimed the lives of citizens was upon the nation, and as a remedy, the enrichments of outdoor life were rediscovered. Like many other ideas, the notion of outdoor education did not bloom from a single advocate but grew from several movements and dedicated individuals. A closer look at two early programs in the United States and the thinking of several early leaders follows.

Round Hill School

Round Hill School of Northampton, Massachusetts, was a school for boys that operated from 1823 to 1834. The curriculum was unique in offering two hours a day of physical education and outdoor activities. Sharing an interest in nature, the outdoors, and hiking, the school's founders, Joseph Cogswell and George Bancroft, located their school on a round hill overlooking the scenic Connecticut River valley within view of the beautiful Berkshire Mountains. Joseph Cogswell is credited as the originator of school camping and outdoor education in the United States. (Bennett, 1974:33-37).

Bennett's research uncovered the following proposal in the school prospectus:

> . . . and certainly in the pleasant days of Spring and Autumn, so far from compelling them to remain at home, we would encourage them [the students] to go abroad and learn to feel the beauty of creation and the benevolence of its Author. Short journeys, whether on foot or by other means of conveyance, might quicken their powers of observation, and by refreshing and strengthening their bodies, prepare their minds for more profitable application (Cogswell & Bancroft, 1823:8-9).

Early after the school's opening in 1823, outdoor activities were made available. Cogswell took six of the students on a 100-mile round-trip journey to Hartford. Changing off the entire way, they either walked or rode horses. Student letters refer to Cogswell leading other excursions to strawberry fields and gardens, on fishing and hunting trips, and on camping expeditions. Students participated extensively in outdoor activities such as skating, coasting, swimming, and horseback riding. Art lessons were sometimes taught at the bank of the river. Crony Village was constructed by the boys by burrowing into the hill and adding a chimney and door. Many evenings were spent around the fire cooking and telling stories. Reports indicate the pupils enjoyed excellent health (Bennett, 1974:33-37).

Offering an excellent education in which camping and outdoor education played an essential part, Round Hill School was described by a student in later years as follows:

> When I left it in 1828 to enter my uncles' Boston office, I was strong, healthy, and self-reliant, though not remarkable in any degree; a fair swimmer, a good shot, and best of all a good rider; and I never can be grateful enough for the advantages which Mr. Cogswell conferred (Bennett, 1974:37).

Boy Scouts of America

The Boy Scout movement (see Chapter 10) took off immediately in the United States and quickly became the nation's largest non-school youth organization. Other outdoor youth organizations of the early 1900s such as Woodcraft Indians, Sons of Daniel Boone, and Boy Pioneers set the stage for the movement's acceptance. Ernest Thompson Seton, who established Woodcraft Indians, had the background and interest in youth to establish him as the logical choice for the position of first Chief Scout of the Boy Scouts of America in 1910. His many volumes on scout-craft became an integral part of scouting and his intelligence and enthusiasm helped turn an idea into reality. The handbook *Boy Scouts of America: A Handbook of Woodcraft, Scouting, and Life-craft* first appeared in 1910, and within the first 30 years of publication sold an estimated seven million copies (Nash, 1970:19). In it, Seton listed nine pertinent principles necessary for achieving the joys of outdoor life. These principles were worded as follows (Nash, 1970:21-22):

1. This movement is essentially for recreation.
2. Camping is the simple life reduced to actual practice, as well as the culmination of the outdoor life.
3. Camps should be self-governing.
4. The campfire is the focal center of all primitive brotherhood. We shall not fail to use its magic powers.
5. Fine character and physique can be developed through the knowledge of *woodcraft pursuits*—riding, hunting, camper-craft, scouting, mountaineering, Indian-craft, Star-craft, signaling, boating, and all good outdoor athletics and sports including sailing, motoring, nature-study, wild animal photography and above all Heroism.
6. Try not to "down the others, but to raise ourselves."

7. Personal achievements will receive decoration.
8. A heroic ideal leads to higher things.
9. The effect of the picturesque is magical. The charm of titles, costumes, ceremony, phrase, dance and song are utilized in all ways.

The Boy Scout movement continues today. Current programs are discussed later in this chapter. Seton, who immigrated to America from Scotland in the 1880s, wrote:

> Sport is the great incentive to Outdoor Life; nature study is the intellectual side of sport. I should like to lead this whole nation into the way of living outdoors for at least a month each year, reviving and expanding a custom that as far back as Moses was deemed essential to the national well-being . . . it is not enough to take men out-of-doors. We must also teach them to enjoy it. . . .
> (Nash, 1970:21).

More Leadership

In 1903 Liberty Hyde Bailey, another man of insight, wrote of the child's need to study nature. Borrowing some ideas from American philosopher, psychologist, and educator John Dewey's progressive education, Bailey wrote:

> Nature-study is not science. It is not knowledge. It is not facts. It is spirit. It is concerned with the child's outlook on the world . . . nature-study is studying things and the reason of things, not about things. It is not reading from nature books. A child was asked if she had ever seen the great dipper. 'Oh, yes,' she replied, 'I saw it in my geography' (Nash, 1970:65-66).

It is perhaps due to the influence of innovative thinkers and educational philosophers that outdoor education evolved. Two people, Lloyd B. Sharp and Julian W. Smith, are especially significant to the development of outdoor education in the United States.

Lloyd Burgess Sharp, known as "L.B." or as "The Chief," was born in Kansas in 1894. He was first called "Chief" by campers, but he eventually earned the title from others because he was an innovator, promoter, and chief in his field. Educated at Columbia University, Sharp received his B.S., M.A., and Ph.D. degrees at a time when Columbia was noted for its progressiveness. For several years he was with the National Recreation Association and taught at Columbia. In 1925 he was named executive director of Life Camps, Inc., and by 1926 he led the organization away from the traditional camping program of centralized camping to decentralized camping with each group responsible for its own program. During the 1930s he continued pioneering in "camping education" at Life Camps. In 1940 Sharp established National Camp for the training of leaders, and by 1944, National Camp and Life Camps, Inc., had published *Extending Education*. Sharp's vision received national exposure in this publication and others, and his books and publications influenced many in the field of outdoor education (Vinal, 1974:45-47).

Many methods and practices that were proven successful in outdoor educational instruction were evolved by Sharp and his associates. Sharp made the original proposition that subjects, topics, and courses that could best be learned outdoors be carried out in their own optimum sphere. This concept was the basis of his writing and teaching (Conrad, (1974:16). Sharp explained (Rillo, 1985:1), "That which ought and can best be taught inside the schoolroom should there be taught, and that which can best be learned through experience, dealing directly with native materials and life situation outside the school, should there be learned."

Julian W. Smith has been referred to as the Dean of American outdoor education. He served as professor of education at Michigan State University and director of the Outdoor Education Project of the American Association for Health, Physical Education and Recreation (now AAHPERD, discussed later in this chapter). Smith's involvement with outdoor education began in 1940. As principal of Lakeview High School (Michigan), Smith arranged for the school to participate in one of the W. K. Kellogg Foundation school camping programs. In 1946 he became the head of a cooperative project between the Michigan Department of Conservation and the Department of Public Instruction to promote outdoor education. The Kellogg Foundation provided partial financial support. During the period from 1946 to 1953, Michigan was known for its innovations in the field of outdoor education and became the nation's primary leader (Donaldson, 1974:59-61).

In 1953 Smith joined the faculty of the then Michigan State College. By 1955 his ambition of the 1940s was realized when his strongly felt need for an umbrella organization to encompass the many fields involved in outdoor education came into being. At that time he became the director of the far-reaching Outdoor Education Project. The project arranged many activities, including three national conferences and a newsletter, *A Newsletter for the Exchange of Ideas on Outdoor Education*. Smith's contributions made the newsletter preeminent among several such publications, and there was evidence that the project impacted and broadened the nation's concept of outdoor education. Eventually the Council on Outdoor Education and Camping was developed under the General Division of AAHPERD after more than 10 years of project status. Because of Smith's efforts, thousands of American youth are better off. Smith proclaimed, "Outdoor education and camping are not frills to be scalloped around the curriculum. In the woods, fields, and streams children can see, feel, hear; they can even smell and taste. Here reality, with all its vividness, becomes both motivation and method for learning" (Donaldson, 1974:59).

Developments

Julian Smith described the significant developments of outdoor education in the United States (1974:27-30). Early development prior to 1940 began with such labels

as field and camping trips, outings, recreation, and camping education. Organized camping, combined with the educational philosophies of Dewey, Kilpatrick, and others whose leadership gave rise to "progressive" education, influenced outdoor education. During the period from 1940 to 1950, resident outdoor schools grew in number, including those in the Battle Creek, Michigan, area conducted at the Clear Lake Camp; San Diego (California) City-County Camp Commission with a program at Cuyamaca; Tyler, Texas; Cleveland Heights, Ohio; and others. What occurred at resident outdoor schools was generally referred to by the term outdoor education during this period. An event of particular significance was the first state legislation, passed in Michigan, which allowed school districts to acquire and operate camps as a segment of a school program. To a great degree, outdoor education was strongly influenced by organized camping at this time, but developments in curriculum, professional training, and programs were strong forces. Near the conclusion of this period a surge of interest in all forms of outdoor pursuits began to take hold.

The 1950s brought rapid growth in resident outdoor schools and greater emphasis on other out-of-classroom experiences. The Outdoor Education Project broadened the concept of outdoor education and further developed teaching of skills, attitudes, and appreciation for satisfying outdoor pursuits. The National Conference on Teacher Education for Outdoor Education was held at the Clear Lake Camp in Michigan in 1953, and the interdisciplinary approach to outdoor education was emphasized. During this period the Taft Field Campus was established by Northern Illinois University with its excellent leaders in outdoor education.

The 1960s brought about growth in a wide variety of outdoor education activities, particularly the use of outdoor settings by elementary schools, teaching of outdoor skills, and the increase in the in-service and pre-service preparation of teachers and leaders. Institutions that developed graduate study in the field included Indiana University, Pennsylvania State University, State University of New York, Northern Colorado University at Greeley, and New York University. Expansion of programs was the result of the influence of such organizations as the Outdoor Recreation Resources Review Commission and the Bureau of Outdoor Recreation and was assisted by federal legislation and a number of federal programs in education. By the late 1960s, terminology began to expand, and an increased concern toward environmental education took root.

Ever since the 1970s educators have recognized the need to provide environmental education programs throughout all academic levels and to integrate the subject with other subject matters. In 1970 public outcry led to passage of the Environmental Education Act, which specified state and federal partnerships in the areas of teacher training, curriculum development, and community education programs. More than 50 percent of the funding never materialized, however, and in 1982 Congress decided not to extend the act. After coming to a virtual standstill during the Reagan administration, new proposals were forwarded by environmentalists for future consideration. These are contained in the Blueprint for the Environment. Also making an impact on outdoor education in the 1980s and 1990s was the formation of the President's Commission on Americans Outdoors. This bipartisan commission was appointed by President Ronald Reagan in 1985 to look ahead for a generation to determine what Americans would want to do outdoors and how appropriate places to do these things could be provided. Since the late 1990s, outdoor education appeared to be underrepresented in the school setting despite its potential (Crawford, 1998:11). Blame has been placed on time constraints, lack of funding, and liability. Creative solutions have resulted. These include staying on campus more often and forming partnerships with other core disciplines to make better use of time and to avoid liability problems connected with field trips. Partnerships with local, city,

county, state parks; federal agencies; sporting-goods stores; university recreation departments or outdoor clubs; graduate programs; non-profit organizations have resulted in transportation, instructors, equipment, and liability advice. Liability waivers are completed for various activities as needed by the school (Rose, 2001:17-18).

Philosophy and Teaching Methodology

The practice of teaching outdoor education evolved as a result of years of experience of devoted individuals, outdoor centers, laboratories, and community agencies. Ahead of its time in teaching interrelationships of various areas of the curriculum with the outdoors and the environment, the movement offered another means to teach and reach children. Through outdoor education, urban children may learn about the earth by experiencing it. Observation is the theme, and the earth is the teacher. For example, students actually see erosion in process. They learn to problem solve and to cooperate with others. Students and teachers interact. With the focus off the individual, some students blossom in ways they never could in the classroom.

The primary goal, legal justification, and unique contribution of outdoor schools are found in the nurturing of understanding outdoor science and conservation. Other goals include social adjustments, work experience, and healthful living. Finally, students learn that life is more than mere existence. It is hoped that they discover things in our world that are beautiful. Whatever the outdoor program, the philosophy for outdoor education may be based on the following four premises (Council on Outdoor Education, 1989:32):

1. A prime goal of outdoor education is to teach a commitment to human responsibility for stewardship or care of the land. The development of a land ethic that commands us to treat the land and all its resources with respect at all times and on all occasions is the first value for

any outdoor education program. It is action-oriented and attitude-developing. It recognizes that whatever is taught in outdoor education must be translated into ethical ecological action.

2. Related to the goal of a land ethic or commitment to stewardship must be the belief in the importance of knowing certain facts or concepts. The cognitive purpose of outdoor education must be that of the interrelationship of all facets of the ecosystem. The interrelationship of natural resources with each other, and with humans and their societal customs, is the underlying curricular objective. The understanding of basic ecological, sociological, and cultural principles is prerequisite to the commitment to an ethic of land stewardship. Concurrently, outdoor education does not mandate specific choices in ecological ethics. . . . It prepares people to choose carefully after weighing the impact of the action on the environment, culture, and humanity.

3. We not only need to know the natural environment for the survival of the species, but we need to know it as a medium through which we spend many hours of leisure. Just teaching people about the interrelationships of the resources will not enhance their leisure hours, nor save them from the miseries encountered in harsh environmental situations. Because we know that humans seek the outdoors for leisure pursuits, it is incumbent upon us to teach the recreationist how to live comfortably in the outdoors and how to recreate with a minimum impact on the environment. The

quality of the outdoor recreation experience is directly related to the quantity of the knowledge about the out-of-doors.

4. A fourth philosophical belief is that the outdoor educational experience extends beyond one field trip, one week at outdoor school, or even a once-a-year event. It should be taught at all levels and pursued throughout life.

Unfortunately many young people today, no matter where they are from, are at risk of never developing positive attitudes and feelings toward the natural environment because so much of their time is spent indoors watching television, riding in cars, and in classrooms (Wilson, 1999:1). As one professor noted: "Education, for the most part, occurs in buildings with lots of squareness and straight lines. They tell no story, offer no clue about how they are maintained and at what ecological cost. . . . Students begin to suspect that the unraveling of the fabric of life on Earth is unreal, unsolvable, or occurring somewhere else" (Sierra Club, 1997:2). Contributions of outdoor education have included the following (Earl V. Pullias, 1974:14) :

1. A healing and growth-producing relationship with the natural world.
2. A promotion of sensitivity.
3. An assistance in the development of habits of withdrawal and renewal which are fundamental to physical, mental, and spiritual health in modern life.
4. To offset dealing with abstractions with simple direct experience.
5. At its best, nurturing of the spirit and bringing forth of communication with the earth.

To be an effective tool in the educational process, outdoor education must be planned, organized, and administered so that teaching and learning take advantage of the outdoor situation. The land itself provides the information and, with the assistance of a qualified teacher, the land does the teaching. Because children come to the out-of-doors to learn, they spend as much time as possible learning in the outdoors by focusing their attention on nature. When inside, the instructor expects the attention of the students.

Sharp helped to mold many of the methods and practices that have proven successful in outdoor teaching. These methods include discovery, inquiry, deliberation, and integration. Learning out-of-doors is a natural process with student and teacher developing a partnership. They observe objects together. Teachers serve as facilitators of the learning process. They must not attempt to be controlling, nor can they expect to have all of the answers. By learning together, students and teachers develop trust and confidence, both of which can often be carried back into the indoor environment. The methodology is simple and direct; it is learning by using the senses.

Discovery learning is the most appropriate method used to teach in outdoor education. Natural curiosity can be aroused in the out-of-doors. More important than knowing answers is the ability to ask questions. Children may be able to provide the answers, and answers can be provided through use of the five senses and through availability of reference materials at the outdoor site and in the classroom. There are various curriculum approaches to outdoor education, as follows (Rillo, 1985: 15-16):

1. **Vertical Articulation** This approach encompasses the use of a broad theme or basic understanding that is introduced at the kindergarten level. Each grade level studies the theme but in a more refined and sophisticated manner.

2. **Horizontal Articulation** In this approach, outdoor activities are selected that correlate with basic concepts of each discipline in the curriculum. The study of art, for example, can be offered through opportunities to sketch in the natural environment.

3. **Modular Approach** This approach uses packaged instructional modules or planned units of study. Modular programs are particularly popular with recreation departments and park systems that organize programs for visiting groups of students. The modular approach is less time-consuming than the other approaches, but it does not allow for the careful curriculum correlation of the other approaches.

As with all programs in a curriculum, the outdoor education program is evaluated by every participant. It is important that the scope is broad-based to include not only the cognitive but also the other outcomes of the program; for example, social development, interpersonal skills, environmental awareness, and responsibility.

OUTDOOR EDUCATION IN SCHOOLS

Implementing the practice of studying in the out-of-doors varies by grade level. To date, outdoor education has had its largest impact upon the elementary school curriculum. Lower grade instructors tend to offer classroom-related field experiences and projects at parks, ponds, school sites, and the like. Teachers in the upper elementary levels and beyond may use camp settings. Students in higher grade levels tend to study the out-of-doors through activity and adventure programs. Some high schools arrange programs through outside agencies (see non-school agencies). Outdoor education programs are also seen in higher education in interesting ways, for example, in interdisciplinary programs.

Objectives specifically related to school camping programs were approved as early as 1949 by the American Association of Health, Physical Education and Recreation at their Boston Convention (Los Angeles City Schools, 1961:4-6). These include the following:

1. Consider the development of the whole child.
2. Ensure children's participation in the total program—planning, executing, evaluation
3. Seek to integrate all of the educational activities around problems inherent in living together outdoors.
4. Make the setting the out-of-doors, and center all of the activities on outdoor traditions.
5. Make complete use of the country's natural resources and outdoor heritage.
6. Base methodology upon discovery, adventure, and direct experience.
7. Stress principles rather than detailed facts.
8. Emphasize the social process of cooperation rather than competition.
9. Make the education experience be essentially a group process.
10. Make the education be essentially an experiential process.

Research done on outdoor education programs for behavior disordered students resulted in a number of positive findings such as improvement in self-concept, social adjustment, academic achievement, and group cohesion. Relationships with peers, parents, teachers, and counselors were improved in some of the programs. Teachers noticed an improved ability to teach specific skills and academic behaviors, and reported that disruptive behavior decreased when they taught in the outdoor environment. Likewise, residential and non-residential programs that use wilderness camping also reported success. Success is escalated when they participated in high-adventure programming that presented a challenge (Lappin, 2000:2-3).

Outdoor Education in Preschool

A day camp program for preschoolers, ages three to five, was developed at a university in Ohio and implemented at a local, private day school. The program, offered one weekend of each season of the school year, was designed to give the children a chance to grow as total individuals through outdoor skills and shared experiences. A second aim was to provide a social interaction between children and adults during leisure time, and a third aim was to train education and recreation leaders from nearby colleges to work with preschoolers and their families in a nontraditional outdoor setting. To foster the development of a natural, curious, creative childhood, children were given activities to encourage outdoor exploration and use of the senses without pressures. Organizers not only discovered that the preschool children "were developmentally ready for sensory learning, but that they wanted to feel and listen" (Shepard & Caruso, 1988:28-19). The children also participated in games that focused on cooperation and sharpened movement skills and coordination.

On camp day, they assemble items in a day pack for their upcoming hike. Staff leaders pack the first-aid kit, but each child must carry an item important to the group as a whole. The hike includes a group trip of 15 to 20 feet into the woods, where opportunities to use the senses abound. Here children begin to develop an environmental vocabulary. A color-coded frame tent is put together, and children learn about campfire safety. They mix their own instant drink, wash their dishes when done, and put them away. The children are also encouraged to read a map and color-coded compass to aid in basic skill development and outdoor vocabulary.

Outdoor Education in Public Schools

Outdoor education programs are not mandated in California, but residential centers throughout the state influence more than 190,000 students a year. Educators and interested citizens of San Diego city and county conducted an experimental community school camp at Cuyamaca State Park in 1946 to test the theory that camping could become an integral part of the educational program. Aims were twofold:

Nontraditional outdoor settings provide a stimulating environment.

first, to make democracy real and understandable through outdoor living, and second, to give every child of appropriate age a camp experience. The sixth grade level was selected for the experimental program, and 1,201 campers plus some 300 parents, teachers, volunteers, and visitors participated in the experience. Afterward, San Diego's elementary school principals met to evaluate the project, voting unanimously to continue and to expand the program (Pumala, 1973:99; San Diego County Office of Education, 1999:1).

San Diego's Outdoor Education Program, the oldest in California, now operates on three sites. Hundreds of sixth grade girls and boys go with their classroom teachers to the outdoor education schools in the mountains near San Diego. Living together in an attractive outdoor setting, children can participate in the four- or five-day residential package where the environment is explored with trained outdoor personnel. Students also take an active part in planning their week, setting standards of behavior, and accepting the responsibilities that are necessary for group outdoor living.

The San Diego County Office of Education is responsible for the administration of the Outdoor Education Program, for providing and maintaining facilities, and for hiring staff. A staff of instructors and support staff consisting of maintenance and kitchen personnel, a nurse, and a clerk, all work under the leadership of the director of outdoor education. The on-site principal and credentialed teachers prepare for a week of living and learning together in a new social and natural environment. Fees for attending are the same for each school and district, although costs to parents may vary, since some districts provide a portion of the cost from annual budgets or through district fund-raising activities. The four-day experience costs less than the five-day, and a county-wide essay competition gives fifth grade students the opportunity to win a full scholarship.

Part of the regular school instructional program, classroom teachers are responsible for correlating indoor classroom learning with outdoor school instruction. The outdoor school curriculum is one of action: exploring, discovering, investigating, evaluating, working, creating, conserving, and sharing. Outdoor classroom activities include studies in life science, astronomy, biology, meteorology, outdoor skills, American Indian lore, recreational activities and crafts. The outdoor environment includes hills, valleys, rivers, clear skies, and plants and animals. Campers learn to use maps, compasses, telescopes, binoculars, microscopes, and magnets while using scientific methods of research: exploring, discovering, collecting, recognizing problems, planning, cooperating, proposing, testing, investigating, and evaluating. In conjunction with work projects, students develop an appreciation for, and an understanding of, the complexity of the environment. They also learn the need to use natural resources wisely to ensure that they are available to provide a good quality of life in the future.

After-School Programs

After-school programs are needed to serve children of all ages. When properly designed, they provide children with a safe environment while shaping attitudes, values, skills, and academic performance. They will only be successful, however, if they have appeal for all stakeholders, including children, parents, teachers, and politicians (Witt, 2001:21). While children generally require some relief from formal learning, many schools are trying to find programs that enrich recreation activities by using them as tools for purposive learning. Outdoor education programs provide rich learning experiences in fun, informal environments and are great ways for park and recreation departments to become critical players in after-school programs.

Higher Education Programs

A private college in the Southwest stresses experiential learning and self-direction within an interdisciplinary curriculum. The college expects its graduates to learn to adapt to a changing world. The process begins upon arrival through the college's Wilderness Orientation Program, which blends recreation, social interaction, and inspired learning. Joining highly qualified student instructors, the novices are divided into groups of ten and led on a three-week outdoor backpacking expedition. Three days are reserved for supervised solitude and contemplation. Groups travel with the uppermost regard for safety and are taught outdoor techniques, campcraft skills, and low-impact camping. As students become acclimated to the Southwestern environment, they are introduced to a variety of physical, social, and cultural conditions in which they learn the process of adaptation. Curiosity, wonder, and appreciation become major stimulants for learning. Personal attributes such as self-reliance, cooperation, self-motivation, and perseverance are encouraged. Working together, students evaluate environmental ethics, reverence for nature, and responsibility to the planet. All group members contribute by teaching basic ecological concepts of local flora, fauna, landscapes, and past and present inhabitants of the area. After returning to campus, academic orientation begins.

One liberal arts college uses an interdisciplinary approach to teach the interconnections between recreation, language, culture, and the environment. It is a goal of the paired courses, "Outdoor Recreation" and "Spanish," to contrast as well as explore the continuities between Latin American values and those of the United States with respect to recreation and leisure. In doing so, the Outdoor Recreation class emphasizes cultures and recreational opportunities of the Southwest and Mexico. The activity-oriented Spanish class uses an innovative technique, called Total Physical Response (TPR), to teach language. The movement and actions taught are associated with outdoor recreation class in order to provide the setting for learning the language while studying the culture and learning about the environment. Laboratory classes and field trips include outdoor activities conducted in Spanish.

A community college near the coast takes advantage of the many touring companies, outdoor equipment businesses, rental supply stores, and federal agencies as resources when offering Outdoor Recreation/Education. For the cost of transportation and, in some rare instances, a minimal group fee, the instructor arranges for the class of 20 to have specialized instructors, equipment, and the opportunity to try kayaking at the bay, SCUBA diving in a pool, deep sea fishing off the coast, freshwater casting at a lake, surfing at the beach, ice skating and broomball on an indoor rink, rock climbing at an indoor facility, orienteering in a national forest, tidepooling at a national park, birding at the wetlands in a national wildlife refuge, and petroglyph hunting and desert hiking at a state park. Learning about the various habitats and the environment becomes a first-hand experience. On campus, other representatives visit the class to share experiences, equipment, safety, and environmental material in other activities, including llama trekking, ballooning, hunting, stargazing, rock hounding, cross-country and downhill skiing, and backpacking. Local trails are used for plant identification. After drawing a specific outdoor location from a hat, each student plans and presents an imaginary trip for four students during their spring break, accounting for transportation, reasonable financing, outdoor activities, environmental awareness, and tours planned in route. Students, who might never have been exposed to these outdoor experiences, refer to the class as one of their best college experiences, and one that they carry with them for the rest of their lives.

A 2,400-acre Outdoor Leadership Center at a Midwestern university serves as a satellite campus. The learning resource has over 1,800 acres of woods and hills for study; a beach and boating facilities for camp programs, experiential and professional development programs; and a rustic retreat and conference facilities for year-round accommodations. Opportunities exist for persons to gain academic credit and practical experience in outdoor education, outdoor recreation, camping administration and leadership, resource management, therapeutic recreation, special education, and other areas. Major programs include outdoor and environmental education for elementary and special education children, adventure and challenge education programs, a full residential summer camping season for children and adults with a variety of disabilities, leadership conferences, seminars, professional development workshops, and weekend retreats. Training opportunities and internships are also available for students from universities throughout the United States.

Graduate Programs

Educational Directories Unlimited lists a variety of graduate programs that specialize in outdoor education. Some lead to the Master of Arts or Master of Science degree in Education. One of these programs is designed for teachers who hold certification in any subject area or grade level. By using an experiential approach to education, the goals are to enhance existing curriculums, expand environmental awareness, and to utilize resources beyond the school building. A graduate program in Outdoor Teacher Education is designed to help classroom teachers, outdoor professionals, such as summer camp and nature center personnel, and youth workers to more effectively use nature in their teaching and outdoor programs by helping them assume leadership roles in outdoor, nature, camping and environmental education. A private college teamed with the Wilderness Learning Center to provide a Master of Arts in Educational Ministries with an emphasis in Leadership, Camp Ministry, and Adventure Education. At one state university, the oldest graduate program in experiential education in the United States grew out of a strong affiliation with Outward Bound and other adventure-based outdoor education programs to offer a Master of Science in Experiential Education.

The Master of Education degree within Health and Physical Education at one state university prepares students as scholars, leaders and educators. Graduate education provides the opportunity to acquire an advanced theoretical and research base for planning and providing education that is culturally sensitive and learner-centered. Value for the health of individuals and communities is a focus of this educational preparation. Students acquire education for the education specialist option or for doctoral study. Other graduate degrees are offered in Outdoor Education, Outdoor Adventure, Wilderness Leadership, Integrated Ecology, and Environmental Education. One private institute that offers a graduate program leading to a M.S. in Environmental Education or Ecological Teaching and Learning encourages students to travel in and study different bioregions of the United States, Canada, Mexico, and Bahamas. Research areas include Systematic Investigation of Local Flora and Fauna; Cultural Perspectives of Human Communities; Learning Communities: Group Dynamics, Ethics and Decision-making; Philosophy of Education; Outdoor Skills and Leadership; Natural History and Ecology; Life Systems and Their Communication; Water Systems: Effects, Interrelationships and Problems; Culture, Spirit and Ethic: A Relationship to the Living Earth; Environmental Psychology; Science and Technology and Their Effects on Nature; Environmental Education and Its Applications; Special Topics in Ecology; Ethics of Water and Land Use; Sustainable Human Ecology; Learning Communities: Communication, Leadership and Advocacy; Methods in Environmental Education; Approaches to Research in Environmental Education; Independent Study in Writing; Independent Study; Practicum in Environmental Education (Educational Directories Unlimited, 2001:1-9).

Extracurricular Activities

The Outdoor Program at a university in the northwest has been active for more than 25 years and serves as a model for other programs across the country. Embracing all aspects of outdoor pursuits and wilderness activities, it brings people from the campus and community together in a wide range of pursuits and environments. Unlike traditional outing clubs, there are no administrative obligations or mandatary meetings. Serving as a cooperative, the program offers those interested in pursuing an outdoor activity a chance to find others with similar plans. Wilderness goals range from learning new skills to extended expeditions all over the world. Several hundred trips are arranged each year, offering a wide range of activities at various skill levels. Most are fairly spontaneous and are arranged by volunteers. All responsibilities, chores, and decisions are borne equally among trip participants who share cooperative costs of gas, food, and equipment rental if necessary. With a variety of resources available, the Outdoor Program can launch just about any trip. Vehicles of all sizes are available through the state motor pool, and a variety of outdoor gear for trips is also available. Resource staff help in any aspect of trip preparation. Trips are open to students, staff, and community. The objectives are cooperative learning and fun. The Outdoor Program provides the community with an outdoor resource center, with libraries and files teeming with valuable resource material.

Typical program activities include backpacking, day hikes, canoeing, kayaking, rafting, bike touring, photography, mountaineering, sail-boarding, ski touring, telemark skiing, winter camping, ocean kayaking, and other self-propelled wilderness activities. On-campus events include films, slide shows, speakers, equipment swaps, equipment sessions, instructional sessions, kayak pool sessions, environmental action projects, and environmental symposiums and conferences.

NON-SCHOOL AGENCY CONTRIBUTIONS TO OUTDOOR EDUCATION

Many nonschool agencies, including nonprofit organizations, federal and state agencies, local recreation and park departments, and special interest groups participate in outdoor education programs that complement the school setting. In some cases these programs actually become part of a school curriculum, or they may serve in the capacity of extracurricular activity. Examples of a few of such offerings are included below.

Boy Scouts of America

The Boy Scouts of America (BSA) teach boys skills for outdoor adventures, with camping playing a vital role in this process. Today, the Family Camping Program, launched in 1984, is designed to give family members ample opportunity to share the outdoor experience. The Boy Scout Conservation Program incorporates educational activities throughout the scout program, which builds an awareness and understanding of wise and intelligent management of natural resources. The Conservation award, initiated as early as 1914, continues to inspire scouts to work constructively for conservation by participating in community decision-making groups, research, individual skill development, the planning process, and the action needed. Follow-up includes unit evaluation of the project—what was learned, what else could have been done, etc.

Passport to High Adventure is a complete package of everything needed to help older Scouts plan and safely guide council and unit high-adventure treks with the counsel of adult leaders. Ultimate goals include the development of teamwork, critical thinking and decision-making skills, and sound judgment (Boy Scouts of America, 2001:1-2). Some Explorer posts specialize in outdoor activities and conservation. Fields of study include camping, hiking, canoeing, ecology, mountaineering, field sports, fishing, conservation education, safety, survival, and proper outdoor living.

Girl Scouts of the U.S.A.

Outdoor activities have always been an integral part of Girl Scouting. Founder Juliette Low rebuffed the notion of the day that ladies do nothing strenuous. She believed that girls would be attracted to the out-of-doors for sports, camping, and nature study. Outdoor education experiences take place from preschool to adult training weekends. Camping experiences and facilities are an important part of the Girl Scouts' outdoor education experience. In Junior Scouting, for example, outdoor education may be divided into camping and campcraft skills, scout ceremonies on outdoor themes in local parks, and various nature and outdoor education activities (Ciraco, et al. 1984:2). For a number of years, the Girl Scouts have worked with the Environmental Protection Agency on environmental issues and projects to promote environmental stewardship. For example, Girl Scouts learn about wetlands management when earning the Water Drop Patch. With EPA's counsel, the new Girl Scout Environmental Health badge will give thousands of girls the opportunity to learn about ways that the environment affects their health (Christie, 2001:1-2).

Young Men's Christian Associations

Outdoor education programs are offered at a number of YMCA units. An example is Camp Cosby, a branch of the Birmingham, Alabama, YMCA, which is located one hour from the city on the wooded shores of a lake formed behind Logan Martin Dam on the Coosa River. Although its site was in a different location, Camp Cosby was set up as a complete outdoor recreation center as early as 1922. In 1981 it opened its small outdoor environmental education program. Starting as an overnight program, it offered canoeing, fishing, and forestry. Growth and interest were phenomenal. Today Camp Cosby Outdoor Environmental Education Program serves more than 80 schools with most students staying for three days and two nights, although some stay for a week (YMCA, 2000:1).

A dramatic part of the outdoor experience is the Living History Program. Held one morning or evening, Y camp staff reenact Alabama's past. One program takes students back to 1810, a time when Alabama was part of the Mississippi Territory and Birmingham was a sparsely populated wilderness. In this manner the students learn history, geography, and basic survival skills. They are taught American Indian sign language and how to use silence and the five senses to enjoy nature. The Underground Railroad is the topic of a more intense program that deals with racism and prejudice by presenting the enslaved Americans' quest for freedom.

Staff are young, energetic teachers and recent graduates from college. Besides participating in Living History, the staff instruct parents, haul canoes, lead song and prayer, and teach students. Teachers from participating schools and some volunteer parents also teach classes, which include water ecology, orienteering, and outdoor skills, among others. A nominal fee that is charged includes food and lodging. The Y offers a number of scholarships, called camperships, and many schools raise money to help send children to camp. The aim is to enable everyone to participate. The success of the outdoor environmental education program at Cosby has also renewed local interest in summer camp.

National Audubon Society

The National Audubon Society Ecology Camps for children, teenagers, families, adults, and teachers are guided by experts, who plan active programs designed to motivate participants so that they will take a closer look at the natural world. Audubon Camp in Maine on Hog Island on Muscongus Bay was established in 1936 as a pioneering experiment in nature education for adult leaders and teachers. Today the original homestead buildings are still on site. Rustic dormitory accommodations house visitors on the 333-acre Todd Wildlife Sanctuary. Children, ages 10 through 14, learn about nature and how they relate to it. Day and evening explorations instill respect and stewardship for the natural environment. Maine youth camps offer marine biology, oceanography, geology, forest ecology, ornithology, and pond life (Audubon Society, 2001:1-3). Adults attend summer camps, too, with subject specialties that include field ornithology, nature photography, bird migration and conservation, natural history of the Maine Coast, kayaking, and other courses.

Sierra Club

More than 100 years ago, John Muir and his fledgling Sierra Club espoused to bring others to the wilderness. Sierra Club *Inner City Outing* (ICO) provides low-income inner city youth with adventure trips into the wilderness with certified volunteers who are trained in recreation, outdoor, and safety skills as well as environmental education. Community agencies such as schools, churches, rehabilitation centers, and outdoor clubs provide most of the outings at no cost to the students, while ICO contributes the needed equipment for a safe trip. First started in 1971 by the San Francisco Bay Chapter, now some 50 groups of ICO volunteers located in cities across the country and Canada conduct as many as 900 outings a year that impact roughly 1,500 at-risk youngsters (Sierra Club, 2001:2). Their greatest challenge today is keeping up with demand.

ICO students leave the ghetto, barrio, and borough to explore places where forest trails replace sidewalks and concrete; sounds of waterfalls and brooks are swapped for ambulance and police car sirens; and a vast constellation of stars have been exchanged for traffic and head-lights. For some, the everyday existence of hopelessness, poverty, and drugs are left behind, at least for a short time, and it is hoped that the mountains can bring a

Rock climbing can be learned in outdoor adventure programs that stress safety and environmental awareness.

Desert environments require backpackers to master specialized skills while learning about the nature and wildlife.

Preparing for this outdoor education adventure in the tropics demands appropriate dress and the right safety equipment.

Girl Scouts gather for a traditional camp meeting at the conclusion of the weekend's activities, where they summarize what has been learned.

mind-set that will help them to aim high and to become stewards of nature. In a like manner, Sierra's *Youth in Wilderness Project* seeks to expand opportunities for low-income youth to experience nature by providing grant money for experiential learning in outdoor settings, and by looking for barriers that keep schools from participating in outdoor education programs. In addition, Sierra Club's Environmental Education Committee has developed a curriculum that focuses on historical and social studies issues for young people. For instance, on John Muir's birthday, the Sierra Club in California encourages all schools to study his impact on the environment, offers a John Muir Day Study Guide to help teachers, and the John Muir Youth Award Program to reward children who take action to protect wild places. The Sierra Club Outings program offers wilderness treks to adventurers of all levels. Each trip, planned by a volunteer with fees charged to just cover the costs, incorporates lessons about natural history and environmental issues via hiking, backpacking, rafting, sailing, and so forth. In Muir's words, "If people in general could be got into the woods, even for once, to hear the trees speak for themselves, all difficulties in the way of forest preservation would vanish" (McManus, 2001:40).

Outward Bound

Outward Bound is an adventure-based educational program whose objective is leadership training and self-discovery through challenging activities in a wilderness setting. The concept was born in 1941 when German U-boats were sinking British merchant ships. It was discovered that the older seamen, who awaited rescue in the frigid waters were more likely to survive than the younger, probably more fit sailors. In his research regarding the reasons for this, Outward Bound founder, Kurt Hahn concluded that it was lack of confidence rather than lack of skill that made the difference. Realizing that confidence comes from experience, the Outward Bound "learn through doing" experience met with success (Outward Bound,

2001:33). Now Outward Bound has a worldwide presence.

Centering on a specific activity, each Outward Bound program offers extensive technical training. Activities include: mountaineering, canoeing, sailing, backpacking, sea kayaking, canyoneering, white water rafting, dog sledding, horse training, coastal trekking, skiing, rock climbing, bicycling, or some combination. Instructors teach the technical skills needed for the particular environment and activities of choice and gradually turn the responsibility over to the participants. Each course offers opportunities to become proficient in basic campcraft, emergency care, wilderness navigation, food planning and preparation, and expedition planning. Care and protection of the environment are emphasized in all courses. During coursework, personal skills in leadership, problem-solving, decision-making, and communication may be augmented. While Outward Bound does not consider itself to be a survival school, time alone or a solo experience is an important part of the program. This time is spent in a natural setting with minimum equipment so that reflection on the course can take place.

Each course has regular onsite safety inspection, and external review teams audit each school's programs. Although students do not have to be athletic or experienced outdoor persons to join in the wilderness challenges, they should be in reasonably good physical condition, because the courses are mentally, physically, and emotionally demanding. Recognizing that the period between adolescence and adulthood is characterized by rapid change, Outward Bound offers programs especially for young men and women from the ages of 16 to 24. Some high school and college programs have formed partnerships with Outward Bound to offer outdoor experiences for their students. College credit is an option if available through individual institutions. Courses are also accessible to youth, families, adults, and professionals through corporate training programs. Some programs are found in urban centers. There is an application available for financial assistance.

U.S. Forest Service

The Forest Service's natural resource and environmental education program emphasizes involving educators, resource professionals, and citizens' groups in developing skills and techniques for teaching others about their environment. Information and involvement programs aim to familiarize the public about natural resource matters on both national and local levels. The Forest Service Woodsy Owl symbolizes their environmental awareness programs and offers solutions for environmental problems. The fanciful creature, known for his request, "Give a Hoot, Don't Pollute, has been America's environmental champion since 1970 (USDA Forest Service, 2001:1-2). Woodsy visits school and after-school centers, providing hand-out materials for children participating in the Conservation Education programs as well as Teacher Education Guides for use with elementary school programs. As he helps to guide stewardship activities, Woodsy has taken on a new motto, "Lend a Hand, Care for the Land."

PROFESSIONAL EDUCATION

Another responsibility of education is to serve the professional who will act as leader, organizer, interpreter, manager, and/or administrator in outdoor settings. While it can be difficult to prescribe specific qualifications for the outdoor education/recreation professional, there are some qualifications that may be expected of all employees working in outdoor-related programs (Ford, 1985:32).

Some of these include:

1. The ability to understand all types of people, and to understand their psychological needs.
2. The ability to understand basic physiological needs such as food, liquid, rest, health, exercise, warmth, and shelter from wind, rain, heat, and cold.
3. A knowledge of basic natural resource understanding such as reading signs of changing weather, and basic concepts of ecology including the interrelationships of plants, animals, rocks, water, air, and humidity.
4. An understanding of one or more of the following: trees, flowers, mammals, birds, insects, reptiles, or rocks.
5. The knowledge of minimum-impact camping.
6. A knowledge of how to help prevent accidents and administer first aid.
7. An ability to lead songs, tell stories, teach games, express a sense of humor, display high energy, and possess an attitude of professionalism.

In summary, the leader needs the ability to see the world and interpret it to others who do not have the knowledge, and at the same time to teach the skills necessary for safe and successful enjoyment of activities in the out-of-doors. The following are examples of some of the organizations and schools that offer professional development opportunities.

American Association for Leisure and Recreation

The American Association for Leisure and Recreation (AALR) is a national nonprofit membership association serving recreation professionals, and one of several associations that make up the American Alliance for Health, Physical Education, Recreation and Dance. Members include practitioners, educators, volunteers, and students who are involved in the widely diverse field of recreation and leisure services. Since its origin in 1938, AALR has remained committed to advancing the recreation profession and enhancing the quality of life of all Americans through the promotion of creative and meaningful leisure and recreation experiences by promoting professional standards, increasing public awareness and support, encouraging professional training, serving as a forum of ideas and exchange, and advancing and publishing scientific knowledge and research. Areas of involvement include aging, aquatics, campus recreation, college/university education, community/school recreation, correctional recreation, ethics, family recreation, management/administration, outdoor adventure, education, and recreation, play, programming, research, therapeutic recreation, tourism and commercial recreation, and wellness.

AALR publishes *Leisure Today* as part of the Alliance's *Journal of Physical Education, Recreation and Dance*. Each article focuses exclusively on timely trends in recreation and leisure services. AALR also publishes the *AALReporter*, a quarterly newsletter that addresses the current events occurring in AALR and serves as a forum for members to express new thoughts and ideas about subjects like outdoor education.

American Camping Association

Founded in 1910, the American Camping Association (ACA), originally named Camp Directors Association of America, is the largest association serving the camping industry. The nonprofit educational organization's more than 5,700 members are composed of all segments of the camp profession who help people experience the out-of-doors, including: camp owners, directors, executives, students, businesses, day and resident camps, private and not-for-profit camps, travel and trip camps, school programs, environmental education centers, special emphasis camps, and agency camps. The association's mission is to enhance the quality of the experience for youth and adults in organized camping. To do so, ACA promotes high professional practices in camp administration and interprets the values of organized camping to the public. ACA is the only organization that accredits all types of summer camps based on up to 300 national standards for health and safety that are recognized by courts of law and government regulations. ACA accreditation is a voluntary process with a 50-year history (ACA, 2001:1). Through the accreditation process, it educates camp owners and directors in the administration of camp operations and

assists the public in selecting camps that meet recognized standards (ACA, 2001:1).

The American Camping Association offers education and training through conferences, educational events, study materials, and mentors. *Camping Magazine*, which debuted in 1926, is published seven times a year. Its certified Camp Director Program is built on education, self-assessment, evaluation, and professional involvement. In partnership with its accredited camps, ACA is sponsoring a first-of-its-kind national appraisal of the effect of camps on American youth. In conclusion it will study top performing camps, thereby establishing an outcome-based program that will impact the future training of camp directors and staff (ACA, 2001:1-2). Committed also to minimum-impact camping, the ACA's Outdoor Living Skills (OLS) training program teaches children and adults outdoor skills with little or no impact on the environment. Depending on the participant's outdoor experience, the OLS program can be taught at five different levels. Each tier offers skills in map and compass reading, preparing and planning a trip, food preparation and storage, knot tying, first aid and safety, environmental hazards, basic ecology, minimum-impact camping, outdoor hazards, and weather (ACA, 2001:1). ACA has OLS training opportunities for program leaders, instructors and trainers throughout most regions of the country.

National Outdoor Leadership School

Since 1965, the National Outdoor Leadership School (NOLS) has taught wilderness skills, conservation, and leadership to more than 50,000 students (NOLS, 2001: 3). Each area of study provides the fundamental knowledge, skills, and experiences essential for Leave No Trace use and enjoyment of a wilderness environment by emphasizing safety, judgment, leadership, teamwork, outdoor skills, and environmental analyzation. Instructors provide hands-on personal instruction that help students develop leadership abilities along with their physical skills. No matter what the topic–group dynamics, risk management, environmental ethics, leadership, managing groups in the outdoors, or natural history–educators will be immersed in the field of outdoor education.

Educator Courses are offered for outdoor recreation specialists, classroom teachers looking for new approaches, or those persons who would like to become wilderness educators. Courses extend unique opportunities for professionals to share ideas and to teach approaches and skills with colleagues and peers in an expedition setting. Ideas are exchanged, and students are encouraged to teach class in an area of expertise. With the assistance of instructors, students alternate functioning as leader. Classes offer expedition planning, equipment selection, student evaluation processes, and college credit. The adult range of ages in 2000 ranged from 25 to 69 (NOLS, 2001:71). *Instructor Courses* are offered to people interested in working as field instructors for NOLS. Other outdoor programs consider applications from IC graduates as well. NOLS also offers *Leadership Semesters Wilderness Leadership Courses*, and *Mountaineering and Skill Courses*. An *Adventure Wilderness Leadership Course* is open to youth ages 14 to 15. All students should be motivated and in good health physically and mentally. Scholarship applications may be forwarded to the international office in Lander, Wyoming.

National Recreation and Park Association

The National Recreation and Park Association (NRPA) is an independent, nonprofit organization established in 1965. It originated as the Playground Association of America in 1911 and became the National Recreation Association in 1926. The association promotes the wise use of leisure, the conservation of natural and human resources, and the extension of the social, health, cultural, and economic benefits of parks and recreation for all Americans. NRPA members, which include park and recreation administrators; planners and supervisors, therapeutic recreation specialists, military personnel, elected and appointed members of public policy boards and commissions, and citizen advocates, are actively involved on all levels with its numerous branches and sections, each of which serves an area of specialized interest in the park and recreation field. Their outreach activities reach professionals and others informed about national affairs that could impact their work and leisure activities. Their annual Congress and Exposition is held each fall and the organization's main publication is *Parks and Recreation*.

National Wildlife Federation

The National Wildlife Federation (NWF) offers outdoor educational opportunities for K-12 teachers, administrators, and outdoor educators. The focus is a multidisciplinary approach to environmental education. Education programs, interpretive activities, and indoor/outdoor adventures are taught by skilled training coordinators from one of the NWF Field Offices. Each program demonstrates how nature studies can be readily incorporated into existing classes in the arts and humanities, global issues and current events, and science by bringing the natural world into the classroom and the classroom out into nature. Continuing education and/or graduate-level credits are available. After school is finished, students receive a NWF tote bag and kit filled with classroom materials and lesson plans, regular program updates, and a quarterly electronic newsletter. Various workshop topics include information about habitats, endangered species, wetlands, the arctic environment, the northern forest, prairies, wolves, smart growth, water quality, disability-related activities, and schoolyard habitats (NWF, 2001:1-2).

In addition, the National Wildlife Federation offers an inclusive class, called *Access Nature*, for all audiences, including students with disabilities. Youth and teens learn about nature as members of their community-based conservation clubs, known as Ranger Rick's EarthSavers (elementary), Teen Adventure (middle school), and Earth Tomorrow (high school). In partnership with the Wilderness Education Institute, NWF offers educational summer camps for youth and teens at Rocky Mountain National Park in Colorado. Family Summit, their week-long environmental discovery program, has unique opportunities available for the entire family. And NWF's educational outdoor adventure program offers participants a chance to see wild places and wildlife from around the world.

Wilderness Education Association

The Wilderness Education Association (WEA), located in Bloomington, Indiana, is committed to promoting outdoor leadership as a profession, improving the safety of adventure travel, and enhancing the conservation of the wild outdoors. Founded in 1977, the WEA believes that professional outdoor leaders must possess knowledge and skills based on sound judgement and decision-making ability and be able to candidly appraise their competencies and weaknesses. Their 18-Point Curriculum for outdoor leadership certification is designed to be used in different courses offered to professional wilderness leaders through the WEA. The 18-point curriculum includes: decision-making and problem-solving, leadership, expedition behavior and group dynamics, environmental ethics, basic camping skills, nutrition and rations planning, equipment/clothing selection and use, weather, health and sanitation, travel techniques, navigation, safety and risk management, emergency procedures and treatment, natural and cultural history, specialized travel and adventure activities, group processing and communication, trip planning, and teacher and transference (WEA, 2001:1). WEA also offers a Wilderness Education workshop to provide children, adults, and professionals an opportunity to explore the basics of outdoor travel.

Student Conservation Association

The Student Conservation Association (SCA) is a nonprofit, educational organization and the oldest provider of national and community service opportunities in conservation, outdoor education, and career training for students and volunteers in the stewardship of our public lands and natural resources. The SCA, headquartered in Charlestown, New Hampshire, operates three national volunteer programs: the Resource Assistance Program for college students and adults 18 and over; the High School Conservation Work Crew Program for youth between the ages of 16 and 19; and the Conservation Career Development Program, designed to encourage youth from under-represented populations to pursue resource management careers. Because SCA participants gain work experience, future employment opportunities are enhanced. In addition SCA published *Earth work*, a magazine for current and future conservation professionals, and operates the Wilderness Work Skills training program offering courses in traditional and contemporary conservation work skills (SCA, 1998:2).

Resource assistants work individually in a professional capacity for approximately 12 to 16 weeks if they are Resource Assistants (RAs) or six months to one year if they are Conservation Associates (CAs). Both complete a variety of resource management duties as members of the resource staff of cooperating agencies, which include the National Park Service, Bureau of Land Management, Forest Service, Fish and Wildlife Service, the U.S. Geological Survey, and the U.S. Navy, Army, and Air Force National Resources Programs, state and local agencies, and private natural resource organizations. Some volunteer positions are open in Canada. Volunteers receive funds to travel to and from a program site, free housing, a subsistence allowance to offset foot expenses. RAs receive a uniform allowance when authorized by the cooperating agency. In return, volunteers work 40 hours a week. The positions offer a variety of tasks, and generally each position has a main theme or subject matter in which the volunteer participates. Some of these subjects are: wildlife and fisheries, forestry recreation management, environmental education, interpretation, visitor assistance, trail maintenance and construction, and backcountry management. Positions may require specific educational background, skill, or experience. Academic or internship credit for field experience is also possible.

INTERNATIONAL PROGRAMS

International outdoor education is probably best characterized by a great diversity in outdoor adventures. The diversity of programs is influenced by the immediate environment, time, and philosophy. While Americans may marvel at schools allowing five-day camp experiences, Bavarian codes endorse camp experiences of two weeks or more. Philosophical goals vary from country to country, and are influenced by earlier expectations. For example, primary goal emphasis varied from a social emphasis in New Zealand and Australia, to a conservation emphasis in Sweden and a physical fitness emphasis in Great Britain (MacKenzie, 1974:155-59). An outdoor education program in Venezuela in the 1990s was influenced by New Yorker Judy Myers, who took children from Maracaibo to the Andes for one week of outdoor camping activities.

As a result of a partnership between the Canadian Space Agency, the Canadian Wildlife Service of Environment Canada, the Canadian Wildlife Federation and National Resources, and Canada Center for Remote Sensing, a web-based project linking space age technology to the conservation of endangered species was launched in 2000. The goal of the *Space for Species* is to allow students in Canada to become actively engaged with the struggles of these special animals by connecting participating classrooms to four at risk species there: the leatherback turtle, polar bear, caribou, and eider duck. Monitoring their migratory cycle on line, it is hoped that students will learn the threats of their existence by tracking a leatherback turtle in its search for jellyfish prey or by following a pregnant polar bear as she searches for a den (Canadian Space Agency, 2001:1). Thinking globally, the Global Environmental and Outdoor Education Council of the Alberta Teacher's Association believes that

young people yearn for more meaning in their lives than an education that will simply help prepare them for a job. Finding that desirable goals lead to desirable outcomes, they strive to teach toward a vision of the world in which "the environment is cared for; human development is sustainable; human rights are protected; cultural diversity is valued and a culture of peace is the norm" (Coumantarakis, 1999:1-2).

North American Association for Environmental Education

North American Association for Environmental Education members believe that education must go beyond consciousness-raising to prepare people to think about environmental stewardship and to work together to try to solve environmental problems. This network of professionals, students, and volunteers working in environmental education throughout North America and in over 55 countries around the world believe that to be truly effective, environmental issues must be integrated into all aspects of the curriculum and into all types of educating institutions for the widest array of audiences. Since 1971, NAAEE, based in Rock Spring, Georgia, has uniquely combined and integrated environmental groups and organizations dedicated to improving education into a balanced approach through its annual conference, publications, and on-line services.

SUMMARY

Outdoor education has a multitude of objectives, some of which include: to help people live in harmony with the natural environment, to establish a basic understanding of others, to utilize an interdisciplinary approach to education, to learn to use all of the senses, to learn in the natural laboratory, and to arouse the natural curiosity of the student. Outdoor education is commonly defined as education in, about, and for the out-of-doors.

In America, outdoor education goes back to the eighteenth and nineteenth centuries when it began to expand in reaction to the industrialization of North America. Among the early advocates were Joseph Cogswell, George Bancroft, Ernest Thompson Seton, Lloyd Burgess Sharp, and Julian Smith. Their efforts resulted in both formal offerings such as Round Hill School and informal ones through youth organizations. Traditional schools became involved in outdoor education through interdisciplinary programs and planned instruction.

As a self-conscious movement in American education, outdoor education experiences have moved from elementary school camping to all age levels and outdoor settings. Preschoolers to adults are enriched by outdoor education courses. No longer a middle-class phenomenon, outdoor education has moved to a greater classspread and to special groups. Schools without camps seek local settings within walking distance. Farms, forests, and gardens offer increasing possibilities. At the college level, centers for outdoor education have been established and extracurricular programs with outdoor orientation bring opportunities to students, staff, and the community. Academic credit is given for students who are planning careers in recreation or education through various undergraduate and graduate institutions.

A number of nonprofit organizations such as the National Audubon Society and the YMCA became involved in providing outdoor education experiences, and other organizations such as the American Camping Association are concerned with the education and training of camp staff. Outward Bound offers courses around the world to those who want to learn practical outdoor skills, self-discovery, and more about the natural environment. The various approaches used to teach outdoor/ environmental education can be shared with others at various conferences put on by professional organizations. One organization, the North American Association for Environmental Education, serves professionals, students, and volunteers from more than 55 countries throughout the world.

REFERENCES

American Camping Association (ACA). (2001). *ACA fact sheet.* [On-line]. Available: http.// www.acacamps.org/media/factset.htm.

American Camping Association (ACA). (2001). *Outdoor living skills.* [On-line]. Available: http:// www.acacamps.org/education/ols.htm.

American Camping Association (ACA). (2001). *Youth development outcomes of the camp experience.* [On-line]. Available: http:// www.acacamps.org/research/grant.htm

Audubon Society. (2001). Audubon camps in Maine. [On-line]. Available: http:// www.audubon.org/educate/cw/maine- kid.html

Bennett, B. (1974). Camping and outdoor education began at Round Hill School. In G. Donldson & O. Goering (Eds.), *Perspectives on outdoor education.* Dubuque, IA: Wm. C. Brown.

Boy Scouts of America (BSA). (2001). *Passport to high adventure.* [On-line]. Available: http:// www.scouting.org/pubs/ptha/index.html

Brown, R. (1998 September/October). Outdoor learning centers: Realistic social studies experience for K-6 students. *The social studies, 89*(5), 199-204.

Canadian Space Agency. (2001). Kids, space and species: Leading the way in wildlife conservation, (pp. 1-3), Ottawa, Canada: Media Relations Office.

Ciraco, C., Davies, G., Findutter, J., Hussey, S., Kennedy, C., Murphy, C., Nye, D., Simpkins, V. & Waite, K. (1984). *Outdoor education in girl scouting.* New York: Girl Scouts of the United States of America.

Christie, E. (2001). Girl Scouts and the Environmental Protection Agency collaborate on new badge. [On-line]. Available: http:// www.girlscouts.org/news/epa.html

Cogswell, J., & Bancroft, G. (1823). *Prospects of a school to be established at Round Hill.* Northampton, MA: Cambridge University Press.

Coles, R. (2000). *Careers in recreation.* Reston, VA: American Association for Leisure and Recreation.

Coumantarakis, S. (1999). *Why Global Education?* [On-line]. Available: http://www.rockies.ca/eoec/ about/why-global.html

Conrad, L. (1974). Lloyd B. Sharp's philosophy of education. In G. Donaldson & O. Goering (Eds.), *Perspectives on outdoor education.* Dubuque, IA: Wm. C. Brown.

Council on Outdoor Education. (1989, February). Outdoor education definition and philosophy. *Journal of Health, Physical Education, Recreation and Dance, 60*(2).

Crawford, S. (1998, August). Should outdoor education be a regular part of physical education programs addressing national standards? *Journal of Physical Education, Recreation, and Dance, 69*(6).

Donaldson, G. (1974). Julian W. Smith. In G. Donaldson & O. Goering (Eds.), *Perspectives on outdoor education.* Dubuque, IA: Wm.C. Brown.

Donaldson, G., & Goering, O., (Eds.). (1974). *Perspectives on outdoor education.* Dubuque, IA: Wm C. Brown.

Educational Directories Unlimited. (2001). Outdoor education graduate schools in the United States. [On-line]. Available: http://www.gradschools.com/listings/all/edu_outdoor.html

Ford, P. (1985). Outdoor education/recreation. In *American Association for Leisure and Recreation Career Information.* Reston, Va: Association of the American Alliance for Health, Physical Education, Recreation and Dance.

Ford, P. (1987). *Outdoor education: Definition and philosophy.* ERIC/Cress. Las Cruces, NM: New Mexico State University (ERIC Document Reproduction Service No. ED 267-941).

Ford, P. (1989). The inseparable links of outdoor education or you can't divide a mobius. *Julian Smith Lecture.* Reston, VA: The Council on Outdoor Education (AAHPERD).

Ford, P. (1989, February). Outdoor education. *Journal of Health, Physical Education, Recreation and Dance, 60*(2).

Gilbert, J., & Chase, C. (1988, May/June). Outdoor education, the malady and the prescription. *Journal of Health, Physical Education, Recreation and Dance, 59*(5).

Lappin, E. (2000). Outdoor education for behavior disordered students, [On-line]. Available: http://www.kidsource.com/kidsource/content2/outdoor.education.1d.k12.3.html

Los Angeles City Schools. (1961). *Outdoor education and school camping.* Los Angeles: In G. Donaldson & O. Goering (Eds.), *Perspectives on Outdoor Education.* Dubuque, IA: Wm. C. Brown.

McManus, R. (2001, May/June). Happy trails. *Sierra. 86*(3) 40-42.

Nash, R. (1970). *The call of the wild* (1900-1916). New York: George Braziller.

National Outdoor Leadership School (NOLS). (2001). *National outdoor leadership school.* Lander, WY: NOLS.

National Wildlife Federation (NWF). (2001). *Workshop topics.* [On-line]. Available: http://www.nwf.org/schoolyardhabitats/workshoptopics.cfm

Outward Bound. (2000). *Pacific crest outward bound.* Portland, OR: Pacific Crest Outward Bound School.

Pullias, E. (1974). Better education for modern man. In G. Donaldson and O. Goering (Eds.), *Perspectives on outdoor education*, Dubuque, IA: Wm. C. Brown.

Pumula, E. (1973). The San Diego California community school camp. In D. Hammerman & W. Hammerman (Eds.), *Outdoor education: A book of readings.* Minneapolis, MN: Burgess.

Rillo, T. (1985). *Outdoor education: Beyond the classroom walls.* Bloomington, IN: Phi Delta Kappa Educational Foundation.

Rose, T. (2001, August). Incorporating the outdoors in physical education. *Journal of Physical Education, Recreation, and Dance, 72*(6),17-18.

San Diego County Office of Education. (1999). Images from the past. [On-line]. Available: http//www.sdcoe.k12.ca.us/outdoored/past/past.html

Shepard, C., & Caruso, V. (1988 January). Kid's play in the great outdoors. *Camping Magazine, 60*(3).

Sierra Club. (1997, November/December). Last words. *Sierra Club Magazine*, 1-3. [On-line]. Available: http://www.sierraclub.org/sierra/199711/last.asp

Sierra Club. (2001). What is inner city outings? [On-line]. Available: http://www.sierraclub.org/education/programs.asp

Smith, J. (1974). Where we have been—What we will become. In G. Donaldson & 0. Goering (Eds.), *Perspectives on outdoor education*. Dubuque, IA: Wm. C. Brown.

Smith, J. (1974). Words, words, words. In G. Donaldson & 0. Goering (Eds.), *Pespectives on outdoor education*. Dubuque, IA: Wm. C. Brown.

Student Conservation Association. (1998). *Resource assistant program*. Charlestown, NH: SCA.

USDA Forest Service. (2001). Woodsy owl. [On-line]. Available: http:www.fs.fed.us/spf/woodsy

Vinal, W. (1974). Still more outdoor leaders I have known. In G. Donaldson & 0. Goering (Eds.), *Perspectives on outdoor education*. Dubuque, IA: Wm. C. Brown.

WEA (2001, February). *National conference on outdoor leadership: Shaping the wave of the profession,* Program, San Diego, CA.

Wilson, R. (1999). *What can I teach my young child about the environment?* [On-line]. Available: http//www.sierraclub.org/education/eear1299.asp

Witt, P. (July). Re-Examining the role of recreation and parks in after-school programs. *Parks & Recreation,* 36(7).

YMCA. (2000). *YMCA Camp Cosby.* [On-line]. Available: http://www.campcosby.org/history.htm

15 OUTDOOR RECREATIONAL ACTIVITIES

America's landscapes include mountains, deserts, woodlands, wetlands, prairies, swamps, and tundra. Its waterways form a web over most of the continent, and its coastline, if stretched, would reach halfway around the world. Its wildlife refuges are unparalleled, and its panoramic vistas are a source of American pride. Approximately 28 percent of the total land area in the United States is in federal ownership, and more than a third of the land is composed of federal, state, regional, county, and municipal property (Betz et al., 1999:40; President's Commission on Americans Outdoors 1987:1). While some of the land is not conducive to recreational pursuits, much of it is open to recreational use. In fact, about 40 percent of all Americans reported a visit to a federally operated recreation site during the last year (Roper Starch, 2000:24). The land available is a living testament of America's commitment to the outdoors, and the benefits it provides seem to be increasing faster than many other uses of our precious land (Pandolfi, 1999:ix).

Americans almost unanimously (90%) agree that outdoor recreation is the best way to be physically active, with two-thirds of the American public (66%) engaged in some type of outdoor recreation at least several times a month. Additionally, more than three-quarters of Americans (78%) are participating in outdoor recreation. This number has been rising for several years and increased 11 points in the last year alone. Incidentally, outdoor recreation is also increasing across all age and income categories. Since those who participate in outdoor recreation consistently report higher satisfaction with their lives, this is likely to have broad societal benefits (Roper Starch, 2000:3-4). Because the public lands are available to all Americans at little cost, if any, it is important that the public sector have up-to-date information detailing demand trends to discern whether recreational opportunities are expanding enough or in appropriate directions to meet increasing needs.

In an analysis, well-known researcher H. Ken Cordell (Cordell et al., 1990:3-4) explains that the demand for outdoor recreation grew after World War II, when the economy grew to support it. At the same time many new families were started, and the population grew rapidly. The quality of automobiles and roads increased, fuel became cheaper, and the average work week declined to 40 hours over five days. Outdoor recreation opportunities became increasingly available to middle- and lower-income groups. Use of the public recreation lands expanded. By the mid-1950s it burgeoned, but many federal recreation sites were deteriorating. Park Service Director Newton Drury responded with Mission 66, a program to rehabilitate facilities and build new ones by 1966. Conservationists, led by Joseph Penfold of the lzaak Walton League, recommended additional action to meet the nation's outdoor recreation needs. The result was congressional action in 1958 establishing the Outdoor Recreation Resources Review Commission (ORRRC). The ORRRC was charged with addressing the nation's outdoor recreation needs to the year 2000 and recommending programs to address those needs. Information was gathered by the commission over a period of three years.

The ORRRC found that outdoor recreation was a major leisure activity growing in importance and that outdoor recreation opportunities were most urgently needed near metropolitan areas. While considerable land was available for outdoor recreation, it was not effectively meeting the need. The ORRRC's recommendations led to creation of the Bureau of Outdoor Recreation (BOR) in 1963 (reorganized into the Heritage Conservation and Recreation Service (HCRS) by the Carter administration) to coordinate national recreation policy and programs, and influenced the development of the Land and Water Conservation Fund (1965), the Wilderness Preservation System (1964), the National Wild and Scenic Rivers System (1968), and the National Trails System (1968) (see Chapter 7, Federal Resources).

In the 1960s and early 1970s, demand for outdoor recreation opportunities dramatically increased again. Government at all levels responded to the demands. With money from the Land and Water Conservation Fund, states, cities, and counties expanded their park and open-space systems. Meanwhile, American society changed significantly. Its population increased by 63 million people and shifted southward and westward; the average American became older; the nation shifted from dependence on traditional heavy industry to high technology, communication, and services; and government, business, and residences became less centralized.

The 1980s brought major changes both in the demand for and the supply of outdoor recreation opportunities. Participation in many activities had surpassed the projections of the ORRRC. A growing population was putting increased pressure on recreation lands while development was subtracting from available open space in and near growing cities and towns. Technology had spawned a host of new activities, from hang gliding, to driving rugged vehicles off-road, to snowmobiling. The population changed toward an older citizenry, more women were working, and there were more single parents. The federal government and many states were finding it difficult to pay for many programs, including outdoor recreation.

A consortium of interest groups went to Laurance Rockefeller, the chairman of the 1960 ORRRC, and urged that he take the lead in stimulating a new ORRRC-like assessment of outdoor recreation trends and needs. He convened with a small group of conservation and recreation leaders. Rockefeller's Outdoor Recreation Policy Review Group concluded that there was evidence that outdoor recreation opportunities were contracting, rather than expanding to meet increasing need. These findings led the group to recommend that a comprehensive federal reappraisal of the nation's recreation policy and resources be made by a new commission patterned after the ORRRC (Cordell et al., 1990:2-4).

When efforts to have Congress enact legislation creating the commission stalled, President Ronald Reagan established, by executive order, the President's Commission on Americans Outdoors (PCAO) in 1985, although the HCRS was abolished and with it the outdoor recreation planning process (Betz, 1999:24). President Reagan then directed the commission to look ahead for a generation and determine what Americans wanted to do outdoors and what was needed to ensure that they have the necessary opportunities. The commission's report, *Americans Outdoors: The Legacy, the Challenge* (1987), although not as extensive as that of the ORRRC, contained more than 60 specific recommendations: it urged the establishment of greenways, described as "corridors of private and public lands and waters to provide people with access to open spaces closest to where they live; it urged communities to shape growth so they could remain attractive places to live and work; and it recommended intensified efforts to maintain the quality of national resources and to increase recreation opportunities on federal lands. Partnerships between government agencies and the private sector were seen as a key to expanding outdoor opportunities. Finally, the commission recommended that Congress establish a dedicated trust fund to provide a minimum of $1 billion a year for outdoor recreation (Cordell et al., 1990:3-4).

ORRRC's recommendation that a national survey about outdoor recreation be conducted every five years resulted in a series of general-population surveys that were coordinated by the National Park Service. These National Recreation Surveys (NRS), which began in 1960, resulted in a series of periodic updates to 1982-83. The survey process continued in 1994-1995 with a new name, the National Survey on Recreation and the Environment (NSRE); a new coordinating sponsor, the Forest Service; other federal sponsors; and a private sponsor, the Sporting Goods Manufacturers Association. In addition, the Forest Service has been conducting assessments since Congress passed the Forest and Rangeland Renewable Resources Planning Act (RPA) in 1974, directing the secretary of agriculture to prepare a Renewable Resources Assessment in 1975, 1979, and every 10 years thereafter. Although not intended to be a national plan, the RPA assessment is highly valued as the most reliable and scientifically sound assessment of outdoor recreation and wilderness in the United States and for its future projections (Betz, 1999: 24-26). The 1998 national outdoor recreation assessment was conducted by Forest Service scientists at the Southern Research Station along with many collaborators and contributors. These findings were published by Sagamore Publishing in a volume entitled *Outdoor Recreation in American Life: A National Assessment of Demand and Supply Trends* (Cordell, 1999). Some of the findings during the 1990s include (Betz, 1999:26-27; Society of Park and Recreation Educators 1999:28).

1. Outdoor recreation opportunities in the United States have increased.
2. Growth in the acreage among the federal estate has been limited, but special designations such as wilderness and national rivers have increased appreciably.
3. State park systems and local park and recreation systems continue to supply increasing numbers of sites.
4. Rural private land available for outdoor recreation use has declined significantly, while public-private partnerships have enabled greenways, scenic byways, and watchable-wildlife programs to burgeon.
5. Americans' outdoor recreation participation has grown rapidly.
6. The top land- and water-based recreation activities were walking, birdwatching, wildlife viewing, biking, sightseeing, family gatherings, visiting a beach or waterside, and swimming in pools, rivers, lakes, or oceans.
7. The fast-growing activities through the year 2050 are expected to be visiting historic places, downhill skiing, snowmobiling, sightseeing, and non-consumptive wildlife activity.
8. The changing and evolving nature of outdoor recreation guarantees that relevant research on experience preferences and motivations will continue.

To increase awareness about the many outdoor activities available, we classify a few examples of them according to their various natural features including land, snow, water, and air. The activities selected are also intended to represent popular,

Table 15.1 Maximum Preferred Demand for Recreational Trips away from Home and Indices of Future Demand Growth to 2040

Resource Category and Activity	Trips in 1987 (millions)	Future Number of Trips as Percentage of 1987 Demand				
		2000	2010	2020	2030	2040
Land						
Wildlife observation and photography	69.5	116	131	146	162	174
Camping in primitive campgrounds	38.1	114	127	140	154	164
Backpacking	26.0	134	164	196	230	255
Nature study	70.8	105	113	120	131	138
Horseback riding	63.2	123	141	160	177	190
Day hiking	91.2	131	161	196	244	293
Photography	42.0	123	143	165	188	205
Visiting prehistoric sites	16.7	133	160	192	233	278
Collecting berries	19.0	113	126	143	166	192
Collecting firewood	30.3	112	124	138	157	178
Walking for pleasure	266.5	116	131	146	164	177
Running/jogging	83.7	133	163	197	234	262
Bicycle riding	114.6	125	148	173	202	222
Driving vehicles or motorcycles off-road	80.2	105	111	118	125	130
Visiting museums or info. centers	9.7	118	136	153	174	188
Attending special events	73.7	114	127	141	157	168
Visiting historic sites	73.1	122	143	169	203	241
Driving for pleasure	421.6	115	128	142	157	167
Family gatherings	74.4	119	135	152	170	182
Sightseeing	292.7	118	136	156	183	212
Picnicking	262.0	108	117	126	136	144
Camping in developed campgrounds	60.6	120	137	155	173	186
Water						
Canoeing/kayaking	39.8	113	126	140	157	169
Stream/lake/ocean swimming	238.8	105	110	117	124	129
Rafting/tubing	8.9	111	136	164	215	255
Rowing/paddling/other boating	61.8	112	124	136	150	159
Motor boating	219.5	106	111	117	123	127
Water skiing	107.5	111	121	131	141	148
Pool swimming	221.0	137	169	205	242	269
Snow and Ice						
Cross-country skiing	9.7	147	177	199	212	195
Downhill skiing	64.3	153	197	247	298	333

Source: H. K. Cordell et al. *An Analysis of the Outdoor Recreation and Wilderness Situation in the United States: 1989–2040.* (U.S. Department of Agriculture, Forest Service, Fort Collins, CO 1990), 44.

growth, high-risk, or high-tech adventures that cross a variety of income levels. A special section, representing viewing and learning activities, follows. The activity section ends with orienteering and camping activities, which are associated with many of the selected activities. Although a few safety tips are included in the activities section, this is not within the scope of this book. A number of courses and books specialize in first aid, outdoor survival skills, and various activities. Anyone who is or becomes interested in participating in the activities in this chapter will find a list of related organizations at the end of the chapter for additional information.

While low-impact suggestions are given, adventurers should always follow the low-impact advice of the local area management officials. Two not-for-profit organizations, *Leave No Trace*, Incorporated and *Tread Lightly!*, Incorporated offer a variety of educational materials that are used by outdoor recreation enthusiasts who want to do their part to diminish their impact on the backcountry while continuing to enjoy their activities in it. Each of these programs, launched by the Forest Service, was based on the same type of premise as their *Smoky the Bear* and *Woodsy Owl* programs, which were designed to reduce the impacts of fire and litter.

The *Leave No Trace* (LNT) education program, developed as an outdoor ethics program for non-motorized users, went into partnership with the National Outdoor Leadership School (NOLS) in 1991 before the program grew into its present model. *Tread Lightly!*, conceived by a Forest Service task force in 1985, provides a focus for educational messages geared toward motorized visitors. Through the years this program steadily added new dimensions to meet the needs of all types of outdoor adventurers. To maximize its effectiveness, the program was transferred to the private sector in 1990. There is, according to a Roper Starch survey, a strong association between outdoor recreation and environmental awareness, and virtually all Americans agree (95%) that outdoor recreation is a good way to increase people's apprecia-

tion for the environment (Roper Starch, 2000:9). For more information about how you can minimize your impact on the land and water, please contact these programs, listed at the end of this chapter.

ADVENTURES ON LAND

Land adventures are those activities that occur primarily on land as opposed to snow, ice, or water. Together these adventures constitute the largest single category of outdoor recreational participation in the country (Cordell et al., 1999:222). Providing a foundation for numerous other outdoor experiences, we highlight hiking and backpacking. Few activities have stormed onto the scene like mountain bicycling, also introduced in this section.

Hiking

Trails for day hikers go through beautiful scenic areas throughout the United States. A hike may simply break up a lengthy vacation drive, lead to another recreational activity, or provide recreation in and of itself. Whatever the purpose, hiking is an outdoor activity for almost everyone. For instance, a two-mile city trail, The Freedom Trail in Boston, attracts two to three million people each year. Trails are also designed for the visually and physically impaired. Other than transportation to a trailhead, little else is needed in order to participate.

A hike often occurs in a natural setting, and is generally longer and more vigorous than a walk. For instance, the United States Census Bureau (2000:262) reports that 77,645,000 individuals disclosed that they participate in exercise walking, as compared to the 27,190,000, who called themselves hikers. Another account taken in the mid-nineties, which included people 16 years and older, established that 133.7 million participated in walking and 47.8 million participated in hiking. There is no doubt that walking is the single most popular activity in the United States and that hiking is the most popular outdoor recreation activity (Cordell et al., 1999:223; Bowker et al., 1999:338). Hiking is pro-

Table 15.2 Essentials for Hiking and Backpacking

Ten Essentials:

- Compass
- Clothing (enough to survive most probable adverse conditions)
- Extra food
- Flashlight
- Fire starter (candle, heat lamp, etc.)

- First aid kit (including moleskin, tape)
- Sunglasses (goggles or clip on)
- Pocket knife
- Map (USGS topographic)
- Waterproof matches (or matches in waterproof container)

Clothing to Wear:

- Socks (either pile or wool), two pair
- Boots
- Long pants (loose fitting and preferably wool)
- Wool or pile gloves or mittens and hat

- Parka or jacket (wind and water resistant)
- Shirts and/or sweaters (have several including a wool or pile one to utilize the layer system)
- Pile cap or sun visor

Additional Items for Day Trips:

- Pack
- Canteen or poly bottle (one quart minimum)
- Emergency shelter (tube tent, space blanket)
- Insect repellent
- Ice axe or walking stick
- Sitting pad (ensolite, etc.)
- Drinking cup
- Handkerchief
- Camera and film

- Plastic bags
- Tissue and/or toilet paper
- Litter bag
- Watch
- Poncho, rain chaps, gaiters or other rain gear
- Hiking shorts
- Sun screen lotion
- Windbreaker (wind and water resistant)

Additional Equipment for Overnight Trips:

- Shelter (tent or tarp)
- Ground cloth
- Sleeping bag in waterproof stuff bag
- Sleeping pad
- Stove and fuel
- Cooking pot
- Water purifying kit
- Long underwear

- Extra flashlight battery and bulb
- Pot gripper
- Eating utensils
- Bag for hanging food
- Nylon cord
- Personal toilet items
- Biodegradable soap
- Rain cover for pack

Other Things that Are Nice to Have:

- Swimsuit
- Camp shoes
- Binoculars

- Towel
- Notebook and pencil

Source: REI, A382:rev. 4/86. (Reprinted with permission.)

jected to increase marginally faster than the population growth to 2050 (Bowker et. al., 1999:338). At little cost, it provides a setting for social interaction with friends, family, or in an organized group. For those who enjoy their solitude it can be done alone, although that is not recommended for safety reasons. On the other hand, groups larger than eight or ten are not recommended either. Because hiking provides many diversions along the trail that occupy the mind, it is known for reducing stress and building self-esteem. Most hikers will say each trail leads to a unique experience.

One of the best cardiovascular exercises, hiking promotes fitness and strengthens muscles. It places less strain on bones and joints than most other aerobic activities, and it is an excellent way to lose weight. While rugged terrains provide excellent conditions for cardiovascular development, hills can be strenuous for beginners or for those who do not walk or hike regularly. For instance, as much energy is needed to hike two miles an hour up a 10-percent grade as hiking four miles an hour on level trail (McKinney, 1998:19). Hikers try to maintain a steady, comfortable pace that is comfortable for them. For more useful horizontal energy, hikers can try lengthening the stride to increase speed by allowing the hips to turn so that the forward leg advances farther while the rear leg swings farther back.

Everyone on the hike ought to be aware of the destination, and whenever there is a fork or change along the trail, all members of the party gather for directions. No one leaves the trail without asking a member of the party to wait. Off-trail hiking, however, is only done where permissible, and with topographical map and compass (see the section on Orienteering). When hiking off-trail in wilderness, with the exception of in the desert, a group should spread out width-wise rather than marching single file. This keeps everyone from tramping over the same ground, which creates undesirable trails. The general rule, however, is to stay on trails. This is always important in the desert, where delicate cryptogamic soil is damaged from the slightest disturbance.

Prior to departure, hikers leave a note at the trailhead, in the car, or with a ranger or friend to provide the intended destination and the expected time of return, but first they prepare for weather, terrain and altitude changes. Even the most healthy and physically fit hikers (backpackers and skiers) need to become acclimated. Regardless of fitness level, altitude can cause discomfort, including shortness of breath, headache, nausea, and dehydration above 5,000 feet. Altitude sickness, also called acute mountain sickness, may begin at 8,000 feet and become more intense at higher levels (McKinney, 1998:19). Beach hiking calls for knowledge of tide changes. Desert monsoons can lead to disaster when hiking in ravines, which are capable of transforming into running rapids with little notice.

Although required equipment (see Table 15.2) varies according to the length of the hike and the other variables mentioned (see Table 15.2), the day hiker always carries water or must plan to treat water found en route with purification tablets or a filter. Food packed in is always packed back out, and trail mix really is great to take along! It is recommended that day hikers bring along an extra meal just in case it is necessary to spend the night (Knight-Ridder, 1998:E-3). A hiking stick is desirable for balance in hilly or rough terrain; some turn to their cross-country ski poles. The soft frameless day pack should be firmly padded at the shoulder straps and have a pocket large enough for a water bottle. A waist or hip band helps to keep the pack stabilized.

Clothing made of natural fibers suitable to existing weather conditions is recommended. Light colors are best in warm climates, and layering is helpful for day hikes. Special precautions are necessary to protect against ultraviolet rays of the sun including protective lotions, hats, sunglasses with UV protection, and a handkerchief around the neck. Loose pants, tucked into the boots or socks, and

A hiker peers down the world famous Grand Canyon.

long-sleeved shirts provide protection in all climates and guard against brambles and brush, poison oak and poison ivy, and insects. For damp, rainy, and cool environments, the breathable, high-tech fabric laminates are hiker friendly, but a water-resistant jacket or poncho accommodates the conditions. Gaiters, attached to the bottom of the boot by a cord, protect boots and lower leggings against rain and snow.

Lightweight hiking boots that have been broken in provide the best protection and traction and are advantageous for longer hikes. Socks that will not bunch or wrinkle help to prevent blisters. Two pairs are recommended. The lighter inside pair moves with the foot and protects the heel. With only one pair of socks, the boots and

Soft packs are better for bushwhacking, scrambling over rock fields, climbing, and skiing.

Backpacking trips are usually planned well ahead of time so that camping reservations and permits can be arranged and maps can be ordered and studied.

the socks tend to move together and rub against the heel. Because tennis shoes absorb heat, they can be particularly uncomfortable in warmer climates, but exercise-walking shoes or running shoes can get the novice started.

Safety

Blisters are the hiker's most common problem. Caused by improperly sized shoes, new or stiff shoes, or temperature extremes, blisters can cause incapacitation. Early signs and symptoms are hot spots or sore areas. Treatment involves changing to dry socks and readjusting the boot lacing. Moleskin is used to protect the sore area or the blister. The hiker can cut a piece of moleskin in the shape of a doughnut, fitting the hole around the injury. Several more doughnuts can be shaped and stacked to keep pressure off of the blister and to help prevent it from breaking. If the blister is large or appears as though it will break, it should be washed and drained before

applying antiseptic and moleskin. To drain a blister, a sterilized needle (heated with a flame) is inserted under the skin just inside the edge of the blister.

The spread of Lyme disease has made it more important for hikers to occasionally check their clothes and skin for small, dark ticks when in heavily infested areas. This is easier to do when light colored fabrics are worn. The skin and hair can also be checked before bathing. If a tick is still moving when found, it likely has not fed. If embedded in the skin, it is slowly lifted off by pulling straight out of the skin with tweezers if handy, trying not to crush the body. Afterward the area is washed and an antiseptic is applied. Lyme disease, a bacterial infection, is usually spread by the nymph deer tick. Although it is too small to see, all ticks grow larger as they fill with blood (Kemper et al., 1999:65-66). Symptoms of Lyme disease are an expanding red rash that may resemble a bull's-eye, fever, headache, fatigue, stiff neck, or muscle and joint pain. A physician can treat Lyme disease with oral antibiotics, which are most beneficial when administered shortly after the infection occurs. The tick can also be saved in a jar for tests if symptoms develop. A vaccine is available for individuals who spend a good amount of time in infected areas. Other means of prevention include pulling socks over pant legs; wearing a hat and long-sleeved shirt; staying in the middle of the trail, applying DEET to exposed areas or to clothing, although care is needed around the mouth and eyes and with children's hands since they tend to put them in their mouths. Lower-concentration products are used for children and pregnant women (Kemper et al., 1999:64-65). Pets should also be checked as soon as possible.

Backpacking

The major difference between backpacking and hiking is that the backpacker can hike deep into the wilderness, carrying essentials in a backpack allowing for overnight outings. The hiker, carrying a lighter day pack, can cover more ground but must return to shelter by nightfall. The increased distance and freedom from civilization can make the burden of the heavier pack worthwhile. Currently an estimated 15 million outdoor enthusiasts across the country participate in backpacking and over the next half century, participation is expected to increase by 26 percent (Bowker et al., 1999:338).

Backpacking trips are usually difficult to arrange on the spur of the moment. Reservations for camping are generally required before, during, and after the trip, and it is important to order and study maps, elevations, and current weather conditions before attempting a trip in the backcountry (see Orienteering in this chapter). Beginners may prefer guided trips, which can be arranged by local outfitters, the American Forestry Association, the Wilderness Society, or the Sierra Club, for example.

The packer's hiking speed should be the same throughout the day. The weight is balanced over the feet or slightly ahead; a bent-over posture is only advisable for steep inclines. When going uphill, the stride may be shortened and should be lengthened when going downhill. Steady, even breathing will help to keep the heart beating at an even pace. Resting is important, but for brief stops the pack is not removed. Instead, the waist belt is released, and the packer bends at the waist until the pack is parallel to the ground. Hands are placed on slightly bent knees to help relieve the strain on the shoulders. These stops only last a couple of minutes so that the muscles will not stiffen as the body cools down. For longer stops, the backpack is removed.

In addition to the day-hiker supplies, the typical backpacker carries other equipment (see Table 15.2). It is advisable for backpackers to underestimate the weight that can be carried and to test their abilities with short trips before an extensive one is undertaken. A rule of thumb is to carry no more than one-third of the body weight when in good condition and no more than one-fourth if out of shape. The ideal weight to carry for comfort and agility is no more than one-fifth of the body weight (Meier, 1980:65). Generally, more enjoyment is equated with less weight. A well-ventilated poncho, readily available in the pack, protects not only the packer but the pack as well, preventing excess water weight to weigh down the pack. Raingear typically consists of a poncho or rain jacket and pants.

Backpacks generally have either external or internal frames. External frames distribute the load more evenly over the back, and the frame allows air to pass between the back and the load. It is suited fine for carrying gear when traveling mostly on trails, but it can throw the packer off balance if there is a need to climb or travel in rough terrain. Internal frames, sometimes called soft packs, have a lower center of gravity and can be worn tighter to the body, making it easier to keep balanced. While they are not as comfortable for carrying heavy loads, the balance and upper body mobility make them better for bushwhacking, scrambling over rock fields, climbing and skiing. There are also frameless packs that need to be packed just right to fit the body and provide stability. With varying degrees of adjustability, they can be checked as luggage. Down-filled sleeping bags are light and compress easily, and small ultra-lightweight tents aid in keeping the weight down.

Backpacks are arranged so that the weight rests on the hips in a balanced fashion. When putting the pack on, one tightens the shoulder straps until the pack is comfortable against the back. The shoulders are hunched while the waist belt is fastened. The waist belt should be cinched tightly until the weight of the pack is held directly on the hips. The shoulders simply lend stability. Outside pockets carry items used throughout the day. Other items can be stored at the bottom of the pack or in an inside compartment. Heavier items are placed high in the pack and as close to the body as possible. This method allows for the heavier equipment to align with the center of gravity, and it keeps the pack from pulling off the shoulders. All equipment is packed inside to prevent snagging trees. To protect items from moisture and make them more accessible, they may be packed together in plastic bags according to their general use.

Safety

Carrying the pack can certainly be depleting on hot summer days, especially when it is humid. Physical exertion and exercise generates heat. As the body heats, the heat is displaced by perspiration, increased respiration, and dissipation through the skin. Hotter conditions make it more difficult for the body to keep cool. Heat stroke and heat exhaustion are disorders that transpire when the body's capability of removing heat is surpassed by the rate at which heat is being generated.

Heat exhaustion transpires when the body cannot sweat enough to keep cool. Signs and symptoms of heat exhaustion include a weak, rapid pulse, headache, muscle cramps, dizziness, nausea, and general weakness. The whole body may feel cool and clammy from perspiration and appear pale, red, or flushed. Since heat exhaustion can lead to heat stroke, a much more serious and life-threatening condition, it is important to terminate the activity, move to a cooler location, drink water, sponge the body with cold water, and lie down if nauseated or dizzy (Kemper, 1999:46).

Heat stroke occurs when the heat-regulating mechanism fails, putting the circulatory system under great strain. In this case, the body stops sweating and the temperature continues to rise, often to 105 degrees or higher. Other symptoms include confusion, delirium, or unconsciousness. The skin is red or flushed and dry, even under the armpits. Emergency treatment is needed to quickly lower the body temperature with cold, wet cloths all over the body or by immersion in cold water. Care is given, however, not to over-cool the body if it falls to 102 degrees. Both heat exhaustion and heat stroke can be prevented by: drinking eight to ten glasses of water per day or more when exercising in hot weather; drinking more liquid than one's thirst requires when exercising strenuously; avoiding strenuous outdoor physical activity during the hottest part of the day; resting often in cool areas on hot days; refraining from sudden changes in temperature; and wearing loose-fitting, light-colored clothing that reflects the sun (Kemper, 1999:46).

As with all outdoor activities, the importance of current first aid knowledge and an adequate first aid kit cannot be emphasized enough. Packers must take care to disinfect water by vigorously boiling for two minutes; adding eight drops of household chlorine bleach to one gallon; adding 20 drops of iodine to one gallon; or following directions on commercial products such as purification tablets or filter.

Low-impact

Hikers and backpackers can help to protect the environment by (also see camping):

1. Blending in.
2. Staying on the trail.
3. Moving off the trail when meeting less mobile trail users.

4. When hiking cross country, spread out, avoid creating trails, and walk on rocks or snow when possible.
5. Follow in one another's footsteps when there is no way to avoid cryptobiotic soil or microbiotic crusts that are unique to arid regions.
5. Selecting campsites that will reduce impact.
6. Packing out what was packed in.
7. Disposing of solid bodily waste properly.

Mountain Bicycling

With their upright handlebars, wide tires, and low gearing, mountain bikes provide cyclists with a non-motorized ability to leave the pavement and enter a world of solitude and beauty. Few activities have exploded on the scene like mountain bicycling. Estimated participation increased, according to the Sporting Goods Manufacturing Association (SGMA), more than 100 percent between 1987 and 1989 from 1.5 million to 3.2 million total user days (Chavez, 1999:245). Today 8,610,000 persons lay claim to mountain bike off-road at least once a year, while another 15,283,000 go mountain biking on-road (U.S. Census Bureau). These numbers may peak, but those who ride may do so more often and go to more places. The majority of these riders, according to profiles, are males who are 30 or more years of age (Chavez, 1999:245-246).

Many of the mountain biking events held in the past few years are attracting hundreds of participants and thousands of viewers (Chavez, 1999:246). Night riding when done with care and with companions may provide a new and different experience. Additionally, a number of recreation sites that were open to other activities are now open to mountain bicyclists. For instance, downhill skiing facilities open to mountain bikes during the off season. Almost overnight mountain bikers discovered roads, trails, and slickrock. Some of the best riding in the world is seen on public lands administered by the BLM in southern Utah. Besides the Moab Slickrock Bike Trails, that have caught international attention, there are thousands of miles of old mining and ranching roads in the area that provide access to some of the most amazing backcountry anywhere. By using no trace etiquette, these and other trails remain open. The popularity of mountain bicycling, however, also led to user conflicts and threats to the environment that caused many trails to close to bikers (IMBA, 2000:1). This rising concern has led many mountain bikers to join clubs and organizations that represent their interests and can help them gain access to various sites (Chavez, 1999:246). These developments also spurred the establishment of the International Mountain Bicycling Association (IMBA), a non-profit, public supported organization that promotes mountain bicycling opportunities that are environmentally sound and socially responsible. Working to keep trails open and in good condition for everyone, the IMBA publicized their six Rules of the Trail in 1988 for land managers to post at trailheads. Today these rules are recognized around the world as the standard code of conduct for mountain bikers (see low-imact below).

Safety

It is always best to ride with two or three riders in backcountry in case of an accident or breakdown. Essential items for backcountry riding include: water bottles, pump, light, tools, and first aid kit. They also carry along the same items as the hiker, such as a whistle, candle, and extra food. Because trail descriptions cannot list every turn, a map and compass are a necessity. Before leaving, it is wise to check the weather and prepare accordingly by bringing along a sweater, wind jacket, rain gear, and bandana. Cyclists generally wear cycling shorts or tights, gloves, sturdy shoes, sunglasses, helmet, and appropriate safety gear. Streams are crossed slowly, at a 90-degree angle. Because bottoms are slippery, walking is preferable. By following the IMBA standard code of conduct below, mountain bicyclers protect their safety as well as their environment.

Low-Impact

The IMBA National Mountain Bike Patrol establishes mountain bikers as land stewards, a much-needed help to over-worked and underbudgeted land mangers who are overwhelmed by recreational demands. As president of the IMBA, Ashley Korenblat explained, "There is a balance between the grace and joy and freedom we all feel from gliding through the woods on our bikes, and the responsibility we have to the land" (Korenblat, 1998:6). Their standard code of conduct encourages mountain bicyclists to protect the trails and themselves by (IMBA, 2000:1-2):

1. Ride on open trails only (by obtaining permits and avoiding closed areas).
2. Leave no trace (by practicing low-impact cycling, considering other riding options when trails are wet and muddy, staying on existing trails, and packing at least as much as was packed in).
3. Control your bicycle (by paying attention and obeying all bicycle speed regulations and recommendations).
4. Always yield the trail (by slowing down, establishing communication, stopping if needed).
5. Never scare animals (by making sudden movements or loud noises—they need extra room and time to adjust; special care when passing; gates left as they were found).
6. Plan ahead (by knowing and preparing equipment, keeping it in good repair; carrying extra supplies, and wearing a helmet and appropriate safety gear).

For low-impact camping information, please see backpacking and camping.

ADVENTURES ON SNOW

Trail adventures continue after leaves have fallen when clean, fresh snow transforms the most humble terrain into a beautiful area ideal for snowshoeing or ski touring and other winter activities. With simple equipment, the adventures below can take place as a brisk outing or as a week-long journey into challenging backcountry, where crowds begin to vanish and the presence of nature intensifies the spirit.

Snowshoeing

By strapping on snowshoes, outdoor adventurers gain access to a winter wonderland of crisp, fresh air and may reach winter wilderness lands that are otherwise inaccessible to skiers because of underbrush or rough terrain. Snowshoes also present a great way to take a look at wildlife from a safe distance. By keeping an appropriate distance, animals are not forced to waste precious energy to run away.

Although invigorating, snowshoeing does not have to be overly strenuous. Even so, the low-impact aerobic activity can burn more calories, 400 to 1000 per hour, than running or cross-country skiing (Potter, 1998 F-12; Lohr, 1999:86). The 2,000-year-old activity originated in the sub-arctic region of what is now Canada among the Inuit (the now-preferred word for people once called Eskimo) and spread to trappers, hunters, loggers, farmers, ice fishermen and fisherwomen, mountaineers, and snowshoe-clad adventurers, who tote their packs into the backcountry. Through the years, modern technology has made the shoes user-friendly. Today's sport snowshoe, constructed from aluminum, rubber, and high-tech materials, are light, durable, and easy to walk on and maintain. As the saying goes, "If you can walk, you can snowshoe." This does not necessarily mean that everyone can do it well, or that they are in condition for it. It does mean that nearly everyone can do it, making it an excellent group activity. If someone seeks a greater challenge, the lead position is a good place to find it. As groups travel single file, leaders take turns doing the more strenuous work of breaking in the trail. Taller leaders need to remember to shorten their normal stride to accommodate anyone shorter following behind.

Flotation, also called buoyancy, is the shoe's ability to allow a person to be supported by the snow. Larger shoes have surface areas that generally provide better flotation, but shoes with smaller surface areas permit a more natural walking gait. New materials have improved the amount of flotation provided by shoes with smaller surface areas. *Decking,* the material that creates the shoe's surface area, is often made of solid sheets of lightweight, tough materials like Hypalon, a rubbery type of nylon known for its resiliency. Vinyl and polyurethane-coated nylon are also used on new models and replace the rawhide webbing strung across the wooden frame on traditional snowshoes. *Bindings* connect boots to snowshoes and differ in style from lace-ups to buckle and ratchet bindings. The *pivot point* is the place where the binding attaches to the frame. *Frames,* made of either traditional wood or lightweight aluminum tubing, come in symmetrical or asymmetrical forms. *Crampons,* also called claws, are spikes that bite into the snowy surface and provide traction in slippery conditions.

Snowshoes are available that are tailored for walking, hiking, and running with different sizes in the walking and hiking lines capable of handling anyone from a child to a person over 300 pounds. When a pack is added it can make a difference, so trying out rented shoes can prove helpful before buying. Ski poles can be carried for balance and for maneuvering in tight spots. The left pole is placed in the snow ahead while the right shoe is carried forward just high enough to lift the front two-thirds of the snowshoe off the snow, dragging the tail behind. The tail pushes the shoe ahead slightly as the traveler steps down, thus allowing more momentum. A rhythmic, rolling gait is established. Other skills are required, including learning to travel on slopes, turning, and recovering from a fall.

For outdoor wear, the polypropylene and fleece garments designed for cross-country skiing work well. Layering allows for weather changes during longer outings and adjustments as the body warms up. Heavy perspiration can cause a quick chill-down later. To transport perspiration away from the body, the first layer, or wicking layer, is composed of long underwear made of synthetic fibers and newer fabric designed to wick the moisture away. Natural fabrics, used in low-exertion activities, do not transport moisture away from the body as readily. The middle layer of clothing, or insulating layer, is composed of wool, fleece, down, or treated materials that trap air around the body to provide warmth. In warmer conditions, the legs do not need this layer. A breathable, waterproof outer layer is best for blocking wind and snow. It should provide enough room for the insulating layer, but not be so big that it allows heat loss. An extra layer of clothing can be carried in a day pack for added warmth when stopping for lunch. Hats, gloves, neck gaiters, balaclava hoods, and headbands add to the comfort. On shorter stints, to accommodate for the generation of body heat from activity, some simply incorporate the "25-degree rule," that is dressing 25 degrees lighter than the weather would normally call for. This does not account for emergencies however.

For the feet, lighter, flexible boots make it easier to snowshoe. Heavier, bulky boots can cause perspiration, which leads to cold feet. Rubber boots do the same, causing the skin to soften and blister easily. In warmer weather, some even use running shoes for quicker travel and running. It is all a matter of comfort. Too many socks tend to cut off circulation, impeding the body's efforts to warm the feet. Wool or blended socks work well with a synthetic liner to help wick away moisture. Gaiters are worn around leggings and boots to help keep the powdery snow from getting inside around the socks.

Snowshoe rentals generally cost less than a lift ticket, and have become popular as a means to getaway from crowds during ski vacations. Guided tours, some offering gourmet lunches, are also available. Meanwhile, cross-country ski centers have become a mecca for snowshoeing, and when ski trails become buried under two feet or more of snow, cross-country skiers may swich to their snowshoes. In parks, such as Adirondack State Park in upstate New

York, there are more than 2,000 miles of snowshoe hiking trails that go through forests of spruce, fir and hardwoods, marshes and swamps, and lakes, rivers, and streams from mid-December until mid-March. At Indian Peaks Wilderness Area in the Rocky Mountains of Colorado in the Arapaho and Roosevelt national forests, snowshoers choose from more than 28 trails of varying difficulty, length, and scenery that pass along mountain lakes, streams, elk, and deer on the way to camping sites or to peak zones, where elevation ranges from 10,000 to 13,500 feet.

Cross-Country Skiing

Many crowded national parks, like Yellowstone and Yosemite, are advocating that the outdoor adventurer take up cross-country skiing for a pristine winter nature experience. The trails are far less crowded in winter and the parks are more peaceful. Cross-country, or Nordic, skiing is exhilarating and far easier to learn than Alpine, or downhill, skiing. Although comparatively new in North America, it originated many centuries ago. In fact, a crude ski unearthed by archaeologists from a Swedish peat bog is estimated to be over 5,000 years old.

Cross-country skiing offers an alternative to the typical summer exploration of crowded parks.

Cross-country skiing may take place on prepared or unprepared trails at parks, golf courses, and at many Alpine ski developments. Bushwhacking, skiing in deep woods and up and down hills, requires precision skills to avoid trees. Wilderness schools offer excellent instruction for backcountry skiing and how to make quick-fix repairs when out in the field. They generally provide lessons in orienteering, snow camping/backpacking, and bushwhacking.

Touring on cross-country skis is simply an extension of walking with the addition of two basic moves: the kick and the glide. The kick occurs as the skier pushes down on one ski, which causes it to grip the snow as the other ski slides or glides forward. The arms swing as if walking, but they carry poles that are placed in the snow in a manner similar to snowshoeing. Poles aid power. As the knee drives ahead, the skier pushes back with the arm and pole on the

same side. Other touring skills include turning, recovering from a fall, sidestepping, climbing in a herringbone pattern, moving downhill, and stopping. None of these skills is too difficult, but practice is needed for them to become natural. Lessons are available through recreational centers, schools and colleges, at ski resorts, and through various outfitters. Like snowshoeing, it is quite possible to learn the basic skills by studying an instructional manual, but the advice of an expert always helps beginners to develop technique and skiers with more experience to excel. Learning on groomed trails also leads to greater success and the chance that the adventurer will develop cross-country skiing as a lifetime sport.

Most skiers select equipment for general touring in groomed areas, but specialized skis, boots, bindings, and poles are available for backcountry and alpine ski touring, telemarking, skate skiing, or racing. Touring skis come in waxable or waxless models. Depending on snow conditions, waxable skis utilize a varying hardness of wax to achieve the grip and glide effect. Because the waxable ski can be adjusted to the weather conditions, they can provide the best performance. Generally speaking, the colder the weather, the harder the wax needed. The results are more significant on dry snow or on a prepared ski track. Waxless skis use a synthetic base to achieve the grip and glide, and they are convenient because they function well in varying snow conditions. For a better glide, glide wax can be applied to the tip and tail sections of the ski. Silicon sprays also help prevent icing. These skis are best suited to soft, new snow or spring snow and in areas where temperatures vary (REI, 1992:2).

In general, longer skis are more stable, but the right length is determined by the skier's weight, height, ability, and the ski design. Providing a hinge between the foot and the ski are the boots. Comfort is the most important feature of the boot. They should flex at the same point where the toes flex. Boots are also designed for touring, mountaineering, and racing. The toe of the boot connects to the ski at the bindings; with the heels unattached. As with snowshoeing, clothing is layered. Pants that do not restrict leg motion are best. Skiers benefit from technological advances in clothing, ski equipment, and ski facilities. Currently technological advancements in ski equipment have achieved an all-time high (Betz et al., 1999:160).

After the boom years of the 1980s, the number of Nordic skiers leveled off in the 1990s, and eventually led to a decline from an estimated 6.5 million to 3.5 million skiers. These years are expected to be followed by a 95 percent increase in participation by the year 2050, with the Rocky Mountain region pulling in a 144 percent participation increase. Meanwhile, the number of commercial cross-country ski areas escalated 51 percent from 1987 to 1996. The recent popularity of snowshoeing brings with it an opportunity for cross-country ski areas to reach out to snowshoers and other trail users. With more than half of the nation's ski centers inviting their skiing customers to rent snowshoes, the industry is constructively working on trail courtesies that will encourage shared trail use. Snowshoers, for example, unknowingly interfere with machine-prepared ski track grooves in the snow (Betz et al., 1999:159-161; Bowker et al., 1999:326).

Safety

Ski centers create comparatively safe alternatives for snow enthusiasts, and the refined trails help them to develop skills, confidence, and preparedness before heading off to local parks, wilderness trails, and the backcountry. Snowmobile trials, maintained by snowmobilers, can be dangerous for snowshoers and cross-country skiers and should not be used unless they are marked for shared trail use. In these cases, great care is necessary, especially among quiet, quick cross-country skiers who run the risk of collisions with snowmobiles at intersections and corners (Betz et al., 1999:161).

The secret of touring safely in the mountains lies in learning how to choose the safest route (Tilton, 1997:5). For instance, the safest routes are usually found on ridgetops, slightly on the windward side from cornices. On the other hand, volcanic peaks above 8,000-10,000 feet present significant hazards. While it is important to always travel with a companion, it is best to find a companion who has traveled the same or similar terrain before. And it is best to always gather as much information about the proposed route of travel as possible. Land managers can usually provide information about avalanche conditions that range from low, moderate, high, and extreme. A low rating means that the route may be taken, although that does not mean there will not be an avalanche. Moderate conditions require extra care, especially on steep snow-covered open slopes and gullies. During high and extreme conditions, the route should not be taken (Tilton, 1997:5; Forest Service, 1994:10)

Before leaving, it is important to know what to do if caught in an avalanche and how others can be helped. An itinerary with information regarding who to contact for search and rescue action is given to someone who will know when and if you returned on time. Even on a day trip, extra food, water, and clothing are taken along, and a sleeping bag can save a life. A collapsible shovel is considered an essential in avalanche territory. Additional basics include an electronic rescue transceivers, avalanche probes and avalanche cord as well as a first aid kit and matches in a waterproof container, candle, fire starter, knife, wide tape for repairs, map, and compass (Tilton, 1997:5; Forest Service, 1994:2).

Because safety always precedes adventure, if dangerous conditions occur, it is best to turn back. Large area slides, called slab avalanches, are often started by victims, while loose snow slides that trap victims are usually triggered by other members of the party if not by natural causes. Dangerous slopes are not traversed, and cornices are not to be disturbed. If dangerous slopes must be crossed, it is advisable to stay high, while avoiding fracture lines and similar snow areas. They are crossed by one person at a time with all party members watching the traveler. The traveler removes ski pole straps and ski safety straps, loosens equipment, and puts on and fastens all clothing. Prudent travelers always watch for evidence of old avalanche paths, recent activity, unusual weather conditions and they listen for sounds of hollow snow or cracks. Although an avalanche can occur in other areas, they are more common at higher elevations; on slopes from 30 to 45 degrees; on convex slopes; and smooth, open slopes. Wind, storms, snowfall, warmer temperature, temperature inversions, and wet snow can create dangerous conditions. (Forest Service, 1994:7-11).

Low-Impact

Snowshoers and cross-country skiers can help to maintain their trails by following these guidelines:

1. Snowshoers stay off of ski tracks.
2. Skiers stay to the right side, and yield to faster skiers and those coming downhill.
3. Skiers get out of the track by lifting their skis parallel and off without disturbing the track.
4. When breaking trail, skiers keep skis wider apart than normal as the trail will narrow with use.
5. Both fill and smooth the trail after a fall.
6. On roads, make the ski track near the edge so snowmobiles can avoid it.

ADVENTURES IN WHITEWATER RIVERS

For thousands of years, the earth's rivers have served as thoroughfares for transportation, exploration, and commerce. Log canoes, reed boats, and crude rafts traversed the rivers past mountains and deserts. The three most common river sport vessels today—the canoe, kayak, and inflatable raft—are descendants of early river history. Each has its own special features and requires independent skills. These modern crafts made of metal, fiberglass, and synthetic material can hit river boulders by the force of currents with little serious damage, enabling skilled adventurers the thrill of moving down fast whitewater currents on rivers just as different as the settings they traverse. Viewing nature from the river offers the enthusiast a unique perspective of the land, its wildlife, and its rare birds, and whitewater boating continues to attract new participants because it offers a degree of risk that challenges the physical and mental skills of the individual and the opportunities to work in groups. Some river craft can be used to explore lakes and wilderness areas, or to reach otherwise impossible terrain for backpacking and for fishing. Outfitters run tours, teach skills, and rent equipment, but the future of whitewater activities depend on the quality and quantity of available opportunities. Overcrowding is a concern on popular whitewater rivers like the Ocoee in Tennessee, the Lower Youghiogheny in Pennsylvania, and the South Fork American in California. Overcrowding can result in quotas and lower the quality of the experience (Cordell et al., 1999:147).

Canoeing

The modern canoe with its fine sturdy workmanship and graceful lines is a descendent of the North American Indian birch-bark canoe (see Figure 15.1). Used for many purposes, the versatile craft is the most popular muscle-powered boat in North America (Cordell, 1999:237; Huser, 1981:32). A good river canoe is designed differently than lake canoes. River canoes generally have higher sides and lack keels, which catch on rocks and reduce maneuverability. A shorter, wider canoe is slower but more maneuverable.

Lakes present the safest way to introduce families to water adventures and skills, and lessons can be arranged at local clubs or recreation organizations such as the YMCA and the Red Cross. For the more challenging adventures on rivers, wise novices join outfitters on a tour. To control and guide a canoe successfully in whitewater, it takes keen concentration and strength for a firm and steady hand. Navigating with a partner is an exercise in teamwork, concentration, and skill. In the slender craft, paddlers fight for control of the river's force by finding safe, exhilarating runs and by battling cross currents to keep the boat from upsetting. The experienced stern paddler in the back of the canoe is responsible for steering and is the master of the "J" stroke, used to keep the canoe on a straight course. The bow paddler paddles on the opposite side, setting the rhythm of the stroke while looking out for rocks or snags. On some trips it is necessary to portage or carry the canoe past shallow or rough waters.

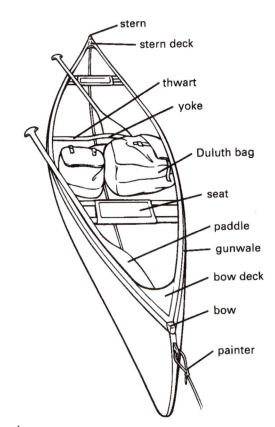

Figure 15.1 Diagram of the components of a typical canoe.

To the joy of paddlers, the route of the Lewis and Clark National Historic Trail includes designated water trail segments where the expedition traveled by canoe, keelboat, or pirogue on the Missouri, Yellowstone, Snake, and Columbia Rivers and their tributaries. Although travelers must cope with a series of dams and impounded lakes in some areas, these segments can be retraced today. In Montana, the Bureau of Land Management administers the 149-mile Upper Missouri National Wild and Scenic River where there are opportunities to retrace a section of the Lewis and Clark route that has changed very little since the Corps of Discovery's exploration. Also exhibiting the river's dynamic character are two stretches—one from Ponca State Park in Nebraska to Gavins Point Dam near Yankton, South Dakota, and a second above Lewis and Clark Lake—administered by the Army

Corps of Engineers through a cooperative effort with the National Park Service (Cordes, 1999:80-81). The Lewis and Clark Bicentennial of 2004-6 promises to only increase adventure opportunities.

Estimates are that more than 20 million individuals 16 years and older participate in canoeing (Leeworthy, 2001:12). Canoeing is projected to increase slightly more than the population growth nationally to 2050, while the number of days spent canoeing is expected to rise 30 percent more than the population growth over the same period. The largest of these increases, about 80 percent, will occur in the North and Pacific Coast regions (Bowker et al., 1999:329).

Kayaking

The kayak is traced back to the Aleutian Inuit of the high Arctic, who built their kayaks by stretching sealskins over driftwood or whalebone frames before rubbing the skins with animal fat to waterproof them. Sleek modern kayaks are designed for challenging whitewater and wilderness touring. They are also used for slalom and river racing, and for lake and ocean adventures. The kayak's exceptional buoyancy allows it to handle fiercer white water. Although faster than a canoe, the longer craft is more difficult to turn. It also lacks the same viewing opportunities provided by the canoe because of the low seating. The low seat, on the other hand, presents outstanding opportunities to view birds and shoreline wildlife. On longer tours, "kayakers" may regret that they do not have as much room for storing camping supplies. They do have the option to travel on their own in a single kayak or with a buddy in a double.

Kayaks are outfitted with seats, foot braces, knee pads, thigh braces, back straps, and grab loops for both bow and stern. The paddler sits in a small cockpit, uses a double-bladed paddle, and is held to the vessel by foot, thigh, and knee braces. A waterproof spray skirt seals in the paddler, protecting against water spray. This can cause the beginner some uncomfortable moments. When the kayak tips, the paddler hangs upside down under the water. For this reason, proper and adequate training is a necessity. While progressing in both directions from either canoe to kayak or kayak to canoe is common, the skills do differ, making lessons and practice sessions essential before rapids are navigated. For instance, control can be tricky in rapids, which seem like waves to the kayaker who sits so close to the water. Because the kayak is so agile, however, the paddler must be in complete control. Skill refinements come only after serious effort and practice. The Nantahala Outdoor Center in Bryson City, North Carolina, offers some 200 clinics for both kayakers and canoeists of various skill and experience levels. Local outfitters schedule lessons and tours as well.

Unlike the designs of a river boat, the newer generation ocean kayak is not designed for speed or maneuverability, but rather for stability and comfort. This larger sea-worthy craft rarely tips over even in moderate to heavy waves. And if it does turn over, the kayaker, who often sits unrestrained in an open deck, is not stuck inside. Recovery by climbing back on board is reportedly easy. Suited for younger or older paddlers alike, as well as people who are physically challenged, these kayaks are billed as unsinkable and self-bailing, meaning that water automatically will drain out. The saying here is that "anyone who can swim can kayak." Ocean kayaking, also known as sea kayaking or bluewater kayak touring, is as different to river kayaking as cross-country is to downhill skiing.

Besides presenting an excellent cardio-vascular workout, kayaking strengthens the arms, shoulders, back muscles, and abdominal muscles, which are very important for low back strength and stability. In turn, isometric pushing of the legs works the hamstrings and thigh muscles. Kayaking also improves balance and coordination. With the popularity of sea kayaking added to statistics, the Outdoor Industry Association found that 6.4 million Americans kayaked in 2000, a whopping 50 percent more than in 1998. Fueling the growth were adventure-seeking middle-

Successful river trips are dependent on the river runner's ability to read hazards and select routes that avoid danger.

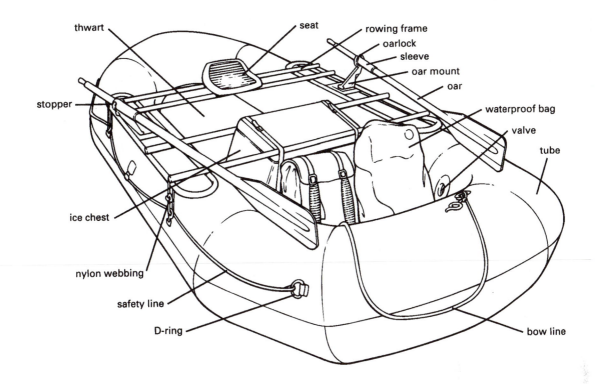

Figure 15.2 Diagram of the typical components of a river raft.

aged adults (Gearon, 2001:14). Interestingly from a carry-over perspective, many of the skills drawn upon for white water paddling are similar to the edge to edge turning and carving techniques used for snow boarding and skiing. Also, the upper body strength and conditioning required for paddling improves upper body endurance for using poles in snowshoeing or cross-country skiing, and overall endurance for mountain biking.

Rafting

Inflatable river rafts, the descendants of life rafts developed for World War II sea rescues, are relatively newer vessels for use with whitewater river running. Rafting, which has undergone dramatic increases in recent years, will undergo a leveling off to some extent to 2015, although sizable increases are expected in Rocky Mountain and Pacific Coast regions (1999:332).

Raft tours provide beginners and others the luxury of traveling through churning rapids with little exertion or any great demands. Rafts are limiting because they only travel downstream, and transportation must be arranged to carry rafters up the river for another run. Ranging in style from inflatables suited for two to larger pontoons capable of holding numerous passengers and equipment, rafts offer a variety of experiences. Exceptionally buoyant, they bounce off boulders and waves that would demolish other boats. Made of puncture-resistant material, the raft is composed of small air chambers that link together. If one chamber is damaged, the remaining flotation chambers retain their buoyancy. A diagram of the typical components of a river raft is shown in Figure 15.2. Rafting is probably safer and easier than other whitewater activities.

Commercial raft trips provide an excellent means to experience river running. Professionals pilot the craft while passengers take a turn at the oars or shift their weight according to command. Guides often prepare meals at rest stops along the river, which provides the guests with additional time for hiking, photography, swimming, and exploration. Incidentally, plastic bags are inadequate protection for cameras. Most people use army surplus ammo boxes, pelican-style camera boxes, and plastic products that enclose cameras. In Yellowstone, float trips down the Yellowstone River provide tourists with outstanding opportunities to view wildlife. A trip in Canyonlands National Park floats past ancient Anasazi ruins and petroglyphs carved in rock. The Upper Gauley in West Virginia races passengers through thrilling, swirling Class V river challenges, not meant for beginners or the faint-of-heart.

River Safety

Successful river trips are dependent on the river runner's ability to read hazards and select routes that avoid danger. Guidebooks, U.S. Geological Survey maps, rangers, and wilderness outfitters are consulted before a downriver adventure is attempted. The ability to swim is essential; life jackets or personal floatation devices (PFDs) are a must; and skillful boat handling is important but not enough. The adventurer needs to know how to read water and weather. Rivers have common features such as wide V-patterns, known as tongues, which point the way downstream between rocks. V-patterns pointing upstream warn of submerged boulders, while a horizontal line indicates that a dam or vertical drop lies ahead. Dangerous water traps called suckholes form when water flows over an obstacle with force causing the flow to reverse at the obstacles' base. These currents may form a hole that can trap a boat. Eddies or pools of calm water that tend to collect debris can be found in the midst of raging streams. They can provide a refuge, a place to relax and judge the next set of rapids (David & Moran, 1983:24). Even before entering the craft, efforts should be made to identify rough water, boulders, and other obstacles from shore.

River running is an exciting risk activity. Life jackets, boating helmets, and protective sport shoes are worn. Rubber wet suits provide protection against hypothermia if the wearer is thrown into cold waters. When capsized, the general rule is to stay with the craft, since it should be able to support the passengers, even when filled with water. Ropes, attached to the craft, allow the boater to hang on with one hand while paddling to shore with the other. Containers for boiling water, safety lines for rescues, extra flotation devices, emergency rations, first aid kits, and extra paddles are all carried along. Clothing items include a wool hat, wool or synthetic sweater, wool socks, gloves, windbreaker, rain parka or paddling jacket, swimsuit, and a change of clothes for after river running. Other items include a hat for shore, suntan lotion, and bug repellent. Equipment is always checked to be sure that it is in good repair, and appropriate repair materials are taken along. All supplies should be placed in waterproof protectors that are strapped to the craft. One should never boat alone. A minimum of three boats and boaters should travel together and maintain visual communication. Local rules are followed.

A river trip is not attempted until the necessary skills are mastered in calm water. Rivers of higher levels are attempted only after lower grades are mastered. A shortened version of the standard rating system used to compare difficulty throughout the world, called The International Rating Scale for Whitewater Rivers, follows:

Class I: Easy. Fast-moving water with a few riffles and small waves. Few or no obstructions with slight risk to swimmers:

Class II: Novice. Easy rapids with obvious channels. Rocks and waves are easily missed by trained paddlers. Some maneuvering is required, but no scouting is necessary. Swimmers are seldom injured.

Class III: Intermediate. Rapids with moderate, irregular waves are capable of swamping an open canoe. Fast current in narrow passages require complex maneuvers. Large waves or strainers can be easily avoided. The inexperienced should scout. Injuries to swimmers are rare and self-rescue possible. Group assistance may be required, however, to avoid long swims.

Class IV: Advanced. Intense, powerful, but predictable rapids with constricted passages that often require precise maneuvering in turbulent waters. There may be large, unavoidable waves and holes. Scouting from shore is necessary. Risk of injury to swimmers is moderate to high, and rescue may be difficult.

Class V: Expert. Extremely long, obstructed, or very violent rapids expose a paddler to added risk. Drops may contain large, unavoidable waves and holes or steep, congested chutes with complex, demanding routes. Rapids may continue for long distances between pools, demanding a high level of fitness. What eddies exist may be small, turbulent, or hard to reach. Rescue is difficult and there is significant hazard to life. Scouting is recommended but may be difficult. Swims are dangerous, and rescue is often difficult even for experts. Proper equipment, extensive experience, and practiced rescue skills are essential.

Class VI: Extreme and Exploratory. These runs have almost never been attempted and often exemplify the extremes of difficulty, unpredictability, and danger. The consequences of errors are very severe and rescue may be impossible. This class is for teams of experts only, at favorable water levels, after close personal inspection and after taking all precautions. After a Class VI rapid has been run many times, the rating may be changed to an appropriate Class V rating.

Low-impact

Each river has different guidelines to follow for minimum-impact techniques that should be observed. On some rivers, campsites are assigned. When a choice may be made, camps are made on non-vegetated sites. Some areas stress making camp below the waterline, so that any possible trace of your passing is washed away with later floods. The following guidelines can help keep campsites in good shape:

1. Everything packed in, is packed out.
2. Since open fires result in ashes, charcoal, partially burnt garbage, and blackened fire rings, pack stoves are used.
3. Dishwashing is done at least 200 feet away from any side streams with small amounts of biodegradable soap. The water is then strained and scattered.
4. Where there are no toilets, there are several commercially available portable toilet-type devices that solve the human waste problems. Otherwise, leak-resistant methods to pack out solid human waste can be devised from ammo cans, heavy duty plastic bags, and Aqua Chem or bleach.
5. By camping only on durable surfaces in remote areas and staying in well-established campsites in popular areas, it is possible to minimize changes to the landscape and prevent the proliferation of unnecessary campsites.
6. If there is no established campsite or no suitable sandy beach for a site, be sure to camp at

least 100 feet from the river, and 200 feet from side streams and springs. Take alternate paths to the river and between tent sites. This will help protect the fragile riverside ecosystem known as the riparian area. Wildlife depend on this zone for food, water, cover, and shelter, and it is a natural travel route for migratory birds and animals.

7. Avoid sites for camping that show slight use. With time and rest, these sites may revert back to their natural appearance if left alone. If not left alone, a certain trampling threshold may be reached from which the area may become barren. It can be reached after only a couple tramplings in one season. Then the site expands and deteriorates rapidly, and non-native and noxious weeds may be encouraged to grow that provide poor forage for wildlife.

8. Prior to leaving, naturalize the area by covering up scuffed up areas with native materials such as pine needles and rake matted grassy areas with a stick to help recovery.

9. Follow the suggestions in the camping section of this chapter for general low-impact camp techniques.

ADVENTURES IN THE OCEAN

The ocean can invade the senses with its unique environment, its own geology, and its life forms. The ocean's mystery is intensified by its moods and contrasts between its wild nature and serenity. It may even be this very characteristic that induces us to explore its depths and its tidepools, and to exhilarate in its challenges.

Skin Diving and SCUBA Diving

Diving underwater dates back to the earliest of times. Eventually human lungs were aided by air-filled animal bladders, and then the development of the air compressor in the early 1800s opened the way for the modern era of underwater sea diving. By 1819, Augustus Siebe of England developed the forerunner of the modern diving outfit. In 1943 Jacques-Yves Cousteau and Emile Gagnan introduced the aqualung, which regulated air automatically in relation to the depth of the diver. By the 1960s SCUBA diving (that is, diving with a Self-Contained Underwater Breathing Apparatus) had become the fastest-growing American activity, and by the 1970s an estimated 10 percent of the population owned some type of diving gear (Fisher & Brown, 1979: 297; Sullivan, 1965: 1-9). Today's bright array of equipment allows the underwater adventurer to explore a unique, fascinating, and peaceful world. In the United States, there are 8.5 million certified SCUBA divers of which 72 percent are male and 28 percent are female. Their average age is 36 and income is $50,000 (PADI, 2001:1). Based on the most recent figures taken in the mid-1990s, it is estimated that 14.5 million United States citizens 16 and over are snorkeling and SCUBA diving, and they take 57.2 million snorkeling/SCUBA diving trips per year (Cordell et al., 1999:231).

Supervised lessons are essential. Many enthusiasts start by trying the older, simpler, and inexpensive skindiving (also called snorkeling, free diving, or breath-hold diving; (Berger, 2000:24). Snorkeling, a popular family activity, teaches valuable SCUBA skills, including breathing through a mouthpiece with a snorkel, and using a mask and fins. By diving down, a snorkeler can explore a reef from top to bottom, much like a SCUBA diver. Free divers, however, can explore only as long as they can hold their breath. The snorkel is not useful for breathing unless the snorkeler returns to the surface of the water where the breathing activity takes place.

Many SCUBA divers prefer shallow dives as well because that is where the light and color are better. They build slowly to deeper depths under the supervision of a teacher, generally on guided dives. SCUBA lessons are available at many ocean resorts, schools and colleges, recreational centers, community organizations, and SCUBA clubs and organizations. Certification is necessary to go on a dive, rent equipment, or fill up an air tank. Participants that decide to pursue certification (or C card) must be at least 12 years of age to enroll in a SCUBA course. Organizations that certify divers and train instructors are included at the end of this chapter. Their requirements for certification are similar, although classroom time, philosophy, and teacher training differ. Most require a physical, swim test, and about 16 to 24 hours of classroom and pool use followed by four or five hours of open-water dives (Berger, 2000:18). Some classes are intensive, while others run over a stretch of time. Some courses do their open-water dives at tropical destinations. Without appropriate attention and reassurance at this phase, divers tend to drop out, finding the ocean dive a traumatic experience. For this reason, it is wise to do some research first and/or to interview instructors to find out the ratio of pupils per teacher at open-water dives. Once certification is obtained, it is important to keep up with skills and/or take a refresher course. Advanced courses are available, and lessons in photography, wreck diving, and night diving are offered through several diving shops and clubs. Cave and ice diving are a few of the diving activities done today.

Safety

Before diving it is important to be in good physical health. A medical examination is highly recommended. All divers should be competent swimmers. A 1974 Los Angeles County SCUBA diving ordinance required that new divers demonstrate the ability to swim continuously for 200 yards without swimming aids; swim 50 feet underwater without swimming aids; swim 50 yards towing another person without swimming aids; float and/or tread water with minimal movement for 10 minutes; and tread water with legs only for 20 seconds (Fisher & Brown, 1979:301).

Using rental gear is generally satisfactory when taking classes or when limited to

a few dives a year. Caution is applied particularly when renting SCUBA gear in some countries, where faulty equipment has led to unfortunate mishaps. To avoid accidents, participants may be required to wear inflatable snorkeling vests and plant dive flags within 50 feet of them and at locations that mark where a diver is. Nylon or Lycra suits provide protection against sunburn and accidental coral encounters and are handy for long swims, when snorkelers become cooler than they realize. Weights worn with a quick-release belt to aid diving are correctly weighted to allow buoyancy at the surface. Before descending, a few breaths are taken prior to holding the breath. Too many, though, can cause hyperventilation. All ascents are made looking up to the surface for boats and other objects. Snorkelers should be aware that a mask on the forehead means distress.

SCUBA instruction includes coverage of many safety measures. For example, how to react to an emergency situation such as an air shortage, or what to do if another diver is stricken in the water. Divers know the location of the nearest decompression chamber, the local rescue telephone numbers, and how to use a diver's flag and underwater distress signals. Signals are listed in the *U.S. Navy Diving Manual*. They do not go beyond their experience or wear gear that they have not been trained to use. In addition, all divers check weather conditions, local tides and currents, and inspect their equipment. Observing the buddy system and joining a diver who knows the local waters is important in unfamiliar areas. Many resorts, charter boats, and SCUBA clubs offer convenient trips with locals who are familiar with the waters. First aid and repair kits are assembled, and divers know how to prevent and respond to hyperthermia, dehydration, heat exhaustion, and heatstroke. They attempt to stay in good shape, and avoid alcohol, cigarettes, and drugs before diving.

The fear of a shark attack is often exaggerated. Among the roughly 360 shark species, only a score appear to attack humans. Humans are a greater danger to sharks, threatening some with extinction.

Shark aggression is not consistent, but attacks are generally more frequent in tropical and subtropical seas and whenever water temperatures are over 70F. Sharks may alter their normal habits and become dangerous when attracted, for example, by blood, flashing lights, colored materials, or splashing water. They tend to sneak up from behind, attacking a nonmoving part (Cahill, 1990). Cousteau equipped his divers with shafts of wood or aluminum over three feet long. Small nails were placed in one end in circular formation. The nails were long enough to be felt, but not so long or sharp as to injure the shark or to aggravate an attack. Cousteau's divers also pioneered the use of cages that divers could climb into if threatened. They also operated in pairs, back-to-back, if an attack seemed probable. Some chemical repellents have received negligible success. Air bubbling from a diver's aqualung has deterred some sharks (Steel, 1985:39-41).

Other dangerous creatures include the great barracuda, octopus, and the killer whale. Groupers swim around rocks, caverns, and old wrecks; the moray eel may lurk beneath rocks and coral; and jellyfish and sea urchins are found in the deep. The stingray, if stepped on, can puncture the foot or leg with its tail, injecting a venom that produces severe pain. All divers must always be aware and cautious. If dangerous predators are seen, it is advisable to keep away and get out of the water. With the proper precautions, diving can be enjoyed for a lifetime.

The Florida Department of Natural Resources recommends the following safeguards:

1. Never dive alone.
2. Participate in appropriate training.
3. Display a diver-down flag when in the water.
4. Be aware of other boats and diver-down flags.
5. Do not dive in narrow channels where you are a hazard to navigation.
6. Avoid direct contact with corals.

Contact may kill them or cause infection or disease, and divers risk an allergic reaction.
7. Don't feed fish, as it often attracts predators such as sharks and barracuda. Certain foods eaten by humans can be unhealthy and often fatal to fish.
8. Be aware of potentially dangerous sea life.
9. A boat operator should remain on board when divers are in the water. Divers should begin the dive by proceeding upcurrent from the boat. Strong currents can carry divers far from the boat.

Low-impact

The Divers Alert Network focuses on diver safety and has a responsible Diver's Code. In this case, "divers take nothing but pictures, and leave nothing but bubbles." All divers can help protect the underwater environment in the following ways (NOAA &PADI, 1993):

1. Dive carefully in fragile ecosystems, such as coral (and avoid silting up the bottom).
2. Be aware of body equipment placement when diving.
3. Keep diving skill sharp with continuing education.
4. Be considerate of aquatic life.
5. Understand and respect underwater life.
6. Resist the urge to collect souvenirs.
7. All hunting laws and restrictions are obeyed. Do not spearfish in areas that other divers are using.
8. Report environmental disturbances or destruction.
9. Be a role model for others.
10. Get involved in local environmental activities and issues.

Windsurfing

Windsurfing or sailboarding quickly developed into a popular outdoor activity throughout the world, and it is estimated that 1.7 million individuals 16 years of age or older participate in the United States (Leeworthy, 2001:12). A combination of sailing, surfing, water-skiing, and hang gliding, its early beginnings are difficult to attribute. The ancient Polynesians and the early surfers deserve credit, but sailor and aeronautical engineer Jim Drake and surfer Hoyle Schweitzer are the 1968 inventors of the Windsurfer that drew their two activities together into a new hybrid. Pioneered in the United States, it was first popularized in Europe, where Europeans produced their own designs. By the 1980s, windsurfing underwent extraordinary growth. Equipment development progressed, racing participation increased, the World Cup tour was initiated, and, as a sport, it was awarded Olympics status at the Los Angeles Games in 1984. Now there are destination resorts all over the world and prime locations, including premiere destinations in Aruba, Hawaii, Florida, and North Carolina. Based on figures from the studies made in the mid-1990s, it is estimated that United States citizens take 5.91 million trips a year in order to windsurf to do so (Cordell et al., 1999:231).

Windsurfing is not confined to the ocean. In fact, calmer waters are recommended for beginners before progressing to wave sailing. The Hood River Event Site on the Columbia River in Oregon is the site of international windsufing events. The park is also available to amateurs. With appropriate instruction and equipment, beginners can learn to windsurf in a few hours. The skills are not difficult to master and are easy to remember. Certified instructors offer individual and group lessons. Lessons are available through local windsurfing shops and schools across the country (see Windsurfing at the end of the chapter). Top professionals also conduct nationwide clinic tours at the prime windsurfing beaches. Because equipment has become much lighter, easier to use, and more reliable, learning has only gotten easier. Requiring finesse more than strength has made windsurfing attractive to all ages and to girls and women. To the surprise of many, a good, basic set-up is relatively inexpensive, and it can be used for a lifetime of general light-wind sailing.

Light-wind windsurfing takes place in winds of 10 knots or under. *Cruising* from point to point is the simplest and most popular form. Freestyle involves putting the board and sail through a series of turns, spins, and maneuvers and is done by all levels of sailors. *High-wind windsurfing*, done in winds over 10 knots and generally at a range from 15 to 25 knots, appeals to some advanced sailors. The most popular style is slalom sailing, where exhilarating runs and high-speed runs are done on slalom boards at speeds up to 40 miles per hour. *Bump-and-jump-sailing* is accomplished when the winds are good and the waters are choppy, and sailors can make spectacular jumps, turns, and loops. The most spectacular and most difficult, *wavesailing*, is practiced on open swells breaking parallel to the beach and when the wind is blowing along the beach or sideshore (Windsurfer, 2000:1-2).

For any wind conditions, windsurfing equipment is composed of five primary pieces: board, sail, mast, boom, and mast base. When a sail, mast, boom and base are put together, it is called a *rig*. The board carries a universal joint capable of swinging completely around, and the universal joint carries the mast to which the sail is attached. Sailors hold on to the boom. Longboards are used for light-wind windsurfing and longboard racing, while smaller more maneuverable boards are used for high-wind windsurfing. Smaller boards go faster, but require more agility and quicker reflexes to handle. Bigger sales are used in lighter wind. Smaller sails with their smaller area to collect wind is needed for strong winds so that the sailor can hang on. Beginners use a smaller sail to learn. Most boards have footstraps, which are used by experts to keep them aboard when traveling at high speeds or for wave jumping and fun boarding. Tandem windsurfing is done on a board for two. A board built for three is called a tridem. Windsurfing boards have also been adapted for use on land, ice, and snow.

Safety

A Progress Chart is available for windsurfers to match their abilities with skill level, including the beginner, novice, intermediate, advanced, expert, and professional. Since one of the greatest dangers is colliding with commercial vessels and swimmers, windsurfers stay clear of motorboats, learn right-of-way rules, avoid swimmers, and avert waves that break on the beach. Windsurfers swim well; learn self-help techniques, including how to recognize hypothermia; sail with others and tell someone where they are; and avoid sailing in poor conditions, including night hours. Simple safety rules follow (windsurfer.com, 2000:1-2):

1. In the rare event that the board and rig are separated, stay with the board for flotation.
2. Prepare for the conditions by wearing a wetsuit, drysuit, buoyancy aid; visor; booties; and sunscreen.
3. Know the sailing site, including boat traffic patterns and weather conditions that will likely be encountered. Check tides and other dangers.
4. Learn the International Distress Signal. If in serious need of help while on the water, sit on the board and raise and lower your arms above your head and down to your sides.
5. Before sailing, learn to read the wind by looking at a flag, tossing some sand, etc., sailing accordingly.

ADVENTURES IN THE AIR

Humans have always envied birds' ability to fly. Outdoor enthusiasts can achieve the feeling of conquering gravity by taking part in adventures in the air. A new world awaits those who dare to soar above. Vistas sweep far below and off to the horizon, while gentle breezes beckon. For those who prefer to have their feet on the ground, gliders, hot-air balloons, and parachutes provide a relaxing backdrop for picnics or as the focus at an outdoor festival or event.

Hang Gliding

According to legend it was Daedalus, held in exile on the island of Crete, who fashioned a set of wings to suspend himself into the air. King Minos told him he would never be permitted to travel by land or sea, but the air was free, so he studied the flight of birds. After devising a set of wings for himself and his son, they flew into the air. His son Icarus flew higher, and higher trying to reach the sun, until the wax holding the feathers to the framework began to melt. Disaster came when the feathers detached and Icarus fell into the sea (Oiney, 1976: 27-28).

Today the dream of flying is accomplished by hang gliders, who launch from mountaintops, ski slopes, and sand dunes. While the majority of pilots fly their entire careers without sustaining a serious injury, great care is required (Mackey & Leonard, 1995:2). Aviation is not very forgiving if a careless judgment is made in error. For this reason, beginners should under no conditions try this high-risk activity without the supervision of a competent certified instructor. The United States Hang Gliding Association (USHGA) certifies hang gliding instructors and schools. This program consists of a standardized set of flying skills corresponding to a series of pilot proficiency rates (Beginner through Master), each carrying a set of recommended operating limitations.

Hang Gliders launch from just about any slope that is relatively free from obstructions, is steeper than about 6 to 1, and faces into the wind. Depending on the flight sight, ideal winds for launching and landing vary from five to 20 miles per hour, but pilots safely launch, fly, and land in winds from zero to 30 (Mackey & Leonard, 1995:2-3). Attached to the underside of their gliders' wings, which look like large triangles, pilots provide the energy for launching and landing with their legs. To launch, they hold on to the control bar and quickly run downhill into the wind. Thus, the expression, "If you can jog while bal-

Certified instructors teach this high-risk activity at schools certified by the United States Hang Gliding Association.

ancing a 50- to 70-pound weight on your shoulders, you can learn to fly!" In actuality, flying does not require great strength, because the straps, not the pilot's arms, hold the pilot up. Long flights in turbulent conditions require a moderate degree of upper-body endurance that generally develops as the pilot progresses through training (Mackey & Leonard, 1995:3).

Once airborne, wind speed is less important, since the pilot controls the speed of the glider. Speed is increased or decreased by pulling the bar forward or backward, respectively. Riding underneath the glider, the pilot hangs from a harness (thus the name "hang" glider) and is capable of controlling the wing with the trapeze, a triangle of tubing that extends straight down under the wing structure in front of the pilot's body. By moving the body to one side, the glider will tilt and turn to the desired direction. To go up and

ride an air draft, the pilot pushes back. Landing judgments are instantaneous as hesitations can prove fatal. For a perfect landing, the glider is in a stall the moment the feet touch the ground. Even so, pilots must start running immediately in order to prevent the forward momentum from pulling them off balance (Dean, 1982: 59-61; Fisher & Brown, 1979:354).

On good days, pilots land when the sun goes down, but flight time is all a matter of conditions and altitude. In summers in the western United States, pilots typically reach altitudes of 5,000 to 10,000 feet AGL and fly over 100 miles, but flights in excess of 300 miles in length and altitudes of well over 17,999 feet MSL have been recorded. Since air temperature tends to fall by about four degrees (F) for every 1000 foot gain in elevation, high altitude pilots that expect to fly over 12 to 14,000 feet in the summer will generally require warm clothing to protect them against exposure (Mackey & Leonard, 1995:3). Safety gear includes high shoes to protect the ankles, knee and elbow protectors, long pants, and a crash helmet. Gliders in the United States are certified for airworthiness by the Hang Glider Manufacturers Association (HGMA).

Although time required for training varies with the student's innate skills and the type of training conditions, most students obtain the first two USHGA ratings, Beginner and Novice, after taking five to ten lessons through a period of three to six months. In one day, a student learns the rudiments of flight. By the end of the primary training process, students are usually flying in moderate altitudes from several hundred to a few thousand feet in relatively mild conditions (Mackey & Leonard, 1995:4-5).

Since flying depends more on balance and endurance than brute strength, hang glider pilots range in age from teens to octagenarians. About 10 to 15 percent of the pilots in the United States are women. Since most pilots range in weight from 90 to 250 pounds, it can be difficult for anyone beyond this range to find equipment, although heavier pilots may use specially designed tandem gliders. Harness and glider modification may be necessary for individuals outside the range of 5 to 6.5 feet tall (Mackey & Leonard, 1995:3-5). One veteran finds that hang gliding appeals to the person who wants to be detached and free to enjoy nature: It's not just I-can-do everything daredevil" (Doll, 1990:C1).

Safety

Instructors usually provide training equipment through the Beginner rating as part of their package. More advanced students obtain their own equipment, a serious and costly endeavor. Instructors generally offer sound advice to get started on the search. Importantly, if used equipment is purchased as a cost-saving measure, it is critical that an experienced pilot familiar with equipment goes along for inspection and approval. Some will have

degraded sails, dented or bent frame parts, kinked wires, rust on the hardware, or are simply difficult to fly safely. Because current aircraft are more nimble and forgiving, purchasing a new glider in the pilot's class and weight range is recommended. These glides are also pre-tuned and test flown to ensure that the glider will fly as close as possible to one that the customer test flew (Meadows, 1994:1-4). Likewise, seeking a good price when selecting a school is secondary to looking for professionalism and skill. Rated pilots do not fly beyond their proficiency rating. Progression to more difficult flying conditions continues under the supervision of more experienced pilots or Observers/ Advanced Instructors (Mackey & Leonard, 1995:4).

Hot-Air Ballooning

Hot-air ballooning began in 1782 in France when two paper makers, Joseph and Etienne Montgolfier, launched the first hot-air balloon. They had noticed burning pieces of paper flying up the chimney and tried to float small bags over the kitchen fire. Later they constructed a much larger bag of paper and linen, filled it with smoke from burning straw, and watched it drift away. By 1783, the first balloonist was lifted from earth. Today's hot-air balloons are highly maneuverable, allowing more adventurers to float in the sky and create a brightly colored scene for viewers below.

Hot-air balloon rallies are held in beautiful locations that allow spectacular views. The world's largest ballooning event, the Albuquerque International Balloon Fiesta, is held in New Mexico every October. As the official ballooning branch of the United States National Aeronautic Association, the Balloon Federation of America (BFA) organizes and operates the United States National Balloon Championships as well as other competitions, and selects United States representative pilots for participation in World Championships and the world's most prestigious gas balloon race, the Coupe Aeronautic Gordon Bennett, also referred to as the Gordon Bennet Cup.

Ballooning equipment is expensive, but once acquired, the only cost remaining is the propane used for an average flight of two hours. The average diameter of a balloon is 55 feet, with a height of 70 feet. The envelope, or bag, is made of nylon or dacron, a very light but very strong material. The envelope can weight from 150 to 300 pounds. The basket weighs from 300 to 700 pounds and the fan from 75 to 150 pounds (BFA, 1999:2). The crew, ideally consisting of the pilot, crew chief, and three other members, work together throughout the flight on the assembly, launch, chase, and landing. After clearing the launch site, they pull the heavy envelope and basket out of the trailer for the *assembly*, and help the pilot install upright poles and set the burner unit in place. Only the pilot can make connections to propane tanks (Carlton, 2000:1). Helping with the *launch*, crew place their weight on the basket, keeping one foot on the ground at all times. After releasing the tie-off rope, the balloon begins its ascent.

Basically a balloon drifts with the wind. The pilot adjusts the altitude by regulating the temperature of the air within the envelope, and higher or lower altitudes may offer wind currents of different directions. The crew chief directs operations on the ground, which starts with the *chase*. The chase involves driving in front of the balloon to look for and get permission for the landing. Most landowners are obliging, but it may be necessary for the crew chief to explain the necessity of an unplanned landing. On a rare occasion that a landowner is especially concerned, this is communicated to the pilot who may elect to fly on. Crew members keep eye contact with the balloon. The pilot can land the balloon without the crew, but they can be very helpful provided that they do not get in front of it. During the *landing* and recovery, crews catch the balloon by the sides or the back as it hits the ground and place their weight on the basket until the pilot tells them to gather in the envelope. Landowners, crew, passengers, and pilot often celebrate the landing together with champaign and soft drinks. Crews are not

The desert provides favorable wind currents for hot-air ballooning.

Rallies present excellent opportunities for the beginning enthusiast to learn about piloting skills since volunteers are frequently needed to offer services (and respond to orders) when the balloons are being prepared for inflation and launching. Preparations begin before sunrise in order to avoid dangerous air turbulence caused later in the day as the sun begins to heat wind currents in the atmosphere. Sunset flights are also popular. Formal rides can be arranged through balloon companies and tours. The balloons can carry from four to eight passengers. Commercial pilots should be FAA licensed and have many hours of flying experience. Balloons have also been used for air safaris in Africa as a means to observe the animals and by risk-taking bungee jumpers who have taken their leap from balloons.

to help a pilot who has had anything alcoholic within eight hours of the flight (BFJ, 1999:1).

Ballooning injuries are infrequent. Fatalities are the exception. Lessons may be arranged through balloon touring companies, schools, or manufacturers. Training includes both practical and theoretical experience. The school's safety record should be checked before lessons are begun. Balloons used for lessons and rental need to be FAA certified. In many countries, instructor ratings are awarded to pilots of sufficient skill and experience. Examiners are appointed by the balloon club on behalf of the national aviation authority to certify that a student has achieved a safe level of competence in practical and theoretical instruction. Flying hours are required to qualify for a license. Medical standards for ballooning are much lower than for aircraft licenses (Wirth, 1980:146). Attire is cotton-based and casual to include long pants and long sleeves, hiking boots, jacket or sweater, and leather gloves (crews also wear gloves because oil from hands will deteriorate nylon). Warmer clothes are generally not needed, because the propane burners, which heat the air inside the balloon, keep the passengers warm in the gondola.

Safety

The BFA provides a long list of crew advice and safety information as much needs to be done to provide a safe trip. Some tips follow (Carlton, 1999:1-2):

1. Do not smoke.
2. Be careful around ropes, and never wrap them around any part of you.
3. Keep hair and loose items away from the fan.
4. Pay attention at all times to your surroundings.
5. Do not get in front of a moving basket.
6. Always keep one foot on the ground unless in the basket.
7. Know where and how to use fire extinguishers.
8. Have a lost balloon phone number.
9. Be aware of hot burners.
10. Follow the pilot's directions.

Skydiving

Panoramic views are enjoyed by skydivers, who claim that the experience of jumping from aircraft is more like flying than falling. Leonardo da Vinci is credited with the design of a parachute that was dropped off the Tower of Pisa in Italy. Since a skydive requires aircraft, this probably did not occur until the 18th century when Frenchman Andre Garnerin jumped out of an air balloon. By the early 20th century, "barnstormers" began stunt flying, which eventually included jumping out of airplanes with parachutes. After World War II, many of the trained ex-paratroopers who wanted to continue jumping organized jumping clubs for small groups of enthusiasts. A jump made from a small airplane for fun was soon known as sport parachuting. A few of these pioneers proved that parachuting was not limited to low-altitude jumps with parachutes that automatically opened by a static line attached to the departure aircraft. This led to *skydiving*, a term that appeared later to define the experience of jumping from an aircraft in flight in order to enjoy the experience of falling free prior to pulling the chute for a safe landing. For skydiving, the record for the longest freefall occurred in 1961 when Colonel Joseph Kittinger, Jr. jumped from a balloon at 102,000 feet, although many-time world champion skydiver Cheryl Steams hopes to break the record (USPA, 2001:1-3). Skydiving quickly became one of the fastest-growing high-risk activities in the United States with an average of over 4,000 jumps a day made for fun and adventure (Dean, 1982:119). During the 1990s, the number of jumps made annually doubled, with more than 350,000 people making about 3.3 million jumps a year. It should be noted here that although some skydivers have become *fixed-object* jumpers using similar equipment, it is a separate and distinct activity (USPA, 2001:4).

There are many reason for skydiving's popularity. Many Americans are looking for more adventurous sports, motion pictures have used skydiving as an underlying theme, and the ability to take air-to-air videos shows how skydiving can be. More importantly, the advancements in equipment and techniques have made parachuting safer. Automatic activation devices reduced fatal accidents, and ram-air parachutes, developed in the 1960s, made landings soft and fun. While traditional round parachutes, often referred to as canopies, offered a slow vertical descent, it was discovered in the 1950s that jumpers could move laterally if holes were cut in the back of the canopy. Ram parachutes, shaped like an aircraft wing or *airfoil,* retain a slow descent and generate lift that makes steering possible when the skydiver distorts the airfoil with special steering lines. By pulling down on both rear steering lines, for example, the canopy could raise its "angle of attack" to the relative wind. Since it also increases drag, which slows the skydiver while momentarily increasing lift, the jumper is allowed to land slowly and gently. School and camps use older, round canopies for supervised children's exercises and games, but they are getting harder to find.

Freefall time depends on the height of the jump or the exit from the airplane to the point where the jumper ends the freefall by pulling the ripcord or cable that holds the parachute pack together, thereby causing the parachute to release. This action prompts a tug to the shoulders as the jumper begins the float to the ground, but landings can be so soft that the jumper remains standing. The higher the airplane the longer the freefall opportunity. Experienced jumpers, sometimes working in groups, make formations in the sky during the freefall. Group jumping is more difficult and dangerous, because there is always a chance that the parachute lines could become entangled. Group skydivers must allow themselves time to move away from each other after the formation in order to open their parachutes.

Despite the inherent dangers, people are attracted to skydiving due to the excitement and adventure. They also find the adventure satisfying because it provides a feeling of accomplishment in overcoming gravity and the basic human fear of falling (Benson, 1979:43). Like hang gliding, sessions are scheduled at parachuting schools and clubs with skilled instructors and sound equipment. Parachute clubs and centers offering lessons are located throughout the United States. Those associated with the United States Parachute Association (USPA) are likely to be a good choice because the courses are taught by certified instructors who must follow basic safety regulations. USPA rules allow minors as young as 16 to skydive with written parental or guardian consent, but schools may set their own standards.

The *static line or instructor-assisted deployment*, where the student jumps and the parachute opens right away automatically, and *harness-hold*, where two USPA Accelerated Freefall Jumpmasters go alongside in freefall holding on until the student opens the parachute, are part of progressive multiple-jump training courses. Instruction for this package commonly includes an orientation, information regarding use of equipment and the inspection of equipment, parachute packing, instruction for malfunction, and drill in emergency procedures. Skill instruction ordinarily entails appropriate techniques for the jump, steering and control, landing preparation, and proper landing falls. Most people who just make one jump make the *tandem* jump, where the student and the instructor jump out, freefall, and land together under the same parachute system. For a tandem jump, the amount of preparation time varies from a few minutes to a full course, depending on the student's objectives and the school's administration strategy. Because more training is needed for multiple jump training, students pay a heftier price. One solo jump can also be accomplished after a day of lessons. Each drop zone sets its own jump training prices based upon its operating costs and the school's objectives. Lessons usually include equipment, and some lessons may include the cost of an airplane for the jump. Students should be prepared for possible delays due to weather conditions or other factors. Typical clothes and sneakers worn for outdoor activities are appropriate. Generally those wishing to purchase equipment start the process with their drop zone's instructional staff or the pro shop at the school or center (USPA, 2001:5-10).

Safety

Skydiving is self-regulated activity, meaning that skydivers voluntarily follow a set of basic safety requirements set by the USPA. While there are some federal rules established by the Federal Aviation Administration, most apply to the aircraft from which skydivers jump. Just as SCUBA diving can become more dangerous at lower depths, skydiving risks can increase with altitude. During the 1990s, the average number of fatalities per year was 30 or approximately one per 111,000 jumps. Very few of these involve student skydivers, even though they compose the bulk of the participants. Injuries are more difficult to estimate since there is no requirement that they be reported or that parachute malfunctions be reported. It is estimated that in 600 to 1,000 random main parachute openings, one will result in malfunction, requiring the reserve parachute. Jumpers can help to control this by design choice, study, inspection and maintenance, packing, putting parachute on properly, being careful with gear in the airplane, and stability on opening (USPA, 2001:2-5). One of the greatest dangers comes from over-confidence, which leads to carelessness.

VIEWING AND LEARNING ACTIVITIES

Viewing and learning activities include bird-watching, rock hounding, tidepooling, plant identification, and photography. They include trips to park nature centers, visitor centers, traditional and outdoor museums, planetariums, and aquariums. They include visits to archeological and historic sites, such as ancient American Indian mounds, battlefields, canals, and other sites that are important to the preservation and understanding of our nation's culture and heritage. Sightseeing, a loosely defined activity, is also a part of this type of participation, which includes driving on a scenic byway or traveling to a city to see the sights.

Bird-watching

The numbers of people actively birdwatching increased a dramatic 155 percent from the mid-1980s to the mid-1990s (Cordell, 1999:242). Today there are some 70 million people in the United States who call themselves birders. About a third of these are serious enough to go out in the field to look for birds, and two-thirds are *residential* or backyard birders (Brandt, 1997:62). Seeking a wide range of experience, one study ranked birders into four groups corresponding with their distinct characteristics. In order of declining behavior interest, they were called undifferentiated birders, outdoor recreationists, generalists and water seekers, and heritage recreationists and comfort seekers (Cordell, 1999:243). Altogether, American bird-watchers, according to a United States Fish and Wildlife report, spent at least $5.2 billion for travel, binoculars, wild-bird seed, and the like. This was close to the total $5.9 billion that sports fans spent that same year on football, baseball, and other sporting events (*Backpacker*, 1996:29).

Some bird-watching field trips are taken to wild and remote places, especially when in search of exotic species. A *pelagic trip* is an ocean or Gulf trip that goes out to sea to find oceanic species. It is also quite possible to identify, attract, and become absorbed by a surprising variety of birds in the backyard. This is where one can often learn to key in on details for species identification, which with practice, generally become more apparent just as the sounds become more distinct. Local clubs or Audubon chapters also schedule field trips that are especially helpful for newcomers. These organizations are located through telephone directories, local natural history museums, nature centers, or outdoor stores specializing in bird-feeding equipment. The National Audubon Society can advise of the nearest local Audubon chapter. Ornithology classes on the science of bird study are also available in many areas.

If there appears to be no organization in the area, birding can be self-taught. Basic abilities include looking and listening. The observer must learn to identify distinct characteristics of the bird being watched. Birds are identified by spotting certain markings or by their behavior, song, size, or shape. Observations are recorded in a notebook and looked up later. Studying a field guide before participating in an excursion is helpful. When birding in a group, someone is usually able to offer an identification when simple descriptions are given. Checklists are often available to keep records of sightings.

Along with the field guide, checklist, and notebook, hiking boots or tennis shoes and binoculars are essential. Birds are usually found with the naked eye. Binoculars are then brought forward for a sharper, closer look by keeping the eyes on the bird. One can also try sweeping an open area or body of water with binoculars. To find the right binoculars, quality optical equipment is matched to particular characteristics of the individual's eyes. It is best to try several binoculars before buying. The buyer usually knows when the chemistry is right, but it is generally better not to sacrifice quality in order to save a few dollars, as the savings could lead to frustration and difficulty later (Brandt, 1997:63).

Standard-size binoculars are generally used, but when bird-watching while hiking or biking, compact or mini binoculars may be favorable. Standard and compact binoculars are also available with a rubber coating to help withstand shock and in some cases water. The basic measure of binoculars is a formula such as 7x35. The first number represents the magnification. With 7 x binoculars objects appear to be seven times closer. For most beginners 6 x, 7 x, or 8 x are adequate and 10 is the maximum. The greater the magnification, the narrower the field of view and the greater the image shake or the unavoidable result of heartbeat and hand shaking. The second number indicates the objective lens diameter in millimeters. The larger the opening, the more light is collected, and the higher the ratio; better binoculars are for low-light use. For example, dividing the first number into the second will result in the binoculars' brightness, or exit pupil. The pair that is 7x35 has an exit pupil of 5, which is acceptable for most conditions. An 8 x 20 has an exit pupil of only 2.5, which would tend to be dark even in bright daylight.

For bird identification, true birders need to see detail, and this is aided by a good pair of binoculars that have high resolution or clarity. Resolution is tested by focusing on an object that has detail or lines. The details should be sharp both near the middle and at the edge of the viewer's field of vision. Another important factor in maximum optical quality is depth of view. Because birds move around, birders do not want to have to constantly refocus. And because birders tend to be very hard on equipment, binoculars should be light but strong or rugged. Waterproof and fogproof is best. A growing line of compact models is also available. More experienced birders sometimes invest in powerful spotting scopes set up on tripods to zero in on birds at long range. On birding trips, leaders will usually have one or two scopes. To care for binoculars, they are cleaned with lens tissues, not with clothes or facial tissue.

Bird-watching is a good daybreak activity, and photographers also find it an excellent time to photograph the birds in their natural surroundings. More experienced birders enjoy capturing birds on film. Hiking, backpacking, bicycling, and boating can be enhanced by a search for various bird species. People from all over the nation and world flock to Everglades National Park in Florida, a bird-watcher's paradise especially for those who want to watch wading birds. More than 100,000 Americans visit Cape May, New Jersey migrations, and about 50,000 avitourists visit the raptor migration "hotspot" every year at Hawk Mountain in Pennsylvania. Some 6,000 made it to High Island, Texas, for a five-week migration, and 80,000 made their way to Grand Island, Nebraska, on the

Platte River to watch for cranes (Cordell et al., 1999:242-243). Biologists, however, attribute a decline in migratory species such as western bluebirds and wood thrushers to loss of vital habitat throughout the Western Hemisphere. If the popular songbird species continues to decline, an important segment of the bird-watching population will be at risk (Backpacker, 1996). Presently it is expected that wildlife watching observation and photographing, including birding, is expected to rise by 61 percent for participants and 97 percent for total participation days by 2050 (Cordell et al., 245).

Safety

Birders must follow the same safety precautions as other adventures, depending on the mode of transportation and length of the trip. According to one authority, the bird watcher on a forest trail must keep one eye on the treetops, and the other eye on the ground (Lotz, 1987:249). Admittedly impossible, the advice calls for watching ahead for snakes, wild animals, puddles, rocks, and other hazards.

Low-Impact

Those interested in birding can volunteer as observers for the annual Christmas Bird Count, Breeding Bird Survey, or Project Feederwatch sponsored locally and nationally by the National Audubon Society, the Fish and Wildlife Service, and other organizations. Birders can help with conservation and education programs, and reduce waste and energy use by reusing and recycling materials. When viewing wildlife experts advise to:

1. Wear natural colors and fade into the scenery.
2. Be considerate by keeping your distance from wildlife and nests, and by letting them be themselves.
3. Leave pets at home.
4. Respect the space of other viewers.
4. Carry out trash.
5. Use existing roads and trails.

6. Report wildlife or environmental abuse.

Rock Art

In the mid-1990s, it was estimated that 1.4 million people 16 and older visited a prehistoric site and 44.1 million visited a historic site (Cordell et al., 1999:223). Archeological and historic sites are important to the preservation and understanding of our nation's heritage. When available for the public to visit and experience personally, they can spark wonder, delight, and reflection. Finding these sites can also be physically demanding. For example, only able hikers can locate some of the rock art sites found in remote desert areas. Some of the nation's best rock art museums are found on federal lands, where canyon walls, caves, and rock faces have depictions of ancient hunting scenes, stars, wildlife, and humanlike figures. Archaeologists interpret the figures as cultural, religious, or ceremonial symbols; astronomical observations; and expressions of the supernatural.

When the drawing is etched onto a rock or chipped away by bone chisels and rock hammers, it is known as a *petroglyph*. More than 15,000 prehistoric and historic American Indian and Hispanic petroglyphs stretch along 17 miles of Albuquerque's West Mesa escarpment at Petroglyph National Monument in New Mexico. Pictures on rock, known as *pictographs*, may display many colors. Pigments formed by the American Indians were made by crushing minerals. When the minerals were mixed with water, red, black, yellow, white, and blue paints could be created. These paints were applied with plant fibers or by spreading the pigment onto a rock by hand. Negative-image pictographs were also created by painting around an object such as a hand (Browning, 1989:37-39). Well-known examples of pictographs are found in El Morro National Monument in New Mexico and in the Virgin Islands National Park. Canyonlands National Park in Utah is known for several striking polychromatic, or multicolored, pictographs. Park interpreters lead day and overnight trips to some of the sites. Some

A natural protective coating on desert boulders called desert varnish once attracted ancient artists who pecked away at the dark surface to create lighter images as seen in the rock pictured. The technique of painting came later.

sites are can only be viewed after a hard climb up a bed of rocks, but at times rock art is reached after a short walk or through a good pair of binoculars.

Safety

Care must be taken when climbing to avoid injuries and site damage. Refer to hiking, backpacking, camping, and birdwatching for tips.

Low-Impact

When it comes to visiting archaeological and historical sites, the fragile and irreplaceable settings demand care and protection. Unauthorized collecting or digging for artifacts is illegal on federal land and many other kinds of public land, as well as on private land without permission. To prevent vandalism at some rock art sites, several archaeologists refused to disclose site locations until more recent years when attitudes among modern archaeologists began to shift toward a belief that greater public awareness of the art's frailty and historical significance are actually a better means of preservation (Browning, 1989:37-39). Unfortunately some rock art sites have also fallen to housing developments and natural wear by flash floods, rock exfoliation, natural erosion, and acid rain. Rock art should only be appreciated by viewing, photographing, or sketching. Direct contact such as chalking, rubbing, tracing, or touching slowly causes it to disappear, and it can make it impossible to use new dating techniques. It is strictly prohibited to take it home or to add one's own art, and substantial fines and penalties are authorized. Re-pecking or re-painting a difficult-to-see image does not restore it, but rather destroys the original. Other things to remember when visitng archeological and historical resources:

1. Stay on the trail and off of middens (trash piles left by original occupants) and still-standing structures.
2. Leave artifacts where they lie.
3. Camp, sleep, cook, and gather wood well away from sites.
4. Report violators.

ORIENTEERING AND CAMPING

Orienteering provides a form of navigation that is used by outdoor travelers who enjoy hiking, backpacking, snowshoeing, cross-country skiing, canoeing, kayaking, cycling, and nature study. When day turns into night, these same adventurers find that a night spent away from the comforts of home can be as refreshing and rewarding as the day's activities. Whether hiking in the mountains, rafting down a white-water river, or snorkeling in the ocean, the night stars, the howls of the coyotes, a warm meal, and a place to rest offer a welcome respite from the activities of the day. These skills can also be basic to survival in the out-of-doors.

Orienteering and Navigation

Nature provides several means of navigation. Before the development of the compass, the North Star, the sun, the winds, moving clouds, and ocean currents served as guides. About 2500 B.C., the Chinese observed that when lodestone was placed on drifting wood that it consistently rotated to the same direction. From this finding, the compass needle, a strip of magnetized steel balanced on a pivot that was free to swing in any direction, came into being. While the Arabs and Vikings used a simple magnetic compass to help them navigate their vessels, the compass probably did not become widely used by Western civilization until the 13th century. Eventually the map and compass became invaluable aides to the adventurer. Putting map and compass skills to use in order to find the correct path is called *orienteering*. Developing effective orienteering techniques requires hands-on experience. By acknowledging that nobody has a perfect

"sense of direction," there is less chance of becoming lost. Whenever one is in unfamiliar surroundings, a map and compass are invaluable, and the same basic skills can be used for land navigation any time of the year. Precautions are taken when noting landmarks, and topographical maps are excellent aides.

The United States Geological Survey (USGS) began topographic and geologic mapping in 1879. Today almost two million natural and manmade features are identified in the USGS topographic map series, available from the USGS. These features make topographic maps extremely useful to professional and recreational map users alike. The first step in reading a map includes learning what the various lines, symbols, and colors mean. Colors, for example, depict the work of humans, water, or the contours of hills and valleys. The shape and steepness of hillsides appear as contour lines—the closer the lines, the steeper the hill. Several forms of measurement may be offered on the scale found on the map. For instance, the degree or percent of slope is a good indicator of the degree of difficulty in traversing the area by foot, ski, or bicycle. It is also a good indicator for snow avalanche hazard. Information on the types of maps produced by the USGS can be found in the USGS *Catalog of Maps*. The *Index Circular*, a reference book that divides each state into sections or quadrangles, is useful in identifying which maps are applicable. Separate maps exist for each quadrangle, which often means that the purchase of more than one map may be necessary. National Forest recreation maps are available from the district ranger, forest supervisor, or regional offices of the Forest Service and several outdoor recreation and conservation organizations also make useful maps.

A compass is a necessary tool for orienting the map to determine direction of travel. The most versatile compass for backcountry travel is the orienteering compass (Figure 15.3) with its rotating transparent plastic base plate allowing for more effortless use with a map. Care is taken that no nearby metallic objects

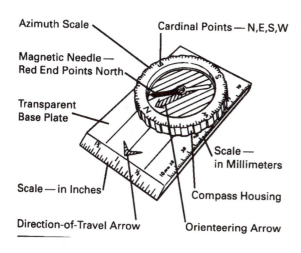

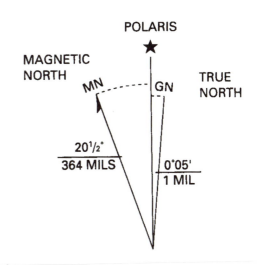

Figure 15.3 Orienteering compass

Figure 15.4 Declination Marker

disturb the needle, causing a false reading. The needle points to magnetic north, not true north. To identify true north, it is necessary to understand declination. *Declination* is defined as the angle between magnetic north and true north. The difference between magnetic north and true north (the declination angle) varies according to geographic location. For example, the declination angle in New Hampshire can be 15 degrees West and in Montana 20 degrees East.

The declination for a given area is generally printed on the map margin adjacent to the north arrow. True north, magnetic north, and declination are shown in Figure 15.4. Not knowing the effect of declination (or variation) could cause travelers to miss their destination point by a wide margin. To travel by map and compass, the map must be oriented to the terrain. The magnetic north arrow on the map points the same direction as the magnetic needle on the compass. The compass is then placed on the map with one long edge of the base plate touching a line between the starting point and the destination. The direction-of-travel arrow on the compass should be pointing in the direction of the destination point. Holding the base plate firmly, the compass housing is rotated until the orienting arrow is in line with the north portion of the compass

needle. To begin the venture, the traveler looks up to see where the direction-of-travel arrow is pointed, finds a landmark that is out as far as the terrain will allow and is in direct line with the travel arrow (Forest Service, 1982:8, 11). From this point, it is the map, not the compass, that is the really important tool.

Orienteering clubs set up local competitions open to everyone for a nominal fee. Orienteers bring a compass and water bottle and wear hiking boots, long pants, and light layers. The challenge lies in how quickly the competitor can find, in correct order, a series of preset control points in a wilderness setting, usually finishing at the point of origin. Cards are punched with unique pin-punches found hanging at the control point. To miss a control spells doom. The sport, which began in Sweden in the early 1900s as a military exercise, was developed in the United States in the 1940s by outdoor enthusiasts. Orienteering events (O-meets), which typically attract 75 to 120 participants, have several different courses that are arranged from novice to expert levels. Beginner courses are usually a mile long. An advanced course could take about two or three hours, with orienteers following contour lines, ridgelines, gullies, bodies of water, stone walls, and other features, all detailed on specially made topographic maps. After the standard

Utilizing observation skills from a high vantage point, this hiker can benefit from orienteering skills when exploring the inhospitable desert.

three-hour time limit, organizers go after anyone who has not finished, while everyone else is checking out their time and where they placed on the results board. High-level regional meets are sanctioned by the United States Orienteering Federation (USOF), while the International Orienteering Federation (IOF) sponsors the World Championships. In Europe, many O-meets attract more than 20,000 people (Wright, 1997:32). The four-season events include Ski-O events, snowshoe meets, and mountain-bike orienteering. Training kits, map and compass games, workshops, and clinics can help beginners to get started. In the United States, nearly five million people participate in orienteering each year.

Safety

By following the trail and carrying a map and compass, hikers will not likely get lost. If they do, there are techniques used with the map and compass to backtrack and to find where they are by selecting two landmarks. On longer wilderness treks, observing nature is more than pleasure. Landmarks are canvassed from the front and back. There is a surprising difference in the appearance of landmarks when backtracking. Making notes mentally and on the map can save the wilderness traveler some anguish later. Nature also provides direction. For example, while the sun and moon only rise in the east and west twice a year, during the equinoxes, they do travel in a general east-west direction. Moss, on the other hand, does not always grow on the north side of a tree, as many people believe. Stars tend to rise in the east and set in the west and move toward your right when you are facing south and to the left when you are facing north. The North Star aligns with Ursa Major, the bright star in the Big Dipper. And then, of course, you can always pick up a Global Positioning System (GPS) unit. GPS units lock on to high-frequency radio signals from some of the 24 GPS satellites and calculate the exact location of the user through triangulation (Drury & Holmlund, 1997:152).

Survival emergencies occur more often when the backcountry orienteer or traveler has been pushing too hard and energy is low or if one has not bothered to take preventative measures to avoid distress situations (see Camping Safety and Survival). The backpacker, for example, should remember that storms and lightning can come on suddenly and unexpectedly. Once signs of lightening appear, the packers drop their packs, remove metal objects, descend high points, get out of water, and stay away from solitary trees and objects. Surprisingly, a forest of shorter trees can be a relatively safe refuge (Breitling, 1984:156-559, 188-89).

When responding to an emergency, panic wastes energy, and most likely there will be other travelers, campers, or rangers in the local area. Resting and waiting is ordinarily the best plan. A good night's sleep is more beneficial than taking a chance on aimless travel. Rescuers will respond to the lapsing of the planned return time and generally begin to search during daylight. They are attracted to signals that make the wilderness traveler larger, louder, and more colorful than usual. The universal distress signal is any kind of signal repeated three times. For example, blasting a whistle three times signals distress. Aircraft can be signaled by using colors that contrast with the natural terrain. An X indicates distress and can be made from bright clothing or lining stones. Flashing a mirror, tin foil, or a tin lid can be seen miles away. While waiting, the traveler must drink enough water to

remain healthy and do everything possible to prevent the loss of moisture through perspiration. Necessary activities are accomplished in cool hours. During the day it can be important to stay in the shade, and if in the desert, it is necessary to move above the desert floor.

Low-Impact

Orienteers can follow low-impact suggestions for hikers and backpackers. They should be sure to (Drury & Holmlund, 1997:170):

1. Keep noise levels down.
2. Stay on trails.
3. Avoid cutting switchbacks.
4. Walk on durable surfaces, such as open rocks, sand and gravel, to minimize trail erosion.
5. Spread out to walk cross-country to avoid creating pathways.
6. Do not crowd wildlife.

Camping

Camping is as old as human existence. In the United States, recreational camping in the great outdoors can probably be traced to the early 1800s when some Americans began to see wilderness for its beauty and as a source of inspiration (McEwen, 1999:89). Later that century, devoted men and women organized outings for young people that resulted in the beginning of organized camping (Meir & Mitchell, 1993:19). After World War II as new technology and increases in disposable income and leisure time improved, people began to flock to the backcountry (Drury & Holmlund, 1997:106). By the 1960s, the majority of the 13 million people 12 years of age and older who reported camping one or more times during the previous 12 months had done so mainly in tents at developed campgrounds with their families. By the mid-1990s, the more than 58 million people, also 12 years of age and older who had participated in camping in the previous 12 months, camped in tents, recreational vehicles, and motor homes. Still representing families, a significant number also represented retirees, singles, and friends. While developed camping grew about 42 percent, others with weather-resistant tents and RVs turned to more primitive settings, creating a 72 percent growth in primitive camping (Cordell et al., 1999:236). We address tent camping below.

The best way to enjoy a night spent under the stars is to be prepared. The first step in setting up camp requires finding the natural advantages of a location. It is far preferable to use existing sites when possible. When it is not, the camper tries to anticipate the unexpected and plans for any dangers such as high winds or floods. The following questions can be asked:

> Is there an established site?
> Is the site close to water?
> Will the site provide shelter?
> Is the land flat?
> Is the area protected; could it flood?
> Are there any dead trees next to the camp site?
> Is the site aesthetically pleasing?
> Does the site offer privacy and interesting scenery?

After the site selection is made, each member of the party takes on different duties, such as clearing a place for the tent, setting it up, getting the water, and cooking. If the camp is laid out properly, an overnight fire will not be missed, and the use of single-burner cookstoves can minimize the negative effects of campfires. Before pitching the tent, sticks and small stones are cleared from the tent site, but leaves, pine needles, or humus remain in place. They serve as a cushion and improve drainage. The tent is pitched on a waterproof ground layering to form a tent floor that will, when combined with a foam pad, protect the bed from moisture. When possible, the back of the tent is positioned on the wind side with the door facing toward the rising sun. This positioning will help to dry the tent and gear better. When it rains, the humidity inside the tent is very high, while the outside temperature is cool. Since moisture will condense on non-breathable surfaces, it is helpful to ventilate by leaving vents, windows, and doors open as much as possible. When bugs are not a problem, the netting is opened as well, since anything that increases air circulation will decrease condensation. On dry days the sleeping bag is unrolled as early as possible to restore it to its original loft. The dining area may be centrally located if bears are not a threat. The cook area needs to be level to prevent stove tip-over, away from pine needles or other inflammable materials, and protected from the wind.

Safety

If bears are around, they can smell food more than two miles away. By learning proper food-storage techniques and following procedures of land managers, backpackers and campers can help protect bears and themselves. Because they are unpredictable, however, there are no hard and fast rules about how to protect oneself. Sites are avoided that are obviously used by bears, such as sites near ripe berry patches and less obvious avalanche chutes where bears like to graze. Tents are pitched at least 150 feet upwind from the cooking area. Food is eaten in one spot, and any spills are cleaned. Food is never eaten or stored in a tent, and cooking clothes are stored like food (Cordes, 2001:62-65). Local procedures are carefully followed, but typically food is placed in waterproof bags and hung at least 12 feet up and at least six feet out in a tree (see Figure 15.5). One recommendation is to place tents near climbable trees, but experts provide varying recommendations for bear encounters. According to one old tale, you can tell a grizzly from a black bear by sneaking up behind the bear and giving it a swift kick. If the bear knocks the tree over and eats you, it's a grizzly. If it climbs up the tree and eats you, it's a black bear (*Backpacker*, 1990:71). Obviously this old tale should not be tested, and information about bear encounters needs to be studied before entering bear country.

In general, every effort is made to stay odor-free by keeping personally clean but shunning scented lotions, soaps, deodorants, and cosmetics. Even before the trip, it

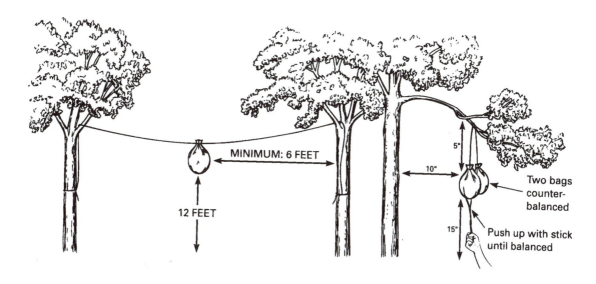

Figure 15.5 Diagram of a suspended food bag.

is important not to use scented water softeners, whose strong, sweet smell attracts bears. And needless to say, carrying dried or freeze-dried food is much safer than food with odors. Noisemakers and flashlights make handy deterrents, and when on the trail, noise is made at blind corners, in thick brush, on windy days, and near running water, where it may be more difficult for a bear to sense human presence. Before and after camp, especially in grizzly country, it is advisable for backpackers to travel in large groups during the middle of the day.

Camps are also not set up near plants with three leaflets, including poison ivy and poison oak. To avoid snakes and poisonous insects, the camper (and hiker) does not: sit or step where it is impossible to see clearly (this includes stepping over logs); put hands inside holes in logs, trees, or rocks; or wander around the camp at night without a flashlight. Boots and clothing are inspected in the morning before putting them on. If a rattler's buzz is heard, stop, find out where the noise came from, then retreat carefully. Normally rattlesnakes strike moving objects. Since they seldom strike very high, leather hiking boots provide protection. Although

there are several hundred varieties of snakes in the United States, only four are poisonous. These are the coral, the rattler, the copperhead, and the cottonmouth, but there are several varieties of each. Corals are found in the south, copperheads in the eastern and southern states, cottonmouth moccasins or water moccasins in swamps and various varieties of rattlers in nearly all of the 50 states (Meier & Mitchell, 1993:334-338).

Winter Camping

With modern equipment designed to function for below-freezing or even in subzero weather, winter can be one of the best times to visit the outdoors. One does not need to fight crowds or insects, but there are special challenges. A solid foundation in basic camping and survival techniques is essential, as well as advanced cold weather skills.

Winter campers need to become familiar with cold-weather techniques, equipment, and local conditions. With night arriving earlier in the winter, camps are set up by mid-afternoon. Cold wind is avoided as much as possible by selecting a shielded site near shorter, younger trees or building a snow windbreak on the weather side of the tent site. While a tree can provide additional protection, snow-laden trees are bypassed since the snow can fall on the tent (Langer, 1973:262 63). To avoid potential avalanche conditions, locations near hills with a gradient of over 25 degrees are avoided. Needles furnish excellent ground covering around the site and prevent the tent from freezing to the ground. If freezing does occur, the tent is detached with boiling water to keep it from ripping. Tents should be waterproof, condensation-resistant, and sturdy in design. Hoop and dome tents are often preferred by winter campers. Snow shelters such as snow domes, snow caves, and igloos can be made and will provide greater insulation than tents. Building methods are discussed in books focused or camping and winter survival.

Equipment can be carried in backpacks or by pulling a toboggan. Wool clothes, hat, and a sleeping bag with a closed-cell pad underneath the bag shield against the chill. Pine needles are collected to insulate the bed. Mummy bags with built-in hoods add protection on cold nights. With down bags, less clothing leads to more comfort. Overdressing causes perspiration, which makes the night and early mornings even colder. Down provides the excellent insulation per carried pound, but it is ineffective insulation when wet. Some bags, insulated with high-tech materials, may be preferable in wet weather. Boots can be wrapped in a plastic bag and placed at the foot of the sleeping bag to keep them warm. Even if a fire is not intended, wood, tinder and kindling are collected for emergencies. Fuel is placed on plastic and kept inside the tent to help it to dry out. Any fires must be carefully planned and tended. Tent heaters are a hazard; more winter camping accidents occur from asphyxiation than from freezing temperatures.

Outer clothing is colorful to allow for more visibility. Brightly colored yarn or cord can be tied to smaller gear to avoid losing it if dropped in snow. Winter supplies include sunglasses to protect against snow blindness, lip balm, and chewing gum. Chewing gum stimulates facial circulation and helps to protect against

frostbite. A six-inch square of l/4-inch plywood is carried for placement under the stove for insulation (Breitling, 1984:355). Winter campers tend to drink less than they should. It is important to drink more fluids to avoid dehydration. Hot liquids warm the body better than hot foods. Water may be collected from streams flowing too swiftly to freeze or by cutting through ice with a hammer and chisel. To melt snow, a few cups of water are placed at the bottom of a pot to create steam. More water results from melting chunks of ice and slab snow than from melting powdered snow. After water is collected it must be purified.

Local outfitters provide organized tours and special equipment to meet the challenges of cold weather. With advances in high-tech materials, more and more enthusiasts are expanding their camping adventures into a year-round activity. The national and state parks, in an effort to provide relief from the crowded summer months, have launched public relations campaigns encouraging winter camping.

Safety

The two most common hazards are frostbite and hypothermia. *Frostbite,* caused by prolonged exposure to cold, is similar to a burn. The body parts most commonly affected by frostbite are ears, nose, hands, and feet. Signs and symptoms may involve a tingling sensation, pain followed by numbness. There is a white or purplish appearance to the skin. To avoid frostbite, the camper stays dry and out of wind in extremely cold temperatures. Layered clothing is worn as described previously in this chapter. Exposed areas of the skin are covered, and smoking and alcohol is bypassed in extreme cold. To treat frostbite, go inside or seek shelter from the wind. Check for signs of hypothermia and treat it first (to be discussed). Small areas are warmed with warm breath and hands or feet are tucked inside warm clothing next to bare skin. The skin is not rubbed, and every effort is made to avoid walking on frostbitten feet. The frostbitten part is elevated and wrapped with blankets or soft material. If possible, it is immersed in warm water from 104 to 108 degrees for 15 to 30 minutes. If blisters appear, they are not broken and a doctor is called. A doctor is also called, and careful rewarming and antibiotic treatment is needed when the skin is white or blue, hard, and cold. Aspirin or acetaminophen may be required if the skin turns red, burns, tingles, or becomes very painful (Kemper, 1999:43).

When the body loses so much heat that it can no longer warm itself, *hypothermia* has occurred. *Hypo* means "low," and *thermia* means "heat." Untreated conditions will result in a continual drop in the body's core temperature until bodily functions cease. Hypothermia can happen at temperatures of 45 degrees or higher when in wet and windy weather or to frail and inactive people if not dressed warmly indoors. Signs and symptoms involve shivering, cold and pale skin, apathy, and impaired judgment. Physical and mental deterioration will continue until the advanced stages, which include cold abdomen, slow pulse and slow breathing, weakness or drowsiness, and confusion. Shivering may stop if body temperature drops below 96 degrees.

Treatment must be immediate for this emergency situation, which can lead to unconsciousness and death. For milder cases, the victim is taken out of the cold or wind, wet clothing is replaced with dry or wool clothes, and warm liquids are provided for them to drink. In more extreme cases, cold, wet clothing is removed and heat is transferred to the victim by wrapping a blanket or sleeping bag around both of you. Warm liquids and high-energy food, such as candy are furnished unless the person is disoriented or unconscious. When medical help is not available and all other home treatments are not working, it is possible to try rewarming the victim in warm water (100 to 105 degrees) as a last resort. This method can cause shock or heart attack, so it is avoided if at all possible. Emergency help is called immediately whenever a person has lost consciousness, remains unconscious, or seems confused; when the victim is a child or older adult regardless of the severity of the symptoms; or if the body temperature does not return to normal after four hours (Kemper, 1999:47-49).

Low-Impact

Campers are quiet and considerate of others and adhere to the following guidelines:

1. Select camping supplies in natural colors that blend with the surroundings. They are less intrusive to another camper's experience.
2. Whenever possible, use existing campsites.
3. A camper should never ditch or build trenches around the tent. Ditches and trenches can start soil erosion and lasting scars will remain.
4. Observe all fire restrictions, and use camp stoves for cooking whenever possible. They are generally preferable to a campfire in terms of impact on the land. Use only fallen timber for a fire, and gather it well away from the camp. Let a fire burn down to a fine ash and ensure it is completely extinguished.
5. Carry water containers to reduce traffic at campsites. Do not wash in streams or lakes. Detergents, toothpaste and soap harm fish and other aquatic life.
6. Do not use evergreen boughs for shelter or beds. Do not cut standing trees.
7. The stay is planned for as few nights as possible to avoid waste accumulation and injury to plants. One night in each campsite is best to avoid impact.
8. Campers try to leave the site in better condition than when it was originally found by restoring the natural appearance of pristine sites and packing everything out that was packed in.

It is our duty to exercise responsible outdoor practices while enjoying outdoor activities.

Camping with Pack Animals

Many adventurers enjoy horse packing in back-country areas. Pack stock groups must be equally conscientious about leaving no trace of their visit. Proper trip planning, selection of camp location, and containment of animals once in camp all demand special attention. In general, the same type of planning is used for a pack stock trip as for a backpacking trip. It is important to check with local officials for trail conditions and to find out whether stock is allowed. Some areas are closed to pack animals due to overuse or fragile environments. The fewer animals taken, the less impact on the land. Keep the group small and carry light-weight equipment to reduce the number of animals needed. On the trail, try to keep stock in single file.

For the horsepacker, the first rule of campsite selection is to think of the stock.

The campsite should be able to accommodate the animals without any damage to the area. After riding into a potential campsite, the packer must decide whether there is enough feed. Consideration should also be given to the wildlife in the area. If the area is overgrazed, pack stock may remove feed otherwise needed by deer and elk during winter months. If grazed, it should be on north or east slopes, which will be snow-covered during the winter, leaving forage for wildlife on exposed south and west slopes. Stock water is another important consideration. A place downstream from camp in a gravelly area where the stream bank can withstand hard use lowers impact, or use buckets. Hitchlines, hobbles, and pickets are all methods of containing pack animals. Hitchlines need to be erected in rocky areas and on good stout trees using tree saver straps. Hobbles prevent horses from moving too fast, and pickets confine them to an area that is only as long as the rope or chain. Pickets should be moved at least twice daily to prevent overgrazing. Temporary corrals are an excellent method of containing pack animals for several days but should be moved frequently. They can be built out of natural timbers, rope, or portable electric fence. Remember to only tie stock to trees and brush for short periods of time, if at all. They may paw up roots or strip the bark by gnawing and fighting the ropes, which can kill the brush or trees.

Feeding pack animals can cause a negative impact on an area. Spreading loose hay on the ground could introduce exotic plant species to an area. Instead, processed weed seed-free feed is packed in, and feed bags are used. This helps prevent overgrazing. Begin feeding stock the weed-seed-free feed 72 hours before the trip to avoid leaving seeds in the manure. National Park Service areas do not allow grazing of stock.

Safety

The nature of traveling with stock requires the utmost care and continual attention to safety precautions. The latest procedures and the local procedures need to be followed at all times. Basic safety precautions include:

1. Check all riding gear for need of repair prior to departure.
2. Carry a first-aid kit for riders and stock.
3. Know the ability of the stock and any limitations.
4. Know the ability of the riders and any limitations.
5. Practice back-country techniques at home.
6. Familiarize the horses with llamas and backpackers prior to departure.
6. Travel single file and do not run the animals.
7. If hikers are encountered, be courteous and talk to them. Explain the safety advantage if they stand on the downhill side of a trail; since horses are

creatures of flight, they will move away from something they are afraid of and this can be dangerous if the horse is on the downhill side.

Low-Impact

Many low-impact techniques have been mentioned above for camping with pack animals. Here are just a few low-impact techniques (USDA Forest Service, n.d.; NOLS, 1997:8-12):

1. Follow all local regulations and permit requirements for use of stock in the back country.
2. Try to camp only one night in each location to protect the area from overuse. If a stay is more than one night at a destination camp, considerable determination and commitment are needed to keep the area of disturbance from growing larger. Picket pins and fence have to be moved again and again to prevent overgrazing and trampling. It is best if extra horses can be sent out of base camp with a friend or member of the party for the length of the extended stay.
3. The general rule is the greater the confinement of horses, the greater the impact. Free-roaming horses grazing on good grassy areas cause little long-term impact. Ideally the horses will only be in the immediate camp area long enough to load and unload. Hobbling of horses causes very little environmental impact. Tree saver straps are needed if a highline is used, and grazing areas should be as large as possible.
4. Pack in weed seed-free feed to avoid the introduction of exotic plants and weeds. Use feed bags and water the stock at established fords, low rocky spot, or in

gravel protected areas. Buckets are an alternative to avoid damage to delicate riparian areas.

5. It takes extra time to naturalize an area from the impact of pack animals. Manure piles need to be scattered to aid decomposition and discourage flies, and as a courtesy to other users. Areas dug up by animal hooves will need to be filled and trampled areas made to look natural.

SUMMARY

Americans' love of nature is reflected in the type, as well as the amount, of outdoor activities they partake. This chapter provides just a glimpse of these activities. The equipment needed for each activity and how to satisfactorily participate in these activities is described. Adventures on land include hiking, backpacking, and mountain biking. Activities in the snow include snowshoeing, and cross-country skiing. White-water rivers of America provide ample opportunities for leisure pursuits, such as canoeing, kayaking, and rafting. On the other hand, the ocean is used for SCUBA diving and wind-surfing. In the air, Americans enjoy hang gliding, hot-air ballooning, and sky diving. Bird-watching and rock art visits are two viewing and educational activities described in more detail here. Orienteering and navigation are necessary for many outdoor pursuits, and camping is an activity that is enjoyed in both winter and summer, and when accompanied by pack animals.

Safety techniques and low-impact techniques were described after activities. Safety must always be a priority in planning and during the activity, and minimizing impact helps to protect the environment by leaving no sign of visitation. Despite overcrowding in wilderness areas, the recreationist can prevent adverse impact by practicing the no-trace ethic. The low-impact ethic advocates leaving wilderness areas in better condition than before

they were visited. By practicing no-trace and low-impact techniques, wilderness visitors can enjoy these beautiful and pristine environments today and tomorrow.

ORGANIZATIONS

Many organizations that support outdoor recreation are shown in Appendix B. The following organizations provide excellent resources for learning proper techniques for the activities cited.

Ballooning

Balloon Federation of America, PO Box 400, Indianola, IA 50125 515-961-8809, FAX: 515-961-3537, www.bfa.net

Bicycling

Adventure Cycling Association, P.O. Box 8308-W, Missoula, MT 59807 (800)755-2453,(406)721-1776,FAX: (406)721-8754, www.advcycling.org

Birding

National Audubon Society; 700 Broadway; New York, NY 10003 212 979 3000, FAX: 212 979 3188, www.audubon.org/

Cornell Laboratory of Ornithology, 159 Sapsucker Woods Road, Ithaca, NY 14850 (607) 254-2473 , www.ornith.cornell.edu/

Camping

American Camping Association, Inc., Bradford Woods, 5000 State Rd. 67 N., Martinsville, IN 46151-7902. 765-342-8456 FAX: 765-342-2065, www.acacamps.org

Association of Independent Camps, 10331 Tarpan Dr., Indianapolis, IN 46256-9792 317-596-8701, FAX: 317-596-8703, www.independentcamps.com.

Christian Camping International, P.O. Box 62189,Colorado Springs, CO 80962-2189 (719) 260-9400, www.gospelcom.net/cci/#

National Camp Association, 610 Fifth Ave. PO Box 5371,New York, NY 10185 1-800-966-CAMP (2267), 212-645-0653, FAX 845-354-5501, www.summercamp.org/

Family Campers and RVers Association, 74 West Genesee St., Skanteles, NY 13152 http://www.fcrv.org

Canoeing, Kayaking, and Rafting

American Canoe Association, 7432 Alban Station Blvd, Suite B-232, Springfield, VA 22150 Phone: (703) 451-0141 FAX: (703) 451-2245, www.acanet.org

American Whitewater Association, 1430 Fenwick Lane, Silver Spring, MD 20910, Phone: 866-BOAT4AW, FAX: 301-589-6121, www.americanwhitewater.org/

National Organization for Rivers, 212 West Cheyenne Mountain Blvd., Colorado Springs, CO 80906 (719) 579-8759. FAX (719) 576-6238, www.nationalrivers.org/

United States Canoe Association, 606 Ross St., Middletown, OH 45042, www.uscanoe.org/

Cross-country skiing and snowshoeing

American Camping Association, Inc., Bradford Woods, Martinsville, IN 46151.

American Hiking Association, 1422 Fenwick Lane, Silver Spring MD 20910 (301) 565-6704, FAX: (301) 565-6714 , www.americanhiking.org

Cross-Country Ski Area Association 259 Bolton Road Winchester, NH 03470 603-239-4341, FAX:603-239-6387, www.xcski.org

Bolton Road Winchester, NH 03470

Far West Ski Association, PMB #121,27525 Puerta Real, Suite 100 Mission Viejo, CA 92691, www.fwsa.org

Professional Ski Instructors of America (PSIA), 133 S. Van Gordon, Suite 101 Lakewood, CO 80228 303-988-0545, 303-988-3005, www.psia.org

The North American Telemark Organization, Box 44, Waitsfield, VT 05673. 800-835-3404, FAX 802-496-5515, www.telemarknato.com/

The Sierra Club, 85 Second St., Second Floor, San Francisco, CA 94105-3441, 415-977-5500, FAX:415-977-5799, www.sierraclub.org

Hang gliding

Hang Glider Manufacturers' Association (HGMA), 137 Oregon St., El Segundo, CA 90245.

United States Hang Gliding Association (USHGA), P.O. Box 1330, Colorado Springs CO 80901 719-632-8300, FAX 719-632-6714, www.ushga.org

Hiking/Backpacking

American Hiking 1422 Fenwick Lane, Silver Spring MD 20910 (301) 565-6704, FAX (301) 565-6714, www.americanhiking.org

American Trails, P.O. Box 11046, Prescott, Arizona 86304-10, (928) 632-1140, Fax: (928) 632-1147, www.AmericanTrails.org

Appalachian Trail Conference, 799 Washington Street, Harpers Ferry, WV 25425, Phone 304-535-6331, FAX (304) 535-2667 www.atconf.org

Appalachian Mountain ClubAMC Main Office, 5 Joy Street, Boston, MA 02108, phone 617-523-0636 FAX 617-523-0722, www.outdoors.org

Rails-to-Trails Conservancy, 1100 17th Street N.W., 10th Floor, Washington, D.C. 20036, 202-331-9696; FAX 202-331-9680, www.railtrails.org

Mountain biking

International Mountain Bike Association (IMBA), 1121 Broadway Ste 203, P.O. Box 7578, Boulder, CO 80306, 888-442-4622, 303-545-9011, FAX: 303-545-9026, www.imba.com

National Mountain Bike Association (NORBA/ USA), P.O. Box 1901, Chandler, AZ 85244.

Orienteering

National Outdoor Leadership School, P.O. 288, Main Street, Lander, WY 82520-3140. (307) 332-5300,   FAX (307) 332-1220, www.nols.edu/NOLSHome.html

Outward Bound, Inc. 1-888-882-6863

http://www.outwardbound.org/

United States Orienteering Federation, P.O. Box 1444, Forest Park, Georgia 30051 http://www.us.orienteering.org/

Map Information U.S. Geological Survey, USGS Information Services, Box 25286 Denver, CO 80225 A free Topographical Map Index Circular for any state east or west of the Mississippi River can be requested 1-888-ASK-USGS (1-888-275-8747), www.usgs.gov

U.S. Geological Survey, Box 25286, Building 810, Federal Center, Denver, CO 80225.

Parachuting

The United States Parachute Association (USPA), 1440 Duke St., Alexandria, VA 22314 703-836-3495, FAX 703-836-2843, www.uspa.org

Rock art

American Rock Art Research Association (ARARA), Arizona State Museum University of Arizona, Tucson, AZ 85721-0026 (520) 621-3999, FAX(520) 621-2976, www.arara.org

The National Pictographic Society, P.O. Box 94, Copperton, UT 84006.

SCUBA Diving

American Association of Certified SCUBA Divers, Inc., 1066 Westover Road, Stanford, CT 06902.

Underwater Society of America, 1701 Lake Ave., Glenview, IL 60025. www.underwater-society.org

For Diver Certification:

Handicapped Scuba Association (certification agency for persons with disabilities) 1104 El Prado, San Clemente CA 92672, 714-498-6128, FAX: 714-498-6128

IDEA (International Diving Education Association), P O Box 8427, Jacksonville FL 32239 904-744-5554, 904-743-5425 NAUI (National Association of Underwater Instructors)9942 Currie Davis Drive, Ste H, Tampa, FL 33619-2667, 813-628-6284, FAX: 813-628-8253, www.naui.org

PADI (Professional Association of Diving Instructors) 1251 East Dyer Road #100, Santa Ana CA 92705 800-729-7234, 714-540-7234 , www.padi.com

PDIC (Professional Diving Instructors Corporation, International) P.O. Box 3633, 1554 Gardner Ave, Scranton PA 18505, 717-342-1480,FAX: 717-342-1276 , www.pdic-intl.com

SSI (Scuba Schools International - SSI merged with the National Association of SCUBA Diving Schools) 2619 Canton Ct, Ft. Collins CO 80525, 800-892-2702, 970-482-0883, FAX: 970-482-6157

YMCA of the USA SCUBA Program, 101 N. Wacker Drive, Chicago, IL 60606 Phone (800) 872-9622, FAX (312) 977-0894, www.ymcascuba.org

Windsurfing

American Windsurfing Industries Association, 10.99 Snowden Road, White Salmon, WA 98672 Phone: 800-963-7873 509-493-9463, FAX: 509-493-9464 fax, www.awia.org/

International Windsurfer Class Association, 1955 W. 190th St., Torrance, CA 90509. www.sailing.org

U.S. Windsurfer Association, www.uswindsurfing.org/index.html

References

Backpacker. (1990, October). Our favorite animal stories. *Backpacker, 18*(2).

Balloon Federation of America (BFA). (1999). *Crew and safety tips*, 1-10. [On-line]. Available: http://www.bfa-jr-balloonist.com/crew.htm

Berger, K. (2000). *SCUBA Diving: A trailside guide*. New York: W.W. Norton & Company.

Betz, C. (1999, January). National outdoor recreation assessments. *Parks & Recreation, 34*(1), 22-31.

Betz, C., English, D. & Cordell, H. K. (1999). Outdoor recreation resources. In H. K. Cordell (Ed.), *Outdoor recreation in American life: A national assessment of demand and supply trends*. Champaign, IL: Sagamore Publishing, Inc.

Benson, R. (1979). *Skydiving*. Minneapolis, MN: Turner Publications.

Bowker, J., English, D., & Cordell, H. K. (1999). Projections of outdoor recreation participation to 2050. In H. K. Cordell *(Ed.), Outdoor recreation in American life: A national assessment of demand and supply trends*. Champaign, IL: Sagamore Publishing, Inc.

Boyle, M. (1997, December 7). Altitude can cause a run-down feeling. *The San Diego Union-Tribune.*

Brandt, A. (1997, January). Crane spotting, *Sky*, 62-63.

Breitling, J. (Ed.). (1984). *Field book*. Irving, TX: Boy Scouts of America.

Browning, T. (1989, September/October). Spirits in stone. *National Parks, 63*, 9-10.

Bureau of Land Management. (1989). Leave no trace. In *Land ethics*. Washington, D.C.: U.S. Government Printing Office.

Cahill, T. (1990, October). Swimming with sharks. *Reader's Digest, 137*, 822.

Carlton, D. (2000). *Assembly*, 1-2, [On-line]. Available: http://www.heritagedevelop.com/crewing/assembly.htm

Carlton, D. (2000). *Safety*, 1-2, [On-line]. Available: http://www.heritagedevelop.com/crewing/safety.htm

Chavez, D. (1999). Mountain biking: A rapidly growing sport. In H. K. Cordell *(Ed.), Outdoor recreation in American life: A national assessment of demand and supply trends*. Champaign, IL: Sagamore Publishing, Inc.

Cordell, H. K, McDonald, B., Teasley, R., Bergstrom, J., Martin, J., Bason, J., & Leeworthy, V. (1999). Outdoor recreation participation trends. In H. K. Cordell *(Ed.), Outdoor recreation in American life: A national assessment of demand and supply trends*. Champaign, IL: Sagamore Publishing, Inc.

Cordell, H. K, Bergstrom, L. Hartmann, L., & English, D. (1990). An analysis of the outdoor recreation and wilderness situation in the United States: 1989-2040. *General technical report RM-189*. Fort Collins, CO: U.S. Department of Agriculture Forest Service.

Cordes, K. (1999). *America's national historic trails*. Norman, OK: University of Oklahoma Press.

Cordes, K. (2001). *America's national scenic trails*. Norman, OK: University of Oklahoma Press.

David, A., & Moran, T. (1983). *River thrill sports*. Minneapolis, MN: Lemer Publications.

Dean, A. (1982). *Wind sports*. Philadelphia, PA: Westminster Press.

Doll, P. (1990, June). Sense the invisible. *Times Advocate*. Escondido, CA: John Armstrong.

Drury, J. & Holmlund, E. (1997). *The camper's guide to outdoor pursuits*. Champaign, IL: Sagamore Publishing, Inc.

Fisher, R., & Brown, L. (Eds.). (1979). *Fodors outdoors America*. New York: David McKay Company.

Florida Department of Natural Resources (Unknow). *Reef guide*. Tallahassee, FL: Florida Department of Natural Resources.

Huser, V. (1981). *River camping*. New York: Dial Press.

International Mountain Bicycling Association (IMBA). (2000). IMBA History - *A chrononology*, 1-4. [On-line]. Available: http://www.imba.com/about history.html

International Mountain Bicycling Association (IMBA). (2000). *Rules of the trail*, 1-2. [On-line]. Available: http://www.imba.com/about/trail_rules.html

Kemper, D. (1999). The healthwise staff, the physicians and staff of Kaiser Permanente. *Kaiser Permanente healthwise handbook*. Boise, ID: Healthwise, Inc.

Knight-Ridder (1998, May 18). Equipping yourself for a day away from civilization, *The San Diego Union-Tribune.*

Korenblat, A. (1998, November). IMBA President responds to mountain bike criticism. *IMBA Trail News, 11*(5) 6.

Leave No Trace (LNT). (1997, July). *Leave no trace outdoor skills & ethics backcountry horse*. Use Vol. 3.2. Lander, WY: National Outdoor Leadership School.

Leeworthy, V. R. (2001). Preliminary estimates from versions 1-6: Coastal recreation participation. *National survey on recreation and the environment (NSRE) 2000*. Silver Spring, MD: U.S. Department of Commerce National Oceanic and Atmospheric Administration.

Lohr, R. (1999, October). Dashing through the snow. *Parks & Recreation, 34*(10), 85-87.

Lotz, A. (1987). *Birding around the world*. New York: Dodd, Mead.

Mackey, B. & Leonard, R. (1995). *Frequently asked questions about hang gliding and paragliding*, 1-8, [On-line]. Available: http://www.ushga.org/faq.asp

McEwen, D. (1999). Camping facilities on public land. In H. K. Cordell *(Ed.), Outdoor recreation in American life: A national assessment of demand and supply trends*. Champaign, IL: Sagamore Publishing, Inc.

McKinney, J. (1998). *Day hiker's guide to southern California*. Santa Barbara, CA:Olympus Press.

Meadows, G. (September). How to buy a used entry-level hang glider. *USHGA Hang Gliding Magazine*,1-4. [On-line]. Available: http://www.ushga.org/article05.asp

Meier, J. (1980). *Backpacking*. Dubuque, IA:Wm. C. Brown.

Meier, J., & Mitchell, A. (1993). *Camp counseling*. Dubuque, IA:WCB Brown & Benchmark

National Oceanic and Atmospheric Administration (NOAA) and Professional Association of Diving Instructors (PADI). (1993). *Ten ways a diver can protect the underwater environment* (brochure). Washington, D.C.:U.S. Government Printing Office 19200.

Oiney, R. (1976). *Hang gliding*. New York: Putnam's Sons.

Professional Association of Diving Instructors (PADI). (2001). *PADI diver statistics*. [On-line]. Available: http//www.padi.com/news/stats/

Potter, E. (1998, February, 1). Snowshoein' it. *The San Diego Union-Tribune*, F-12.

President's Commission on Americans Outdoors. (1987). *Americans and the outdoors*. Washington, D.C.: National Geographic Society.

Robb, G. (1986). Risk recreation and special populations. In *The President's Commission on American outdoors, A literature review*. Washington, D.C.: U.S. Government Printing Office.

REI (1992). *Cross-Country skis FYI*, brochure P195; rev.2/92.

Society of Park and Recreation Educators (1999, January). Research into action: What's hot in outdoor recreation. *Parks & Recreation, 34*(1), 28.

Steel, R. (1985). *Sharks of the world*. New York: Blanford Press.

Sullivan, G. (1965). *Skin and SCUBA diving*. New York: Frederick Fell.

Tilton, B. (1997). Avalanche Safety: Choosing the Safest Route." *Continental Divide Trail News* 2:1 (Winter):5.

United States Census Bureau. (2000). *Statistical abstract of the United States*. Lantham, MD:Bernam Press.

USDA Forest Service. (1993). *Horse sense*, Pamphlet R1-93-23.

USDA Forest Service. (1994). *Winter safety guide*. Washington, D.C.: Government Printing Office R1 94-1

Windsurfer.com. (2000). *Basic lesson, 1-2*, [On-line]. Available: http://www.windsurfer.com/newsite/biginners/lesson.cfm.

Windsurfer.com. (2000). *Many spects,1-2*, [On-line]. Available: http://www.windsurfer.com/newsite/beginners/aspects.cfm.

Wirth, D. (1980). *Ballooning*. New York:Random House.

Wright, B. (1997, June). Hate asking directions? *Women's Sports + Fitness, 19*(5), 31-33.

16 *THE ENVIRONMENT*___

Outdoor survival skills have been lost for the most part by urban populations. The hostile natural environment once feared by the pioneers has been developed and industrialized, eliminating the need for use of outdoor skills on a daily basis. Today, wilderness survival instincts are satisfied by outdoor enthusiasts in wilderness and nature preserves. The return to these skills by recreationists tends to stimulate sensitivity to the protection of nature and its survival. One survey shows that an overwhelming 95 percent of the respondents who spend time outdoors and participate in outdoor recreation activities understand the importance of environmental protection (Roper Starch, 2000:2). Three aspects of this relationship follow (Atkinson, 1990:47):

1. Leisure activities that focus on the appreciation of the natural (nature walking, canoeing, outdoor photography) appear to have a greater impact on one's environmental concern and one's likelihood to behave in a pro-environmental fashion when contrasted with activities that are more consumptive of energy or natural resources.

2. Recreationists may possess stronger attitudes about aspects of the environment on which their leisure activity is dependent (clean water for fishing, clean air for ballooning, etc.).

3. Pro-environmental attitudes of recreationists do not always translate into sound environmental behavior. Some recreationists in their enthusiasms and efforts to see and experience remote or desirable public lands are guilty of damaging some of our most fragile ecosystems.

Increasingly, chemicals, agriculture, and urban development place tremendous pressure on our natural resources. Because it is difficult to measure the state of the natural environment, and because many environmental issues seem invisible and distant, Americans are increasingly dependent on conservation groups, public laws, the media, museums, zoos, parks, and nature centers for information regarding the condition of the natural world. Outdoor enthusiasts, for instance, experience nature first hand, thereby giving them a unique opportunity to share their knowledge, experiences, and interpretations to their recreational societies to keep them abreast of environmental issues affecting their activity. The American Hiking Society finds that the longer multiple environmental impacts go unobserved, the more likely they will accelerate ecological damage. In recognizing that trails offer the potential to act as indicators of a community's ecological health, they recommend that trail managers assign dependable volunteer hikers to observe the ecosystems in their regions. Any changes observed are reported to trail managers who will then describe the changes to scientists and environmental advocates.

Outdoor leaders must understand basic concepts of environmental conservation. For not only do they teach others to enjoy the wonders of the natural world, they also teach them how to preserve nature and to develop outdoor ethics. When tested by the National Environmental Education Training Foundation and Roper Starch Worldwide, only one out of three Americans received a passing grade on their environmental knowledge (EPA, 1999b:1). When people at leisure interact with the natural environment, three ingredients characterize the interaction, especially when they are simultaneously exposed to the leadership of a role model (Chase, 1990:55-56):

1. *Direct experience* provides a reference point to view the effect of leisure on the natural environment and may nurture empathy for other users and an environmental conscience.
2. *Cognition,* enhanced by direct experience, provides for short-term and long-term betterment of the environment due to a strengthened knowledge base.
3. *Ethics,* positively influenced by cognition, produce an immediate betterment in the form of awareness of the aesthetic appeal of a natural environment that is free of debris and other traces of the user. Long-term betterment results through responsible management grounded in an ethical framework.

THE ENVIRONMENTAL MOVEMENT

Early environmentalists, like Henry David Thoreau, George Perkins Marks, and John Muir, provided the foundation for the environmental movement (Sessions, 1995:164-165). And President Theodore Roosevelt propelled the first wave of the conservation campaign when he announced in his first State of the Union that natural resource issues were "the most vital international problems of the United States." A second wave resulted when President Franklin D. Roosevelt set up the Civilian Conservation Corps and encouraged scientists to think holistically. The conservation-minded scientists, like Aldo Leopold, influenced the public to look at the broader picture of the interaction between people and the environment. When Rachel Carson's 1962 book *Silent Spring* came out, it served as a mandate for a cause that was waiting to happen. Adding fuel to the fire, Stewart L. Udall, secretary of the Interior from 1961 to 1969, predicted an environmental crisis in his 1963 book *The Quiet Crisis.* When a series of environmental accidents followed, such as a fire on the polluted Cuyahoga River in Cleveland and an oil spill off California in the Santa Barbara Harbor, a third wave took place. Citizens were aroused into action and environmental laws, such as the Federal Clean Air Act of 1963, Wilderness Act of 1964, Land and Water Conservation Fund Act of 1965, National Wildlife Refuge System Administration Act of 1966, Wild and Scenic Rivers Act of 1968, and the National Environmental Policy Act of 1969 were passed (Moody, 2000:14, 24; Williams, 2000:144).

On April 22, 1970, environmentalists led by Senator Gaylord Nelson, called the father of Earth Day, were drawn together for a series of environmental teach-ins across the nation that were coordinated by Denis Hayes, who now heads the Earth Day Network. The next year, President Richard Nixon signed the law creating the United States Environmental Protection Agency (EPA). In 1973, Congress passed the Endangered Species Act, one of the most comprehensive laws ever enacted to prevent the extinction of imperiled life. That same year, the debate over the last frontier in Alaska began. The Alaska Lands Act was signed in December 1980 as one of President Jimmy Carter's last official acts, although oil drilling in the Alaska National Wildlife Refuge is still debated today. During the 1980s, memberships in environmental and conservation organizations soared. By the 1990s, there were more than 10,000 nonprofit environmental groups in the United States, according to the Conservation Fund. They ranged from traditional land and wildlife conservation or nature education groups to hybrids of health and pollution control organizations (Moody, 2000:14-15).

When more than 200 million people in 140 countries participated in Earth Day 1990, Hayes announced that he believed that the environmental movement was the most successful social movement in the United States (Moody, 2000:14-15). With support from 95 percent of all Americans and 96 percent of parents, environmental education in schools became the norm (EPA, 1999b:2). By 1996, President William Clinton protected 1.9 million acres of Utah redrock as the Grand Staircase-Escalante National Monument. In his second term, he proposed permanent protection for more than 58 million acres of wild, roadless national forests, and before leaving office had designated or expanded by presidential proclamation more than 22 national monuments (Pope, 2001:16). Earth Day 2000 attracted an estimated 500 million people—25 times the number of those who took part in the first Earth Day in 1970—to activities that focused on the roots of environmental awareness in America, which began with the American Indians.

Environmental Approaches

Environmentalists are generally divided into two basic philosophical groups. *Reformists* believe that environmental problems are resolved through technology, increased governmental and industrial expenditures, and ceaseless public vigilance and legal action. Their critics maintain that they do not reach the root causes of the ecocrisis, thereby failing to turn the tide of global environmental destruction. These *deep environmentalists* do not believe in a technological fix, but, instead, focus on an entirely new social and economic value system that they believe will help prevent environmental deterioration. Concluding that a decrease in the consumption of the earth's resources is essential, they support a move from an anthropocentric to a spiritual/ecocentric value orientation (Capra, 1995:20-21; Sessions, 1995 xxi).

The *anthropocentric* orientation, also known as *shallow* ecology, views humans as above or outside of nature. Under this orientation, the wilderness is preserved in a piecemeal fashion based on rationales like aesthetics and recreation. The motivation to protect entire ecosystems and maintain ecosystem integrity was fundamentally ignored and compromises became the norm (Sessions, 1995:6). In the holistic *ecocentric* orientation, wilderness areas are much more than aesthetic or recreational spaces. They are also seen as essential components in the newer ecological concept of an unfinished system of interconnected nature preserves that will provide habitat for wide-ranging or sensitive wilderness-dependent species (Foreman, 1995:50-56; Sessions, 1995:6). Like the American Indians, these environmentalists believe that society must live in harmony with all living things (Capra, 1995:20-21). They hold contrasting positions on issues such as pollution, resources, human overpopulation, cultural diversity and appropriate technology, land and sea ethics, and education and the scientific enterprise (Naess, 1995:71-74). For example, the shallow approach views conservation of resources for future generations of humans, whereas the *deep* approach takes this a step further. Although they recognize the need to use resources to satisfy vital needs, they will not come into conflict with the vital needs of nonhumans in order to satisfy non-vital needs. While it is believed that the deep ecology approach will last well into the twenty-first century, one question looms in the horizon. How much irreversible global ecological destruction will result before existing trends can be significantly reversed (Sessions, 1995:xxi)? Critics of the deep movement insist that no matter how one feels about the environment, it is the political actors who will make the decision to destroy or protect it (Slater, 2001:52).

At the Interior's 2001 Conference on the Environment, *The Path Before Us: Environmental Stewardship for the 21st Century*, participants were exposed to both philosophies. Technological training was offered and American Indians explained their view of the earth and the environment (Mathews, 2001:8). Whichever philosophy or combination of philosophies is endorsed, solutions to environmental problems are vital. Worldwatch Institute, an environment research group, warns government officials that many global ecosystems are in danger (Dunphy, 2001:25). Several environmental issues affecting outdoor recreation follow, but further study of these issues will be required. Future leaders will be expected to educate others and sensitize the public to problems related to the use and enjoyment of nature.

THE NATURE OF ECOSYSTEMS

All organisms share an evolutionary history and an ecological kinship. An *ecosystem* is a community of all living organisms that function together in a particular environment. This includes every plant, insect, aquatic animal, bird, or land species (including humans) that forms a complex web of interdependency. An action taken at any level in the food chain has a potential domino effect on every other occupant of that system. This could include the use of pesticides, for example. *Ecology* is the study of these relationships within the environment (EPA, 1996:52).

Ecological relationships are manifested in physiochemical settings of nonliving, or *abiotic,* environmental substances and gradients. These groups consist of basic inorganic elements and compounds such as oxygen, water, carbon dioxide, and an array of organic compounds, the by-products of organism activity. Also included are physical factors and gradients such as moisture, winds, currents, tides, and solar radiation. *Biotic* components, or the living components, such as plants, animals, and microbes, interplay against the abiotic backdrop (EPA, 1996:52; Kormondy, 1984:1-2,159). These relationships are so intricate, however, that only the most obvious mysteries have been unraveled. The following cycles exhibit noteworthy relationships:

1. **The Food Chain Cycle**
   A sequence of organisms, each of which uses the next, lower member of the sequence as a food source. Plants flourish by receiving energy from the sun and nutrients from the soil. Smaller animals consume the plants, larger animals feed on the smaller, and so on. Upon their deaths the bodies decompose and return to the soil, where plants absorb the fresh nutrients, thus completing the chain.

2. **The Oxygen-Carbon Cycle**
   Similar to the food chain cycle, the oxygen-carbon cycle generates life. Animals consume oxygen and exhale carbon dioxide. Carbon dioxide is also produced when plants and animals decay and when fuels are burned. Plants use carbon dioxide to produce oxygen. Sunlight, the source of all energy, works with the photosynthetic pigments such as green chlorophyll in plants to combine carbon from the air with water to originate sugars that plants use for food. This process, *photosynthesis*, or making something from light, allows for the production of oxygen.

3. **The Water Cycle**
   Plants and animals depend on water, which permits foods and gases to pass through the cells

of plants and animals. Relying on the sun for power, water circulates through the environment in a cycle. The sun's heat evaporates water from the aquatic ecosystems. The vapors form clouds, and when the air cools or becomes filled with moisture, the vapor falls as rain, snow, sleet, or hail. Plants use the water soaked into the soil. Some water becomes part of the groundwater supply, forming springs and wells, which eventually returns to lakes and oceans where it can evaporate, continuing the cycle.

In general, there are two major types of ecosystems: aquatic and terrestrial with subdivisions that will be discussed in this chapter. *Aquatic ecosystems* are distinguished as freshwater, estuarine, and marine ecosystems, while *terrestrial ecosystems* include forests, tundra, savanna, grasslands, and desert. Very large ecosystems are sometimes referred to as *ecoregions*. In recent years, policymakers have become more cognizant of the significance of preserving the natural diversity in these physical environments (Loomis, Bonetti, & Echohawk, 1999:351). And since ecosystems do not stop at traditional boundary lines, active partnerships between the federal agencies and the federal, state, and public agencies with private industry have become extremely important.

Ecosystem management (EM) is an environmentally sensitive, socially responsible, and scientifically sound way to manage the nation's public land so that the environment will be healthy, diverse, and productive. EM also means trying to restore damaged resources to a healthy condition. When healthy, ecosystems provide clean, clear water; furnish habitat for fish, wildlife, and plants; offer way stations for migratory birds; help purify the air and prevent soil erosion; supply rich, fertile, and productive soils; turn over higher water tables; afford greener streamside area; allow for more songbirds; clean streambanks; create buffers for flooding; present better fishing and hunting; result in a more resilient mix of native plants; effect increased productivity; produce healthier livestock; and encourage disease-free forests. Healthy ecosystems also help to ensure that future generations will have the opportunity to draw social, aesthetic, and spiritual benefits from the land. Recognizing the importance of healthy ecosystems, Americans are showing an increased concern for air and water pollution (Roper Starch, 2000:5).

NATURE CHANGING

Nature changes constantly, and these alterations are essential for living things to thrive. For example, a forest matures gradually, taking hundreds or even thousands of years to develop. In an area starting as a pond, soil washes in from hillsides and collects along the edges. Wind carries grass seeds which take root in the soil. As the grass grows and dies, it mats and decays, producing a nutrient-rich bed for larger plants. Frogs and fish find protection among the plants, and insects lay eggs on the leaves. These plants and animals eventually expire, decay, and build a more fertile soil which ultimately becomes home to bushes and small trees. As the plants decay, they form additional earth for larger trees which gradually grow into a stand or forest. The pond disappears and the forest, which has developed through the long process of succession, has a vast number of plants and animals within it. Diversity in the forest acts as a buffer against drastic change, allowing an area to adjust slowly to new conditions. If one tree species is destroyed, for instance, another may take over. Should a solitary species exist in an area, any threat would endanger the entire forest.

Rapid natural changes also occur from forest fires or volcanic eruptions. Destruction by forest fire allows for a continuing process of succession. Humans, too, have the ability to alter the earth. We may suit our needs, rather than adapting our needs to existing conditions. While not intending to harm the environment, outdoor recreationists have an impact. Steps taken to minimize this impact such as the no-trace ethic are addressed in Chapter 15, Outdoor Recreational Activities.

Climate Change

Never free from change, the earth's atmosphere varies in composition and temperature. In the last two centuries, though, the composition of the atmosphere has undergone disturbing changes. A dramatic increase in carbon dioxide (CO_2), caused by the burning of fossil fuels and the clearing and burning of forests for agriculture, has resulted in greater quantities of carbon dioxide into the atmosphere than can be removed by photosynthesis on land or by diffusion in the oceans. Scientists are concerned that the growing burden of carbon dioxide and other gasses will enhance a warming trend. Most are in near-unanimous agreement that the world has warmed about 1 degree Fahrenheit in the past 140 years, and the United Nations-sponsored Inter-governmental Panel on Climate Change (IPCC) projects an increase in average global temperatures of 3 to 10.4 degrees Fahrenheit this century (Watson & Weisman, 2000:1A; Gelbspan, 2001:63).

Climate change, commonly used inter-changeably with *global warming* and the *greenhouse effect*, refers to the buildup of human-made gases in the atmosphere that trap the sun's heat, causing changes in weather patterns on a global scale. The effects include changes in rainfall pattern, sea level rise, potential droughts, habitat loss, and heat stress. The greenhouse gases of most concern are carbon dioxide, meth-ane, and nitrous oxides (EPA, 1996:48; EPA, 1998b:1). Carbon dioxide is respon-sible for about 83 percent of greenhouse gases. Methane (CH_4) results from agricul-tural activities, landfills, and other sources. Nitrous oxide (NO_4), known as laughing gas, includes everything from nitrogen based fertilizer to manure from farm animals (Watson & Weisman, 2001:2:A). It has also been learned that some catalytic converters, used to reduce smog from cars,

rearrange compounds to form nitrous oxide. The EPA calculates that production of nitrous oxide from vehicles rose by nearly 50 percent between 1990 and 1996 as older cars without converters have neared extinction. This is of special concern because emissions are increasing rapidly, and nitrous oxide is 300 times more potent than carbon dioxide (Wald, 1998:A-7). If greenhouse gases in the atmosphere double, the earth could warm up by 1.5 to 4.5 degrees by the year 2050 (EPA, 1996:48).

Half of the glacial ice in the Alps has melted in the past century, the sea has risen half a foot, and the temperature in the Antarctic Peninsula has gone up three degrees since the 1940s, according to environmental author John J. Berger, who suggests that global warming may also be responsible for increasingly severe weather, including more extreme El Nino cycles in the Pacific and a record number of hurri-canes in the Atlantic (Schildgen, 2001:85). If global rainfall patterns shift, it could cause deserts to expand, rich farmland to suffer droughts, heavier flooding, ice sheets to melt, oceans to expand, loss of habitat, the disappearance of endangered species, heat-related death, and the increase of infectious diseases like malaria (Rauber, 2001:64). To stabilize the climate, human-ity needs to cut greenhouse gas emissions (Gelbspan, 2001:63). On the question of global warming and the nation's responsi-bility, 57 percent of respondents polled in a nationwide survey favor reducing carbon dioxide emissions as a national responsibil-ity (NPCA, 2001:12).

Taking Initiative

Approaches for tackling global warming and air pollution follow:

Kyoto Protocol

In 1992, 150 countries signed the *Frame-work Convention on Climate Change (FCCC)*, which has the objective of stabiliz-ing the concentration of greenhouse gases in the atmosphere at levels that would prevent dangerous interference with the climate system. Parties to the FCCC formulated the *Kyoto Protocol* at a 1997 conference held in Kyoto, Japan. The Kyoto Protocol includes greenhouse gas emission targets for industrialized countries for the period of 2008-2012. The average reduction target for all industrialized countries for this period is five percent below 1990 emission levels. This target varies across countries to account for differing circumstances, with the United States' target being a seven percent reduction below 1990 levels. The Kyoto Protocol also provides for market-based measures, such as international emissions trading with other countries, to help them meet their commitments at the lowest possible cost (EPA, 1998c:2). Supporters of the proposal believe that the United States' compliance costs are modest and will be offset by savings from sharply declining energy use. Opponents believe that compliance would be too costly, and that similar demands should be placed on developing nations (Watson & Weisman, 2001:2A).

Climate Action Plan

The United States adopted a *Climate Action Plan (CCAP)* in 1993 to reduce greenhouse gas emissions. Thousands of companies and nonprofit organizations are working together to effectively reduce their emissions. The Plan involves more than 40 programs implemented by the Department of agriculture, the Department of Energy, and the EPA. By 1997, these voluntary programs reduced green house gas emissions by more than 15 million tons of carbon, while partners saved over one billion dollars from energy bill savings (EPA, 1998c:2).

Clean Air Act

The Clean Air Act of 1970 is the comprehensive federal law that regulates air emissions from area, stationary, and mobile sources. This law authorizes the EPA to establish National Ambient Air Quality Standard (NAAQS) to protect public health and the environment. The goal of the Act was to set and achieve NAAQS in every state by 1975. The setting of maximum pollutant standards was coupled with

directing the states to develop state implementation plans (SIP's) applicable to appropriate industrial sources in the state. In 1977 the Act was amended primarily to set new dates for achieving attainment of NAAQS since many areas of the country had failed to meet the deadlines (EPA, 1996:1). The 1990 amendments to the Clean Air Act in large part were intended to address problems such as acid rain, ground-level ozone, stratospheric ozone depletion, and air pollutants commonly called toxic air pollutants.

Since Congress passed the amendments, EPA has issued air standards which when fully implemented will reduce one million tons of toxic air emissions each year. Despite continued improvements in air quality, approximately 107 million people still live in counties where monitored data show unhealthy air for one or more of the six principal pollutants: carbon monoxide, lead, nitrogen dioxide, ozone, particulate matter, and sulfur dioxide. While many of the more industrialized areas have high pollution levels due to increased use of motor vehicles and local industries in their vicinity, some rural locations are also experiencing increased air pollution levels (EPA, 1998c:1).

AIR POLLUTION AND ACID RAIN IN RECREATION AREAS

When travelers were asked if they had ever been adversely affected by air quality at a vacation destination, 47 percent of the respondents to one survey answered yes (Mark Clements Research, 1996:22). Visitors should not assume that air quality in our treasured national parks is better than in surrounding towns and cities. Park Service officials at dozens of national parks, monuments, and wilderness areas have been monitoring air quality since an amendment was added to the Clean Air Act in 1977. Some national parks have even experienced high air pollution concentrations as a result of pollutants being transported many miles from their original source. Ground-level ozone concentrations in remote locations of the Great Smoky

Mountains National Park in Tennessee and North Carolina, for example, have increased nearly 20 percent over the last 10 years (EPA, 1998c:1). It also kills and damages leaves, forcing them to fall off the plants too soon or become spotted or brown. These effects can significantly decrease the natural beauty of national parks, forests, and recreation areas.

Ozone, an odorless, colorless gas, can be good or bad depending on where it is found. In the earth's upper atmophere—10 to 12 miles about the earth's surface—it forms a protective layer that shields us from the sun's damaging ultraviolet rays. Because this *good ozone* is gradually being destroyed by human-made chemicals, we are more susceptible to sunburn and skin cancers when we participate in outdoor activities. As such, suntan lotion and sunglasses are highly recommended. Near ground level, in the lower atmosphere, *bad ozone* forms when pollutants react chemically in the presence of sunlight. This can happen frequently during summer months when outdoor adventurers are more likely to head to natural areas for summer trips. Ozone exposure irritates the respiratory system and can become painful, especially for those who actively participate in outdoor recreational activities. If this condition occurs frequently, the lung may change permanently in a way that could cause long-term health effects and a lower quality of life.

In the western United States, the typical visual range is 60 miles or about one-half what it would be without human-made air pollution. In most of the East, the typical visual range is 15 to 30 miles or about one-third of the visual range under natural conditions. The *haze* is caused when sunlight encounters tiny pollution particles in the air. Some of the light is absorbed by particles, while other light is scattered away before it reaches an observer. More pollutants mean more absorption and scattering of light, which reduces the clarity and color of what is seen. From the rim of the Grand Canyon in Arizona, colors sometimes appear faded and rock formations can become indistinguishable to the dismay of outdoor nature photographers and other visitors. Natural sources of air pollution come from sources such as windblown dust, and soot from wildfires. Human-made sources come from motor vehicles, electric utility, industrial fuel burning, manufacturing operations, and other sources (EPA, 1999a:2).

While some haze-causing particles are directly emitted to the air, others are formed when gases emitted to the air form particles as they are carried many miles from the source of pollutants. Air pollution caused by distant power plants, smelters, and automobiles obscure views in some of America's most scenic national parks, forests, and wilderness areas, attesting to the fact that smog has been creeping into our most cherished lands. One research physicist even estimates that visibility is impaired in every national park as much as 80 to 90 percent of the time (Associated Press, 1990). *Smog,* literally a blend of smoke and fog, from the Los Angeles basin is blamed for muddying views and crippling plants in Joshua Tree National Monument, 120 miles away. In 1997, EPA proposed a new regional haze program to address visibility impairment in national parks and wilderness areas. Where such impairment is caused by numerous sources located over broad regions, states are encouraged to coordinate with each other to develop strategies that will improve visibility.

Meanwhile acid deposition, blamed for visibility in the Okefenokee National Wildlife Area in Florida, Boundary Waters Canoe Area in Minnesota, and Upper Buffalo Wilderness Area, places severe stress on many ecosystems. Lakes and bodies of water have increased in acidity, a special concern for anglers. Many of the forests enjoyed by recreationists have been damaged, particularly in the Northeast and at high elevations. *Acid deposition* occurs when emissions of sulfur and nitrogen compounds and other substances form acid compounds. These compounds fall to the Earth in either dry (gas and particles) or wet forms (rain, snow, and fog), known as *acid rain*. Some of these substances are carried by the wind across state lines and national borders (EPA, 1999c:3). Before falling to the earth, they contribute to the poor visibility and impact public health. Besides raising the acid levels in soils and various bodies of water, acid rain also speeds the decay of buildings, statues, and sculptures that are part of our national heritage.

Soil degradation, which causes slower growth, injury or death of forests, impacts Shenandoah and Great Smoky Mountain national parks. Since the thinner soils cannot buffer or neutralize the acid rainwater, nutrients and minerals are washed away before trees and other plants can use them to grow. At the same time, the acid rain causes the release of substances that are toxic to trees and plants. These substances are washed into the watershed. Acidification has taken place in the lakes and streams in Adirondack Park and Catskill Forest Preserve in New York, Shenandoah National Park in the Appalachian Mountains in Virginia, and other recreation areas. A National Surface Water Survey showed that acid rain had caused acidity in 75 percent of the lakes and about 50 percent of the acid streams surveyed. The Canadian government estimates that 14,000 lakes in eastern Canada are acidic (EPA, 2001a:1-2). High acidic levels cause declines in the fish population and species diversity. Some acid lakes have no fish. In higher elevations—even where soil is buffeted—acid clouds and fog blanket trees and strip them of their leaves and needles. The goal of EPA's Acid Rain Program, established by the Clean Air Act, is to reduce levels of sulfates, nitrates, and ground-level ozone to improve health, benefit water quality in lakes and streams, reduce damage to trees, and enhance the beauty of our country's scenic vistas, including those in national parks and forests (EPA, 1999c:13-18; EPA, 1998a:1).

AQUATIC ECOSYSTEMS AND OUTDOOR RECREATION

Water, an odorless, tasteless, substance, covers more than 70 percent of the earth's surface, making *aquatic ecosystems* the earth's most dominate feature. Distinguished on the basis of their salt content, they include freshwater, estuarine, and marine systems. Only about three percent of earth's water is fresh with 66 percent of that in solid form, found in ice caps and glaciers. Most of the earth's water, 97 percent, is saltwater found in oceans. That means only about one percent of the earth's water is available for use by people and land animals (Evergreen Project, 1998:1). This fresh water is acquired in streams, rivers, ponds, lakes, and in the ground. A small amount is found as vapor in the atmosphere.

Water that returns to earth as precipitation runs off the surface of the land, flowing downhill into streams, rivers, ponds, and lakes to eventually reach the ocean or larger lake. A *watershed* is the region in which a common set of streams and rivers work together to do this. Since a watershed includes the larger river and all of its tributaries, a watershed may be large or small. Smaller watersheds are usually part of larger ones. The Mississippi River watershed, for example, covers much of the Midwest and some of the West, including the Rockies. On the way to the ocean, the larger river not only carries the water that runs into streams and rivers from the surface, but also water that has filtered through soil and drains into the same streams and rivers. These processes of *surface runoff* and *infiltration* are important to aquatic ecosystems because the water supplies them. Anything that is not a natural element of the system is a type of pollution. Some types of water pollution can be traced directly to a particular factory or industrial plant. Other types are more difficult to monitor because they come from widespread sources. These include fertilizers spread on fields, runoff of livestock wastes, soil resulting from erosion, pesticides sprayed on lawn and crops, and materials washed from streets into storm drains (Evergreen Project, 1998:1). These pollutants choke the rivers and streams, which should be healthy sources of life.

Freshwater Ecosystems

Some lakes are the source for some rivers, and some rivers end in lakes. Since both are freshwater and flow in and out of each other, they share similar characteristics. These characteristics allow some aquatic life to move in and out of both habitats, whereas others prefer only one environment. Freshwater ecosystems are distinguished as *lotic* or *lentic*, with running water or still water, respectively. Waterfalls are associated with lotic ecosystems. Running fresh-water streams (springs, creeks, brooks) and rivers may vary on their course from narrow and shallow and relatively rapid to increasingly broad, deep, and slow moving. Most streams are characterized by a repeating sequence of rapids and pools (lentic systems) that decrease in frequency downstream. Chemically lentic environments are rich in oxygen upstream. Downstream, where the water becomes more sluggish, oxygen level tends to drop. With a continual addition of nutrients en route, there is also an increase of nutrient levels downstream. Lentic ecosystems, including pools, ponds, bogs, and lakes, vary considerably in their physical, chemical, and biological characteristics (Kormondy, 1984:183).

Human-made dams across rivers control river flow, improve navigation, regulate flooding, or produce hydroelectric power. Water is also used to dilute and remove municipal and industrial waste, for irrigation, cooling purposes, transportation, and recreation. With each use, there is also opportunity for abuse. For example, municipalities and industries have polluted freshwater lakes chemically and thermally. After water is used to irrigate fields, it is frequently returned with chemical residues from fertilizers. Oil and refuse is left behind by ships. And many enthusiastic recreational users commonly ignore basic sanitary and antipollution practices to the detriment of the waters enjoyed. Others believe that public waters can be used as they see fit. To improve water pollution, the *Federal Water Pollution Control Act of 1972* set the basic structure for regulating discharges of pollutants into waters. The Clean Water Act (CWA) followed as a 1977 amendment to the Federal Water Pollution Control Act. The law, focusing on toxic substances, gave EPA the authority to set effluent standards on an industry-by-industry basis and continued the requirements to set water quality standards for all contaminants in surface waters. It also makes it unlawful to discharge any pollutant into navigable waters without a permit. In 1987, when CWA was reauthorized, it condoned citizen suit provisions and funded sewage treatments plants (EPA, 1998c:73). The CWA provides for the delegation by EPA of many permitting, administrative, and enforcement aspects of the law to state governments which EPA oversees.

Inevitably environmental choices will have to be made as sources of water are exploited. Poor water quality has vastly affected recreational pursuits. One survey disclosed that more than half of the respondents had to forego swimming at a vacation destination because of the water quality (Mark Clements Research, 1996:22). For the continuation of water recreation activities, recreation and park professionals are becoming more knowledgeable and defensive of the resource, and educate others about the resource to modify behaviors and attitudes. Managers are making long-term plans, remembering that they are working with a living system whose health is at risk from human factors. These plans address water quality, habitat health and capacity, commercial and residential development, economic impact, and recreation use (Caneday & Neal, 1996:56).

Environmental Impacts on Freshwater Sportfishing

Nearly 20 percent of the Bass Club respondents, composed primarily of anglers, identified pollution as a constraint to participation (Cordell et al, 1997:78). The Bass Club is one of the seven market segments defined by the National Survey on Recreation and the Environment (NSRE). In an attempt to ensure environmental safety of fish habitats, fishing organizations, such as the Bass Anglers

Sportsman Society (BASS) has made this a primary goal. BASS resurrected the 1899 Refuse Act in 1970, filing lawsuits against more than 200 polluters. They created Anglers for Clean Water, and they organized affiliated clubs into 25 federations that work with state agencies on pollution problems. Working together fishing organizations like this lobbied to pass and protect key provisions to the 1984 Wallop-Breaux Amendment to the Dingell-Johnson Sportfish Restoration Act. This brought more than one billion dollars from additional taxes on motorboat fuel and fishing tackle into state fish and wildlife agencies for management programs, which include safeguarding endangered species, catching poachers and polluters, protecting birds and marine life from oil spills, stocking streams, and staving off commercial development in animal habitats (Cordell et al, 1999:310-311). Anglers are also looking for ways to help species that are hurt by dams when using rivers to spawn.

While dams on rivers provide clean, pollution-free energy, they can harm the environment (Evergreen Project, 1998:1). For years salmon have been fighting dams and other diversions built on rivers. Some dams have even taken on names such as "Fish-Killer" dam because swirling waters and backwash have disoriented their delicate homing mechanisms. In the Northwest, sockeye salmon and trout populations have dropped from 16 million to 2.5 million since hydroelectric plants were built on the Columbia River (Evergreen Project, 1998:1). Salmon, for instance, leave the ocean to return to the freshwater stream where they were first hatched to breed, lay their eggs, and die. About the same time that they are traveling upstream, young salmon, called smolts, are trying to make it down the Columbia River to the ocean. When human-made fish ladders—concrete waterways that guide the salmon above the dam—are available, only a small percentage of the adults headed upstream are stopped by the dam. After the trip, however, some are too tired to spawn. Others are taken by predators who take advantage of the situation by

waiting to feed on them at the bottom of the dam. More lethal are the turbines that kill smolts headed downstream. As they are forced through the powerhouses at high pressure and speed their swim bladders explode. Moreover, reservoirs flood the gravel bars where salmon spawn, thereby increasing the time it takes smolts to move from streams to the ocean. This also gives predators more time to attack. Heat upstream increases mortality as well (Montaigne, 2001:25). As salmon disappear, hatcheries have bred the wildness out of them, inhibiting genetic diversity. Anglers complain that beautiful fish have been replaced with "just another dumb fish." Likewise, some of the fish caught off the Columbia at a Willamette River Superfund site show high levels of deformity that may result from agricultural and industrial pollutants.

Experts agree that the only real safeguard against extinction is to restore the salmon's natural spawning grounds and stream dynamics. One free-flowing stretch of the Columbia on the Hanford Ranch, where an estimated 30,000 salmon spawn, was protected from development when it was declared a national monument by President Clinton. Furthermore, a passionate commitment among citizens' groups and anglers is helping to heal streams and restore some fish runs. Courts have recognized the salmon's need for water as equal to human need. The Northwest Power Planning Council was established in 1980 to help coordinate conservation efforts. Fish and power were given equal priority, causing a modest salmon recovery on the Columbia River. Fish ladders were added and turbine intakes screened. Deflectors were fitted on spillways, helping to speed young salmon downstream around some dams—approximately eight to ten percent are killed at each dam and pool (Montaigne, 2001:25). To lower death rates, the National Marine Fisheries Service (NMFS) and the Army Corps of Engineers began barging three-quarters of all salmon and steelhead smolts to release points in the 1970s. Unfortunately, only a little over one percent make their way back to spawn. It is debated whether some of the dams should be dismantled to create a free-flowing lower Snake River in order to rebuild commercial and sportfishing industries. A new economy based on tourism, angling, and recreation could be worth hundreds of millions annually, but such a move would eliminate or restrict those who depend on dams for their livelihood, including farmers and barge operators.

California populations of steelhead trout have dropped by more than 90 percent. They, too, are born in freshwater streams and migrate to the ocean to live as adults. Unlike salmon, they make numerous trips to their freshwater origins to spawn. By the mid-1960s, dams had blocked access to tributary spawning beds and dried some streams. Other streams were uninhabitable due to logging, mining, agriculture, and other developments. Many waters were simply overfished. To anglers, they represent the pinnacle of freshwater fishing, and they want to save them. The turnabout came when anglers became concerned that wild strains of trout were disappearing. Where southern coast populations have been listed as endangered, many anglers and concerned citizens support the removal of Rindge Dam at Malibu Canyon. The dam, built 70 years ago to impound water for a ranch, silted up in only 20 years. Removal of the dam is estimated to cost about $18 million, but it would free eight miles of prime spawning habitat for steelhead and be beneficial for Pacific lamprey, another anadromous fish (Slack, 1998:6-7).

Working with state biologists, small groups of anglers have helped to develop management programs that protect remaining wild trout populations. Some states have developed wild trout programs, setting restrictions on tackle and catch limits, including *catch-and-release programs* or the gentle handling to resuscitate and release fish back into the waters. *Resuscitation* includes sweeping the fish back and forth through the water with wet hands to restore oxygen to its gills after its long struggle on the line. Few states, however, have laws to protect designated wild trout streams from poor land-use practices, and existing laws are not broad enough.

Preservation is possible when the public demands it. In Nueltin Lake in central Canada on the border between Manitoba and the Northwest Territories, one trend-setting law increased clientele. Here the "big one" must be returned. This is a departure from standard angling ethics, which allow anglers to keep all or most of the big fish caught, returning the little ones. Unless participating in catch-and-release programs, the vast majority of anglers still follow the standard ethic, assuming that the small fish will replace the larger ones in future years. Part of the practice revolves around sportsmanship: smaller fish are easier to catch, while the larger fish is smarter and more worthy. Minimum-size regulations, however, have added to the rapid depletion of large native fish in the more popular fresh-water lakes and streams. In New York state, for example, the largest brook trout ever caught was in 1908, weighing eight pounds, eight ounces, and the largest northern pike was caught in 1940, weighing 46 pounds, two ounces. Today nothing approaches these sizes. The theory that the small fish will grow to the size of the larger has not proven true. Typically smaller fish make up at least 90 percent of the population (Hope, 1990:57-58). Because they are protected, they tend to remain small or stunted due to lack of food. In addition, trophy fish have the capacity to reproduce more big fish. In many North American waterways, large fish have essentially been angled out, leaving lakes and rivers with little or no genetic potential.

It is quite possible that angling laws will need to change direction if we expect to have any big fish left (Hope, 1990:50). Additional safeguards at Nueltin include allowing only the trained guides to resuscitate the fish. Anglers may not pose too long for trophy shots or use any lure except live bait. All multiple hooks must be removed and replaced with a barbless single hook to ensure a quick and easy release. No fish may be weighed with the traditional, damaging jaw scale. Instead, the length-girth conversion system is used to calculate the weight. Following the experiment, Manitoba became the first province or state in North America to pass a law requiring barbless hooks for all of its sportfishing. Many of its lakes and rivers follow either *no-trophy* or *one-trophy* rules. Several states and provinces, including Wyoming, Montana, Minnesota, and Ontario, are basing most of their sportfishing laws or policies to protect big fish. On the Atlantic coast, from North Carolina to Newfoundland, maximum-size laws regulate the taking of two imperiled species, the striped bass and the Atlantic salmon (Hope, 1990:50). New moral pressures can help to establish a new code so that future generations can go fishing in North America.

Estuaries and Wetlands

An *estuary* is a complex ecosystem defined more by salinity than geographical boundaries. The partially enclosed body of water is formed where freshwater from rivers and streams flows into the ocean, mixing with the salty seawater. Estuaries and lands surrounding them are places of transition from land to sea, and from fresh to saltwater. Although influenced by the tides, they are protected from the full force of ocean waves, winds, and storms by the reefs, barrier islands, or fingers of land, mud, or sand that define an estuary's seaward boundary. Estuaries come in all shapes and sizes and are often known as bays, lagoons, harbors, inlets, sounds, and sloughs (EPA, 2001b:1-3). Nonetheless, not all bodies by those names are estuaries. It is the mixing of waters, not the name, that defines an estuary. Familiar examples include San Francisco Bay (California), South Slough (Oregon), Indian River Lagoon (Florida), Galveston Bay (Texas), North Inlet/Winyah Bay (South Carolina), Boston Harbor (Massachusetts), and Long Island Sound (New York and Connecticut).

The tidal sheltered waters of estuaries support unique communities of plants and animals that are especially adapted for life at the margin of the sea. These estuarine environments are among the most produc-tive on earth, creating more organic matter each year than comparably sized areas of forest, grassland, or agricultural land. Many different habitat types are found in and around estuaries, including shallow open waters, freshwater and salt marshes, sandy beaches, mud and sand flats, rocky shores, oyster reefs, mangrove forests, river deltas, tidal pools, sea grass and kelp beds, and wooded swamps (EPA,2001c:1). The productivity and variety of estuarine habitats foster an abundance and diversity of wildlife, including shore birds, fish, crabs and lobsters, clams and shellfish, reptiles, and marine mammals that make their homes in and around estuaries. These animals are linked to one another and to an assortment of specialized plants and microscopic organisms through complex food webs and other interactions. Estuarine environments also provide ideal spots for migratory birds to rest and protected places for species of fish and shellfish to spawn.

These critical living resources also provide Americans with vast aesthetic, recreational, economical opportunities while reducing polluted runoff and controlling flooding. Photography, swimming, boating, birdwatching, and fishing are just a few of the outdoor activities enjoyed. In fact, the average American spends 10 recreational days on the coast each year, where approximately 25,000 recreational facilities along the nation's coasts await them (see also Marine Ecosystems below). To illustrate, estuaries provide habitat for 80 to 90 percent the country's recreational fish catch and more than 75 percent of the nation's commercial catch. In just one estuarine system, Massachusetts and Cape Cod Bays, commercial and recreational fishing generate about $240 million per year. In that same estuary, shipping and marinas bring in 1.86 billion per year, and tourism and beach-going yield $1.5 billion per year. Nationwide coastal recreation and tourism generate about $8 to $12 billion annually (EPA, 2001c:2).

As our population grows around these already populated coastal areas, where roughly 110 million Americans or about half of the United States population live, the demands imposed on our estuarine and marine ecosystems have increased tremendously (EPA, 2001c:4). Decisions to convert natural resource wetlands to real estate by filling them to create waterfront lots or dredging them to make canals or otherwise interfering with normal tidal circulation by draining, impounding, or diking are the subject of extensive controversy. Additionally, abundant pollution from discharges of domestic and industrial wastes can cause serious deterioration of their functions. Stresses caused by overuse and unchecked land use have resulted in unsafe drinking water, beach and shellfish bed closings, harmful algal blooms, unproductive fisheries, fish kills, wildlife loss, excessive nutrient pollution, and loss of habitat (EPA, 2001c: 2-3). San Francisco Bay has lost 95 percent of its associated wetlands, while Chesapeake Bay—the largest estuary in the United States—has lost 90 percent of its seagrass meadows. Louisiana's estuaries lose about 25,000 acres of coastal marshes annually to development (Lord, 1998:38).

The National Estuary Program (NEP) is designed to restore and protect America's nationally significant estuaries. Through its approach of inclusive, community-based planning and action on the watershed level, the NEP is an important initiative toward conserving estuarine resources. Under the coastal Zone Management Act of 1972, as amended, NOAA protects and studies estuarine areas through a network of 25 reserves. The National Estuary Program, administered by the EPA, was established in 1987 by amendments to the Clean Water Act. This program encourages federal, state, and local communities to work together to maintain estuaries as a whole system, protecting their chemical, physical, biological, economic, recreational, and aesthetic properties and values. In the future, communities will need to make every effort to prevent or limit disruptive activities, control pollution, restore former saltwater wetlands as possible, and define the boundaries of their natural resources.

Wetlands, a collective term for marshes, swamps, bogs, prairie potholes, and similar areas found in generally flat vegetated areas, in depressions in the landscape, and between dry land and water along the edges of streams, rivers, lakes, and, of course, coastline, vary widely because of regional and local differences in soils, topography, climate, hydrology, water chemistry, vegetation, and other factors, including human disturbance. They can be large or very small, wet at all times, or look completely dry most of the time. Overall, they fall into two general categories, the coastal or tidal wetlands already mentioned and inland or non-tidal wetlands (EPA, 2001c:1).

The coastal wetlands that fringe many estuaries provide crucial habitat for wildlife and perform other valuable services. As the water drained from the uplands flows through fresh and salt marshes, much of the sediments, nutrients, and other pollutants that were carried in the water are filtered out. This filtration process creates cleaner and clearer water, which benefits people and marine life. Wetland plants and soils also act as a natural buffer between the land and ocean, absorbing flood waters and dissipating storm surges. This protects upland organisms as well as valuable real estate from storm and flood damage. Salt marsh grasses and other estuarine plants also help prevent erosion and stabilize the shoreline. The wetland vegetation removes silt, toxic chemicals, and nutrients from coastal water. If wetland vegetation were eliminated, the food supply, and thus the carrying capacity of the coastal ecosystem, would be greatly reduced. Besides the *coastal wetlands,* which include unvegetated mud flats or sand flats, tidal salt marshes with grasses and grasslike plants, and mangrove swamps with salt-loving shrubs or trees that are linked to our nation's estuaries, some tidal freshwater wetlands form beyond the upper edges of tidal salt marshes (EPA, 2001c:1). This is where the influence of salt water ends and inland wetlands begin.

Inland wetlands are most common on floodplains along rivers (riparian wetlands), in isolated depressions surrounded by dry land (playas, basins, and potholes, for example), along the margins of lakes and ponds, and in other low-lying areas where the groundwater intercepts the soil surface or where precipitation sufficiently saturates the soil (vernal pools and bogs). Inland wetlands include marshes and wet meadows dominated by herbaceous plants, swamps dominated by shrubs, and wooded swamps dominated by trees. Certain types of inland wetlands are common to particular regions of the country. These include bogs and fens of the northeastern and north-central states and Alaska; wet meadows or wet prairies in the Midwest; inland saline and alkaline marshes and riparian wetlands of the arid and semiarid west; prairie potholes of Iowa, Minnesota, and the Dakotas; alpine meadows of the west; playa lakes of the southwest and Great Plains; bottomland hardwood swamps of the south; pocosins and Carolina Bays of the southeast coastal states; tundra wetlands of Alaska (EPA, 2001c:1-2). Many of these are seasonal or wet only periodically, particularly in the arid and semiarid West. The quantity of water and the timing of its presence in part determine the functions of a wetland.

Found from the tundra to the tropic and on every continent except Antarctica, wetlands are among the most productive ecosystems in the world, comparable to rain forests and coral reefs. Yet, because they have been regarded as wastelands, sources of mosquitos, odors, and disease, more than half of America's original wetlands have been destroyed since the days that European settlement began. In the United States, an estimated 220 million acres of wetlands that existed in the lower 48 during the 1600s fell to the estimated 103.3 million acres of wetlands by the mid-1980s. In Alaska, there is an estimated 170-200 million acres of wetlands, while Hawaii has another 52,000 acres (EPA, 2001c:1). The years from the mid-1950s to the mid-1970s brought much of the loss—about 458,000 acres a year—as wetlands were drained, filled, or used to dispose of household and industrial waste (Watson, 1999:12A).

Realizing that these losses helped lead the way to declining bird populations, for example, and increased flood and drought damages, we now know that wetlands provide values that no other ecosystem can. These include natural water quality improvement, natural products for our use, flood and shoreline erosion control, habit protection for wildlife, and opportunities for outdoor recreation and aesthetic gratifications. Wetlands, particularly on America's National Wildlife Refuges, offer wildlife and plant life observation, birding, photography, hunting, fishing, canoeing, sightseeing, and hiking on trails and boardwalks. Wetland management districts were created in 1962 as the Fish and Wildlife Service's land acquisition program accelerated because of increasing Duck Stamp sales. Wetland management staff also manage wetland easements and work with willing private landowners who protect their wetlands. Protecting wetlands also protects our welfare and saves money. In performing their filtering function, a 1990 study showed that without the Congaree Bottomland Hardwood Swamp, a national monument in South Carolina, the area would need a $5 million waste water treatment plant. In addition to improving water quality through filtering, some wetlands maintain stream flow during dry periods, and several replenish groundwater that many depend on for drinking. Wetlands also store carbon within their plant communities and soil instead of releasing it to the atmosphere as carbon dioxide, thus helping moderate global climate.

The federal government protects wetlands through regulations (such as Section 404 of the Clean Water act and watershed protection initiatives), economic incentives and disincentives, cooperative programs, and acquisitions for national wildlife refuges. Beyond the federal level, a number of states have enacted laws to regulate activities in wetlands, and some counties and towns have adopted local wetlands protection ordinances or have changed the way development is permitted. Most coastal states have significantly reduced losses of coastal wetlands through protective laws. Few states, however, have laws specifically regulating activities in inland wetlands, although some states and local governments have non-regulatory programs that help protect wetlands. Recently, partnerships to manage whole watersheds have developed among federal, state, tribal, and local governments; non-profit organizations; and private landowners. The goal of these partnerships is to implement comprehensive, integrated watershed protection approaches that recognize the inter-connectedness of water, land, and wetlands resources for more complete solutions to wetland degradation (see Using Technology for Habitat Protection in this chapter). Finally public efforts in conjunction with states, local governments, and private citizens to educate the public are helping (EPA, 2001c:1-2). With citizen support for wetlands conservation initiatives, wetland loss is slowing to about 100,000 acres per year, but many environmentalists believe that much more needs to be done (Watson, 1999:12A). On the international level the Convention on Wetlands of International Importance held in Ramsar, Iran in 1971 provides a framework for the conservation of wetlands worldwide.

Marine Ecosystems

Standing on the bluffs above any ocean we see beautiful, vast, seemingly limitless water. At its deepest spot in the Mariana Trench, it reaches a depth of 36,198 feet. The concentration of nutrients in the ocean is low. Its salt content if dried would cover all of the continents to a depth of about five feet. Unlike land and freshwater ecosystems, the sea is continuous and is in circulation via the major surface currents. Waves cause the water to oscillate back and forth. The rise and fall of the water level is caused by tides that are related to the gravitational effects of the moon and the sun.

As boundless as they seem, oceans receive enough of the world's waste to have raised public alarm concerning safety of outdoor activities, such as swimming, surfing, and fishing. Shifting sands, foul water, and human-made follies present

threats to coasts. With more people living near and visiting beaches, tons of trash make their way into the ocean. In a one-day beach cleanup held by the California Coastal Commission, 10 tons of trash and 52,000 cigarette butts were collected. Most trash left on all beaches is from beachgoers who do not use trash cans. In one survey by the Center for Marine Conservation, plastic trash was found to be the number-one source of debris on beaches from Miami to Long Beach. Incoming tides from northern New Jersey to Long Island have washed up a nauseating array of waste including drug paraphernalia, medical debris, and balls of sewage 2 inches thick (Perry, 1990:11).

Environmentalists have identified the nation's most significant marine debris problem to be so called "offshore icebergs." Upon closer inspection these icebergs are collages of discarded cups, containers, bottles, and straws. This plastic trash is posing serious problems to wildlife. Undigestible plastic bags are confused for jellyfish and are eaten by whales, dolphins, and turtles. Gulls and other birds eat broken foam cups, eventually choking. Fish become wedged in the plastic rings used for beer and soda cans and are sliced as they grow. Sprawling icebergs, perhaps more aptly termed "trashbergs," are caused by collections of trash flushed into oceans from storm drains, creeks, and rivers (Murphy, 1990:8). Great volumes of sewage pollute beaches. Storm drains bring motor oil, garbage, pesticides, and untreated animal waste directly to beaches. Swimming near drains has resulted in skin rashes and eye and ear infections. Waste-water flow has endangered several bird species and led to warnings not to eat bottom-dwelling fish caught off ocean piers.

Problems worsen with the oil spills from old shore tankers. The largest oil spill in the United States released 37,000 tons of crude oil that affected marine life through western Prince William Sound just below Valdez, Alaska, the Gulf of Alaska, and lower Cook Inlet, passing Kenai Fjords National Park on its way south to contaminate Katmai National Park. Pristine coastlines off Africa, Asia, Europe, and

Standing on the bluffs above any ocean we see a beautiful, vast, seemingly limitless water.

Beach homes with their own individual ladders mar the natural scenery and encourage cliff erosion.

South America and those near the earth's poles have been sadly blighted. Oil continues to clog the ocean. In addition to oil from accidents, tankers dump oil into seas, mostly from flushing oily residue from empty tanks. The toll on wildlife is tragic. Although much remains unknown about the possible long-term effects of spills, it is estimated 3,500 to 5,500 sea otters may have died as a direct consequence of the grounding of the Exxon Valdez (Fair & Becker, 2000:336,341). Other contaminants include industrial chemical, toxic algal blooms, metals, and pesticides.

Chronic stress effects from environmental contaminants have caused widespread concern, particularly as mass mortalities are on the rise. Coastal waters are nearing their capacity to absorb civilian waste. More than 700 dolphins died mysteriously along the Atlantic coast. Many that washed ashore had snouts, flippers, and tails pocked with blisters and craters. In the Gulf of Maine, harbor seals were rated with the highest pesticide level of any U.S. mammal on land or water. From Portland, Maine, to Morehead City, North Carolina, lobsters and crabs were found with gaping holes in their shells. At least 400 California sea lions died during 1998. Fish have been reported with rotted fins and ulcerous lesions. Fragile kelp beds, rivaled only by coral reefs and tropical forests for their biological diversity, are yielding to a hybrid of pollution, dredging, overfishing, and natural change. Coral reefs, habitation to one-third of the world's marine species, are rapidly succumbing to pollution. Bottom-trawling for fish, and other human activities are also responsible. Sophisticated electronic devises are used to spot faster larger boats, impacts of hatchery-destroying pollution, and loss of coastal habitat, yet, marine species in 15 of the world's 17 largest fisheries are in trouble (Fair & Becker, 2000:339; Time, 1988:45-47; Johnson, 2000:G-2; Lord, 1998:36,38; Larkin, 1999:83).

Other mortalities come from indirect threats. Dolphins are entangled in tuna nets, noise and acoustic influences ranging from ship traffic, ocean experimentation, to recreational whale watching. The broadest attack to sea creatures could come from global warming. The Intergovernmental Panel on Climate Change says sea levels could rise about 34 inches this century (Papciak, 2001:82). There could also be increasing sea-surface temperatures and more frequent and severe storms. Greater precipitation would lead to more runoff of pollution and nutrient-laden soil and water into coastal waters. An increasing ultraviolet-B radiation caused by ozone depletion might well damage or kill fish eggs and larvae. This would reduce the productivity of plankton (collection of minute organisms that animals feed on), the source of 70 percent of the planet's oxygen (Lord, 1998:38-39). Some bodies of water have already been almost totally depleted of oxygen—a huge dead zone is adrift in the Gulf of Mexico.

With problems lying miles from the ocean where contaminants enter streams and rivers, corrective action is needed on a national scale. Six-pack rings are made of substances that decompose upon exposure to the ultraviolet light in sunshine. Previously unregulated storm drains are now regulated in some regions. In areas where sewage disposal has undergone upgraded treatment, scientists have measured a concurrent drop in the pollution level on beaches even though sewage is dumped in greater volume. Other positive steps toward diminishing marine pollution include legislation that places cleanup costs of oil spills on oil companies rather than on taxpayers. Commitments have been made to bar offshore drilling, particularly in areas where environmental risks outweigh potential energy benefits. The Clean Air Act impacts ocean vessels, cruise ships, and sewage discharges. And as stewards of the ocean, NOAA is developing computer equipment that can track the potential direction of oil and chemical spills. NOAA also researches, monitors, and assesses toxic red tides, damaging storms,

pollution, and coastal development; works on environmental issues with coastal and ocean experts in other countries and forms international agreements and treaties; makes efforts to balance competing public needs and interests in the use and enjoyment of living marine resources while preserving their biological integrity; protects National Marine Sanctuaries; and works with various partners and volunteers on projects that will embrace their ocean ethic—to preserve, protect, and respect our nation's marine environment.

Coral Reefs and Human Activity

The nation's most extensive living coral reef and third longest barrier reef in the world is adjacent to the 126-mile island chain of the Florida Keys. To protect some of the world's northernmost coral reefs, the nation's and world's first undersea park was established in 1960. The boundaries of John Pennekamp Coral Reef State Park were changed at a later date, placing most of the reefs within an adjacent federal preserve referred to as the Sanctuary. Alarmingly, three freighters ran aground in the area within a 17-day period in 1989, this, and previous concerns for the environment, led to a proposal that all of the reefs from Biscayne to Dry Tortugas national parks be designated the Florida Keys National Marine Sanctuary in 1990.

Although all ships were off-limits, people using the reef can also have an adverse impact of reef resources. An initial influx of recreational boats, divers, and swimmers put pressure on the underwater environment. With five of its most popular reefs attracting nearly 3,000 people a day to generate about $1.6 billion from recreational uses, it had become one of the most popular recreational destinations in the world (Jameson, et al, 2000:4). With the popularity came destruction. Incompetent boat operators crashed into reefs and coral. Portions of reef were broken by impact of boat anchors, and boaters polluted the water with litter, sewage, and petroleum products. They drug hooks, fishing line, and nets across the coral reefs. Lobster traps were placed on reefs and recovered from them. Boats running through shallow water, disturbed and suspended silts with their propellers, while snorkelers and divers kicked up sediment that block essential sunlight. Thousands of swimmers, snorkelers, and divers routinely bumped, scraped, and stood on coral. Their suntan oil inadvertently harmed and killed sensitive corals. Souvenir specimen collecting and spear fishing continued, even where unlawful. Overfishing removed important species that ate the algae growing on corals, causing it to overgrow. Today more than four million domestic and foreign visitors drive, fly, or cruise to the area, especially "during season" from November to April (NOAA, 2001:1-2).

Besides recreational and commercial fishing activities taking a toll, nature can intrude on coral as well. Waves stirred by hurricanes may cause damage, as will fluctuations in water temperatures. While reefs usually recover from these natural disturbances, there is concern that global warming has and will increase hurricane action that can rip coral reefs apart. The destruction from human-made pollution, however, can be devastating. Coral reefs, the largest constructions formed by living organisms, are developed by small marine animals called polyps. After a polyp dies, it leaves deposits of calcium carbonate behind for other polyps to build upon. When nutrient levels surge from improperly treated sewage, atmospheric deposition, agricultural and urban runoff, and cleaning products high in phosphate, they over-stimulate the growth of aquatic plants and algae. The algae eventually overcome and smother polyps. This, in turn, impacts the fish and other aquatic organisms, leading to a decrease in biodiversity and alterations in the use of the water for fishing and swimming. Coral reefs are also vulnerable to the introduction of a wide variety of toxic substances from runoff, mining activities, organic chemicals, metals, pesticides, and herbicides, which cause scarring, death, or reproductive failure in fish, shellfish, and other marine organisms. Because of this pollution, some water quality experts believe that the Florida

Reef Tract could become the first in the world to be killed by humans. Worldwide if present conditions continue, NOAA predicts that 70 percent of the coral reefs will disappear by the year 2050 (Hymon, 2001:19). To save the reefs, they must be given time to repair. This calls for immediate and drastic changes.

Among other responses to the difficulties, NOAA called for the designation of an ecological reserve. After establishing a working group of representatives from federal and state agencies, as well as scientists and representatives of the commercial fishing, recreational angling, sportdiving, and environmental communities, a no-take Ecological Reserve went into effect July 1, 2001 in the westernmost waters of the Florida Keys National Marine Sanctuary. The Sanctuary's network of 23 *no-take zones,* established in 1997, exclude fishing to increase the natural production of the local marine habitat. The Tortugas Ecological Reserve is broken into two sections. Tortugas North, west of Dry Tortugas National Park, contains some of the most spectacular and pristine coral reefs in the North America. Tortugas South, located southwest of the park, includes critical spawning grounds. Beside regulations that prohibit the taking of all marine life, the reserve in Tortugas North, for example, restricts vessel discharges and engine exhaust, and prohibits anchoring and the use of mooring buoys by vessels more than 100 feet in combined length. While snorkeling and diving is permitted, these activities require a simple no-cost, phone-in permit to ensure that all vessels have access to mooring buoys, ease enforcement, and assist in monitoring visitor impacts (NOAA, 2001:1). It is believed that the reserve will also help scientists evaluate what is happening outside of the reserve. Because the ecosystem does not recognize political boundaries, NOAA suggests that the no-take zone incorporate the areas adjacent to the reefs that are controlled by Dry Tortugas National Park as well. The park already prohibits commercial fishing, but questions concerning a ban on recreational fishing caused park officials to consider the delicate role that they play between protection and recreation. After receiving overwhelming support, the NPS designated 42 percent of the park's waters a Research Natural Area, which prohibits fishing and limits public access. This is the first time that action of this nature has taken place to protect marine habitat in a national park (Daerr, 2001:16). The plan to protect coral reefs, fish, and sea grasses, will not impact recreational fishing and other uses in a large portion of the park. Together the national park and the Tortugas Ecological Reserve is now the third largest protected marine area in the world. This action may encourage other states and national parks to work together to protect coral reefs. With traditionally little to say about how parks' waters or adjacent areas are fished, six of the nation's ten national parks with coral reefs currently allow commercial fishing. And seven are operating under general management plans that were written in 1983 or earlier, before the collapse of many of the world's reefs (Hymon, 2001:22).

Other sources of protection are found in the Clean Water Act, the River and Harbors Act, and the Coastal Zone Management Act. Additionally, EPA's Watershed Approach employs an integrated approach to maintain the nation's waters, including coral reefs. The EPA and other federal agencies are also developing guidance programs for runoff of pollutants, marine debris monitoring, discharge regulation, and water quality standards. The International Coral Reef Initiative (ICRI) coordinates information, bringing higher visibility to the need for coral reef ecosystem preservation throughout the world. For the International Year of the Ocean in 1998, President Clinton issued Executive Order 13089 on Coral Reef Protection, which directs federal agencies to protect coral reef ecosystems to the extent feasible, and instructs particular agencies to develop coordinated, science-based plans to restore damaged reefs as well as mitigate current and future impacts on reefs in the United States and the world. One restoration project was necessi-

tated after a 4,000-year-old portion of the Florida Reef Tract was damaged in the 1994 grounding of the University of Miami's *R/V Columbus Iselin*. The university's payment of $3.76 million in natural resource damage claims spurred a 1999 reconstruction plan that is making use of state-of-the-art materials that will attempt to enhance recolonization and help support the reef from further deterioration (NOAA, 1999:2-5). In early stages are attempts to grow coral in nurseries and coral transplants. If current conditions continue, however, they will lead to the degradation of most of the world's reef sources during this century.

TERRESTRIAL ECOSYSTEMS

Terrestrial ecosystems, which may be divided into forests, savannas, grasslands, tundra, and desert, are generally distinguished on the basis of the predominant type of vegetation such as trees or grass. An interaction of temperature and rainfall is significant to the type of vegetation grown. For example, grasslands might be sustained in regions with low rainfall coupled with low temperatures or with high rainfall combined with higher temperatures. Soil and vegetation are intimate parts of the same ecosystem. *Forests*, found in humid climates, feature trees that form a canopy over the ground. A *savanna* consists of a mixture of forest and grassland associated with a tropical climate. *Grasslands* are dominated by grass and found in semiarid climatic zones. *Tundra* is limited to herbs and shrubs and is located in cold climates, including arctic, subarctic, and high mountains. The *desert* originates in arid regions where generally low herbs and shrubs form a disconnected cover. Each is a resource to be protected and enjoyed. Some are discussed in more detail.

Forests

Tropical forests play a vital role in regulating the global climate. Disappearance of forests is regarded by many environmental experts as the most serious global environmental problem faced today. They believe that carbon dioxide must be kept in bal-

Rain forest can be found in Olympic National Park in Washington.

ance to help prevent a significant warming of the earth this century. Major carbon dioxide emissions are created by the burning of trees and vegetation from cut forests as well as the burning of fossil fuels. Forests have the capacity to absorb huge quantities of carbon dioxide through photosynthesis. Yet, statistics indicate that global emissions, fires, and deforestation are increasing (United Nations Environmental Programme, 1999: 4-10):

1. **Global emissions of carbon dioxide reached a new high of nearly 23,900 million tons in 1996, nearly four times the 1950 total.** Although North Americans have reduced emissions of many air pollutants during the last 20 years, the region is the largest per capita contributor to greenhouse gasses in the world. This is primarily the result of high-energy consumption.

2. **Forest fires appear to be happening more frequently and with greater intensity due to unfavorable weather conditions and land use practices.** In Indonesia, for example, about one million hectares of national forests were destroyed by fires that burned for several months from September 1997.

3. **The world has lost 80 percent of its original forests.** Remaining old-growth forests found primarily in the Amazon rainforest, Central Africa, Southeast Asia, Canada, and the Russian Federation are in jeopardy from logging, mining, and development. The depletion and destruction of forest resources in Latin American countries, particularly in the Amazon basin, and the related threat to biodiversity continues. During 1990 to 1995, about three percent of the natural forest cover was lost. Africa lost 39 million hectares of tropical forest during the 1980s, and another 10 million by 1995. Increasing habitat fragmentation in Southeast Asia has depleted the wide variety of forest products that were once the main source of food, medicine, and income for indigenous people. In Canada, British Columbia's forests have been treated as if they were endless, leaving clear-cuts behind as large as several hundred acres (Rauber, 2001:58-59). Commercial forestry has depleted and fragmented boreal forests, especially in the European Arctic, where regeneration is slow due to the harshness of the climate.

Preservation of the World's Largest Trees

Environmental groups convinced 400 corporations and several cities to phase out the sale or use of wood from old-growth forests. As consumer pressure mounted, the government of British Columbia announced an immediate moratorium on logging in the 3.5-million-acre Great Bear Rainforest, thereby devising the largest rainforest conservation measure in North American history (Sierra Club, 2001:23). Classic old-growth forests contain redwoods, cedars, Douglas fir, hemlock, or spruce. At a minimum, these forests contain eight large trees that are older than 300 years or more than 40 inches in diameter at chest height per acre. In the United States, there are only 4.3 million acres of old-growth forests left. About one-third of those protected are in designated public lands. Originally redwoods composed the greatest old-growth forest on earth. Today, much like the loss of old-growth Douglas fir, only about four percent remain (PBS, 1999:2). These lingering redwood giants are found mostly in parks, like Redwood National Park in northern California. While the coastal redwood towers over all other trees in the world, its cousin the Giant Sequoia grows larger in diameter and bulk. The tree that once grew all over North America is protected in central California in Yosemite, Sequoia, and Kings Canyon National Parks and Giant Sequoia National Monument, where hikers, campers, horseback riders, skiers, and anglers can gaze up at their majesty. If left to grow, Sequoias reach heights of 300 feet and live 500 to 700 years. That is only a portion of the potential age of the coast redwood, which can survive to be 2,000 years old.

In 1850, redwood "gold" lured loggers away from the depleted eastern forest. In an expanding nation, the need for wood products grew rapidly. With new machinery, chain saws, large trucks, and the bulldozer, logging activity accelerated even further after World War II. The old-growth or "virgin" forests began to disappear with alarming speed during the 1950s and 1960s, leaving behind overcut, eroding landscapes. Sensing the need for protection of the rapidly diminishing redwood forest, concerned citizens became active in setting aside redwood lands as local, state, and national parks. Redwood National Park, was established in 1968 to preserve superlative prime coast redwood forests along the coastline and rivers of northern California. After park establishment, however, extensive logging continued on private timberlands around this narrow corridor. Large scale logging of the unstable, highly erosive Redwood Creek watershed increased landsliding and surface erosion far above pre-logging levels. Besides directly altering the landscape and causing soil compaction, loss of topsoil, destruction of ground cover, elimination of shade, and massive changes to small drainages, the logging activities also produced cumulative downstream impacts. These included increased streamside landslides, elevated and wild streambeds, greater bank erosion, higher winter stream discharge, and lower summer discharge. These physical changes of the stream system jeopardized the associated plant and animal communities, and a heightened watertable directly threatened the Tall Trees Grove and other trees growing on alluvial terraces adjacent to Redwood Creek.

As a result of these problems, in March 1978 Congress expanded the existing 58,000-acre Redwood National Park by an additional 48,000 acres. Realizing that land-use practices adjoining the park can damage resources within, Congress made a landmark decision by establishing a 30,000-acre Park Protection Zone upstream in the Redwood Creek watershed. Of the 48,000 acres of new park lands, only about 9,000 acres were old-growth redwoods. Since most of the area was recently logged land, Congress authorized $33 million for Redwood National Park to rehabilitate overcut forestlands, with a major emphasis on erosion control as part of the park's expansion. This watershed rehabilitation program has a long-term goal of speeding the recovery of natural forest, stream systems, and life communities, while protecting park values and outdoor recreation opportunities.

California redwoods are the tallest living things on earth.

With most of the old growth cut by companies on lands they owned in the 1960s, public sources were needed to meet high demands for lumber.

Rehabilitation begins with the reduction of excessive erosion and creek siltation resulting from past timber harvesting and road building, and by replanting forests and shaping their regrowth. Years will pass before evidence of logging disappears and streams are fully recovered, but in Redwood National Park lies the unique challenge and opportunity to perpetuate and restore one of nature's most majestic natural systems.

Clearcutting and the Spotted Owl

Clear-cutting is the practice of removing all standing timber from a given area, typically 80-120 acres. Multiple clear-cuts are separated by narrow strips of timber several hundred feet in width. The consequences of clear-cutting vary according to terrain, soil conditions, weather patterns, and species. When all trees are cleared, there are no nutrients from dead rotting trees to benefit the soil. New growth is often weak and spindly as a result. Clear-

cuts also tend to spoil rivers and destroy fisheries. One specialist claims, "After a clear-cut it takes two or three years for the soil-supporting rootlet to rot away. Then the headwalls just fall into the rivers, sluice them out and settle into the lower reaches, sending the water braiding over or under wide, fish-proof deltas" (Williams, 1990:7). One such deluge of forest soil slid out from under a clear-cut at the source of Gwynn Creek in Oregon's Siuslaw National Forest's Mapleton District, the district containing the best public steelhead and salmon water south of Alaska. Sliding for four miles, the soil crossed Pacific Coast Highway 101, where it merged with the sea. Instantly it obliterated fish habitat and abolished fish life (Williams, 1990:8).

Several creatures depend on original, uncut ancient forest. In the Pacific Northwest, the northern spotted owl dwells in the old and dead trees of the rain forests. When the July 23, 1990 announcement that the spotted owl was listed as threatened, it came under the protection of the federal Endangered Species Act. A heated debate among environmentalists and the timber industry followed. To environmentalists, who were opposed to overharvesting and the unalterable loss of old-growth forests, the spotted owl was seen as a barometer to determine the integrity and health of the ancient forest ecosystem and the hundreds of species dependent on it for all or part of their needs. It became a symbol of an era when acres of primeval forest blanketed much of the continent and natural events were the controlling fate of the forest and its creatures. Now, the spotted owl's listing brought public attention to the 95 percent decline of these forests (Forests Forever, 1990:1). To the timber industry, the spotted owl's protection meant loss of work as prime timberland was set aside as protected habitat by the Forest Service. With most of the old growth cut by companies on lands they owned in the 1960s, these public sources were needed to meet high demands for lumber (Yuskavitch, 2001:42). They saw trees as a renewable resource, noting that Americans rely on thousands of wood products daily.

As public attention turned to the owl, and not to the fish in the same areas, an authority at Oregon State University observed that the timber industry was doing everything possible to keep it that way. With the spotlight on the owl, the issue of impacts to fisheries stayed in the background. Even if a forest that is unfit for a spotted owl is unfit for wild salmonoid, it was believed that there would be less public sympathy for an owl that few had seen or ever heard of than for fish and water (Williams, 1990:8). For many, though, economic issues were outweighed by the ecological survival, and the Northern spotted owl became an endearing mascot in the struggles to save the Northwest's old-growth forest. The dispute between timber companies, environmental groups, and federal agencies deferred to the Northwest Forest Plan that was implemented in 1994.

In seeking to find a solution to the controversies surrounding forest management, President Clinton held a 1993 Forest Conference in Portland, Oregon. After a Forest Ecosystem Management Assessment Team (FEMAT) was established to develop options for the management of federal forest ecosystems, a revolutionary plan was selected. The plan conserves not only the owls, but all species found in old-growth forests on federal lands within the spotted owls' range, from bears to fish to bryophtes. According to the habitat-based conservation strategy, much of the land—some 7.5 million acres—was designated as late-successional reserves. In those areas, federal land managers from the Forest Service and the Bureau of Land Management will primarily take a hands-off approach, with the goal of nurturing remaining stands of old growth by working together to preserve ecosystems common to their jurisdictions (Yuskavitch, 2001:43). Although logging restrictions were imposed, in part, because of the northern spotted owl, the regional economy began booming. Three years after curtailment of logging in federal forests, Oregon posted its lowest unemployment rate in a generation (United States Fish and Wildlife Service, 1998:1-2). As for the owl, its struggle for life continues. While data collected from 1985 to 1993 show that the spotted owl's population dropped 4.5 percent a year, it is expected to do so until the decline reaches equilibrium with available habitat (National Audubon Society, 1997:18-19; Yuskavitch, 2001:44).

While loggers saw mill jobs disappear and environmentalists watched hundreds of thousands of acres of forest in the Northwest disappear, both parties agreed that Americans needed to be concerned about consumption and explore new ways to minimize the use of trees. Georgia-Pacific (1990:1) reported that the United States had the world's highest rate of paper use, assaying that each American was using the equivalent of a 100-foot tree each year. If waste is cut and trees are saved, more trees will be left behind for outdoor recreation. See Figure 16.1 and 16.2 to compare total timber harvest with recreation use on national forests.

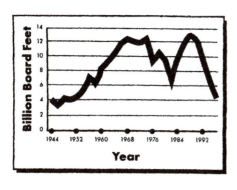

Figure 16.1 Total timber harvest on national forests.

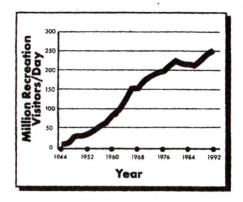

Figure 16.2 Recreation use on national forests.

Forest Fires

Fire is important and necessary to a wide range of natural ecosystems. The chaparral and giant Sequoias of California, prairies of the Midwest, the bogs of the Southeast, and the lodge-pole pines of Yellowstone National Park all depend on periodic fires. One type of lodge-pole cone opens and releases its seed only after exposure to heat. Other environmental conditions are created by burns: dead branches and pine needles are cleared, sunlight and nutrients allow new trees to grow and flourish, and grasses and herbs grow providing new food sources for wildlife. In the spring that follows a fire, wild flowers bloom profusely, and by summer the vegetation is well on its way to recovery so that deer can feed on nutritious, succulent new shoots and grasses.

For years, the Forest Service, Bureau of Land Management, the National Park Service, and state parks believed that fires should be prevented at all costs to preserve our nation's forests. In 1945, the creation of Smokey the Bear played a vital role in the National Forest Service fire prevention campaign. When Smokey's messages began, hundred of thousands of acres of American forests were consumed by human-caused wildfires every year. Since that time, it is estimated that this message helped reduce these fires by as much as 97 percent (Forest Service, 1998:1). Smokey's communique did not distinguish between natural and hu-

man-made fires, however. In time, it became apparent that wildland fires were getting larger and burning hotter, faster, and more frequently. Overgrown vegetation that had accumulated unnaturally in areas where fire was kept out, provided fuel for unprecedented, raging fires (BLM, 1997:1). Researchers soon learned that all fires are not evil. In stark contrast, *fire suppression* was perceived as unnatural by the 1970s. Instead, *natural fires* in remote locations that did not threaten life, property, or critical natural and cultural resources were allowed to burn when weather conditions were right. Under the right conditions, *let-it-burn* practices in wildlands preserve natural systems and allow for higher biological diversity. Since fires tend to jump rather than to burn cleanly over the landscape, interesting variety and diversity can result.

True natural wildfire occurrences, like those caused from lightning, happen infrequently. These fires are referred to as *prescribed natural fires,* meaning that they are within the limits prescribed by the fire-management plan under specific burning conditions. In contrast, unwanted or unplanned fires, including those resulting from children playing with matches, improper campfire care, cigarettes, motorcycles without spark arresters, or from sparks from welding and construction equipment, are contained immediately because they are burning outside of prescribed guidelines (Romme & Despain,

1989:39). *Prescribed burns* are fires that are deliberately set in a particular forest area by foresters and wildfire managers to reduce fuel build up, stimulate wildlife habitat and runoff, and control large-scale wildfires. Prescribed burns are particularly important to recreational areas of parks and forests where human use is high, thereby thwarting the risk of a large unnatural fire that could cause harm to persons and property. These "friendly fires," should generally not exceed the natural fire frequency, intensity, and seasonality, as determined by replicate studies on the ecosystem involved, however, or the impacts can be harmful.

Prescribed burns can become wildfires that burn out of control. As a result of the Cerro Grande wildfire that started as a prescribed burn at Bandelier National Monument in New Mexico, more than 48,000 acres of the Santa Fe National Forest were burned and 200 homes were destroyed (NPCA, 2000:13). In 1988, the great fire in Yellowstone was a result of years of fire suppressions, drought-like conditions, high winds, and high temperatures. Fires continued for weeks early that summer, but controversy mounted when the wind-driven flames moved in on the historic Old Faithful Inn and the towns of West Yellowstone, Cooke City, and Silver Gate by late summer. Notwithstanding the efforts of some 10,000 civilian and military firefighters, nearly a million acres of the entire Yellowstone territory burned, and timber and homes worth billions of dollars were destroyed (Jeffery, 1989:258). In the charred areas today is a lush carpet of green with young pines that have taken root after the lodgepoles' cones exploded in the intense heat, but after each of these firestorms, fire management policies in wilderness environments were reviewed.

Among other recommendations, interagency coordination, stronger public input, and careful planning and preparation around high-value developments and recreational resources have taken high priorities. It also became clear that remaining tracts of wilderness are small in comparison to the times when fires moved

freely, making it compelling for humans, not nature, to be the primary managers (Romme & Despain, 1989:46). During the investigation of Bandelier National Monument/Santa Fe National Forest wildfire, it was recommended that once a prescribed fire becomes a wildfire, the blaze should be suppressed as quickly as possible even if it requires mechanical means using chainsaws and bulldozers, which could be the cause of future controversies (Los Alamos, 2000:13). Traditionally, policy that dictates action after fires varies between the Forest Service and the National Park Service. Customarily, the Forest Service will respond by rapidly clearing fire-killed trees and planting new ones. The Park Service generally responds as it would to any other natural forest process, that is, the remains are best left alone for scientists and park visitors to study and observe unless the damage requires rehabilitation. The Forest service and other big land management agencies must consider the production of resources such as timber on their lands, except in wilderness areas, while the national parks are managed under policies that protect and preserve all native species in their natural habitat.

Grasslands

Familiar garden lawns and grassy urban parks are human-made, but the world's fast-disappearing native grassland is as natural as forests or deserts. Generally requiring a moisture level somewhere between the humid climate that supports a forest and the dry climate that supports a desert, grasslands are most often found in semiarid climates. Summer drought is long enough to prevent most tree and shrub growth, but not severe enough to prohibit growth of bounteous grass and forbs (broad-leaf herbs). Sometimes given other names in other countries, grasslands are found in all continents except Antarctica. In the United States, grasslands extended west from the Appalachians to the Rocky Mountains through a relatively flat land known as the Interior Plains. These grasslands of central North America are divided into three major types, including the *tallgrass prairie* toward the east and the *shortgrass prairie* in the west. Between them is a middle section composed of both types. This *mixed prairie* is found in most of the Dakotas, much of Nebraska and Kansas, the central part of Oklahoma, and parts of north-central Texas. The transition from tall to short grass correlates with an increased aridity, reduced rainfall, and increased evaporation. Other grassland varieties exist in the Southwest, the Far West, and the East. Collectively these grassland ecosystems, which once covered more than half of the land surface of the contiguous United States, provide homes to more than 7,500 plant and animal species (Hoofnagle 2001:1).

Boundaries between the various grassland types were difficult to define because they were bordered by transition zones. Influenced by precipitation, the transition zone between tallgrass and mixed grass prairie, for instance, could retreat from tallgrass to mixed prairie during years of decreased precipitation. During the great drought of 1933 to 1939, scientists documented an eastward retraction of 100 to 150 miles on the tallgrass prairie's western border (Brown, 1997:32). Roughly, tallgrass prairie once stretched from Ohio and Michigan across large portions of the Midwest to the eastern edges of Kansas, Nebraska, South Dakota, and North Dakota, where it extended northward into Canada and south over northern Texas. Nutrients from the grasses produced a dark rich soil that was perfect for agriculture. Victims of their own lushness, farms, roads, industry, and development caused original grasslands to vanish from many states. Some of the native grasses were replaced with other species, including corn on the tallgrass prairie and wheat on the mixed prairie, known as the Great Plains. Where the grasslands were too dry for crop production, they were eaten by sheep and cows. This was particularly the case in the shortgrass prairie, which was never considered to be attractive for agriculture in the way that the tallgrass and mixed grass prairies were. Since only portions of this land were plowed, short-

grass prairie is less altered today than are the other two prairie systems (Brown, 1997:61). Countless acres have suffered from overgrazing, however. While some areas have been permanently degraded, others still have the capacity to recover. The shortgrass prairie, also known as the Great Plains and the High Plains, occupies eastern Wyoming, much of Montana, eastern Colorado, western Kansas, the Oklahoma panhandle, northern Texas, and eastern New Mexico.

North American prairies are thought to date back to Micene times beginning 35 million years ago. Vast areas had grass so thick and tall that pioneers on horseback feared getting lost in them. They were full of bobcats, wolves, deer, elk, rabbits, prairie dogs, and bison. Swarms of birds hovered above in search of food, while winds encouraged the spread of fire. Within a relatively short span, pioneers changed this wild, native land to a country of farms, ranches, railroads, and towns, but conservationists are mobilizing to save remaining grasslands. Tall grass prairie is preserved in the Flint Hills region of Kansas in Tallgrass Prairie National Preserve and in Nebraska's Homestead National Monument of America. Other smaller regions are scattered throughout the Midwest. When a one-acre swatch of virgin grassland was going to be destroyed to mine gravel, for instance, an experimental transplant was made by the Illinois chapter of the Nature Conservancy in an attempt to preserve it. The cooperative effort emphasizes the rarity of the once prodigious prairies, while demonstrating society's awareness of the need to save an endangered environment and ecosystem. Illinois, the Prairie State, was once nearly four-fifths prairie. In an unlikely partnership, the Sierra Club joined the National Rifle Association to protect the Texas Katy Prairie, the winter home for millions of waterfowl (Sierra Club, 2001:60). Furthermore, grasses are also conserved by the Bureau of Land Management at Fort Meade Recreation Area in South Dakota, and prairie landscaping along highways and around homes has resulted in the restoration and recreation of tallgrass prairies. A pocket of shortgrass prairie is reserved in Canada's Grasslands National Park in Saskatchewan.

National Grasslands

Today's National Grasslands, administered by the Forest Service, also present a scene of quiet beauty. Culminating more than two decades of conservation, these public lands were given permanent status as a National Grassland System on June 20, 1960. Prior to that these lands were known as Land Utilization Projects, or LU lands. They were purchased by the federal government from homesteaders who were facing bankruptcy and foreclosure due to drought and depression in America's heartland during the 1930s. Continual cultivation, excessive grazing, recurrent dry years, and relentless wind had changed sod to dust. The land purchase program brought about a basic change in land use that was better suited to the dry, windy plains. Farms and ranches that remained had been, in general, larger and better able to operate economically. The areas purchased were slowly rehabilitated and became summer pastures. Sheep and cattle became the chief agricultural product in grass country, and grass resumed its rightful place as the dominant resource in the western plains.

Under leadership of the Soil Conservation Service, grazing associations and Soil Conservation Districts were organized who leased the new public ranges under controls guaranteeing range improvement and conservation. Land Utilization Project managers led the way in demonstrating conservation techniques and practices toward a fully restored range. Now, the Land Utilization Projects on the plains have become the National Grasslands and a part of the National Forest System. These lands continue to support stable grassland agriculture, while supporting other resources such as outdoor recreation in a manner that will blend and remain beneficial for generations of the future. Just one of 20 National Grassland sites, the Little Missouri National Grassland in North Dakota offers trails with special programs for hikers, campgrounds, canoeing, hunting, fishing, and wildlife and scenic tours. In Colorado, Comanche National Grassland has hiking and horseback riding, Prairie Chicken viewing, wildflowers, picnicking, camping, and 22 miles of the Santa Fe National Historic Trail.

Deserts

For many people, deserts conjure an image of lifeless sand dunes shimmering in waves of heat. Appearing barren, deserts seem to be forsaken. Yet the clear skies, the distant horizons, and the starry nights may represent the same appeal that oceans or mountains bring to others. Deserts, covering about one-third of the earth's land area, occur from vicinities close to the poles down to expanses near the Equator. These arid regions may be hot or cold, but they are always dry. Surprisingly, sand covers only about 20 percent of the earth's deserts. Nearly 50 percent of desert surfaces are plains where wind and runoff have removed the fine-grained material, leaving exposed loose gravel. The remaining surfaces of arid lands are composed of uncovered bedrock outcrops, desert soils, and fluvial deposits including alluvial fans, playas, desert lakes, and oases (USGS, 1996:3, 22-23). Some of these features can be seen in Guadalupe Mountains and Arches national parks in Texas and Utah, at Anza-Borrego Desert State Park in California, along the Pyramid Lake National Scenic Byway through Pyramid the Lake Indian Reservation in Nevada, and at numerous other desert parks and recreational lands.

In the harshest *dry desert*, such as the Atacama of northern Chile, the terrain is essentially barren. Only a few small, isolated plants are able to survive. The *shrub deserts* of the American west are a different story. In fact, the Sonoran Desert, the home of Saguaro National Park near Tucson, Arizona, has the most complex desert vegetation on earth. Although the living conditions are still severe, the shrub desert is far from uninhabited. Its plants and animals possess highly specialized

An intaglio or geoglyph, in the Mojave Desert near Blyth, California is marred by dirt bikes that rode over the ancient sand drawings a few years ago. The Tread Lightly! Guide to Responsible Trail Biking *encourages* Leave No Trace *principles and inspires trail etiquette.*

abilities and mechanisms for survival. The diverse plant life, which covers roughly 10 to 20 percent of the ground (more around dry river beds), varies from cactus with their shallow root systems to plants with long tap roots that can anchor the soil and control erosion. Some plants have evolved into water-storing succulents, while others have developed reduced leaf size or drop them altogether in dry conditions. Overall, the stems and leaves of plants help lower the surface velocity of winds that carry sand away. Most of the desert mammals are nocturnal, burrowing during the day.

Deserts also contain valuable mineral deposits that were formed in the arid environment or that were exposed by erosion. A paved trail in Death Valley National Park in California passes the old refinery and one of the famous "20-mule team" borax wagons used to haul loads of the precious material across the desert.

Balance between preservation and use, including mining, ranching, and landfills is an important factor for desert properties such as Grand Canyon-Parashant National Monument in Arizona, Grand Staircase-Escalante National Monument in Utah, and Joshua Tree National Park in California. And because deserts are dry, they present ideal places for human artifacts and fossils to be preserved, like the fossils of gigantic fish dinosaurs found at Berlin-Ichthyosaur State Park in Nevada.

Misuse of these fragile environments is a serious and growing problem (USGS, 1996:4), especially in the transition zone from the arid desert to more humid environments. These delicate areas are easily stressed by overgrazing and the hooves of livestock, which causes the desertification of productive land. As vegetation is lost, local arid climates are encouraged. The same problem can occur far from natural

Giant saguaro cacti, unique to the Sonoran Desert, sometimes reach a height of 50 feet in the cactus forest of Saguaro National Monument near Tucson, Arizona.

Desert Running

Because the desert is a fragile ecosystem, when abused it is damaged long-term. Desert ecologists estimate that it can take up to 200 years for some of the destroyed habitat to recover (Lance, 2001:8). Recreationists traveling on dirt bikes and off-road vehicles scar the desert and can kill the plants and animals. The compacted soil erodes rapidly and will not absorb water or insulate the roots against temperature extremes. The loss of plant life in turn devastates other dependent life forms. In a race on BLM land in the Mojave Desert, scientists reported a 90 percent drop in small-mammal populations. The noise of approximately 1,200 motorcycles and all-terrain vehicles (ATV) were extremely damaging to animal life. Because desert animals have adapted to a normally quiet habitat, some have developed an acute sense of hearing. After the race, kangaroo rats were found weaving in circles; their bleeding ears burst from the noise pollution. Other animals were found crushed or buried alive in their burrows (California, 1989:105). Tracks were seen on the cracked shells of desert tortoises, which were placed on the federal list of endangered species in 1989 on emergency status.

Attempts to stop the race were met with severe opposition from participants. After a study revealed the extensive damage to plants and wildlife, the BLM canceled the race. Though bitterly opposed by environmentalists, the race was resumed from 1982 to 1990 when it was once again canceled for environmental reasons. Over 100 motorcyclists demonstrated for the American right to use the nation's public lands (Warren, 1990:A3). Now more than 100,000 ATV enthusiasts from across the Southwest converge on the Imperial Sand Dunes Recreation Area in California, making the dunes the most-used public land in the nation on Thanksgiving weekend. This is the date that represents the beginning of the eight-month season that brings 500,000 participants to the area. Conservationists are concerned that the event is altering the fragile desert and endangering species that exist nowhere

deserts if the land is not properly managed. This is the same process that occurred when parts of the grasslands of the Great Plains turned into a "Dust Bowl" in the 1930s. The greatly improved methods of agriculture and land and water management there have prevented that disaster from recurring, but increased pressure on marginal lands and desert environments encourages erosion and loss. Overgrazing made the Rio Puerco basin of central New Mexico one of the most eroded river basins of the American West. Recreationally, off-road vehicle activity significantly increases soil loss in the delicate desert environment. In just a few seconds, soils that took hundreds of years to develop are destroyed (USGS, 1996:54-56).

else. Off-roaders say that they, too, feel like an endangered species (Associated Press, 1998:A-25-26).

Certainly, one survey shows that there may be major differences between the perceptions of land managers and participants. After participation in the Moab Easter Jeep Safari, 90 percent of the participants who responded to a survey conducted for the BLM believed that the physical impacts from their activity were acceptable or low. This could be the result of the relatively resilient appearing nature of the redrock country, or because they feared that an impact statement could cause land managers to close existing trails. When asked about specific resource impacts, 52 percent did indicate soil erosion. Open-ended comments, on the other hand, showed that many respondents believed that most impacts were caused by mountain bikers and dispersed campers, not OHVers. Sixty-two percent listed four-wheelers going off established trails as a major management problem. Most of the respondents participate in other outdoor activities as well, and they bring significant revenue to the local community for various services (Reiter, Blahna, & Von Koch, 1997:1-4).

In California, dune buggy and sand rail registration have increased 96 percent (California State Parks, 2001:5). These and other OVA enthusiasts require recreational space. When Congress passed the California Desert Protection Act of 1994 that formed Death Valley and Joshua Tree national parks and Mojave National Preserve, some of the land that was previously available for off-highway recreation activities was closed. In 1999, the state received funding from the Recreation Trails Program administered by the Federal Highway Administration for trails construction. Funds were used to form the Off-Road PALs Program, which promotes safe, responsible off-road riding and opportunities for at-risk youth to off-road in state parks. The state's vehicular recreation areas are located in varied and unique settings. With some areas available for use, other more sensitive regions are restricted, including desert archeological sites. The vehicle tire tracks left on the Mojave Desert *Intaglios* (large desert drawings made by Indian peoples centuries ago) caused permanent scars. *Tred Lightly!*, originally launched by the Forest Service in 1985 to help protect public and private land, was transferred to the private sector to maximize its effectiveness. Now a nonprofit organization, Tred Lightly!, educates the public on "low-impact" principles related to outdoor recreational activities, including ATV and Four Wheeling. Hikers and people on mountain bicycles are also advised to stay on trails to avoid damaging delicate dessert soil.

NOISE POLLUTION

Besides the noise pollution impacts on desert animals cited above, humans suffer from noise pollution. The peacefulness and quietude that many visitors seek in parks are lost to low-flying military jets, helicopters, automobiles, and ORVs. Sailors complain about motorboats and personal watercraft (PWCs), also known as jet skis. Cross-country skiers barely tolerate noisy snowmobiles. Hikers and anglers contend with noise from swamp buggies, airboats, and other mechanized equipment. Each seek their own space. A report presented to the President's Commission on Americans Outdoors (Williams & Jacobs, 1986:M20) noted psychological annoyance depends on many factors: the extent of interference with communication, relaxation, and sleep; the settings in which the noise occurs; the importance of the activities interrupted; and the time of exposure. A standard of 70 decibels is sufficient to protect hearing loss. However, about half of the people exposed to noise at this level over a period of time became highly dissatisfied.

Because attitudes of the perceiver affect the assessment of annoyance, noise levels are likely to be evaluated much more critically in outdoor recreation settings than in urban settings where adaptations to noise levels have been made. Complaints mount when noisy equipment is also linked to more conspicuous and measurable disturbances such as air or water pollution, wildlife disruption, environmental destruction, property loss, or personal injury. Restrictions, stricter guidelines, permits, and bans are being applied. When restrictions are too soft, damages may result that might otherwise have been controlled. ORV users suffer the public relations loss that comes with the repercussions. Hunters reported the mosaic scars that covered the fragile land in Big Cypress National Preserve (Wilkinson, 2001:38). Funds for patrols needed to prevent future illegal incursions are often required after extreme occurrences. In the meantime, ORV lobbys demand access to public lands, and managers strive to find low-impact ways to allow high-impact activity that will not disturb others. The nonprofit organization American Trails helps all trail groups resolve discord by working together.

WILDLIFE

No one knows exactly why some animals and plants flourish for thousands of years while others vanish within a relatively short time. But those species that do survive exhibit a common trait: adaptability. The animal or plant that is able to change its requirements to fit changes in its environment holds the vital key to survival. Conversely, animals and plants that are highly specialized can be more vulnerable to extinction. The black-footed ferret of the Great Plains, for instance, feeds almost entirely on the prairie dog, making it precariously dependent on an extremely narrow resources or habitats. In some cases plants and animals will become extinct for reasons not fully understood by science. Others may die out regardless of what we can do for them (USFWS, 1998:2). Extinction remains a fact of life on earth, but the species of the world are becoming increasingly endangered. It is estimated that one-third of the world's species could be gone in the next 20 years (Fetter, 2001:6). A disregard for the many human-made factors contributing to the destruction of our natural world could soon cause us to find our own survival in question. The

greatest causes of extinction related to human activity is the loss of habitat and fragmentation, pollution, commercial exploitation, edification, and the introduction of exotic species.

Loss of Habitat

Destruction, degradation, and the fragmentation of habitat are currently the leading causes of extinction for both plants and animals. Clear-cutting forests near rivers can cause excessive erosion, and the increased silt in the waterways can suffocate fish. This caused the Michigan grayling, a trout-like sport fish, to become extinct in the 1920s. Habitat protection on federal and private lands may enhance recovery efforts for the red-cockaded woodpecker. Once abundant throughout the Southeast, it began a rapid decline as humans altered its pine forest habitat for a variety of uses, primarily timber harvest and agriculture. In 1970, the species was listed as endangered under a precursor to the 1978 endangered species law. Their current population, estimated to be 10,000 to 14,000 birds, is fragmented into isolated islands of populations ranging from Florida to Virginia and west to eastern Texas. Working closely with the United States Fish and Wildlife Service (USFWS), the Forest Service is striving to preserve colonies, and the Georgia-Pacific Company established a landmark conservation agreement with the Fish and Wildlife Service to save the woodpecker on approximately four million acres of company land (Fish & Wildlife Service, 1998:1).

Pollution

Endangered species often serve as indicators of environmental problems that may also affect people. A good example is freshwater mussels. Several mussels are endangered in large part due to pollution of the waterways where they live. Contamination commonly results from agricultural pesticide runoff, municipal sewage disposal, and industrial waste discharge (USFWS, 1998:1). Since people depend on the nation's waterways for sources of food and water, and as popular places for recreational activities, our own health and well-being are in jeopardy when these areas become polluted. Interest in opening up the Arctic National Wildlife Refuge in northern Alaska to oil drilling has resulted in the mobilization of thousands of Americans who fear that, despite new technology, the distinctive wildlife nursery for polar bears and caribou herds; wetland nesting grounds for millions of snow geese, sandhill cranes, red-throated loons, and other bird species; and the year round home of muskoxen, grizzlies, wolves, foxes, golden eagles, and snowy owls will be turned into a polluted oil field with potential for oil spills (Mitchell, 2001:53).

Commercial Exploitation

Many early laws passed to protect animals and plants were poorly written and inadequately enforced. They made it relatively easy for rare, native plants such as some cactus, carnivorous plants, orchids, and others to pass into commercial trade. The demand for exotic pets, such as parrots and other wild birds, has caused many of these species to become endangered. In the early 1900s, there were reported sightings of flocks of thick-billed parrots numbering in the thousands in the Chiricahua Mountains of Arizona. Although their range once spanned from Venezuela in South America to Arizona and New Mexico, they are now clinging to existence in northwest Mexico. After their confiscation from a pet smuggling ring by the United States Fish and Wildlife Service in the 1980s, 26 thick-billed parrots were released back into the Chiricahua Mountains, located in Coronado National Forest. Reintroduction was not successful, however, because they had not learned the necessary flock structure and behavior that would allow them to protect one another and because of a severe drought. Captive-breeding programs hope to reintroduce them into the wild in Mexico, where 4,000 acres of the birds' most important nesting sites have been rescued from proposed logging operations (Casey, 2000:18-19, 21). Additionally, some Asian cultures consider animal parts, such as those of bear species, rhinoceros, and tiger, to have medicinal powers. The illegal wildlife trade is a very lucrative business, and the demand for these animals parts is a growing threat to their very survival. Elephants and sea turtles are also endangered due in large part to the demand for ivory and turtle shell for jewelry and other wildlife products (USFWS, 1998:1-2).

Edification

Some animal species have joined humans in a population explosion. Human-made edifices (structures of especially imposing appearance) such as agricultural developments, dams, reservoirs, drainage schemes, interstate highways, and buildings have aided the evolution. Certain species that adapt well to these structures are known as edification species. Edification species have had a negative effect on general wildlife diversity by causing species turnover and replacement. In New England's coastal islands, herring gull eggs were once collected to near extinction. The gulls began to make a comeback in the 1950s when their central edifice became the sanitary landfill. They grew as they fed in cities and dumps. Nesting on offshore islets, they ate the eggs and chicks of smaller species and crowded out larger ones. Biological diversity tumbled until gull population control became mandatory. In the 1960s their nests were eradicated and greater control of landfills and fish-processing practices reduced their food base. Afterward other seabirds began nesting in greater numbers on coastal islets (Lazell, 1989:20-23). Likewise, buildings offer sanctuary for raccoons. Expanding its regional range to lakes and shores in the north where wildlife are unaccustomed to the marauders, the raccoons eat summer garbage and winter under summer cottages. Capable of living off their fat during winter, they have anxiously consumed the eggs and chicks of nesting loons in the spring.

Exotic Species

Invasive species have been purposefully, carelessly, and unwittingly introduced around the globe since Polynesian seafarers began transporting rats to Pacific islands via dugout canoes more than 1,500 years ago. In the Hawaiian Islands rats introduced by sailing ships, have played havoc with nesting birds. When mongooses were imported to control the rats, they turned on the nesting birds instead and were a serious factor in bringing the nene goose to near extinction. Second only to habitat destruction, non-native species can, if uncontrolled, increase and become a threat to other species of wildlife. During the last century, more than 4,500 foreign species have established a foothold in the United States (Nature Conservancy, 1999:8). In addition, diseases and parasites, introduced by international trade, have caused disasters in United States forests. Since its introduction into Massachusetts from Europe in 1869, the gypsy moth has spread to 17 states in the Northeast and the District of Columbia where it is a major threat to hardwoods (USFWS, 2000:6). Carrying out policy to eradicate noxious or exotic plant and animal species on public lands is not always easy politically. In the Grand Canyon National Park, burros released by early prospectors had almost completely displaced the desert bighorn sheep by overgrazing. Because park managers were charged with protecting the habitat, they ordered that the burrows be shot. Associated with preservation and not destruction, the action led to public outcry. With increasing conservation, recreation, wildlife preservation, and pressures from conservation groups, the Bureau of Land Management faces issues with cattle.

Endangered Species Act

In early 1973, an international conference on endangered species took place in Washington, D.C. The meeting resulted in the formation of the Convention on International Trade in Endangered Species of Wild Fauna and Flora (CITES), a 130-nation agreement designed to prevent species from becoming endangered or extinct because of international trade. To meet some of the agreement's provisions, the United States needed new legislation. By the end of that year, one of the most com-

prehensive laws ever enacted by any country to prevent the extinction of imperiled life was enacted (Hogan, 1999:G-5). Upon passing the Endangered Species Act (ESA), Congress not only recognized a concern that many of the nation's native plants and animals were in decline, but that the rich natural heritage was of "esthetic, ecological, educational, recreation, and scientific value to the Nation and its people" (USFWS, 2001:1).

The ultimate goal of ESA is to conserve the ecosystems upon which endangered and threatened species are dependent and to conserve and recover species so they no longer need protection under the Act. *Endangered* means a species is in danger of extinction throughout all or a significant portion of its range. *Threatened* means a species is likely to become endangered within the foreseeable future. All species of plants and animals, except pest insects, are eligible for listing based on the best scientific and commercial data available. After a species is listed, it becomes protected by federal law. Of the 1,244 United States species listed, 508 are animals and 736 are plants. Groups with the most listed species are (in order) plants, birds, fishes, mammals, and clams/mussels (USFWS, 2001:1). A listed species cannot be taken, which includes killing, harming, or harassing. The law also provides species protection by requiring federal agencies to ensure activities that they conduct, authorize, or fund do not jeopardize the continued existence of listed species. When prudent and determinable, this includes the designation of critical habitat as they affect federal agency actions or federally funded or permitted activities. Federal agencies, in turn, consult with the USFWS and the National Marine Fisheries Service (the two federal agencies responsible for administering the law) to allow their projects to go forward at the same time species are protected. This action alone is sometimes enough to save a species from extinction and start it back on the road to recovery. As such, the law has been a catalyst in the way Americans approach land use decisions.

Still, the number of listed species

continue to grow, creating controversy between economic growth and the preservation of imperiled wildlife and its habitat. As the human population grows and spreads, there is less room for plants and animals. Adversaries complain that since its inception only five species have been removed from the list because they have recovered sufficiently enough to no longer need protection (Hogan, 1999:G-5). Supporters credit the law with blocking the extinction of species, finding that just as it takes time for species to become endangered, it also takes time for them to recover. When the Northwest Forest Plan was implemented, for example, the object was to prevent the acceleration of the decline of the spotted owl by preserving old-growth forests on federal lands within its range. While preserving, rather than clear-cutting these stands should slow the decline. The decline is expected to continue until the new growth in clear-cut areas of the old-growth forests reach sufficient stature to allow for a possible recovery. This could take 20 to 50 years, but the newly planted stands may well begin to support juveniles, just as they did years ago when fires burned some areas of the forest. Supporters, in turn, grow concerned about a backlog of candidate species that are losing their habitat while USFWS reviews an overwhelming number of petitions for the list (Martin, 2001:1; *New York Times,* 2002:2). It is believed that each day of delay increases the possibility of extinctions.

Species protection is also achieved through partnerships with the states and non-federal landowners. Other laws to protect species include the Marine Mammal Protection Act, the Migratory Bird Treaty Act, and the Anadromous Fish Conservation Act. The Lacey Act makes it a federal crime for any person to import, export, transport, sell, receive, acquire, possess, or purchase any fish, wildlife, or plant taken, possessed, transported or sold in violation of any federal, state, foreign or Indian tribal law, treaty, or regulation.

Habitat Protection

The greatest protection of biological diversity is in the preservation of various habitats or ecosystems. Here they draw upon resources available in the ecosystem to which they also contribute. A holistic habitat protection approach helps protect the species before they reach critical stages, requiring the individual attention of a species-by-species approach. Through habitat protection, the individual listing process might even be eventually phased out. The theory holds that by saving habitats, more species could, in the long run, be saved; and by scaling down the listing process more resources would be available to help protect habitats (Norton, 1987:266-70). The Northwest Forest Plan was considered revolutionary because it did not seek to mange the lands just for the threatened spotted owl, but for all species found in old-growth forests on federal lands within the threatened species' range (Yuskavitch, 2001:43).

Some animals who venture outside park boundaries require habitat protection. For example, hunters shoot bison that wander out of Yellowstone National Park, home of the nation's last free-roaming herd. National attention was directed to the problem in 1989 when a harsh winter drove 800 of the herd over the park's northern boundary to find grass to eat, thereby providing ranchers and hunters with the opportunity to kill more than half of the celebrated northern herd. Critics cite this case to illustrate the arbitrary nature of national park and public lands borders which often ignore natural boundaries, such as ridgelines and watersheds, slicing through the natural boundaries of animal habitats.

Artificial Habitats

Zoos, wild animal parks, wildlife research centers, and marine mammal research centers contribute to animal comebacks. Zoos, sometimes criticized for capturing and exploiting animals, have rescued some species from extinction, like the California condor, black-footed ferret, Arabian oryx, and red wolf. Others, such as the bighorn sheep, would be rapidly declining if it were not for contributions from Species Survival Plans (SSPs). The SSP is a cooperative breeding and conservation program designed to preserve endangered species through captive breeding and gene pool management. The program, established and maintained by the American Zoo and Aquarium Association (AZA), brings together more than 180 AZA accredited zoos and aquariums to manage more than 100 species of mammals, birds, amphibians, reptiles, fish, and invertebrates (Zoological Society of San Diego, 2001:21). If AZA decides that a captive-breeding program can aid the recovery of an endangered species, an SSP is established, and participating programs manage and exchange their animals in the best interest of the species, including selection of a mate, determining the desired number of offspring, and strategies for habitat preservation in the wild. SSPs also support public education, supportive research, and reintroduction to the wild. Barasingha deer, tree kangaroos, clouded leopards, and giant pandas are just some of the species the AZA is working with.

Using Technology for Habitat Restoration

Nearly one-third of the nation's endangered and threatened species live only in wetlands, and nearly half use them at some point in their lives. Many other animals and plants depend on wetland habitats for survival (EPA, 2001c:2). For instance, some fish and shellfish, various birds, and certain mammals must have coastal wetlands to survive. Yet in California, 90 percent of the state's coastal wetlands have been lost in just 150 years (Lafee, 2001:F1). Likewise, inland wetlands are needed by many animals and plants such as wood ducks, muskrat, cattails, and swamp rose. For others, including striped bass, peregrine falcon, otter, deer, and black bear wetland habitats provide important food, water, or shelter. Song birds and hawks use

them to feed, nest, and raise their young. Migratory waterfowl use coastal and inland wetlands as resting, feeding, or nesting grounds for a least part of the year. For these reasons, an international agreement to protect wetland habitats of international importance was developed. In some cases, migratory birds are so completely dependent on certain wetlands that they would become extinct if they were destroyed (EPA, 2001c:2-3).

Although we have not been able to restore a fully functional ecosystem, technology and scientific innovations are helping where protection came too late. A case in point is Florida's watershed. The vital water system of southern Florida consists of three essential elements: the Kissimmee River, Lake Okeechobee, and the Everglades. About a century ago, the freshwater system of Florida nurtured an ecosystem unique to the earth. Water flowed from a chain of lakes into the Kissimmee River. It carried water through the savanna to Lake Okeechobee, an area higher than the expanse to the south. Periodically the lake would overflow, moving south across the saw-grass of the Everglades, over the then-undrawn boundaries of big Cypress National Preserve and Everglades National Park. This flowing water in part evaporated, contributing moisture for rain in a constantly reviewing cycle. But after the Civil War, an environmental onslaught began as efforts were undertaken to contain the flood-prone lake. By the turn of the century, a network of locks, dams, and canals was established for flood control. Farming was tried, but the topsoil dried to a powder or decomposed. Nutrients that were released flowed into the Everglades. The United States Army Corps of Engineers strengthened dikes and dug more channels to tame the flooding water system. Finally, plumbing projects of the 1940s changed the water wilderness. As the population grew, water was further tapped for human needs, greatly affecting nesting and wading birds, whose numbers declined dramatically. High concentrations of mercury were found in fish, egrets, and Florida panthers. Cattails began to take

These red mangroves with massive exposed root systems fringe the waterways of the Everglades and filter material washed from the land, trapping debris and sediment. Mangrove roots provide nursery grounds to many species of fish and invertebrates, and near Key Largo, are the habitat for the endangered American crocodile.

over thousands of acres of former saw-grass marsh. Alligator nests flooded when excess summer water could no longer spread over larger areas. During dry periods the region was parched. Indicator species—the Florida panther and the alligator—almost became extinct as a result of the environmental degradation (Cordes, 2001: 99-100).

By the 1980s polluted Lake Okeechobbee burst into blooms of blue-green algae, perhaps nature's desperate call for help. The situation now threatened other forms of life in the lake. To save the unusual ecosystem, a commitment to restore a more natural flow of water was necessary. Water managers responded to requests for help, and a computer program was designed to imitate seasonal rainfall conditions. Annual water deliveries were made for the appropriate distribution of water allotments. A levee was breached to assist the restoration of natural water flow. Successful rehabilitation of the Kissimmee was effected by engineers, and waterfowl began to return. Other changes were devised to keep manure nutrients from Lake Okeechobee, and laws were enacted for pollution reduction and environmental restoration. In 1991, the state settled a lawsuit by agreeing to acquire 37,000 acres of farmland that released phosphorus and could serve as a natural filter to remove contaminants from farms (Cordes, 2001:100). The experiment is still in progress, and time will tell how the wildlife will fare. Hikers pass through Big Cypress National Preserve, and visit the marshes on the Florida National Scenic Trail.

Partnerships Protecting Wildlife

Approximately one-third of all federally listed species dwell on national forests and grasslands. And more than 2,500 sensitive species, those requiring special management to prevent their loss, are also found on these lands. This means that the national forest and grasslands harbor the greatest diversity of wildlife under any single ownership nationwide (see Figure 16.3). The Forest Service believes that partnerships are critical in their effort to maintain the ecosystems essential for supporting healthy populations of wildlife. Since 1986, their Challenge Cost-Share Program has provided the means for the Forest Service and the private sector to share management and financial costs for projects on the national forests that help to restore wildlife and fish habitat. Anglers, hunters, birders, off-highway vehicle users, ranchers, miners, utility companies, educational institutions, conservation groups, and other recreation users are among the 3,400 partners working with the Forest Service in various programs to aid wildlife and their habitats (Williams, 2000: 137). With cooperative efforts, there is hope that the decline in forest habitat as shown in Figure 16.4 will cease. Programs such as *Get Wild, Every Species Counts, Rise to the Future, and NatureWatch* help the Forest Service to inventory and improve habitats; recover and conserve rare species; coordinate aquatic habitat management goals, plans, and programs; and provide enhanced recreational opportunities for the public.

HARMONY WITH NATURE

With approximately six billion inhabitants in the world, tremendous demands are placed on the environment. We can hardly afford to waste, pollute, or abuse it. Still, the signs of environmental abuse are all around us. In our abundance, we became careless, acquisitive, and wasteful, causing severe environmental stress. Sometimes we do not understand how the environment will respond to our actions. Nonetheless, our landfills are choking with the tons of garbage dumped every day. Acid rain caused by automobile and factory emissions is killing our forests and polluting our lakes. Sewage and industrial pollution are fouling rivers and oceans. Inappropriate methods of farming, mining, logging, and manufacturing are eroding land, poisoning water, and threatening wildlife. Yet, there is hope for our planet.

With restraint, technology, consideration, diligence, partnerships, and mindful management we are capable of slowing and perhaps even reversing much of the damage. In many instances, tourism dollars are replacing older economies as outdoor adventurers and nature enthusiasts make new and often improved demands of the environment. And the more time we spend outside, the more we seem to learn about our need to live in harmony with nature. With the passage of the National Environmental Policy Act of 1969, the enhancement of harmony between people and their environment became a national policy. As a direct result, the Council on Environmental Quality was established which required that all federal agencies prepare reports on the environmental impact of all major planned programs. Like the American Indians, a growing number of Americans are finding that the earth is sacred. The majority of respondents to a nationwide poll, 69 percent, support tougher laws or restricting enforcement of existing environmental laws (NPCA, 2001:12). One of the most powerful orations addressing the environment that has ever been made follows. In his 1854 address to the American people who had offered to buy a large portion of American Indian land, Chief Seattle stressed ecological values and harmony with nature.

> How can you buy or sell the sky, the warmth of the land? The idea is strange to us.
>
> If we do not own the freshness of the air and the sparkle of the water, how can you buy them?

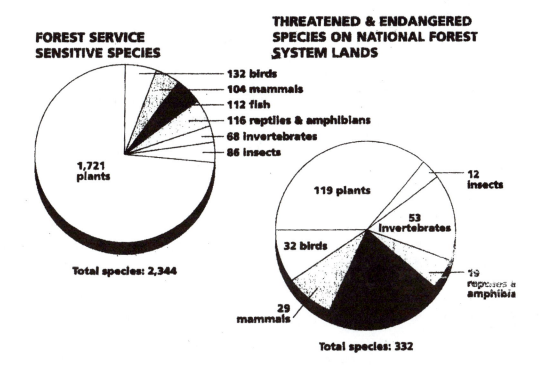

FOREST SERVICE SENSITIVE SPECIES

- 132 birds
- 104 mammals
- 112 fish
- 116 reptiles & amphibians
- 68 invertebrates
- 86 insects
- 1,721 plants

Total species: 2,344

THREATENED & ENDANGERED SPECIES ON NATIONAL FOREST SYSTEM LANDS

- 119 plants
- 12 insects
- 53 invertebrates
- 32 birds
- 19 reptiles & amphibia
- 29 mammals

Total species: 332

Figure 16.3 Threatened & Endangered Species on National Forest System Lands.

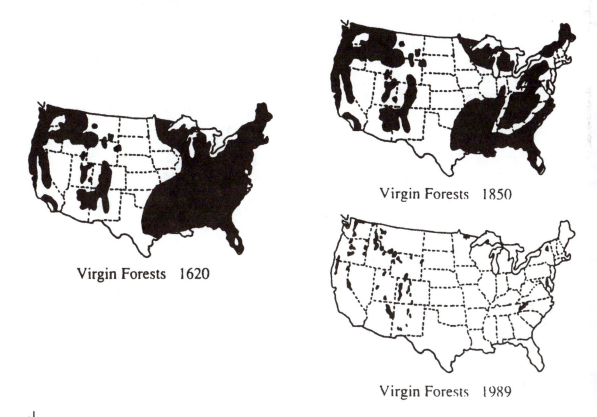

Virgin Forests 1620

Virgin Forests 1850

Virgin Forests 1989

Figure 16.4 Forest decline, 1620-1989, in continental United States.

THE EARTH IS SACRED

Every part of this earth is sacred to my people. Every shining pine needle, every sandy shore, every mist in the dark woods, every clearing and humming insect is holy in the memory and experience of my people. The sap which courses through the trees carries the memories of the red man.

The white man's dead forget the country of their birth when they go to walk among the stars. Our dead never forget this beautiful earth, for it is the mother of the red man.

We are part of the earth and it is part of us. The perfumed flowers are our sisters; the deer, the horse, the great eagle, these are our brothers. The rocky crests, the juices in the meadow, the body heat of the pony, and man—all belong to the same family.

THINGS TO REMEMBER

So, when the Great Chief in Washington sends word that he wishes to buy our land, he asks much of us. The Great Chief sends word he will reserve us a place so that we can live comfortably to ourselves.

He will be our father and we will be his children. So we will consider your offer to buy our land.

But it will not be easy. For this land is sacred to us.

This shining water that moves in the streams and rivers is not just water but the blood of our ancestors.

If we sell you land, you must remember that it is sacred, and you must teach your children that it is sacred and that each ghostly reflection in the clear water of the lakes tells of events and memories in the life of my people.

The water's murmur is the voice of my father's father.

GIVE THE RIVERS KINDNESS

The rivers are our brothers, they quench our thirst. The rivers carry our canoes, and feed our children. If we sell you our land, you must remember, and teach your children that the rivers are our brothers, and yours, and you must henceforth give the rivers the kindness you would give any brother.

We know that the white man does not understand our ways. One portion of land is the same to him as the next, for he is a stranger who comes in the night and takes from the land whatever he needs.

The earth is not his brother, but his enemy, and when he has conquered it, he moves on.

He leaves his father's grave behind, and he does not care. He kidnaps the earth from his children, and he does not care.

His father's grave, and his children's birthright, are forgotten. He treats his mother, the earth, and his brother, the sky, as things to be bought, plundered, sold like sheep or bright beads.

His appetite will devour the earth and leave behind only a desert.

I do not know. Our ways are different from your ways.

The sight of your cities pains the eyes of the red man. But perhaps it is because the red man is a savage and does not understand.

There is no quiet place in the white man's cities. No place to hear the unfurling of leaves in spring, or the rustle of an insect's wings.

But perhaps it is because I am a savage and do not understand.

The clatter only seems to insult the ears. And what is there to life if a man cannot hear the lonely cry of the whippoorwill or the arguments of the frogs around a pond at night? I am a red man and do not understand.

The Indian prefers the soft sound of the wind darting over the face of a pond and the smell of the wind itself, cleaned by a midday rain, or scented with the pinon pine.

THE AIR SHARES ITS SPIRIT

The air is precious to the red man, for all things share the same breath—the beast, the tree, the man, they all share the same breath.

The white man does not seem to notice the air he breathes. Like a man dying for many days, he is numb to the stench.

But if we sell you our land, you must remember that the air is precious to us, that the air shares its spirit with all the life it supports. The wind that gave our grandfather his first breath also receives his last sigh.

And if we sell you our land, you must keep it apart and sacred, as a place where even the white man can go to taste the wind that is sweetened by the meadow's flowers.

TREAT THE BEASTS AS BROTHERS

So we will consider your offer to buy our land. If we decide to accept, I will make one condition: the white man must treat the beasts of this land as his brothers.

I am a savage and I do not understand any other way.

I have seen a thousand rotting buffaloes on the prairie, left by the white man who shot them from a passing train.

I am a savage and I do not understand how the smoking iron horse can be more important than the buffalo that we kill only to stay alive.

What is man without the beasts? If all the beasts were gone, man would die from a great loneliness of spirit.

For whatever happens to the beasts, soon happens to man. All things are connected.

TEACH YOUR CHILDREN

You must teach your children that the ground beneath their feet is the ashes of your grandfathers. So that they will respect the land, tell your children that the earth is rich with the lives of our kin.

Teach your children that we have taught our children, that the earth is our mother.

Whatever befalls the earth befalls the sons of the earth. If men spit upon the ground, they spit upon themselves.

This we know: The earth does not belong to man; man belongs to the earth. This we know.

All things connectd like the blood which unites one family. All things are connected.

Whatever befalls the earth befalls the sons of the earth. Man did not weave the web of life: he is merely a strand in it. Whatever he does to the web, he does to himself.

Even the white man, whose God walks and talks with him as friend to friend, cannot be exempt from the common destiny.

We may be brothers after all.

We shall see.

One thing we know, which the white man may one day discover—our God is the same God. You may think now that you own Him as you wish to own our land; but you cannot. He is the God of man, and His compassion is equal for the red man and the white.

This earth is precious to Him, and to harm the earth is to heap contempt on its Creator. The whites too shall pass; perhaps sooner than all other tribes. Contaminate your bed, and you will one night suffocate in you own waste. But in your perishing you will shine brightly, fired by the strength of the God who brought you to this land and for some special purpose gave you dominion over this land and over the red man.

That destiny is a mystery to us, for we do not understand when the buffalo are all slaughtered, the wild horses are tamed, the secret corners of the forest heavy with scent of many men, and the view of the ripe hills blotted by talking wires.

Where is the thicket? Gone.

Where is the eagle? Gone.

The end of living and the beginning of survival.

If we sell you our land, love it as we have loved it. Care for it as we have cared for it. Hold in your mind the memory of the land as it is when you take it. And with all your strength, with all you mind, with all your heart, preserve it for your children and love it . . . as God loves us all.

Summary

Human activities, including outdoor recreation, also impact the environment. Air pollution has caused havoc in national parks even with the passage of the Clean Air Act. The destruction to the freshwater aquatic system is seen in the extinction and near extinction of many fish. This has impacted fishing and fishing ethics. Another area affected by human activities are the estuarine and marine systems. "Trashbergs" are reducing life at an alarming rate. Coral reefs along the Florida keys could become the first in the world to be killed by humans.

Forests and trees are disappearing at an alarming rate, the recreational values of which are gone forever. But most important is the impact of the unwise timber harvesting on the environment, which results in the loss of wildlife and creates a dangerous level of global warming. Ancient forests support established ecosystems.

Prairie lands may be the most endangered terrestrial ecosystem, while the desert is extremely fragile. Steps are being taken to reduce damage.

References

Associated Press. (1998, December 4). Off-roaders Annual Invasion of Dunes has Trills and Spills. *San Diego Union-Tribune.*

Associated Press. (1990, November 24). Study Finds Sharp Rise in Ozone Damage to Yosemite Pine Trees. *Los Angeles Times.*

Atkinson, G. (1990, April). Outdoor Recreation's Contribution to Environmental Attitudes *Leisure Today.* 14-16.

Balog, J. (1990, April). A Personal Vision of Vanishing Wildlife. *National Geographic.* 177(4).

Brown, L. (1997). *Grasslands.* New York: National Audubon Society.

Bureau of Land Management. (1997). *Using Fire to Manage Public Lands* (BLM/RS/GI- 97/001-9210).

California Magazine. (1989, December). Vanishing California.

California State Parks. (2001, Spring). Off-Highway Recreation Trends. *The Green Sticker* 16, 5.

Caneday, L., & R. Neal. Can We Go to the Lake? A Case for the Future. *Parks & Recreation* 31(8),52-56.

Capra, R. (1995). Deep Ecology: A new paradigm. In Sessions, G. (Ed.), *Deep ecology for the 21st century.* (pp. 19-25). Boston, MA: Shambhala Publications, Inc. .

Casey, S. (2000). A Noisy Struggle to Survive. *ZooNooz, LXXIII*(7):17-21.

Chase, C. (1990). Cognition, Ethics and Direct Experience. *Journal of Physical Education, Recreation and Dance 61*(4)

Cordell, H.K. (1999). Outdoor Recreation Participation Trends. In H. K. Cordell (Ed.), *Recreation in American life: A national assessment of demand and supply trends.* (pp. 219-321) Champaign, IL: Sagamore Publishing.

Cordell, H.K. (1997, April). *Emerging markets for outdoor recreation in the United States: A report to the Sporting Goods Manufacturers Association and the Outdoor Products Council.* Athens, GA: USDA Forest Service.

Cordes, K. (2001). *America's national scenic trails.* (pp. 99-100). Norman: University of Oklahoma Press,

Daerr, E. (2001). Regional Report. *National Parks 75*(9-10),16.

Duffey, E. (1975). *Grassland lift.* Madrid, Spain: The Dunbury Press.

Dunphy, H. (2001, January 14). Environment Group Warns of Worldwide Ecological Decline. Associated Press, *The San Diego Union-Tribune.*

Duplaix, N. (1990, July). Paying the Price, *National Geographic 178*(1).

Environmental Protection Agency. (2001a). *Effects of Acid Rain: Lakes & Streams.* [On-line]. Available: http://www.epa.gov/airmarkt/acidrain/effects/surfacewater.html.

Environmental Protection Agency. (2001b). *About Estuaries.* [On-line]. Available: http://www.epa.gov/OWOW/estuaries/about1.htm

Environmental Protection Agency. (2001c). *America's Wetlands.* [On-line]. Available: http://www.epa.gov/OWOW/wetlands/vital/people.html.

Environmental Protection Agency. (1999a, April). *Haze* . Washington, D.C.: EPA-456/F-99- 001.

Environmental Protection Agency. (1999b, January). *Key Findings of America's Environmental Knowledge, Attitudes and Behaviors.* Washington, D.C.: EPA-171-F-98-019.

Environmental Protection Agency. (1999c, November). *Progress Report on the EPA Acid Rain Program* . Washington, D.C.: EPA430-R-99-011.

Environmental Protection Agency. (1998a, December). *Acid Rain* . Washington, D.C.: EPA Office of Air & Radiation.

Environmental Protection Agency. (1998b, December). *Global warming and climate change.* Washington, D.C.: EPA Office of Air & Radiation.

Environmental Protection Agency. (1998c, December). *Highlights.* Washington, D.C.: EPA Office of Air & Radiation.

Environmental Protection Agency. (1996, September). *Guide to environmental issues.* Washington, D.C.: EPA-520/B-94-001 9/1996.

Evergreen Project. (1998). What is a Watershed? [On-line]. Available: http://mbgnet.mobot.org/fresh/index.htm.

Fair, P., & P. Becker. (2000). Review of Stress in Marine Mammals. *Journal of Aquatic Ecosystem Stress and Recovery 7*, 335-354.

Fetter, T. (2001). Message from the President. *ZooNooz, LXXIV* (6).

Foreman D. (1995). The New Conservation Movement. In G. Sessions (Ed.), *Deep ecology for the 21st century* (50-56). Boston, MA: Shambhala Publications, Inc.

Forests Forever. (1990). *California Forest Facts.* Ukiah, CA.

Forest Service. (2000). *America's forests 1999 health update.* Washington, D.C.: USDA 757.

Forest Service. (1998). *Rx fire!* Washington, D.C.: USDA.

Gelbspan, R. (2001). A Modest Proposal to Stop Global Warming. *Sierra 86*(3).

Hogan, D. (1999, January 3). Endangered Species Act at 25. *The San Diego Union-Tribune*, G-5.

Hoofnagle, S. America's Grasslands. *Habitats 4*(3):1.

Hope, J. (May/June). Radical Fishing. *Mother Earth News,* 123.

Hymon, S. (Unknown). Bringing Up Coral. *National Parks 75*(9-10): 19-22.

Jameson, S. et al. (2000). *Charting a Course Toward Diagnostic Monitoring: A Continuing Review of Coral Reef Attributes and a Research Strategy for Creating Coral Reed Indexes of Biotic Integrity* (for the Environmental Protection Agency). (pp.1-9).The Plains, VA: Coral Seas Inc.:

Jeffery, D. (1989, February). Yellowstone: The great fires of 1988. *National Geographic 175*:2

Johnson, C. (2000, February 13). Disappearing Forest. *North County Times:* G- 1,G-2.

Kormondy, E. (1984). *Concepts of ecology.* Englewood Cliffs, NJ: Prentice Hall.

Lafee, S. (May 2). True Lagoon. *San Diego Union-Tribune*, F1.

Lance, V. (2001). Disease in Desert Tortoises: Is it Affecting Long-Term Survival? *ZooNooz, LXXIV*(9),8-9.

Larkin, P. (Ed.). (1999). *Sustainable seas expeditions.* Santa Barbara, CA: NOAA.

Lazell, Jr., J. (1989). Wildlife. *National Parks, 65*, 9-10.

Loomis, J., K. Bonetti, & C. Echohawk. (1999). Demand For and Supply of Wilderness. In H. K. Cordell, (Ed.), *Outdoor recreation in American life*: *A national assessment of demand and supply trends* . Champaign, IL: Sagamore Publishing.

Lord, N. (1998). Our Only Ocean. *Sierra 83*(4):35-39.

Mark Clements Research, Inc. (1996, September). Readers Poll: Travel and the Environment." *Conde Nast Traveler,* 22.

Martin, G. (2001, April). Bush Proposal Imperils Part of Species Act. *San Francisco Chronicle*, 11,1.

Mathews, A. (Unknown). The 2001 Conference on the Environment: Practicing What We Preach. *People, Land, & Water 8*(3),8.

Miller, K. (2000, August). A Call for Review of Large Dams. *River Monitor.* 1(4),3.

Mitchell, J. (2001). Arctic National Wildlife Refuge. *National Geographic 200*(2),48-55.

Montaigne, F. (2001). A River Dammed. *National Geographic 199*(4),1-33.

National Audubon Society. (1997). Whither the Spotted Owl. *Audubon 99*(2),18-19.

National Oceanic and Atmospheric Administration (NOAA). (1999). The Project. [On-line]. Available: http://www.sanctuaries.nos.noaaa.gov/special/columbus/project.html.

National Parks and Conservation Association. (2001). Energy and Environment. *National Parks 75*(9-10),12.

National Parks and Conservation Association. (2000). Los Alamos Causes Fire Policy Change. *National Parks 74*(9-10),13.

National Parks and Conservation Association. (1990). Clean Air Bill on Move at Last. *National Parks 64(5-6)*.

National Park Service. (1981). *Redwood National Park, California*. Washington D.C.; U.S. Government Printing Office.

Nature Conservancy (The). (1999). Pathways of Invasion. *Nature Conservancy 49*(4).

Norton, B. (1987). *Why preserve natural variety?* Princeton, NJ: Princeton University Press.

New York Times (The). (2001, April 14). "A threatened act." *The New York Times*, 2.

Papciak, M. (2001). "Endless bummer." *Sierra 86*(3):82-83.

PBS. (1999). *"Spotted Owl/Old Growth Forests."* [On-line] Available: http://www.pbs.org/ktca/newtons/11/oldgrwth.html.

Pope, C. (2001). The new conquerors. *Sierra 86*(4):16-17.

Rauber, P. (2001). Life in a Warmer World. *Sierra 86*(3),64.

Reiter, D., D. Blahna, & R. Von Koch. (1997). *Off-highway vehicle four-wheeler survey of 1997 Moab Easter Jeep Safari participants.* Logan, UT: IORT:1-4.

Romme, W., & D. Despain. (1989, November). The Yellowstone Fires. *Scientific American 261*,5.

Roper Starch for the Recreation Roundtable. (2000). *Outdoor recreation in America 2000: Addressing key societal concerns.* Washington, D.C.: Roper Starch.

San Francisco Examiner. (1990). The Culprit Isn't the Owl But Japan. June 30.

Schildgen, B. (2001). Beating the Heat: Why and How We Must Combat Global Warming. *Sierra 83*(3).

Sector, B. (1989, November 19.). Saguaro rustlers taming population of a desert king. *Los Angeles Times.*

Sessions, G. (Ed.). (1995). *Deep ecology for the 21st century.* Boston, MA: Shambhala Publications, Inc.

Sierra Club. (2001). Strange Bedfellows or Natural Allies? *Sierra, 86*(4), 60-61.

Sierra Club. (2001). Updates. *Sierra, 86*(4):23.

Slack, G. (1998, Winter). Dammed if we don't. *Headwaters*, 6-7.

Slater, D. (2001). Moments of Truth. *Sierra 86*(4):48-57.

Unknown (1988, August 1). The dirty seas. *Time,* 132,(5), Pg. *44-50.*

United Nations Environment Programme. (1999). *Overview Geo-2000.* Nairobi, Kenya: UNEP.

United States Fish & Wildlife Service. (2001). *ESA Basics.* [On-line]. Available: http:// endangered.fws.gov/.

United States Fish & Wildlife Service. (1998). *Endangered species general information.* [On-line]. Available: http://www.fws.gov.

United States Fish and Wildlife Service. (1998). Myths and Realities of the Endangered Species Act. [On-line]. Available: http://www.fws.gov/ r9endspplendspp.html.

United States Geological Survey. (1996). *Deserts: Geology and resources.* Washington, D.C.GPO 421-577.

Wald, M. (1998, May 29). EPA says catalytic converter growing cause of global warming. *San Diego Union Tribune,* A-7.

Warren, J. (1990, November *25.*). Bikers kick up dust over canceled desert run. *Los Angeles Times.*

Watson, T., & J. Weisman. (2001, July 16). Six ways to combat global warming. *USA Today.* 1A-2A.

Watson, T. (1999, June 8). Wetlands preservation plan draws a groundswell of support, Critics. *USA Today.* 12A.

Wilkinson, T. (2001). On the beaten path. *National Parks 75*(3-4).

Williams, D., & G. Jacobs. (1986). Off-site resource development conflicts in *The President's Commission on Americans Outdoors, A Literature Review.*

Williams, G. (2000). *The USDA Forest Service-The First Century.* Washington, D.C.: USDA Forest Service FS-650.

Williams, T. (1990, March). Clearcutting spoils Rivers, Destroys Fisheries. *Forest Voice, 2,*1.

*Youtz, G. (1987). *If we sell you our land.* Tacoma, WA: Pacific Lutheran University.

Yuskavitch, J. (2001, March/April). Bye bye Birdie? *Forest Magazine,* 41-45.

Zoological Society of San Diego. (2001). What is a species survival plan? *ZooNooz, LXXII*(7).

*Note: According to Gregory Youtz (If We Sell You Our Land, Tacoma, WA: Pacific Lutheran University, 1987, pp. 1-3), Chief Seattle is also referred to as Chief Sealth of the Puget Sound area. Dr. Henry Smith published his version of the speech in the *Seattle Sunday Star* in 1877, 30 years after it was made. Smith reported that the speech was given to Governor Isaac Stevens at the beginning of treaty negotiations. It is unclear exactly who took notes at the speech, but it is possible that Seattle's native tongue, Lushootseed, had to be translated into Chinook, and then into English. Smith may have reconstructed the speech over 30 years after the fact from his notes or Stevens' notes. Thus the exact words may have been lost (Youtz 1987:1-3).

EPILOGUE

Climb the mountains and get their good tidings. Nature's peace will flow into you as sunshine flows into trees. The winds will blow their own freshness into you, and the storms their energy, while cares will drop off the autumn leaves.

John Muir

Nature provided human beings with plants and game, which became the source for our primary need for protection and survival. Today, a new picture emerged in that contemporary psychology showed us that there is more to life than mere survival and safety. For instance, belonging is an important human need, so is the need for expression. Outdoor pursuits are becoming increasingly significant as means to fulfill some of our secondary needs. This volume begins by describing the relationship between outdoor pursuits and human needs along with the work of those who helped us understand that relationship.

The psychological impetus for outdoor pursuits is tempered by the many socioeconomic factors that should be taken into consideration. Yet it seems that the enjoyment of outdoor pursuits cuts through all social strata in many, if not all, human societies. Having reached a new height in its offerings of outdoor opportunities, the American society can well afford them. Other nations have followed suit, and it is becoming clear that the need for outdoor pursuits is there and more opportunities should be provided.

But the earth's natural resources are not limitless, even if some of these resources are renewable. Many of the earth's resources have been exhausted in our quest for survival and safety. The additional quest for outdoor pursuits is adding to the problems that plague the environment. Prudent use can be achieved through the wise management of outdoor recreation resources as well as through formal and informal education. Only then will the future of outdoor recreation be protected.

STATE AGENCIES INVOLVED IN OUTDOOR RECREATION

State	Agencies with Principal Responsibilities in Outdoor Recreation	Agencies with Limited Responsibilities in Outdoor Recreation

Alabama	Department of Conservation
	  Division of Water Safety
	  Division of State Parks, Monuments, and Historical Sites
	  Division of Game and Fish
	  Division of Seafoods
	  Division of Outdoor Recreation
		Mound State Monument
		Department of Highways

Alaska	Department of Natural Resources	
Arizona	Game and Fish Commission State Parks Board Outdoor Recreation Coordinating Commission	Highway Commission Economic Planning Development Board
Arkansas	State Planning Commission Game and Fish Commission Parks, Recreation, and Travel Commission	Ozarks Regional Commission (joint federal-state agency) Geological Commission Forestry Commission Industrial Development Commission State Highway Department
California	Resources Agency Department of Parks and Recreation Division of Beaches and Parks Division of Recreation Division of Small Craft Harbors Department of Conservation Division of Forestry Department of Fish and Game Department of Water Resources	Department of Public Works Bureau of Health Education, Physical Education and Recreation State Lands Commission Water Pollution Control Department of Health
Colorado	Department of Natural Resources Division of Game, Fish and Parks	State Historical Society Department of Highways State Board of Land Commissioners
Connecticut	Park and Forest Commission Board of Fisheries and Game	State Highway Department State Department of Health Water Resources Commission State Development Commission

State	Agencies with Principal Responsibilities in Outdoor Recreation	Agencies with Limited Responsibilities in Outdoor Recreation
Delaware	Board of Game and Fish Commissioners State Park Commission	State Archives Commission State Forestry Department State Highway Department State Developmental Department State Board of Health Water and Air Resources Commission Soil and Water Conservation Commission
Florida	Outdoor Recreational Development Council Board of Parks and Historic Memorials Game and Fresh Water Fish Commission	Board of Forestry Board of Conservation State Road Department Development Commission Trustees of the Internal Improvement Fund Board of Archives and History
Georgia	Department of State Parks State Game and Fish Commission Jekyll Island State Park Authority	Stone Mountain Memorial Association State Highway Department Lake Lanier Islands Development Authority North Georgia Mountains Commission
Hawaii	Department of Land and Natural Resources State Parks Division Fish and Game Division Forestry Division	Marinas and Small Boat Harbors
Idaho	State Park Board Fish and Game Commission	State Forestry Department Department of Highways Department of Aeronautics State Department of Commerce and Development State Historical Society State Land Department
Illinois	Department of Conservation Division of Parks and Memorials Division of Game Division of Fisheries Division of Forestry	Department of Public Works and Buildings Department of Registration and Education Department of Public Health Illinois State Youth Commission Department of Business and Economic Development

State	Agencies with Principal Responsibilities in Outdoor Recreation	Agencies with Limited Responsibilities in Outdoor Recreation

Indiana	Department of Natural Resources
	  Division of Fish and Game
	  Division of Forestry
	  Division of State Parks
	  Division of Reservoir Management
		State Highway Department
		Department of Recreation
		Great Lakes Park Training Institute
		State Health Department
		State Commission on Aging and the Aged and the Governor's Youth Council
		Wabash Valley Commission
		  Department of Commerce and Public Relations
		Indiana Flood Control-Water Resources Commission
		Governor's Advisory Committee on Recreation

Iowa	State Conservation Commission
	  Division of Administration
	  Division of Fish and Game
	  Division of Land and Waters
		State Soil Conservation Committee
		Iowa Development Commission
		State Highway Commission
		Office of Planning and Programming

Kansas	State Park and Resources Authority Forestry, Fish and Game Commission Joint Council on Recreation	State Highway Commission State Recreation Consultant State Historical Society Department of Economic Development Water Resources Board

Kentucky	Department of Conservation
	  Division of Forestry
	  Division of Soil and Water Resources
	  Division of Strip Mining and Reclamation
	  Flood Control and Water Usage Board
	Department of Fish and Wildlife Resources
	Department of Parks
		Department of Public Safety
		Department of Public Information
		Kentucky Highway Department
		State Historical Society

Louisiana	State Parks and Recreation Commission Wildlife and Fisheries Commission	Department of Highways Department of Public Works Department of Commerce and Industries State Land Office Louisiana Tourist Development Commission
Maine	Department of Inland Fisheries and Game State Park Commission Baxter State Park Authority Maine Forest Service	Atlantic Sea Run Salmon Commission Department of Sea and Shore Fisheries Water Improvement Commission Department of Economic Development State Highway Commission Department of Health and Welfare

State	Agencies with Principal Responsibilities in Outdoor Recreation	Agencies with Limited Responsibilities in Outdoor Recreation
Maryland	Board of Natural Resources Department of Forests and Parks Department of Game and Inland Fish Department of Tidewater Fisheries Department of Research and Education	Department of Geology, Mines, and Water Resources Water Pollution Control Commission State Roads Commission Department of Economic Development

Massachusetts	Department of Natural Resources
	  Division of Fisheries
	  Division of Water Resources
	  Division of Forests and Parks
	  Division of Marine Fisheries
	  Division of Law Enforcement
	Metropolitan District Commission
	  Parks Engineering Division
	Department of Public Works
		Department of Public Health
		Department of Commerce
		Department of Correction
		Youth Service Board

Michigan	Department of Natural Resources
	  Office of Administration
	  Field Administration Division
	  Fish and Fisheries Division
	  Forestry Division
	  Game Division
	  Geological Survey Division
	  Lands Division
	  Parks and Recreation Division
	State Waterways Commission
	Huron-Clinton Metropolitan Authority
	Mackinac Island State Park Commission
		Michigan Tourist Council
		State Highway Department
		Department of Health
		Department of Social Welfare
		Michigan Water Resources Commission
		Department of Public Instruction

Minnesota	Department of Conservation
	  Division of Forestry
	  Division of Game and Fish
	  Division of Parks and Recreation
	  Division of Enforcement and Field Service
		Department of Highways
		Historical Society
		Iron Range Resources and Rehabilitation Commission
		Pollution Control Agency
		State Planning Agency
		Minnesota Resources Commission
		Minnesota-Wisconsin Boundary Area Commission
		Department of Economic Development

Mississippi	Mississippi Game and Fish Commission State Park Commission	Highway Department State Board of Health Mississippi Forestry Commission Pearl River Valley Water Supply District Water Resources Board Yellow Creek Watershed Authority Pearl River Industrial Commission
Missouri	State Conservation Commission State Park Board	State Highway Commission Division of Commerce and Industrial Development Bi-State Development Agency

State	Agencies with Principal Responsibilities in Outdoor Recreation	Agencies with Limited Responsibilities in Outdoor Recreation
Montana	State Fish and Game Commission State Highway Commission Park Division	Board of Land Commissioners Office of State Forester State Highway Department Board of Health State Historical Society State Water Conservation Board
Nebraska	Game and Parks Commission	Department of Health Department of Roads State Historical Society

Nevada	Department of Conservation and
	   Natural Resources
	Fish and Game Commission
		Department of Economic
		   Development
		Department of Highways
		State Museum
		Division of Forestry

New Hampshire	Department of Resources and
	   Economic Development
	   Division of Parks
	Fish and Game Department
	State Advisory Commission
		Natural Resources Council
		Water Resources Board
		Water Pollution Commission
		State Historical Commission
		Department of Public Works and
		   Highways

New Jersey	Department of Conservation and
	   Economic Development
	   Division of Fish and Game
	   Division of Resource
	      Development
	   Division of Water Policy and
	      Supply
	   Division of State and Regional
	      Planning
		State Department of Health
		Department of Highways

New Mexico	Department of Game and Fish
	State Park and Recreation
	   Commission
	State Planning Office
		State Highway Department
		Department of Development
		Department of Public Health and
		   Welfare
		Museum of New Mexico
		Department of Education

New York	Department of Conservation
	   Division of Lands and Forests
	   Division of Parks
	   Division of Saratoga Springs
	      Reservation
	   New York State Historic Trust
	   Division of Fish and Game
	   Division of Water Resources
	   Division of Motor Boats
	   Division of Conservation
	      Education
	   Lake George Park Commission
	   Water Resources Commission
		Department of Health
		Department of Public Works
		Department of Education

State	Agencies with Principal Responsibilities in Outdoor Recreation	Agencies with Limited Responsibilities in Outdoor Recreation

North Carolina	State Recreation Commission
	Department of Conservation and
	   Development
	     State Parks Division
	     Travel and Promotion Division
	Wildlife Resources Commission
	Department of Archives and History
	     Historical Sites Division
	State Planning Task Force on
	   Recreation
		Kerr Reservoir Development
		   Commission
		State Highway Commission
		Department of Water and Air
		   Resources
		Coastal Plains Regional Commission
		Appalachian Regional Commission
		Department of Conservation and
		   Development
		     Community Planning Division
		     Forestry Division
		Seashore Commission
		State Board of Health

North Dakota	State Outdoor Recreation Agency State Park Service State Game and Fish Department	State Water Commission State Health Department State Historical Society State Soil Conservation Committee State Highway Department State Travel Department Economic Development Commission

Ohio	Department of Natural Resources
	   Division of Parks and Recreation
	   Division of Wildlife
	   Division of Watercraft
	   Division of Forestry and
	     Reclamation
		Department of Highways
		Department of Industrial and
		   Economic Development
		Department of Health
		Department of Correction
		Department of Public Works
		Historical Society
		Muskingum Conservancy District

Oklahoma	Oklahoma Planning and Resources Board Wildlife Conservation Commission	State Highway Department Grand River Dam Authority

Oregon	State Highway Commission
	   State Parks and Recreation
	     Division
	State Game Commission
	State Committee on Natural
	   Resources
	State Fish Commission
	State Department of Forestry
		Department of Geology and Mineral
		   Industries
		State Water Resources Board
		State Marine Board
		State Engineer
		Sanitary Authority
		Columbia River Gorge Commission

Pennsylvania	Department of Forests and Water
	   State Forester
	   Water and Power Resources
	     Board
	State Fish Commission
	State Game Commission
		Department of Commerce
		Department of Health
		Department of Internal Affairs
		Military Reservation Commission
		Department of Highways
		Historical and Museum Commission

Rhode Island	Department of Natural Resources
	   Division of Parks and Recreation
	   Division of Forestry
	   Division of Fish and Game
	   Division of Harbors and Rivers
		Department of Health
		State Development Council

State	Agencies with Principal Responsibilities in Outdoor Recreation	Agencies with Limited Responsibilities in Outdoor Recreation
South Carolina	Wildlife Resources Department Forestry Commission Department of Parks, Recreation, and Tourism	Highway Department State Board of Health Water Pollution Control Authority State Development Board State Budget and Control Board Public Service Authority

South Dakota	Department of Game, Fish, and Parks
	  Game Division
	  Fisheries Division
	  Parks Division
	  Custer State Park
		Commissioner of School and Public Lands
		Department of Highways
		Department of History
		Water Resources Commission
		State Planning Commission

Tennessee	Department of Conservation
	  Division of Parks
	  Division of Information and Tourist Promotion
	Game Commission
	Fish Commission
		State Planning Commission
		Department of Highways

Texas	State Parks and Wildlife Commission	The Daughters of the Republic of Texas Battleship Texas Commission State Highway Department

Utah	Department of Natural Resources
	  Division of Parks and Recreation
	  Division of Fish and Game
	  Outdoor Recreation Assistance Agency
		State Road Commission
		Tourist and Publicity Council
		Utah National Guard
		State Land Division
		State Historical Society

Vermont	Department of Forests and Parks Fish and Game Department Natural Resources Interagency Committee State Recreation Commission	Department of Highways State Health Department Water Conservation Board State Development Corporation

Virginia	Department of Conservation and Economic Development
	  Division of Forestry
	  Division of Parks
	Commission of Game and Inland Fisheries
	Commission of Outdoor Recreation
	Interagency Committee on Recreation
		Department of Highways
		Breaks Interstate Park Commission
		Water Control Board
		Department of Health
		Commission of Fisheries
		Agencies Administering Historic Sites
		Historic Landmark Commission

Washington	Department of Natural Resources State Parks and Recreation Commission Department of Game Interagency committee for Outdoor Recreation Department of Fisheries	Highway Department Department of Health Pollution Control Commission Department of Commerce and Economic Development Planning and Community Affairs Agency Department of Water Resources

State	Agencies with Principal Responsibilities in Outdoor Recreation	Agencies with Limited Responsibilities in Outdoor Recreation

West Virginia	Department of Natural Resources
	    Division of Game and Fish
	    Division of Forestry
	    Division of Parks and Recreation
	    Division of Water Resources
	    Division of Reclamation
	Public Lands Corporation
		State Road Commission
		Department of Commerce
		Office of Federal-State Relations

ORGANIZATIONS INVOLVED IN OUTDOOR RECREATION

Adirondack Mountain Club
814 Goggins Road
Lake George, New York 12845
www.adk.org

America Outdoors
PO Box 10847
Knoxville, Tennessee 37939
www.americaoutdoors.org

American Alpine Club
710 10th Street
Suite 100
Golden, Colorado 80401
www.americanalpineclub.org

American Alliance for Health,
Physical Education, Recreation, and Dance
900 Association Drive
Reston, Virginia 22091
www.aahperd.org

American Blind Skiing Foundation
610 South William Street
Mount Prospect, Illinois 60056
www.absf.org

American Camping Association
Bradford Woods
Martinsville, Indiana 46151
www.aca-camps.org

American Canoe Association
7432 Alban Station Boulevard
Suite B-232
Springfield, Virginia 22150
www.acanet.org

American Casting Association
1773 Lance End Lane
Fenton, Missouri 63026
www.americancastingassoc.org

American Cross Country Skiers
PO Box 604
Bend, Oregon 97709
www.xcskiworld.org

American Forests
PO Box 2000
Washington, DC 20013
www.americanforests.org

American Hiking Society
1422 Fenwick Lane
Silver Spring, Maryland 20910
www.americanhiking.org

American Ski Club Association
393 S. Harlan #120
Lakewood, Colorado 80226
www.wzone.com/mall/asca

American Sportfishing Association
1033 North Fairfax Street #200
Alexandria, Virginia 22314
www.asafishing.org

American Trails
PO Box 491797
Redding, California 96049
www.americantrails.org

American Whitewater Association
1430 Fenwick Lane
Silver Spring, Maryland 20910
www.awa.org

Americans for Our Heritage
and Recreation
1615 M Street NW
Washington, DC 20036
www.ahrinfo.org

Association for Challenge Course
Technology
PO Box 970
Purcellville, Virginia 20134
www.acctinfo.org

Association of Outdoor Recreation
and Education
PO Box 1829
Boulder, Colorado 80306
www.aore.org

Association for Experiential Education
2305 Canyon Boulevard
Suite 100
Boulder, Colorado 80302
www.aee.org

Association of Jewish Sponsored Camps
130 E. 59th Street
New York, New York 10022
www.jewishcamps.org

Blue Water Sportfishing Association, Inc.
PO Box 611997
Port Huron, Michigan 48061
www.bluewatersportfishing.net

Boy Scouts of America
PO Box 152079
Irving, Texas 75015
www.scouting.org

Botanical Society of America
Missouri Botanical Garden
Saint Louis, Missouri 63166
www.botany.org/bsa

Canadian Parks and Recreation Association
tion
216-1600 James Naismith Drive
Gloucester, ON K1B 5N4
www.cpra.ca

Christian Camping International/USA
PO Box 62189
Colorado Springs, Colorado 60189
www.cciusa.org
Coalition for Education in the Outdoors
PO Box 2000
Cortland, New York 13045
www.cortland.edu

Ducks Unlimited, Incorporated
One Waterfowl Way
Memphis, Tennessee
www.ducks.org

Family Campers and Rivers Association
74 West Genessee Street
Skanteles, New York 13152
www.fcrv.org

Greater Yellowstone Coalition
PO Box 1874
Bozeman, Montana 59715
www.greateryellowston.org

Handicapped Scuba Association
1104 El Prado
San Clemente, CA 92672
www.hsascuba.com

International Game Fish Association
300 Gulf Stream Way
Dania Beach, Florida
www.igfa.org

International Hunter Education Association
tion
PO Box 490
Wellington, Colorado 80549-0490
www.ihea.com

International Hunting Land Association
PO Box 416
Johnstown, Pennsylvania 15907
www.hunt4land.org

International Mountain Bicycling
Association
PO Box 7578
Boulder, Colorado 80306
www.imba.com

International Windsurfer Class Association
1955 West 190th Street
Torrance, California 90509
www.sailing.org

Izaak Walton League of America
IWLA Conservation Center
707 Conservation Lane
Gaithersburg, Maryland 20807
www.iwla.org

Girl Scouts of the USA
830 Third Avenue and 51st Street
New York, New York 10022
www.gsusa.org

Leave No Trace
PO Box 997
Boulder, Colorado 80306
www.lnt.org

National Association of Competitive
Mounted Orienteering
503 171st Avenue SE
Tenino, Washington 98589
www.nacmo.com

National Association of Conservation
Districts
509 Capitol Court NE
Washington, DC 20002
www.nacdnet.org

National Association of State Outdoor
Recreation
Liaison Officers
PO Box 731
Richmond, VA 23206
www.house.gov/boelert/nasorla.htm

National Association of State Park Directors
9894 East Holden Place
Tucson, Arizona 85748
www.NASPD.org

National Association of State Foresters
444 North Capitol Street NW
Suite 540
Washington, DC 2001
www.stateforesters.org

National Association of Therapeutic
Wilderness Camps
4270 Hambrick Way
Stone Mountain, Georgia 30083
www.natwc.org

National Association of Underwater
Instructors
9942 Curie Drive
Suite H
Tamps, Florida
www.naui.org

National Audubon Society
950 Third Avenue
New York, New York 10003
www.audubon.org

National Camp Association
610 5th Avenue
PO Box 5371
New York, New York 10185
www.summercamp.org

National Center for Therapeutic Riding
PO Box 434
Burtonsville, Maryland 20866
www.netriding.org

National Organization for Rivers
212 West Cheyenne Mountain Boulevard
Colorado Springs, Colorado 80906
www.nors.org

National Outdoor Leadership School
288 West Main Street
Lander, Wyoming 82520
www.nols.edu

National Parks Conservation Association
1300 19th Street NW
Washington, DC 20036
www.npca.org

National Park Foundation
1101 17th Street NW
Suite 1102
Washington, DC 20036
www.nationalparks.org

National Recreation and Park Association
22377 Belmont Ridge Road
Ashburn, Virginia 20148
www.nrpa.org

National Society for Experiential
Education
1703 North Beauregard Street
Suite 400
Alexandria, Virginia 22311
www.nsee.org

National Trust for Historic Preservation
1785 Massachusetts Avenue NW

Washington, DC 20036
www.nationaltrust.org

National Wildlife Federation
1400 10th Street NW
Washington, DC 20036
www.nwf.org

National Wildlife Refuge Association
1010 Wisconsin Avenue NW
Suite 200
Washington, DC 20007
www.refugenet.com

Natural Areas Association
PO Box 1504
Bend, Oregon 97709
www.naturalarea.org

North American Riding
for the Handicapped Association
PO Box 33150
Denver, Colorado 80233
www.narha.org

North American Association for
Environmental Education
1825 Connecticut Avenue NW
Washington, DC 20009
www.naaee.org

North American Gamebird Association
1214 Brooks Avenue
Raleigh, NC 27607
www.naga.org

Outdoor Recreation Coalition
of America
PO Box 1319
Boulder, CO 80304
www.orca.org

Outdoor Writers Association of America
27 Fort Missoula Road
Suite 1
Missoula, Montana 59804
www.owaa.org

Outward Bound
100 Mystery Point Road
Garrison, New York 10524
www.outwardbound.org

Professional Association of Diving Instructors
30151 Thomas

Rancho Santa Margarita, California 92688
www.padi.com

Rails-to-Trails Conservancy
1100 17th Street NW
10th Floor
Washington, DC
www.railtrails.org

Sierra Club
85 2nd Street, 2nd Floor
San Francisco, California 94105
www.sierraclub.org

Society of American Foresters
5400 Governor Lane
Bethesda, Maryland 20814
www.safnet.org

Sportsmen for Fish and Wildlife
PO Box 95970
South Jordon, Utah 84095
www.sfwsfh.org

Student Conservation Association
PO Box 550
Charlestown, New Hampshire 03603
www.sca-inc.org

The Access Fund
PO Box 17010
Boulder, Colorado 80308
www.accessfund.org

The American Canyoneering Association
2625 South Plaza Drive
Suite 400
Tempe, Arizona 85282
www.canyoneering.net

The National Speoleological Society
2813 Cave Avenue
Huntsville, Alabama
www.caves.org

The Nature Conservancy
4245 Fairfax Drive
Suite 100
Arlington, Virginia 22203
www.tnc.org

The North American Telemark Organization
PO Box 44
Waitsfield, Vermont 05673
www.telemarknato.com

The Wilderness Society
900 17th Street NW
Washington, DC 20006
www.wilderness.org

The Wildlife Legislative Fund of America
801 Kingsmill Parkway
Columbus, Ohio 43229
www.wlfa.org

Trout Unlimited
1500 Wilson Boulevard
Suite 310
Arlington, Virginia
www.tu.org

Underwater Society of America
1701 Lake Avenue
Glenview, Illinois 60025
www.underwatersociety.org.

USA Equestrian
4047 Iron Works Parkway
Lexington, KY 40511
www.equestrian.org

United States Canoe Association
606 Ross Street
Middletown, Ohio 45055
www.usca-canoe-kayak.org

United States Hang Gliding Association
PO Box 1330
Colorado Springs, CO 80901
www.ushga.org

United States Orienteering Federation
PO Box 1444
Forest Park, Georgia 30051
www.us.orienteering.org

United States Parachute Association
1440 Duke Street
Alexandria, Virginia 22314
www.uspa.org

United States Snowshoe Association
678 County Route 25
Corinth, New York 12822
www.snowshoeracing.com

United States Sportsmen's Alliance
801 Kingsmill Parkway
Columbus, Ohio
www.wlfa.org

United States Windsurfing Association
PO Box 978
Hood River, OR 97031
www.uswindsurfing.org

Wilderness Education Association
PO Box 158897
Nashville, Tennessee 37215
www.wildernesseducation.org

Wilderness Inquiry
808 14th Avenue SE
Minneapolis, MN 55414
www.wildernessinquiry.org

Wilderness Medical Society
3595 East Fountain Boulevard
Suite A-1
Colorado Springs, Colorado 80910
www.wms.org

Wilderness Trust
61 Route 9W
Palisades, New York 10964
www.pti.org

Wilderness Watch
PO Box 9175
Missoula, Montana
www.wildernesswatch.org

Wildlife Management Institute
1101 14th Street NW
Suite 801
Washington, DC 20005
www.wildlifemanagementinstitute.org

Wildlife Society
5410 Grosvenor Lane
Bethesda, Maryland 20814
www.wildlife.org

Women Outdoors
55 Talbot Avenue
Medford, Massachusetts 02155
www.women-outdoors.org

Wooden Canoe Heritage Association
PO Box 226
Blue Mountain Lake, New York 12812
www.wcha.org

Young Men's Christian Association
101 North Wacker Drive
Chicago, Illinois 60606
www.ymca.net

Young Women's Christian Association
Empire State Building
350 Fifth Avenue
Suite 301
New York, New York 10118
www.ywca.org

FEDERAL AGENCIES INVOLVED IN OUTDOOR RECREATION

DEPARTMENT OF AGRICULTURE

USDA Forest Service
Sidney R. Yates Federal Building
201 14th Street, SW at Indepen
dence Ave., SW
Washington, DC 20250
Regional Offices
Northern (Montana, Northern
Idaho, North Dakota, and
Northwestern South Dakota)
Federal Building, P.O. Box 7669,
Missoula, MT 59807
Rocky Mountain (Colorado, Kansas,
Nebraska, South Dakota, and
Wyoming)
P.O. Box 25127, Lakewood, CO
80225; 740 Simms Street,
Golden, CO 80401
Southwestern (Arizona and New
Mexico)
333 Broadway, SE, Albuquerque,
NM 87102
Intermountain (Southern Idaho,
Nevada, Utah, and Western
Wyoming)
Federal Building 324, 25th Street
Ogden, UT 84401
Pacific Southwest (California,
Hawaii, Guam, and Trust
Territories of the Pacific Islands)
1323 Club Drive, Vallejo, CA
94592;

Pacific Northwest (Oregon and
Washington)
333 SW First Avenue, Portland,
Oregon 97204
Southern (Alabama, Arkansas,
Florida, Georgia, Kentucky,
Louisiana, Mississippi, North
Carolina, Oklahoma, Puerto
Rico, South Caroline,
Tennessee, Texas, Virgin Islands,
and Virginia)
1720 Peachtree Road NW,
Atlanta, GA 30309
Eastern (Illinois, Indiana, Iowa,
Maine Maryland, Massachusetts,
Michigan, Minnesota, Missouri,
New Hampshire, New Jersey,
New York, Ohio, Pennsylvania,
Rhode Island, Vermont, West
Virginia, Wisconsin)
310 W. Wisconsin Avenue, Mil-
waukee, WI 53203
Alaska
Federal Office Building
709 W. 9th Street, Anchorage, AK
99801-1807

DEPARTMENT OF THE ARMY

Army Corps of Engineers
Office of the Chief of Engineers
441 G Street NW
Washington, D.C. 20314

Divisions:

Mississippi Valley: P.O. Box 80,
Vicksburg, MS 39181

North Atlantic: 302 General Lee
Avenue, Fort Hamilton Military
Community, Brooklyn, NY
11252

Great Lake and Ohio River: P.O.
Box 1159, Cincinnati, OH
45201

Pacific Ocean: Building 230,
Fort Shafter, HI 96858

South Atlantic: Room 9M15, 60
Forsyth Street SW, Atlanta, GA
30303

Southwestern: 1100 Commerce Street,
Dallas, TX 75242

DEPARTMENT OF COMMERCE

National Oceanic and Atmospheric Administration

Sanctuaries and Reserves
Division
1305 East-West Highway, 12th
Floor
Silver Spring, MD 20910

National Marine Fisheries Service

Office of Constituent Services
1315 East-West Highway, 14th
Floor
Silver Spring, MD 20910

DEPARTMENT OF THE INTERIOR

Bureau of Indian Affairs

Office of Public Affairs
1849 C Street NW
Washington, D.C. 20240

Bureau of Land Management

Recreation Group
1849 C Street NW
Washington, D.C. 20240

Denver Service Center
Center Federal Center, Building 50
Denver, C0

State Directors:

Alaska
222 West 7th Avenue #13,
Anchorage, 99513

Arizona
222 North Central Avenue,
Phoenix, 85004

California
Room E-2841, 2800 Cottage Way
Sacramento, 95825

Colorado
2850 Youngfield Street,
Lakewood, 80215

Idaho
1387 South Vinnell Way,
Boise, ID 83709

Montana
5001 Southgate Drive,
Billings, MT 59101

New Mexico (including Kansas,
Oklahoma, and Texas)
1474 Rodeo Road, Santa Fe, NM
87505

Oregon and Washington
333 SW First Avenue,
Portland, 97204

Utah
324 South State Street, 4th Floor
Salt Lake City, 84111

Wyoming
5353 Yellowstone,
Cheyenne, 82003

Eastern States Office
7450 Boston Boulevard,
Springfield, VA 22153

Bureau of Reclamation

1849 C Street NW
Washington DC 20240-0001

Regional Offices:

Great Plains
P.O. Box 36900
Billings, MT 59107-6900

Lower Colorado
400 Railroad Avenue
Boulder City, NV 89005-2422

Mid Pacific
Federal Office Building
2800 Cottage Way
Sacramento CA 95825-1898

Pacific Northwest
1150 North Curtis Road, Suite 100
Boise, Idaho 83706-1234

Upper Colorado
125 South State Street, Room 6107
Salt Lake City, UT 84138-1102

National Park Service

1849 C Street NW
Washington, DC 20240

Regional Offices

Alaska Area Region
2525 Gambell St. RM 107
Anchorage, AK 99503

Midwest Region
1709 Jackson St.
Omaha, NE 68102

Intermountain Region
12795 Alameda Pkwy
Denver, CO 80225

Pacific West Region
One Jackson Center
1111 Jackson Street, Suite 700
Oakland, CA 94607

Northeast Region
U.S. Custom House 200 Chestnut St.,
Fifth Floor
Philadelphia, PA 19106

National Capital Region
1100 Ohio Dr., SW
Washington D.C. 20242

Southeast Region
100 Alabama St. SW
1924 Building
Atlanta, GA 30303

U.S. Fish and Wildlife Service

1849 C Street, NW
Washington, DC 20240

Regional Offices

Region 1: Washington, Oregon,
California, Nevada, Idaho, Hawaii
911 NE 11th Avenue
Portland, Oregon 97232-4181

Region 2: New Mexico, Arizona,
Oklahoma, Texas
P.O. Box 1306
Albuquerque, New Mexico 87103

Region 3: Minnesota, Indiana, Missouri,
Michigan, Wisconsin, Ohio, Illinois,
Iowa

Federal Building, Fort Snelling
Twin Cities, Minnesota 55111

Region 4: Kentucky, Arkansas, Tennes
see, North Carolina, South Caro
lina, Georgia, Alabama, Missis
sippi, Louisiana, Florida, Virgin
Islands, Puerto Rico
1875 Century Boulevard
Atlanta, Georgia 30345

Region 5: Virginia, West Virginia,
Maryland, Pennsylvania, New
York, Delaware, New Jersey,
Connecticut, Maine, Massachu
setts, Vermont, New Hamp
shire, Rhode Island
300 Westgate Center Drive
Hadley, Massachusetts 01035

Region 6: Colorado, Montana,
Nebraska, Utah, Wyoming,
Kansas, North Dakota, South
Dakota
P.O. Box 25486
Denver, Colorado 80025

Region 7: Alaska
1011 East Tudor Road
Anchorage, Alaska 99503

DEPARTMENT OF TRANSPORTATION

Federal Highway Administration
National Scenic Byways Program
400 Seventh Street, SW
Room 3222, HEPM
Washington, DC 20590

INDEPENDENT AGENCY

Tennessee Valley Authority
400 W. Summit Hill Dr.
Knoxville, TN 37902-1499
Phone: 865-632-2101

APPENDIX D

FEDERAL LAWS RELATED TO OUTDOOR RECREATION

Forest Reserve Act (Creative Act of National Forests) ch. 561	1891	USFS
Organic Administration Act-National Forests ch. 2	1897	USFS
Weeks Law ch. 186	1911	USFS
Multiple Use-Sustained Yield Act P.L. 86-517	1960	USFS
Forest and Rangeland Renewable Resources Planning Act P.L. 93-378	1974	USFS
Eastern Wilderness Act P.L. 93-622	1975	USFS
National Forest Management Act P.L. 94-388	1976	USFS
Yellowstone National Park Act ch. 24	1897	NPS
Antiquities Act ch. 3060	1906	NPS
National Park Service Act ch. 408	1916	NPS
Historic Sites Act ch. 593	1935	NPS
Bureau of Outdoor Recreation Organic Act P.L. 88-29	1963	NPS
Land and Water Conservation Fund Act P.L. 88-578	1965	NPS
National Historic Preservation Act P.L. 89-665	1966	NPS
Golden Gate National Recreation Area Act P.L. 92-589	1972	NPS
National Historic Preservation Fund (Title II of Land and Water Conservation Fund Act Amendments) P.L. 94-422	1976	NPS
Omnibus Parks and Public Lands Management Act P.L. 104-333	1996	NPS
Migratory Bird Conservation Act ch. 257	1929	FWS
Migratory Bird Hunting Stamp Act ch. 71	1934	FWS
Federal Aid to Wildlife Restoration Act ch. 899	1937	FWS
Fish Restoration and Management Projects Act ch. 658	1950	FWS
Fish and Wildlife Act (Fish and Wildlife Service Establishment) ch. 1036	1956	FWS
Refuge Recreation Act P.L. 87-714	1962	FWS
National Wildlife Refuge System Administration Act (Organic Act) P.L. 93-205	1966	FWS
National Wildlife Refuge System Administration Act P.L. 105-57)	1997	FWS

O&C Sustained Yield Forestry Act ch. 876 (P.L. 405 of 75th Congress)	1937 BLM	

Federal Property and Administrative
Services Act (Surplus Property Act)
(first passed 1926)   1954
ch. 263 (P.L. 387)   BLM

Federal Land Policy and Management Act
(BLM Organic Act)   1976
P.L. 94-579   BLM

National Marine Sanctuaries Act   1972
Title III   NOAA

National Marine Sanctuaries Act   1996
P.L. 104-283   NOAA

National Marine Sanctuaries Amendment Act
P.L. 106-513   2000
                                                                 NOAA

Intermodal Surface Transportation Efficiency
Act (ISTEA)   1996
P.L. 102-240   FHWA

Transportation Equity Act for the 21st Century
(TEA-21)   1991
P.L. 105-178   FHWA

Housing and Community Development Act 1974
P.L. 93-383   HUD

Watershed Protection and Flood
Prevention Act   1954
P.L. 566   SCS

Federal Water Projects Recreation Act   1965
P.L. 89-72   COE, B. Recl.

Federal Water Pollution Control Act
Amendments   1972
P.L. 92-500

Coastal Zone Management Act   1972
P.L. 92-583

Wilderness Act   1964
P.L. 88-577

National Trails System Act   1968
P.L. 90-543, P.L. 98-11   1983

Wild and Scenic Rivers Act   1968
P.L. 90-542

National Environmental Policy Act   1969
P.L. 91-190

Environmental Education Act   1970
P.L. 91-516

Alaska Native Claims Settlement Act   1971
P.L. 92-203

Alaska National Interest Lands
Conservation Act   1980
P.L. 96-487

Endangered Species Act   1973
P.L. 93-205   1983

Public Lands-Local Government Funds Act or
"Payment In Lieu of Taxes" Act   1976
P.L. 94-579   USFS, BLM

California Desert Protection Act   1994
P.L. 104-333   NPS, BLM, USFS, FWS

Index

12–13
emergence of, 9–11
and the human tendency to play, 5–7
and the human tendency to ritualize, 6–7
impact of improved transportation systems on, 13
increased free time and, 12
protecting the future of, 459
psychological benefits of, 75–76
social mobility and, 13–14
outdoor recreational activities
availability of, 359
growth in demand for, 1945 to present, 359–61
organizations advocating low-impact practices, 363
popularity of, 359
predicted future demand growth, 362
see also specific activities
Outdoor Recreation Resources Review Commission (ORRRC), 292–93
Outward Bound, 68, 350

P
park rangers, 120
peers, as agents for outdoor pursuits, 84, 85–86
performing arts sites, 155
permits, user, 318–20
personality traits, and the leisure experience, 62–64
personal outdoor recreation resources
houseboats, RVs, and SUVs, 224–25
primary residences, 223–24
private lands, 225
second homes, 224
physically challenged persons, outdoor experiences for, 96–97
Pinchot, Gifford, 49–52, 133
planning outdoor recreation
importance of, 290
key principles for, 291
local government plans, 299
methods of public involvement, 290
national plans
Nationwide Outdoor Recreation Plan of 1973, 294–95
Nationwide Outdoor Recreation Plan of 1979, 295–98
Outdoor Recreation Resources Review Commission (ORRRC), 292–93
pre-1960s, 292
Public Land Law Review Commission Report (1970), 293–94
single project plans, 299–300

state plans, 298–99
steps in the planning process, 290–91
play
definition of, 8
and outdoor recreation, 5–7
and ritual, 6–7
preservation
history/evolution of, 9–11, 279–82
as a land management philosophy, 133
preservation organizations, 230–32
private organization outdoor recreation resources
boat and yacht clubs, 226
hiking and mountaineering clubs, 226–27
sport and athletic clubs, 226
sportspersons clubs, 226
professional development opportunities, 351–55
project planning, 299–300
Public Land Law Review Commission Report (1970), 293–94

R
Rails-to-Trails Conservancy, 232
range managers, 120
RARE, 232
recreation, definition of, 5, 8
recreation specialists, 120–22
religion, as a basic social institution, 79–80
residence, leisure pursuits and, 91
resorts, 242–43
resources, outdoor recreation. see commercial outdoor recreation resources; employee recreation programs; industrial land, outdoor recreation on; local governments, and outdoor recreation; personal outdoor recreation resources; private organization outdoor recreation resources; semipublic organization outdoor recreation resources; state government, and outdoor recreation; specific federal agencies
risk management
definitions of legal terms, 323–24
enforcing laws, 323
guidelines for, 322–23
liability
keeping liability concerns in perspective, 326–27
protection for trespassers vs. licensees vs. invitees, 325–26
proving negligence, 324–25
sovereign immunity and, 324
waivers/releases, 326
ritual
definition of, 7

forms of, 7
and play, 6–7
river rafting
low-impact, 381–82
overview of, 379–80
river rating scale, 380–81
safety considerations, 380
support organizations, 407
river recreation, managing, 321–22
rock art viewing
low-impact, 395–96
overview of, 394–95
safety considerations, 395
support organizations, 408
Roosevelt, Theodore, 147
Round Hill School, 334–35
Rousseau, Jean-Jacques, 24–25

S
salaries, state natural resources personnel, 122–24
Scenic Byways program, 177–78
school, as a socializing agent for leisure, 81
schoolmates, as agents for outdoor pursuits, 86
SCUBA diving. see skin diving and SCUBA diving
scuba diving instructors, 121
semipublic organization outdoor recreation resources
preservation organizations, 230–32
youth-serving organizations, 227–30
Sharp, Lloyd Burgess, 336
Sierra Club, The, 231, 347–48, 350
signs, 314
ski areas, 237–42
ski instructors, 121
skin diving and SCUBA diving
low-impact, 384
overview of, 382–83
safety considerations, 383–84
support organizations, 408
skydiving
overview of, 390–92
safety considerations, 392
support organizations, 408
Smith, Julian W., 336–37
snowshoeing, 371–73, 407
social institutions
economic system, 80
family, 79
government, 80
religion, 79–80
technology, 80
socialization
agents for socialization into leisure activities, 81–82
age of socialization into leisure activities, 81
leisure as a socializing agent, 82
as a means of learning leisure roles, 80
socially deviant individuals,

About the Authors _____

Authors Hilmi Ibrahim and Kathleen Cordes enjoy their professions and writing about it. Besides writing Outdoor Recreation: Enrichment for a Lifetime with Sagamore Publishing, they have teamed to write three editions of Applications in Recreation and Leisure (McGraw-Hill, 2002, 1999, 1996), Parks, Recreation and Leisure Service Management (Eddie Bowers, 2002), and Outdoor Recreation (Brown and Benchmark,1993). The Chinese translation of their book Applications in Recreation and Leisure was released in 2000. Both have served on the editorial board of Leisure Today, contributed independent articles for publication, and volunteered their time as feature editors.

For his outstanding contributions, Ibrahim received the American Association for Leisure and Recreation's highest recognition, the Honor Award. Ibrahim, Professor of Physical Education and Recreation at Whittier College in California, obtained his BA from the American University in Cairo and pursued his graduate studies on a Fullbright Scholarship at Indiana University (Doctorate in Recreation) and later at California State University (MA in Sociology). His research in leisure and sport has been published in the Research Quarterly for Exercise and Sport on temperament, prejudice, recreation preference, personality, and self-concept; the International Review of Modern Sociology on inner-other directedness and leisure, and leisure among Saudi males; in Society and Leisure (Prague) on societal differentiation and leisure inclination; and in the Journal of Leisure Research on leisure behavior of the contemporary Egyptians as compared to twelve other nationals.

Other books by Ibrahim include Sport and Society; Leisure: An Introduction with Fred Martin; Leisure: Emergence and Expansion with Jay Shiever; Leisure: A Psychological Approach with Rick Crandall (Hwong); and Leisure in Society (Wm. C. Brown). Ibrahim has been instrumental in educational exchanges between students and intellectuals in Egypt and North America.

Cordes, who served as the Executive Director for the American Association for Leisure and Recreation, received their Outstanding Achievement Award in 2001 and their Merit Service Award in 1997. She is the recipient of the Distinguished Service to Recreation Award from the California Association for Health, Physical Education, and Recreation (CAHPERD) and the CAHPERD Southern District's Outstanding Teacher Award. Cordes received her undergraduate and graduate degrees from Indiana University and Ball State University and is Professor Emeritus from Miramar College in San Diego. She was previously a tenured member of the faculty at Whittier College. While on the faculty at the University of Notre Dame in Indiana, she became the first woman to coach a Notre Dame varsity sport—tennis. At Saint Mary's College, Cordes served as Director of Athletics and Recreation. Her book, America's National Historic Trails (University of Oklahoma Press,1999) was posted on the University Press Best Seller List and was followed by America's National Scenic Trails (2001). America's Millennium Trails: Pathways for the 21st Century (AALR/2002) with Jane Lammers is an official project of the White House Millennium Council. Cordes has presented her published papers at international and national symposiums.